Routing Protocols
Companion Guide

Cisco Networking Academy

Cisco Press

800 East 96th Street
Indianapolis, Indiana 46240 USA

Routing Protocols Companion Guide

Cisco Networking Academy

Copyright© 2014 Cisco Systems, Inc.

Published by:
Cisco Press
800 East 96th Street
Indianapolis, IN 46240 USA

Printed in the United States of America

First Printing February 2014

Library of Congress Control Number: 2013957291

ISBN-13: 978-1-58713-323-7

ISBN-10: 1-58713-323-7

Warning and Disclaimer

This book is designed to provide information about the Cisco Networking Academy Routing Protocols course. Every effort has been made to make this book as complete and as accurate as possible, but no warranty or fitness is implied.

The information is provided on an "as is" basis. The authors, Cisco Press, and Cisco Systems, Inc. shall have neither liability nor responsibility to any person or entity with respect to any loss or damages arising from the information contained in this book or from the use of the discs or programs that may accompany it.

The opinions expressed in this book belong to the author and are not necessarily those of Cisco Systems, Inc.

This book is part of the Cisco Networking Academy® series from Cisco Press. The products in this series support and complement the Cisco Networking Academy curriculum. If you are using this book outside the Networking Academy, then you are not preparing with a Cisco trained and authorized Networking Academy provider.

For more information on the Cisco Networking Academy or to locate a Networking Academy, Please visit www.cisco.com/edu.

ılıılıı
CISCO.

Publisher
Paul Boger

Associate Publisher
Dave Dusthimer

Business Operation Manager, Cisco Press
Jan Cornelssen

Executive Editor
Mary Beth Ray

Managing Editor
Sandra Schroeder

Development Editor
Ellie C. Bru

Project Editor
Mandie Frank

Copy Editor
Bill McManus

Technical Editor
Bruce Brumley

Editorial Assistant
Vanessa Evans

Designer
Mark Shirar

Composition
Tricia Bronkella

Indexer
Brad Herriman

Proofreader
Debbie Williams

Trademark Acknowledgements

All terms mentioned in this book that are known to be trademarks or service marks have been appropriately capitalized. Cisco Press or Cisco Systems, Inc., cannot attest to the accuracy of this information. Use of a term in this book should not be regarded as affecting the validity of any trademark or service mark.

Special Sales

For information about buying this title in bulk quantities, or for special sales opportunities (which may include electronic versions; custom cover designs; and content particular to your business, training goals, marketing focus, or branding interests), please contact our corporate sales department at corpsales@pearsoned.com or (800) 382-3419.

For government sales inquiries, please contact governmentsales@pearsoned.com.

For questions about sales outside the U.S., please contact international@pearsoned.com.

Feedback Information

At Cisco Press, our goal is to create in-depth technical books of the highest quality and value. Each book is crafted with care and precision, undergoing rigorous development that involves the unique expertise of members from the professional technical community.

Readers' feedback is a natural continuation of this process. If you have any comments regarding how we could improve the quality of this book, or otherwise alter it to better suit your needs, you can contact us through email at feedback@ciscopress.com. Please make sure to include the book title and ISBN in your message.

We greatly appreciate your assistance.

Americas Headquarters
Cisco Systems, Inc.
170 West Tasman Drive
San Jose, CA 95134-1706
USA
www.cisco.com
Tel: 408 526-4000
800 553-NETS (6387)
Fax: 408 527-0883

Asia Pacific Headquarters
Cisco Systems, Inc.
168 Robinson Road
#28-01 Capital Tower
Singapore 068912
www.cisco.com
Tel: +65 6317 7777
Fax: +65 6317 7799

Europe Headquarters
Cisco Systems International BV
Haarlerbergpark
Haarlerbergweg 13-19
1101 CH Amsterdam
The Netherlands
www-europe.cisco.com
Tel: +31 0 800 020 0791
Fax: +31 0 20 357 1100

Cisco has more than 200 offices worldwide. Addresses, phone numbers, and fax numbers are listed on the Cisco Website at **www.cisco.com/go/offices.**

About the Contributing Authors

Rick Graziani teaches computer science and computer networking courses at Cabrillo College in Aptos, California. Prior to teaching, Rick worked in the information technology field for Santa Cruz Operation, Tandem Computers, and Lockheed Missiles and Space Corporation. He holds an M.A. in Computer Science and Systems Theory from California State University Monterey Bay. Rick is also a member of the Curriculum Development team for the Cisco Networking Academy since 1999.

Rick has authored multiple books for Cisco Press and multiple online courses for the Cisco Networking Academy. Rick is the author of the Cisco Press book *IPv6 Fundamentals* and has presented on IPv6 at several Cisco Academy conferences.

When Rick is not working, he is most likely surfing at one of his favorite Santa Cruz surf breaks.

Bob Vachon is a professor in the Computer Systems Technology program at Cambrian College in Sudbury, Ontario, Canada, where he teaches networking infrastructure courses. He has more than 30 years of work and teaching experience in the computer networking and information technology field.

Since 2001, Bob has collaborated as team lead, lead author, and subject matter expert on various CCNA, CCNA-S, and CCNP projects for Cisco and the Cisco Networking Academy. He also co-authored *Accessing the WAN, CCNA Exploration Companion Guide* and authored *CCNA Security (640-554) Portable Command Guide*.

In his downtime, Bob enjoys playing the guitar, shooting darts or pool, and either working in his gardens or white-water canoe tripping.

Contents at a Glance

Contents

Icons Used in This Book

IP Phone

Phone

Cisco
CallManager

100BaseT
Hub

Wireless
Router

Route/Switch
Processor

Cisco
ASA 5500

Printer

Cisco 5500
Family

Access
Point

Router

Workgroup
Switch

PC

Laptop

Modem

Headquarters

Branch
Office

File/
Application
Server

Hub

Network Cloud

Line: Ethernet

Command Syntax Conventions

The conventions used to present command syntax in this book are the same conventions used in the IOS Command Reference. The Command Reference describes these conventions as follows:

- **Boldface** indicates commands and keywords that are entered literally as shown. In actual configuration examples and output (not general command syntax), boldface indicates commands that are manually input by the user (such as a **show** command).

- *Italic* indicates arguments for which you supply actual values.

- Vertical bars (|) separate alternative, mutually exclusive elements.

- Square brackets ([ ]) indicate an optional element.

- Braces ({ }) indicate a required choice.

- Braces within brackets ([{ }]) indicate a required choice within an optional element.

Introduction

Routing Protocols Companion Guide is the official supplemental textbook for the Cisco Network Academy CCNA Routing Protocols course. Cisco Networking Academy is a comprehensive program that delivers information technology skills to students around the world. The curriculum emphasizes real-world practical application, while providing opportunities for you to gain the skills and hands-on experience needed to design, install, operate, and maintain networks in small- to medium-sized businesses, as well as enterprise and service provider environments.

As a textbook, this book provides a ready reference to explain the same networking concepts, technologies, protocols, and devices as the online curriculum. This book emphasizes key topics, terms, and activities and provides some alternate explanations and examples as compared with the course. You can use the online curriculum as directed by your instructor and then use this Companion Guide's study tools to help solidify your understanding of all the topics.

Who Should Read This Book

The book, as well as the course, is designed as an introduction to routing protocols for those pursuing careers as network professionals as well as those who need only an introduction to routing protocols for professional growth. Topics are presented concisely, starting with the most fundamental concepts and progressing to a comprehensive understanding of routing protocols. The content of this text provides the foundation for additional Cisco Academy courses, and preparation for the CCENT and CCNA Routing and Switching certifications.

Book Features

The educational features of this book focus on supporting topic coverage, readability, and practice of the course material to facilitate your full understanding of the course material.

Topic Coverage

The following features give you a thorough overview of the topics covered in each chapter so that you can make constructive use of your study time:

- **Objectives:** Listed at the beginning of each chapter, the objectives reference the core concepts covered in the chapter. The objectives match the objectives stated in the corresponding chapters of the online curriculum; however, the question format in the Companion Guide encourages you to think about finding the answers as you read the chapter.

- **"How-to" feature:** When this book covers a set of steps that you need to perform for certain tasks, the text lists the steps as a how-to list. When you are studying, the icon helps you easily refer to this feature as you skim through the book.

- **Notes:** These are short sidebars that point out interesting facts, timesaving methods, and important safety issues.

- **Chapter summaries:** Each chapter includes a summary of the chapter's key concepts. It provides a synopsis of the chapter and serves as a study aid.

- **"Practice" section:** The end of each chapter includes a full list of all the Labs, Class Activities, and Packet Tracer Activities to refer back to for study time.

Readability

The following features have been updated to assist your understanding of the networking vocabulary:

- **Key terms:** Each chapter begins with a list of key terms, along with a page-number reference from inside the chapter for each key term. The key terms are listed in the order in which they are explained in the chapter. This handy reference allows you to find a term, flip to the page where the term appears, and see the term used in context. The Glossary defines all the key terms.

- **Glossary:** This book contains an all-new Glossary with approximately 175 terms.

Practice

Practice makes perfect. This new Companion Guide offers you ample opportunities to put what you learn into practice. You will find the following features valuable and effective in reinforcing the instruction that you receive:

- **Check Your Understanding Questions and answer key:** Updated review questions are presented at the end of each chapter as a self-assessment tool. These questions match the style of questions that you see in the online course. Appendix A, "Answers to the 'Check Your Understanding' Questions," provides an answer key to all the questions and includes an explanation of each answer.

- **Labs and activities:** Throughout each chapter, you will be directed back to the online course to take advantage of the activities created to reinforce concepts. In addition, the end of each chapter includes a "Practice" section that collects a list of all the labs and activities to provide practice with the topics introduced in that chapter. The labs and class activities are available in the companion *Routing Protocols Lab Manual* (ISBN 978-1-58713-322-0). The Packet Tracer Activities PKA files are found in the online course.

- **Page references to online course:** After each heading, you will see, for example, (1.1.2.3). This number refers to the page number in the online course so that you can easily jump to that spot online to view a video, practice an activity, perform a lab, or review a topic.

Lab Manual

The supplementary book *Routing Protocols Lab Manual*, by Cisco Press (ISBN 978-1-58713-322-0), contains all the labs and class activities from the course.

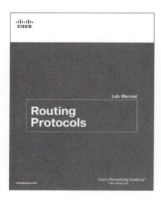

Practice and Study Guides

Additional Study Guide exercises, activities, and scenarios are available in the new *CCENT Practice and Study Guide* (978-158713-345-9) and *CCNA Routing and Switching Practice and Study Guide* (978-158713-344-2) books by Allan Johnson. Each Practice and Study Guide coordinates with the recommended curriculum sequence—the CCENT book follows the course outlines for *Introduction to Networks* and *Routing and Switching Essentials*, and the CCNA book follows the course outlines for *Scaling Networks* and *Connecting Networks*.

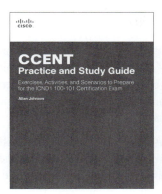
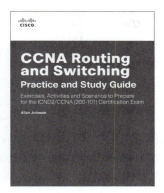

About Packet Tracer Software and Activities

Interspersed throughout the chapters you'll find many activities to work with the Cisco Packet Tracer tool. Packet Tracer allows you to create networks, visualize how packets flow in the network, and use basic testing tools to determine whether the network would work. When you see this icon, you can use Packet Tracer with the listed file to perform a task suggested in this book. The activity files are available in the course. Packet Tracer software is available only through the Cisco Networking Academy website. Ask your instructor for access to Packet Tracer.

How This Book Is Organized

This book corresponds closely to the Cisco Networking Academy Routing Protocols course and is divided into 10 chapters, one appendix, and a glossary of key terms:

- **Chapter 1, "Routing Concepts":** Introduces initial router configuration, directly connected networks, static routing, and dynamic routing protocols. The process of packet forwarding is also reviewed, including the path determination and switching functions.

- **Chapter 2, "Static Routing":** Introduces the use of static routes and the role they play in modern networks. This chapter describes the advantages, uses, and configuration of IPv4 and IPv6 static routes using next-hop IP addresses and exit interfaces. Floating static routes and summary routes are also discussed. The chapter includes a review of VLSM and CIDR.

- **Chapter 3, "Routing Dynamically":** Examines the purpose of dynamic routing protocols and compares their use to static routing. Distance vector and link-state routing protocols are discussed, along with the IP routing table. RIP and RIPng routing protocols are introduced as a foundation for understanding other routing protocols discussed in this book. This chapter serves as an introduction to terms and concepts that are examined more fully in later chapters.

- **Chapter 4, "EIGRP":** Introduces the routing protocol EIGRP. EIGRP is a Cisco-proprietary, advanced distance vector routing protocol. This chapter describes the basic features and operations of EIGRP, EIGRP packet formats, and how the composite metric is calculated by EIGRP. The concepts and operations of DUAL (Diffusing Update Algorithm) are discussed, and how DUAL determines best path and loop-free back up paths. This chapter includes the basic configuration and verification of EIGRP for IPv4 and EIGRP for IPv6.

- **Chapter 5, "EIGRP Advanced Configurations and Troubleshooting":** This chapter includes the configuration and verification of advanced EIGRP features such as automatic summarization, manual summarization, default route propagation, EIGRP authentication of routing updates, and fine-tuning EIGRP interfaces. The components of troubleshooting EIGRP are discussed along with neighbor and routing table issues.

- **Chapter 6, "Single-Area OSPF":** Introduces the link-state routing protocol OSPF. Single-area OSPF operations are discussed, including how routers achieve convergence in an OSPF network, the OSPF metric of cost, OSPF messages, and the use of the OSPF router ID. This chapter includes the configuration and verification of single-area OSPFv2 (OSPF for IPv4) and OSPFv3 (OSPF for IPv6).

- **Chapter 7, "Adjust and Troubleshoot Single-Area OSPF":** Focuses on advanced features of OSPF. The OSPF DR/BDR election process is discussed along with OSPF link-state advertisements, propagating a default route with an OSPF routing domain, neighbor adjacencies, modifying OSPF interface settings to improve network performance, and configuring OSPF authentication. This chapter includes troubleshooting OSPF missing route entries for OSPFv2 and OSPFv3.

- **Chapter 8, "Multiarea OSPF":** Examines the purpose and advantages of multiarea OSPF. Multiarea OSPF link-state advertisements are discussed along with implementing multiarea OSPF. This chapter includes the configuration and verification of multiarea OSPFv2 and OSPFv3.

- **Chapter 9, "Access Control Lists":** Examines how access control lists (ACLs) are used to filter traffic in IPv4 and IPv6 networks. The use of wildcard masks for IPv4 ACLs is discussed along with the guidelines for creating ACLs and the placement of ACLs. The configuration and verification of IPv4 standard named and extended ACLs (both named and numbered) are discussed. The use of ACLs to limit debug output and secure VTY access is demonstrated. The configuration and verification of IPv6 ACLs are also examined.

- **Chapter 10, "IOS Images and Licensing":** Explains the IOS image and naming conventions for IOS 12.4 and IOS 15. The IOS 15 licensing process is discussed along with how to install an IOS 15 software image license.

- **Appendix A, "Answers to the 'Check Your Understanding' Questions":** Lists the answers to the "Check Your Understanding" review questions that are included at the end of each chapter.

- **Glossary:** Provides you with definitions for all the key terms identified in each chapter.

CHAPTER 1

Routing Concepts

Objectives

Upon completion of this chapter, you will be able to answer the following questions:

- What are the primary functions and features of a router?

- How do you connect devices for a small routed network?

- Can you configure basic settings on a router to route between two directly connected networks?

- How can you verify connectivity between two networks that are directly connected to a router?

- How do routers encapsulate and de-encapsulate packets when switching packets between directly connected interfaces?

- How do routers determine the best path?

- How do routers build a routing table of directly connected networks?

- How do routers build a routing table using static routes?

- How do routers build a routing table using a dynamic routing protocol?

Key Terms

This chapter uses the following key terms. You can find the definitions in the Glossary.

Introduction (1.0.1.1)

Networks allow people to communicate, collaborate, and interact in many ways. Networks are used to access web pages, talk using IP telephones, participate in video conferences, compete in interactive gaming, shop using the Internet, complete online coursework, and more.

At the core of the network is the router. A router connects one network to another network. The router is responsible for the delivery of packets across different networks. The destination of the IP packet might be a web server in another country or an email server on the local-area network.

The router uses its routing table to determine the best path to use to forward a packet. It is the responsibility of the routers to deliver those packets in a timely manner. The effectiveness of internetwork communications depends, to a large degree, on the ability of routers to forward packets in the most efficient way possible.

When a host sends a packet to a device on a different IP network, the packet is forwarded to the default gateway because a host device cannot communicate directly with devices outside of the local network. The *default gateway* is the destination that routes traffic from the local network to devices on remote networks. It is often used to connect a local network to the Internet.

This chapter will also answer the question, "What does a router do with a packet received from one network and destined for another network?" Details of the routing table will be examined, including connected, static, and dynamic routes.

Because the router can route packets between networks, devices on different networks can communicate. This chapter will introduce the router, its role in the networks, its main hardware and software components, and the routing process.

Class Activity 1.0.1.2: Do We Really Need a Map?

This modeling activity asks you to research travel directions from source to destination. Its purpose is to compare those types of directions to network routing directions.

Scenario

Using the Internet and Google Maps, located at http://maps.google.com, find a route between the capital city of your country and some other distant town or between two places within your own city. Pay close attention to the driving or walking directions Google Maps suggests.

Notice that in many cases, Google Maps suggests more than one route between the two locations you chose. It also allows you to put additional constraints on the route, such as avoiding highways or tolls.

Copy at least two route instructions supplied by Google Maps for this activity. Place your copies into a word processing document and save it for use with the next step.

Open the .pdf accompanying this modeling activity and complete it with a fellow student. Discuss the reflection questions listed on the .pdf and record your answers.

Be prepared to present your answers to the class.

Initial Configuration of a Router (1.1)

A router is essentially a special-purpose computer with an internetwork operating system optimized for the purpose of routing and securing networks. This section will examine the functions of a router and how a router determines the best path. It will also review the command-line interface (CLI) commands required to configure the base settings of a router.

Characteristics of a Network (1.1.1.1)

Networks have had a significant impact on our lives. They have changed the way we live, work, and play.

Networks allow us to communicate, collaborate, and interact in ways we never did before. We use the network in a variety of ways, including web applications, IP telephony, video conferencing, interactive gaming, electronic commerce, education, and more.

There are many terms, key structures, and performance-related characteristics that are referred to when discussing networks. These include:

- **Topology:** There are physical and logical topologies. The *physical topology* is the arrangement of the cables, network devices, and end systems. It describes how the network devices are actually interconnected with wires and cables. The *logical topology* is the path over which the data is transferred in a network. It describes how the network devices appear connected to network users.

- **Speed:** Speed is a measure of the data rate in bits per second (b/s) of a given link in the network.

- **Cost:** Cost indicates the general expense for purchasing of network components, and installation and maintenance of the network.

- **Security:** Security indicates how protected the network is, including the information that is transmitted over the network. The subject of security is important, and techniques and practices are constantly evolving. Consider security whenever actions are taken that affect the network.

- *Availability*: Availability is a measure of the probability that the network is available for use when it is required.

- *Scalability*: Scalability indicates how easily the network can accommodate more users and data transmission requirements. If a network design is optimized to only meet current requirements, it can be very difficult and expensive to meet new needs when the network grows.

- *Reliability*: Reliability indicates the dependability of the components that make up the network, such as the routers, switches, PCs, and servers. Reliability is often measured as a probability of failure or as the mean time between failures (MTBF).

These characteristics and attributes provide a means to compare different networking solutions.

Note

While the term "speed" is commonly used when referring to the network bandwidth, it is not technically accurate. The actual speed that the bits are transmitted does not vary over the same medium. The difference in bandwidth is due to the number of bits transmitted per second, not how fast they travel over wire or wireless medium.

Why Routing? (1.1.1.2)

How does clicking a link in a web browser return the desired information in mere seconds? Although there are many devices and technologies collaboratively working together to enable this, the primary device is the router. Stated simply, a router connects one network to another network.

Communication between networks would not be possible without a router determining the best path to the destination and forwarding traffic to the next router along that path. The router is responsible for the routing of traffic between networks.

Video

Video 1.1.1.2: Routers Route Packets

Go to the online course and play the animation of a packet being sent through a Cisco 1841 router from sender to receiver.

When a packet arrives on a router interface, the router uses its routing table to determine how to reach the destination network. The destination of the IP packet might be a web server in another country or an email server on the local-area network. It is the responsibility of routers to deliver those packets efficiently. The effectiveness of internetwork communications depends, to a large degree, on the ability of routers to forward packets in the most efficient way possible.

Routers Are Computers (1.1.1.3)

Most network capable devices (i.e., computers, tablets, and smartphones) require the following components to operate:

- Central processing unit (CPU)
- Operating system (OS)
- Memory and storage (RAM, ROM, NVRAM, Flash, hard drive)

A router is essentially a specialized computer. It requires a CPU and memory to temporarily and permanently store data to execute operating system instructions, such as system initialization, routing functions, and switching functions.

Note

Cisco devices use the Cisco Internetwork Operating System (IOS) as the system software.

Routers store data using:

- *Random Access Memory (RAM)*: Provides temporary storage for various applications and processes, including the running IOS, the running configuration file, various tables (i.e., IP routing table, Ethernet ARP table), and buffers for packet processing. RAM is referred to as volatile because it loses its contents when power is turned off.

- *Read-Only Memory (ROM)*: Provides permanent storage for bootup instructions, basic diagnostic software, and a limited IOS in case the router cannot load the full featured IOS. ROM is firmware and referred to as non-volatile because it does not lose its contents when power is turned off.

- *Non-Volatile Random Access Memory (NVRAM)*: Provides permanent storage for the startup configuration file (startup-config). NVRAM is non-volatile and does not lose its contents when power is turned off.

- *Flash*: Provides permanent storage for the IOS and other system-related files. The IOS is copied from flash into RAM during the bootup process. Flash is non-volatile and does not lose its contents when power is turned off.

Table 1-1 provides a summary of the types of router memory, their volatility, and examples of what is stored in each.

Table 1-1   Router Memory

Memory	Volatile/Non-Volatile	Stores
RAM	Volatile	■ Running IOS ■ Running configuration file ■ IP routing and ARP tables ■ Packet buffer
ROM	Non-volatile	■ Bootup instructions ■ Basic diagnostic software ■ Limited IOS
NVRAM	Non-volatile	■ Startup configuration file
Flash	Non-volatile	■ IOS file ■ Other system files

Unlike a computer, a router does not have video adapters or sound card adapters. Instead, routers have specialized ports and network interface cards to interconnect devices to other networks. Figure 1-1 displays the back panel of a Cisco 1941 ISRG2 and identifies those special ports and interfaces.

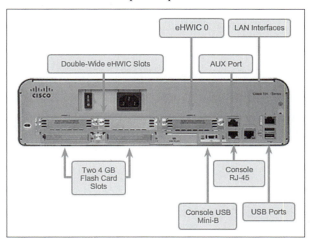

Figure 1-1   Back Panel of a 1941 ISRG2

Routers Interconnect Networks (1.1.1.4)

Most users are unaware of the presence of numerous routers on their own network or on the Internet. Users expect to be able to access web pages, send emails, and download music, regardless of whether the server accessed is on their own network or on another network. Networking professionals know that it is the router that is responsible for forwarding packets from network to network, from the original source to the final destination.

A router connects multiple networks, which means that it has multiple interfaces that each belong to a different IP network. When a router receives an IP packet on one interface, it determines which interface to use to forward the packet to the destination. The interface that the router uses to forward the packet may be the final destination, or it may be a network connected to another router that is used to reach the destination network.

Video 1.1.1.4: Routers Connect

Go to the online course and play the animation of a packet being sent through two Cisco routers. R1 and R2 are responsible for receiving the packet on one network and forwarding the packet out another network toward the destination network.

Each network that a router connects to typically requires a separate interface. These interfaces are used to connect a combination of both local-area networks (LANs) and wide-area networks (WANs). LANs are commonly Ethernet networks that contain devices, such as PCs, printers, and servers. WANs are used to connect networks over a large geographical area. For example, a WAN connection is commonly used to connect a LAN to the Internet service provider (ISP) network.

Notice that each site in Figure 1-2 requires the use of a router to interconnect to other sites. Even the Home Office requires a router. In this topology, the router located at the Home Office is a specialized device that performs multiple services for the home network.

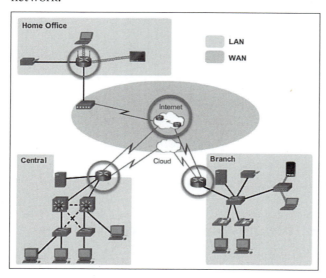

Figure 1-2   Sample Routed Topology

Routers Choose Best Paths (1.1.1.5)

The primary functions of a router are to:

- Determine the best path to send packets
- Forward packets toward their destination

The router uses its routing table to determine the best path to use to forward a packet. When the router receives a packet, it examines the destination address of the packet and uses the routing table to search for the best path to that network. The routing table also includes the interface to be used to forward packets for each known network. When a match is found, the router encapsulates the packet into the data link frame of the outgoing or exit interface, and the packet is forwarded toward its destination.

It is possible for a router to receive a packet that is encapsulated in one type of data link frame, and to forward the packet out of an interface that uses a different type of data link frame. For example, a router may receive a packet on an Ethernet interface, but must forward the packet out of an interface configured with the Point-to-Point Protocol (PPP). The data link encapsulation depends on the type of interface on the router and the type of medium to which it connects. The different data link technologies that a router can connect to include Ethernet, PPP, Frame Relay, DSL, cable, and wireless (802.11, Bluetooth).

Video

Video 1.1.1.5: How the Router Works

Go to the online course and play the animation of a packet being sent through two routers from sender to receiver.

Note

Routers use static routes and dynamic routing protocols to learn about remote networks and build their routing tables.

Packet Forwarding Mechanisms (1.1.1.6)

Routers support three packet-forwarding mechanisms:

- *Process switching*: An older packet-forwarding mechanism still available for Cisco routers. When a packet arrives on an interface, it is forwarded to the control plane, where the CPU matches the destination address with an entry in its routing table, and then determines the exit interface and forwards the packet. It is important to understand that the router does this for every packet, even if the destination is the same for a stream of packets. This process-switching mechanism is very slow and rarely implemented in modern networks. Figure 1-3 illustrates how packets are process-switched.

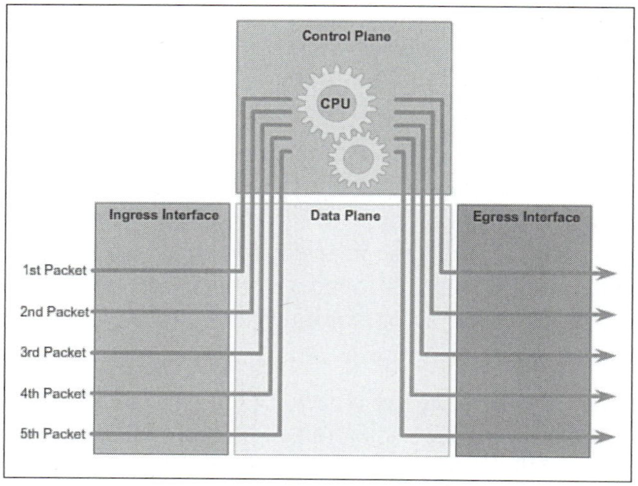

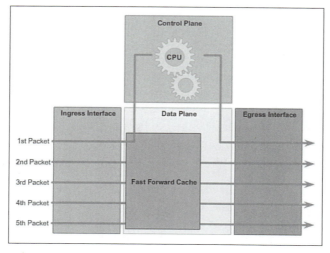

Figure 1-3   Process Switching

- *Fast switching*: This is a common packet-forwarding mechanism which uses a fast-switching cache to store next-hop information. When a packet arrives on an interface, it is forwarded to the control plane, where the CPU searches for a match in the fast-switching cache. If it is not there, it is process-switched and forwarded to the exit interface. The flow information for the packet is also stored in the fast-switching cache. If another packet going to the same destination arrives on an interface, the next-hop information in the cache is re-used without CPU intervention. Figure 1-4 illustrates how packets are fast-switched.

Figure 1-4   Fast Switching

- *Cisco Express Forwarding (CEF)*: CEF is the most recent and preferred Cisco IOS packet-forwarding mechanism. Like fast switching, CEF builds a Forwarding Information Base (FIB) and an adjacency table. However, the table entries are not packet-triggered like fast switching but change-triggered such as when something changes in the network topology. Therefore, when a network has converged, the FIB and adjacency tables contain all the information a router would have to consider when forwarding a packet. The FIB contains pre-computed reverse lookups and next-hop information for routes, including the interface and Layer 2 information. Cisco Express Forwarding is the fastest forwarding mechanism and the preferred choice on Cisco routers. Figure 1-5 illustrates how packets are forwarded using CEF.

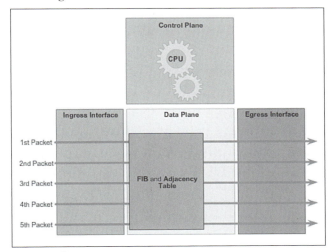

Figure 1-5 Cisco Express Forwarding

Figures 1-3 to 1-5 illustrate the differences between the three packet-forwarding mechanisms. Assume a traffic flow consisting of five packets all going to the same destination. As shown in Figure 1-3, with process switching, each packet must be processed by the CPU individually. Contrast this with fast switching, as shown in Figure 1-4. With fast switching, notice how only the first packet of a flow is process-switched and added to the fast-switching cache. The next four packets are quickly processed based on the information in the fast-switching cache. Finally, in Figure 1-5, CEF builds the FIB and adjacency tables, after the network has converged. All five packets are quickly processed in the data plane.

A common analogy used to describe the three packet-forwarding mechanisms is as follows:

- Process switching solves a problem by doing math long hand, even if it is the identical problem.

- Fast switching solves a problem by doing math long hand one time and remembering the answer for subsequent identical problems.

- CEF solves every possible problem ahead of time in a spreadsheet.

Activity 1.1.1.7: Identify Router Components

Go to the online course to perform this practice activity.

Packet Tracer Activity 1.1.1.8: Using Traceroute to Discover the Network

The company you work for has acquired a new branch location. You asked for a topology map of the new location, but apparently one does not exist. However, you have username and password information for the new branch's networking devices and you know the web address for the new branch's server. Therefore, you will verify connectivity and use the **tracert** command to determine the path to the location. You will connect to the edge router of the new location to determine the devices and networks attached. As a part of this process, you will use various **show** commands to gather the necessary information to finish documenting the IP addressing scheme and create a diagram of the topology.

Lab 1.1.1.9: Mapping the Internet

In this lab, you will complete the following objectives:

- Part 1: Determine Network Connectivity to a Destination Host
- Part 2: Trace a Route to a Remote Server Using Tracert

Connect Devices (1.1.2)

In this section, you will see how accessing a network involves connecting hosts and infrastructure devices with IP addresses, subnet masks, and default gateways. This section will also introduce how to configure the initial settings of a switch.

Connect to a Network (1.1.2.1)

Network devices and end users typically connect to a network using a wired Ethernet or wireless connection. Refer to the sample reference topology in Figure 1-6. The LANs in the figure serve as an example of how users and network devices could connect to networks.

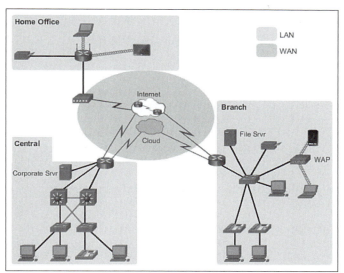

Figure 1-6   Sample LAN and WAN Connections

Home Office devices can connect as follows:

- Laptops and tablets connect wirelessly to a home router.

- A network printer connects using an Ethernet cable to the switch port on the home router.

- The home router connects to the service provider cable modem using an Ethernet cable.

- The cable modem connects to the Internet service provider (ISP) network.

The Branch site devices connect as follows:

- Corporate resources (i.e., file servers and printers) connect to Layer 2 switches using Ethernet cables.

- Desktop PCs and voice over IP (VoIP) phones connect to Layer 2 switches using Ethernet cables.

- Laptops and smartphones connect wirelessly to wireless access points (WAPs).

- The WAPs connect to switches using Ethernet cables.

- Layer 2 switches connect to an Ethernet interface on the edge router using Ethernet cables. An edge router is a device that sits at the edge or boundary of a network and routes between that network and another, such as between a LAN and a WAN.

- The edge router connects to a WAN service provider (SP).

- The edge router also connects to an ISP for backup purposes.

The Central site devices connect as follows:

- Desktop PCs and VoIP phones connect to Layer 2 switches using Ethernet cables.

- Layer 2 switches connect redundantly to multilayer Layer 3 switches using Ethernet fiber-optic cables (orange connections).

- Layer 3 multilayer switches connect to an Ethernet interface on the edge router using Ethernet cables.

- The corporate website server is connected using an Ethernet cable to the edge router interface.

- The edge router connects to a WAN SP.

- The edge router also connects to an ISP for backup purposes.

In the Branch and Central LANs, hosts are connected either directly or indirectly (via WAPs) to the network infrastructure using a Layer 2 switch.

Default Gateways (1.1.2.2)

To enable network access, devices must be configured with IP address information to identify the appropriate:

- *IP address*: Identifies a unique host on a local network

- *Subnet mask*: Identifies with which network subnet the host can communicate

- **Default gateway**: Identifies the router to send a packet to when the destination is not on the same local network subnet

When a host sends a packet to a device that is on the same IP network, the packet is simply forwarded out of the host interface to the destination device.

When a host sends a packet to a device on a different IP network, then the packet is forwarded to the default gateway, because a host device cannot communicate directly with devices outside of the local network. The default gateway is the destination that routes traffic from the local network to devices on remote networks. It is often used to connect a local network to the Internet.

The default gateway is usually the address of the interface on the router connected to the local network. The router maintains routing table entries of all connected networks as well as entries of remote networks, and determines the best path to reach those destinations.

For example, if PC1 sends a packet to the Web Server located at 172.16.1.99, it would discover that the Web Server is not on the local network and it, therefore, must send the packet to the Media Access Control (MAC) address of its default gateway. The packet protocol data unit (PDU) in Figure 1-7 identifies the source and destination IP and MAC addresses.

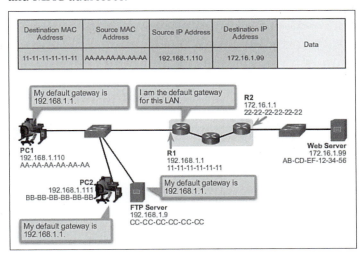

Figure 1-7   Getting the Pieces to the Correct Network

A router is also usually configured with its own default gateway. This is sometimes known as the Gateway of Last Resort.

Document Network Addressing (1.1.2.3)

When designing a new network or mapping an existing network, document the network. At a minimum, the documentation should identify:

- Device names
- Interfaces used in the design
- IP addresses and subnet masks
- Default gateway addresses

This information is captured by creating two useful network documents:

- *Topology diagram*: Provides a visual reference that indicates the physical connectivity and logical Layer 3 addressing. Often created using software, such as Microsoft Visio.

- *Addressing table*: A table that captures device names, interfaces, IPv4 addresses, subnet masks, and default gateway addresses.

Figure 1-8 displays the sample topology diagram, while Table 1-2 provides a sample addressing table for the topology.

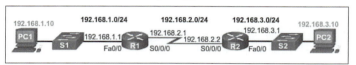

Figure 1-8   Documenting Network Addressing

Table 1-2   Addressing Table

Device	Interface	IP Address	Subnet Mask	Default Gateway
R1	Fa0/0	192.168.1.1	255.255.255.0	N/A
	S0/0/0	192.168.2.1	255.255.255.0	N/A
R2	Fa0/0	192.168.3.1	255.255.255.0	N/A
	S0/0/0	192.168.2.2	255.255.255.0	N/A
PC1	N/A	192.168.1.10	255.255.255.0	192.168.1.1
PC2	N/A	192.168.3.10	255.255.255.0	192.168.3.1

Enable IP on a Host (1.1.2.4)

A host can be assigned its IP address information in one of two ways. A host can get a:

- *Statically Assigned IP Address*: The host is manually assigned the correct IP address, subnet mask, and default gateway. The DNS server IP address can also be configured.

- *Dynamically Assigned IP Address*: IP address information is provided by a server using the Dynamic Host Configuration Protocol (DHCP). The DHCP server provides a valid IP address, subnet mask, and default gateway for end devices. Other information may be provided by the server.

Figures 1-9 and 1-10 provide static and dynamic IPv4 address configuration examples.

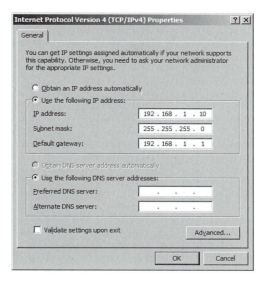

Figure 1-9   Statically Assigning an IP Address

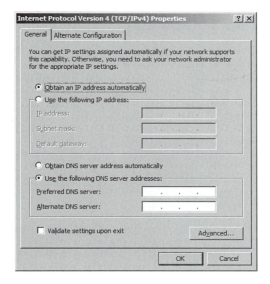

Figure 1-10   Dynamically Assigning an IP Address

Statically assigned addresses are commonly used to identify specific network resources, such as network servers and printers. They can also be used in smaller networks with few hosts. However, most host devices acquire their IPv4 address information by accessing a DHCP server. In large enterprises, dedicated DHCP servers providing services to many LANs are implemented. In a smaller branch or small office setting, DHCP services can be provided by a Cisco Catalyst switch or a Cisco ISR.

Device LEDs (1.1.2.5)

Host computers connect to a wired network using a network interface and RJ-45 Ethernet cable. Most network interfaces have one or two LED link indicators next to the interface. Typically, a green LED means a good connection while a blinking green LED indicates network activity.

If the link light is not on, then there may be a problem with either the network cable or the network itself. The switch port where the connection terminates would also have an LED indicator lit. If one or both ends are not lit, try a different network cable.

Note

The actual function of the LEDs varies between computer manufacturers.

Similarly, network infrastructure devices commonly use multiple LED indicators to provide a quick status view. For example, a Cisco Catalyst 2960 switch has several status LEDs to help monitor system activity and performance. These LEDs are generally lit green when the switch is functioning normally and lit amber when there is a malfunction.

Cisco ISRs use various LED indicators to provide status information. The LEDs on the router help the network administrator conduct some basic troubleshooting. Each device has a unique set of LEDs. Consult the device-specific documentation for an accurate description of the LEDs.

The LEDs of the Cisco 1941 router shown in Figure 1-11 are explained in Table 1-3.

Figure 1-11   Cisco 1941 LEDs

Table 1-3   Description of the Cisco 1941 LEDs

#	Port	LED	Color	Description
1	GE0/0 and GE0/1	S (Speed)	1 blink + pause	Port operating at 10 Mb/s
			2 blink + pause	Port operating at 100 Mb/s
			3 blink + pause	Port operating at 1000 Mb/s
		L (Link)	Green	Link is active
			Off	Link is inactive
2	Console	EN	Green	Port is active
			Off	Port is inactive
3	USB	EN	Green	Port is active
			Off	Port is inactive

Console Access (1.1.2.6)

In a production environment, infrastructure devices are commonly accessed remotely using Secure Shell (SSH) or HyperText Transfer Protocol Secure (HTTPS). Console access is really only required when initially configuring a device, or if remote access fails.

Console access requires:

- *Console cable*: RJ-45-to-DB-9 console cable
- *Terminal emulation software*: Tera Term, PuTTY, HyperTerminal

The cable is connected between the serial port of the host and the console port on the device. Most computers and notebooks no longer include built-in serial ports. If the host does not have a serial port, the USB port can be used to establish a console connection. A special USB-to-RS-232 compatible serial port adapter is required when using the USB port.

The Cisco ISR G2 supports a USB serial console connection. To establish connectivity, a USB Type-A to USB Type-B (mini-B USB) is required, as well as an operating system device driver. This device driver is available from http://www.cisco.com. Although these routers have two console ports, only one console port can be active at a time. When a cable is plugged into the USB console port, the RJ-45 port becomes inactive. When the USB cable is removed from the USB port, the RJ-45 port becomes active.

Table 1-4 summarizes the console connection requirements, while Figure 1-12 displays the various ports and cables required.

Table 1-4   Console Connection Requirements

Port on Computer	Cable Required	Port on ISR	Terminal Emulation
Serial Port	RJ-45 to DB-9 Console Cable	RJ-45 Console Port	Tera Term PuTTY
USB Type-A Port	USB to RS-232 compatible serial port adapter ■ Adapter may require a software driver RJ-45 to DB-9 Console Cable		
	USB Type-A to USB Type-B (Mini-B USB) ■ A device driver is required and available from Cisco.com	USB Type-B (Mini-B USB)	

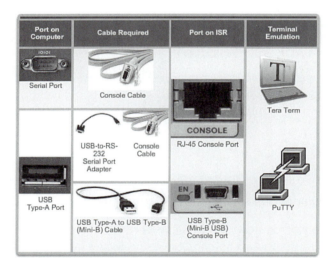

Figure 1-12   Ports and Cables

Enable IP on a Switch (1.1.2.7)

Network infrastructure devices require IP addresses to enable remote management. Using the device IP address, the network administrator can remotely connect to the device using Telnet, SSH, HTTP, or HTTPS.

A switch does not have a dedicated interface to which an IP address can be assigned. Instead, the IP address information is configured on a virtual interface called a *switched virtual interface (SVI).*

The steps to configure the basic settings on a switch are as follows:

Step 1. Name the device.

Step 2. Configure the SVI. This makes the switch accessible for network management.

Step 3. Enable the SVI.

Step 4. Configure the default gateway for the switch. Packets generated by the switch and destined for an address other than its management network segment will be forwarded to this address. This default gateway is used by the switch only for the packets it generates, not any hosts connected to the switch.

For example, the following commands would configure the management VLAN interface and default gateway of switch S1 shown in Figure 1-13.

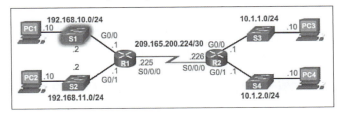

Figure 1-13 Configuring the SVI of S1

```
S1(config)# interface vlan 1
S1(config-if)# ip address 192.168.10.2 255.255.255.0
S1(config-if)# no shutdown
%LINK-5-CHANGED: Interface Vlan1, changed state to up
S1(config-if)# exit
S1(config)#
S1(config)# ip default-gateway 192.168.10.1
S1(config)#
```

In the example, the switch SVI is configured and enabled with the IP address 192.168.10.2/24 and a default gateway of the router located at 192.168.10.1. Packets generated by the switch and destined for an address outside of the 192.168.1.0/24 network segment will be forwarded to this address. In the example, the address is that of the G0/0 interface of R1.

Activity 1.1.2.7: Configure the Management SVI on S2

Go to the online course to use the Syntax Checker in the second graphic to configure the S2 Layer 2 switch.

Activity 1.1.2.8: Document an Addressing Scheme

Go to the online course to perform this practice activity.

Packet Tracer Activity 1.1.2.9: Documenting the Network

Your job is to document the addressing scheme and connections used in the Central portion of the network. You will need to use a variety of commands to gather the required information.

Basic Settings on a Router (1.1.3)

The basic addressing and configuration of Cisco devices was covered in either the Introduction to Networks or Network Basics course. However, we will spend some time reviewing these topics as well as preparing you for the hands-on lab experience in this course.

Configure Basic Router Settings (1.1.3.1)

Cisco routers and Cisco switches have many similarities. They support a similar modal operating system, similar command structures, and many of the same commands. In addition, both devices have similar initial configuration steps.

When initially configuring a Cisco switch or router, the following steps should be executed:

Step 1. Name the device. This changes the router prompt and helps distinguish the device from others.

Step 2. Secure management access. Specifically, secure the privileged EXEC, user EXEC, and Telnet access, and encrypt passwords to their highest level.

Step 3. Configure a banner. Although optional, this is a recommended step to provide legal notice to anyone attempting to access the device.

Step 4. Save the configuration.

For example, the following commands would configure the basic settings for router R1 shown in Figure 1-14.

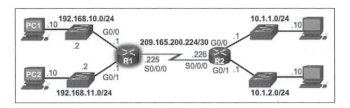

Figure 1-14 Configuring the Basic Settings of R1

```
Router# configure terminal
Enter configuration commands, one per line.  End with CNTL/Z.
Router(config)# hostname R1
R1(config)#
R1(config)# enable secret class
R1(config)#
R1(config)# line console 0
R1(config-line)# password cisco
R1(config-line)# login
R1(config-line)# exit
R1(config)#
R1(config)# line vty 0 4
R1(config-line)# password cisco
R1(config-line)# login
R1(config-line)# exit
R1(config)#
R1(config)# service password-encryption
R1(config)#
R1(config)# banner motd $ Authorized Access Only! $
R1(config)# end
R1#
R1# copy running-config startup-config
Destination filename [startup-config]?
Building configuration...
[OK]
R1#
```

Interactive Graphic

Activity 1.1.3.1: Configure Basic Settings on R2

Go to the online course to use the Syntax Checker in the fifth graphic to configure basic settings on R2.

Configure an IPv4 Router Interface (1.1.3.2)

One distinguishing feature between switches and routers is the type of interfaces supported by each. For example, Layer 2 switches support LANs and, therefore, have multiple FastEthernet or Gigabit Ethernet ports.

Routers support LANs and WANs and can interconnect different types of networks; therefore, they support many types of interfaces. For example, G2 ISRs have one or two integrated Gigabit Ethernet interfaces and *High-Speed WAN Interface Card (HWIC)* slots to accommodate other types of network interfaces, including serial, DSL, and cable interfaces.

To be available, an interface must be:

- **If using IPv4, configured with an address and a subnet mask**: Use the **ip address** *ip-address subnet-mask* interface configuration command.

- **Activated**: By default, LAN and WAN interfaces are not activated (**shutdown**). To enable an interface, it must be activated using the **no shutdown** command. (This is similar to powering on the interface.) The interface must also be connected to another device (a hub, a switch, or another router) for the physical layer to be active.

Optionally, the interface could also be configured with a short description. It is good practice to configure a description on each interface. The description text is limited to 240 characters. On production networks, a description can be helpful in troubleshooting by providing information about the type of network to which the interface is connected. If the interface connects to an ISP or service carrier, it is helpful to enter the third-party connection and contact information.

Depending on the type of interface, additional parameters may be required. For example, in the lab environment, the serial interface connecting to the serial cable end labeled DCE must be configured with the **clock rate** command.

Note

Accidentally using the **clock rate** command on a DTE interface generates a "%Error: This command applies only to DCE interface" message.

How To

The steps to configure an IPv4 interface on a router are:

Step 1.   Add a description. Although optional, it is a necessary component for documenting a network.

Step 2.   Configure the IPv4 address.

Step 3.   Configure a clock rate on Serial interfaces. This is only necessary on the DCE device in our lab environment and does not apply to Ethernet interfaces.

Step 4.   Enable the interface.

For example, the following commands would configure the three directly connected interfaces of router R1 shown in Figure 1-14 (in the previous section):

```
R1(config)# interface gigabitethernet 0/0
R1(config-if)# description Link to LAN 1
R1(config-if)# ip address 192.168.10.1 255.255.255.0
R1(config-if)# no shutdown
R1(config-if)# exit
R1(config)#
R1(config)# interface gigabitethernet 0/1
R1(config-if)# description Link to LAN 2
R1(config-if)# ip address 192.168.11.1 255.255.255.0
R1(config-if)# no shutdown
R1(config-if)# exit
R1(config)#
R1(config)# interface serial 0/0/0
R1(config-if)# description Link to R2
R1(config-if)# ip address 209.165.200.225 255.255.255.252
R1(config-if)# clock rate 128000
R1(config-if)# no shutdown
R1(config-if)# exit
R1(config)#
```

Interactive Graphic

Activity 1.1.3.2: Configure the R2 Interfaces

Go to the online course to use the Syntax Checker in the fourth graphic to configure the R2 interfaces.

Configure an IPv6 Router Interface (1.1.3.3)

Configuring an IPv6 interface is similar to configuring an interface for IPv4. Most IPv6 configuration and verification commands in the Cisco IOS are very similar to their IPv4 counterparts. In many cases, the only difference uses **ipv6** in place of **ip** in commands.

An IPv6 interface must be:

- **Configured with IPv6 address and subnet mask:** Use the **ipv6 address** *ipv6-address/prefix-length* [**link-local** | **eui-64**] interface configuration command.

- **Activated:** The interface must be activated using the **no shutdown** command.

Note

An interface can generate its own IPv6 link-local address without having a global unicast address by using the **ipv6 enable** interface configuration command.

Unlike IPv4, IPv6 interfaces will typically have more than one IPv6 address. At a minimum, an IPv6 device must have an IPv6 link-local address but will most likely also have an IPv6 global unicast address. IPv6 also supports the ability for an interface to have multiple IPv6 global unicast addresses from the same subnet. The following commands can be used to statically create a global unicast or link-local IPv6 address:

- **ipv6 address** *ipv6-address/prefix-length*: Creates a global unicast IPv6 address as specified.

- **ipv6 address** *ipv6-address/prefix-length* **eui-64**: Configures a global unicast IPv6 address with an interface identifier (ID) in the low-order 64 bits of the IPv6 address using the EUI-64 process.

- **ipv6 address** *ipv6-address/prefix-length* **link-local**: Configures a static link-local address on the interface that is used instead of the link-local address that is automatically configured when the global unicast IPv6 address is assigned to the interface or enabled using the **ipv6 enable** interface command. Recall, the **ipv6 enable** interface command is used to automatically create an IPv6 link-local address whether or not an IPv6 global unicast address has been assigned.

How To

The steps to configure an IPv6 interface on a router are:

Step 1.   Add a description. Although optional, it is a necessary component for documenting a network.

Step 2.   Configure the IPv6 global unicast address. Configuring a global unicast address automatically creates a link-local IPv6 address.

Step 3.   Configure a link-local unicast address which automatically assigns a link-local IPv6 address and overrides any previously assigned address.

Step 4.   Configure a clock rate on Serial interfaces. This is only necessary on the DCE device in our lab environment and does not apply to Ethernet interfaces.

Step 5.   Enable the interface.

In the example topology shown in Figure 1-15, R1 must be configured to support the following IPv6 global network addresses:

- 2001:0DB8:ACAD:0001:/64 (2001:DB8:ACAD:1::/64)

- 2001:0DB8:ACAD:0002:/64 (2001:DB8:ACAD:2::/64)

- 2001:0DB8:ACAD:0003:/64 (2001:DB8:ACAD:3::/64)

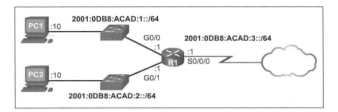

Figure 1-15   IPv6 Topology

When the router is configured using the **ipv6 unicast-routing** global configuration command, the router begins sending ICMPv6 Router Advertisement messages out the interface. This enables a PC connected to the interface to automatically config-ure an IPv6 address and to set a default gateway without needing the services of a DHCPv6 server. Alternatively, a PC connected to the IPv6 network can get its IPv6 address statically assigned, as shown in Figure 1-16. Notice that the default gate-way address configured for PC1 is the IPv6 global unicast address of the R1 Gigabit Ethernet 0/0 interface.

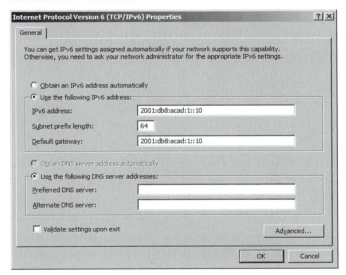

Figure 1-16   Statically Assign an IPv6 Address to PC1

For example, the following commands would configure the IPv6 global unicast address-es of the three directly connected interfaces of the R1 router shown in Figure 1-15:

```
R1# configure terminal
R1(config)# interface gigabitethernet 0/0
R1(config-if)# description Link to LAN 1
R1(config-if)# ipv6 address 2001:db8:acad:1::1/64
R1(config-if)# no shutdown
R1(config-if)# exit
R1(config)#
```

```
R1(config)# interface gigabitethernet 0/1
R1(config-if)# description Link to LAN 2
R1(config-if)# ipv6 address 2001:db8:acad:2::1/64
R1(config-if)# no shutdown
R1(config-if)# exit
R1(config)#
R1(config)# interface serial 0/0/0
R1(config-if)# description Link to R2
R1(config-if)# ipv6 address 2001:db8:acad:3::1/64
R1(config-if)# clock rate 128000
R1(config-if)# no shutdown
R1(config-if)#
```

Interactive Graphic

Activity 1.1.3.3: Configure the R2 Interfaces

Go to the online course to use the Syntax Checker in the sixth graphic to configure the IPv6 global unicast addresses on the R2 router.

Configure an IPv4 Loopback Interface (1.1.3.4)

Another common configuration of Cisco IOS routers is enabling a loopback interface.

The *loopback interface* is a logical interface internal to the router. It is not assigned to a physical port and can therefore never be connected to any other device. It is considered a software interface that is automatically placed in an "up/up" state, as long as the router is functioning.

The loopback interface is useful in testing and managing a Cisco IOS device because it ensures that at least one interface will always be available. For example, it can be used for testing purposes, such as testing internal routing processes, by emulating networks behind the router.

Additionally, the IPv4 address assigned to the loopback interface can be significant to processes on the router that use an interface IPv4 address for identification purposes, such as the Open Shortest Path First (OSPF) routing process. By enabling a loopback interface, the router will use the always available loopback interface address for identification, rather than an IP address assigned to a physical port that may go down.

How To

The steps to configure a loopback interface on a router are:

Step 1. Create the loopback interface using the **interface loopback** *number* global configuration command.

Step 2. Add a description. Although optional, it is a necessary component for documenting a network.

Step 3. Configure the IP address.

For example, the following commands configure a loopback interface of the R1 router shown in Figure 1-14 (shown earlier in the chapter):

```
R1# configure terminal
R1(config)# interface loopback 0
R1(config-if)# ip address 10.0.0.1 255.255.255.0
R1(config-if)# exit
R1(config)#
```

A loopback interface is always enabled and therefore does not require a **no shutdown** command. Multiple loopback interfaces can be enabled on a router. The IPv4 address for each loopback interface must be unique and unused by any other interface.

Packet Tracer
☐ Activity

Packet Tracer Activity 1.1.3.5: Configuring IPv4 and IPv6 Interfaces

Routers R1 and R2 each have two LANs. Your task is to configure the appropriate addressing on each device and verify connectivity between the LANs.

Verify Connectivity of Directly Connected Networks (1.1.4)

The first task to undertake once the basic settings and interfaces are configured is to verify and validate the configured settings. This is an important step and should be done before any other configurations are added to the router.

Verify Interface Settings (1.1.4.1)

There are several **show** commands that can be used to verify the operation and configuration of an interface. The following three commands are especially useful to quickly identify an interface status:

- **show ip interface brief**: Displays a summary for all interfaces, including the IPv4 address of the interface and current operational status.

- **show ip route**: Displays the contents of the IPv4 routing table stored in RAM. In Cisco IOS 15, active interfaces should appear in the routing table with two related entries identified by the code 'C' (Connected) or 'L' (Local). In previous IOS versions, only a single entry with the code 'C' will appear.

- **show running-config interface** *interface-id*: Displays the commands configured on the specified interface.

Figure 1-17 displays the output of the **show ip interface brief** command.

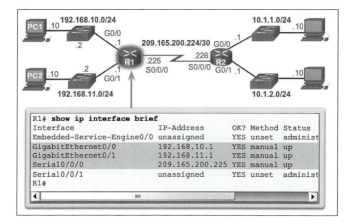

Figure 1-17   Display Interface Summaries

The output reveals that the LAN interfaces and the WAN link are all activated and operational as indicated by the Status of "up" and Protocol of "up." A different output would indicate a problem with either the configuration or the cabling.

Note

The entire output of the **show ip interface brief** command in Figure 1-17 can be viewed in the online course on page 1.1.4.1 graphic number 1.

Note

In Figure 1-17, the Embedded-Service-Engine0/0 interface is displayed because Cisco ISRs G2 have dual-core CPUs on the motherboard. The Embedded-Service-Engine0/0 interface is outside the scope of this course.

Figure 1-18 displays the output of the **show ip route** command.

```
R1# show ip route
Codes: L - local, C - connected, S - static, R - RIP, M - mo

<output omitted>

Gateway of last resort is not set

      192.168.10.0/24 is variably subnetted, 2 subnets, 2 ma
C        192.168.10.0/24 is directly connected, GigabitEther
L        192.168.10.1/32 is directly connected, GigabitEther
      192.168.11.0/24 is variably subnetted, 2 subnets, 2 ma
C        192.168.11.0/24 is directly connected, GigabitEther
L        192.168.11.1/32 is directly connected, GigabitEther
      209.165.200.0/24 is variably subnetted, 2 subnets, 2 m
```

Figure 1-18   Verify the IPv4 Routing Table

Note

The entire output of the **show ip route** command in Figure 1-18 can be viewed in the online course on page 1.1.4.1 graphic number 2.

Notice the three directly connected network entries and the three local host route interface entries. A local host route has an administrative distance of 0. It also has a /32 mask for IPv4, and a /128 mask for IPv6. The local host route is for routes on the router owning the IP address. It is used to allow the router to process packets destined to that IP.

Figure 1-19 displays the output of the **show running-config interface** command. The output displays the current commands configured on the specified interface.

```
R1# show running-config interface gigabitEthernet 0/0
Building configuration...

Current configuration : 128 bytes
!
interface GigabitEthernet0/0
 description Link to LAN 1
 ip address 192.168.10.1 255.255.255.0
 duplex auto
 speed auto
end

R1#
```

Figure 1-19   Verify an Interface Configuration

The following two commands are used to gather more detailed interface information:

- **show interfaces:** Displays interface information and packet flow count for all interfaces on the device

- **show ip interface:** Displays the IPv4-related information for all interfaces on a router

Interactive
Graphic

Activity 1.1.4.1: Verify Router Interfaces

Go to the online course to use the Syntax Checker in the fourth and fifth graphics to verify the interfaces of the R2 router.

Verify IPv6 Interface Settings (1.1.4.2)

The commands to verify the IPv6 interface configuration are similar to the commands used for IPv4.

The **show ipv6 interface brief** command in Figure 1-20 displays a summary for each of the interfaces.

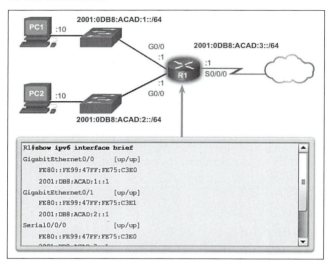

Figure 1-20 Verify the R1 IPv6 Interface Status

Note

The entire output of the **show ipv6 interface brief** command in Figure 1-20 can be viewed in the online course on page 1.1.4.2 graphic number 1.

The "up/up" output on the same line as the interface name indicates the Layer 1/Layer 2 interface state. This is the same as the Status and Protocol columns in the equivalent IPv4 command.

The output displays two configured IPv6 addresses per interface. One address is the IPv6 global unicast address that was manually entered. The other address, which begins with FE80, is the link-local unicast address for the interface. A link-local address is automatically added to an interface whenever a global unicast address is assigned. An IPv6 network interface is required to have a link-local address, but not necessarily a global unicast address.

The **show ipv6 interface gigabitethernet 0/0** command output shown in Figure 1-21 displays the interface status and all of the IPv6 addresses belonging to the interface. Along with the link-local address and global unicast address, the output includes the multicast addresses assigned to the interface, beginning with prefix FF02.

```
R1#show ipv6 interface gigabitEthernet 0/0
GigabitEthernet0/0 is up, line protocol is up
  IPv6 is enabled, link-local address is FE80::32F7:DFF:FEA3:DA0
  No Virtual link-local address(es):
  Global unicast address(es):
    2001:DB8:ACAD:1::1, subnet is 2001:DB8:ACAD:1::/64
  Joined group address(es):
    FF02::1
    FF02::1:FF00:1
```

Figure 1-21   Verify the IPv6 Configuration on R1 G0/0

> **Note**
>
> The entire output of the **show ipv6 interface** command in Figure 1-21 can be viewed in the online course on page 1.1.4.2 graphic number 2.

The **show ipv6 route** command shown in Figure 1-22 can be used to verify that IPv6 networks and specific IPv6 interface addresses have been installed in the IPv6 routing table. The **show ipv6 route** command will only display IPv6 networks, not IPv4 networks.

```
<output omitted>

C   2001:DB8:ACAD:1::/64 [0/0]
     via GigabitEthernet0/0, directly connected
L   2001:DB8:ACAD:1::1/128 [0/0]
     via GigabitEthernet0/0, receive
C   2001:DB8:ACAD:2::/64 [0/0]
     via GigabitEthernet0/1, directly connected
L   2001:DB8:ACAD:2::1/128 [0/0]
```

Figure 1-22   Verify the R1 IPv6 Routing Table

> **Note**
>
> The entire output of the **show ipv6 route** command in Figure 1-22 can be viewed in the online course on page 1.1.4.2 graphic number 3.

Within the routing table, a 'C' next to a route indicates that this is a directly connected network. When the router interface is configured with a global unicast address and is in the "up/up" state, the IPv6 prefix and prefix length is added to the IPv6 routing table as a connected route.

The IPv6 global unicast address configured on the interface is also installed in the routing table as a local route, as indicated with an 'L' next to the route entry. The local route has a /128 prefix. Local routes are used by the routing table to efficiently process packets with the interface address of the router as the destination.

The **ping** command for IPv6 is identical to the command used with IPv4 except that an IPv6 address is used. As shown in Figure 1-23, the **ping** command is used to verify Layer 3 connectivity between R1 and PC1.

```
R1#ping 2001:db8:acad:1::10
Type escape sequence to abort.
Sending 5, 100-byte ICMP Echos to 2001:DB8:ACAD:1::10, timeout is 2
seconds:
!!!!!
Success rate is 100 percent (5/5)
R1#
```

Figure 1-23   Verify Connectivity on R1

Other useful IPv6 verification commands include:

- **show interface**
- **show ipv6 routers**

Filter Show Command Output (1.1.4.3)

Commands that generate multiple screens of output are, by default, paused after 24 lines. At the end of the paused output, the --More-- text displays. Pressing Enter displays the next line and pressing the spacebar displays the next set of lines. Use the **terminal length** *number* command to specify the number of lines to be displayed. A value of 0 (zero) prevents the router from pausing between screens of output.

Another very useful feature that improves the user experience in the command-line interface (CLI) is the filtering of **show** output. Filtering commands can be used to display specific sections of output. To enable the filtering command, enter a pipe (l) character after the **show** command and then enter a filtering parameter and a filtering expression.

The filtering parameters that can be configured after the pipe include:

- **section:** Shows entire section that starts with the filtering expression
- **include:** Includes all output lines that match the filtering expression
- **exclude:** Excludes all output lines that match the filtering expression
- **begin:** Shows all the output lines from a certain point, starting with the line that matches the filtering expression

Note

Output filters can be used in combination with any **show** command.

Figures 1-24 through 1-27 provide examples of the various output filters. The example in Figure 1-24 uses the pipe character and the **section** keyword.

```
R1# show running-config | section line vty
line vty 0 4
 password 7 030752180500
 login
 transport input all
R1#
```

Figure 1-24   Filter **show** Commands by Section

The example in Figure 1-25 uses the pipe character and the **include** keyword.

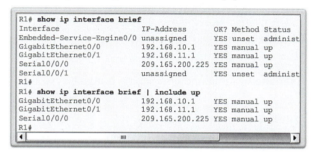

```
R1# show ip interface brief
Interface                  IP-Address       OK? Method Status
Embedded-Service-Engine0/0 unassigned       YES unset  administ
GigabitEthernet0/0         192.168.10.1     YES manual up
GigabitEthernet0/1         192.168.11.1     YES manual up
Serial0/0/0                209.165.200.225 YES manual up
Serial0/0/1                unassigned       YES unset  administ
R1#
R1# show ip interface brief | include up
GigabitEthernet0/0         192.168.10.1     YES manual up
GigabitEthernet0/1         192.168.11.1     YES manual up
Serial0/0/0                209.165.200.225 YES manual up
R1#
```

Figure 1-25   Filter **show** Commands by Common Keyword

Note

The entire output of the **show ip interface brief** command in Figure 1-25 can be viewed in the online course on page 1.1.4.3 graphic number 2.

The example in Figure 1-26 uses the pipe character and the **exclude** keyword.

```
R1# show ip interface brief
Interface                  IP-Address       OK? Method Status
Embedded-Service-Engine0/0 unassigned       YES unset  administ
GigabitEthernet0/0         192.168.10.1     YES manual up
GigabitEthernet0/1         192.168.11.1     YES manual up
Serial0/0/0                209.165.200.225 YES manual up
Serial0/0/1                unassigned       YES unset  administ

R1# show ip interface brief | exclude unassigned
Interface                  IP-Address       OK? Method Status
GigabitEthernet0/0         192.168.10.1     YES manual up
GigabitEthernet0/1         192.168.11.1     YES manual up
Serial0/0/0                209.165.200.225 YES manual up

R1#
```

Figure 1-26   Filter **show** Commands to Exclude Rows of Output

> **Note**
>
> The entire output of the **show ip interface brief** command in Figure 1-26 can be viewed in the online course on page 1.1.4.3 graphic number 3.

The example in Figure 1-27 uses the pipe character and the **begin** keyword.

```
R1# show ip route | begin Gateway
Gateway of last resort is not set

      192.168.10.0/24 is variably subnetted, 2 subnets, 2 masks
C        192.168.10.0/24 is directly connected, GigabitEthernet0/0
L        192.168.10.1/32 is directly connected, GigabitEthernet0/0
      192.168.11.0/24 is variably subnetted, 2 subnets, 2 masks
C        192.168.11.0/24 is directly connected, GigabitEthernet0/1
L        192.168.11.1/32 is directly connected, GigabitEthernet0/1
      209.165.200.0/24 is variably subnetted, 2 subnets, 2 masks
C        209.165.200.224/30 is directly connected, Serial0/0/0
L        209.165.200.225/32 is directly connected, Serial0/0/0
R1#
```

Figure 1-27   Filter **show** Commands Beginning from a Keyword

Activity 1.1.4.3: Filter Command Output

Go to the online course to use the Syntax Checker in the fifth graphic to practice how to filter command output on the R1 router.

Command History Feature (1.1.4.4)

The command history feature is useful, because it temporarily stores the list of executed commands to be recalled.

To recall commands in the history buffer, press **Ctrl+P** or the **Up Arrow** key. The command output begins with the most recent command. Repeat the key sequence to recall successively older commands. To return to more recent commands in the history buffer, press **Ctrl+N** or the **Down Arrow** key. Repeat the key sequence to recall successively more recent commands.

By default, command history is enabled and the system captures the last 10 command lines in its history buffer. Use the **show history** privileged EXEC command to display the contents of the buffer.

It is also practical to increase the number of command lines that the history buffer records during the current terminal session only. Use the **terminal history size** user EXEC command to increase or decrease the size of the buffer.

For example, the following displays a sample of the **terminal history size** and **show history** commands:

```
R1# terminal history size 200
R1#
R1# show history
  show ip interface brief
  show interface g0/0
  show ip interface g0/1
  show ip route
  show ip route 209.165.200.224
  show running-config interface s0/0/0
  terminal history size 200
  show history
R1#
```

Activity 1.1.4.4: Adjusting the Command History

Go to the online course to use the Syntax Checker in the second graphic to adjust and list the command history output on the R1 router.

Packet Tracer Activity 1.1.4.5: Configuring and Verifying a Small Network

In this activity, you will configure a router with basic settings including IP addressing. You will also configure a switch for remote management and configure the PCs. After you have successfully verified connectivity, you will use **show** commands to gather information about the network.

Lab 1.1.4.6: Configuring Basic Router Settings with IOS CLI

In this lab, you will complete the following objectives:

- Part 1: Set Up the Topology and Initialize Devices
- Part 2 Configure Devices and Verify Connectivity
- Part 3: Display Router Information
- Part 4: Configure IPv6 and Verify Connectivity

Lab 1.1.4.7: Configuring Basic Router Settings with CCP

In this lab, you will complete the following objectives:

- Part 1: Set Up the Topology and Initialize Devices
- Part 2: Configure Devices and Verify Connectivity
- Part 3: Configure Router to Allow CCP Access
- Part 4: (Optional) Install and Set Up CCP on PC-A
- Part 5: Configure R1 Settings Using CCP
- Part 6: Use CCP Utilities

Routing Decisions (1.2)

The key to understanding the role of a router in the network is to understand that a router is a Layer 3 device responsible for forwarding packets. However, a router also operates at Layers 1 and 2.

Router Switching Function (1.2.1.1)

A primary function of a router is to forward packets toward their destination. This is accomplished by using a switching function, which is the process used by a router to accept a packet on one interface and forward it out of another interface. A key responsibility of the switching function is to encapsulate packets in the appropriate data link frame type for the outgoing data link.

> **Note**
>
> In this context, the term "switching" literally means moving packets from source to destination and should not be confused with the function of a Layer 2 switch.

After the router has determined the exit interface using the path determination function, the router must encapsulate the packet into the data link frame of the outgoing interface.

What does a router do with a packet received from one network and destined for another network? The router performs the following three major steps:

Step 1. De-encapsulates the Layer 3 packet by removing the Layer 2 frame header and trailer.

Step 2. Examines the destination IP address of the IP packet to find the best path in the routing table.

Step 3.   If the router finds a path to the destination, it encapsulates the Layer 3 packet into a new Layer 2 frame and forwards the frame out the exit interface.

As shown in Figure 1-28, devices have Layer 3 IPv4 addresses and Ethernet interfaces have Layer 2 data link addresses. For example, PC1 is configured with IPv4 address 192.168.1.10 and an example MAC address of 0A-10. As a packet travels from the source device to the final destination device, the Layer 3 IP addresses do not change. However, the Layer 2 data link addresses change at every hop as the packet is de-encapsulated and re-encapsulated in a new frame by each router. It is very likely that the packet is encapsulated in a different type of Layer 2 frame than the one in which it was received. For example, an Ethernet encapsulated frame might be received by the router on a FastEthernet interface, and then processed to be forwarded out of a serial interface as a Point-to-Point Protocol (PPP) encapsulated frame.

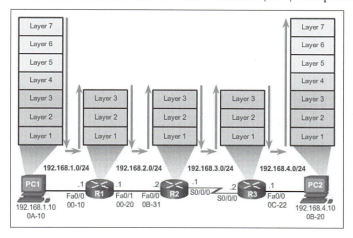

Figure 1-28   Encapsulating and De-Encapsulating Packets

Send a Packet (1.2.1.2)

In the animation in the online course, PC1 is sending a packet to PC2.

Video 1.2.1.2: PC1 Sends a Packet to PC2

Go to the online course and play the animation of a packet being sent from PC1 to PC2.

PC1 must determine if the destination IPv4 address is on the same network. PC1 determines its own subnet by doing an **AND** operation on its own IPv4 address and subnet mask. This produces the network address that PC1 belongs to. Next, PC1 does this same **AND** operation using the packet destination IPv4 address and the PC1 subnet mask.

If the destination network address is the same network as PC1, then PC1 does not use the default gateway. Instead, PC1 refers to its ARP cache for the MAC address of the device with that destination IPv4 address. If the MAC address is not in the cache, then PC1 generates an ARP request to acquire the address to complete the packet and send it to the destination. If the destination network address is on a different network, then PC1 forwards the packet to its default gateway.

To determine the MAC address of the default gateway, PC1 checks its ARP table for the IPv4 address of the default gateway and its associated MAC address.

If an ARP entry does not exist in the ARP table for the default gateway, PC1 sends an ARP request. Router R1 sends back an ARP reply. PC1 can then forward the packet to the MAC address of the default gateway, the Fa0/0 interface of router R1.

A similar process is used for IPv6 packets. Instead of the ARP process, IPv6 address resolution uses ICMPv6 Neighbor Solicitation and Neighbor Advertisement messages. IPv6-to-MAC address mappings are kept in a table similar to the ARP cache, called the neighbor cache.

Forward to the Next Hop (1.2.1.3)

The following processes take place when R1 receives the Ethernet frame from PC1:

1. R1 examines the destination MAC address, which matches the MAC address of the receiving interface, FastEthernet 0/0. R1, therefore, copies the frame into its buffer.

2. R1 identifies the Ethernet Type field as 0x800, which means that the Ethernet frame contains an IPv4 packet in the data portion of the frame.

3. R1 de-encapsulates the Ethernet frame.

4. Because the destination IPv4 address of the packet does not match any of the directly connected networks of R1, R1 consults its routing table to route this packet. R1 searches the routing table for a network address that would include the destination IPv4 address of the packet as a host address within that network. In this example, the routing table has a route for the 192.168.4.0/24 network. The destination IPv4 address of the packet is 192.168.4.10, which is a host IPv4 address on that network.

The route that R1 finds to the 192.168.4.0/24 network has a next-hop IPv4 address of 192.168.2.2 and an exit interface of FastEthernet 0/1. This means that the IPv4 packet is encapsulated in a new Ethernet frame with the destination MAC address of the IPv4 address of the next-hop router.

Because the exit interface is on an Ethernet network, R1 must resolve the next-hop IPv4 address with a destination MAC address using ARP:

1. R1 looks up the next-hop IPv4 address of 192.168.2.2 in its ARP cache. If the entry is not in the ARP cache, R1 would send an ARP request out of its FastEthernet 0/1 interface and R2 would send back an ARP reply. R1 would then update its ARP cache with an entry for 192.168.2.2 and the associated MAC address.

2. The IPv4 packet is now encapsulated into a new Ethernet frame and forwarded out the FastEthernet 0/1 interface of R1.

The animation in the online course illustrates how R1 forwards the packet to R2.

Video

Video 1.2.1.3: R1 Forwards the Packet to R2

Go to the online course and play the animation of a packet being sent through three routers from sender to receiver.

Packet Routing (1.2.1.4)

The following processes take place when R2 receives the frame on its Fa0/0 interface:

1. R2 examines the destination MAC address, which matches the MAC address of the receiving interface, FastEthernet 0/0. R2, therefore, copies the frame into its buffer.

2. R2 identifies the Ethernet Type field as 0x800, which means that the Ethernet frame contains an IPv4 packet in the data portion of the frame.

3. R2 de-encapsulates the Ethernet frame.

4. Because the destination IPv4 address of the packet does not match any of the interface addresses of R2, R2 consults its routing table to route this packet. R2 searches the routing table for the destination IPv4 address of the packet using the same process R1 used.

5. The routing table of R2 has a route to the 192.168.4.0/24 network, with a next-hop IPv4 address of 192.168.3.2 and an exit interface of Serial 0/0/0. Because the exit interface is not an Ethernet network, R2 does not have to resolve the next-hop IPv4 address with a destination MAC address.

6. The IPv4 packet is now encapsulated into a new data link frame and sent out the Serial 0/0/0 exit interface.

When the interface is a point-to-point (P2P) serial connection, the router encapsulates the IPv4 packet into the proper data link frame format used by the exit interface (HDLC, PPP, etc.). Because there are no MAC addresses on serial interfaces, R2 sets the data link destination address to an equivalent of a broadcast (MAC address: FF:FF:FF:FF:FF:FF).

The animation in the online course illustrates how R2 forwards the packet to R3.

Video

Video 1.2.1.4: R2 Forwards the Packet to R3

Go to the online course and play the animation of a packet being sent from R2 to R3.

Reach the Destination (1.2.1.5)

The following processes take place when the frame arrives at R3:

1. R3 copies the data link PPP frame into its buffer.

2. R3 de-encapsulates the data link PPP frame.

3. R3 searches the routing table for the destination IPv4 address of the packet. The routing table has a route to a directly connected network on R3. This means that the packet can be sent directly to the destination device and does not need to be sent to another router.

Because the exit interface is a directly connected Ethernet network, R3 must resolve the destination IPv4 address of the packet with a destination MAC address:

1. R3 searches for the destination IPv4 address of the packet in its Address Resolution Protocol (ARP) cache. If the entry is not in the ARP cache, R3 sends an ARP request out of its FastEthernet 0/0 interface. PC2 sends back an ARP reply with its MAC address. R3 then updates its ARP cache with an entry for 192.168.4.10 and the MAC address that is returned in the ARP reply.

2. The IPv4 packet is encapsulated into a new Ethernet data link frame and sent out the FastEthernet 0/0 interface of R3.

3. When PC2 receives the frame, it examines the destination MAC address, which matches the MAC address of the receiving interface, its Ethernet network interface card (NIC). PC2, therefore, copies the rest of the frame into its buffer.

4. PC2 identifies the Ethernet Type field as 0x800, which means that the Ethernet frame contains an IPv4 packet in the data portion of the frame.

5. PC2 de-encapsulates the Ethernet frame and passes the IPv4 packet to the IPv4 process of its operating system.

The animation in the online course illustrates how R3 forwards the packet to PC2.

Video

Video 1.2.1.5: R3 Forwards the Packet to PC2

Go to the online course and play the animation of a packet being sent from R3 to PC2.

Interactive Graphic

Activity 1.2.1.6: Match Layer 2 and Layer 3 Addressing

Go to the online course to perform this practice activity.

Path Determination (1.2.2)

This section discusses the best path to send packets, load balancing, and the concept of administrative distance.

Routing Decisions (1.2.2.1)

A primary function of a router is to determine the best path to use to send packets. To determine the best path, the router searches its routing table for a network address that matches the destination IP address of the packet.

The routing table search results in one of three path determinations:

- *Directly connected network*: If the destination IP address of the packet belongs to a device on a network that is directly connected to one of the interfaces of the router, that packet is forwarded directly to the destination device. This means that the destination IP address of the packet is a host address on the same network as the interface of the router.

- *Remote network*: If the destination IP address of the packet belongs to a remote network, then the packet is forwarded to another router. Remote networks can only be reached by forwarding packets to another router.

- **No route determined:** If the destination IP address of the packet does not belong to either a connected or remote network, the router determines if there is a Gateway of Last Resort available. A *Gateway of Last Resort* is set when a default route is configured on a router. If there is a default route, the packet is forwarded to the Gateway of Last Resort. If the router does not have a default route, then the packet is discarded. If the packet is discarded, the router sends an ICMP Unreachable message to the source IP address of the packet.

The logic flowchart in Figure 1-29 illustrates the router packet-forwarding decision process.

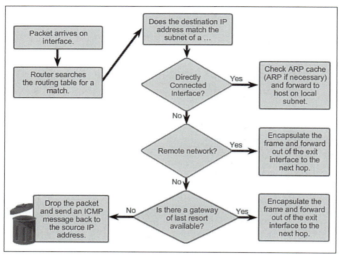

Figure 1-29   Packet Forwarding Decision Process

Best Path (1.2.2.2)

Determining the best path involves the evaluation of multiple paths to the same destination network and selecting the optimum or shortest path to reach that network. Whenever multiple paths to the same network exist, each path uses a different exit interface on the router to reach that network.

The best path is selected by a routing protocol based on the value or metric it uses to determine the distance to reach a network. A *metric* is the quantitative value used to measure the distance to a given network. The *best path* to a network is the path with the lowest metric.

Dynamic routing protocols typically use their own rules and metrics to build and update routing tables. The routing algorithm generates a value, or a metric, for each path through the network. Metrics can be based on either a single characteristic or several characteristics of a path. Some routing protocols can base route selection on multiple metrics, combining them into a single metric.

The following lists some dynamic protocols and the metrics they use:

- **Routing Information Protocol (RIP)** : Hop count

- **Open Shortest Path First (OSPF):** Cisco routers use a cost based on cumulative bandwidth from source to destination

- **Enhanced Interior Gateway Routing Protocol (EIGRP):** Bandwidth, delay, load, reliability

The animation in the online course highlights how the path may be different depending on the metric being used.

Video

Video 1.2.2.2: Hop Count vs. Bandwidth as a Metric

Go to the online course and play the animation showing how a network path may be different depending on the metric being used.

Load Balancing (1.2.2.3)

What happens if a routing table has two or more paths with identical metrics to the same destination network?

When a router has two or more paths to a destination with equal cost metrics, then the router forwards the packets using both paths equally. This is called *equal cost load balancing.* The routing table contains the single destination network, but has multiple exit interfaces, one for each equal cost path. The router forwards packets using the multiple exit interfaces listed in the routing table.

If configured correctly, load balancing can increase the effectiveness and performance of the network. Equal cost load balancing can be configured to use both dynamic routing protocols and static routes.

By default, Cisco routers can load balance up to four equal cost paths. The maximum number of equal cost paths depends on the routing protocol and IOS version.

EIGRP supports equal cost load balancing and is also the only routing protocol to support *unequal cost load balancing*. Unequal cost load balancing is when a router distributes traffic over network interfaces, even those that are different distances from the destination address.

Note

EIGRP supports unequal cost load balancing by using the `variance` command.

The animation in the online course provides an example of equal cost load balancing.

Video

Video 1.2.2.3: Equal Cost Load Balancing

Go to the online course and play the animation showing an example of equal cost load balancing

Administrative Distance (1.2.2.4)

It is possible for a router to be configured with multiple routing protocols and static routes. If this occurs, the routing table may have more than one route source for the same destination network. For example, if both RIP and EIGRP are configured on a router, both routing protocols may learn of the same destination network. However, each routing protocol may decide on a different path to reach the destination based on that routing protocol's metrics. RIP chooses a path based on hop count, whereas EIGRP chooses a path based on its composite metric. How does the router know which route to use?

Cisco IOS uses what is known as the *administrative distance* (AD) to determine the route to install into the IP routing table. The AD represents the "trustworthiness" of the route; the lower the AD, the more trustworthy the route source. For example, a static route has an AD of 1, whereas an EIGRP-discovered route has an AD of 90. Given two separate routes to the same destination, the router chooses the route with the lowest AD. When a router has the choice of a static route and an EIGRP route, the static route takes precedence. Similarly, a directly connected route with an AD of 0 takes precedence over a static route with an AD of 1.

Table 1-5 lists various routing protocols and their associated ADs.

Table 1-5   Default Administrative Distances

Route Source	Administrative Distance
Connected	0
Static	1
EIGRP summary route	5
External BGP	20
Internal EIGRP	90
IGRP	100
OSPF	110
IS-IS	115
RIP	120
External EIGRP	170
Internal BGP	200
Unknown	255

Activity 1.2.2.5: Order the Steps in the Packet Forwarding Process

Go to the online course to perform these four practice activities.

Router Operation (1.3)

The primary function of a router is to forward packets toward their destination network, the destination IP address of the packet. To do this, a router needs to search the routing information stored in its routing table. In the following sections, you will learn how a router builds the routing table. Then, you will learn the three basic routing principles.

Analyze the Routing Table (1.3.1)

A good understanding of routing tables is crucial for any network administrator.

The Routing Table (1.3.1.1)

The *routing table* of a router stores information about:

- **Directly connected routes:** These routes come from the active router interfaces. Routers add a directly connected route when an interface is configured with an IP address and is activated.

- **Remote routes:** These are remote networks connected to other routers. Routes to these networks can be either statically configured or dynamically configured using dynamic routing protocols.

Specifically, a routing table is a data file in RAM that is used to store route information about directly connected and remote networks. The routing table contains network or next-hop associations. These associations tell a router that a particular destination can be optimally reached by sending the packet to a specific router that represents the next hop on the way to the final destination. The next-hop association can also be the outgoing or exit interface to the next destination.

Figure 1-30 identifies the directly connected networks and remote networks of router R1.

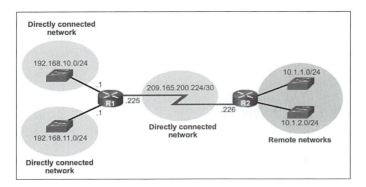

Figure 1-30   Directly Connected and Remote Network Routes

Routing Table Sources (1.3.1.2)

On a Cisco IOS router, the **show ip route** command can be used to display the IPv4 routing table of a router. A router provides additional route information, including how the route was learned, how long the route has been in the table, and which specific interface to use to get to a predefined destination.

Entries in the routing table can be added as:

- **Local Route interfaces:** Added when an interface is configured and active. This entry is only displayed in IOS 15 or newer for IPv4 routes and all IOS releases for IPv6 routes.

- **Directly connected interfaces:** Added to the routing table when an interface is configured and active.

- **Static routes:** Added when a route is manually configured and the exit interface is active.

- **Dynamic routing protocol:** Added when routing protocols that dynamically learn about the network, such as EIGRP or OSPF, are implemented and networks are identified.

The sources of the routing table entries are identified by a code. The code identifies how the route was learned. For instance, common codes include:

- **L:** Identifies the address assigned to a router's interface. This allows the router to efficiently determine when it receives a packet for the interface instead of being forwarded.

- **C:** Identifies a directly connected network.

- **S**: Identifies a static route created to reach a specific network.
- **D**: Identifies a dynamically learned network from another router using EIGRP.
- **O**: Identifies a dynamically learned network from another router using the OSPF routing protocol.

Note

Other codes are beyond the scope of this chapter.

Figure 1-31 shows a sample routing table of R1.

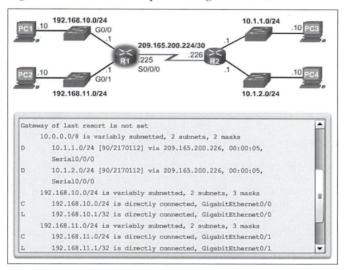

```
Gateway of last resort is not set
    10.0.0.0/8 is variably subnetted, 2 subnets, 2 masks
D      10.1.1.0/24 [90/2170112] via 209.165.200.226, 00:00:05,
       Serial0/0/0
D      10.1.2.0/24 [90/2170112] via 209.165.200.226, 00:00:05,
       Serial0/0/0
    192.168.10.0/24 is variably subnetted, 2 subnets, 3 masks
C      192.168.10.0/24 is directly connected, GigabitEthernet0/0
L      192.168.10.1/32 is directly connected, GigabitEthernet0/0
    192.168.11.0/24 is variably subnetted, 2 subnets, 3 masks
C      192.168.11.0/24 is directly connected, GigabitEthernet0/1
L      192.168.11.1/32 is directly connected, GigabitEthernet0/1
```

Figure 1-31   Routing Table of R1

Note

The entire output of the **show ip route** command in Figure 1-31 can be viewed in the online course on page 1.3.1.2.

Remote Network Routing Entries (1.3.1.3)

As a network administrator, it is imperative to know how to interpret the content of an IPv4 and IPv6 routing table. Figure 1-32 displays an IPv4 routing table entry on R1 for the route to remote network 10.1.1.0.

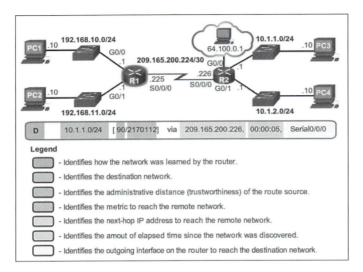

Figure 1-32   Remote Network Entry Identifiers

The entry identifies the following information:

- **Route source:** Identifies how the route was learned.

- **Destination network:** Identifies the address of the remote network.

- **Administrative distance:** Identifies the trustworthiness of the route source. Lower values indicate preferred route source.

- **Metric:** Identifies the value assigned to reach the remote network. Lower values indicate preferred routes.

- **Next-hop:** Identifies the IPv4 address of the next router to forward the packet to.

- **Route timestamp:** Identifies how much time has passed since the route was learned.

- **Outgoing interface:** Identifies the exit interface to use to forward a packet toward the final destination.

Activity 1.3.1.4: Interpret the Content of a Routing Table Entry

Go to the online course to perform this practice activity.

Directly Connected Routes (1.3.2)

How does a router add its interfaces to the routing table? Well, whenever an interface is configured with an IP address and enabled, it is automatically added as a directly connected network.

Directly Connected Interfaces (1.3.2.1)

A newly deployed router, without any configured interfaces, has an empty routing table, as shown in Figure 1-33.

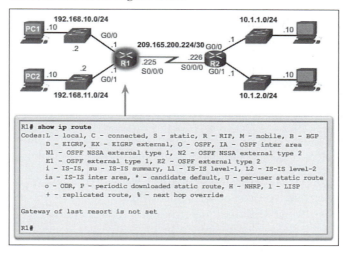

Figure 1-33   Empty Routing Table

Before the interface state is considered "up/up" and added to the IPv4 routing table, the interface must:

- Be assigned a valid IPv4 or IPv6 address
- Be activated with the **no shutdown** command
- Receive a carrier signal from another device (router, switch, host, etc.)

When the interface is up, the network of that interface is added to the routing table as a directly connected network.

Directly Connected Route Table Entries (1.3.2.2)

An active, properly configured, directly connected interface actually creates two routing table entries. Figure 1-34 displays the IPv4 routing table entries on R1 for the directly connected network 192.168.10.0.

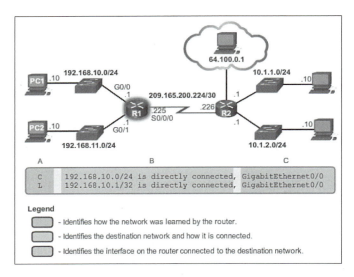

Figure 1-34   Directly Connected Network Entry Identifiers

The routing table entry for directly connected interfaces is simpler than the entries for remote networks. The entries contain the following information:

- **Route source:** Identifies how the route was learned. Directly connected interfaces have two route source codes. 'C' identifies a directly connected network. 'L' identifies the IPv4 address assigned to the router's interface.

- **Destination network:** The address of the remote network.

- **Outgoing interface:** Identifies the exit interface to use when forwarding packets to the destination network.

Note

Prior to IOS 15, local route routing table entries (L) were not displayed in the IPv4 routing table. Local route (L) entries have always been a part of the IPv6 routing table.

Directly Connected Examples (1.3.2.3)

When directly connected interfaces are enabled, Layer 1 and 2 informational messages are automatically generated.

For example, configuring the following commands on R1 would enable the directly connected Gigabit Ethernet 0/0 interface and generate the following messages:

```
R1(config)# interface gigabitethernet 0/0
R1(config-if)# description Link to LAN 1
R1(config-if)# ip address 192.168.10.1 255.255.255.0
```

```
R1(config-if)# no shutdown
R1(config-if)# exit
R1(config)#
*Jan 30 22:04:47.551: %LINK-3-UPDOWN: Interface GigabitEthernet0/0, changed state to
   down
R1(config)#
*Jan 30 22:04:50.899: %LINK-3-UPDOWN: Interface GigabitEthernet0/0, changed state to
   up
*Jan 30 22:04:51.899: %LINEPROTO-5-UPDOWN: Line protocol on Interface
   GigabitEthernet0/0, changed state to up
R1(config)#
```

As each interface is enabled, the routing table automatically adds the connected ('c')
and local ('L') entries.

The following provides an example of the routing table with the directly connected
interfaces of R1 configured and activated:

```
R1# show ip route | begin Gateway
Gateway of last resort is not set


     192.168.10.0/24 is variably subnetted, 2 subnets, 2 masks
C       192.168.10.0/24 is directly connected, GigabitEthernet0/0
L       192.168.10.1/32 is directly connected, GigabitEthernet0/0
     192.168.11.0/24 is variably subnetted, 2 subnets, 2 masks
C       192.168.11.0/24 is directly connected, GigabitEthernet0/1
L       192.168.11.1/32 is directly connected, GigabitEthernet0/1
     209.165.200.0/24 is variably subnetted, 2 subnets, 2 masks
C       209.165.200.224/30 is directly connected, Serial0/0/0
L       209.165.200.225/32 is directly connected, Serial0/0/0
R1#
```

Interactive Graphic

Activity 1.3.2.3: Configure and Activate the Interfaces on R2

Go to the online course to use the Syntax Checker in the fifth graphic to configure
the interfaces of the R2 router.

Directly Connected IPv6 Example (1.3.2.4)

Enabling directly connected IPv6 interfaces also generates Layer 1 and Layer 2 informational messages.

For example, configuring the following commands on R1 would enable the directly
connected IPv6 Gigabit Ethernet 0/0 interface and generate the following messages:

```
R1(config)# ipv6 unicast-routing
R1(config)# interface gigabitethernet 0/0
R1(config-if)# description Link to LAN 1
```

```
R1(config-if)# ipv6 address 2001:db8:acad:1::1/64
R1(config-if)# no shutdown
R1(config-if)# exit
*Feb  3 21:38:37.279: %LINK-3-UPDOWN: Interface GigabitEthernet0/0, changed state to
  down
*Feb  3 21:38:40.967: %LINK-3-UPDOWN: Interface GigabitEthernet0/0, changed state to
  up
*Feb  3 21:38:41.967: %LINEPROTO-5-UPDOWN: Line protocol on Interface
  GigabitEthernet0/0, changed state to up
R1(config)#
```

The following provides an example of the routing table with the directly connected interfaces of R1 configured and activated:

```
R1# show ipv6 route
IPv6 Routing Table - default - 5 entries
Codes: C - Connected, L - Local, S - Static, U - Per-user Static route
       B - BGP, R - RIP, H - NHRP, I1 - ISIS L1
       I2 - ISIS L2, IA - ISIS interarea, IS - ISIS summary, D - EIGRP
       EX - EIGRP external, ND - ND Default, NDp - ND Prefix, DCE - Destination
       NDr - Redirect, O - OSPF Intra, OI - OSPF Inter, OE1 - OSPF ext 1
       OE2 - OSPF ext 2, ON1 - OSPF NSSA ext 1, ON2 - OSPF NSSA ext 2
C   2001:DB8:ACAD:1::/64 [0/0]
     via GigabitEthernet0/0, directly connected
L   2001:DB8:ACAD:1::1/128 [0/0]
     via GigabitEthernet0/0, receive
C   2001:DB8:ACAD:2::/64 [0/0]
     via GigabitEthernet0/1, directly connected
L   2001:DB8:ACAD:2::1/128 [0/0]
     via GigabitEthernet0/1, receive
L   FF00::/8 [0/0]
     via Null0, receive
R1#
```

When the **show ipv6 route** command reveals a 'c' next to a route, that indicates that this is a directly connected network. An 'L' indicates the local route. In an IPv6 network, the local route has a /128 prefix. Local routes are used by the routing table to efficiently process packets with a destination address of the interface of the router.

Notice that there is also a route installed to the FF00::/8 network. This route is required for multicast routing.

Figure 1-35 displays how the **show ipv6 route** command can be combined with a specific network destination to display the details of how that route was learned by the router.

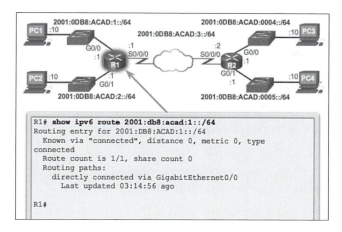

Figure 1-35   Show the IPv6 Route Entry

The following displays how connectivity to R2 can be verified using the **ping** command:

```
R1# ping 2001:db8:acad:3::2
Type escape sequence to abort.
Sending 5, 100-byte ICMP Echos to 2001:DB8:ACAD:3::2, timeout is 2 seconds:
!!!!!
Success rate is 100 percent (5/5), round-trip min/avg/max = 12/13/16 ms
R1#
```

Notice what happens when the G0/0 LAN interface of R2 is the target of the **ping** command:

```
R1# ping 2001:db8:acad:4::1
Type escape sequence to abort.
Sending 5, 100-byte ICMP Echos to 2001:DB8:ACAD:4::1, timeout is 2 seconds:

% No valid route for destination
Success rate is 0 percent (0/1)
R1#
```

The pings are unsuccessful. This is because R1 does not have an entry in the routing table to reach the 2001:DB8:ACAD:4::/64 network.

R1 requires additional information to reach a remote network. Remote network route entries can be added to the routing table using either:

- Static routing
- Dynamic routing protocols

| Packet Tracer |
| ☐ **Activity** |

Packet Tracer Activity 1.3.2.5: Investigating Directly Connected Routes

The network in the activity is already configured. You will log in to the routers and use **show** commands to discover and answer the questions below about the directly connected routes.

Statically Learned Routes (1.3.3)

Routers can dynamically learn about remote networks using a routing protocol or statically. Statically learned routes must be manually configured by an administrator. This topic introduces how to enter remote routes manually.

Static Routes (1.3.3.1)

After directly connected interfaces are configured and added to the routing table, then static or dynamic routing can be implemented.

Static routes are manually configured. They define an explicit path between two networking devices. Unlike a dynamic routing protocol, static routes are not automatically updated and must be manually reconfigured if the network topology changes. The benefits of using static routes include improved security and resource efficiency. Static routes use less bandwidth than dynamic routing protocols, and no CPU cycles are used to calculate and communicate routes. The main disadvantage to using static routes is the lack of automatic reconfiguration if the network topology changes.

There are two common types of static routes in the routing table:

■ Static route to a specific network

■ Default static route

A static route can be configured to reach a specific remote network. IPv4 static routes are configured using the **ip route** *network mask* {*next-hop-ip* | *exit-intf*} global configuration command. A static route is identified in the routing table with the code 's'.

A default static route is similar to a default gateway on a host. The default static route specifies the exit point to use when the routing table does not contain a path for the destination network.

A default static route is useful when a router has only one exit point to another router, such as when the router connects to a central router or service provider.

To configure an IPv4 default static route, use the **ip route 0.0.0.0 0.0.0.0** {*exit-intf* | *next-hop-ip*} global configuration command.

Figure 1-36 provides a simple scenario of how default and static routes can be applied.

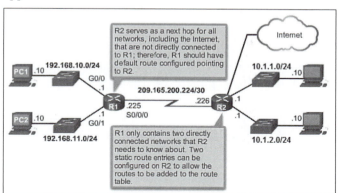

Figure 1-36   Static and Default Route Scenario

Static Route Examples (1.3.3.2)

Figure 1-37 shows the configuration of an IPv4 default static route on R1 to the Serial 0/0/0 interface. Notice that the configuration of the route generated an 's*' entry in the routing table. The 's' signifies that the route source is a static route, while the asterisk (*) identifies this route as a possible candidate to be the default route. In fact, it has been chosen as the default route as evidenced by the line that reads, "Gateway of last resort is 0.0.0.0 to network 0.0.0.0."

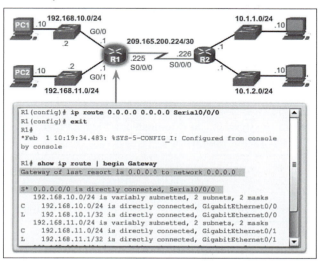

Figure 1-37   Entering and Verifying a Static Default Route

Note

The entire output of the **show ip route** command in Figure 1-37 can be viewed in the online course on page 1.3.3.2 graphic number 1.

Figure 1-38 shows the configuration of two static routes from R2 to reach the two LANs on R1. The route to 192.168.10.0/24 has been configured using the exit interface while the route to 192.168.11.0/24 has been configured using the next-hop IPv4 address. Although both are acceptable, there are some differences in how they operate. For instance, notice how different they look in the routing table. Also notice that because these static routes were to specific networks, the output indicates that the Gateway of Last Resort is not set.

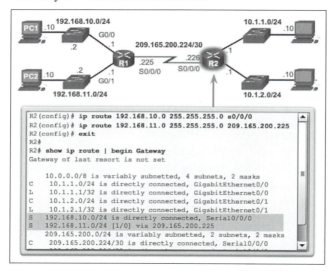

Figure 1-38   Entering and Verifying Static Routes

Note

The entire output of the **show ip route** command in Figure 1-38 can be viewed in the online course on page 1.3.3.2 graphic number 2.

Note

Static and default static routes are discussed in detail in the next chapter.

Interactive Graphic

Activity 1.3.3.2: Entering and Verifying the Static and Default Routes on R1 and R2

Go to the online course to use the Syntax Checker in the third and fourth graphics to configure a default static route on router R1 and a static route on router R2.

Static IPv6 Route Examples (1.3.3.3)

Like IPv4, IPv6 supports static and default static routes. They are used and configured like IPv4 static routes.

To configure a default static IPv6 route, use the **ipv6 route ::/0** {*ipv6-address* | *inter-
face-type interface-number*} global configuration command.

The following configures a default static route on R1 exiting out of the Serial 0/0/0
interface:

```
R1(config)# ipv6 route ::/0 s0/0/0
R1(config)# exit
R1#
```

Notice in the following output that the default static route configuration generated
an 's' entry in the routing table. The 's' signifies that the route source is a static route.
Unlike the IPv4 static route, there is no asterisk (*) or Gateway of Last Resort explicitly identified.

```
R1# show ipv6 route
IPv6 Routing Table - default - 8 entries
Codes: C - Connected, L - Local, S - Static, U - Per-user Static route
       B - BGP, R - RIP, H - NHRP, I1 - ISIS L1
       I2 - ISIS L2, IA - ISIS interarea, IS - ISIS summary, D - EIGRP
       EX - EIGRP external, ND - ND Default, NDp - ND Prefix, DCE - Destination
       NDr - Redirect, O - OSPF Intra, OI - OSPF Inter, OE1 - OSPF ext 1
       OE2 - OSPF ext 2, ON1 - OSPF NSSA ext 1, ON2 - OSPF NSSA ext 2
S    ::/0 [1/0]
     via Serial0/0/0, directly connected
C    2001:DB8:ACAD:1::/64 [0/0]
     via GigabitEthernet0/0, directly connected
L    2001:DB8:ACAD:1::1/128 [0/0]
     via GigabitEthernet0/0, receive
C    2001:DB8:ACAD:2::/64 [0/0]
     via GigabitEthernet0/1, directly connected
L    2001:DB8:ACAD:2::1/128 [0/0]
     via GigabitEthernet0/1, receive
C    2001:DB8:ACAD:3::/64 [0/0]
     via Serial0/0/0, directly connected
L    2001:DB8:ACAD:3::1/128 [0/0]
     via Serial0/0/0, receive
L    FF00::/8 [0/0]
     via Null0, receive
```

Like IPv4, static routes are routes explicitly configured to reach a specific remote network. Static IPv6 routes are configured using the **ipv6 route** *ipv6-prefix/prefix-length* {*ipv6-address | interface-type interface-number*} global configuration command.

The following example configures two static routes from R2 to reach the two LANs on R1:

```
R2(config)# ipv6 route 2001:DB8:ACAD:1::/64 2001:DB8:ACAD:3::1
R2(config)# ipv6 route 2001:DB8:ACAD:2::/64 s0/0/0
R2(config)# ^Z
R2#
```

The route to the 2001:0DB8:ACAD:2::/64 LAN is configured with an exit interface, while the route to the 2001:0DB8:ACAD:1::/64 LAN is configured with the next-hop IPv6 address. The next-hop IPv6 address can be either an IPv6 global unicast or link-local address.

The following output displays the routing table with the new static routes installed:

```
R2# show ipv6 route
IPv6 Routing Table - default - 9 entries
Codes: C - Connected, L - Local, S - Static, U - Per-user Static route
       B - BGP, R - RIP, H - NHRP, I1 - ISIS L1
       I2 - ISIS L2, IA - ISIS interarea, IS - ISIS summary, D - EIGRP
       EX - EIGRP external, ND - ND Default, NDp - ND Prefix, DCE - Destination
       NDr - Redirect, O - OSPF Intra, OI - OSPF Inter, OE1 - OSPF ext 1
       OE2 - OSPF ext 2, ON1 - OSPF NSSA ext 1, ON2 - OSPF NSSA ext 2
S   2001:DB8:ACAD:1::/64 [1/0]
     via 2001:DB8:ACAD:3::1
S   2001:DB8:ACAD:2::/64 [1/0]
     via Serial0/0/0, directly connected
C   2001:DB8:ACAD:3::/64 [0/0]
     via Serial0/0/0, directly connected
L   2001:DB8:ACAD:3::2/128 [0/0]
     via Serial0/0/0, receive
C   2001:DB8:ACAD:4::/64 [0/0]
     via GigabitEthernet0/0, directly connected
L   2001:DB8:ACAD:4::1/128 [0/0]
     via GigabitEthernet0/0, receive
C   2001:DB8:ACAD:5::/64 [0/0]
     via GigabitEthernet0/1, directly connected
L   2001:DB8:ACAD:5::1/128 [0/0]
     via GigabitEthernet0/1, receive
```

```
L    FF00::/8 [0/0]
       via Null0, receive
R2#
```

The following confirms remote network connectivity to the 2001:0DB8:ACAD:4::/64 LAN on R2 from R1:

```
R1# ping 2001:db8:acad:4::1
Type escape sequence to abort.
Sending 5, 100-byte ICMP Echos to 2001:DB8:ACAD:4::1, timeout is 2 seconds:
!!!!!
Success rate is 100 percent (5/5), round-trip min/avg/max = 12/13/16 ms
R1#
```

Dynamic Routing Protocols (1.3.4)

You just saw how a router can be manually configured with static routes to reach remote networks. In this section you will see how a dynamic routing protocol can be used to achieve the same result.

Dynamic Routing (1.3.4.1)

Dynamic routing protocols are used by routers to share information about the reachability and status of remote networks. Dynamic routing protocols perform several activities, including network discovery and maintaining routing tables.

Network discovery is the ability of a routing protocol to share information about the networks that it knows about with other routers that are also using the same routing protocol. Instead of depending on manually configured static routes to remote networks on every router, a dynamic routing protocol allows the routers to automatically learn about these networks from other routers. These networks, and the best path to each, are added to the routing table of the router, and identified as a network learned by a specific dynamic routing protocol.

During network discovery, routers exchange routes and update their routing tables. Routers have converged after they have finished exchanging and updating their routing tables. Routers then maintain the networks in their routing tables.

Figure 1-39 provides a simple scenario of how two neighboring routers would initially exchange routing information. In this simplified message exchange, R1 introduces itself and the networks it can reach. R2 responds and provides R1 with its networks.

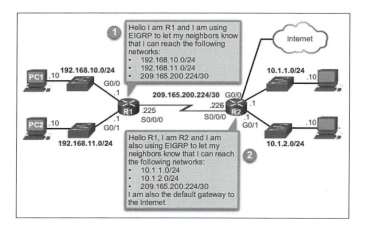

Figure 1-39   Dynamic Routing Scenario

IPv4 Routing Protocols (1.3.4.2)

A router running a dynamic routing protocol does not only make a best path determination to a network, it also determines a new best path if the initial path becomes unusable (or if the topology changes). For these reasons, dynamic routing protocols have an advantage over static routes. Routers that use dynamic routing protocols automatically share routing information with other routers and compensate for any topology changes without involving the network administrator.

Cisco ISR routers can support a variety of dynamic IPv4 routing protocols, including:

- **EIGRP**: Enhanced Interior Gateway Routing Protocol
- **OSPF**: Open Shortest Path First
- **IS-IS**: Intermediate System-to-Intermediate System
- **RIP**: Routing Information Protocol

To determine which routing protocols are supported by the IOS, use the **router ?** command in global configuration mode as shown in Figure 1-40.

> **Note**
>
> The focus of this course is on EIGRP and OSPF. RIP will be discussed only for legacy reasons; the other routing protocols supported by the IOS are beyond the scope of the CCNA certification.

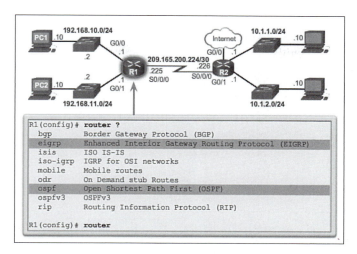

Figure 1-40   Supported IPv4 Routing Protocols

IPv4 Dynamic Routing Examples (1.3.4.3)

In this dynamic routing example, assume that R1 and R2 have been configured to support the dynamic routing protocol EIGRP. The routers also advertise directly connected networks. R2 advertises that it is the default gateway to other networks.

The output in Figure 1-41 displays the routing table of R1 after the routers have exchanged updates and converged.

```
R1# show ip route | begin Gateway
Gateway of last resort is 209.165.200.226 to network 0.0.0.0

D*EX  0.0.0.0/0 [170/2297856] via 209.165.200.226, 00:07:29, Serial0/0/0
      10.0.0.0/24 is subnetted, 2 subnets
D        10.1.1.0 [90/2172416] via 209.165.200.226, 00:07:29, Serial0/0/0
D        10.1.2.0 [90/2172416] via 209.165.200.226, 00:07:29, Serial0/0/0
      192.168.10.0/24 is variably subnetted, 2 subnets, 2 masks
C        192.168.10.0/24 is directly connected, GigabitEthernet0/0
L        192.168.10.1/32 is directly connected, GigabitEthernet0/0
      192.168.11.0/24 is variably subnetted, 2 subnets, 2 masks
C        192.168.11.0/24 is directly connected, GigabitEthernet0/1
L        192.168.11.1/32 is directly connected, GigabitEthernet0/1
      209.165.200.0/24 is variably subnetted, 2 subnets, 2 masks
C        209.165.200.224/30 is directly connected, Serial0/0/0
L        209.165.200.225/32 is directly connected, Serial0/0/0
R1#
```

Figure 1-41   Verifying Dynamic Routes

Along with the connected and link-local interfaces, there are three 'D' entries in the routing table:

- The entry beginning with 'D*EX' identifies that the source of this entry was EIGRP ('D'). The route is a candidate to be a default route ('*'), and the route is an external route ('EX') forwarded by EIGRP.

■ The other two 'D' entries are routes installed in the routing table based on the update from R2 advertising its LANs.

IPv6 Routing Protocols (1.3.4.4)

As shown in Figure 1-42, ISR routers can support dynamic IPv6 routing protocols, including:

■ RIPng (RIP next generation)

■ OSPFv3

■ EIGRP for IPv6

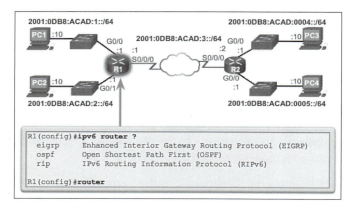

Figure 1-42   Supported IPv6 Routing Protocols

Support for dynamic IPv6 routing protocols is dependent on hardware and IOS version. Most of the modifications in the routing protocols are to support the longer IPv6 addresses and different header structures.

To enable IPv6 routers to forward traffic, you must configure the **ipv6 unicast-routing** global configuration command.

IPv6 Dynamic Routing Examples (1.3.4.5)

Routers R1 and R2 have been configured with the dynamic routing protocol EIGRP for IPv6. (This is the IPv6 equivalent of EIGRP for IPv4.)

To view the routing table on R1, enter the **show ipv6 route** command, as shown in the following output. The output displays the routing table of R1 after the routers have exchanged updates and converged. Along with the connected and local routes, there are two 'D' entries (EIGRP routes) in the routing table.

```
R1# show ipv6 route
IPv6 Routing Table - default - 9 entries
Codes: C - Connected, L - Local, S - Static, U - Per-user Static route
       B - BGP, R - RIP, H - NHRP, I1 - ISIS L1
       I2 - ISIS L2, IA - ISIS interarea, IS - ISIS summary, D - EIGRP
       EX - EIGRP external, ND - ND Default, NDp - ND Prefix, DCE - Destination
       NDr - Redirect, O - OSPF Intra, OI - OSPF Inter, OE1 - OSPF ext 1
       OE2 - OSPF ext 2, ON1 - OSPF NSSA ext 1, ON2 - OSPF NSSA ext 2
C    2001:DB8:ACAD:1::/64 [0/0]
     via GigabitEthernet0/0, directly connected
L    2001:DB8:ACAD:1::1/128 [0/0]
     via GigabitEthernet0/0, receive
C    2001:DB8:ACAD:2::/64 [0/0]
     via GigabitEthernet0/1, directly connected
L    2001:DB8:ACAD:2::1/128 [0/0]
     via GigabitEthernet0/1, receive
C    2001:DB8:ACAD:3::/64 [0/0]
     via Serial0/0/0, directly connected
L    2001:DB8:ACAD:3::1/128 [0/0]
     via Serial0/0/0, receive
D    2001:DB8:ACAD:4::/64 [90/2172416]
     via FE80::D68C:B5FF:FECE:A120, Serial0/0/0
D    2001:DB8:ACAD:5::/64 [90/2172416]
     via FE80::D68C:B5FF:FECE:A120, Serial0/0/0
L    FF00::/8 [0/0]
     via Null0, receive
R1#
```

Summary (1.4)

Class Activity 1.4.1.1: We Really Could Use a Map!

Scenario

Use the Ashland and Richmond routing tables shown in the file provided with this activity.

With the help of a classmate, draw a network topology using the information from the tables.

To assist you with this activity, follow these guidelines:

- Start with the Ashland router—use its routing table to identify ports and IP addresses/networks.
- Add the Richmond router—use its routing table to identify ports and IP addresses/networks.
- Add any other intermediary and end devices as specified by the tables.

In addition, record answers from your group to the reflection questions provided with this activity.

Be prepared to share your work with another group and/or the class.

This chapter introduced the router. The main purpose of a router is to connect multiple networks and forward packets from one network to the next. This means that a router typically has multiple interfaces. Each interface is a member or host on a different IP network.

Cisco IOS uses what is known as the administrative distance (AD) to determine the route to install into the IP routing table. The routing table is a list of networks known by the router. The routing table includes network addresses for its own interfaces, which are the directly connected networks, as well as network addresses for remote networks. A remote network is a network that can only be reached by forwarding the packet to another router.

Remote networks are added to the routing table in one of two ways: either by the network administrator manually configuring static routes or by implementing a dynamic routing protocol. Static routes do not have as much overhead as dynamic routing protocols; however, static routes can require more maintenance if the topology is constantly changing or is unstable.

Dynamic routing protocols automatically adjust to changes without any intervention from the network administrator. Dynamic routing protocols require more CPU processing and also use a certain amount of link capacity for routing updates and messages. In many cases, a routing table will contain both static and dynamic routes.

Routers make their primary forwarding decision at Layer 3, the network layer. However, router interfaces participate in Layers 1, 2, and 3. Layer 3 IP packets are encapsulated into a Layer 2 data link frame and encoded into bits at Layer 1. Router interfaces participate in Layer 2 processes associated with their encapsulation. For example, an Ethernet interface on a router participates in the ARP process like other hosts on that LAN.

The Cisco IP routing table is not a flat database. The routing table is actually a hierarchical structure that is used to speed up the lookup process when locating routes and forwarding packets.

Components of the IPv6 routing table are very similar to the IPv4 routing table. For instance, it is populated using directly connected interfaces, static routes, and dynamically learned routes.

Practice

The following activities provide practice with the topics introduced in this chapter. The Labs and Class Activities are available in the companion *Routing Protocols Lab Manual* (978-1-58713-322-0). The Packet Tracer Activities PKA files are found in the online course.

Class Activities

Class Activity 1.0.1.2: Do We Really Need a Map?

Class Activity 1.4.1.1: We Really Could Use a Map!

Labs

Lab 1.1.1.9: Mapping the Internet

Lab 1.1.4.6: Configuring Basic Router Settings with IOS CLI

Lab 1.1.4.7: Configuring Basic Router Settings with CCP

Packet Tracer
Activity

Packet Tracer Activities

Packet Tracer Activity 1.1.1.8: Using Traceroute to Discover the Network

Packet Tracer Activity 1.1.2.9: Documenting the Network

Packet Tracer Activity 1.1.3.5: Configuring IPv4 and IPv6 Interfaces

Packet Tracer Activity 1.1.4.5: Configuring and Verifying a Small Network

Packet Tracer Activity 1.3.2.5: Investigating Directly Connected Routes

Check Your Understanding Questions

Complete all the review questions listed here to test your understanding of the topics and concepts in this chapter. The appendix, "Answers to the 'Check Your Understanding' Questions," lists the answers.

1. Which of the following matches a router component with its function?

    A. Flash: Permanently stores the bootstrap program

    B. ROM: Permanently stores the startup configuration file

    C. NVRAM: Permanently stores the operating system image

    D. RAM: Stores the routing tables and ARP cache

2. Which command can a technician use to determine whether router serial ports have IP addresses that are assigned to them?

    A. **show interfaces ip brief**

    B. **show controllers all**

    C. **show ip config**

    D. **show ip interface brief**

3. Which of the following commands will set and automatically encrypt the privileged EXEC mode password to "quiz"?

    A. R1(config)# **enable secret quiz**

    B. R1(config)# **password secret quiz**

    C. R1(config)# **enable password secret quiz**

    D. R1(config)# **enable secret password quiz**

4. Which routing principle is correct?

    A. If one router has certain information in its routing table, all adjacent routers have the same information.

    B. Routing information about a path from one network to another implies routing information about the reverse, or return, path.

    C. Every router makes its routing decisions alone, based on the information it has in its own routing table.

    D. Every router makes its routing decisions based on the information it has in its own routing table and the information in its neighbor routing tables.

5. What two tasks do dynamic routing protocols perform? (Choose two.)

    A. Discover hosts

    B. Update and maintain routing tables

    C. Propagate host default gateways

    D. Network discovery

    E. Assign IP addressing

6. A network engineer is configuring a new router. The interfaces have been configured with IP addresses and activated, but no routing protocols or static routes have been configured yet. What routes are present in the routing table?

    A. Default routes

    B. Remote network routes

    C. Directly connected routes

    D. No route as the routing table is empty

7. Which statements are correct regarding how a router forwards packets? (Choose two.)

    A. If the packet is destined for a remote network, the router forwards the packet out all interfaces that might be a next hop to that network.

    B. If the packet is destined for a directly connected network, the router forwards the packet out the exit interface indicated by the routing table.

    C. If the packet is destined for a remote network, the router forwards the packet based on the information in the router host table.

    D. If the packet is destined for a remote network, the router sends the packet to the next-hop IP address in the routing table.

    E. If the packet is destined for a directly connected network, the router forwards the packet based on the destination MAC address.

    F. If the packet is destined for a directly connected network, the router forwards the packet to the switch on the next-hop VLAN.

8. Which command is used to explicitly configure a local IPv6 address on a router interface?

    A. **ipv6 enable**

    B. **ipv6 address** *ipv6-address/prefix-length*

    C. **ipv6 address** *ipv6-address/prefix-length* **eui-64**

    D. **ipv6 address** *ipv6-address/prefix-length* **link-local**

9. Which statement is true regarding metrics used by routing protocols?

    A. A metric is the quantitative value that a routing protocol uses to measure a given route.

    B. A metric is a Cisco-proprietary means to convert distances to a standard unit.

    C. Metrics represent a composite value of the amount of packet loss occurring for all routing protocols.

    D. Metrics are used by the router to determine whether a packet has an error and should be dropped.

10. The network administrator configured the **ip route 0.0.0.0 0.0.0.0 serial 0/0/0 command** on the router. How will this command appear in the routing table, assuming that the Serial 0/0/0 interface is up?

    A. D 0.0.0.0/0 is directly connected, Serial0/0/0

    B. S* 0.0.0.0/0 is directly connected, Serial0/0/0

    C. S* 0.0.0.0/0 [1/0] via 192.168.2.2

    D. C 0.0.0.0/0 [1/0] via 192.168.2.2

11. How many equal-cost paths can a dynamic routing protocol use for load balancing by default?

    A. 2

    B. 3

    C. 4

    D. 6

12. What two statements correctly describe the concepts of administrative distance and metric? (Choose two.)

    A. Administrative distance refers to the trustworthiness of a particular route.

    B. A router first installs routes with higher administrative distances in its routing table.

    C. Routes with the smallest metric to the destination indicate the best path.

    D. Metrics are used by the router to determine whether a packet has an error and should be dropped.

    E. The metric is always determined based on hop count.

13. When a packet travels from router to router to its destination, what address continually changes from hop to hop?

   A.   Source and destination Layer 2 address

   B.   Source Layer 3 address

   C.   Destination Layer 3 address

   D.   Destination port

14. Describe the internal router hardware components, and outline the purpose of each.

15. Describe the router bootup process from power on to final configuration.

16. What are two important functions that a router performs?

17. Describe the steps necessary to configure basic settings on a router.

18. Describe the importance of the routing table. What purposes does it serve?

19. What are the three basic ways a router learns about networks?

20. What three pieces of information must be configured on a host to forward packets to remote networks? (Choose three.)

   A.   Clock rate

   B.   Default gateway

   C.   DHCP server address hostname

   D.   DNS server address

   E.   IP address

   F.   Subnet mask

21. A serial interface has been configured with an IP address and the clock rate. However, the **show ip interface brief** command indicates that the interface is administratively down. What must be done to correct the problem?

22. What type of IPv6 address must be configured on an IPv6-enabled interface?

23. When a computer is pinging another computer for the first time, which type of message does it send first to determine the MAC address of the other device?

CHAPTER 2

Static Routing

Objectives

Upon completion of this chapter, you will be able to answer the following questions:

- What are the advantages and disadvantages of static routes?

- Can you explain the purpose of different types of static routes?

- Can you configure IPv4 and IPv6 static routes by specifying a next-hop address?

- How is legacy classful addressing used in network implementation?

- What is the purpose of CIDR in replacing classful addressing?

- How do you design and implement a hierarchical addressing scheme?

- How do you configure an IPv4 and IPv6 summary network address to reduce the number of routing table entries?

- Can you configure a floating static route to provide a backup connection?

- How does a router process packets when a static route is configured?

- How do you troubleshoot common static and default route configuration issues?

Key Terms

This chapter uses the following key terms. You can find the definitions in the Glossary.

stub network   *page 77*

summary static route page   *80*

floating static route   *page 81*

recursive lookup   *page 86*

fully specified static route   *page 89*

quad-zero route   *page 93*

stub router   *page 106*

summary route   *page*   *128*

route summarization   *page 128*

Introduction (2.0.1.1)

Routing is at the core of every data network, moving information across an internetwork from source to destination. Routers are the devices responsible for the transfer of packets from one network to the next.

Routers learn about remote networks either dynamically, using routing protocols, or manually, using static routes. In many cases, routers use a combination of both dynamic routing protocols and static routes. This chapter focuses on static routing.

Static routes are very common and do not require the same amount of processing and overhead as dynamic routing protocols.

In this chapter, sample topologies will be used to configure IPv4 and IPv6 static routes and to present troubleshooting techniques. In the process, several important IOS commands and the resulting output will be examined. An introduction to the routing table using both directly connected networks and static routes will be included.

This chapter will also contrast classful routing and the widely implemented classless routing methods. It will cover Classless Inter-Domain Routing (CIDR) and the variable-length subnet mask (VLSM) methods. CIDR and VLSM have helped conserve the IPv4 address space using subnetting and summarization techniques.

Class Activity 2.0.1.2: Which Way Should We Go?

A huge sporting event is about to take place in your city. To attend the event, you make concise plans to arrive at the sports arena on time to see the entire game.

There are two routes you can take to drive to the event:

- **Highway route:** It is easy to follow and fast driving speeds are allowed.
- **Alternative, direct route:** You found this route using a city map. Depending on conditions, such as the amount of traffic or congestion, this just may be the way to get to the arena on time!

With a partner, discuss these options. Choose a preferred route to arrive at the arena in time to see every second of the huge sporting event.

Compare your optional preferences to network traffic, which route would you choose to deliver data communications for your small- to medium-sized business? Would your network route be the fastest, easiest route or the alternative, direct route? Justify your choice.

Complete the modeling activity .pdf and be prepared to justify your answers to the class or with another group.

Static Routing Implementation (2.1)

As previously stated, static routes are widely used in networks today. Static routes are used in networks of all sizes, and are used along with a dynamic routing protocol. For this reason, a good understanding of static routes is a requirement for implementing routing on a network.

Reach Remote Networks (2.1.1.1)

A router can learn about remote networks in one of two ways:

- **Manually:** Remote networks are manually entered into the route table using static routes.

- **Dynamically:** Remote routes are automatically learned using a dynamic routing protocol.

Figure 2-1 provides a sample scenario of static routing. Figure 2-2 provides a sample scenario of dynamic routing using EIGRP.

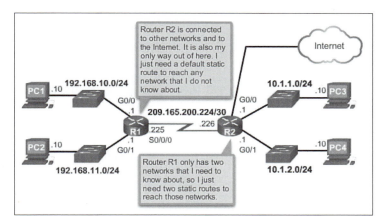

Figure 2-1 Static and Default Route Scenario

A network administrator can manually configure a static route to reach a specific network. Unlike a dynamic routing protocol, static routes are not automatically updated and must be manually reconfigured any time the network topology changes. A static route does not change until the administrator manually reconfigures it.

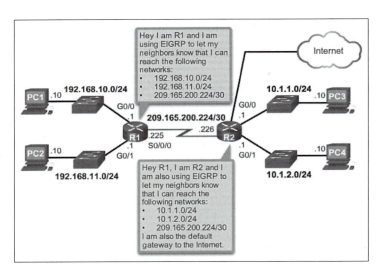

Figure 2-2 Dynamic Routing Scenario

Why Use Static Routing? (2.1.1.2)

Static routing provides some advantages over dynamic routing, including:

- Static routes are not advertised over the network, resulting in better security.

- Static routes use less bandwidth than dynamic routing protocols, as routers do not exchange routes.

- No CPU cycles are used to calculate and communicate routes.

- The path a static route uses to send data is known.

Static routing has the following disadvantages:

- Initial configuration and maintenance is time-consuming.

- Configuration can be error-prone, especially in large networks.

- Administrator intervention is required to maintain changing route information.

- Does not scale well with growing networks; maintenance becomes cumbersome.

- Requires complete knowledge of the whole network for proper implementation.

In Table 2-1, dynamic and static routing features are compared. Notice that the advantages of one method are the disadvantages of the other.

Table 2-1   Dynamic Routing Versus Static Routing

	Dynamic Routing	**Static Routing**
Configuration Complexity	Generally independent of the network size	Increases with the network size
Topology Changes	Automatically adapts to topology changes	Administrator intervention required
Scaling	Suitable for simple and complex topologies	Suitable for simple topologies
Security	Less secure	More secure
Resource Usage	Uses CPU, memory, link bandwidth	No extra resources needed
Predictability	Route depends on the current topology	Route to destination is always the same

Static routes are useful for smaller networks with only one path to an outside network. They also provide security in a larger network for certain types of traffic or links to other networks that need more control. It is important to understand that static and dynamic routing are not mutually exclusive. Rather, most networks use a combination of dynamic routing protocols and static routes. This may result in the router having multiple paths to a destination network via static routes and dynamically learned routes. However, the administrative distance (AD) of a static route is 1. Therefore, a static route will take precedence over all dynamically learned routes.

When to Use Static Routes (2.1.1.3)

Static routing has three primary uses:

- Providing ease of routing table maintenance in smaller networks that are not expected to grow significantly.

- Routing to and from stub networks. A *stub network* is a network accessed by a single route, and the router has only one neighbor.

- Using a single default route to represent a path to any network that does not have a more specific match with another route in the routing table. Default routes are used to send traffic to any destination beyond the next upstream router.

Figure 2-3 shows an example of a stub network connection and a default route connection. Notice in the figure that any network attached to R1 would only have one way to reach other destinations, whether to networks attached to R2, or to destinations beyond R2. This means that network 172.16.3.0 is a stub network and R1 is a stub router. Running a routing protocol between R2 and R1 is a waste of resources.

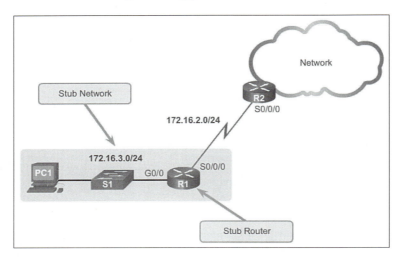

Figure 2-3 Stub Networks and Stub Routers

In this example, a static route can be configured on R2 to reach the R1 LAN. Additionally, because R1 has only one way to send out non-local traffic, a default static route can be configured on R1 to point to R2 as the next hop for all other networks.

Interactive Graphic

Activity 2.1.1.4: Identify the Advantages and Disadvantages of Static Routing

Go to the online course to perform this practice activity.

Static Route Applications (2.1.2.1)

Static routes are most often used to connect to a specific network or to provide a Gateway of Last Resort for a stub network. They can also be used to:

- Reduce the number of routes advertised by summarizing several contiguous networks as one static route

- Create a backup route in case a primary route link fails

The following types of IPv4 and IPv6 static routes will be discussed:

- Standard static route

- Default static route

- Summary static route

- Floating static route

Standard Static Route (2.1.2.2)

Both IPv4 and IPv6 support the configuration of static routes. Static routes are useful when connecting to a specific remote network.

Figure 2-4 shows that R2 can be configured with a static route to reach the stub network 172.16.3.0/24.

Note

The example is highlighting a stub network, but in fact, a static route can be used to connect to any network.

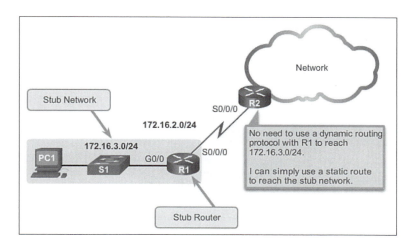

Figure 2-4   Connecting to a Stub Network

Default Static Route (2.1.2.3)

A default static route is a route that matches all packets. A default route identifies the gateway IP address to which the router sends all IP packets that it does not have a learned or static route for. A default static route is simply a static route with 0.0.0.0/0 as the destination IPv4 address. Configuring a default static route creates a Gateway of Last Resort.

Note

All routes that identify a specific destination with a larger subnet mask take precedence over the default route.

Default static routes are used:

- When no other routes in the routing table match the packet destination IP address. In other words, when a more specific match does not exist. A common use is when connecting a company's edge router to the ISP network.

- When a router has only one other router to which it is connected. This condition is known as a stub router.

Refer to Figure 2-5 for a sample scenario of implementing default static routing.

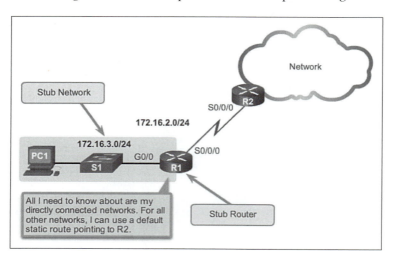

Figure 2-5 Connecting to a Stub Router

Summary Static Route (2.1.2.4)

To reduce the number of routing table entries, multiple static routes can be summarized into a single *summary static route* if:

- The destination networks are contiguous and can be summarized into a single network address.

- The multiple static routes all use the same exit interface or next-hop IP address.

In Figure 2-6, R1 would require four separate static routes to reach the 172.20.0.0/16 to 172.23.0.0/16 networks. Instead, one *summary static route* can be configured and still provide connectivity to those networks.

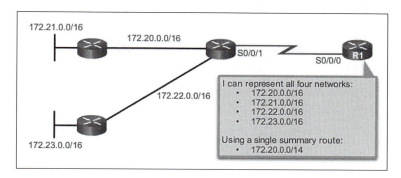

Figure 2-6 Using One Summary Static Route

Floating Static Route (2.1.2.5)

Another type of static route is a *floating static route*. Floating static routes are static routes that are used to provide a backup path to a primary static or dynamic route, in the event of a link failure. The floating static route is only used when the primary route is not available.

To accomplish this, the floating static route is configured with a higher administrative distance than the primary route. Recall that the administrative distance represents the trustworthiness of a route. If multiple paths to the destination exist, the router will choose the path with the lowest administrative distance.

For example, assume that an administrator wants to create a floating static route as a backup to an EIGRP-learned route. The floating static route must be configured with a higher administrative distance than EIGRP. EIGRP has an administrative distance of 90. If the floating static route is configured with an administrative distance of 95, the dynamic route learned through EIGRP is preferred to the floating static route. If the EIGRP-learned route is lost, the floating static route is used in its place.

In Figure 2-7, the Branch router typically forwards all traffic to the HQ router over the private WAN link. In this example, the routers exchange route information using EIGRP. A floating static route, with an administrative distance of 91 or higher, could be configured to serve as a backup route. If the private WAN link fails and the EIGRP route disappears from the routing table, the router selects the floating static route as the best path to reach the HQ LAN.

Interactive Graphic

Activity 2.1.2.6: Identify the Type of Static Route

Go to the online course to perform this practice activity.

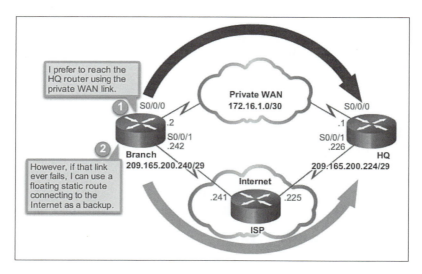

Figure 2-7 Configuring a Backup Route

Configure Static and Default Routes (2.2)

Recall that a router can learn about remote networks in one of two ways:

- Manually, from configured static routes

- Automatically, from a dynamic routing protocol

This chapter focuses on configuring static routes. Dynamic routing protocols are introduced in the next chapter. Even with the implementation of a dynamic routing protocol, static routes are also commonly used.

Configure IPv4 Static Routes (2.2.1)

Routers can be configured for both IPv4 and IPv6 static routes. This section will focus on the configuration of IPv4 static routes. IPv4 static routes are manually configured routing entries for reaching IPv4 networks. The configuration of IPv6 static routes is covered later in this chapter.

ip route Command (2.2.1.1)

Static routes are configured using the **ip route** global configuration command. The syntax of the command is:

```
Router(config)# ip route network-address subnet-mask { ip-address | interface-type
interface-number [ ip-address ]} [ distance ] [ name name ] [ permanent ] [ tag tag ]
```

The following parameters are required to configure static routing:

- *network-address*: Destination network address of the remote network to be added to the routing table; often this is referred to as the prefix.
- *subnet-mask*: Subnet mask, or just mask, of the remote network to be added to the routing table. The subnet mask can be modified to summarize a group of networks.

One or both of the following parameters must also be used:

- *ip-address*: The IP address of the connecting router to use to forward the packet to the remote destination network. Commonly referred to as the next hop.
- *interface-type interface-number or exit-intf*: The outgoing interface to use to forward the packet to the next hop.

As shown in Table 2-2, the command syntax commonly used is **ip route** *network-address subnet-mask* {*ip-address* | *exit-intf*}.

The *distance* parameter is used to create a floating static route by setting an administrative distance that is higher than a dynamically learned route.

Table 2-2   iproute Command Syntax

Parameter	Description
network-address	Destination network address of the remote network to be added to the routing table.
subnet-mask	- Subnet mask of the remote network to be added to the routing table. - The subnet mask can be modified to summarize a group of networks.
ip-address	- Commonly referred to as the next-hop router's IP address. - Typically used when connecting to a broadcast media (i.e., Ethernet). - Commonly creates a recursive lookup.
exit-intf	- Use the outgoing interface to forward packets to the destination network. - Also referred to as a directly attached static route. - Typically used when connecting in a point-to-point configuration.

Note

The remaining parameters are not relevant for this chapter or for CCNA studies.

Next-Hop Options (2.2.1.2)

Figure 2-8 and the subsequent outputs display the topology and the routing tables of R1, R2, and R3. Notice that each router has entries only for directly connected networks and their associated local addresses. None of the routers have any knowledge of any networks beyond their directly connected interfaces.

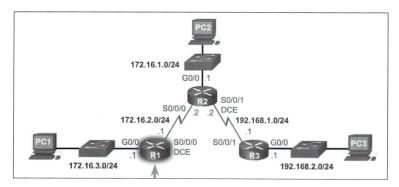

Figure 2-8 Verify the Routing Table of R1, R2, R3

```
R1# show ip route | begin Gateway
Gateway of last resort is not set
      172.16.0.0/16 is variably subnetted, 4 subnets, 2 masks
C        172.16.2.0/24 is directly connected, Serial0/0/0
L        172.16.2.1/32 is directly connected, Serial0/0/0
C        172.16.3.0/24 is directly connected, GigabitEthernet0/0
L        172.16.3.1/32 is directly connected, GigabitEthernet0/0
R1#

R2# show ip route | begin Gateway
Gateway of last resort is not set
      172.16.0.0/16 is variably subnetted, 4 subnets, 2 masks
C        172.16.1.0/24 is directly connected, GigabitEthernet0/0
L        172.16.1.1/32 is directly connected, GigabitEthernet0/0
C        172.16.2.0/24 is directly connected, Serial0/0/0
L        172.16.2.2/32 is directly connected, Serial0/0/0
      192.168.1.0/24 is variably subnetted, 2 subnets, 2 masks
C        192.168.1.0/24 is directly connected, Serial0/0/1
L        192.168.1.2/32 is directly connected, Serial0/0/1
R2#

R3# show ip route | include C
Codes: L - local, C - connected, S - static, R - RIP, M - mobile, B - BGP
C        192.168.1.0/24 is directly connected, Serial0/0/1
C        192.168.2.0/24 is directly connected, GigabitEthernet0/0
R3#
```

For example, R1 has no knowledge of networks:

- 172.16.1.0/24: LAN on R2

- 192.168.1.0/24: Serial network between R2 and R3

- 192.168.2.0/24: LAN on R3

Figure 2-9 displays a successful ping from R1 to R2. Figure 2-10 displays an unsuccessful ping to the R3 LAN. This is unsuccessful because R1 does not have an entry in its routing table for the R3 LAN network.

```
R1# ping 172.16.2.2
Type escape sequence to abort.
Sending 5, 100-byte ICMP Echos to 172.16.2.2, timeout is 2 seconds:
!!!!!
Success rate is 100 percent (5/5), round-trip min/avg/max = 12/13/16
ms
R1#
```

Figure 2-9 Verify Connectivity from R1 to R2

```
R1# ping 192.168.2.1
Type escape sequence to abort.
Sending 5, 100-byte ICMP Echos to 192.168.2.1, timeout is 2 seconds:
.....
Success rate is 0 percent (0/5)
R1#
```

Figure 2-10 Verify Connectivity from R1 to R3 LAN

The next hop can be identified by an IP address, exit interface, or both. How the destination is specified creates one of the three following route types:

- **Next-hop route:** Only the next-hop IP address is specified.

- **Directly connected static route:** Only the router exit interface is specified.

- **Fully specified static route:** The next-hop IP address and exit interface are specified.

Configure a Next-Hop Static Route (2.2.1.3)

In a next-hop static route, only the next-hop IP address is specified. The output interface is derived from the next hop. For example, in Figure 2-11, three next-hop static routes are configured on R1 using the IP address of the next hop, R2.

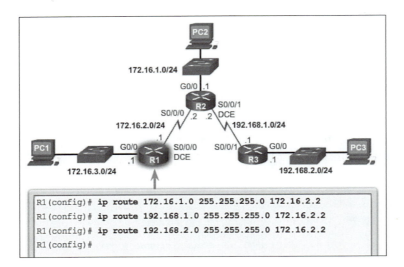

Figure 2-11 Configuring Next-Hop Static Routes on R1

Before any packet is forwarded by a router, the routing table process must determine the exit interface to use to forward the packet. This is known as route resolvability. The route resolvability process will vary depending upon the type of forwarding mechanism being used by the router. CEF (Cisco Express Forwarding) is the default behavior on most platforms running IOS 12.0 or later.

Figure 2-12 details the basic packet forwarding process in the routing table for R1 without the use of CEF. When a packet is destined for the 192.168.2.0/24 network, R1:

1. Looks for a match in the routing table and finds that it has to forward the packets to the next-hop IPv4 address 172.16.2.2, as indicated by the label 1 in Figure 2-12. Every route that references only a next-hop IPv4 address and does not reference an exit interface must have the next-hop IPv4 address resolved using another route in the routing table with an exit interface.

2. R1 must now determine how to reach 172.16.2.2; therefore, it searches a second time for a 172.16.2.2 match. In this case, the IPv4 address matches the route for the directly connected network 172.16.2.0/24 with the exit interface Serial 0/0/0, as indicated by the label 2 in Figure 2-12. This lookup tells the routing table process that this packet is forwarded out of that interface.

It actually takes two routing table lookup processes to forward any packet to the 192.168.2.0/24 network. When the router performs multiple lookups in the routing table before forwarding a packet, it is performing a process known as a *recursive lookup*. Because recursive lookups consume router resources, they should be avoided when possible.

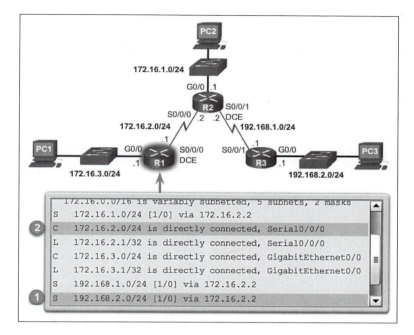

Figure 2-12 Verify the Routing Table of R1

A recursive static route is valid (that is, it is a candidate for insertion in the routing table) only when the specified next hop resolves, either directly or indirectly, to a valid exit interface.

Note

CEF provides optimized lookup for efficient packet forwarding by using two main data structures stored in the data plane: an FIB (Forwarding Information Base), which is a copy of the routing table, and an adjacency table that includes Layer 2 addressing information. By combining the information from these two tables, CEF eliminates the need for recursive lookup for next-hop IP address lookups. In other words, a static route using a next-hop IP address requires only a single lookup when CEF is enabled on the router.

Configure a Directly Connected Static Route (2.2.1.4)

When configuring a static route, another option is to use the exit interface to specify the next-hop address. In older IOS versions, prior to CEF, this method is used to avoid the recursive lookup problem.

In Figure 2-13, three directly connected static routes are configured on R1 using the exit interface. The routing table for R1 in Figure 2-14 shows that when a packet is destined for the 192.168.2.0/24 network, R1 looks for a match in the routing table, and finds that it can forward the packet out of its Serial 0/0/0 interface. No other lookups are required.

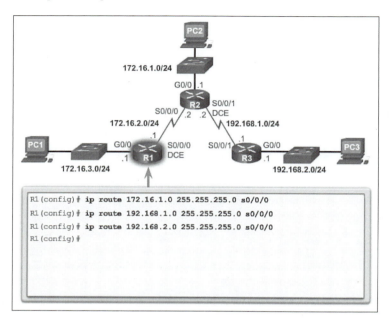

```
R1(config)# ip route 172.16.1.0 255.255.255.0 s0/0/0
R1(config)# ip route 192.168.1.0 255.255.255.0 s0/0/0
R1(config)# ip route 192.168.2.0 255.255.255.0 s0/0/0
R1(config)#
```

Figure 2-13 Configure Directly Connected Static Routes on R1

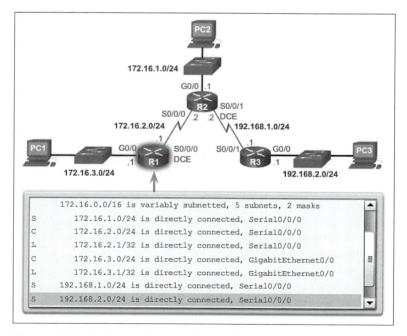

```
      172.16.0.0/16 is variably subnetted, 5 subnets, 2 masks
S         172.16.1.0/24 is directly connected, Serial0/0/0
C         172.16.2.0/24 is directly connected, Serial0/0/0
L         172.16.2.1/32 is directly connected, Serial0/0/0
C         172.16.3.0/24 is directly connected, GigabitEthernet0/0
L         172.16.3.1/32 is directly connected, GigabitEthernet0/0
S      192.168.1.0/24 is directly connected, Serial0/0/0
S      192.168.2.0/24 is directly connected, Serial0/0/0
```

Figure 2-14 Verify the Routing Table of R1

Notice how the routing table looks different for the route configured with an exit interface than the route configured with a recursive entry.

Configuring a directly connected static route with an exit interface allows the routing table to resolve the exit interface in a single search, instead of two searches. Although the routing table entry indicates "directly connected," the administrative distance of the static route is still 1. Only a directly connected interface can have an administrative distance of 0.

Note

For point-to-point interfaces, you can use static routes that point to the exit interface or to the next-hop address. For multipoint/broadcast interfaces, it is more suitable to use static routes that point to a next-hop address.

Interactive Graphic

Activity 2.2.1.4 Part 1: Configure Directly Connected Static Routes on R2

Go to the online course to use the Syntax Checker in the third graphic to configure a static route to the 172.16.3.0/24 network using exit interface S0/0/0.

Interactive Graphic

Activity 2.2.1.4 Part 2: Configure Directly Connected Static Routes on R3

Go to the online course to use the Syntax Checker in the fourth graphic to configure static routes to the 172.16.1.0/24, 172.16.2.0/24, and 172.16.3.0/24 networks using the exit interface S0/0/1.

Although static routes that use only an exit interface on point-to-point networks are common, the use of the default CEF forwarding mechanism makes this practice unnecessary.

Configure a Fully Specified Static Route (2.2.1.5)

In a *fully specified static route*, both the output interface and the next-hop IP address are specified. This is another type of static route that is used in older IOS versions, prior to CEF. This form of static route is used when the output interface is a multi-access interface and it is necessary to explicitly identify the next hop. The next hop must be directly connected to the specified exit interface.

Suppose that the network link between R1 and R2 is an Ethernet link and that the GigabitEthernet 0/1 interface of R1 is connected to that network, as shown in Figure 2-15. CEF is not enabled. To eliminate the recursive lookup, a directly connected static route can be implemented using the following command:

```
R1(config)# ip route 192.168.2.0 255.255.255.0 GigabitEthernet 0/1
```

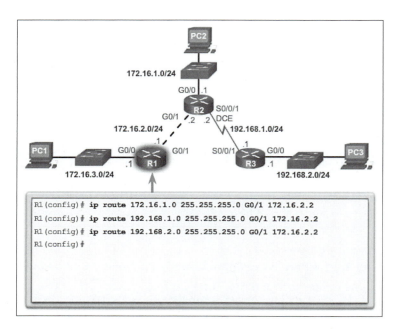

Figure 2-15 Configure Fully Specified Static Routes on R1

However, this may cause unexpected or inconsistent results. The difference between an Ethernet multi-access network and a point-to-point serial network is that a point-to-point network has only one other device on that network, the router at the other end of the link. With Ethernet networks, there may be many different devices sharing the same multi-access network, including hosts and even multiple routers. By only designating the Ethernet exit interface in the static route, the router will not have sufficient information to determine which device is the next-hop device.

R1 knows that the packet needs to be encapsulated in an Ethernet frame and sent out the GigabitEthernet 0/1 interface. However, R1 does not know the next-hop IPv4 address and therefore it cannot determine the destination MAC address for the Ethernet frame.

Depending upon the topology and the configurations on other routers, this static route may or may not work. It is recommended that when the exit interface is an Ethernet network, a fully specified static route is used including both the exit interface and the next-hop address.

As shown in Figure 2-16, when forwarding packets to R2, the exit interface is GigabitEthernet 0/1 and the next-hop IPv4 address is 172.16.2.2.

Note

With the use of CEF, a fully specified static route is no longer necessary. A static route using a next-hop address should be used.

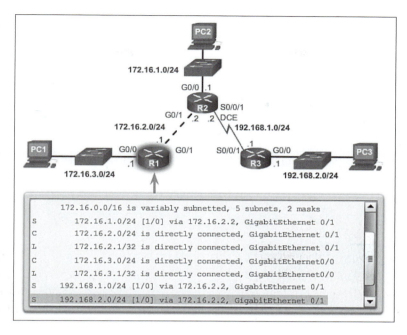

172.16.1.0/24

172.16.2.0/24

192.168.1.0/24

172.16.3.0/24

192.168.2.0/24

```
       172.16.0.0/16 is variably subnetted, 5 subnets, 2 masks
S         172.16.1.0/24 [1/0] via 172.16.2.2, GigabitEthernet 0/1
C         172.16.2.0/24 is directly connected, GigabitEthernet 0/1
L         172.16.2.1/32 is directly connected, GigabitEthernet 0/1
C         172.16.3.0/24 is directly connected, GigabitEthernet0/0
L         172.16.3.1/32 is directly connected, GigabitEthernet0/0
S      192.168.1.0/24 [1/0] via 172.16.2.2, GigabitEthernet 0/1
S      192.168.2.0/24 [1/0] via 172.16.2.2, GigabitEthernet 0/1
```

Figure 2-16 Verify the Routing Table of R1

Interactive Graphic

Activity 2.2.1.5 Part 1: Configure Fully Specified Static Routes on R2

Go to the online course to use the Syntax Checker in the third graphic to configure a static route to the 172.16.3.0/24 network using the exit interface/next-hop pair: G0/1 172.16.2.1.

Interactive Graphic

Activity 2.2.1.5 Part 2: Configure Fully Specified Static Routes on R3

Go to the online course to use the Syntax Checker in the fourth graphic to configure a static route to the 172.16.1.0/24, 172.16.2.0/24, and 172.16.3.0/24 networks using the exit interface S0/0/1 and next-hop address 192.168.1.2.

Verify a Static Route (2.2.1.6)

Along with **ping** and **traceroute**, useful commands to verify static routes include:

- **show ip route**
- **show ip route static**
- **show ip route** *network*

Figure 2-17 displays sample output of the **show ip route static** command. In the example, the output is filtered using the pipe and **begin** parameter. The output reflects the use of static routes using the next-hop address.

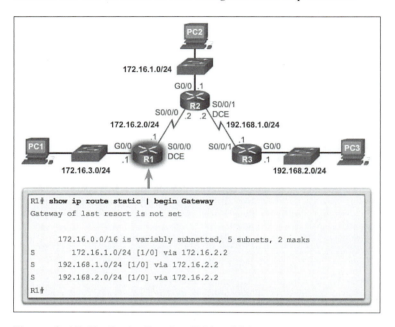

Figure 2-17 Verify the Routing Table of R1

The following displays sample output of the **show ip route 192.168.2.1** command:

```
R1# show ip route 192.168.2.1
Routing entry for 192.168.2.0/24
   Known via "static", distance 1, metric 0
   Routing Descriptor Blocks:
      *172.16.2.2
         Route metric is 0, traffic share count is 1
R1#
```

The following output verifies the **ip route** configuration in the running configuration with the output filtered using the pipe and **section** parameter:

```
R1# show running-config | section ip route
ip route 172.16.1.0  255.255.255.0  172.16.2.2
ip route 192.168.1.0  255.255.255.0  172.16.2.2
ip route 192.168.2.0  255.255.255.0  172.16.2.2
R1#
```

Interactive
Graphic

Activity 2.2.1.6 Part 1: Verify the Static Routing Settings on R2

Go to the online course to use the Syntax Checker in the third graphic to display only the static routes in the routing table of R2.

Interactive
Graphic

Activity 2.2.1.6 Part 2: Verify the Static Routing Settings on R3

Go to the online course to use the Syntax Checker in the third graphic to display only the static routes in the routing table of R3.

Configure IPv4 Default Routes (2.2.2)

If a router does not have a route entry in its routing table for a destination network, a default route entry can be used to forward packets to another router. The use of a static default route is common with dynamic routing protocols and will be discussed in later chapters.

Default Static Route (2.2.2.1)

A default route is a static route that matches all packets. Rather than storing all routes to all networks in the routing table, a router can store a single default route to represent any network that is not in the routing table.

Routers commonly use default routes that are either configured locally or learned from another router, using a dynamic routing protocol. A default route is used when no other routes in the routing table match the destination IP address of the packet. In other words, if a more specific match does not exist, then the default route is used as the Gateway of Last Resort.

Default static routes are commonly used when connecting:

- An edge router to a service provider network
- A stub router (a router with only one upstream neighbor router)

As shown in Table 2-3, the command syntax for a default static route is similar to any other static route, except that the network address is **0.0.0.0** and the subnet mask is **0.0.0.0**. The basic command syntax of a default static route is:

- **ip route 0.0.0.0 0.0.0.0** { *ip-address* | *exit-intf* }

Note

An IPv4 default static route is commonly referred to as a *quad-zero route*.

Table 2-3   Default Static Route Syntax

Parameter	Description
0.0.0.0	Matches any network address.
0.0.0.0	Matches any subnet mask.
ip-address	■ Commonly referred to as the next-hop router's IP address. ■ Typically used when connecting to a broadcast media (i.e., Ethernet).
exit-intf	■ Use the outgoing interface to forward packets to the destination network. ■ Also referred to as a directly attached static route.

Configure a Default Static Route (2.2.2.2)

R1 can be configured with three static routes to reach all of the remote networks in the example topology. However, R1 is a stub router because it is only connected to R2. Therefore, it would be more efficient to configure a default static route.

The example in Figure 2-18 configures a default static route on R1. With the configuration shown in the example, any packets not matching more specific route entries are forwarded to 172.16.2.2.

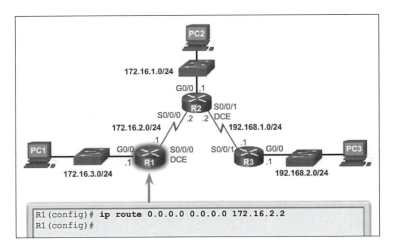

Figure 2-18   Configuring a Default Static Route

Verify a Default Static Route (2.2.2.3)

In Figure 2-19, the **show ip route static** command output displays the contents of the routing table. Note the asterisk (*) next to the route with code 's'. As displayed in the

Codes table in Figure 2-19, the asterisk indicates that this static route is a candidate default route, which is why it is selected as the Gateway of Last Resort.

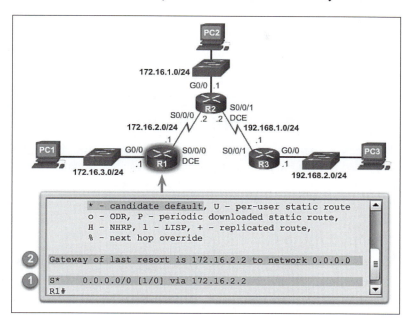

Figure 2-19 Verifying the Routing Table of R1

The key to this configuration is the /0 mask. Recall that the subnet mask in a routing table determines how many bits must match between the destination IP address of the packet and the route in the routing table. A binary 1 indicates that the bits must match. A binary 0 indicates that the bits do not have to match. A /0 mask in this route entry indicates that none of the bits are required to match. The default static route matches all packets for which a more specific match does not exist.

Packet Tracer Activity 2.2.2.4: Configuring IPv4 Static and Default Routes

In this activity, you will configure static and default routes. A static route is a route that is entered manually by the network administrator to create a route that is reliable and safe. There are four different static routes that are used in this activity: a recursive static route, a directly connected static route, a fully specified static route, and a default route.

Lab 2.2.2.5: Configuring IPv4 Static and Default Routes

In this lab, you will complete the following objectives:

- Part 1: Set Up the Topology and Initialize Devices
- Part 2: Configure Basic Device Settings and Verify Connectivity
- Part 3: Configure Static Routes
- Part 4: Configure and Verify a Default Route

Configure IPv6 Static Routes (2.2.3)

This section focuses on the configuration of IPv6 static routes. IPv6 static routes are similar to IPv4 static routes. IPv4 static routes are manually configured routes for reaching IPv4 networks, whereas IPv6 static routes are configured for reaching IPv6 networks.

The **ipv6 route** Command (2.2.3.1)

Static routes for IPv6 are configured using the **ipv6 route** global configuration command. Table 2-4 shows the simplified version of the command syntax:

```
Router(config)# ipv6 route ipv6-prefix/prefix-length { ipv6-address | exit-intf }
```

Table 2-4   IPv6 Command Syntax

Parameter	Description
ipv6-prefix	Destination network address of the remote network to be added to the routing table.
prefix-length	Prefix length of the remote network to be added to the routing table.
ipv6-address	■ Commonly referred to as the next-hop router's IP address. ■ Typically used when connecting to a broadcast media (i.e., Ethernet).
exit-intf	■ Use the outgoing interface to forward packets to the destination network. ■ Also referred to as a directly attached static route. ■ Typically used when connecting in a point-to-point configuration.

Most of the parameters are identical to the IPv4 version of the command. IPv6 static routes can also be implemented as:

- Standard IPv6 static route
- Default IPv6 static route

- Summary IPv6 static route

- Floating IPv6 static route

As with IPv4, these routes can be configured as recursive, directly connected, or fully specified.

The **ipv6 unicast-routing** global configuration command must be configured to enable the router to forward IPv6 packets. Figure 2-20 displays the enabling of IPv6 unicast routing.

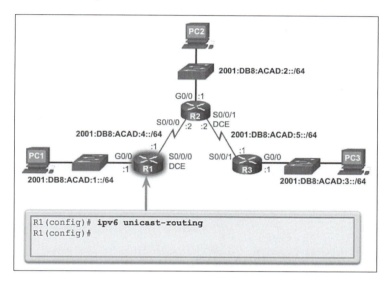

Figure 2-20 Enabling IPv6 Unicast Routing

**Interactive
Graphic**

Activity 2.2.3.1 Part 1: Enabling IPv6 Unicast Routing on R2

Go to the online course to use the Syntax Checker in the third graphic to enable IPv6 unicast routing on R2.

**Interactive
Graphic**

Activity 2.2.3.1 Part 2: Enabling IPv6 Unicast Routing on R3

Go to the online course to use the Syntax Checker in the third graphic to enable IPv6 unicast routing on R3.

Next-Hop Options (2.2.3.2)

The following example displays the routing tables of R1, R2, and R3. Each router has entries only for directly connected networks and their associated local addresses.

None of the routers have any knowledge of any networks beyond their directly connected interfaces.

```
R1# show ipv6 route
<output omitted>
C    2001:DB8:ACAD:1::/64 [0/0]
     via GigabitEthernet0/0, directly connected
L    2001:DB8:ACAD:1::1/128 [0/0]
     via GigabitEthernet0/0, receive
C    2001:DB8:ACAD:4::/64 [0/0]
     via Serial0/0/0, directly connected
L    2001:DB8:ACAD:4::1/128 [0/0]
     via Serial0/0/0, receive
L    FF00::/8 [0/0]
     via Null0, receive
R1#

R2# show ipv6 route
<output omitted>
C    2001:DB8:ACAD:2::/64 [0/0]
     via GigabitEthernet0/0, directly connected
L    2001:DB8:ACAD:2::1/128 [0/0]
     via GigabitEthernet0/0, receive
C    2001:DB8:ACAD:4::/64 [0/0]
     via Serial0/0/0, directly connected
L    2001:DB8:ACAD:4::2/128 [0/0]
     via Serial0/0/0, receive
C    2001:DB8:ACAD:5::/64 [0/0]
     via Serial0/0/1, directly connected
L    2001:DB8:ACAD:5::2/128 [0/0]
     via Serial0/0/1, receive
L    FF00::/8 [0/0]
     via Null0, receive
R2#

R3# show ipv6 route
<output omitted>
C    2001:DB8:ACAD:3::/64 [0/0]
     via GigabitEthernet0/0, directly connected
L    2001:DB8:ACAD:3::1/128 [0/0]
     via GigabitEthernet0/0, receive
C    2001:DB8:ACAD:5::/64 [0/0]
     via Serial0/0/1, directly connected
L    2001:DB8:ACAD:5::1/128 [0/0]
     via Serial0/0/1, receive
L    FF00::/8 [0/0]
     via Null0, receive
R3#
```

For example, R1 has no knowledge of networks:

- 2001:DB8:ACAD:2::/64: LAN on R2

- 2001:DB8:ACAD:5::/64: Serial network between R2 and R3

- 2001:DB8:ACAD:3::/64: LAN on R3

Figure 2-21 displays a successful ping from R1 to R2. And the subsequent output shows an unsuccessful ping to the R3 LAN. This is unsuccessful because R1 does not have an entry in its routing table for that network.

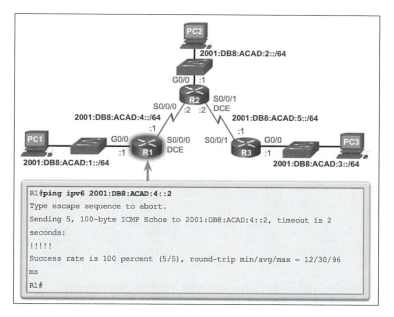

Figure 2-21 Verify Connectivity from R1 to R2

```
R1# ping ipv6 2001:DB8:ACAD:3::1
Type escape sequence to abort.
Sending 5, 100-byte ICMP Echos to 2001:DB8:ACAD:3::1, timeout is 2 seconds:

% No valid route for destination
Success rate is 0 percent (0/1)
R1#
```

The next hop can be identified by an IPv6 address, exit interface, or both. How the destination is specified creates one of three route types:

- **Next-hop static IPv6 route:** Only the next-hop IPv6 address is specified.

- **Directly connected static IPv6 route:** Only the router exit interface is specified.

- **Fully specified static IPv6 route:** The next-hop IPv6 address and exit interface are specified.

Configure a Next-Hop Static IPv6 Route (2.2.3.3)

In a next-hop static route, only the next-hop IPv6 address is specified. The output interface is derived from the next hop. For instance, in Figure 2-22, three next-hop static routes are configured on R1.

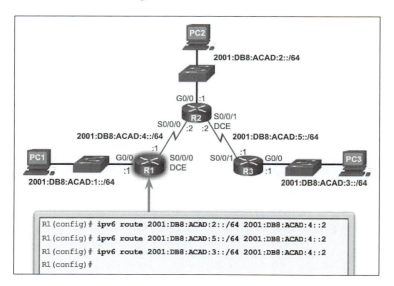

Figure 2-22 Configure Next-Hop Static IPv6 Routes

As with IPv4, before any packet is forwarded by the router, the routing table process must resolve the route to determine the exit interface to use to forward the packet. The route resolvability process will vary depending upon the type of forwarding mechanism being used by the router. CEF is the default behavior on most platforms running IOS 12.0 or later.

Figure 2-23 details the basic packet forwarding route resolvability process in the routing table for R1 without the use of CEF. When a packet is destined for the 2001:DB8:ACAD:3::/64 network, R1:

1. Looks for a match in the routing table and finds that it has to forward the packets to the next-hop IPv6 address 2001:DB8:ACAD:4::2. Every route that references

only a next-hop IPv6 address and does not reference an exit interface must have the next-hop IPv6 address resolved using another route in the routing table with an exit interface.

2. R1 must now determine how to reach 2001:DB8:ACAD:4::2; therefore, it searches a second time looking for a match. In this case, the IPv6 address matches the route for the directly connected network 2001:DB8:ACAD:4::/64 with the exit interface Serial 0/0/0. This lookup tells the routing table process that this packet is forwarded out of that interface.

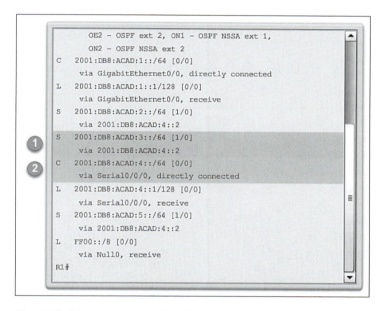

Figure 2-23 Verifying an IPv6 Next-Hop Lookup

Therefore, it actually takes two routing table lookup processes to forward any packet to the 2001:DB8:ACAD:3::/64 network. When the router has to perform multiple lookups in the routing table before forwarding a packet, it is performing a process known as a recursive lookup.

A recursive static IPv6 route is valid (that is, it is a candidate for insertion in the routing table) only when the specified next hop resolves, either directly or indirectly, to a valid exit interface.

Activity 2.2.3.3 Part 1: Configure Next-Hop Static IPv6 Routing on R2

Go to the online course to use the Syntax Checker in the third graphic to configure an IPv6 route to network 2001:DB8:ACAD:1::/64 using the next-hop address 2001:DB8:ACAD:4::1.

Interactive Graphic

Activity 2.2.3.3 Part 2: Configure Next-Hop Static IPv6 Routing on R3

Go to the online course to use the Syntax Checker in the fourth graphic to configure an IPv6 route to networks 2001:DB8:ACAD:1::/64, 2001:DB8:ACAD:2::/64, and 2001:DB8:ACAD:4::/64 using the next-hop address 2001:DB8:ACAD:5::2.

Configure a Directly Connected Static IPv6 Route (2.2.3.4)

When configuring a static route on point-to-point networks, an alternative to using the next-hop IPv6 address is to specify the exit interface. This is an alternative used in older IOS versions or whenever CEF is disabled, to avoid the recursive lookup problem.

For instance, in Figure 2-24, three directly connected static routes are configured on R1 using the exit interface.

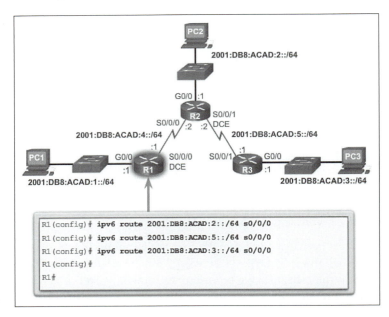

Figure 2-24 Configure Directly Connected Static IPv6 Routes on R1

The IPv6 routing table for R1 in the following output shows that when a packet is destined for the 2001:DB8:ACAD:3::/64 network, R1 looks for a match in the routing table and finds that it can forward the packet out of its Serial 0/0/0 interface. No other lookups are required.

```
R1# show ipv6 route
IPv6 Routing Table - default - 8 entries
Codes: C - Connected, L - Local, S - Static, U - Per-user Static route
       B - BGP, R - RIP, I1 - ISIS L1, I2 - ISIS L2
       IA - ISIS interarea, IS - ISIS summary, D - EIGRP, EX - EIGRP external
       ND - ND Default, NDp - ND Prefix, DCE - Destination, NDr - Redirect
       O - OSPF Intra, OI - OSPF Inter, OE1 - OSPF ext 1, OE2 - OSPF ext 2
       ON1 - OSPF NSSA ext 1, ON2 - OSPF NSSA ext 2
C    2001:DB8:ACAD:1::/64 [0/0]
     via GigabitEthernet0/0, directly connected
L    2001:DB8:ACAD:1::1/128 [0/0]
     via GigabitEthernet0/0, receive
S    2001:DB8:ACAD:2::/64 [1/0]
     via Serial0/0/0, directly connected
S    2001:DB8:ACAD:3::/64 [1/0]
     via Serial0/0/0, directly connected
C    2001:DB8:ACAD:4::/64 [0/0]
     via Serial0/0/0, directly connected
L    2001:DB8:ACAD:4::1/128 [0/0]
     via Serial0/0/0, receive
S    2001:DB8:ACAD:5::/64 [1/0]
     via Serial0/0/0, directly connected
L    FF00::/8 [0/0]
     via Null0, receive
R1#
```

Notice how the routing table looks different for the route configured with an exit interface than the route configured with a recursive entry.

Configuring a directly connected static route with an exit interface allows the routing table to resolve the exit interface in a single search instead of two searches. Recall that with the use of the CEF forwarding mechanism, static routes with an exit interface are considered unnecessary. A single lookup is performed using a combination of the FIB and adjacency table stored in the data plane.

Interactive Graphic

Activity 2.2.3.4 Part 1: Configure Directly Connected Static IPv6 Routes on R2

Go to the online course to use the Syntax Checker in the third graphic to configure an IPv6 route to network 2001:DB8:ACAD:1::/64 using exit interface S0/0/0.

Interactive Graphic

Activity 2.2.3.4 Part 2: Configure Directly Connected Static IPv6 Routes on R3

Go to the online course to use the Syntax Checker in the fourth graphic to configure an IPv6 route to the 2001:DB8:ACAD:1::/64, 2001:DB8:ACAD:2::/64, and 2001:DB8:ACAD:4::/64 networks using exit interface S0/0/1.

Configure a Fully Specified Static IPv6 Route (2.2.3.5)

In a fully specified static route, both the output interface and the next-hop IPv6 address are specified. Similar to fully specified static routes used with IPv4, this would be used if CEF were not enabled on the router and the exit interface was on a multi-access network. With CEF, a static route using only a next-hop IPv6 address would be the preferred method even when the exit interface is a multi-access network.

Unlike IPv4, there is a situation in IPv6 when a fully specified static route must be used. If the IPv6 static route uses an IPv6 link-local address as the next-hop address, a fully specified static route including the exit interface must be used. Figure 2-25 shows an example of a fully qualified IPv6 static route using an IPv6 link-local address as the next-hop address.

The reason a fully specified static route must be used is because IPv6 link-local addresses are not contained in the IPv6 routing table. Link-local addresses are only unique on a given link or network. The next-hop link-local address may be a valid address on multiple networks connected to the router. Therefore, it is necessary that the exit interface be included.

In Figure 2-25, a fully specified static route is configured using R2's link-local address as the next-hop address. Notice that IOS requires that an exit interface be specified.

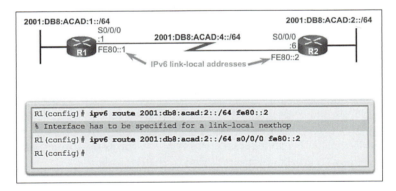

Figure 2-25 Configure a Fully Specified Static IPv6 Route on R1

The following output shows the IPv6 routing table entry for this route. Notice that both the next-hop link-local address and the exit interface are included.

```
R1# show ipv6 route static    being 2001:DB8:ACAD:2::/64
S   2001:DB8:ACAD:2::/64 (1/0)
      via FE80::2, Serial0/0/0
```

Activity 2.2.3.5: Configure a Fully Specified IPv6 Route on R2

Go to the online course to use the Syntax Checker in the third graphic to configure a fully specified static IPv6 route to the R1 LAN using the R1 link-local address as the next-hop address.

Verify IPv6 Static Routes (2.2.3.6)

Along with **ping** and **traceroute**, useful commands to verify static routes include:

- **show ipv6 route**
- **show ipv6 route static**
- **ipv6 route** *network*

The following displays sample output of the **show ipv6 route static** command. The output reflects the use of static routes using next-hop global unicast addresses.

```
R1# show ipv6 route static
IPv6 Routing Table - default - 8 entries
Codes: C - Connected, L - Local, S - Static, U - Per-user Static route
       B - BGP, R - RIP, I1 - ISIS L1, I2 - ISIS L2
       IA - ISIS interarea, IS - ISIS summary, D - EIGRP, EX - EIGRP external
       ND - ND Default, NDp - ND Prefix, DCE - Destination, NDr - Redirect
       O - OSPF Intra, OI - OSPF Inter, OE1 - OSPF ext 1, OE2 - OSPF ext 2
       ON1 - OSPF NSSA ext 1, ON2 - OSPF NSSA ext 2
S   2001:DB8:ACAD:2::/64 [1/0]
      via 2001:DB8:ACAD:4::2, Serial0/0/0
S   2001:DB8:ACAD:3::/64 [1/0]
      via 2001:DB8:ACAD:4::2, Serial0/0/0
S   2001:DB8:ACAD:5::/64 [1/0]
      via 2001:DB8:ACAD:4::2, Serial0/0/0
R1#
```

The following output displays sample output from the **show ip route 2001:DB8:ACAD:3::1** command:

```
R1# show ipv6 route 2001:0DB8:ACAD:3::1
Routing entry for 2001:DB8:ACAD:3::/64
  Known via "static", distance 1, metric 0
  Route count is 1/1, share count 0
  Routing paths:
    2001:DB8:ACAD:4::2, Serial0/0/0
      Last updated 00:19:11 ago
R1#
```

The following output verifies the **ipv6 route** configuration in the running configuration with the output filtered using the pipe and **section** parameter:

```
R1# show running-config | section ipv6 route
ipv6 route 2001:DB8:ACAD:2::/64 Serial0/0/0 2001:DB8:ACAD:4::2
ipv6 route 2001:DB8:ACAD:3::/64 Serial0/0/0 2001:DB8:ACAD:4::2
ipv6 route 2001:DB8:ACAD:5::/64 Serial0/0/0 2001:DB8:ACAD:4::2
R1#
```

Configure IPv6 Default Routes (2.2.4)

Similar to IPv4, an IPv6 default route entry can be used to forward packets to another router when there is not a specific IPv6 route in the IPv6 routing table.

Default Static IPv6 Route (2.2.4.1)

A default route is a static route that matches all packets. Instead of routers storing routes for all of the networks in the Internet, they can store a single default route to represent any network that is not in the routing table.

Routers commonly use default routes that are either configured locally or learned from another router, using a dynamic routing protocol. They are used when no other routes match the packet's destination IP address in the routing table. In other words, if a more specific match does not exist, then use the default route as the Gateway of Last Resort.

Default static routes are commonly used when connecting:

- A company's edge router to a service provider network.

- A router with only an upstream neighbor router. The router has no other neighbors and is, therefore, referred to as a *stub router*.

As shown in Table 2-5, the command syntax for a default static route is similar to any other static route, except that the ipv6-prefix/prefix-length is ::/0, which matches all routes.

The basic command syntax of a default static route is:

- **ipv6 route ::/0** { *ipv6-address* | *exit-intf* }

Table 2-5   Default Static IPv6 Route Syntax

Parameter	Description
::/0	Matches any IPv6 prefix regardless of prefix length.
ipv6-address	■ Commonly referred to as the next-hop router's IP address. ■ Typically used when connecting to a broadcast media (i.e., Ethernet).
exit-intf	■ Use the outgoing interface to forward packets to the destination network. ■ Also referred to as a directly attached static route.

Configure a Default Static IPv6 Route (2.2.4.2)

R1 can be configured with three static routes to reach all of the remote networks in our topology. However, R1 is a stub router because it is only connected to R2. Therefore, it would be more efficient to configure a default static IPv6 route.

The example in Figure 2-26 displays a configuration for a default static IPv6 route on R1.

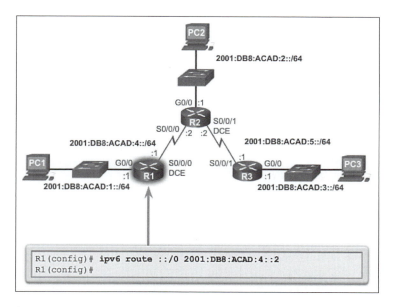

Figure 2-26 Default Static IPv6 Route Syntax

Verify a Default Static Route (2.2.4.3)

In the following output, the **show ipv6 route static** command output displays the contents of the routing table:

```
R1# show ipv6 route static
IPv6 Routing Table - default - 6 entries
Codes: C - Connected, L - Local, S - Static, U - Per-user Static route
       B - BGP, R - RIP, I1 - ISIS L1, I2 - ISIS L2
       IA - ISIS interarea, IS - ISIS summary, D - EIGRP, EX - EIGRP external
       ND - ND Default, NDp - ND Prefix, DCE - Destination, NDr - Redirect
       O - OSPF Intra, OI - OSPF Inter, OE1 - OSPF ext 1, OE2 - OSPF ext 2
       ON1 - OSPF NSSA ext 1, ON2 - OSPF NSSA ext 2
S   ::/0 [1/0]
      via 2001:DB8:ACAD:4::2, Serial0/0/0
R1#
```

Unlike IPv4, IPv6 does not explicitly state that the default IPv6 is the Gateway of Last Resort.

The key to this configuration is the ::/0 mask. Recall that the ipv6 prefix-length in a routing table determines how many bits must match between the destination IP address of the packet and the route in the routing table. The ::/0 mask indicates that none of the bits are required to match. As long as a more specific match does not exist, the default static IPv6 route matches all packets.

The following output displays a successful ping to the R3 LAN interface:

```
R1# ping 2001:0DB8:ACAD:3::1
Type escape sequence to abort.
Sending 5, 100-byte ICMP Echos to 2001:DB8:ACAD:3::1, timeout is 2 seconds:
!!!!!
Success rate is 100 percent (5/5), round-trip min/avg/max = 28/28/28 ms
R1#
```

Packet Tracer Activity 2.2.4.4: Configuring IPv6 Static and Default Routes

In this activity, you will configure IPv6 static and default routes. A static route is a route that is entered manually by the network administrator to create a route that is reliable and safe. There are four different static routes used in this activity: a recursive static route; a directly connected static route; a fully specified static route; and a default route.

Lab 2.2.4.5: Configuring IPv6 Static and Default Routes

In this lab, you will complete the following objectives:

- Part 1: Build the Network and Configure Basic Device Settings
- Part 2: Configure IPv6 Static and Default Routes

Review of CIDR and VLSM (2.3)

Recall that VLSM (variable-length subnet mask) subnetting is similar to the traditional subnetting. The difference is that with VLSM, the network is first subnetted, and then subnets are subnetted again. This can occur in several iterations. CIDR (Classless Inter-Domain Routing) was introduced by IETF in 1993 to replace class network assignments. VLSM and CIDR helped make the allocation of the limited IPv4 address space more efficient.

Classful Addressing (2.3.1)

Although CIDR and classless addressing obsoleted classful addressing, an understanding of classful addressing is still important. Routing protocols such as RIP and EIGRP can both be configured to summarize on classful network boundaries. The IPv4 routing table is also structured in a classful hierarchy.

Classful Network Addressing (2.3.1.1)

Released in 1981, RFC 790 and RFC 791 describe how IPv4 network addresses were initially allocated based on a classification system. In the original specification of IPv4, the authors established the classes to provide three different sizes of networks for large, medium, and small organizations. As a result, class A, B, and C addresses were defined with a specific format for the high order bits. High order bits are the far left bits in a 32-bit address.

As shown in Table 2-6:

- **Class A addresses begin with 0:** Intended for large organizations; includes all addresses from 0.0.0.0 (**0**0000000) to 127.255.255.255 (**0**1111111). The 0.0.0.0 address is reserved for default routing and the 127.0.0.0 address is reserved for loopback testing.

- **Class B addresses begin with 10:** Intended for medium-to-large organizations; includes all addresses from 128.0.0.0 (**10**000000) to 191.255.255.255 (**10**111111).

- **Class C addresses begin with 110:** Intended for small-to-medium organizations; includes all addresses from 192.0.0.0 (**110**00000) to 223.255.255.255 (**110**11111).

The remaining addresses were reserved for multicasting and future uses:

- **Class D Multicast addresses begin with 1110:** Multicast addresses are used to identify a group of hosts that are part of a multicast group. This helps reduce the amount of packet processing that is done by hosts, particularly on broadcast media (i.e., Ethernet LANs). Routing protocols such as RIPv2, EIGRP, and OSPF use designated multicast addresses (RIP = 224.0.0.9, EIGRP = 224.0.0.10, OSPF = 224.0.0.5, and 224.0.0.6).

- **Class E Reserved IP addresses begin with 1111:** These addresses were reserved for experimental and future use.

Table 2-6   High Order Bits

Class	High Order Bits	Start	End
Class A	0xxxxxxx	0.0.0.0	127.255.255.255
Class B	10xxxxxx	128.0.0.0	191.255.255.255
Class C	110xxxxx	192.0.0.0	223.255.255.255
Class D (Multicast)	111xxxx	224.0.0.0	239.255.255.255
Class E (Reserved)	1111xxxx	240.0.0.0	255.255.255.255

Links:

"**Internet Protocol,**" http://www.ietf.org/rfc/rfc791.txt

"**IPv4 Multicast Address Space Registry,**" http://www.iana.org/assignments/multicast-addresses

Classful Subnet Masks (2.3.1.2)

As specified in RFC 790, each network class has a default subnet mask associated with it.

As shown in Figure 2-27, class A networks used the first octet to identify the network portion of the address. This is translated to a 255.0.0.0 classful subnet mask. Because only 7 bits were left in the first octet (remember, the first bit is always 0), this made 2 to the 7th power, or 128 networks. The actual number is 126 networks, because there are two reserved class A addresses (i.e., 0.0.0.0/8 and 127.0.0.0/8). With 24 bits in the host portion, each class A address had the potential for over 16 million individual host addresses.

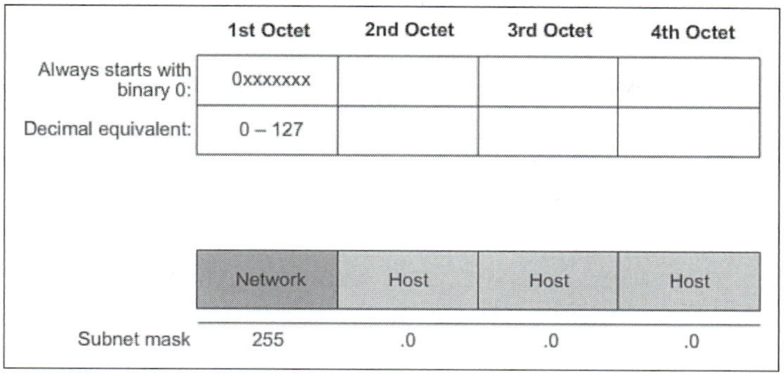

	1st Octet	2nd Octet	3rd Octet	4th Octet
Always starts with binary 0:	0xxxxxxx			
Decimal equivalent:	0 – 127			
	Network	Host	Host	Host
Subnet mask	255	.0	.0	.0

Figure 2-27 Class A Networks

As shown in Figure 2-28, class B networks used the first two octets to identify the network portion of the network address. With the first two bits already established as 1 and 0, 14 bits remained in the first two octets for assigning networks, which resulted in 16,384 class B network addresses. Because each class B network address contained 16 bits in the host portion, it controlled 65,534 addresses. (Recall that two addresses were reserved for the network and broadcast addresses.)

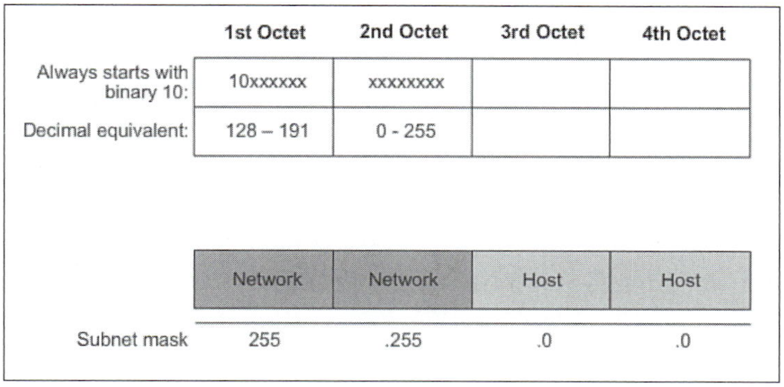

	1st Octet	2nd Octet	3rd Octet	4th Octet
Always starts with binary 10:	10xxxxxx	xxxxxxxx		
Decimal equivalent:	128 – 191	0 - 255		
	Network	Network	Host	Host
Subnet mask	255	.255	.0	.0

Figure 2-28 Class B Networks

As shown in Figure 2-29, class C networks used the first three octets to identify the network portion of the network address. With the first three bits established as 1 and 1 and 0, 21 bits remained for assigning networks for over 2 million class C networks. But, each class C network only had 8 bits in the host portion, or 254 possible host addresses.

An advantage of assigning specific default subnet masks to each class is that it made routing update messages smaller. Classful routing protocols do not include the subnet mask information in their updates. The receiving router applies the default mask based on the value of the first octet, which identifies the class.

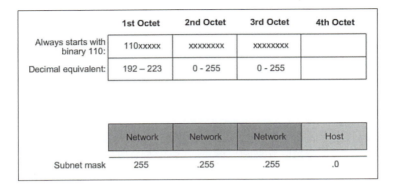

	1st Octet	2nd Octet	3rd Octet	4th Octet
Always starts with binary 110:	110xxxxx	xxxxxxxx	xxxxxxxx	
Decimal equivalent:	192 – 223	0 - 255	0 - 255	
	Network	Network	Network	Host
Subnet mask	255	.255	.255	.0

Figure 2-29 Class C Networks

Classful Routing Protocol Example (2.3.1.3)

Using classful IP addresses meant that the subnet mask of a network address could be determined by the value of the first octet, or more accurately, the first three bits of the address. Routing protocols, such as RIPv1, only need to propagate the network address of known routes and do not need to include the subnet mask in the routing update. This is due to the router receiving the routing update determining the subnet mask simply by examining the value of the first octet in the network address, or by applying its ingress interface mask for subnetted routes. The subnet mask was directly related to the network address.

In Figure 2-30, R1 sends an update to R2. In the example, R1 knows that subnet 172.16.1.0 belongs to the same major classful network as the outgoing interface. Therefore, it sends an RIP update to R2 containing subnet 172.16.1.0. When R2 receives the update, it applies the receiving interface subnet mask (/24) to the update and adds 172.16.1.0 to the routing table.

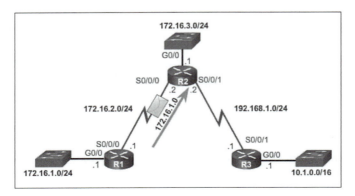

Figure 2-30 Classful Routing Update: R1 to R2

In Figure 2-31, R2 sends an update to R3. When sending updates to R3, R2 summarizes subnets 172.16.1.0/24, 172.16.2.0/24, and 172.16.3.0/24 into the major classful network 172.16.0.0. Because R3 does not have any subnets that belong to 172.16.0.0, it applies the classful mask for a class B network, which is /16.

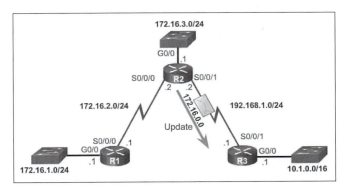

Figure 2-31 Classful Routing Update: R2 to R3

Classful Addressing Waste (2.3.1.4)

The classful addressing specified in RFCs 790 and 791 resulted in a tremendous waste of address space. In the early days of the Internet, organizations were assigned an entire classful network address from the A, B, or C class.

As illustrated in Figure 2-32:

- Class A had 50% of the total address space. However, only 126 organizations could be assigned a class A network address. Ridiculously, each of these organizations could provide addresses for up to 16 million hosts. Very large organizations were allocated entire class A address blocks. Some companies and governmental organizations still have class A addresses. For example, General Electric owns 3.0.0.0/8, Apple Computer owns 17.0.0.0/8, and the U.S. Postal Service owns 56.0.0.0/8.

- Class B had 25% of the total address space. Up to 16,384 organizations could be assigned a class B network address, and each of these networks could support up to 65,534 hosts. Only the largest organizations and governments could ever hope to use all 65,000 addresses. Like class A networks, many IP addresses in the class B address space were wasted.

- Class C had 12.5% of the total address space. Many more organizations were able to get class C networks, but were limited in the total number of hosts that they could connect. In fact, in many cases, class C addresses were often too small for most midsize organizations.

- Classes D and E are used for multicasting and reserved addresses.

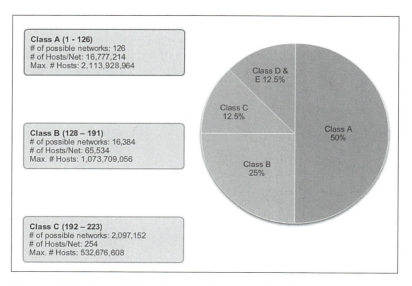

Figure 2-32 Classful IP Address Allocation = Inefficient

The overall result was that the classful addressing was a very wasteful addressing scheme. A better network addressing solution had to be developed. For this reason, Classless Inter-Domain Routing (CIDR) was introduced in 1993.

CIDR (2.3.2)

To help solve the limitation of the IPv4 address space, at least for a relatively short term, CIDR replaced classful addressing to make the distribution of IPv4 addresses more efficient.

Classless Inter-Domain Routing (2.3.2.1)

Just as the Internet was growing at an exponential rate in the early 1990s, so was the size of the routing tables that were maintained by Internet routers under classful IP addressing. For this reason, the IETF introduced CIDR in RFC 1517 in 1993.

CIDR replaced the classful network assignments, and address classes (A, B, and C) became obsolete. Using CIDR, the network address is no longer determined by the value of the first octet. Instead, the network portion of the address is determined by the subnet mask, also known as the network prefix, or prefix length (i.e., /8, /19, etc.).

ISPs are no longer limited to a /8, /16, or /24 subnet mask. They can now more efficiently allocate address space using any prefix length, starting with /8 and larger (i.e., /8, /9, /10, etc.). Figure 2-33 shows how blocks of IP addresses can be assigned to a network based on the requirements of the customer, ranging from a few hosts to hundreds or thousands of hosts.

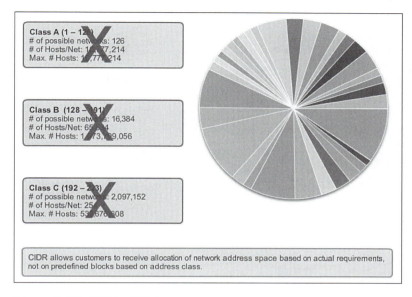

Figure 2-33 CIDR = Efficient

CIDR also reduces the size of routing tables and manages the IPv4 address space more efficiently using:

- **Route summarization:** Also known as prefix aggregation, routes are summarized into a single route to help reduce the size of routing tables. For instance, one summary static route can replace several specific static route statements.

- **Supernetting:** Occurs when the route summarization mask is a smaller value than the default traditional classful mask.

Note

A supernet is always a route summary, but a route summary is not always a supernet.

Classless Inter-Domain Routing (2.3.2.2)

In Figure 2-34, notice that ISP1 has four customers, and that each customer has a variable amount of IP address space. The address space of the four customers can be summarized into one advertisement to ISP2. The 192.168.0.0/20 summarized or aggregated route includes all the networks belonging to Customers A, B, C, and D. This type of route is known as a supernet route. A supernet summarizes multiple network addresses with a mask that is smaller than the classful mask.

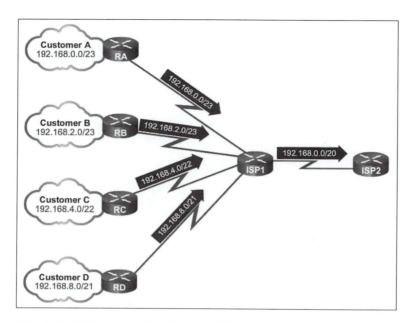

Figure 2-34 Summarizing Supernet Routes

Determining the summary route and subnet mask for a group of networks can be done in the following three steps:

How To

Step 1.   List the networks in binary format.

Step 2.   Count the number of far left matching bits. This identifies the prefix length or subnet mask for the summarized route.

Step 3.   Copy the matching bits and then add zero bits to the rest of the address to determine the summarized network address.

The summarized network address and subnet mask can now be used as the summary route for this group of networks.

Summary routes can be configured by both static routes and classless routing protocols.

Note

If a routing table contains both a summarized route and a more specific route, a route with a longer subnet mask (prefix length), the more specific route is always preferred.

Static Routing CIDR Example (2.3.2.3)

Creating smaller routing tables makes the routing table lookup process more efficient, because there are fewer routes to search. If one static route can be used instead of multiple static routes, the size of the routing table is reduced. In many cases, a single static route can be used to represent dozens, hundreds, or even thousands of routes.

Summary CIDR routes can be configured using static routes. This helps to reduce the size of routing tables.

In Figure 2-35, R1 has been configured to reach the identified networks in the topology. Although acceptable, it would be more efficient to configure a summary static route.

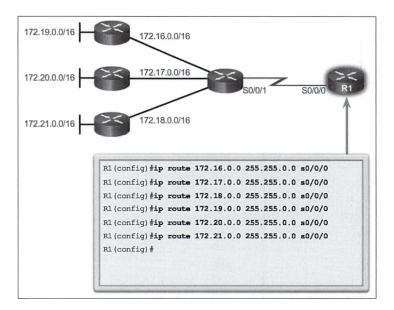

Figure 2-35 Six Static Routes

Figure 2-36 provides a solution using CIDR summarization. The six static route entries could be reduced to a 172.16.0.0/13 entry. The example removes the six static route entries and replaces them with a summary static route.

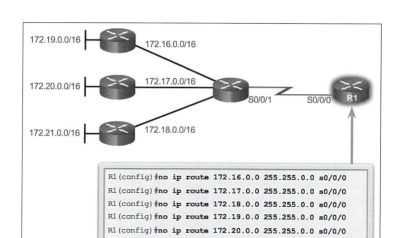

Figure 2-36 One Summary Static Route

Classless Routing Protocol Example (2.3.2.4)

Classful routing protocols cannot send supernet routes. This is because the receiving router automatically applies the default classful subnet mask to the network address in the routing update. If the topology in Figure 2-37 contained a classful routing protocol, then R3 would only install 172.16.0.0/16 in the routing table.

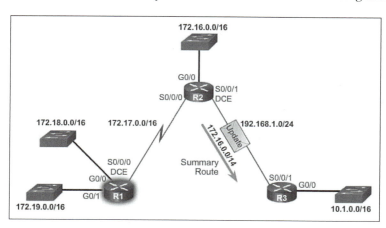

Figure 2-37 Classless Routing Update

Propagating VLSM and supernet routes requires a classless routing protocol such as RIPv2, OSPF, or EIGRP. Classless routing protocols advertise network addresses with their associated subnet masks. With a classless routing protocol, R2 can summarize networks 172.16.0.0/16, 172.17.0.0/16, 172.18.0.0/16, and 172.19.0.0/16, and advertise a supernet summary static route 172.16.0.0/14 to R3. R3 then installs the supernet route 172.16.0.0/14 in its routing table.

Note

When a supernet route is in a routing table, for example, as a static route, a classful routing protocol does not include that route in its updates.

VLSM (2.3.3)

Along with CIDR, VLSM helped more efficiently allocate the IPv4 address space. VLSM permits network administrators to subnet one or more specific subnets, allowing for different sized subnets. With VLSM, network administrators are no longer required to create a one-size-fits-all subnet.

Fixed-Length Subnet Masking (2.3.3.1)

With fixed-length subnet masking (FLSM), the same number of addresses is allocated for each subnet. If all the subnets have the same requirements for the number of hosts, these fixed-size address blocks would be sufficient. However, most often that is not the case.

Note

FLSM is also referred to as traditional subnetting.

The topology shown in Figure 2-38 requires that network address 192.168.20.0/24 be subnetted into seven subnets: one subnet for each of the four LANs (Buildings A to D), and one for each of the three WAN connections between routers.

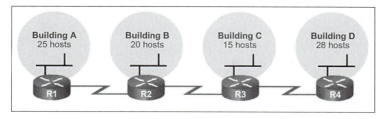

Figure 2-38 Network Topology: Basic Subnets

Figure 2-39 highlights how traditional subnetting can borrow 3 bits from the Host portion in the last octet to meet the subnet requirement of seven subnets. For example, under the Host portion, the Subnet portion highlights how borrowing 3 bits creates 8 subnets, while the Host portion highlights 5 host bits providing 30 usable host IP addresses per subnet. This scheme creates the needed subnets and meets the host requirement of the largest LAN.

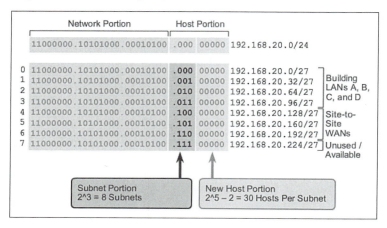

Figure 2-39 Basic Subnet Scheme

Although this traditional subnetting meets the needs of the largest LAN and divides the address space into an adequate number of subnets, it results in significant waste of unused addresses.

For example, only two addresses are needed in each subnet for the three WAN links. Because each subnet has 30 usable addresses, there are 28 unused addresses in each of these subnets. As shown in Figure 2-40, this results in 84 unused addresses (28 × 3). Further, this limits future growth by reducing the total number of subnets available. This inefficient use of addresses is characteristic of traditional subnetting of classful networks.

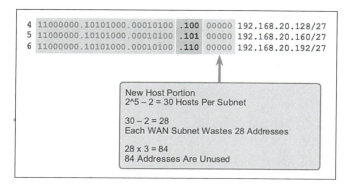

Figure 2-40 Unused Addresses on WAN Subnets

Applying a traditional subnetting scheme to this scenario is not very efficient and is wasteful. In fact, this example is a good model for showing how subnetting a subnet can be used to maximize address utilization. Subnetting a subnet, or using variable-length subnet masking (VLSM), was designed to avoid wasting addresses.

Variable-Length Subnet Masking (2.3.3.2)

In traditional subnetting the same subnet mask is applied for all the subnets. This means that each subnet has the same number of available host addresses.

As illustrated in Figure 2-41, traditional subnetting creates subnets of equal size. Each subnet in a traditional scheme uses the same subnet mask.

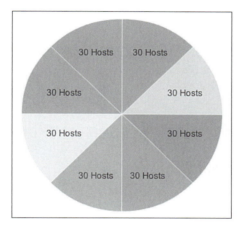

Figure 2-41 Traditional Subnetting Creates Equal Sized Subnets

With VLSM the subnet mask length varies depending on how many bits have been borrowed for a particular subnet, thus the "variable" part of variable-length subnet mask. As shown in Figure 2-42, VLSM allows a network space to be divided into unequal parts.

VLSM subnetting is similar to traditional subnetting in that bits are borrowed to create subnets. The formulas to calculate the number of hosts per subnet and the number of subnets created still apply. The difference is that subnetting is not a single-pass activity. With VLSM, the network is first subnetted, and then the subnets are subnetted again. This process can be repeated multiple times to create subnets of various sizes.

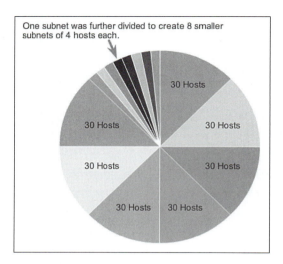

One subnet was further divided to create 8 smaller subnets of 4 hosts each.

30 Hosts

30 Hosts

30 Hosts

30 Hosts

30 Hosts

30 Hosts

30 Hosts

30 Hosts

Figure 2-42 Subnets of Varying Sizes

VLSM in Action (2.3.3.3)

VLSM allows the use of different masks for each subnet. After a network address is subnetted, those subnets can be further subnetted. VLSM is simply subnetting a subnet. VLSM can be thought of as sub-subnetting.

Figure 2-43 shows the network 10.0.0.0/8 that has been subnetted using the subnet mask of /16, which makes 256 subnets; that is, 10.0.0.0/16, 10.1.0.0/16, 10.2.0.0/16, and so forth through 10.255.0.0/16. Four of these /16 subnets are displayed in Figure 2-43. Any of these /16 subnets can be subnetted further.

Figure 2-43 shows four subnets, subnetted a second time using three different subnet masks:

- The 10.1.0.0/16 subnet is subnetted again with the /24 mask.

- The 10.2.0.0/16 subnet is subnetted again with the /24 mask.

- The 10.3.0.0/16 subnet is subnetted again with the /28 mask

- The 10.4.0.0/16 subnet is subnetted again with the /20 mask.

Individual host addresses are assigned from the addresses of sub-subnets. For example, Figure 2-43 shows the 10.1.0.0/16 subnet divided into /24 subnets. The 10.1.4.10 address would now be a member of the more specific subnet 10.1.4.0/24.

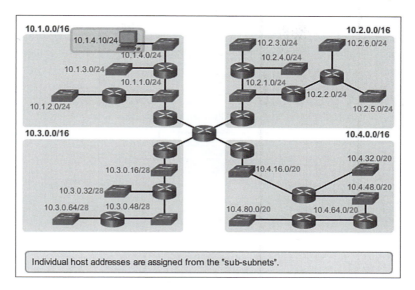

Figure 2-43 VLSM Subnets

Subnetting Subnets (2.3.3.4)

Another way to view the VLSM subnets is to list each subnet and its sub-subnets.

In Figure 2-44, the 10.0.0.0/8 network is the starting address space and is subnetted with a /16 mask. Borrowing 8 bits (going from /8 to /16) creates 256 subnets that range from 10.0.0.0/16 to 10.255.0.0/16.

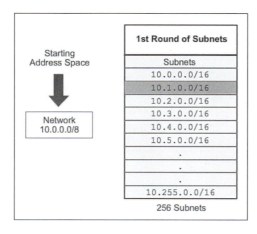

Figure 2-44 Subnetting 10.0.0.0/8 to 10.0.0.0/16

In Figure 2-45, the 10.1.0.0/16 subnet is further subnetted by borrowing 8 more bits. This creates 256 subnets with a /24 mask. This mask allows 254 host addresses per subnet. The subnets ranging from 10.1.0.0/24 to 10.1.255.0/24 are subnets of the subnet 10.1.0.0/16.

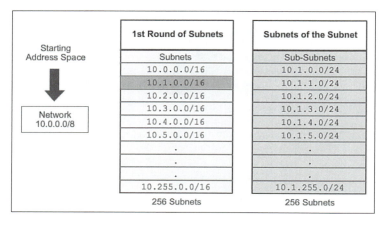

Figure 2-45 Subnetting 10.1.0.0/16 to 10.1.0.0/24

In Figure 2-46, the 10.2.0.0/16 subnet is also further subnetted with a /24 mask allowing 254 host addresses per subnet. The subnets ranging from 10.2.0.0/24 to 10.2.255.0/24 are subnets of the subnet 10.2.0.0/16.

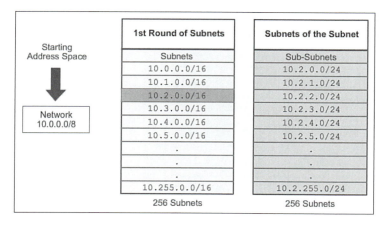

Figure 2-46 Subnetting 10.2.0.0/16 to 10.2.0.0/24

In Figure 2-47, the 10.3.0.0/16 subnet is further subnetted with a /28 mask, thus creating 4,096 subnets and allowing 14 host addresses per subnet. The subnets ranging from 10.3.0.0/28 to 10.3.255.240/28 are subnets of the subnet 10.3.0.0/16.

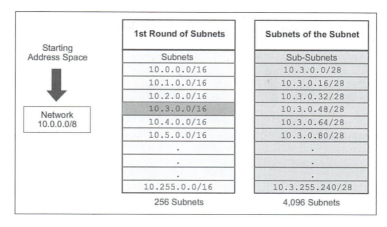

Figure 2-47 Subnetting 10.3.0.0/16 to 10.3.0.0/28

In Figure 2-48, the 10.4.0.0/16 subnet is further subnetted with a /20 mask, thus creating 16 subnets and allowing 4,094 host addresses per subnet. The subnets ranging from 10.4.0.0/20 to 10.4.240.0/20 are subnets of the subnet 10.4.0.0/16. These /20 subnets are big enough to subnet even further, allowing more networks.

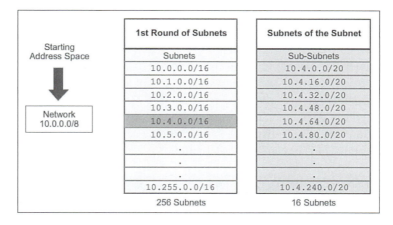

Figure 2-48 Subnetting 10.4.0.0/16 to 10.4.0.0/20

VLSM Example (2.3.3.5)

Careful consideration must be given to the design of a network addressing scheme. For example, the sample topology in Figure 2-49 requires seven subnets.

Using traditional subnetting, the first seven address blocks are allocated for LANs and WANs, as shown in Figure 2-50. This scheme results in 8 subnets with 30 usable addresses each (/27). While this scheme works for the LAN segments, there are many wasted addresses in the WAN segments.

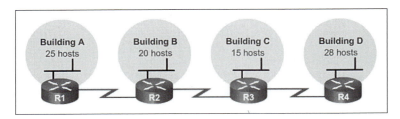

Figure 2-49 Basic Topology

	/27 Network	Hosts
Building A	.0	.1 - .30
Building B	.32	.33 - .62
Building C	.64	.65 - .94
Building D	.96	.97 - .126
WAN R1 – R2	.128	.129 - .158
WAN R2 – R3	.160	.161 - .190
WAN R3 – R4	.192	.193 - .222
Unused	.224	.225 - .254

Figure 2-50 Subnetting 192.168.20.0/24 to 192.168.20.0/27

If an addressing scheme is designed for a new network, the address blocks can be assigned in a way that minimizes waste and keeps unused blocks of addresses contiguous. It can be more difficult to do this when adding to an existing network.

As shown in Figure 2-51, to use the address space more efficiently, /30 subnets are created for WAN links. To keep the unused blocks of addresses together, the last /27 subnet is further subnetted to create the /30 subnets. The first 3 subnets were assigned to WAN links, creating subnets 192.168.20.224/30, 192.168.20.228/30, and 192.168.20.232/30. Designing the addressing scheme in this way leaves three unused /27 subnets and five unused /30 subnets.

	/27 Network	Hosts
Building A	.0	.1 - .30
Building B	.32	.33 - .62
Building C	.64	.65 - .94
Building D	.96	.97 - .126
Unused	.128	.129 - .158
Unused	.160	.161 - .190
Unused	.192	.193 - .222
	.224	.225 - .254

	/30 Network	Hosts
WAN R1–R2	.224	.225 - .226
WAN R2–R3	.228	.229 - .230
WAN R3–R4	.232	.233 - .234

Figure 2-51 Subnetting 192.168.20.224/27 to 192.168.20.224/30

The next four CLI outputs display sample configurations on all four routers to implement the VLSM addressing scheme.

Configuring VLSM on R1:

```
R1(config)# interface gigabitethernet 0/0
R1(config-if)# ip address 192.168.20.1 255.255.255.224
R1(config-if)# exit
R1(config)# interface serial 0/0/0
R1(config-if)# ip address 192.168.20.225 255.255.255.252
R1(config-if)# end
R1#
```

Configuring VLSM on R2:

```
R2(config)# interface gigabitethernet 0/0
R2(config-if)# ip address 192.168.20.33 255.255.255.224
R2(config-if)# exit
R2(config)# interface serial 0/0/0
R2(config-if)# ip address 192.168.20.226 255.255.255.252
R2(config-if)# exit
R2(config)# interface serial 0/0/1
R2(config-if)# ip address 192.168.20.229 255.255.255.252
R2(config-if)# end
R2#
```

Configuring VLSM on R3:

```
R3(config)# interface gigabitethernet 0/0
R3(config-if)# ip address 192.168.20.65 255.255.255.224
R3(config-if)# exit
R3(config)# interface serial 0/0/0
R3(config-if)# ip address 192.168.20.230 255.255.255.252
R3(config-if)# exit
R3(config)# interface serial 0/0/1
R3(config-if)# ip address 192.168.20.233 255.255.255.252
R3(config-if)# end
R3#
```

Configuring VLSM on R4:

```
R4(config)# interface gigabitethernet 0/0
R4(config-if)# ip address 192.168.20.97 255.255.255.224
R4(config-if)# exit
R4(config)# interface serial 0/0/0
R4(config-if)# ip address 192.168.20.234 255.255.255.252
R4(config-if)# end
R4#
```

Packet Tracer Activity 2.3.3.6: Designing and Implementing a VLSM Addressing Scheme

In this activity, you are given a network address to develop a VLSM addressing scheme for the network shown in the included topology.

Lab 2.3.3.7: Designing and Implementing Addressing with VLSM

In this lab, you will complete the following objectives:

- Part 1: Examine the Network Requirements
- Part 2: Design the VLSM Address Scheme
- Part 3: Cable and Configure the IPv4 Network

Configure Summary and Floating Static Routes (2.4)

Summary static routes can be used to help minimize the number of static routes in the routing table. Using summary static routes can also make management of a large number of static routes easier and less prone to errors. Floating static routes can be used as a backup route for another static route or a dynamic routing protocol.

Configure IPv4 Summary Routes (2.4.1)

A single IPv4 static *summary route* can be used to replace multiple static routes when those routes can be summarized with a common prefix length. The configuration of a summary static route is similar to the configuration of other IPv4 static routes.

Route Summarization (2.4.1.1)

Route summarization, also known as route aggregation, is the process of advertising a contiguous set of addresses as a single address with a less-specific, shorter subnet mask. CIDR is a form of route summarization and is synonymous with the term supernetting.

CIDR ignores the limitation of classful boundaries, and allows summarization with masks that are smaller than that of the default classful mask. This type of summarization helps reduce the number of entries in routing updates and lowers the number of entries in local routing tables. It also helps reduce bandwidth utilization for routing updates and results in faster routing table lookups.

In Figure 2-52, R1 requires a summary static route to reach networks in the range of 172.20.0.0/16 to 172.23.0.0/16.

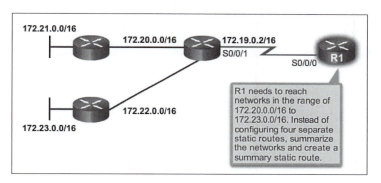

Figure 2-52 Basic Topology

Calculate a Summary Route (2.4.1.2)

Summarizing networks into a single address and mask can be done in three steps, as shown in Figure 2-53:

Step 1.   List the networks in binary format. Figure 2-53 lists networks 172.20.0.0/16 to 172.23.0.0/16 in binary format.

Step 2.   Count the number of far left matching bits to determine the mask for the summary route. Figure 2-53 highlights the 14 far left matching bits. This is the prefix, or subnet mask, for the summarized route: /14 or 255.252.0.0.

Step 3.   Copy the matching bits and then add zero bits to determine the summarized network address. Figure 2-53 shows that the matching bits with zeros at the end results in the network address 172.20.0.0. The four networks—172.20.0.0/16, 172.21.0.0/16, 172.22.0.0/16, and 172.23.0.0/16—can be summarized into the single network address and prefix 172.20.0.0/14.

Figure 2-54 displays R1 configured with a summary static route to reach networks 172.20.0.0/16 to 172.23.0.0/16.

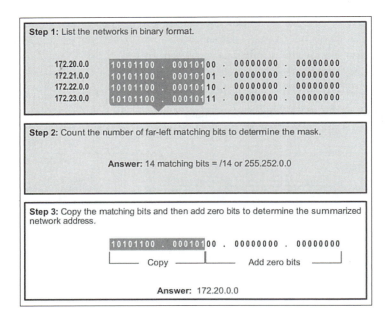

Figure 2-53 Calculating a Route Summary

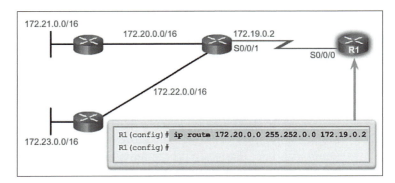

Figure 2-54 One Summary Static Route

Summary Static Route Example (2.4.1.3)

Multiple static routes can be summarized into a single static route if:

- The destination networks are contiguous and can be summarized into a single network address.

- The multiple static routes all use the same exit interface or next-hop IP address.

Consider the example in Figure 2-55. All routers have connectivity using static routes.

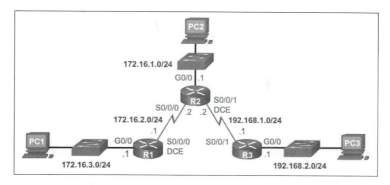

Figure 2-55 Basic Topology

The following output displays the static routing table entries for R3. Notice that it has three static routes that can be summarized because they share the same two first octets.

```
R3# show ip route static | begin Gateway
Gateway of last resort is not set
        172.16.0.0/24 is subnetted, 3 subnets
S          172.16.1.0 is directly connected, Serial0/0/1
S          172.16.2.0 is directly connected, Serial0/0/1
S          172.16.3.0 is directly connected, Serial0/0/1
R3#
```

Figure 2-56 displays the steps to summarize those three networks:

Step 1.   Write out the networks to summarize in binary.

Step 2.   To find the subnet mask for summarization, start with the far left bit, work to the right, finding all the bits that match consecutively until a column of bits that do not match is found, identifying the summary boundary.

Step 3.   Count the number of far left matching bits; in our example, it is 22. This number identifies the subnet mask for the summarized route as /22 or 255.255.252.0.

Step 4.   To find the network address for summarization, copy the matching 22 bits and add all 0 bits to the end to make 32 bits.

After the summary route is identified, replace the existing routes with the one summary route.

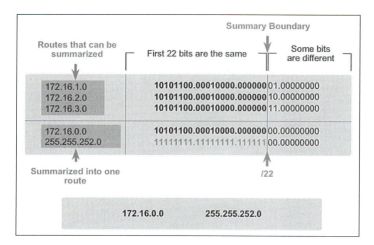

Figure 2-56 Summarize the Networks

The following output shows how the three existing routes are removed and then the new summary static route is configured:

```
R3(config)# no ip route 172.16.1.0 255.255.255.0 s0/0/1
R3(config)# no ip route 172.16.2.0 255.255.255.0 s0/0/1
R3(config)# no ip route 172.16.3.0 255.255.255.0 s0/0/1
R3(config)# ip route 172.16.0.0 255.255.252.0 s0/0/1
R3(config)#
```

The following output confirms that the summary static route is in the routing table of R3:

```
R3# show ip route static | begin Gateway
Gateway of last resort is not set
      172.16.0.0/22 is subnetted, 1 subnets
S        172.16.0.0 is directly connected, Serial0/0/1
R3#
```

Activity 2.4.1.4: Determine the Summary Network Address and Prefix

Go to the online course to perform this practice activity.

Packet Tracer Activity 2.4.1.5: Configuring IPv4 Route Summarization – Scenario 1

In this activity, you will calculate and configure summary routes. Route summarization, also known as route aggregation, is the process of advertising a contiguous set of addresses as a single address.

Packet Tracer Activity 2.4.1.6: Configuring IPv4 Route Summarization – Scenario 2

In this activity, you will calculate and configure summary routes. Route summarization, also known as route aggregation, is the process of advertising a contiguous set of addresses as a single address. After calculating summary routes for each LAN, you must summarize a route which includes all networks in the topology in order for the ISP to reach each LAN.

Configure IPv6 Summary Routes (2.4.1)

Similar to IPv4, a single IPv6 static summary route can be used to replace multiple IPv6 static routes with a common prefix length. The calculation and configuration of an IPv6 summary static route is similar to the configuration of an IPv4 static summary route.

Summarize IPv6 Network Addresses (2.4.2.1)

Aside from the fact that IPv6 addresses are 128 bits long and written in hexadecimal, summarizing IPv6 addresses is actually similar to the summarization of IPv4 addresses. It just requires a few extra steps due to the abbreviated IPv6 addresses and hex conversion.

Multiple static IPv6 routes can be summarized into a single static IPv6 route if:

- The destination networks are contiguous and can be summarized into a single network address.
- The multiple static routes all use the same exit interface or next-hop IPv6 address.

Refer to the network in Figure 2-57. R1 currently has four static IPv6 routes to reach networks 2001:DB8:ACAD:1::/64 to 2001:DB8:ACAD:4::/64.

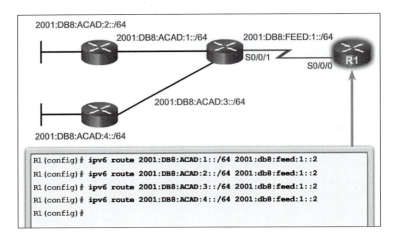

Figure 2-57 Basic Topology

The following output displays the IPv6 static routes installed in the IPv6 routing table:

```
R1# show ipv6 route static
IPv6 Routing Table - default - 7 entries
Codes: C - Connected, L - Local, S - Static, U - Per-user Static route
       B - BGP, R - RIP, I1 - ISIS L1, I2 - ISIS L2
       IA - ISIS interarea, IS - ISIS summary, D - EIGRP, EX - EIGRP external
       ND - ND Default, NDp - ND Prefix, DCE - Destination, NDr - Redirect
       O - OSPF Intra, OI - OSPF Inter, OE1 - OSPF ext 1, OE2 - OSPF ext 2
       ON1 - OSPF NSSA ext 1, ON2 - OSPF NSSA ext 2
S   2001:DB8:ACAD:1::/64 [1/0]
     via 2001:DB8:FEED:1::2
S   2001:DB8:ACAD:2::/64 [1/0]
     via 2001:DB8:FEED:1::2
S   2001:DB8:ACAD:3::/64 [1/0]
     via 2001:DB8:FEED:1::2
S   2001:DB8:ACAD:4::/64 [1/0]
     via 2001:DB8:FEED:1::2
R1#
```

Calculate IPv6 Network Addresses (2.4.2.2)

Summarizing IPv6 networks into a single IPv6 prefix and prefix length can be done in seven steps as shown in Figures 2-58 to 2-64:

Step 1. List the network addresses (prefixes) and identify the part where the addresses differ.

Step 2. Expand the IPv6 if it is abbreviated.

Step 3. Convert the differing section from hex to binary.

Step 4. Count the number of far left matching bits to determine the prefix length for the summary route.

Step 5. Copy the matching bits and then add zero bits to determine the summarized network address (prefix).

Step 6. Convert the binary section back to hex.

Step 7. Append the prefix of the summary route (result of Step 4).

```
2001:0DB8:ACAD:1::/64

2001:0DB8:ACAD:2::/64

2001:0DB8:ACAD:3::/64

2001:0DB8:ACAD:4::/64
```

Figure 2-58 Identify the Part Where the Addresses Differ

```
2001:0DB8:ACAD:0001::/64

2001:0DB8:ACAD:0002::/64

2001:0DB8:ACAD:0003::/64

2001:0DB8:ACAD:0004::/64
```

Figure 2-59 Identify the Part Where the Addresses Differ – Expanded View

```
2001:0DB8:ACAD:0000000000000001::/64

2001:0DB8:ACAD:0000000000000010::/64

2001:0DB8:ACAD:0000000000000011::/64

2001:0DB8:ACAD:0000000000000100::/64
```

Figure 2-60 Convert the Section from Hex to Binary

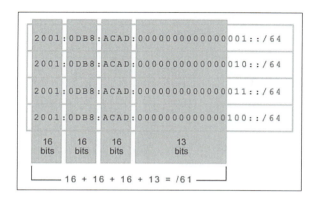

Figure 2-61 Count the Number of Far Left Matching Bits

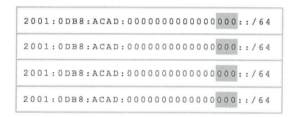

Figure 2-62 Add Zero Bits to Determine the Summarized Network Address

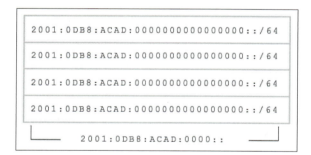

Figure 2-63 Convert the Binary Section Back to Hex

```
2001:0DB8:ACAD:0000000000000000::/64

2001:0DB8:ACAD:0000000000000000::/64

2001:0DB8:ACAD:0000000000000000::/64

2001:0DB8:ACAD:0000000000000000::/64
```
```
          2001:0DB8:ACAD:0000::/61
                     or
          2001:DB8:ACAD:0::/61
                     or
          2001:DB8:ACAD::/61
```

Figure 2-64 Count the Number of Far Left Matching Bits

Configure an IPv6 Summary Address (2.4.2.3)

After the summary route is identified, replace the existing routes with the single summary route.

Figure 2-65 displays how the four existing routes are removed and then the new summary static IPv6 route is configured.

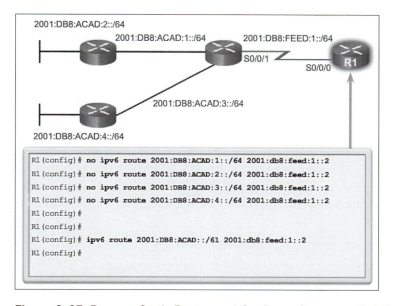

Figure 2-65 Remove Static Routes and Configure Summary IPv6 Route

The following output confirms that the summary static route is in the routing table of R1:

```
R1# show ipv6 route static
IPv6 Routing Table - default - 4 entries
Codes: C - Connected, L - Local, S - Static, U - Per-user Static route
       B - BGP, R - RIP, I1 - ISIS L1, I2 - ISIS L2
       IA - ISIS interarea, IS - ISIS summary, D - EIGRP, EX - EIGRP external
       ND - ND Default, NDp - ND Prefix, DCE - Destination, NDr - Redirect
       O - OSPF Intra, OI - OSPF Inter, OE1 - OSPF ext 1, OE2 - OSPF ext 2
       ON1 - OSPF NSSA ext 1, ON2 - OSPF NSSA ext 2
S   2001:DB8:ACA8::/45 [1/0]
      via 2001:DB8:FEED:1::2
R1#
```

Packet Tracer Activity 2.4.2.4: Configuring IPv6 Route Summarization

In this activity, you will calculate, configure, and verify a summary route for all the networks R1 can access through R2. R1 is configured with a loopback interface. Instead of adding a LAN or another network to R1, we can use a loopback interface to simplify testing when verifying routing.

Lab 2.4.2.5: Calculating Summary Routes with IPv4 and IPv6

In this lab, you will complete the following objectives:

- Part 1: Calculate IPv4 Summary Routes
- Part 2: Calculate IPv6 Summary Routes

Configure Floating Static Routes (2.4.3)

There may be times when a primary route fails due to physical layer problems, hardware issues, a misconfiguration, or many other reasons. A floating static route can be used as a backup route when there is a secondary path available.

Floating Static Routes (2.4.3.1)

Floating static routes are static routes that have an administrative distance greater than the administrative distance of another static route or dynamic routes. They are very useful when providing a backup to a primary link, as shown in Figure 2-66.

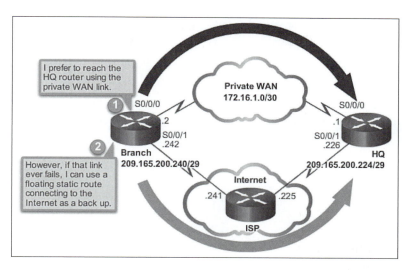

Figure 2-66 Why Configure a Floating Static Route?

By default, static routes have an administrative distance of 1, making them preferable to routes learned from dynamic routing protocols. For example, the administrative distances of some common dynamic routing protocols are:

- EIGRP = 90
- IGRP = 100
- OSPF = 110
- IS-IS = 115
- RIP = 120

The administrative distance of a static route can be increased to make the route less desirable than that of another static route or a route learned through a dynamic routing protocol. In this way, the static route "floats" and is not used when the route with the better administrative distance is active. However, if the preferred route is lost, the floating static route can take over, and traffic can be sent through this alternate route.

A floating static route can be used to provide a backup route to multiple interfaces or networks on a router. It is also encapsulation independent, meaning it can be used to forward packets out any interface, regardless of encapsulation type.

An important consideration of a floating static route is that it is affected by convergence time. A route that is continuously dropping and re-establishing a connection can cause the backup interface to be activated unnecessarily.

Configure a Floating Static Route (2.4.3.2)

IPv4 static routes are configured using the **ip route** global configuration command and specifying an administrative distance. If no administrative distance is configured, the default value (1) is used.

Refer to the topology in Figure 2-67. In this scenario, the preferred route from R1 is to R2. The connection to R3 should be used for backup only.

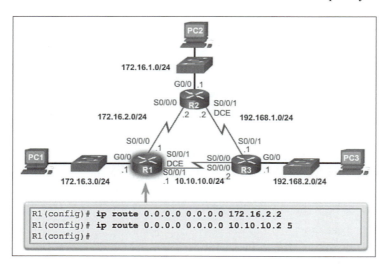

Figure 2-67 Configure a Floating Static Route to R3

R1 is configured with a default static route pointing to R2. Because no administrative distance is configured, the default value (1) is used for this static route. R1 is also configured with a floating static default pointing to R3 with an administrative distance of 5. This value is greater than the default value of 1 and, therefore, this route floats and is not present in the routing table, unless the preferred route fails.

The following output verifies that the default route to R2 is installed in the routing table. Note that the backup route to R3 is not present in the routing table.

```
R1# show ip route static | begin Gateway
Gateway of last resort is 0.0.0.0 to network 0.0.0.0
S*    0.0.0.0/0 [1/0] via 172.16.2.2
R1#
```

Activity 2.4.3.2: Configure a Default Static Route on R3

Go to the online course to use the Syntax Checker in the third graphic to configure a default route using the next-hop address 192.168.1.2.

Test the Floating Static Route (2.4.3.3)

Because the default static route on R1 to R2 has an administrative distance of 1, traffic from R1 to R3 should go through R2. The output in Figure 2-68 confirms that traffic between R1 and R3 flows through R2.

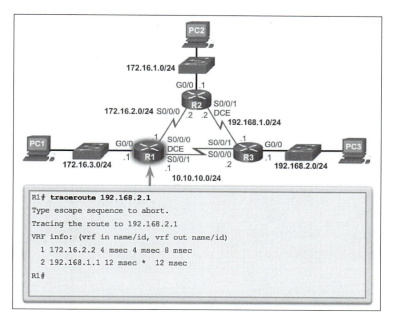

Figure 2-68 Verify the Path to the R3 LAN

What would happen if R2 failed? To simulate this failure, both serial interfaces of R2 are shut down, as shown in the following output:

```
R2(config)# int s0/0/0
R2(config-if)# shut
*Feb 21 16:33:35.939: %LINK-5-CHANGED: Interface Serial0/0/0, changed state to admin-
    istratively down
*Feb 21 16:33:36.939: %LINEPROTO-5-UPDOWN: Line protocol on Interface Serial0/0/0,
    changed state to down
R2(config-if)# int s0/0/1
R2(config-if)# shut
R2(config-if)#
*Feb 21 16:33:42.543: %LINK-5-CHANGED: Interface Serial0/0/1, changed state to admin-
    istratively down
*Feb 21 16:33:43.543: %LINEPROTO-5-UPDOWN: Line protocol on Interface Serial0/0/1,
    changed state to down
```

Notice in the following output that R1 automatically generates messages indicating that the serial interface to R2 is down. A look at the routing table verifies that the default route is now pointing to R3 using the floating static default route configured for next-hop 10.10.10.2.

```
*Feb 21 16:35:58.435: %LINK-3-UPDOWN: Interface Serial0/0/0, changed state to down
*Feb 21 16:35:59.435: %LINEPROTO-5-UPDOWN: Line protocol on Interface Serial0/0/0,
   changed state to down
R1#
R1# show ip route static | begin Gateway
Gateway of last resort is 0.0.0.0 to network 0.0.0.0
S*    0.0.0.0/0 [5/0] via 10.10.10.2
R1#
```

The output confirms that traffic now flows directly between R1 and R3:

```
R1# traceroute 192.168.2.1
Type escape sequence to abort.
Tracing the route to 192.168.2.1
VRF info: (vrf in name/id, vrf out name/id)
  1 10.10.10.2 4 msec 4 msec *
R1#
```

Note

Configuring IPv6 floating static routes is outside of the scope of this chapter.

Packet Tracer
Activity

Packet Tracer Activity 2.4.3.4: Configuring a Floating Static Route

In this activity, you will configure a floating static route. A floating static route is used as a backup route. It has a manually configured administrative distance greater than that of the primary route and therefore would not be in the routing table until the primary route fails. You will test failover to the backup route, and then restore connectivity to the primary route.

Troubleshoot Static and Default Route Issues (2.5)

Now that you have learned how to configure different types of static routes, this section discusses how to troubleshoot some of the common problems you might encounter. Troubleshooting exercises are an excellent method to help better understand network protocols and configurations. When a static route is no longer needed, that static route should be deleted from the running and startup configuration files.

Packet Processing with Static Routes (2.5.1)

Now that you have configured static routes, you need to learn about the process that a packet goes through as it is forwarded by a router.

Static Routes and Packet Forwarding (2.5.1.1)

The following example describes the packet forwarding process with static routes.

Examine Figure 2-69, where PC1 is sending a packet to PC3:

1. The packet arrives on the FastEthernet 0/0 interface of R1.

2. R1 does not have a specific route to the destination network, 192.168.2.0/24; therefore, R1 uses the default static route.

3. R1 encapsulates the packet in a new frame. Because the link to R2 is a point-to-point link, R1 adds an "all 1s" address for the Layer 2 destination address.

4. The frame is forwarded out of the Serial 0/0/0 interface. The packet arrives on the Serial 0/0/0 interface on R2.

5. R2 de-encapsulates the frame and looks for a route to the destination. R2 has a static route to 192.168.2.0/24 out of the Serial 0/0/1 interface.

6. R2 encapsulates the packet in a new frame. Because the link to R3 is a point-to-point link, R2 adds an "all 1s" address for the Layer 2 destination address.

7. The frame is forwarded out of the Serial 0/0/1 interface. The packet arrives on the Serial 0/0/1 interface on R3.

8. R3 de-encapsulates the frame and looks for a route to the destination. R3 has a connected route to 192.168.2.0/24 out of the FastEthernet 0/0 interface.

9. R3 looks up the ARP table entry for 192.168.2.10 to find the Layer 2 Media Access Control (MAC) address for PC3. If no entry exists, R3 sends an Address Resolution Protocol (ARP) request out of the FastEthernet 0/0 interface, and PC3 responds with an ARP reply, which includes the PC3 MAC address.

10. R3 encapsulates the packet in a new frame with the MAC address of the FastEthernet 0/0 interface as the source Layer 2 address and the MAC address of PC3 as the destination MAC address.

11. The frame is forwarded out of the FastEthernet 0/0 interface. The packet arrives on the network interface card (NIC) interface of PC3.

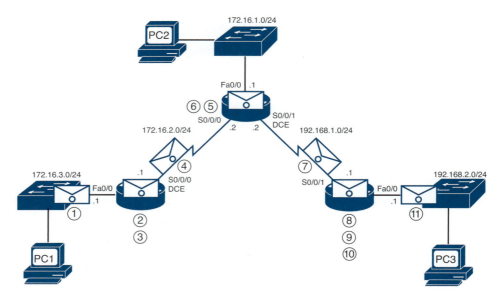

Figure 2-69 Static Routes and Packet Forwarding

Troubleshoot IPv4 Static and Default Route Configuration (2.5.2)

Troubleshooting is a skill that develops as you gain experience. It is always best to look for the most obvious and simplest issues first, such as an interface still in shutdown mode or an interface with the wrong IP address. After these items have been verified, begin looking for more complicated possibilities like an error in the static route configuration.

Troubleshooting a Missing Route (2.5.2.1)

When end-to-end connectivity is a problem, begin by making sure that you can ping your own interface and other devices on your own directly connected networks. When this has been verified, begin testing connectivity to remote networks from other devices.

Networks are subject to forces that can cause their status to change quite often:

- An interface fails.

- A service provider drops a connection.

- Links become oversaturated.

- An administrator enters a wrong configuration.

When there is a change in the network, connectivity may be lost. Network administrators are responsible for pinpointing and solving the problem. To find and solve these issues, a network administrator must be familiar with tools to help isolate routing problems quickly.

Common IOS troubleshooting commands include:

- **ping**

- **traceroute**

- **show ip route**

- **show ip interface brief**

- **show cdp neighbors detail**

Figure 2-70 displays the result of an extended ping from the source interface of R1 to the LAN interface of R3. An extended ping is when the source interface or source IP address is specified.

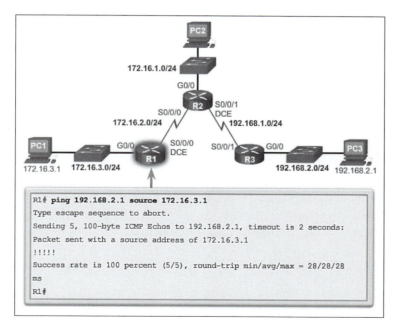

Figure 2-70 Extended Ping

The following output displays the result of a traceroute from R1 to the R3 LAN:

```
R1# traceroute 192.168.2.1
Type escape sequence to abort.
Tracing the route to 192.168.2.1
VRF info: (vrf in name/id, vrf out name/id)
  1 172.16.2.2 4 msec 4 msec 8 msec
  2 192.168.1.1 12 msec 12 msec *
R1#
```

The following output displays the routing table of R1:

```
R1# show ip route | begin Gateway
Gateway of last resort is not set
      172.16.0.0/16 is variably subnetted, 5 subnets, 2 masks
S        172.16.1.0/24 [1/0] via 172.16.2.2
C        172.16.2.0/24 is directly connected, Serial0/0/0
L        172.16.2.1/32 is directly connected, Serial0/0/0
C        172.16.3.0/24 is directly connected, GigabitEthernet0/0
L        172.16.3.1/32 is directly connected, GigabitEthernet0/0
S     192.168.1.0/24 [1/0] via 172.16.2.2
S     192.168.2.0/24 [1/0] via 172.16.2.2
R1#
```

The following output provides a quick status of all interfaces on the router:

```
R1# show ip interface brief
Interface                    IP-Address      OK? Method Status                Protocol
Embedded-Service-Engine0/0 unassigned      YES unset  administratively down down
GigabitEthernet0/0           172.16.3.1      YES manual up                    up
GigabitEthernet0/1           unassigned      YES unset  administratively down down
Serial0/0/0                  172.16.2.1      YES manual up                    up
Serial0/0/1                  unassigned      YES unset  administratively down down
R1#
```

The **show cdp neighbors** command in the following output provides a list of directly connected Cisco devices. This command validates Layer 2 (and therefore Layer 1) connectivity. For example, if a neighbor device is listed in the command output, but it cannot be pinged, then Layer 3 addressing should be investigated.

```
R1# show cdp neighbors
Capability Codes: R - Router, T - Trans Bridge, B - Source Route Bridge
                  S - Switch, H - Host, I - IGMP, r - Repeater, P - Phone,
                  D - Remote, C - CVTA, M - Two-port Mac Relay

Device ID      Local Intrfce    Holdtme    Capability  Platform  Port ID
netlab-cs5     Gig 0/0          156            S I     WS-C2960- Fas 0/1
R2             Ser 0/0/0        153          R S I     CISCO1941 Ser 0/0/0
R1#
```

Solve a Connectivity Problem (2.5.2.2)

Finding a missing (or misconfigured) route is a relatively straightforward process, if the right tools are used in a methodical manner.

For instance, in this example, the user at PC1 reports that he cannot access resources on the R3 LAN. This can be confirmed by pinging the LAN interface of R3 using the LAN interface of R1 as the source (see Figure 2-71). The results show that there is no connectivity between these LANs.

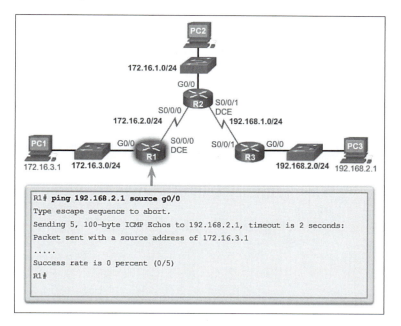

Figure 2-71 Verify Connectivity to the R3 LAN

A traceroute in the following output reveals that R2 is not responding as expected. For some reason, R2 forwards the traceroute back to R1. R1 returns it to R2. This loop would continue until the time to live (TTL) value decrements to zero, in which case, the router would then send an Internet Control Message Protocol (ICMP) Destination Unreachable message to R1.

```
R1# traceroute 192.168.2.1
Type escape sequence to abort.
Tracing the route to 192.168.2.1
VRF info: (vrf in name/id, vrf out name/id)
  1 172.16.2.2 4 msec 4 msec 8 msec
  2 172.16.2.1 12 msec 12 msec 12 msec
  3 172.16.2.2 12 msec 8 msec 8 msec
  4 172.16.2.1 20 msec 16 msec 20 msec
  5 172.16.2.2 16 msec 16 msec 16 msec
```

```
  6 172.16.2.1 20 msec 20 msec 24 msec
  7 172.16.2.2 20 msec
R1#
```

The next step is to investigate the routing table of R2, because it is the router displaying a strange forwarding pattern. Using the **show ip route | begin Gateway** command, the routing table in the following output reveals that the 192.168.2.0/24 network is configured incorrectly. A static route to the 192.168.2.0/24 network has been configured using the next-hop address 172.16.2.1. Using the configured next-hop address, packets destined for the 192.168.2.0/24 network are sent back to R1. It is clear from the topology that the 192.168.2.0/24 network is connected to R3, not R1. Therefore, the static route to the 192.168.2.0/24 network on R2 must use next-hop 192.168.1.1, not 172.16.2.1.

```
R2# show ip route | begin Gateway
Gateway of last resort is not set
      172.16.0.0/16 is variably subnetted, 5 subnets, 2 masks
C       172.16.1.0/24 is directly connected, GigabitEthernet0/0
L       172.16.1.1/32 is directly connected, GigabitEthernet0/0
C       172.16.2.0/24 is directly connected, Serial0/0/0
L       172.16.2.2/32 is directly connected, Serial0/0/0
S       172.16.3.0/24 1/0] via 172.16.2.1
      192.168.1.0/24 is variably subnetted, 2 subnets, 2 masks
C       192.168.1.0/24 is directly connected, Serial0/0/1
L       192.168.1.2/32 is directly connected, Serial0/0/1
S     192.168.2.0/24 [1/0] via 172.16.2.1
R2#
```

The following shows output from the running configuration that reveals the incorrect **ip route** statement. The incorrect route is removed and the correct route is then entered.

```
R2# show running-config | section ip route
ip route 172.16.3.0 255.255.255.0 172.16.2.1
ip route 192.168.2.0 255.255.255.0 172.16.2.1
R2#
R2# conf t
Enter configuration commands, one per line.  End with CNTL/Z.
R2(config)# no ip route 192.168.2.0 255.255.255.0 172.16.2.1
R2(config)# ip route 192.168.2.0 255.255.255.0 192.168.1.1
R2(config)#
```

The following output verifies that R1 can now reach the LAN interface of R3. As a last step in confirmation, the user on PC1 should also test connectivity to the 192.168.2.0/24 LAN.

```
R1# ping 192.168.2.1 source g0/0
Type escape sequence to abort.
Sending 5, 100-byte ICMP Echos to 192.168.2.1, timeout is 2 seconds:
Packet sent with a source address of 172.16.3.1
!!!!!
Success rate is 100 percent (5/5), round-trip min/avg/max = 28/28/28 ms
R1#
```

Packet Tracer Activity 2.5.2.3: Solving the Missing Route

In this activity, PC1 reports that it cannot access resources at Server. Locate the problem, decide on an appropriate solution, and resolve the issue.

Packet Tracer Activity 2.5.2.4: Troubleshooting VLSM and Route Summarization

In this activity, the network is already addressed using VLSM and configured with static routes. But there is a problem. Locate the issue or issues, determine the best solution, implement the solution, and verify connectivity.

Lab 2.5.2.5: Troubleshooting Static Routes

In this lab, you will complete the following objectives:

- Part 1: Build the Network and Configure Basic Device Settings
- Part 2: Troubleshoot Static Routes in an IPv4 Network
- Part 3: Troubleshoot Static Routes in an IPv6 Network

Summary (2.6)

Class Activity 2.6.1.1: Make it Static

Go to the online course to perform this practice activity.

As the use of IPv6 addressing becomes more prevalent, it is important for network administrators to be able to direct network traffic between routers.

To prove that you are able to direct IPv6 traffic correctly and review the IPv6 default static route curriculum concepts, use the topology as shown in the .pdf file provided specifically for this activity.

Work with a partner to write an IPv6 statement for each of the three scenarios. Try to write the route statements without the assistance of completed labs, Packet Tracer files, etc.

Scenario 1

IPv6 default static route from R2 directing all data through your S0/0/0 interface to the next-hop address on R1.

Scenario 2

IPv6 default static route from R3 directing all data through your S0/0/1 interface to the next-hop address on R2.

Scenario 3

IPv6 default static route from R2 directing all data through your S0/0/1 interface to the next-hop address on R3.

When complete, get together with another group and compare your written answers. Discuss any differences found in your comparisons.

Packet Tracer Activity 2.6.1.2: Packet Tracer Skills Integration Challenge

The network administrator asked you to implement IPv4 and IPv6 static and default routing in the test environment shown in the topology. Configure each static and default route as directly connected.

In this chapter, you learned how IPv4 and IPv6 static routes can be used to reach remote networks. Remote networks are networks that can only be reached by forwarding the packet to another router. Static routes are easily configured. However, in large networks, this manual operation can become quite cumbersome. Static routes are still used, even when a dynamic routing protocol is implemented.

Static routes can be configured with a next-hop IP address, which is commonly the IP address of the next-hop router. When a next-hop IP address is used, the routing table process must resolve this address to an exit interface. On point-to-point serial links, it is usually more efficient to configure the static route with an exit interface. On multi-access networks, such as Ethernet, both a next-hop IP address and an exit interface can be configured on the static route.

Static routes have a default administrative distance of 1. This administrative distance also applies to static routes configured with a next-hop address, as well as an exit interface.

A static route is only entered in the routing table if the next-hop IP address can be resolved through an exit interface. Whether the static route is configured with a next-hop IP address or exit interface, if the exit interface that is used to forward that packet is not in the routing table, the static route is not included in the routing table.

Using CIDR, several static routes can be configured as a single summary route. This means fewer entries in the routing table and results in a faster routing table lookup process. CIDR also manages the IPv4 address space more efficiently.

VLSM subnetting is similar to traditional subnetting in that bits are borrowed to create subnets. With VLSM, the network is first subnetted, and then the subnets are subnetted again. This process can be repeated multiple times to create subnets of various sizes.

The ultimate summary route is a default route, configured with a 0.0.0.0 network address and a 0.0.0.0 subnet mask for IPv4, and the prefix/prefix-length ::/0 for IPv6. If there is not a more specific match in the routing table, the routing table uses the default route to forward the packet to another router.

A floating static route can be configured to back up a main link by manipulating its administrative value.

Practice

The following activities provide practice with the topics introduced in this chapter. The Labs and Class Activities are available in the companion *Routing Protocols Lab Manual* (978-1-58713-322-0). The Packet Tracer Activities PKA files are found in the online course.

 ## Class Activities

Class Activity 2.0.1.2: Which Way Should We Go?

Class Activity 2.6.1.1: Make it Static

Labs

Lab 2.2.2.5: Configuring IPv4 Static and Default Routes

Lab 2.2.4.5: Configuring IPv6 Static and Default Routes

Lab 2.3.3.7: Designing and Implementing IPv4 Addressing with VLSM

Lab 2.4.2.5: Calculating Summary Routes with IPv4 and IPv6

Lab 2.5.2.5: Troubleshooting Static Routes

Packet Tracer Activities

Packet Tracer Activity 2.2.2.4: Configuring IPv4 Static and Default Routes

Packet Tracer Activity 2.2.4.4: Configuring IPv6 Static and Default Routes

Packet Tracer Activity 2.3.3.6: Designing and Implementing a VLSM Addressing Scheme

Packet Tracer Activity 2.4.1.5: Configuring IPv4 Route Summarization – Scenario 1

Packet Tracer Activity 2.4.1.6: Configuring IPv4 Route Summarization – Scenario 2

Packet Tracer Activity 2.4.2.4: Configuring IPv6 Route Summarization

Packet Tracer Activity 2.4.3.4: Configuring a Floating Static Route

Packet Tracer Activity 2.5.2.3: Solving the Missing Route

Packet Tracer Activity 2.5.2.4: Troubleshooting VLSM and Route Summarization

Packet Tracer Activity 2.6.1.2: Packet Tracer Skills Integration Challenge

Check Your Understanding Questions

Complete all the review questions listed here to test your understanding of the topics and concepts in this chapter. The appendix, "Answers to the 'Check Your Understanding' Questions," lists the answers.

1. Refer to Figure 2-72. Which two commands must be configured to allow communications between the 192.168.10/24 and 10.0.0.0/8 networks? (Choose two.)

Figure 2-72 Topology for Quiz Question 1

A.   A(config)# **ip route 10.0.0.0 255.0.0.0 172.16.40.2**

B.   A(config)# **ip route 10.0.0.0 255.0.0.0 s0/0/0**

C.   A(config)# **ip route 10.0.0.0 255.0.0.0 10.0.0.1**

D.   B(config)# **ip route 192.168.1.0 255.255.255.0 172.16.40.1**

E.   B(config)# **ip route 192.168.1.0 255.255.255.0 172.16.40.2**

F.   B# **ip route 192.168.1.0 255.255.255.0 192.168.1.1**

2. Which two statements are true concerning configuring static routes using next-hop addresses? (Choose two.)

A.   Next-hop addresses can only be used with IPv4 static routes. They cannot be used for IPv6 static routes.

B.   When configuring a static route with a next-hop address, the exit interface must also be included in the configuration.

C.   Routers configured with static routes using a next-hop address must either have the exit interface listed in the route or have another route with the network of the next hop and an associated exit interface.

D.   With CEF enabled, there is no need for a recursive lookup when using static routes with next-hop addresses.

3. Which of the following are three characteristics of a static route? (Choose three.)

A.   Less memory and processing requirements than a dynamic routing protocol

B.   Ensures that there is always a path available

C.   Used to dynamically find the best path to a destination network

D.   Used for routers that connect to stub networks

E.   Used to indicate a default route or a Gateway of Last Resort

F.   Reduces configuration time on large networks

4. Which global configuration command configures an IPv4 static default route using the next-hop address 10.0.0.1?

A.   Router(config)# **ip route 0.0.0.0/0 10.0.0.1**

B.   Router(config)# **ip route 0.0.0.0 10.0.0.1**

C.   Router(config)# **ipv4 route 0.0.0.0 0.0.0.0 10.0.0.1**

D.   Router(config)# **ip route 0.0.0.0 0.0.0.0 10.0.0.1**

5. Which global configuration command configures an IPv6 static default route using the next-hop address 2001:DB8:ACAD:1::1?

   A. Router(config)# **ipv6 route 0.0.0.0 0.0.0.0 2001:DB8:ACAD:1::1**

   B. Router(config)# **ip route 0/0 2001:DB8:ACAD:1::1**

   C. Router(config)# **ipv6 route ::/0 2001:DB8:ACAD:1::1**

   D. Router(config)# **ip route ::/0 2001:DB8:ACAD:1::1**

6. True/False: A static route configured with an exit interface has an administrative distance of 0, the same as a directly connected network.

7. Summarize the following addresses using the shortest valid subnet mask:

   10.0.12.0

   10.0.13.0

   10.0.14.0

   10.0.15.0

8. What type of static route can be configured to be a backup route in case the primary route fails?

   A. Floating static route

   B. Default route

   C. Backup static route

   D. Summary route

9. True/False: Static routes are commonly configured along with a dynamic routing protocol.

10. Which command will only display the IPv6 static routes in the IPv6 routing table?

   A. Router# **show ip route static**

   B. Router# **show ip static route**

   C. Router# **show ipv6 route static**

   D. Router# **show static ipv6 route**

CHAPTER 3

Routing Dynamically

Objectives

Upon completion of this chapter, you will be able to answer the following questions:

- What is the purpose of dynamic routing protocols?

- How does dynamic routing compare with static routing?

- How do dynamic routing protocols share route information and achieve convergence?

- What are the differences between the categories of dynamic routing protocols?

- How does the algorithm used by distance vector routing protocols determine the best path?

- What are the different types of distance vector routing protocols?

- How do you configure the RIP routing protocol?

- How do you configure the RIPng routing protocol?

- How does the algorithm used by link-state routing protocols determine the best path?

- How do link-state routing protocols use information sent in link-state updates?

- What are the advantages and disadvantages of using link-state routing protocols?

- How do you determine the source route, administrative distance, and metric for a given route?

- How do you explain the concept of a parent/child relationship in a dynamically built routing table?

- How do you describe the differences between the IPv4 route lookup process and the IPv6 route lookup process?

- Can you determine which route will be used to forward a packet upon analyzing a routing table?

Key Terms

This chapter uses the following key terms. You can find the definitions in the Glossary.

Introduction (3.0.1.1)

The data networks that we use in our everyday lives to learn, play, and work range from small, local networks to large, global internetworks. At home, a user may have a router and two or more computers. At work, an organization may have multiple routers and switches servicing the data communication needs of hundreds or even thousands of PCs.

Routers forward packets by using information in the routing table. Routes to remote networks can be learned by the router in two ways: static routes and dynamic routes.

In a large network with numerous networks and subnets, configuring and maintaining static routes between these networks requires a great deal of administrative and operational overhead. This operational overhead is especially cumbersome when changes to the network occur, such as a down link or implementing a new subnet. Implementing dynamic routing protocols can ease the burden of configuration and maintenance tasks and give the network scalability.

This chapter introduces dynamic routing protocols. It explores the benefits of using dynamic routing protocols, how different routing protocols are classified, and the metrics routing protocols use to determine the best path for network traffic. Other topics covered in this chapter include the characteristics of dynamic routing protocols and how the various routing protocols differ. Network professionals must understand the different routing protocols available in order to make informed decisions about when to use static or dynamic routing. They also need to know which dynamic routing protocol is most appropriate in a particular network environment.

Class Activity 3.0.1.2: How Much Does This Cost?

This modeling activity illustrates the network concept of routing cost.

You will be a member of a team of five students who travel routes to complete the activity scenarios. One digital camera or bring your own device (BYOD) with camera, a stopwatch, and the student file for this activity will be required per group. One person will function as the photographer and event recorder, as selected by each group. The remaining four team members will actively participate in the following scenarios.

A school or university classroom, hallway, outdoor track area, school parking lot, or any other location can serve as the venue for these activities.

Activity 1

The tallest person in the group establishes a start and finish line by marking 15 steps from start to finish, indicating the distance of the team route. Each student will take 15 steps from the start line toward the finish line and then stop on the 15th step—no further steps are allowed.

Note

Not all of the students may reach the same distance from the start line due to their height and stride differences. The photographer will take a group picture of the entire team's final location after taking the 15 steps required.

Activity 2

A new start and finish line will be established; however, this time, a longer distance for the route will be established than the distance specified in Activity 1. No maximum steps are to be used as a basis for creating this particular route. One at a time, students will walk the new route from beginning to end twice.

Each team member will count the steps taken to complete the route. The recorder will time each student and, at the end of each team member's route, record the time that it took to complete the full route and how many steps were taken, as recounted by each team member and recorded on the team's student file.

After both activities have been completed, teams will use the digital picture taken for Activity 1 and their recorded data from Activity 2 file to answer the reflection questions.

Group answers can be discussed as a class, time permitting.

Dynamic Routing Protocols (3.1)

Dynamic routing protocols play an important role in today's networks. The following sections describe several important benefits that dynamic routing protocols provide. In many networks, dynamic routing protocols are typically used with static routes.

The Evolution of Dynamic Routing Protocols (3.1.1.1)

Dynamic routing protocols have been used in networks since the late 1980s. One of the first routing protocols was *Routing Information Protocol (RIP)*. RIP version 1 (RIPv1) was released in 1988, but some of the basic algorithms within the protocol were used on the *Advanced Research Projects Agency Network (ARPANET)* as early as 1969.

As networks evolved and became more complex, new routing protocols emerged. The RIP routing protocol was updated to accommodate growth in the network environment, into RIPv2. However, the newer version of RIP still does not scale to the larger network implementations of today. To address the needs of larger networks, two advanced routing protocols were developed: *Open Shortest Path First (OSPF)* and *Intermediate System-to-Intermediate System (IS-IS)*. Cisco developed the *Interior Gateway Routing Protocol (IGRP)* and *Enhanced IGRP (EIGRP)*, which also scales well in larger network implementations.

Additionally, there was the need to connect different internetworks and provide routing between them. The *Border Gateway Protocol (BGP)* is now used between Internet service providers (ISPs). BGP is also used between ISPs and their larger private clients to exchange routing information.

Table 3-1 classifies the protocols.

Table 3-1   Routing Protocol Classification

	Interior Gateway Protocols				Exterior Gateway Protocols
	Distance Vector		Link-State		Path Vector
IPv4	RIPv2	EIGRP	OSPFv2	IS-IS	BGP-4
IPv6	RIPng	EIGRP for IPv6	OSPFv3	IS-IS for IPv6	MBGP

With the advent of numerous consumer devices using IP, the IPv4 addressing space is nearly exhausted; thus, IPv6 has emerged. To support the communication based on IPv6, newer versions of the IP routing protocols have been developed, as shown by the IPv6 row in Table 3-1.

RIP is the simplest of dynamic routing protocols and is used in this section to provide a basic level of routing protocol understanding.

Purpose of Dynamic Routing Protocols (3.1.1.2)

Routing protocols are used to facilitate the exchange of routing information between routers. A routing protocol is a set of processes, algorithms, and messages that are used to exchange routing information and populate the routing table with the routing protocol's choice of best paths. The purpose of dynamic routing protocols includes:

- Discovery of remote networks

- Maintaining up-to-date routing information

- Choosing the best path to destination networks

- Ability to find a new best path if the current path is no longer available

The main components of dynamic routing protocols include:

- *Data structures*: Routing protocols typically use tables or databases for their operations. This information is kept in RAM.

- *Routing protocol messages*: Routing protocols use various types of messages to discover neighboring routers, exchange routing information, and perform other tasks to learn and maintain accurate information about the network.

- *Algorithm*: An algorithm is a finite list of steps used to accomplish a task. Routing protocols use algorithms for facilitating routing information and for best path determination.

Figure 3-1 highlights the data structures, routing protocol messages, and routing algorithm used by EIGRP.

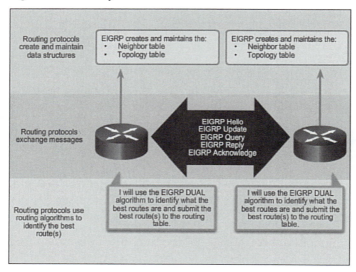

Figure 3-1   Components of Routing Protocols

The Role of Dynamic Routing Protocols (3.1.1.3)

Routing protocols allow routers to dynamically share information about remote networks and automatically add this information to their own routing tables.

Video

Video 3.1.1.3: Routers Dynamically Share Updates

Go to the online course and play the animation of three routers sharing updates dynamically.

Routing protocols determine the best path, or route, to each network. That route is then added to the routing table. A primary benefit of dynamic routing protocols is that routers exchange routing information when there is a topology change. This exchange allows routers to automatically learn about new networks and also to find alternate paths when there is a link failure to a current network.

Compared to static routing, dynamic routing protocols require less administrative overhead. However, the expense of using dynamic routing protocols is dedicating part of a router's resources for protocol operation, including CPU time and network link bandwidth. Despite the benefits of dynamic routing, static routing still has its place. There are times when static routing is more appropriate and other times when dynamic routing is the better choice. Networks with moderate levels of complexity may have both static and dynamic routing configured.

Interactive Graphic

Activity 3.1.1.4: Identify Components of a Routing Protocol (EIGRP)

Go to the online course to perform these three practice activities.

Dynamic versus Static Routing (3.1.2)

Routing tables can contain directly connected, manually configured static routes and routes learned dynamically using a routing protocol. Network professionals must understand when to use static or dynamic routing. This section compares static routing and dynamic routing.

Using Static Routing (3.1.2.1)

Before identifying the benefits of dynamic routing protocols, consider the reasons why network professionals use static routing. Dynamic routing certainly has several advantages over static routing; however, static routing is still used in networks today. In fact, networks typically use a combination of both static and dynamic routing.

Static routing has several primary uses, including:

- Providing ease of routing table maintenance in smaller networks that are not expected to grow significantly.

- Routing to and from a stub network, which is a network with only one default route out and no knowledge of any remote networks.

- Accessing a single default route (which is used to represent a path to any network that does not have a more specific match with another route in the routing table).

Figure 3-2 provides a sample static routing scenario.

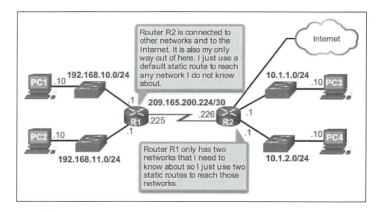

Figure 3-2   Static Routing Scenario

Static Routing Scorecard (3.1.2.2)

Static routing is easy to implement in a small network. Static routes stay the same, which makes them fairly easy to troubleshoot. Static routes do not send update messages and, therefore, require very little overhead.

The disadvantages of static routing include:

- They are not easy to implement in a large network.
- Managing the static configurations can become time consuming.
- If a link fails, a static route cannot reroute traffic.

Table 3-2 highlights the advantages and disadvantages of static routing.

Table 3-2   Static Routing Advantages and Disadvantages

Advantages	Disadvantages
Easy to implement in a small network.	Suitable for simple topologies or for special purposes such as a default static route.
Very secure. No advertisements are sent, unlike with dynamic routing protocols.	Configuration complexity increases dramatically as the network grows. Managing the static configurations in large networks can become time consuming.
It is very predictable, as the route to the destination is always the same.	If a link fails, a static route cannot reroute traffic. Therefore, manual intervention is required to re-route traffic.
No routing algorithm or update mechanisms are required. Therefore, extra resources (CPU and memory) are not required.	

Using Dynamic Routing Protocols (3.1.2.3)

Dynamic routing protocols help the network administrator manage the time-consuming and exacting process of configuring and maintaining static routes.

Imagine maintaining the static routing configurations for the seven routers in Figure 3-3.

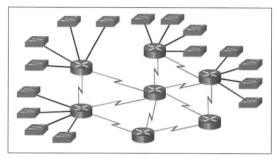

Figure 3-3   Small Dynamic Routing Scenario

What if the company grew and now has four regions and 28 routers to manage, as shown in Figure 3-4? What happens when a link goes down? How do you ensure that redundant paths are available?

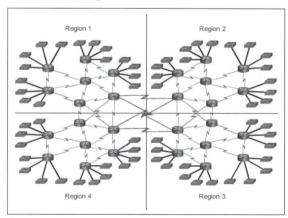

Figure 3-4   Large Dynamic Routing Scenario

Dynamic routing is the best choice for large networks like the one shown in Figure 3-4.

Dynamic Routing Scorecard (3.1.2.4)

Dynamic routing protocols work well in any type of network consisting of several routers. They are scalable and automatically determine better routes if there is a change in the topology. Although there is more to the configuration of dynamic routing protocols, they are simpler to configure in a large network.

There are disadvantages to dynamic routing. Dynamic routing requires knowledge of additional commands. It is also less secure than static routing because the interfaces identified by the routing protocol send routing updates out. Routes taken may differ between packets. The routing algorithm uses additional CPU, RAM, and link bandwidth.

Table 3-3 highlights the advantages and disadvantages of dynamic routing.

Table 3-3   Dynamic Routing Advantages and Disadvantages

Advantages	Disadvantages
Suitable in all topologies where multiple routers are required.	Can be more complex to initially implement.
Generally independent of the network size.	Less secure due to the broadcast and multicast routing updates. Additional configuration settings such as passive interfaces and routing protocol authentication are required to increase security.
Automatically adapts topology to reroute traffic if possible.	Route depends on the current topology.
	Requires additional resources such as CPU, memory, and link bandwidth.

Notice how dynamic routing addresses the disadvantages of static routing.

Interactive Graphic

Activity 3.1.2.5: Compare Static and Dynamic Routing

Go to the online course to perform this practice activity.

Routing Protocol Operating Fundamentals (3.1.3)

All routing protocols basically perform the same tasks. They all exchange routing updates and converge to build routing tables that are used by the router to make packet forwarding decisions. This section provides an overview of routing protocol fundamentals.

Dynamic Routing Protocol Operation (3.1.3.1)

All routing protocols are designed to learn about remote networks and to quickly adapt whenever there is a change in the topology. The method that a routing protocol uses to accomplish this depends upon the algorithm it uses and the operational characteristics of that protocol.

In general, the operations of a dynamic routing protocol can be described as follows:

1. The router sends and receives routing messages on its interfaces.

2. The router shares routing messages and routing information with other routers that are using the same routing protocol.

3. Routers exchange routing information to learn about remote networks.

4. When a router detects a topology change, the routing protocol can advertise this change to other routers.

Video

Video 3.1.3.1: Routing Protocol Operation

Go to the online course and play the animation of two routers sharing routing updates.

Cold Start (3.1.3.2)

All routing protocols follow the same patterns of operation. When a router powers up, it knows nothing about the network topology. It does not even know that there are devices on the other end of its links. The only information that a router has is from its own saved configuration file stored in NVRAM.

After a router boots successfully, it applies the saved configuration. If the IP addressing is configured correctly, then the router initially discovers its own directly connected networks.

Video

Video 3.1.3.2: Directly Connected Networks Detected

Go to the online course to view an animation of the initial discovery of connected networks for each router.

Notice how the routers proceed through the boot process and then discover any directly connected networks and subnet masks. This information is added to their routing tables as follows:

- R1 adds the 10.1.0.0 network available through interface FastEthernet 0/0 and adds 10.2.0.0 available through interface Serial 0/0/0.

- R2 adds the 10.2.0.0 network available through interface Serial 0/0/0 and adds 10.3.0.0 available through interface Serial 0/0/1.

- R3 adds the 10.3.0.0 network available through interface Serial 0/0/1 and adds 10.4.0.0 available through interface FastEthernet 0/0.

With this initial information, the routers then proceed to find additional route sources for their routing tables.

Network Discovery (3.1.3.3)

After initial boot up and discovery, the routing table is updated with all directly connected networks and the interfaces those networks reside on.

If a routing protocol is configured, the next step is for the router to begin exchanging routing updates to learn about any remote routes.

The router sends an update packet out all interfaces that are enabled on the router. The update contains the information in the routing table, which currently comprises all directly connected networks.

At the same time, the router also receives and processes similar updates from other connected routers. Upon receiving an update, the router checks it for new network information. Any networks that are not currently listed in the routing table are added.

Figure 3-5 depicts an example topology setup between three routers, R1, R2, and R3. Notice that only the directly connected networks are listed in each router's respective routing table.

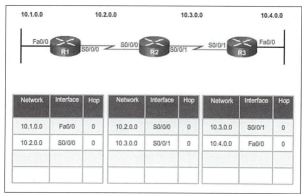

Figure 3-5   Initial Routing Table Before Exchange

Based on this topology, a listing of the different updates that R1, R2, and R3 send and receive during initial convergence is provided:

R1:

- Sends an update about network 10.1.0.0 out the Serial 0/0/0 interface
- Sends an update about network 10.2.0.0 out the FastEthernet 0/0 interface
- Receives update from R2 about network 10.3.0.0 and increments the hop count by 1
- Stores network 10.3.0.0 in the routing table via Serial 0/0/0 with a metric of 1

R2:

- Sends an update about network 10.3.0.0 out the Serial 0/0/0 interface
- Sends an update about network 10.2.0.0 out the Serial 0/0/1 interface
- Receives an update from R1 about network 10.1.0.0 and increments the hop count by 1
- Stores network 10.1.0.0 in the routing table via Serial 0/0/0 with a metric of 1
- Receives an update from R3 about network 10.4.0.0 and increments the hop count by 1
- Stores network 10.4.0.0 in the routing table via Serial 0/0/1 with a metric of 1

R3:

- Sends an update about network 10.4.0.0 out the Serial 0/0/1 interface
- Sends an update about network 10.3.0.0 out the FastEthernet 0/0 interface
- Receives an update from R2 about network 10.2.0.0 and increments the hop count by 1
- Stores network 10.2.0.0 in the routing table via Serial 0/0/1 with a metric of 1

Figure 3-6 displays the routing tables after the initial exchange.

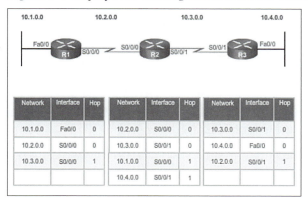

Figure 3-6   Routing Table After Initial Exchange

Video

Video 3.1.3.3: Initial Exchange

Go to the online course and play the animation of R1, R2, and R3 starting the initial exchange.

After this first round of update exchanges, each router knows about the connected networks of its directly connected neighbors. However, did you notice that R1 does not yet know about 10.4.0.0 and that R3 does not yet know about 10.1.0.0? Full knowledge and a converged network do not take place until there is another exchange of routing information.

Exchanging the Routing Information (3.1.3.4)

At this point the routers have knowledge about their own directly connected networks and about the connected networks of their immediate neighbors. Continuing the journey toward convergence, the routers exchange the next round of periodic updates. Each router again checks the updates for new information.

After initial discovery is complete, each router continues the convergence process by sending and receiving the following updates.

R1:

- Sends an update about network 10.1.0.0 out the Serial 0/0/0 interface

- Sends an update about networks 10.2.0.0 and 10.3.0.0 out the FastEthernet 0/0 interface

- Receives an update from R2 about network 10.4.0.0 and increments the hop count by 1

- Stores network 10.4.0.0 in the routing table via Serial 0/0/0 with a metric of 2

- Same update from R2 contains information about network 10.3.0.0 with a metric of 1. There is no change; therefore, the routing information remains the same.

R2:

- Sends an update about networks 10.3.0.0 and 10.4.0.0 out of Serial 0/0/0 interface

- Sends an update about networks 10.1.0.0 and 10.2.0.0 out of Serial 0/0/1 interface

- Receives an update from R1 about network 10.1.0.0. There is no change; therefore, the routing information remains the same.

- Receives an update from R3 about network 10.4.0.0. There is no change; therefore, the routing information remains the same.

R3:

- Sends an update about network 10.4.0.0 out the Serial 0/0/1 interface

- Sends an update about networks 10.2.0.0 and 10.3.0.0 out the FastEthernet 0/0 interface

- Receives an update from R2 about network 10.1.0.0 and increments the hop count by 1

- Stores network 10.1.0.0 in the routing table via Serial 0/0/1 with a metric of 2

- Same update from R2 contains information about network 10.2.0.0 with a metric of 1. There is no change; therefore, the routing information remains the same.

Figure 3-7 displays the routing tables after the routers have converged.

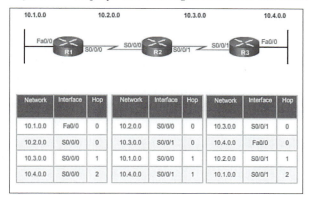

Figure 3-7   Routing Table After Convergence

Video 3.1.3.4: Next Update

Go to the online course and play an animation of R1, R2, and R3 sending the latest routing table to their neighbors.

Distance vector routing protocols typically implement a routing loop prevention technique known as split horizon. Split horizon prevents information from being sent out the same interface from which it was received. For example, R2 does not send an update containing the network 10.1.0.0 out of Serial 0/0/0, because R2 learned about network 10.1.0.0 through Serial 0/0/0.

After routers within a network have converged, the router can then use the information within the route table to determine the best path to reach a destination. Different routing protocols have different ways of calculating the best path.

Achieving Convergence (3.1.3.5)

The network has converged when all routers have complete and accurate information about the entire network, as shown in Figure 3-7. *Convergence* is the time it takes routers to share information, calculate best paths, and update their routing tables. A network is not completely operable until the network has converged; therefore, most networks require short convergence times.

Convergence is both collaborative and independent. The routers share information with each other, but must independently calculate the impacts of the topology change on their own routes. Because they develop an agreement with the new topology independently, they are said to converge on this consensus.

Convergence properties include the speed of propagation of routing information and the calculation of optimal paths. The speed of propagation refers to the amount of time it takes for routers within the network to forward routing information.

As shown in Figure 3-8, routing protocols can be rated based on the speed to convergence; the faster the convergence, the better the routing protocol. Generally, older protocols, such as RIP, are slow to converge, whereas modern protocols, such as EIGRP and OSPF, converge more quickly.

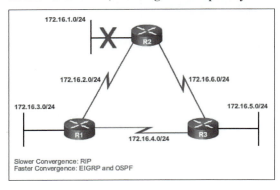

Figure 3-8   Converging

Packet Tracer Activity 3.1.3.6: Investigating Convergence

This activity will help you identify important information in routing tables and witness the process of network convergence.

Types of Routing Protocols (3.1.4)

Table 3-1 showed how routing protocols can be classified according to various characteristics. This section gives an overview of the most common IP routing protocols. Most of these routing protocols will be examined in detail in other chapters. For now, this section gives a very brief overview of each protocol.

Classifying Routing Protocols (3.1.4.1)

Routing protocols can be classified into different groups according to their characteristics. Specifically, routing protocols can be classified by their:

- **Purpose:** Interior Gateway Protocol (IGP) or Exterior Gateway Protocol (EGP)

- **Operation:** Distance vector protocol, link-state protocol, or path-vector protocol

- **Behavior:** Classful (legacy) or classless protocol

For example, IPv4 routing protocols are classified as follows:

- **RIPv1 (legacy):** IGP, distance vector, classful protocol

- **IGRP (legacy):** IGP, distance vector, classful protocol developed by Cisco (deprecated from 12.2 IOS and later)

- **RIPv2:** IGP, distance vector, classless protocol

- **EIGRP:** IGP, distance vector, classless protocol developed by Cisco

- **OSPF:** IGP, link-state, classless protocol

- **IS-IS:** IGP, link-state, classless protocol

- **BGP:** EGP, path-vector, classless protocol

The *classful routing protocols*, RIPv1 and IGRP, are legacy protocols and are only used in older networks. These routing protocols have evolved into the *classless routing protocols*, RIPv2 and EIGRP, respectively. Link-state routing protocols are classless by nature.

Figure 3-9 displays a hierarchical view of dynamic routing protocol classification.

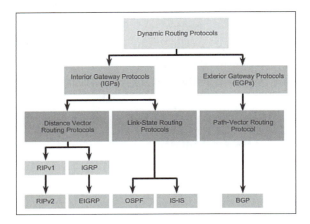

Figure 3-9   Routing Protocol Classification

IGP and EGP Routing Protocols (3.1.4.2)

An *autonomous system (AS)* is a collection of routers under a common administration such as a company or an organization. An AS is also known as a routing domain. Typical examples of an AS are a company's internal network and an ISP's network.

The Internet is based on the AS concept; therefore, two types of routing protocols are required:

- *Interior Gateway Protocols (IGP)*: Used for routing within an AS. It is also referred to as intra-AS routing. Companies, organizations, and even service providers use an IGP on their internal networks. IGPs include RIP, EIGRP, OSPF, and IS-IS.

- *Exterior Gateway Protocols (EGP)*: Used for routing between autonomous systems. It is also referred to as inter-AS routing. Service providers and large companies may interconnect using an EGP. The Border Gateway Protocol (BGP) is the only currently viable EGP and is the official routing protocol used by the Internet.

Note

Because BGP is the only EGP available, the term EGP is rarely used; instead, most engineers simply refer to BGP.

The example in Figure 3-10 provides simple scenarios highlighting the deployment of IGPs, BGP, and static routing.

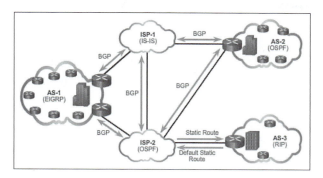

Figure 3-10   IGP versus EGP Routing Protocols

There are five individual autonomous systems in the scenario:

- **ISP-1**: This is an AS and it uses IS-IS as the IGP. It interconnects with other autonomous systems and service providers using BGP to explicitly control how traffic is routed.

- **ISP-2**: This is an AS and it uses OSPF as the IGP. It interconnects with other autonomous systems and service providers using BGP to explicitly control how traffic is routed.

- **AS-1**: This is a large organization and it uses EIGRP as the IGP. Because it is multihomed (i.e., connects to two different service providers), it uses BGP to explicitly control how traffic enters and leaves the AS.

- **AS-2**: This is a medium-sized organization and it uses OSPF as the IGP. It is also multihomed; therefore, it uses BGP to explicitly control how traffic enters and leaves the AS.

- **AS-3**: This is a small organization with older routers within the AS; it uses RIP as the IGP. BGP is not required because it is single-homed (i.e., connects to one service provider). Instead, static routing is implemented between the AS and the service provider.

Note

BGP is beyond the scope of this course and is not discussed in detail.

Distance Vector Routing Protocols (3.1.4.3)

Distance vector means that routes are advertised by providing two characteristics:

- **Distance**: Identifies how far it is to the destination network and is based on a metric such as the hop count, cost, bandwidth, delay, and more

- **Vector:** Specifies the direction of the next-hop router or exit interface to reach the destination

For example, in Figure 3-11, R1 knows that the distance to reach network 172.16.3.0/24 is one hop and that the direction is out of the interface Serial 0/0/0 toward R2.

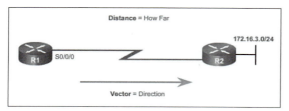

Figure 3-11   The Meaning of Distance Vector

A router using a *distance vector routing protocol* does not have the knowledge of the entire path to a destination network. Distance vector protocols use routers as sign posts along the path to the final destination. The only information a router knows about a remote network is the distance or metric to reach that network and which path or interface to use to get there. Distance vector routing protocols do not have an actual map of the network topology.

There are four distance vector IPv4 IGPs:

- **RIPv1:** First generation legacy protocol
- **RIPv2:** Simple distance vector routing protocol
- **IGRP:** First generation Cisco proprietary protocol (obsolete and replaced by EIGRP)
- **EIGRP:** Advanced version of distance vector routing

Link-State Routing Protocols (3.1.4.4)

In contrast to distance vector routing protocol operation, a router configured with a *link-state routing protocol* can create a complete view or topology of the network by gathering information from all of the other routers.

To continue our analogy of sign posts, using a link-state routing protocol is like having a complete map of the network topology. The sign posts along the way from source to destination are not necessary, because all link-state routers are using an identical map of the network. A link-state router uses the link-state information to create a topology map and to select the best path to all destination networks in the topology.

RIP-enabled routers send periodic updates of their routing information to their neighbors. Link-state routing protocols do not use periodic updates. After the network has converged, a link-state update is only sent when there is a change in the topology. For example, in Figure 3-12, the link-state update is sent when the 172.16.3.0 network goes down.

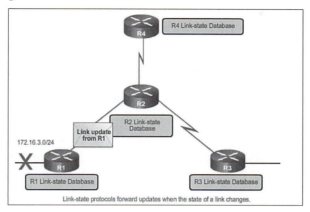

Figure 3-12   Link-State Protocol Operation

Video

Video 3.1.4.4: Link-State Protocol Operation

Go to the online course and play the animation to see how a link-state update is only sent when the 172.16.3.0 network goes down.

Link-state protocols work best in situations where:

- The network design is hierarchical, usually occurring in large networks
- Fast convergence of the network is crucial
- The administrators have good knowledge of the implemented link-state routing protocol

There are two link-state IPv4 IGPs:

- **OSPF:** Popular standards-based routing protocol
- **IS-IS:** Popular in provider networks

Classful Routing Protocols (3.1.4.5)

The biggest distinction between classful and classless routing protocols is that classful routing protocols do not send subnet mask information in their routing updates. Classless routing protocols include subnet mask information in the routing updates.

The two original IPv4 routing protocols developed were RIPv1 and IGRP. They were created when network addresses were allocated based on classes (i.e., class A, B, or

C). At that time, a routing protocol did not need to include the subnet mask in the routing update, because the network mask could be determined based on the first octet of the network address.

> **Note**
>
> Only RIPv1 and IGRP are classful. All other IPv4 and IPv6 routing protocols are classless. Classful addressing has never been a part of IPv6.

The fact that RIPv1 and IGRP do not include subnet mask information in their updates means that they cannot provide variable-length subnet masks (VLSMs) and Classless Inter-Domain Routing (CIDR).

Classful routing protocols also create problems in discontiguous networks. A discontiguous network is when subnets from the same classful major network address are separated by a different classful network address.

To illustrate the shortcoming of classful routing, refer to the topology in Figure 3-13.

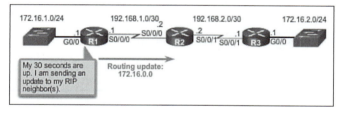

Figure 3-13   R1 Forwards a Classful Update to R2

Notice that the LANs of R1 (172.16.1.0/24) and R3 (172.16.2.0/24) are both subnets of the same class B network (172.16.0.0/16). They are separated by different classful network addresses (192.168.1.0/30 and 192.168.2.0/30).

When R1 forwards an update to R2, RIPv1 does not include the subnet mask information with the update; it only forwards the class B network address 172.16.0.0.

R2 receives and processes the update. It then creates and adds an entry for the class B 172.16.0.0/16 network in the routing table, as shown in Figure 3-14.

```
R2# show ip route | begin Gateway
Gateway of last resort is not set

R       172.16.0.0/16 [120/1] via 192.168.1.1, 00:00:11,
        Serial0/0/0
        192.168.1.0/24 is variably subnetted, 2 subnets,
        2 masks
C          192.168.1.0/30 is directly connected, Serial0/0/0
L          192.168.1.2/32 is directly connected, Serial0/0/0
        192.168.2.0/24 is variably subnetted, 2 subnets, .
        2 masks
C          192.168.2.0/30 is directly connected, Serial0/0/1
L          192.168.2.2/32 is directly connected, Serial0/0/1
R2#
```

Figure 3-14   R2 Adds the Entry for 172.16.0.0 via R1

When R3 forwards an update to R2, it also does not include the subnet mask information and therefore only forwards the classful network address 172.16.0.0.

R2 receives and processes the update and adds another entry for the classful network address 172.16.0.0/16 to its routing table, as shown in Figure 3-15. When there are two entries with identical metrics in the routing table, the router shares the load of the traffic equally among the two links. This is known as load balancing.

```
R2# show ip route | begin Gateway
Gateway of last resort is not set

R       172.16.0.0/16 [120/1] via 192.168.2.1, 00:00:14,
                         Serial0/0/1
                       [120/1] via 192.168.1.1, 00:00:16,
                         Serial0/0/0
        192.168.1.0/24 is variably subnetted, 2 subnets,
        2 masks
C          192.168.1.0/30 is directly connected, Serial0/0/0
L          192.168.1.2/32 is directly connected, Serial0/0/0
        192.168.2.0/24 is variably subnetted, 2 subnets,
        2 masks
C          192.168.2.0/30 is directly connected, Serial0/0/1
L          192.168.2.2/32 is directly connected, Serial0/0/1
R2#
```

Figure 3-15   R2 Adds the Entry for 172.16.0.0 via R3

Discontiguous networks have a negative impact on a network. For example, a ping to 172.16.1.1 would return "U.U.U" because R2 would forward the first ping out its Serial 0/0/1 interface toward R3, and R3 would return a Destination Unreachable (U) error code to R2. The second ping would exit out of R2's Serial 0/0/0 interface toward R1, and R1 would return a successful code (.). This pattern would continue until the **ping** command is done.

Classless Routing Protocols (3.1.4.6)

Modern networks no longer use classful IP addressing and the subnet mask cannot be determined by the value of the first octet. The classless IPv4 routing protocols (RIPv2, EIGRP, OSPF, and IS-IS) all include the subnet mask information with the network address in routing updates. Classless routing protocols support VLSM and CIDR.

IPv6 routing protocols are classless. The distinction whether a routing protocol is classful or classless typically only applies to IPv4 routing protocols. All IPv6 routing protocols are considered classless because they include the prefix-length with the IPv6 address.

Figures 3-16 through 3-18 illustrate how classless routing solves the issues created with classful routing.

In the *discontiguous network* design of Figure 3-16, the classless protocol RIPv2 has been implemented on all three routers. When R1 forwards an update to R2, RIPv2 includes the subnet mask information with the update 172.16.1.0/24.

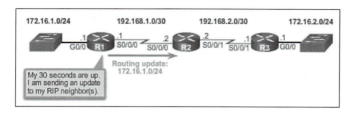

Figure 3-16   R1 Forwards a Classless Update to R2

In Figure 3-17, R2 receives, processes, and adds two entries in the routing table. The first line displays the classful network address 172.16.0.0 with the /24 subnet mask of the update. This is known as the parent route. The second entry displays the VLSM network address 172.16.1.0 with the exit and next-hop address. This is referred to as the child route. Parent routes never include an exit interface or next-hop IP address.

```
R2# show ip route | begin Gateway
Gateway of last resort is not set

        172.16.0.0/24 is subnetted, 1 subnets
R          172.16.1.0 [120/1] via 192.168.1.1, 00:00:06,
            Serial0/0/0
        192.168.1.0/24 is variably subnetted, 2 subnets,
        2 masks
C          192.168.1.0/30 is directly connected, Serial0/0/0
L          192.168.1.2/32 is directly connected, Serial0/0/0
R2#
```

Figure 3-17   R2 Adds the Entry for the 172.16.1.0/24 Network via R1

When R3 forwards an update to R2, RIPv2 includes the subnet mask information with the update 172.16.2.0/24.

R2 receives, processes, and adds another child route entry 172.16.2.0/24 under the parent route entry 172.16.0.0, as shown in Figure 3-18.

```
R2# show ip route | begin Gateway
Gateway of last resort is not set

        172.16.0.0/24 is subnetted, 2 subnets
R          172.16.1.0 [120/1] via 192.168.1.1, 00:00:03,
            Serial0/0/0
R          172.16.2.0 [120/1] via 192.168.2.1, 00:00:03,
            Serial0/0/1
        192.168.1.0/24 is variably subnetted, 2 subnets,
        2 masks
C          192.168.1.0/30 is directly connected, Serial0/0/0
L          192.168.1.2/32 is directly connected, Serial0/0/0
        192.168.2.0/24 is variably subnetted, 2 subnets,
        2 masks
C          192.168.2.0/30 is directly connected, Serial0/0/1
L          192.168.2.2/32 is directly connected, Serial0/0/1
R2#
```

Figure 3-18   Entry for the 172.16.2.0/24 Network via R3

A ping from R2 to 172.16.1.1 would now be successful.

Routing Protocol Characteristics (3.1.4.7)

Routing protocols can be compared based on the following characteristics:

- **Speed of convergence:** Speed of convergence defines how quickly the routers in the network topology share routing information and reach a state of consistent knowledge. The faster the convergence, the more preferable the protocol. Routing loops can occur when inconsistent routing tables are not updated due to slow convergence in a changing network.

- **Scalability:** Scalability defines how large a network can become, based on the routing protocol that is deployed. The larger the network is, the more scalable the routing protocol needs to be.

- **Classful or classless (use of VLSM):** Classful routing protocols do not include the subnet mask and cannot support *variable-length subnet mask (VLSM)*. Classless routing protocols include the subnet mask in the updates. Classless routing protocols support VLSM and better route summarization.

- **Resource usage:** Resource usage includes the requirements of a routing protocol such as memory space (RAM), CPU utilization, and link bandwidth utilization. Higher resource requirements necessitate more powerful hardware to support the routing protocol operation, in addition to the packet forwarding processes.

- **Implementation and maintenance:** Implementation and maintenance describes the level of knowledge that is required for a network administrator to implement and maintain the network based on the routing protocol deployed.

Table 3-4 summarizes the characteristics of each routing protocol.

Table 3-4   Comparing Routing Protocols

	Distance Vector			Link-State		
	RIPv1	**RIPv2**	**IGRP**	**EIGRP**	**OSPF**	**IS-IS**
Speed of Convergence	Slow	Slow	Slow	Fast	Fast	Fast
Scalability – Size of Network	Small	Small	Small	Large	Large	Large
Use of VLSM	No	Yes	No	Yes	Yes	Yes
Resource Usage	Low	Low	Low	Medium	High	High
Implementation and Maintenance	Simple	Simple	Simple	Complex	Complex	Complex

Routing Protocol Metrics (3.1.4.8)

There are cases when a routing protocol learns of more than one route to the same destination. To select the best path, the routing protocol must be able to evaluate and differentiate between the available paths. This is accomplished through the use of routing *metrics*.

A metric is a measurable value that is assigned by the routing protocol to different routes based on the usefulness of that route. In situations where there are multiple paths to the same remote network, the routing metrics are used to determine the overall "cost" of a path from source to destination. Routing protocols determine the best path based on the route with the lowest cost.

Different routing protocols use different metrics. The metric used by one routing protocol is not comparable to the metric used by another routing protocol. Two different routing protocols might choose different paths to the same destination.

For example, assume that PC1 wants to send a packet to PC2. In Figure 3-19, the RIP routing protocol has been enabled on all routers and the network has converged. RIP makes a routing protocol decision based on the least number of hops. Therefore, when the packet arrives on R1, the best route to reach the PC2 network would be to send it directly to R2 even though the link is much slower that all other links.

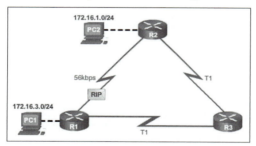

Figure 3-19   RIP Uses Shortest Hop Count Path

In Figure 3-20, the OSPF routing protocol has been enabled on all routers and the network has converged. OSPF makes a routing protocol decision based on the best bandwidth. Therefore, when the packet arrives on R1, the best route to reach the PC2 network would be to send it to R3, which would then forward it to R2.

Video

Video 3.1.4.8: Routing Protocols and Their Metrics

Go to the online course and play the animation showing that RIP would choose the path with the least number of hops, whereas OSPF would choose the path with the highest bandwidth.

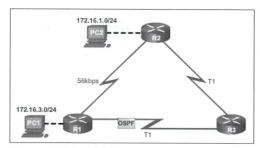

Figure 3-20   OSPF Uses Faster Links

Interactive
Graphic

Activity 3.1.4.9: Classify Dynamic Routing Protocols

Go to the online course to perform this practice activity.

Interactive
Graphic

Activity 3.1.4.10: Compare Routing Protocols

Go to the online course to perform this practice activity.

Interactive
Graphic

Activity 3.1.4.11: Match the Metric to the Protocol

Go to the online course to perform this practice activity.

Distance Vector Dynamic Routing (3.2)

This section describes the characteristics, operations, and functionality of distance vector routing protocols. Understanding the operation of distance vector routing is critical to enabling, verifying, and troubleshooting these protocols.

Distance Vector Technologies (3.2.1.1)

Distance vector routing protocols share updates between neighbors. Neighbors are routers that share a link and are configured to use the same routing protocol. The router is only aware of the network addresses of its own interfaces and the remote network addresses it can reach through its neighbors. Routers using distance vector routing are not aware of the network topology.

Some distance vector routing protocols send periodic updates. For example, RIP sends a periodic update to all of its neighbors every 30 seconds. RIP does this even if the topology has not changed; it continues to send updates. RIPv1 reaches all of its neighbors by sending updates to the all-hosts IPv4 address of 255.255.255.255, a broadcast.

The broadcasting of periodic updates is inefficient because the updates consume bandwidth and consume network device CPU resources. Every network device has to process a broadcast message. RIPv2 and EIGRP, instead, use multicast addresses so that only neighbors that need updates will receive them. EIGRP can also send a unicast message to only the affected neighbor. Additionally, EIGRP only sends an update when needed, instead of periodically.

As shown in Figure 3-21, the two modern IPv4 distance vector routing protocols are RIPv2 and EIGRP. RIPv1 and IGRP are listed only for historical accuracy.

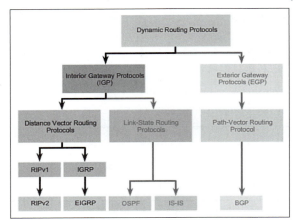

Figure 3-21   Distance Vector Routing Protocols

Distance Vector Algorithm (3.2.1.2)

At the core of the distance vector protocol is the routing algorithm. The algorithm is used to calculate the best paths and then send that information to the neighbors.

The algorithm used for the routing protocols defines the following processes:

- Mechanism for sending and receiving routing information
- Mechanism for calculating the best paths and installing routes in the routing table
- Mechanism for detecting and reacting to topology changes

Video

Video 3.2.1.2: Routers Route Packets

Go to the online course and play the animation to see how the RIP routing protocol adds and deletes routes from a routing table.

In the animation in the online course, R1 and R2 are configured with the RIP routing protocol. The algorithm sends and receives updates. Both R1 and R2 then glean new information from the update. In this case, each router learns about a new network. The algorithm on each router makes its calculations independently and updates the routing table with the new information. When the LAN on R2 goes down, the algorithm constructs a triggered update and sends it to R1. R1 then removes the network from the routing table.

Different routing protocols use different algorithms to install routes in the routing table, send updates to neighbors, and make path determination decisions. For example:

- RIP uses the Bellman-Ford algorithm as its routing algorithm. It is based on two algorithms developed in 1958 and 1956 by Richard Bellman and Lester Ford, Jr.

- IGRP and EIGRP use the Diffusing Update Algorithm (DUAL) routing algorithm developed by Dr. J.J. Garcia-Luna-Aceves at SRI International.

Interactive Graphic

Activity 3.2.1.3: Identify Distance Vector Terminology

Go to the online course to perform this practice activity.

Types of Distance Vector Routing Protocols (3.2.2)

There are two main distance vector routing protocols. This section highlights similarities and differences between RIP and EIGRP.

Routing Information Protocol (3.2.2.1)

The Routing Information Protocol (RIP) was a first generation routing protocol for IPv4 originally specified in RFC 1058. It is easy to configure, making it a good choice for small networks.

RIPv1 has the following key characteristics:

- Routing updates are broadcasted (255.255.255.255) every 30 seconds.

- The hop count is used as the metric for path selection.

- A hop count greater than 15 hops is deemed infinite (too far). That 15th hop router would not propagate the routing update to the next router.

In 1993, RIPv1 evolved to a classless routing protocol known as RIP version 2 (RIPv2). RIPv2 introduced the following improvements:

- **Classless routing protocol:** It supports VLSM and CIDR, because it includes the subnet mask in the routing updates.

- **Increased efficiency:** It forwards updates to multicast address 224.0.0.9, instead of the broadcast address 255.255.255.255.

- **Reduced routing entries:** It supports manual route summarization on any interface.

- **Secure:** It supports an authentication mechanism to secure routing table updates between neighbors.

Table 3-5 summarizes the differences between RIPv1 and RIPv2.

Table 3-5   RIPv1 versus RIPv2

Characteristics and Features	RIPv1	RIPv2
Metric	Both use hop count as a simple metric. The maximum number of hops is 15.	
Updates Forwarded to Address	255.255.255.255	224.0.0.9
Supports VLSM	No	Yes
Supports CIDR	No	Yes
Supports Summarization	No	Yes
Supports Authentication	No	Yes

RIP updates are encapsulated into a UDP segment, with both source and destination port numbers set to UDP port 520.

In 1997, the IPv6-enabled version of RIP was released. RIPng is based on RIPv2. It still has a 15-hop limitation and the administrative distance is 120.

Enhanced Interior Gateway Routing Protocol (3.2.2.2)

The Interior Gateway Routing Protocol (IGRP) was the first proprietary IPv4 routing protocol, developed by Cisco in 1984. It used the following design characteristics:

- Bandwidth, delay, load, and reliability are used to create a composite metric.

- Routing updates are broadcast every 90 seconds, by default.

In 1992, IGRP was replaced by Enhanced IGRP (EIGRP). Like RIPv2, EIGRP also introduced support for VLSM and CIDR. EIGRP increases efficiency, reduces routing updates, and supports secure message exchange.

Table 3-6 summarizes the differences between IGRP and EIGRP.

Table 3-6   IGRP versus EIGRP

Characteristics and Features	IGRP	EIGRP
Metric	Both use a composite metric based on bandwidth and delay. Reliability and load can also be included in the metric calculation if configured.	
Updates Forwarded to Address	255.255.255.255	224.0.0.10
Supports VLSM	No	Yes
Supports CIDR	No	Yes
Supports Summarization	No	Yes
Supports Authentication	No	Yes

EIGRP also introduced:

- *Bounded triggered updates*: It does not send periodic updates. Only routing table changes are propagated, whenever a change occurs. This reduces the amount of load the routing protocol places on the network. Bounded triggered updates means that EIGRP only sends to the neighbors that need it. It uses less bandwidth, especially in large networks with many routes.

- *Hello keepalive mechanism*: A small Hello message is periodically exchanged to maintain adjacencies with neighboring routers. This means a very low usage of network resources during normal operation, instead of the periodic updates.

- **Maintains a topology table**: Maintains all the routes received from neighbors (not only the best paths) in a topology table. DUAL can insert backup routes into the EIGRP topology table.

- **Rapid convergence:** In most cases, it is the fastest IGP to converge because it maintains alternate routes, enabling almost instantaneous convergence. If a primary route fails, the router can use the alternate route identified. The switchover to the alternate route is immediate and does not involve interaction with other routers.

- **Multiple network layer protocol support:** EIGRP uses Protocol Dependent Modules (PDM), which means that it is the only protocol to include support for protocols other than IPv4 and IPv6, such as legacy IPX and AppleTalk.

Activity 3.2.2.3: Compare RIP and EIGRP

Go to the online course to perform this practice activity.

Packet Tracer Activity 3.2.2.4: Comparing RIP and EIGRP Path Selection

PCA and PCB need to communicate. The path that the data takes between these end devices can travel through R1, R2, and R3, or it can travel through R4 and R5. The process by which routers select the best path depends on the routing protocol. We will examine the behavior of two distance vector routing protocols, Enhanced Interior Gateway Routing Protocol (EIGRP) and Routing Information Protocol version 2 (RIPv2).

RIP and RIPng Routing (3.3)

Although the use of RIP has decreased in the past decade, it is still important to your networking studies because it might be encountered in a network implementation. As well, understanding how RIP operates and knowing its implementation will make learning other routing protocols easier.

Configuring the RIP Protocol (3.3.1)

In this section, you will learn how to configure, verify, and troubleshoot RIPv2.

Router RIP Configuration Mode (3.3.1.1)

Although RIP is rarely used in modern networks, it is useful as a foundation for understanding basic network routing. For this reason, this section provides a brief overview of how to configure basic RIP settings and to verify RIPv2.

Refer to the reference topology in Figure 3-22 and the addressing table in Table 3-7.

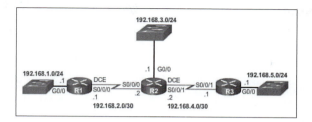

Figure 3-22 RIP Reference Topology

Table 3-7 Addressing Table

Device	Interface	IP Address	Subnet Mask
R1	G0/0	192.168.1.1	255.255.255.0
	S0/0/0	192.168.2.1	255.255.255.0
R2	G0/0	192.168.3.1	255.255.255.0
	S0/0/0	192.168.2.2	255.255.255.0
	S0/0/1	192.168.4.2	255.255.255.0
R3	G0/0	192.168.5.1	255.255.255.0
	S0/0/1	192.168.4.1	255.255.255.0

In this scenario, all routers have been configured with basic management features and all interfaces identified in the reference topology are configured and enabled. There are no static routes configured and no routing protocols enabled; therefore, remote network access is currently impossible. RIPv2 is used as the dynamic routing protocol.

To enable RIP, use the **router rip** command to enter router configuration mode, as shown in the following output. This command does not directly start the RIP process. Instead, it provides access to the router configuration mode where the RIP routing settings are configured.

```
R1# conf t
Enter configuration commands, one per line. End with CNTL/Z.
R1(config)# router rip
R1(config-router)#
```

To disable and eliminate RIP, use the **no router rip** global configuration command. This command stops the RIP process and erases all existing RIP configurations.

Figure 3-23 displays a partial list of the various RIP commands that can be configured. This section covers the two highlighted commands as well as **network**, **passive-interface**, and **version**.

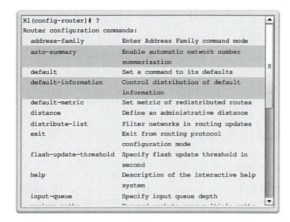

Figure 3-23   RIP Configuration Options

Advertising Networks (3.3.1.2)

By entering the RIP router configuration mode, the router is instructed to run RIP. But the router still needs to know which local interfaces it should use for communication with other routers, as well as which locally connected networks it should advertise to those routers.

To enable RIP routing for a network, use the **network** *network-address* router configuration mode command. Enter the classful network address for each directly connected network. This command:

- Enables RIP on all interfaces that belong to a specific network. Associated interfaces now both send and receive RIP updates.

- Advertises the specified network in RIP routing updates sent to other routers every 30 seconds.

Note

If a subnet address is entered, the IOS automatically converts it to the classful network address. Remember RIPv1 is a classful routing protocol for IPv4. For example, entering the **network 192.168.1.32** command would automatically be converted to **network 192.168.1.0** in the running configuration file. The IOS does not give an error message, but instead corrects the input and enters the classful network address.

In the following command sequence, the **network** command is used to advertise the R1 directly connected networks.

```
R1(config)# router rip
R1(config-router)# network 192.168.1.0
R1(config-router)# network 192.168.2.0
R1(config-router)#
```

Activity 3.3.1.2: Advertising the R2 and R3 Networks

Go to the online course to use the Syntax Checker in the second graphic to configure a similar configuration on R2 and R3.

Examining Default RIP Settings (3.3.1.3)

The output of the **show ip protocols** command in Figure 3-24 displays the IPv4 routing protocol settings currently configured on the router.

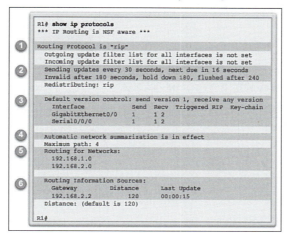

Figure 3-24   Verifying RIP Settings on R1

This output confirms that:

1. RIP routing is configured and running on router R1.

2. The values of various timers; for example, the next routing update is sent by R1 in 16 seconds.

3. The version of RIP configured is currently RIPv1.

4. R1 is currently summarizing at the classful network boundary.

5. The classful networks are advertised by R1. These are the networks that R1 includes in its RIP updates.

6. The RIP neighbors are listed, including their next-hop IP address, the associated AD that R2 uses for updates sent by this neighbor, and when the last update was received from this neighbor.

Note

This command is also very useful when verifying the operations of other routing protocols (i.e., EIGRP and OSPF).

The **show ip route** command displays the RIP routes installed in the routing table. In Figure 3-25, R1 now knows about the highlighted networks.

```
R1# show ip route | begin Gateway
Gateway of last resort is not set

      192.168.1.0/24 is variably subnetted, 2 subnets, 2 masks
C        192.168.1.0/24 is directly connected, GigabitEthernet0/0
L        192.168.1.1/32 is directly connected, GigabitEthernet0/0
      192.168.2.0/24 is variably subnetted, 2 subnets, 2 masks
C        192.168.2.0/24 is directly connected, Serial0/0/0
L        192.168.2.1/32 is directly connected, Serial0/0/0
R        192.168.3.0/24 [120/1] via 192.168.2.2, 00:00:24, Serial0/0/0
R        192.168.4.0/24 [120/1] via 192.168.2.2, 00:00:24, Serial0/0/0
R        192.168.5.0/24 [120/2] via 192.168.2.2, 00:00:24, Serial0/0/0
R1#
```

Figure 3-25   Verifying RIP Routes on R1

Activity 3.3.1.3: Advertising the R2 and R3 Networks

Go to the online course to use the Syntax Checker in the third graphic to verify the R2 and R3 RIP settings and routes.

Enabling RIPv2 (3.3.1.4)

By default, when a RIP process is configured on a Cisco router, it is running RIPv1, as shown in the following output:

```
R1# show ip protocols
*** IP Routing is NSF aware ***

Routing Protocol is "rip"
  Outgoing update filter list for all interfaces is not set
  Incoming update filter list for all interfaces is not set
  Sending updates every 30 seconds, next due in 16 seconds
  Invalid after 180 seconds, hold down 180, flushed after 240
  Redistributing: rip
  Default version control: send version 1, receive any version
    Interface            Send  Recv  Triggered RIP  Key-chain
    GigabitEthernet0/0    1     1 2
    Serial0/0/0           1     1 2
```

```
Automatic network summarization is in effect
Maximum path: 4
Routing for Networks:
   192.168.1.0
   192.168.2.0
Routing Information Sources:
   Gateway          Distance      Last Update
   192.168.2.2           120      00:00:15
Distance: (default is 120)

R1#
```

However, even though the router only sends RIPv1 messages, it can interpret both RIPv1 and RIPv2 messages. A RIPv1 router ignores the RIPv2 fields in the route entry.

Use the **version 2** router configuration mode command to enable RIPv2, as shown in Figure 3-26.

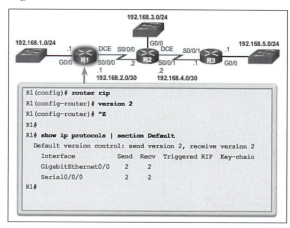

Figure 3-26   Enable and Verify RIPv2 on R1

Notice how the **show ip protocols** command verifies that R2 is now configured to send and receive version 2 messages only. The RIP process now includes the subnet mask in all updates, making RIPv2 a classless routing protocol.

Note

Configuring **version 1** enables RIPv1 only, while configuring **no version** returns the router to the default setting of sending version 1 updates but listening for version 1 or version 2 updates.

The following output verifies that there are no RIP routes still in the routing table:

```
R1# show ip route | begin Gateway
Gateway of last resort is not set

      192.168.1.0/24 is variably subnetted, 2 subnets, 2 masks
C        192.168.1.0/24 is directly connected, GigabitEthernet0/0
L        192.168.1.1/32 is directly connected, GigabitEthernet0/0
      192.168.2.0/24 is variably subnetted, 2 subnets, 2 masks
C        192.168.2.0/24 is directly connected, Serial0/0/0
L        192.168.2.1/32 is directly connected, Serial0/0/0
R1#
```

There are no RIP routes because R1 is now only listening for RIPv2 updates. R2 and R3 are still sending RIPv1 updates. Therefore, the **version 2** command must be configured on all routers in the routing domain.

Activity 3.3.1.4: Enable and Verify RIPv2 on R2 and R3

Go to the online course to use the Syntax Checker in the fourth graphic to enable RIPv2 on R2 and R3.

Disabling Auto Summarization (3.3.1.5)

As shown in Figure 3-27, RIPv2 automatically summarizes networks at major network boundaries by default, just like RIPv1.

```
R1# show ip protocols
*** IP Routing is NSF aware ***

Routing Protocol is "rip"
 Outgoing update filter list for all interfaces is not set
 Incoming update filter list for all interfaces is not set
 Sending updates every 30 seconds, next due in 16 seconds
 Invalid after 180 seconds, hold down 180, flushed after
 240
 Redistributing: rip
 Default version control: send version 2, receive version 2
    Interface          Send  Recv  Triggered RIP  Key-chain
    GigabitEthernet0/0   1    1 2
    Serial0/0/0          1    1 2
 Automatic network summarization is in effect
 Maximum path: 4
 Routing for Networks:
    192.168.1.0
    192.168.2.0
 Routing Information Sources:
    Gateway         Distance      Last Update
    192.168.2.2        120        00:00:15
 Distance: (default is 120)
R1#
```

Figure 3-27   Verify RIPv2 Route Summarization

To modify the default RIPv2 behavior of *automatic summarization*, use the **no auto-summary** router configuration mode command as shown in the following command sequence:

```
R1(config)# router rip
R1(config-router)# no auto-summary
R1(config-router)# end
R1#
*Mar 10 14:11:49.659: %SYS-5-CONFIG_I: Configured from console by console
R1# show ip protocols | section Automatic
  Automatic network summarization is not in effect
R1#
```

This command has no effect when using RIPv1. When automatic summarization has been disabled, RIPv2 no longer summarizes networks to their classful address at boundary routers. RIPv2 now includes all subnets and their appropriate masks in its routing updates. The **show ip protocols** output now states that automatic network summarization is not in effect.

> **Note**
>
> RIPv2 must be enabled before automatic summarization is disabled.

Interactive Graphic

Activity 3.3.1.5: Disable Automatic Summarization on R2 and R3

Go to the online course to use the Syntax Checker in the third graphic to disable automatic summarization on R2 and R3.

Configuring Passive Interfaces (3.3.1.6)

By default, RIP updates are forwarded out all RIP-enabled interfaces. However, RIP updates really only need to be sent out interfaces connecting to other RIP-enabled routers.

For instance, refer to the topology in Figure 3-22. RIP sends updates out of its Gigabit Ethernet 0/0 interface even though no RIP device exists on that LAN. R1 has no way of knowing this and, as a result, sends an update every 30 seconds. Sending out unneeded updates on a LAN impacts the network in three ways:

- **Wasted bandwidth:** Bandwidth is used to transport unnecessary updates. Because RIP updates are either broadcasted or multicasted, switches also forward the updates out all ports.

- **Wasted resources:** All devices on the LAN must process the update up to the transport layers, at which point the devices will discard the update.

- **Security risk:** Advertising updates on a broadcast network is a security risk. RIP updates can be intercepted with packet sniffing software. Routing updates can be modified and sent back to the router, corrupting the routing table with false metrics that misdirect traffic.

To address these problems, an interface can be configured to stop sending routing updates. This is referred to as configuring a *passive interface*. Use the **passive-interface** router configuration command to prevent the transmission of routing updates through a router interface but still allow that network to be advertised to other routers. The command stops routing updates out the specified interface. However, the network that the specified interface belongs to is still advertised in routing updates that are sent out other interfaces.

There is no need for R1, R2, and R3 to forward RIP updates out of their LAN interfaces. The configuration in Figure 3-28 identifies the R1 Gigabit Ethernet 0/0 interface as passive.

```
R1(config)# router rip
R1(config-router)# passive-interface g0/0
R1(config-router)# end
R1#
R1# show ip protocols | begin Default
  Default version control: send version 2, receive version 2
    Interface          Send  Recv  Triggered RIP  Key-chain
    Serial0/0/0         2     2
  Automatic network summarization is not in effect
  Maximum path: 4
  Routing for Networks:
    192.168.1.0
    192.168.2.0
  Passive Interface(s):
    GigabitEthernet0/0
  Routing Information Sources:
    Gateway         Distance      Last Update
    192.168.2.2        120        00:00:06
  Distance: (default is 120)

R1#
```

Figure 3-28 Configuring and Verifying a Passive Interface on R1

The **show ip protocols** command is then used to verify that the Gigabit Ethernet interface was passive. Notice that the Gigabit Ethernet 0/0 interface is no longer listed as sending or receiving version 2 updates, but instead is now listed under the Passive Interface(s) section. Also notice that the network 192.168.1.0 is still listed under Routing for Networks, which means that this network is still included as a route entry in RIP updates that are sent to R2.

Note

All routing protocols support the **passive-interface** command.

Activity 3.3.1.6: Configuring and Verifying a Passive Interface on R2 and R3

Go to the online course to use the Syntax Checker in the third graphic to configure a passive interface on R2 and R3.

As an alternative, all interfaces can be made passive using the **passive-interface default** command. Interfaces that should not be passive can be re-enabled using the **no passive-interface** command.

Propagating a Default Route (3.3.1.7)

In the topology in Figure 3-29, R1 is single-homed to a service provider. Therefore, all that is required for R1 to reach the Internet is a *default static route* going out of the Serial 0/0/1 interface.

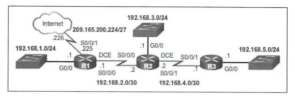

Figure 3-29   Propagating a Default Route on R1

Similar default static routes could be configured on R2 and R3, but it is much more scalable to enter it one time on the edge router R1 and then have R1 propagate it to all other routers using RIP. To provide Internet connectivity to all other networks in the RIP routing domain, the default static route needs to be advertised to all other routers that use the dynamic routing protocol.

To propagate a default route, the edge router must be configured with:

- A default static route using the **ip route 0.0.0.0 0.0.0.0** *exit-intf next-hop-ip* command.

- The **default-information originate** router configuration command. This instructs R1 to originate default information, by propagating the static default route in RIP updates.

The example in Figure 3-30 configures a fully specified default static route to the service provider, and then the route is propagated by RIP. Notice that R1 now has a Gateway of Last Resort and default route installed in its routing table.

```
R1(config)# ip route 0.0.0.0 0.0.0.0 S0/0/1 209.165.200.226
R1(config)# router rip
R1(config-router)# default-information originate
R1(config-router)# ^Z
R1#
*Mar 10 23:33:51.801: %SYS-5-CONFIG_I: Configured from console by
console
R1# show ip route | begin Gateway
Gateway of last resort is 209.165.200.226 to network 0.0.0.0

S*    0.0.0.0/0 [1/0] via 209.165.200.226, Serial0/0/1
      192.168.1.0/24 is variably subnetted, 2 subnets, 2 masks
C        192.168.1.0/24 is directly connected, GigabitEthernet0/0
L        192.168.1.1/32 is directly connected, GigabitEthernet0/0
      192.168.2.0/24 is variably subnetted, 2 subnets, 2 masks
C        192.168.2.0/24 is directly connected, Serial0/0/0
L        192.168.2.1/32 is directly connected, Serial0/0/0
R     192.168.3.0/24 [120/1] via 192.168.2.2, 00:00:08,
Serial0/0/0
R     192.168.4.0/24 [120/1] via 192.168.2.2, 00:00:08,
Serial0/0/0
R     192.168.5.0/24 [120/2] via 192.168.2.2, 00:00:08,
Serial0/0/0
      209.165.200.0/24 is variably subnetted, 2 subnets, 2 masks
C        209.165.200.0/24 is directly connected, Serial0/0/1
```

Figure 3-30   Configuring and Verifying a Default Route on R1

Activity 3.3.1.7: Verifying the Gateway of Last Resort on R2 and R3

Go to the online course to use the Syntax Checker in the third graphic to verify that the default route has been propagated to R2 and R3.

Packet Tracer Activity 3.3.1.8: Configuring RIPv2

Although RIP is rarely used in modern networks, it is useful as a foundation for understanding basic network routing. In this activity, you will configure a default route, configure RIP version 2 with appropriate network statements and passive interfaces, and verify full connectivity.

Configuring the RIPng Protocol (3.3.2)

In this section, you will learn how to configure, verify, and troubleshoot RIPng.

Advertising IPv6 Networks (3.3.2.1)

As with its IPv4 counterpart, RIPng is rarely used in modern networks. It is also useful as a foundation for understanding basic network routing. For this reason, this section provides a brief overview of how to configure basic *RIPng*.

Refer to the reference topology in Figure 3-31.

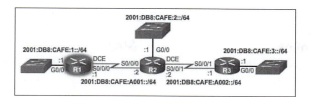

Figure 3-31   Enabling RIPng on the R1 Interfaces

In this scenario, all routers have been configured with basic management features and all interfaces identified in the reference topology are configured and enabled. There are no static routes configured and no routing protocols enabled; therefore, remote network access is currently impossible.

To enable an IPv6 router to forward IPv6 packets, **ipv6 unicast-routing** must be configured.

Unlike RIPv2, RIPng is enabled on an interface and not in router configuration mode. In fact, there is no **network** *network-address* command available in RIPng. Instead, use the **ipv6 rip** *domain-name* **enable** interface configuration command.

In the following output, IPv6 unicast routing is enabled and the Gigabit Ethernet 0/0 and Serial 0/0/0 interfaces are enabled for RIPng using the domain name RIP-AS:

```
R1(config)# ipv6 unicast-routing
R1(config)#
R1(config)# interface gigabitethernet 0/0
R1(config-if)# ipv6 rip RIP-AS enable
R1(config-if)# exit
R1(config)#
R1(config)# interface serial 0/0/0
R1(config-if)# ipv6 rip RIP-AS enable
R1(config-if)# no shutdown
R1(config-if)#
```

Interactive Graphic

Activity 3.3.2.1: Enabling RIPng on the R2 and R3 Interfaces

Go to the online course to use the Syntax Checker in the second graphic to enable RIPng on the R2 and R3 interfaces.

The process to propagate a default route in RIPng is identical to RIPv2 except that an IPv6 default static route must be specified. For example, assume that R1 had an Internet connection from a Serial 0/0/1 interface to IP address 2001:DB8:FEED:1::1/64. To propagate a default route, R1 would have to be configured with:

- A default static route using the **ipv6 route 0::/0 2001:DB8:FEED:1::1** global configuration command.

- The **ipv6 rip** *domain-name* **default-information originate** interface configuration mode command. For example, the Serial 0/0/1 interface of R1 would have to be configured with the **ipv6 rip RIP-AS default-information originate** command. This would instruct R1 to be the source of the default route information and propagate the default static route in RIPng updates sent out of the RIPng-enabled interfaces.

Examining the RIPng Configuration (3.3.2.2)

In Figure 3-32, the **show ipv6 protocols** command does not provide the same amount of information as its IPv4 counterpart.

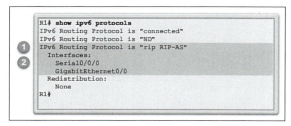

Figure 3-32   Verifying RIPng Settings on R1

However, the command does confirm the following parameters:

1. That RIPng routing is configured and running on router R1.

2. The interfaces configured with RIPng.

The **show ipv6 route** command displays the routes installed in the routing table as shown in Figure 3-33. The output confirms that R1 now knows about the highlighted RIPng networks.

```
R1# show ipv6 route
IPv6 Routing Table - default - 8 entries
Codes: C - Connected, L - Local, S - Static, U - Per-user
Static route
       B - BGP, R - RIP, I1 - ISIS L1, I2 - ISIS L2
       IA - ISIS interarea, IS - ISIS summary, D - EIGRP,
       EX - EIGRP external, ND - ND Default,
       NDp - ND Prefix, DCE - Destination, NDr - Redirect,
       O - OSPF Intra, OI - OSPF Inter, OE1 - OSPF ext 1,
       OE2 - OSPF ext 2, ON1 - OSPF NSSA ext 1,
       ON2 - OSPF NSSA ext 2
C   2001:DB8:CAFE:1::/64 [0/0]
     via GigabitEthernet0/0, directly connected
L   2001:DB8:CAFE:1::1/128 [0/0]
     via GigabitEthernet0/0, receive
R   2001:DB8:CAFE:2::/64 [120/2]
     via FE80::FE99:47FF:FE71:78A0, Serial0/0/0
R   2001:DB8:CAFE:3::/64 [120/3]
     via FE80::FE99:47FF:FE71:78A0, Serial0/0/0
C   2001:DB8:CAFE:A001::/64 [0/0]
     via Serial0/0/0, directly connected
L   2001:DB8:CAFE:A001::1/128 [0/0]
     via Serial0/0/0, receive
R   2001:DB8:CAFE:A002::/64 [120/2]
```

Figure 3-33   Verifying Routes on R1

Notice that the R2 LAN is advertised as two hops away. This is because there is a difference in the way RIPv2 and RIPng calculate the hop counts. With RIPv2 (and RIPv1), the metric to the R2 LAN would be one hop. This is because the metric (hop count) that is displayed in the IPv4 routing table is the number of hops required to reach the remote network (counting the next-hop router as the first hop). In RIPng, the sending router already considers itself to be one hop away; therefore, R2 advertises its LAN with a metric of 1. When R1 receives the update, it adds another hop count of 1 to the metric. Therefore, R1 considers the R2 LAN to be two hops away. Similarly it considers the R3 LAN to be three hops away.

Appending the **rip** keyword to the command as shown in Figure 3-34 only lists RIPng networks.

```
R1# show ipv6 route rip
IPv6 Routing Table - default - 8 entries
Codes: C - Connected, L - Local, S - Static, U - Per-user
Static route
       B - BGP, R - RIP, I1 - ISIS L1, I2 - ISIS L2
       IA - ISIS interarea, IS - ISIS summary, D - EIGRP,
       EX - EIGRP external, ND - ND Default,
       NDp - ND Prefix, DCE - Destination, NDr - Redirect,
       O - OSPF Intra, OI - OSPF Inter, OE1 - OSPF ext 1,
       OE2 - OSPF ext 2, ON1 - OSPF NSSA ext 1,
       ON2 - OSPF NSSA ext 2
R   2001:DB8:CAFE:2::/64 [120/2]
     via FE80::FE99:47FF:FE71:78A0, Serial0/0/0
R   2001:DB8:CAFE:3::/64 [120/3]
     via FE80::FE99:47FF:FE71:78A0, Serial0/0/0
R   2001:DB8:CAFE:A002::/64 [120/2]
     via FE80::FE99:47FF:FE71:78A0, Serial0/0/0
R1#
```

Figure 3-34   Verifying RIPng Routes on R1

Interactive Graphic

Activity 3.3.2.2: Verifying RIPng Settings and Routes on R2 and R3

Go to the online course to use the Syntax Checker in the fourth graphic to verify RIPng settings and routes on R2 and R3.

Packet Tracer ☐ Activity

Packet Tracer Activity 3.3.2.3: Configuring RIPng

RIPng (RIP Next Generation) is a distance vector routing protocol for routing IPv6 addresses. RIPng is based on RIPv2 and has the same administrative distance and 15-hop limitation. This activity will help you become more familiar with RIPng.

Lab 3.3.2.4: Configuring RIPv2

In this lab, you will complete the following objectives:

- Part 1: Build the Network and Configure Basic Device Settings
- Part 2: Configure and Verify RIPv2 Routing

- Part 3: Configure IPv6 on Devices
- Part 4: Configure and Verify RIPng Routing

Link-State Dynamic Routing (3.4)

Distance vector routing protocols are thought to be simple to understand, whereas link-state routing protocols have the reputation of being very complex, even intimidating. However, link-state routing protocols and concepts are not difficult to understand. In many ways, the link-state process is simpler to understand than distance vector concepts.

Link-State Routing Protocol Operation (3.4.1)

This section describes the characteristics, operations, and functionality of link-state routing protocols. Understanding the operation of link-state routing is critical to enabling, verifying, and troubleshooting these protocols.

Shortest Path First Protocols (3.4.1.1)

Link-state routing protocols are also known as shortest path first protocols and are built around Edsger Dijkstra's shortest path first (SPF) algorithm. The SPF algorithm is discussed in more detail in a later section.

The IPv4 link-state routing protocols are shown Figure 3-35:

- Open Shortest Path First (OSPF)
- Intermediate System-to-Intermediate System (IS-IS)

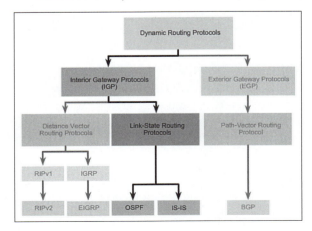

Figure 3-35   Link-State Routing Protocols

Link-state routing protocols have the reputation of being much more complex than their distance vector counterparts. However, the basic functionality and configuration of link-state routing protocols is equally straightforward.

Just like RIP and EIGRP, basic OSPF operations can be configured using the:

- **router ospf** *process-id* global configuration command

- **network** command to advertise networks

Dijkstra's Algorithm (3.4.1.2)

All link-state routing protocols apply *Dijkstra's algorithm* to calculate the best path route. The algorithm is commonly referred to as the *shortest path first (SPF)* algorithm. This algorithm uses accumulated costs along each path, from source to destination, to determine the total cost of a route.

In Figure 3-36, each path is labeled with an arbitrary value for cost.

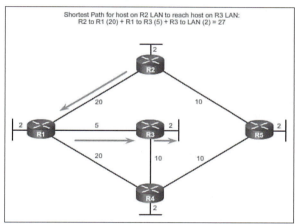

Figure 3-36   Dijkstra's Shortest Path First Algorithm

The cost of the shortest path for R2 to send packets to the LAN attached to R3 is 27. Specifically, the cost is R2 to R1 (20) plus R1 to R3 (5) plus R3 to LAN (2). Each router determines its own cost to each destination in the topology. In other words, each router calculates the SPF algorithm and determines the cost from its own perspective.

Note

The focus of this section is on cost, which is determined by the SPF tree. For this reason, the graphics throughout this section show the connections of the SPF tree, not the topology. All links are represented with a solid black line.

SPF Example (3.4.1.3)

The table in Figure 3-37 displays the shortest path and the accumulated cost to reach the identified destination networks from the perspective of R1.

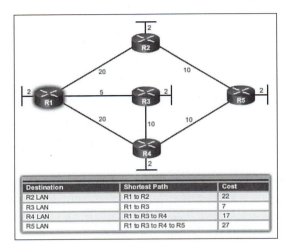

Destination	Shortest Path	Cost
R2 LAN	R1 to R2	22
R3 LAN	R1 to R3	7
R4 LAN	R1 to R3 to R4	17
R5 LAN	R1 to R3 to R4 to R5	27

Figure 3-37   R1 SPF Tree

The shortest path is not necessarily the path with the least number of hops. For example, look at the path to the R5 LAN. It might be assumed that R1 would send directly to R4 instead of to R3. However, the cost to reach R4 directly (22) is higher than the cost to reach R4 through R3 (17).

Observe the shortest path for each router to reach each of the LANs, as shown in Tables 3-8 through 3-11.

Table 3-8   R2 SPF Tree

Destination	Shortest Path	Cost
R1 LAN	R2 to R1	22
R3 LAN	R2 to R1 to R3	27
R4 LAN	R2 to R5 to R4	22
R5 LAN	R2 to R5	12

Table 3-9   R3 SPF Tree

Destination	Shortest Path	Cost
R1 LAN	R3 to R1	7
R2 LAN	R3 to R1 to R2	27
R4 LAN	R3 to R4	12
R5 LAN	R3 to R4 to R5	22

Table 3-10   R4 SPF Tree

Destination	Shortest Path	Cost
R1 LAN	R4 to R3 to R1	17
R2 LAN	R4 to R5 to R2	22
R3 LAN	RR4 to R3	12
R5 LAN	R4 to R5	12

Table 3-11   R5 SPF Tree

Destination	Shortest Path	Cost
R1 LAN	R5 to R4 to R3 to R1	27
R2 LAN	R5 to R2	12
R3 LAN	R5 to R4 to R3	22
R4 LAN	R5 to R4	12

Link-State Updates (3.4.2)

Link-state updates (LSUs) are the packets used for OSPF routing updates. This section discusses how OSPF exchanges LSUs to discover the best routes.

Link-State Routing Process (3.4.2.1)

So exactly how does a link-state routing protocol work? With link-state routing protocols, a link is an interface on a router. Information about the state of those links is known as link-states.

All routers in an OSPF area will complete the following generic link-state routing process to reach a state of convergence:

1. Each router learns about its own links and its own directly connected networks. This is done by detecting that an interface is in the up state.

2. Each router is responsible for meeting its neighbors on directly connected networks. Link-state routers do this by exchanging Hello packets with other link-state routers on directly connected networks.

3. Each router builds a *link-state packet (LSP)* containing the state of each directly connected link. This is done by recording all the pertinent information about each neighbor, including neighbor ID, link type, and bandwidth.

4. Each router floods the LSP to all neighbors. Those neighbors store all LSPs received in a database. They then flood the LSPs to their neighbors until all routers in the area have received the LSPs. Each router stores a copy of each LSP received from its neighbors in a local database.

5. Each router uses the database to construct a complete map of the topology and computes the best path to each destination network. Like having a road map, the router now has a complete map of all destinations in the topology and the routes to reach them. The SPF algorithm is used to construct the map of the topology and to determine the best path to each network.

Note

This process is the same for both OSPF for IPv4 and OSPF for IPv6. The examples in this section refer to OSPF for IPv4.

Link and Link-State (3.4.2.2)

The first step in the link-state routing process is that each router learns about its own links, its own directly connected networks. When a router interface is configured with an IP address and subnet mask, the interface becomes part of that network.

Refer to the topology in Figure 3-38. For purposes of this discussion, assume that R1 was previously configured and had full connectivity to all neighbors. However, R1 lost power briefly and had to restart.

During boot up R1 loads the saved startup configuration file. As the previously configured interfaces become active, R1 learns about its own directly connected networks. Regardless of the routing protocols used, these directly connected networks are now entries in the routing table.

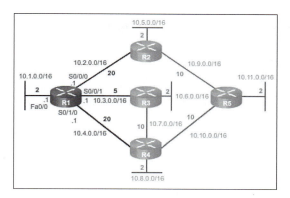

Figure 3-38   R1 Links

As with distance vector protocols and static routes, the interface must be properly configured with an IPv4 address and subnet mask, and the link must be in the up state before the link-state routing protocol can learn about a link. Also, like distance vector protocols, the interface must be included in one of the **network** router configuration statements before it can participate in the link-state routing process.

Figure 3-38 shows R1 linked to four directly connected networks:

- FastEthernet 0/0: 10.1.0.0/16
- Serial 0/0/0: 10.2.0.0/16
- Serial 0/0/1: 10.3.0.0/16
- Serial 0/1/0: 10.4.0.0/16

As shown in Figures 3-39 through 3-42, the link-state information includes:

- The interface's IPv4 address and subnet mask
- The type of network, such as Ethernet (broadcast) or Serial point-to-point link
- The cost of that link
- Any neighbor routers on that link

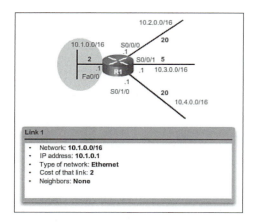

Figure 3-39   Link-State of Interface Fa0/0

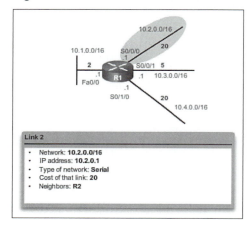

Figure 3-40   Link-State of Interface S0/0/0

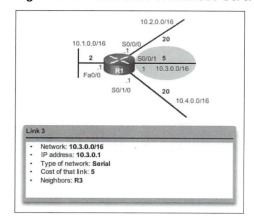

Figure 3-41   Link-State of Interface S0/0/1

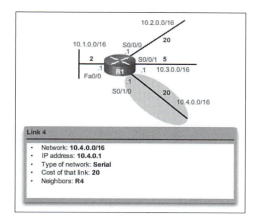

Figure 3-42   Link-State of Interface S0/1/0

Note

Cisco's implementation of OSPF specifies the OSPF routing metric as the cost of the link based on the bandwidth of the outgoing interface. For the purposes of this chapter, we are using arbitrary cost values to simplify the demonstration.

Say Hello (3.4.2.3)

The second step in the link-state routing process is that each router is responsible for meeting its neighbors on directly connected networks.

Routers with link-state routing protocols use a Hello protocol to discover any neighbors on their links. A neighbor is any other router that is enabled with the same link-state routing protocol.

In Figure 3-43, R1 sends Hello packets out its links (interfaces) to discover if there are any neighbors.

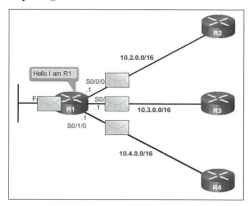

Figure 3-43   R1 Sends Hello Packets

In Figure 3-44, R2, R3, and R4 reply to the Hello packet with their own Hello packets because these routers are configured with the same link-state routing protocol. There are no neighbors out the FastEthernet 0/0 interface. Because R1 does not receive a Hello on this interface, it does not continue with the link-state routing process steps for the FastEthernet 0/0 link.

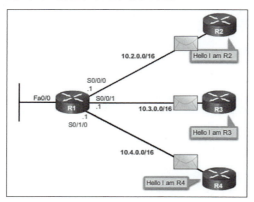

Figure 3-44   R2, R3, and R4 Reply with Hello Packets

Video

Video 3.4.2.3: Neighbor Discovery—Hello Packets

Go to the online course and play the animation to view the link-state neighbor discovery process with Hello packets.

When two link-state routers learn that they are neighbors, they form an adjacency. These small Hello packets continue to be exchanged between two adjacent neighbors and serve as a keepalive function to monitor the state of the neighbor. If a router stops receiving Hello packets from a neighbor, that neighbor is considered unreachable and the adjacency is broken.

Building the Link-State Packet (3.4.2.4)

The third step in the link-state routing process is that each router builds an LSP containing the state of each directly connected link.

After a router has established its adjacencies, it can build its LSPs that contain the link-state information about its links. A simplified version of the LSP from R1 displayed in Figure 3-45 would contain the following:

1. R1; Ethernet network 10.1.0.0/16; Cost 2

2. R1 -> R2; Serial point-to-point network; 10.2.0.0/16; Cost 20

3. R1 -> R3; Serial point-to-point network; 10.3.0.0/16; Cost 5

4. R1 -> R4; Serial point-to-point network; 10.4.0.0/16; Cost 20

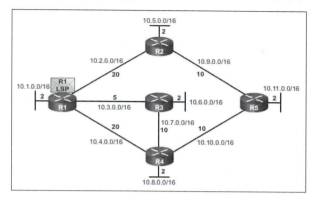

Figure 3-45   Building the LSP

Flooding the LSP (3.4.2.5)

The fourth step in the link-state routing process is that each router floods the LSP to all neighbors, who then store all LSPs received in a database.

Each router floods its link-state information to all other link-state routers in the routing area as shown in Figure 3-46.

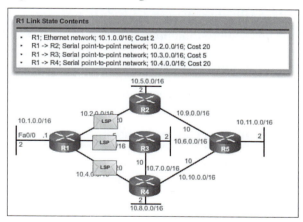

Figure 3-46   R1 Floods Its LSP

Whenever a router receives an LSP from a neighboring router, it immediately sends that LSP out all other interfaces except the interface that received the LSP. This process creates a flooding effect of LSPs from all routers throughout the routing area.

Video

Video 3.4.2.5: Routers Route Packets
Go to the online course and play the animation to view the LSP flooding.

In the animation, the LSPs are flooded almost immediately after being received without any intermediate calculations. Link-state routing protocols calculate the SPF algorithm after the flooding is complete. As a result, link-state routing protocols reach convergence very quickly.

Remember that LSPs do not need to be sent periodically. An LSP only needs to be sent:

- During initial startup of the routing protocol process on that router (e.g., router restart)
- Whenever there is a change in the topology (e.g., a link going down or coming up, a neighbor adjacency being established or broken)

In addition to the link-state information, other information is included in the LSP, such as sequence numbers and aging information, to help manage the flooding process. This information is used by each router to determine if it has already received the LSP from another router or if the LSP has newer information than what is already contained in the link-state database. This process allows a router to keep only the most current information in its link-state database.

Building the Link-State Database (3.4.2.6)

The final step in the link-state routing process is that each router uses the database to construct a complete map of the topology and computes the best path to each destination network.

Eventually, all routers receive an LSP from every other link-state router in the routing area. These LSPs are stored in the link-state database.

Table 3-12 displays the link-state database content of R1.

Table 3-12   Link-State Database

R1 Link-states:
Connected to network 10.1.0.0/16, cost = 2
Connected to R2 on network 10.2.0.0/16, cost = 20
Connected to R3 on network 10.2.0.0/16, cost = 5
Connected to R4 on network 10.3.0.0/16, cost = 20

R2 Link-states:

Connected to network 10.5.0.0/16, cost = 2

Connected to R1 on network 10.2.0.0/16, cost = 20

Connected to R5 on network 10.9.0.0/16, cost = 10

R3 Link-states:

Connected to network 10.6.0.0/16, cost = 2

Connected to R1 on network 10.3.0.0/16, cost = 5

Connected to R4 on network 10.7.0.0/16, cost = 10

R4 Link-states:

Connected to network 10.8.0.0/16, cost = 2

Connected to R1 on network 10.4.0.0/16, cost = 20

Connected to R3 on network 10.7.0.0/16, cost = 10

Connected to R5 on network 10.10.0.0/16, cost = 10

R5 Link-states:

Connected to network 10.11.0.0/16, cost = 2

Connected to R2 on network 10.9.0.0/16, cost = 10

Connected to R4 on network 10.10.0.0/16, cost = 10

As a result of the flooding process, R1 has learned the link-state information for each router in its routing area. Notice that R1 also includes its own link-state information in the link-state database.

With a complete link-state database, R1 can now use the database and the shortest path first (SPF) algorithm to calculate the preferred path or shortest path to each network, resulting in the SPF tree.

Building the SPF Tree (3.4.2.7)

Each router in the routing area uses the link-state database and SPF algorithm to construct the *SPF tree*.

For example, using the link-state information from all other routers, R1 can now begin to construct an SPF tree of the network. To begin, the SPF algorithm interprets each router's LSP to identify networks and associated costs.

The SPF algorithm then calculates the shortest paths to reach each individual network, resulting in the SPF tree as shown in Figure 3-47. R1 now has a complete topology view of the link-state area.

Note

The entire process can be viewed in the online course on page 3.4.2.7 in Figures 1 through 6.

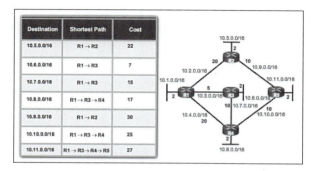

Figure 3-47   Resulting SPF Tree of R1

Each router constructs its own SPF tree independently from all other routers. To ensure proper routing, the link-state databases used to construct those trees must be identical on all routers.

Adding OSPF Routes to the Routing Table (3.4.2.8)

Using the shortest path information determined by the SPF algorithm, these paths can now be added to the routing table. Figure 3-48 shows the routes that have now been added to R1's IPv4 routing table.

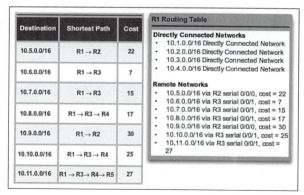

Figure 3-48   Populate the Routing Table

The routing table also includes all directly connected networks and routes from any other sources, such as static routes. Packets are now forwarded according to these entries in the routing table.

**Interactive
Graphic**

Activity 3.4.2.9: Building the Link-State Database and SPF Tree
Go to the online course to perform this practice activity.

Why Use Link-State Routing Protocols? (3.4.3)

This section discusses the advantages of using link-state routing protocols and compares the two types of link-state routing protocols.

Why Use Link-State Protocols? (3.4.3.1)

There are several advantages of link-state routing protocols compared to distance vector routing protocols.

- **Builds a topological map:** Link-state routing protocols create a topological map, or SPF tree of the network topology. Because link-state routing protocols exchange link-states, the SPF algorithm can build an SPF tree of the network. Using the SPF tree, each router can independently determine the shortest path to every network.

- **Fast convergence:** When receiving an LSP, link-state routing protocols immediately flood the LSP out all interfaces except for the interface from which the LSP was received. In contrast, RIP needs to process each routing update and update its routing table before flooding the routing update out other interfaces.

- *Event-driven updates*: After the initial flooding of LSPs, link-state routing protocols only send out an LSP when there is a change in the topology. The LSP contains only the information regarding the affected link. Unlike some distance vector routing protocols, link-state routing protocols do not send periodic updates.

- **Hierarchical design:** Link-state routing protocols use the concept of areas. Multiple areas create a hierarchical design to networks, allowing for better route aggregation (summarization) and the isolation of routing issues within an area.

Link-state protocols also have a few disadvantages compared to distance vector routing protocols:

- **Memory requirements:** Link-state protocols require additional memory to create and maintain the link-state database and SPF tree.

- **Processing requirements:** Link-state protocols can also require more CPU processing than distance vector routing protocols. The SPF algorithm requires more CPU time than distance vector algorithms such as Bellman-Ford, because link-state protocols build a complete map of the topology.

- **Bandwidth requirements:** The flooding of link-state packets can adversely affect the available bandwidth on a network. This should only occur during initial start-up of routers, but can also be an issue on unstable networks.

Link-State Protocols Support Multiple Areas (3.4.3.2)

Modern link-state routing protocols are designed to minimize the effects on memory, CPU, and bandwidth. The use and configuration of multiple areas can reduce the size of the link-state databases. Multiple areas can also limit the amount of link-state information flooding in a routing domain and send LSPs only to those routers that need them. When there is a change in the topology, only those routers in the affected area receive the LSP and run the SPF algorithm. This can help isolate an unstable link to a specific area in the routing domain.

For example, in Figure 3-49, there are three separate routing domains: area 1, area 0, and area 51.

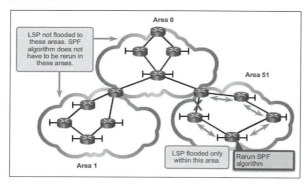

Figure 3-49   Create Areas to Minimize Router Resource Usage

If a network in area 51 goes down, the LSP with the information about this downed link is only flooded to other routers in that area. Only those routers in area 51 need to update their link-state databases, rerun the SPF algorithm, create a new SPF tree, and update their routing tables. Routers in other areas learn that this route is down, but this is done with a type of LSP that does not cause them to rerun their SPF algorithm. Routers in other areas can update their routing tables directly.

Protocols that Use Link-State (3.4.3.3)

There are only two link-state routing protocols, OSPF and IS-IS.

Open Shortest Path First (OSPF) is the most popular implementation. It was designed by the Internet Engineering Task Force (IETF) OSPF Working Group. The development of OSPF began in 1987 and there are two current versions in use:

- **OSPFv2**: OSPF for IPv4 networks (RFC 1247 and RFC 2328)

- *OSPFv3*: OSPF for IPv6 networks (RFC 2740)

> **Note**
>
> With the OSPFv3 Address Families feature, OSPFv3 includes support for both IPv4 and IPv6.

IS-IS was designed by International Organization for Standardization (ISO) and is described in ISO 10589. The first incarnation of this routing protocol was developed at Digital Equipment Corporation (DEC) and is known as DECnet Phase V. Radia Perlman was the chief designer of the IS-IS routing protocol.

IS-IS was originally designed for the OSI protocol suite and not the TCP/IP protocol suite. Later, Integrated IS-IS, or Dual IS-IS, included support for IP networks. Although IS-IS has been known as the routing protocol used mainly by ISPs and carriers, more enterprise networks are beginning to use IS-IS.

OSPF and IS-IS share many similarities and also have many differences. There are many pro-OSPF and pro-IS-IS factions who discuss and debate the advantages of one routing protocol over the other. Both routing protocols provide the necessary routing functionality.

The Routing Table (3.5)

As a network administrator, it is important to know the routing table in depth when troubleshooting network issues. Understanding the structure and lookup process of the routing table will help you diagnose any routing table issue, regardless of your level of familiarity with a particular routing protocol. For example, you might encounter a situation in which the routing table has all of the routes you would expect to see, but packet forwarding is not performing as expected. Knowing how to step through the lookup process of a destination IP address for a packet will enable you to determine whether the packet is being forwarded as expected, if and why the packet is being sent elsewhere, or whether the packet has been discarded.

Parts of an IPv4 Route Entry (3.5.1)

A routing table consists of directly connected networks and routes learned statically or dynamically. This section examines these two types of routing table entries.

Routing Table Entries (3.5.1.1)

The topology displayed in Figure 3-50 is used as the reference topology for this section.

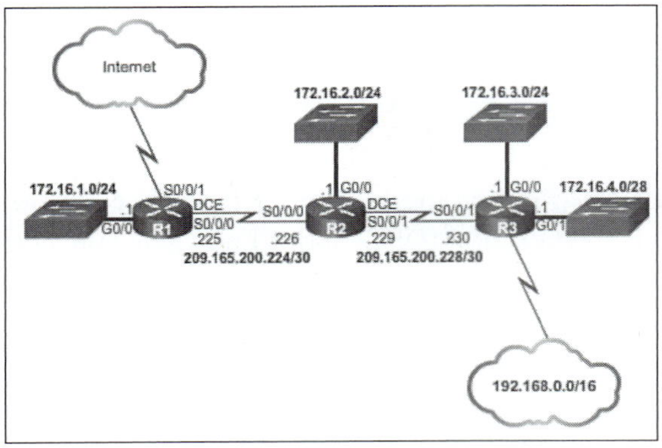

Figure 3-50   Reference Topology

Notice that in the topology:

- R1 is the edge router that connects to the Internet. Therefore, it is propagating a default static route to R2 and R3.

- R1, R2, and R3 contain discontiguous networks separated by another classful network.

- R3 is also introducing a 192.168.0.0/16 supernet route.

Figure 3-51 displays the IPv4 routing table of R1 with directly connected, static, and dynamic routes.

```
R1# show ip route | begin Gateway
Gateway of last resort is 209.165.200.234 to network 0.0.0.0

S*   0.0.0.0/0 [1/0] via 209.165.200.234, Serial0/0/1
                     is directly connected, Serial0/0/1
      172.16.0.0/16 is variably subnetted, 5 subnets, 3 masks
C        172.16.1.0/24 is directly connected, GigabitEthernet0/0
L        172.16.1.1/32 is directly connected, GigabitEthernet0/0
R        172.16.2.0/24 [120/1] via 209.165.200.226, 00:00:12, Serial0/0/0
R        172.16.3.0/24 [120/2] via 209.165.200.226, 00:00:12, Serial0/0/0
R        172.16.4.0/28 [120/2] via 209.165.200.226, 00:00:12, Serial0/0/0
R    192.168.0.0/16 [120/2] via 209.165.200.226, 00:00:03, Serial0/0/0
      209.165.200.0/24 is variably subnetted, 5 subnets, 2 masks
C        209.165.200.224/30 is directly connected, Serial0/0/0
L        209.165.200.225/32 is directly connected, Serial0/0/0
R        209.165.200.228/30 [120/1] via 209.165.200.226, 00:00:12,
                     Serial0/0/0
C        209.165.200.232/30 is directly connected, Serial0/0/1
L        209.165.200.233/30 is directly connected, Serial0/0/1
R1#
```

Figure 3-51   Routing Table of R1

Note

The routing table hierarchy in Cisco IOS was originally implemented with the classful routing scheme. Although the routing table incorporates both classful and classless addressing, the overall structure is still built around this classful scheme.

Directly Connected Entries (3.5.1.2)

As highlighted in Figure 3-52, the routing table of R1 contains three directly connected networks. Notice that two routing table entries are automatically created when an active router interface is configured with an IP address and subnet mask.

```
R1# show ip route | begin Gateway
Gateway of last resort is 209.165.200.234 to network 0.0.0.0

S*  0.0.0.0/0 [1/0] via 209.165.200.234, Serial0/0/1
             is directly connected, Serial0/0/1
     172.16.0.0/16 is variably subnetted, 5 subnets, 3 masks
C       172.16.1.0/24 is directly connected, GigabitEthernet0/0
L       172.16.1.1/32 is directly connected, GigabitEthernet0/0
R       172.16.2.0/24 [120/1] via 209.165.200.226,00:00:12, Serial0/0/0
R       172.16.3.0/24 [120/2] via 209.165.200.226, 00:00:12, Serial0/0/0
R       172.16.4.0/28 [120/2] via 209.165.200.226, 00:00:12, Serial0/0/0
R       192.168.0.0/16 [120/2] via 209.165.200.226, 00:00:03, Serial0/0/0
     209.165.200.0/24 is variably subnetted, 5 subnets, 2 masks
C       209.165.200.224/30 is directly connected, Serial0/0/0
L       209.165.200.225/32 is directly connected, Serial0/0/0
R       209.165.200.228/30 [120/1] via 209.165.200.226, 00:00:12, Serial0/0/0
C       209.165.200.232/30 is directly connected, Serial0/0/1
L       209.165.200.233/32 is directly connected, Serial0/0/1
R1#
```

Figure 3-52   Directly Connected Interfaces of R1

Figure 3-53 displays one of the routing table entries on R1 for the directly connected network 172.16.1.0. These entries were automatically added to the routing table when the GigabitEthernet 0/0 interface was configured and activated.

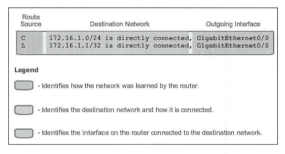

Figure 3-53   Directly Connected Routes of R1

The entries contain the following information:

- **Route source:** Identifies how the route was learned. Directly connected interfaces have two route source codes. C identifies a directly connected network. Directly connected networks are automatically created whenever an interface is configured with an IP address and activated. L identifies that this is a local route. Local routes are automatically created whenever an interface is configured with an IP address and activated.

- **Destination network:** The address of the remote network and how that network is connected.

- **Outgoing interface:** Identifies the exit interface to use when forwarding packets to the destination network.

Note

Local routing table entries did not appear in routing tables prior to IOS release 15.

A router typically has multiple interfaces configured. The routing table stores information about both directly connected and remote routes. As with directly connected networks, the route source identifies how the route was learned. For instance, common codes for remote networks include:

- **S:** Identifies that the route was manually created by an administrator to reach a specific network. This is known as a static route.

- **D:** Identifies that the route was learned dynamically from another router using the EIGRP routing protocol.

- **O:** Identifies that the route was learned dynamically from another router using the OSPF routing protocol.

- **R:** Identifies that the route was learned dynamically from another router using the RIP routing protocol.

Remote Network Entries (3.5.1.3)

Figure 3-54 displays an IPv4 routing table entry on R1 for the route to remote network 172.16.4.0 on R3.

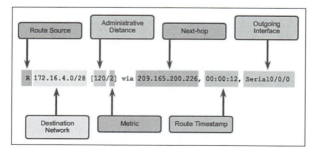

Figure 3-54   Remote Network Route Entry on R1

The entry identifies the following information:

- **Route source:** Identifies how the route was learned.

- **Destination network:** Identifies the address of the remote network.

- **Administrative distance:** Identifies the trustworthiness of the route source.

- **Metric:** Identifies the value assigned to reach the remote network. Lower values indicate preferred routes.

- **Next hop:** Identifies the IPv4 address of the next router to forward the packet to.

- **Route timestamp:** Identifies from when the route was last heard.

- **Outgoing interface:** Identifies the exit interface to use to forward a packet toward the final destination.

Interactive Graphic

Activity 3.5.1.4: Identify Parts of an IPv4 Routing Table Entry

Go to the online course to perform this practice activity.

Dynamically Learned IPv4 Routes (3.5.2)

The structure or format of the routing table might seem obvious until you take a closer look. Understanding the structure of the routing table will help you verify and troubleshoot routing issues because you will understand the routing table lookup process.

Routing Table Terms (3.5.2.1)

A dynamically built routing table provides a great deal of information, as shown in Figure 3-55. Therefore, it is crucial to understand the output generated by the routing table. Special terms are applied when discussing the contents of a routing table.

```
R1#show ip route | begin Gateway
Gateway of last resort is 209.165.200.234 to network 0.0.0.0

S*    0.0.0.0/0 [1/0] via 209.165.200.234, Serial0/0/1
                is directly connected, Serial0/0/1
      172.16.0.0/16 is variably subnetted, 5 subnets, 3 masks
C        172.16.1.0/24 is directly connected, GigabitEthernet0/0
L        172.16.1.1/32 is directly connected, GigabitEthernet0/0
R        172.16.2.0/24 [120/1] via 209.165.200.226, 00:00:12,
           Serial0/0/0
R        172.16.3.0/24 [120/2] via 209.165.200.226, 00:00:12,
           Serial0/0/0
R        172.16.4.0/28 [120/2] via 209.165.200.226, 00:00:12,
           Serial0/0/0
R     192.168.0.0/16 [120/2] via 209.165.200.226, 00:00:03,
         Serial0/0/0
      209.165.200.0/24 is variably subnetted, 5 subnets, 2 masks
C        209.165.200.224/30 is directly connected, Serial0/0/0
L        209.165.200.225/32 is directly connected, Serial0/0/0
R        209.165.200.228/30 [120/1] via 209.165.200.226, 00:00:12,
           Serial0/0/0
C        209.165.200.232/30 is directly connected, Serial0/0/1
L        209.165.200.233/32 is directly connected, Serial0/0/1
R1#
```

Figure 3-55   Routing Table of R1

The Cisco IP routing table is not a flat database. The routing table is actually a hierarchical structure that is used to speed up the lookup process when locating routes and forwarding packets. Within this structure, the hierarchy includes several levels.

Routes are discussed in terms of:

- Ultimate route

- Level 1 route

- Level 1 parent route

- Level 2 child routes

Ultimate Route (3.5.2.2)

An *ultimate route* is a routing table entry that contains either a next-hop IPv4 address or an exit interface. Directly connected, dynamically learned, and local routes are ultimate routes.

In Figure 3-56, the highlighted areas are examples of ultimate routes. Notice that all of these routes specify either a next-hop IPv4 address or an exit interface.

```
R1# show ip route | begin Gateway
Gateway of last resort is 209.165.200.234 to network 0.0.0.0

S*    0.0.0.0/0 [1/0] via 209.165.200.234, Serial0/0/1
               is directly connected, Serial0/0/1
      172.16.0.0/16 is variably subnetted, 5 subnets, 3 masks
C         172.16.1.0/24 is directly connected, GigabitEthernet0/0
L         172.16.1.1/32 is directly connected, GigabitEthernet0/0
R         172.16.2.0/24 [120/1] via 209.165.200.226, 00:00:12,
             Serial0/0/0
R         172.16.3.0/24 [120/2] via 209.165.200.226, 00:00:12,
             Serial0/0/0
R         172.16.4.0/28 [120/2] via 209.165.200.226, 00:00:12,
             Serial0/0/0
R     192.168.0.0/16 [120/2] via 209.165.200.226, 00:00:03,
         Serial0/0/0
      209.165.200.0/24 is variably subnetted, 5 subnets, 2 masks
C         209.165.200.224/30 is directly connected, Serial0/0/0
L         209.165.200.225/32 is directly connected, Serial0/0/0
R         209.165.200.228/30 [120/1] via 209.165.200.226, 00:00:12,
             Serial0/0/0
C         209.165.200.232/30 is directly connected, Serial0/0/1
L         209.165.200.233/32 is directly connected, Serial0/0/1
R1#
```

Figure 3-56   Ultimate Routes of R1

Level 1 Route (3.5.2.3)

A *level 1 route* is a route with a subnet mask equal to or less than the classful mask of the network address. Therefore, a level 1 route can be a:

- **Network route:** A network route has a subnet mask equal to that of the classful mask.

- *Supernet route*: A supernet route is a network address with a subnet mask less than the classful mask, for example, a summary address.

- **Default route**: A default route is a static route with the address 0.0.0.0/0.

The source of the level 1 route can be a directly connected network, static route, or a dynamic routing protocol.

Figure 3-57 highlights how level 1 routes are also ultimate routes.

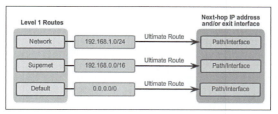

Figure 3-57 Sources of Level 1 Routes

Figure 3-58 highlights level 1 routes.

```
R1# show ip route | begin Gateway
Gateway of last resort is 209.165.200.234 to network
0.0.0.0

S*    0.0.0.0/0 [1/0] via 209.165.200.234, Serial0/0/1
         is directly connected, Serial0/0/1
      172.16.0.0/16 is variably subnetted, 5 subnets, 3
masks
C        172.16.1.0/24 is directly connected,
GigabitEthernet0/0
L        172.16.1.1/32 is directly connected,
GigabitEthernet0/0
R        172.16.2.0/24 [120/1] via 209.165.200.226,
00:00:12, Serial0/0/0
R        172.16.3.0/24 [120/2] via 209.165.200.226,
00:00:12, Serial0/0/0
R        172.16.4.0/28 [120/2] via 209.165.200.226,
00:00:12, Serial0/0/0
R     192.168.0.0/16 [120/2] via 209.165.200.226, 00:00:03,
Serial0/0/0
      209.165.200.0/24 is variably subnetted, 5 subnets, 2
masks
C        209.165.200.224/30 is directly connected,
Serial0/0/0
```

Figure 3-58 Example of Level 1 Routes

Level 1 Parent Route (3.5.2.4)

As illustrated in Figure 3-59, a **level 1 parent route** is a level 1 network route that is subnetted. A parent route can never be an ultimate route.

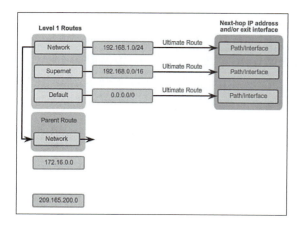

Figure 3-59   Level 1 Parent Route

Figure 3-60 highlights the level 1 parent routes in the routing table of R1. The routing table basically provides a heading for the specific subnets it contains. Each entry displays the classful network address, the number of subnets, and the number of different subnet masks that the classful address has been subdivided into.

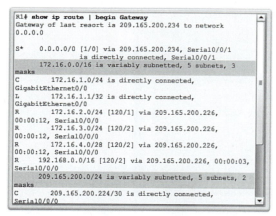

Figure 3-60   Level 1 Parent Routes of R1

Level 2 Child Route (3.5.2.5)

A *level 2 child route* is a route that is a subnet of a classful network address. As illustrated in Figure 3-61, a level 1 parent route is a level 1 network route that is subnetted.

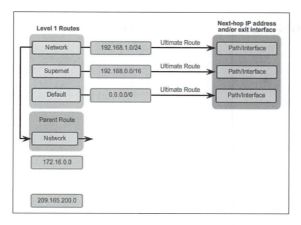

Figure 3-61   Level 2 Child Routes

A level 1 parent route contains level 2 child routes, as shown in Figure 3-62.

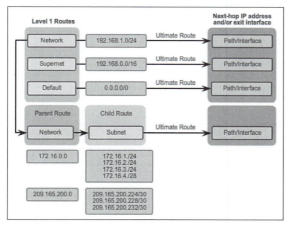

Figure 3-62   Child Routes Are Ultimate Routes

Like a level 1 route, the source of a level 2 route can be a directly connected network, a static route, or a dynamically learned route. Level 2 child routes are also ultimate routes.

> **Note**
>
> The routing table hierarchy in Cisco IOS has a classful routing scheme. A level 1 parent route is the classful network address of the subnet route. This is the case even if a classless routing protocol is the source of the subnet route.

Figure 3-63 highlights the level 2 child routes in the routing table of R1.

```
R1#show ip route | begin Gateway
Gateway of last resort is 209.165.200.234 to network
0.0.0.0

S*    0.0.0.0/0 [1/0] via 209.165.200.234, Serial0/0/1
               is directly connected, Serial0/0/1
        172.16.0.0/16 is variably subnetted, 5 subnets, 3
masks
C        172.16.1.0/24 is directly connected,
GigabitEthernet0/0
L        172.16.1.1/32 is directly connected,
GigabitEthernet0/0
R        172.16.2.0/24 [120/1] via 209.165.200.226,
00:00:12, Serial0/0/0
R        172.16.3.0/24 [120/2] via 209.165.200.226,
00:00:12, Serial0/0/0
R        172.16.4.0/28 [120/2] via 209.165.200.226,
00:00:12, Serial0/0/0
R      192.168.0.0/16 [120/2] via 209.165.200.226, 00:00:03,
Serial0/0/0
        209.165.200.0/24 is variably subnetted, 5 subnets, 2
masks
C        209.165.200.224/30 is directly connected,
Serial0/0/0
```

Figure 3-63   Example of Level 2 Child Routes

Note

The entire output in Figure 3-63 can be viewed in the online course on page 3.5.2.5 graphic number 3.

Interactive Graphic

Activity 3.5.2.6: Identify Parent and Child IPv4 Routes

Go to the online course to perform this practice activity.

The IPv4 Route Lookup Process (3.5.3)

Now that you understand the structure of the routing table, this section will help you understand the routing table lookup process.

Route Lookup Process (3.5.3.1)

When a packet arrives on a router interface, the router examines the IPv4 header, identifies the destination IPv4 address, and proceeds through the router lookup process.

In Figure 3-64, the router examines level 1 network routes for the best match with the destination address of the IPv4 packet.

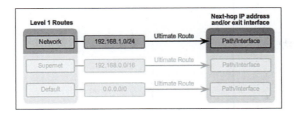

Figure 3-64   Match Level 1 Routes

Specifically, the router proceeds as follows:

1. If the best match is a level 1 ultimate route, then this route is used to forward the packet.

2. If the best match is a level 1 parent route, proceed to the next step.

   In Figure 3-65, the router examines child routes (the subnet routes) of the parent route for a best match.

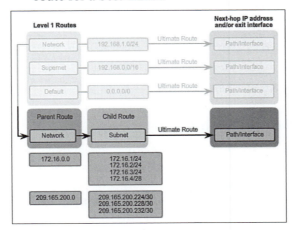

Figure 3-65   Match Level 2 Child Routes

3. If there is a match with a level 2 child route, that subnet is used to forward the packet.

4. If there is not a match with any of the level 2 child routes, proceed to the next step.

   In Figure 3-66, the router continues searching level 1 supernet routes in the routing table for a match, including the default route, if there is one.

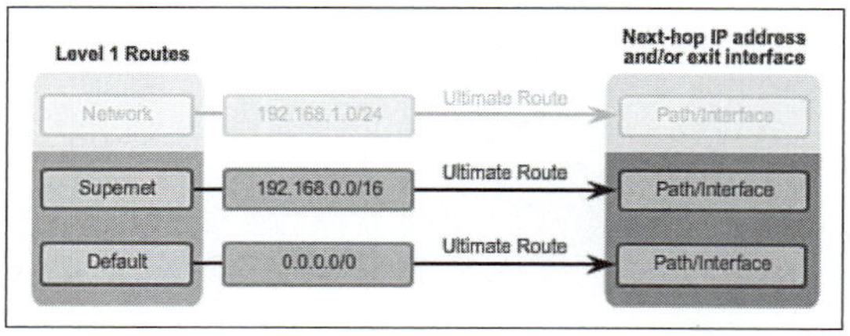

Figure 3-66   Match Supernet and Then Default Route

5. If there is now a lesser match with a level 1 supernet or default routes, the router uses that route to forward the packet.

6. If there is not a match with any route in the routing table, the router drops the packet.

Note

A route referencing only a next-hop IP address and not an exit interface must be resolved to a route with an exit interface. A recursive lookup is performed on the next-hop IP address until the route is resolved to an exit interface.

Best Route = Longest Match (3.5.3.2)

What is meant by the router must find the best match in the routing table? Best match is equal to the longest match.

For there to be a match between the destination IPv4 address of a packet and a route in the routing table, a minimum number of far left bits must match between the IPv4 address of the packet and the route in the routing table. The subnet mask of the route in the routing table is used to determine the minimum number of far left bits that must match. Remember that an IPv4 packet only contains the IPv4 address and not the subnet mask.

The best match is the route in the routing table that has the most number of far left matching bits with the destination IPv4 address of the packet. The route with the greatest number of equivalent far left bits, or the longest match, is always the preferred route.

In Figure 3-67, a packet is destined for 172.16.0.10.

The router has three possible routes that match this packet: 172.16.0.0/12, 172.16.0.0/18, and 172.16.0.0/26. Of the three routes, 172.16.0.0/26 has the longest match and is therefore chosen to forward the packet. Remember, for any of these routes to be considered a match there must be at least the number of matching bits indicated by the subnet mask of the route.

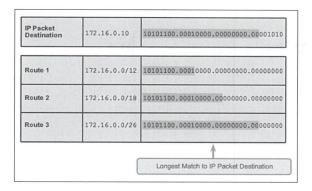

Figure 3-67   Matches for Packets Destined to 172.16.0.10

Interactive
Graphic

Activity 3.5.3.3: Determine the Longest Match Route

Go to the online course to perform this practice activity.

Analyze an IPv6 Routing Table (3.5.4)

The IPv6 routing table shares many similarities with the IPv4 routing table. It also consists of directly connected networks and routes learned statically or dynamically. However, the entries are displayed somewhat differently than IPv4 entries. This section examines the IPv6 routing table.

IPv6 Routing Table Entries (3.5.4.1)

Components of the IPv6 routing table are very similar to the IPv4 routing table. For instance, it is populated using directly connected interfaces, static routes, and dynamically learned routes.

Because IPv6 is classless by design, all routes are effectively level 1 ultimate routes. There is no level 1 parent of level 2 child routes.

The topology displayed in Figure 3-68 is used as the reference topology for this section.

Notice that in the topology:

- R1, R2, and R3 are configured in a full mesh topology. All routers have redundant paths to various networks.

- R2 is the edge router and connects to the ISP; however, a default static route is not being advertised.

- EIGRP for IPv6 has been configured on all three routers.

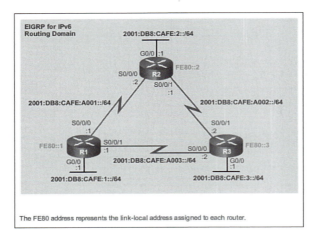

The FE80 address represents the link-local address assigned to each router.

Figure 3-68 Reference IPv6 Topology

Directly Connected Entries (3.5.4.2)

The routing table of R1 is displayed in Figure 3-69 using the **show ipv6 route** command. Although the command output is displayed slightly differently than in the IPv4 version, it still contains the relevant route information.

```
R1# show ipv6 route
<output omitted>

C    2001:DB8:CAFE:1::/64 [0/0]
       via GigabitEthernet0/0, directly connected
L    2001:DB8:CAFE:1::1/128 [0/0]
       via GigabitEthernet0/0, receive
D    2001:DB8:CAFE:2::/64 [90/3524096]
       via FE80::3, Serial0/0/1
D    2001:DB8:CAFE:3::/64 [90/2170112]
       via FE80::3, Serial0/0/1
C    2001:DB8:CAFE:A001::/64 [0/0]
       via Serial0/0/0, directly connected
L    2001:DB8:CAFE:A001::1/128 [0/0]
       via Serial0/0/0, receive
D    2001:DB8:CAFE:A002::/64 [90/3523840]
       via FE80::3, Serial0/0/1
C    2001:DB8:CAFE:A003::/64 [0/0]
       via Serial0/0/1, directly connected
L    2001:DB8:CAFE:A003::1/128 [0/0]
       via Serial0/0/1, receive
L    FF00::/8 [0/0]
       via Null0, receive
R1#
```

Figure 3-69 IPv6 Routing Table of R1

Figure 3-70 highlights the connected network and local routing table entries of the directly connected interfaces. The three entries were added when the interfaces were configured and activated.

```
R1# show ipv6 route
<output omitted>

C   2001:DB8:CAFE:1::/64 [0/0]
      via GigabitEthernet0/0, directly connected
L   2001:DB8:CAFE:1::1/128 [0/0]
      via GigabitEthernet0/0, receive
D   2001:DB8:CAFE:2::/64 [90/3524096]
      via FE80::3, Serial0/0/1
D   2001:DB8:CAFE:3::/64 [90/2170112]
      via FE80::3, Serial0/0/1
C   2001:DB8:CAFE:A001::/64 [0/0]
      via Serial0/0/0, directly connected
L   2001:DB8:CAFE:A001::1/128 [0/0]
      via Serial0/0/0, receive
D   2001:DB8:CAFE:A002::/64 [90/3523840]
      via FE80::3, Serial0/0/1
C   2001:DB8:CAFE:A003::/64 [0/0]
      via Serial0/0/1, directly connected
L   2001:DB8:CAFE:A003::1/128 [0/0]
      via Serial0/0/1, receive
L   FF00::/8 [0/0]
      via Null0, receive
R1#
```

Figure 3-70   Directly Connected Routes on R1

As shown in Figure 3-71, directly connected route entries display the following information:

- **Route source:** Identifies how the route was learned. Directly connected interfaces have two route source codes (C identifies a directly connected network while L identifies that this is a local route).

- **Directly connected network:** The IPv6 address of the directly connected network.

- **Administrative distance:** Identifies the trustworthiness of the route source. IPv6 uses the same distances as IPv4. A value of 0 indicates the best, most trustworthy source.

- **Metric:** Identifies the value assigned to reach the remote network. Lower values indicate preferred routes.

- **Outgoing interface:** Identifies the exit interface to use when forwarding packets to the destination network.

Note

The serial links have reference bandwidths configured to observe how EIGRP metrics select the best route. The reference bandwidth is not a realistic representation of modern networks. It is used only to provide a visual sense of link speed.

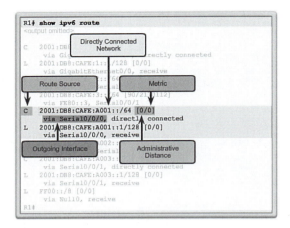

Figure 3-71   Directly Connected Routes on R1

Remote IPv6 Network Entries (3.5.4.3)

Figure 3-72 highlights the routing table entries for the three remote networks (i.e., R2 LAN, R3 LAN, and the link between R2 and R3). The three entries were added by the EIGRP.

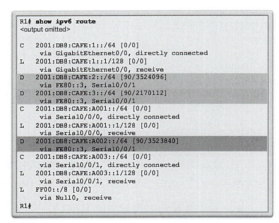

Figure 3-72   Remote Networks Entries on R1

Figure 3-73 displays a routing table entry on R1 for the route to remote network 2001:DB8:CAFE:3::/64 on R3.

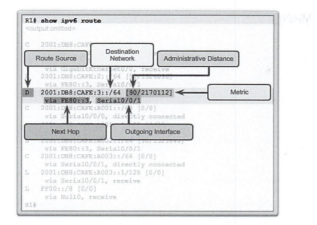

Figure 3-73   Remote Networks Entries on R1

The entry identifies the following information:

- **Route source:** Identifies how the route was learned. Common codes include O (OSPF), D (EIGRP), R (RIP), and S (Static route).

- **Destination network:** Identifies the address of the remote IPv6 network.

- **Administrative distance:** Identifies the trustworthiness of the route source. IPv6 uses the same distances as IPv4.

- **Metric:** Identifies the value assigned to reach the remote network. Lower values indicate preferred routes.

- **Next hop:** Identifies the IPv6 address of the next router to forward the packet to.

- **Outgoing interface:** Identifies the exit interface to use to forward a packet toward the final destination.

When an IPv6 packet arrives on a router interface, the router examines the IPv6 header and identifies the destination IPv6 address. The router then proceeds through the following router lookup process.

The router examines level 1 network routes for the best match with the destination address of the IPv6 packet. Just like IPv4, the longest match is the best match. For example, if there are multiple matches in the routing table, the router chooses the route with the longest match. A match is made by matching the far left bits of the packet's destination IPv6 address with the IPv6 prefix and prefix-length in the IPv6 routing table.

Activity 3.5.4.4: Identify Parts of an IPv6 Routing Table Entry

Go to the online course to perform this practice activity.

Summary (3.6)

Class Activity 3.6.1.1: IPv6 Details, Details...

After studying the concepts presented in this chapter concerning IPv6, you should be able to read a routing table easily and interpret the IPv6 routing information listed within it.

With a partner, use the IPv6 routing table diagram and the .pdf provided with this activity.

Record your answers to the Reflection questions.

Then compare your answers with, at least, one other group from the class.

Dynamic routing protocols are used by routers to facilitate the exchange of routing information between routers. The purpose of dynamic routing protocols includes: discovery of remote networks, maintaining up-to-date routing information, choosing the best path to destination networks, and ability to find a new best path if the current path is no longer available. While dynamic routing protocols require less administrative overhead than static routing, they do require dedicating part of a router's resources for protocol operation, including CPU time and network link bandwidth.

Networks typically use a combination of both static and dynamic routing. Dynamic routing is the best choice for large networks and static routing is better for stub networks.

Routing protocols are responsible for discovering remote networks, as well as maintaining accurate network information. When there is a change in the topology, routing protocols propagate that information throughout the routing domain. The process of bringing all routing tables to a state of consistency, where all of the routers in the same routing domain or area have complete and accurate information about the network, is called convergence. Some routing protocols converge faster than others.

Routing protocols can be classified as either classful or classless, as distance vector or link-state, and as an Interior Gateway Protocol or an Exterior Gateway Protocol.

Distance vector protocols use routers as "sign posts" along the path to the final destination. The only information a router knows about a remote network is the distance or metric to reach that network and which path or interface to use to get there. Distance vector routing protocols do not have an actual map of the network topology.

A router configured with a link-state routing protocol can create a complete view or topology of the network by gathering information from all of the other routers.

Metrics are used by routing protocols to determine the best path or shortest path to reach a destination network. Different routing protocols may use different metrics. Typically, a lower metric means a better path. Metrics can be determined by hops, bandwidth, delay, reliability, and load.

Routers sometimes learn about multiple routes to the same network from both static routes and dynamic routing protocols. When a router learns about a destination network from more than one routing source, Cisco routers use the administrative distance value to determine which source to use. Each dynamic routing protocol has a unique administrative value, along with static routes and directly connected networks. The lower the administrative value, the more preferred the route source. A directly connected network is always the preferred source, followed by static routes and then various dynamic routing protocols.

The **show ip protocols** command displays the IPv4 routing protocol settings currently configured on the router. For IPv6, use **show ipv6 protocols**.

With link-state routing protocols such as OSPF, a link is an interface on a router. Information about the state of those links is known as link-states. All link-state routing protocols apply Dijkstra's algorithm to calculate the best path route. The algorithm is commonly referred to as the shortest path first (SPF) algorithm. This algorithm uses accumulated costs along each path, from source to destination, to determine the total cost of a route.

Practice

The following activities provide practice with the topics introduced in this chapter. The Labs and Class Activities are available in the companion *Routing Protocols Lab Manual* (978-1-58713-322-0). The Packet Tracer Activities PKA files are found in the online course.

Class Activities

Class Activity 3.0.1.2: How Much Does This Cost?

Class Activity 3.6.1.1: IPv6 Details, Details...

Lab

Lab 3.3.2.4: Configuring RIPv2

Packet Tracer Activities

Packet Tracer Activity 3.1.3.6: Investigating Convergence

Packet Tracer Activity 3.2.2.4: Comparing RIP and EIGRP Path Selection

Packet Tracer Activity 3.3.1.8: Configuring RIPv2

Packet Tracer Activity 3.3.2.3: Configuring RIPng

Check Your Understanding Questions

Complete all the review questions listed here to test your understanding of the topics and concepts in this chapter. The appendix, "Answers to the 'Check Your Understanding' Questions," lists the answers.

1. What are two advantages of static routing over dynamic routing? (Choose two.)

   A. The configuration is less error prone.

   B. Static routing is more secure because routers do not advertise routes.

   C. Growing the network usually does not present a problem.

   D. No computing overhead is involved.

   E. The administrator has less work maintaining the configuration.

2. Match the description to the proper routing protocol.

   Routing protocols:
   RIP
   IGRP
   OSPF
   EIGRP
   BGP

   Description:
   A. Path vector exterior routing protocol:

   B. Cisco advanced interior routing protocol:

   C. Link-state interior routing protocol:

   D. Distance vector interior routing protocol:

   E. Cisco distance vector interior routing protocol:

3. Which statement best describes convergence on a network?

   A. The amount of time required for routers to share administrative configuration changes, such as password changes, from one end of a network to the other end

   B. The time required for the routers in the network to update their routing tables after a topology change has occurred

   C. The time required for the routers in one autonomous system to learn routes to destinations in another autonomous system

   D. The time required for routers running disparate routing protocols to update their routing tables

4. Dynamic routing protocols perform which two tasks? (Choose two.)

   A. Assign IP addressing

   B. Discover hosts

   C. Network discovery

   D. Propagate host default routes

   E. Update and maintain routing tables

5. Which of the following parameters are used to calculate metrics? (Choose two.)

   A. Hop count

   B. Uptime

   C. Bandwidth

   D. Convergence time

   E. Administrative distance

6. Which routing protocol has the most trustworthy administrative distance by default?

   A. EIGRP internal routes

   B. IS-IS

   C. OSPF

   D. RIPv1

   E. RIPv2

7. Which command will show the administrative distance of routes?

   A. **show interfaces**

   B. **show ip route**

   C. **show ip interfaces**

   D. **debug ip routing**

8. When do directly connected networks appear in the routing table?

   A. When they are included in a static route

   B. When they are used as an exit interface

   C. As soon as they are addressed and operational at Layer 2

   D. As soon as they are addressed and operational at Layer 3

   E. Always when a **no shutdown** command is issued

9. Router R1 is using the RIPv2 routing protocol and has discovered multiple unequal paths to reach a destination network. How will Router R1 determine which path is the best path to the destination network?

   A. Lowest metric

   B. Highest metric

   C. Lowest administrative distance

   D. Highest administrative distance

   E. By load-balancing between up to four paths

10. Which of the following will trigger the sending of a link-state packet by OSPF? (Choose two.)

   A. A change in the topology

   B. A link to a neighbor router has become congested

   C. The initial startup of the routing protocol process

   D. The router update timer expiring

11. After examining its routing table for a best match with the destination address, which route will a router use to forward an IPv4 packet?

   A. A level 1 child route

   B. A level 1 parent route

   C. A level 1 ultimate route

   D. A level 2 supernet route

   E. A level 2 parent route

12. What is different between IPv6 routing table entries and IPv4 routing table entries?

   A. By design IPv6 is classless, so all routes are effectively level 1 ultimate routes.

   B. Unlike IPv4, IPv6 does not use static routes to populate the routing table.

   C. IPv6 routing tables include local route entries, which IPv4 routing tables do not.

   D. The selection of IPv6 routes is based on the shortest matching prefix, unlike IPv4 route selection, which is based on the longest matching prefix.

13. Enter the proper administrative distance for each routing protocol.

   A. eBGP:

   B. EIGRP (Internal):

   C. EIGRP (External):

   D. IS-IS:

   E. OSPF:

   F. RIP:

14. Designate the following characteristics as belonging to either a classful routing protocol or a classless routing protocol.

   A. Does not support discontiguous networks:

   B. EIGRP, OSPF, and BGP:

   C. Sends subnet mask information in routing updates:

   D. Supports discontiguous networks:

   E. RIP version 1 and IGRP:

   F. Does not send subnet mask in its routing updates:

   G. Allows for use of both 172.16.1.0/26 and 172.16.1.128/27 subnets in the same topology:

15. Explain why static routing might be preferred over dynamic routing.

16. What are four ways of classifying dynamic routing protocols?

17. What are the most common metrics used in IP dynamic routing protocols?

18. What is administrative distance, and why is it important?

19. What is the purpose of a passive interface?

CHAPTER 4

EIGRP

Objectives

Upon completion of this chapter, you will be able to answer the following questions:

- What are the features of EIGRP?
- What are the functions and operations of the EIGRP routing protocol?
- Can you describe the different EIGRP packet formats?
- How is the composite metric used by EIGRP calculated?
- What are the concepts and operation of DUAL?
- What commands are used to configure and verify basic EIGRP operations for IPv4 and IPv6?

Key Terms

This chapter uses the following key terms. You can find the definitions in the Glossary.

protocol-dependent modules (PDMs) page 242

Reliable Transport Protocol (RTP) page 243

TLV page 251

Hold time page 253

autonomous system page 257

loopback address page 261

wildcard mask page 266

adjacency page 277

reference bandwidth page 289

successor page 293

feasible distance (FD) page 294

feasible successor page 295

feasibility condition page 295

reported distance page 295

topology table page 298

passive state page 298

active state page 298

DUAL Finite State Machine page 302

link-local address page 311

Introduction (4.0.1)

Enhanced Interior Gateway Routing Protocol (EIGRP) is an advanced distance vector routing protocol developed by Cisco Systems. As the name suggests, EIGRP is an enhancement of another Cisco routing protocol, IGRP (Interior Gateway Routing Protocol). IGRP is an older classful, distance vector routing protocol, now obsolete since IOS 12.3.

EIGRP is a distance vector routing protocol that includes features found in link-state routing protocols. EIGRP is suited for many different topologies and media. In a well-designed network, EIGRP can scale to include multiple topologies and can provide extremely quick convergence times with minimal network traffic.

This chapter introduces EIGRP and provides basic configuration commands to enable it on a Cisco IOS router. It also explores the operation of the routing protocol and provides more detail on how EIGRP determines best path.

Class Activity 4.0.1.2: Classless EIGRP

EIGRP was introduced as a distance vector routing protocol in 1992. It was originally designed to work as a proprietary protocol on Cisco devices only. In 2013, EIGRP became a multi-vendor routing protocol, meaning that it can be used by other device vendors in addition to Cisco.

Complete the reflection questions which accompany the PDF file for this activity. Save your work and be prepared to share your answers with the class.

Characteristics of EIGRP (4.1)

EIGRP was initially released in 1992 as a proprietary protocol available only on Cisco devices. In 2013, Cisco released a basic functionality of EIGRP as an open standard to the IETF as an informational RFC. This means that other networking vendors can now implement EIGRP on their equipment to interoperate with both Cisco and non-Cisco routers running EIGRP. However, advanced features of EIGRP, such as EIGRP stub, needed for the Dynamic Multipoint Virtual Private Network (DMVPN) deployment, will not be released to the IETF. As an informational RFC, Cisco will continue to maintain control of EIGRP.

Basic Features of EIGRP (4.1.1)

EIGRP includes features of both link-state and distance vector routing protocols. As shown in Table 4-1, EIGRP is still based on the key distance vector routing protocol principle, in which information about the rest of the network is learned from directly connected neighbors.

Table 4-1   Types of Routing Protocols

	Interior Gateway Protocols				Exterior Gateway Protocols
	Distance Vector		Link-State		Path Vector
IPv4	RIPv2	EIGRP	OSPFv2	IS-IS	BGP-4
IPv6	RIPng	EIGRP for IPv6	OSPFv3	IS-IS for IPv6	MBGP

Note

IGRP, a distance vector IGP, is not included in Table 4-1 because it is now obsolete.

Features of EIGRP (4.1.1.1)

EIGRP is an advanced distance vector routing protocol that includes features not found in other distance vector routing protocols like RIP and IGRP.

Diffusing Update Algorithm

As the computational engine that drives EIGRP, the Diffusing Update Algorithm (DUAL) resides at the center of the routing protocol. DUAL guarantees loop-free and backup paths throughout the routing domain. Using DUAL, EIGRP stores all available backup routes for destinations so that it can quickly adapt to alternate routes when necessary.

Establishing Neighbor Adjacencies

EIGRP establishes relationships with directly connected routers that are also enabled for EIGRP. Neighbor adjacencies are used for routing and to track the status of these neighbors.

Reliable Transport Protocol

The Reliable Transport Protocol (RTP) is unique to EIGRP and provides delivery of EIGRP packets to neighbors. RTP and the tracking of neighbor adjacencies set the stage for DUAL.

Partial and Bounded Updates

EIGRP uses the terms *partial* and *bounded* when referring to its updates. Unlike RIP, EIGRP does not send periodic updates and route entries do not age out. The term partial means that the update only includes information about the route changes, such as a new link or a link becoming unavailable. The term bounded refers to the propagation of partial updates that are sent only to those routers that the changes affect. This minimizes the bandwidth that is required to send EIGRP updates.

Equal and Unequal Cost Load Balancing

EIGRP supports equal cost load balancing and unequal cost load balancing, which allows administrators to better distribute traffic flow in their networks.

> **Note**
>
> The term *hybrid routing protocol* is used in some older documentation to define EIGRP. However, this term is misleading because EIGRP is not a hybrid between distance vector and link-state routing protocols. EIGRP is solely a distance vector routing protocol; therefore, Cisco no longer uses this term to refer to it.

Protocol-Dependent Modules (4.1.1.2)

EIGRP has the capability for routing several different protocols including IPv4 and IPv6 using *protocol-dependent modules (PDMs)*. Although now obsolete, EIGRP also used PDMs to route Novell's IPX and Apple Computer's AppleTalk network layer protocols.

The PDMs are responsible for network layer protocol-specific tasks. An example is the EIGRP module, which is responsible for sending and receiving EIGRP packets that are encapsulated in IPv4. The EIGRP module is also responsible for parsing EIGRP packets and informing DUAL of the new information that is received. EIGRP asks DUAL to make routing decisions, but the results are stored in the IPv4 routing table. Also, EIGRP PDMs are responsible for redistributing routes that are learned by other routing protocols.

PDMs are responsible for the specific routing tasks for each network layer protocol, including:

- Maintaining the neighbor and topology tables of EIGRP routers that belong to that protocol suite

- Building and translating protocol-specific packets for DUAL

- Interfacing DUAL to the protocol-specific routing table
- Computing the metric and passing this information to DUAL
- Implementing filtering and access lists
- Performing redistribution functions to and from other routing protocols

When a router discovers a new neighbor, it records the neighbor's address and interface as an entry in the neighbor table. One neighbor table exists for each protocol-dependent module, such as IPv4. EIGRP also maintains a topology table. The topology table contains all destinations that are advertised by neighboring routers. There is also a separate topology and routing table for each PDM, as shown in Figure 4-1.

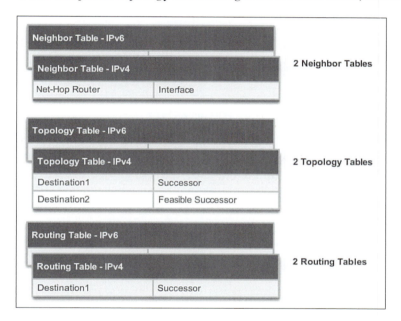

Figure 4-1   EIGRP Protocol-Dependent Modules (PDMs)

Reliable Transport Protocol (4.1.1.3)

EIGRP uses *Reliable Transport Protocol (RTP)* for the delivery and reception of EIGRP packets. EIGRP was designed as a network layer–independent routing protocol; because of this design EIGRP cannot use the services of UDP or TCP. This allows EIGRP to be used for protocols other than those from the TCP/IP protocol suite, such as IPX and AppleTalk. Figure 4-2 conceptually shows how RTP operates.

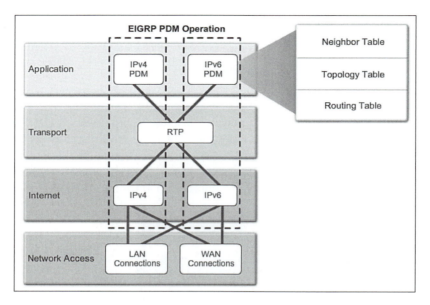

Figure 4-2   EIGRP Replaces TCP with RTP

Although "reliable" is part of its name, RTP includes both reliable delivery and unreliable delivery of EIGRP packets, similar to TCP and UDP, respectively. Reliable RTP requires an acknowledgment to be returned by the receiver to the sender. An unreliable RTP packet does not require an acknowledgment. For example, an EIGRP Update packet is sent reliably over RTP and requires an acknowledgment. An EIGRP Hello packet is also sent over RTP, but unreliably. This means that EIGRP Hello packets do not require an acknowledgment.

RTP can send EIGRP packets as unicast or multicast.

- Multicast EIGRP packets for IPv4 use the reserved IPv4 multicast address 224.0.0.10.

- Multicast EIGRP packets for IPv6 are sent to the reserved IPv6 multicast address FF02::A.

Authentication (4.1.1.4)

Like other routing protocols, EIGRP can be configured for authentication. RIPv2, EIGRP, OSPF, IS-IS, and BGP can each be configured to authenticate their routing information, as shown in Figure 4-3.

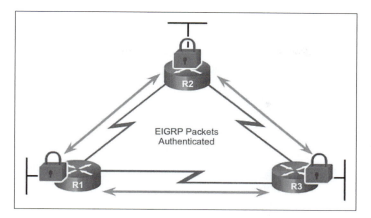

Figure 4-3   Authentication

It is a good practice to authenticate transmitted routing information. Doing so ensures that routers only accept routing information from other routers that have been configured with the same password or authentication information.

Note

Authentication does not encrypt the EIGRP routing updates.

Types of EIGRP Packets (4.1.2)

This section introduces the types of EIGRP packets used to discover neighbors, form adjacencies, and exchange routing updates.

EIGRP Packet Types (4.1.2.1)

EIGRP uses five different packet types, some in pairs. EIGRP packets are sent using either RTP reliable or unreliable delivery and can be sent as a unicast, multicast, or sometimes both. EIGRP packet types are also called EIGRP packet formats or EIGRP messages.

Table 4-2 lists and describes the five EIGRP packet types.

Table 4-2   EIGRP Packet Types

Packet Type	Description	Delivery
Hello	Used to discover other EIGRP routers in the network.	■ Sent with unreliable delivery ■ Multicast (on most network types)

Packet Type	Description	Delivery
Acknowledgment	Used to acknowledge the receipt of any EIGRP packet.	■ Sent with unreliable delivery ■ Unicast
Update	Used to convey routing information to known destinations.	■ Sent with reliable delivery ■ Unicast or multicast
Query	Sent by a router advertising that a route is in active state and the originator is requesting alternate path information from its neighbors. Used to request specific information from a neighbor router.	■ Sent with reliable delivery ■ Unicast or multicast
Reply	Use to respond to a query.	■ Sent with unreliable delivery ■ Unicast

Figure 4-4 shows that EIGRP messages are typically encapsulated in IPv4 or IPv6 packets. EIGRP for IPv4 messages use IPv4 as the network layer protocol. The IPv4 Protocol field uses 88 to indicate the data portion of the packet is an EIGRP for IPv4 message. EIGRP for IPv6 messages are encapsulated in IPv6 packets using the Next Header field of 88. Similar to the Protocol field for IPv4, the IPv6 Next Header field indicates the type of data carried in the IPv6 packet.

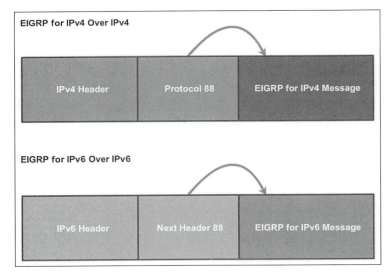

Figure 4-4   EIGRP Messages Are Sent over IP

EIGRP Hello Packets (4.1.2.2)

EIGRP uses small Hello packets to discover other EIGRP-enabled routers on directly connected links. Hello packets are used by routers to form EIGRP neighbor adjacencies, also known as neighbor adjacencies.

EIGRP Hello packets are sent as IPv4 or IPv6 multicasts, and use RTP unreliable delivery. This means that the receiver does not reply with an acknowledgment packet.

- The reserved EIGRP multicast address for IPv4 is 224.0.0.10.

- The reserved EIGRP multicast address for IPv6 is FF02::A.

EIGRP routers discover neighbors and establish adjacencies with neighbor routers using the Hello packet. On most networks, EIGRP Hello packets are sent multicast every five seconds. However, on multipoint, nonbroadcast multiple access (NBMA) networks, such as X.25, Frame Relay, and Asynchronous Transfer Mode (ATM) interfaces with access links of T1 (1.544 Mb/s) or slower, Hello packets are sent unicast every 60 seconds.

EIGRP also uses Hello packets to maintain established adjacencies. An EIGRP router assumes that as long as it receives Hello packets from a neighbor, the neighbor and its routes remain viable.

EIGRP uses a Hold timer to determine the maximum time the router should wait to receive the next Hello before declaring that neighbor as unreachable. By default, the hold time is three times the Hello interval, or 15 seconds on most networks and 180 seconds on low-speed NBMA networks. If the hold time expires, EIGRP declares the route as down and DUAL searches for a new path by sending out queries. Figure 4-5 shows the default Hello intervals and Hold times for both types of networks.

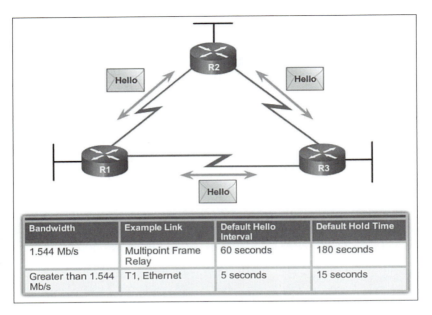

Bandwidth	Example Link	Default Hello Interval	Default Hold Time
1.544 Mb/s	Multipoint Frame Relay	60 seconds	180 seconds
Greater than 1.544 Mb/s	T1, Ethernet	5 seconds	15 seconds

Figure 4-5   Default Hello Intervals and Hold Times for EIGRP

EIGRP Update and Acknowledgment Packets (4.1.2.3)

EIGRP Update packets are sent reliably, meaning they require an acknowledgment packet to be returned by the destination router.

EIGRP Update Packets

EIGRP sends Update packets to propagate routing information. Update packets are sent only when necessary. EIGRP updates contain only the routing information needed and are sent only to those routers that require it.

Unlike RIP (another distance vector routing protocol), EIGRP does not send periodic updates and route entries do not age out. Instead, EIGRP sends incremental updates only when the state of a destination changes. This may include when a new network becomes available, an existing network becomes unavailable, or a change occurs in the routing metric for an existing network.

As previously stated, EIGRP uses the terms partial and bounded when referring to its updates. The term partial means that the update only includes information about the route changes. The term bounded refers to the propagation of partial updates that are sent only to those routers that the changes affect.

By sending only the routing information that is needed, only to those routers that need it, EIGRP minimizes the bandwidth that is required to send EIGRP updates.

EIGRP Update packets use reliable delivery, which means the sending router requires an acknowledgment. Update packets are sent as a multicast when required by multiple routers, or as a unicast when required by only a single router. In Figure 4-6, because the links are point-to-point, the updates are sent as unicasts.

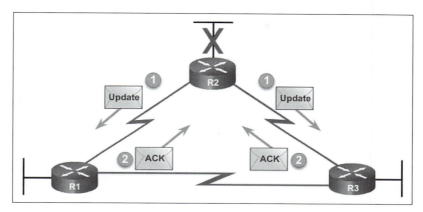

Figure 4-6   EIGRP Update and Acknowledgment Messages

EIGRP Acknowledgment Packets

EIGRP sends Acknowledgment (ACK) packets when reliable delivery is used. An EIGRP acknowledgment is an EIGRP Hello packet without any data. RTP uses reliable delivery for EIGRP update, query, and reply packets. EIGRP acknowledgment packets are always sent as an unreliable unicast. Unreliable delivery makes sense; otherwise, there would be an endless loop of acknowledgments.

In Figure 4-6, R2 has lost connectivity to the LAN attached to its Gigabit Ethernet interface. R2 immediately sends an update to R1 and R3 noting the downed route. R1 and R3 respond with an acknowledgment to let R2 know that they have received the update.

> **Note**
>
> Some documentation refers to the Hello and acknowledgment as a single type of EIGRP packet.

EIGRP Query and Reply Packets (4.1.2.4)

EIGRP uses query and reply packets to discover alternate path information from its neighbors when the primary route has failed and there isn't a backup route in the topology table. Query and reply packets are introduced here but discussed in more detail later in this chapter.

EIGRP Query Packets

DUAL uses query and reply packets when searching for networks and other tasks. Queries and replies use reliable delivery. Queries can use multicast or unicast, whereas replies are always sent as unicast.

In Figure 4-7, R2 has lost connectivity to the LAN and it sends out queries to all EIGRP neighbors searching for any possible routes to the LAN. Because queries use reliable delivery, the receiving router must return an EIGRP acknowledgment. The acknowledgment informs the sender of the query that it has received the query message. To keep this example simple, acknowledgments were omitted in the graphic.

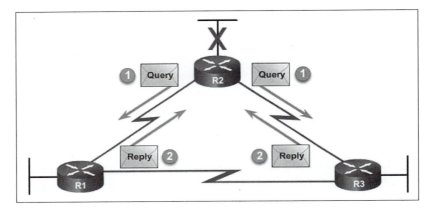

Figure 4-7   EIGRP Query and Reply Messages

EIGRP Reply Packets

All neighbors must send a reply, regardless of whether or not they have a route to the downed network. Because replies also use reliable delivery, routers such as R2 must send an acknowledgment.

It may not be obvious why R2 would send out a query for a network it knows is down. Actually, only R2's interface that is attached to the network is down. Another router could be attached to the same LAN and have an alternate path to this same network. Therefore, R2 queries for such a router before completely removing the network from its topology table.

Activity 4.1.2.5: Identify the EIGRP Packet Type

Go to the online course to perform this practice activity.

Video Demonstration 4.1.2.6: Observing EIGRP Protocol Communications

Go to the online course to view this video or go to the following link: http://www.youtube.com/watch?feature=player_embedded&v=s1ufXw4g5jU

EIGRP Messages (4.1.3)

This section discusses the encapsulation of EIGRP packets, including the packet header and the EIGRP message.

Encapsulating EIGRP Messages (4.1.3.1)

The data portion of an EIGRP message is encapsulated in a packet. This data field is called type, length, value (*TLV*). The types of TLVs relevant to this course are EIGRP parameters, IP internal routes, and IP external routes.

The EIGRP packet header is included with every EIGRP packet, regardless of its type. The EIGRP packet header and TLV are then encapsulated in an IPv4 packet. In the IPv4 packet header, the protocol field is set to 88 to indicate EIGRP, and the IPv4 destination address is set to the multicast 224.0.0.10. If the EIGRP packet is encapsulated in an Ethernet frame, the destination MAC address is also a multicast address, 01-00-5E-00-00-0A.

Figure 4-8 illustrates this encapsulation process starting with the Data Link Ethernet Frame. EIGRP for IPv4 is encapsulated in an IPv4 packet. EIGRP for IPv6 would use a similar type of encapsulation. EIGRP for IPv6 is encapsulated using an IPv6 header. The IPv6 destination address would be the multicast address FF02::A and the next header field would be set to 88.

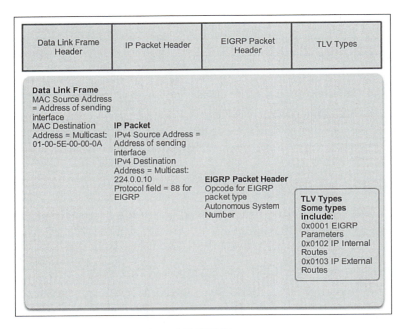

Figure 4-8 Encapsulation of EIGRP Messages

EIGRP Packet Header and TLV (4.1.3.2)

Every EIGRP message includes the header, as shown in Figure 4-9. Important fields include the Opcode field and the Autonomous System Number field. Opcode specifies the EIGRP packet type as follows:

- Update

- Query

- Reply

- Hello

The autonomous system number specifies the EIGRP routing process. Unlike RIP, multiple instances of EIGRP can run on a network; the autonomous system number is used to track each running EIGRP process.

Figure 4-10 shows the EIGRP parameter's TLV. The EIGRP parameter's message includes the weights that EIGRP uses for its composite metric. By default, only bandwidth and delay are weighted. Both are weighted equally; therefore, the K1 field for bandwidth and the K3 field for delay are both set to one (1). The other K values are set to zero (0).

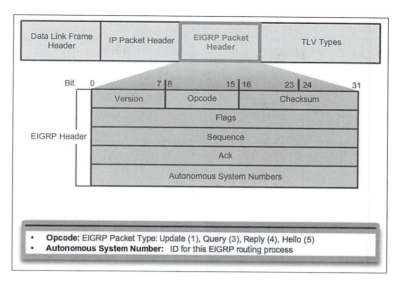

Figure 4-9   EIGRP Packet Header

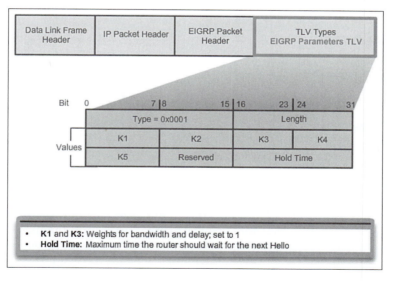

Figure 4-10   EIGRP Parameters

The *Hold Time* is the amount of time the EIGRP neighbor receiving this message should wait before considering the advertising router to be down.

Figure 4-11 shows the IP Internal Routes TLV. The IP internal message is used to advertise EIGRP routes within an autonomous system. Important fields include the metric fields (delay and bandwidth), the subnet mask field (prefix length), and the destination field.

Delay is calculated as the sum of delays from source to destination in units of 10 microseconds. Bandwidth is the lowest configured bandwidth of any interface along the route.

The subnet mask is specified as the prefix length or the number of network bits in the subnet mask. For example, the prefix length for the subnet mask 255.255.255.0 is 24, because 24 is the number of network bits.

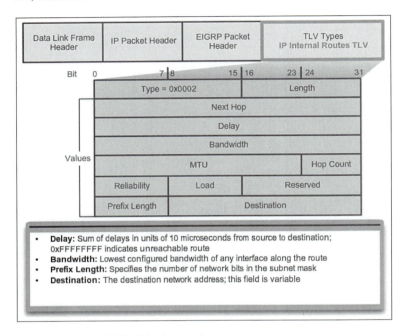

Figure 4-11 EIGRP TLV: Internal

The Destination field stores the address of the destination network. Although only 24 bits are shown in Figure 4-11, this field varies based on the value of the network portion of the 32-bit network address. For example, the network portion of 10.1.0.0/16 is 10.1; therefore, the Destination field stores the first 16 bits. Because the minimum length of this field is 24 bits, the remainder of the field is padded with zeros. If a network address is longer than 24 bits (192.168.1.32/27, for example), then the Destination field is extended for another 32 bits (for a total of 56 bits) and the unused bits are padded with zeros.

Figure 4-12 shows the IP External Routes TLV. The IP external message is used when external routes are imported into the EIGRP routing process. In this chapter, we will import or redistribute a default static route into EIGRP. The top half of the IP External Routes TLV includes fields to track the external source of the route. Notice that the bottom half of the IP External Routes TLV includes all the fields used by the IP Internal Routes TLV.

Note

The maximum transmission unit (MTU) is not a metric used by EIGRP. The MTU is included in the routing updates, but it is not used to determine the routing metric.

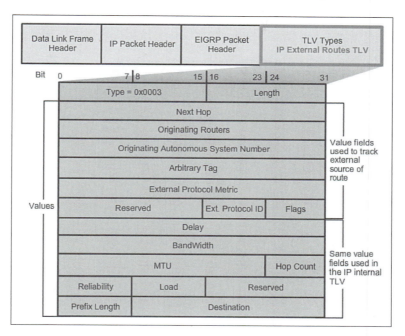

Figure 4-12   EIGRP TLV: External

Configuring EIGRP for IPv4 (4.2)

This section discusses the basics of EIGRP configuration. There are many similarities with the commands used in configuring other routing protocols such as OSPF.

Configuring EIGRP with IPv4 (4.2.1)

We will begin by configuring EIGRP for IPv4 and then, later in this chapter, configure EIGRP for IPv6. Many of the commands used to configure and verify EIGRP for IPv6 are very similar to those used when configuring EIGRP for IPv4.

EIGRP Network Topology (4.2.1.1)

Figure 4-13 displays the topology that is used in this course to configure EIGRP for IPv4. The types of serial interfaces and their associated bandwidths may not necessarily reflect the more common types of connections found in today's networks. The bandwidths of the serial links used in this topology were chosen to help explain the calculation of the routing protocol metrics and the process of best path selection.

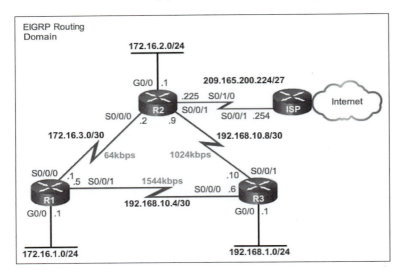

Figure 4-13   EIGRP for IPv4 Topology

The routers in the topology have a starting configuration, including addresses on the interfaces. There is currently no static routing or dynamic routing configured on any of the routers.

The following output shows the interface configurations for the three EIGRP routers in the topology. Only routers R1, R2, and R3 are part of the EIGRP routing domain. The ISP router is used as the routing domain's gateway to the Internet.

```
R1# show running-config
<output omitted>
!
interface GigabitEthernet0/0
 ip address 172.16.1.1 255.255.255.0
!
interface Serial0/0/0
 ip address 172.16.3.1 255.255.255.252
 clock rate 64000
!
interface Serial0/0/1
 ip address 192.168.10.5 255.255.255.252
```

```
R2# show running-config
<output omitted>
!
interface GigabitEthernet0/0
 ip address 172.16.2.1 255.255.255.0
!
interface Serial0/0/0
 ip address 172.16.3.2 255.255.255.252
!
interface Serial0/0/1
 ip address 192.168.10.9 255.255.255.252
 clock rate 64000
!
interface Serial0/1/0
 ip address 209.165.200.225 255.255.255.224

R3# show running-config
<output omitted>
!
interface GigabitEthernet0/0
 ip address 192.168.1.1 255.255.255.0
!
interface Serial0/0/0
 ip address 192.168.10.6 255.255.255.252
 clock rate 64000
!
interface Serial0/0/1
 ip address 192.168.10.10 255.255.255.252
```

Autonomous System Numbers (4.2.1.2)

EIGRP uses the **router eigrp** *autonomous-system* command to enable the EIGRP process. The autonomous system number referred to in the EIGRP configuration is not associated with the Internet Assigned Numbers Authority (IANA) globally assigned autonomous system numbers used by external routing protocols.

So what is the difference between the IANA globally assigned autonomous system number and the EIGRP autonomous system number?

An IANA globally assigned *autonomous system* is a collection of networks under the administrative control of a single entity that presents a common routing policy to the Internet. In Figure 4-14, companies A, B, C, and D are all under the administrative control of ISP1. ISP1 presents a common routing policy for all of these companies when advertising routes to ISP2.

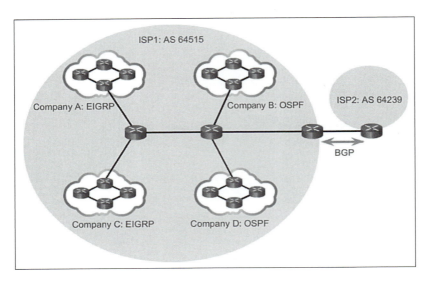

Figure 4-14   Autonomous Systems

The guidelines for the creation, selection, and registration of an autonomous system are described in RFC 1930. Global autonomous system numbers are assigned by IANA, the same authority that assigns IP address space. The local regional Internet registry (RIR) is responsible for assigning an autonomous system number to an entity from its block of assigned autonomous system numbers. Prior to 2007, autonomous system numbers were 16-bit numbers ranging from 0 to 65,535. Today, 32-bit autonomous system numbers are assigned, increasing the number of available autonomous system numbers to over 4 billion.

Usually Internet service providers (ISPs), Internet backbone providers, and large institutions connecting to other entities require an autonomous system number. These ISPs and large institutions use the exterior gateway routing protocol, Border Gateway Protocol (BGP), to propagate routing information. BGP is the only routing protocol that uses an actual autonomous system number in its configuration.

The vast majority of companies and institutions with IP networks do not need an autonomous system number, because they are controlled by a larger entity, such as an ISP. These companies use interior gateway protocols, such as RIP, EIGRP, OSPF, and IS-IS, to route packets within their own networks. They are one of many independent and separate networks within the autonomous system of the ISP. The ISP is responsible for the routing of packets within its autonomous system and between other autonomous systems.

The autonomous system number used for EIGRP configuration is only significant to the EIGRP routing domain. It functions as a process ID to help routers keep track of multiple, running instances of EIGRP. This is required because it is possible to have more than one instance of EIGRP running on a network. Each instance of EIGRP can be configured to support and exchange routing updates for different networks.

The Router EIGRP Command (4.2.1.3)

The Cisco IOS includes the processes to enable and configure several different types of dynamic routing protocols. The **router** global configuration mode command is used to begin the configuration of any dynamic routing protocol. The topology shown in Figure 4-15 is used to demonstrate this command.

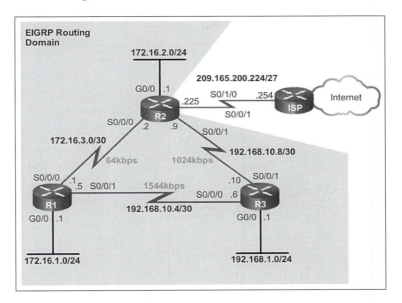

Figure 4-15   EIGRP for IPv4 Topology

As shown in Figure 4-16, when followed by a question mark (**?**), the **router** global configuration mode command lists all the available routing protocols supported by this specific IOS release running on the router.

The following global configuration mode command is used to enter the router configuration mode for EIGRP and begin the configuration of the EIGRP process:

```
Router(config)# router eigrp autonomous-system
```

The *autonomous-system* argument can be assigned to any 16-bit value between the number 1 and 65,535. All routers within the EIGRP routing domain must use the same autonomous system number.

```
R1#conf t
Enter configuration commands, one per line.  End with CNTL/Z.
R1(config)#router ?
  bgp        Border Gateway Protocol (BGP)
  eigrp      Enhanced Interior Gateway Routing Protocol (EIGRP)
  isis       ISO IS-IS
  iso-igrp   IGRP for OSI networks
  mobile     Mobile routes
  odr        On Demand stub Routes
  ospf       Open Shortest Path First (OSPF)
  ospfv3     OSPFv3
  rip        Routing Information Protocol (RIP)

R1(config)#router
```

Figure 4-16   Router Configuration Command

The following shows the configuration of the EIGRP process on routers R1, R2, and R3. Notice that the prompt changes from a global configuration mode prompt to router configuration mode.

```
R1(config)# router eigrp 1
R1(config-router)#


R2(config)# router eigrp 1
R2(config-router)#


R3(config)# router eigrp 1
R3(config-router)#
```

In this example, **1** identifies this particular EIGRP process running on this router. To establish neighbor adjacencies, EIGRP requires all routers in the same routing domain to be configured with the same autonomous system number. In the example, that same EIGRP is enabled on all three routers using the same autonomous system number of **1**.

Note

Both EIGRP and OSPF can support multiple instances of each routing protocol, although this type of multiple routing protocol implementation is not usually needed or recommended.

The **router eigrp** *autonomous-system* command does not start the EIGRP process itself. The router does not start sending updates. Rather, this command only provides access to configure the EIGRP settings.

To completely remove the EIGRP routing process from a device, use the **no router eigrp** *autonomous-system* global configuration mode command, which stops the EIGRP process and removes all existing EIGRP router configurations.

EIGRP Router ID (4.2.1.4)

The EIGRP router ID is used to uniquely identify each router in the EIGRP routing domain. The router ID is used in both EIGRP and OSPF routing protocols, although the role of the router ID is more significant in OSPF.

In EIGRP IPv4 implementations, the use of the router ID is not that apparent. EIGRP for IPv4 uses the 32-bit router ID to identify the originating router for redistribution of external routes. The need for a router ID becomes more evident in the discussion of EIGRP for IPv6. While the router ID is necessary for redistribution, the details of EIGRP redistribution are beyond the scope of this curriculum. For purposes of this curriculum, it is only necessary to understand what the router ID is and how it is derived.

Cisco routers derive the router ID based on three criteria, in the following precedence:

1. Use the IPv4 address configured with the **eigrp router-id** router configuration mode command.

2. If the router ID is not configured, the router chooses the highest IPv4 address of any of its loopback interfaces.

3. If no loopback interfaces are configured, the router chooses the highest active IPv4 address of any of its physical interfaces.

If the network administrator does not explicitly configure a router ID using the **eigrp router-id** command, EIGRP generates its own router ID using either a loopback or physical IPv4 address. A *loopback address* is a virtual interface and is automatically in the up state when configured. The interface does not need to be enabled for EIGRP, meaning that it does not need to be included in one of the EIGRP network commands. However, the interface must be in the up/up state.

Using the previously described criteria, Figure 4-17 shows the default EIGRP router IDs that are determined by the routers' highest active IPv4 address.

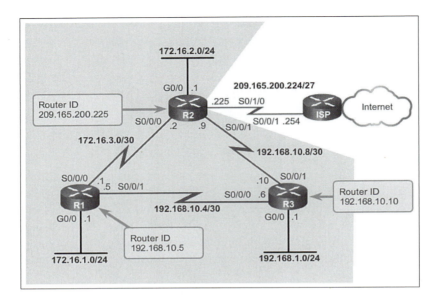

Figure 4-17   Topology with Default EIGRP Router IDs

The **eigrp router-id** command is used to configure the router ID for EIGRP. Some versions of IOS will accept the command **router-id**, without first specifying **eigrp**. The running-config, however, will display **eigrp router-id** regardless of which command is used.

Configuring the EIGRP Router ID (4.2.1.5)

The **eigrp router-id** command is used to configure the EIGRP router ID and takes precedence over any loopback or physical interface IPv4 addresses. The command syntax is:

```
Router(config)# router eigrp autonomous-system
Router(config-router)# eigrp router-id ipv4-address
```

The IPv4 address that is used to indicate the router ID is actually any 32-bit number displayed in dotted-decimal notation.

The router ID can be configured with any IPv4 address with two exceptions: 0.0.0.0 and 255.255.255.255. The router ID should be a unique 32-bit number in the EIGRP routing domain; otherwise, routing inconsistencies can occur.

The following shows the configuration of the EIGRP router ID for routers R1 and R2 using the **router eigrp** *autonomous-system* command:

```
R1(config)# router eigrp 1
R1(config-router)# eigrp router-id 1.1.1.1

R2(config)# router eigrp 1
R2(config-router)# eigrp router-id 2.2.2.2
```

Loopback Address Used as the Router ID

Another option to specify the EIGRP router ID is to use an IPv4 loopback address. The advantage of using a loopback interface, instead of the IPv4 address of a physical interface, is that unlike physical interfaces, it cannot fail. There are no actual cables or adjacent devices on which the loopback interface depends for being in the up state. Therefore, using a loopback address for the router ID can provide a more consistent router ID than using an interface address.

If the **eigrp router-id** command is not used and loopback interfaces are configured, EIGRP chooses the highest IPv4 address of any of its loopback interfaces. The following commands are used to enable and configure a loopback interface:

```
Router(config)# interface loopback number
Router(config-if)# ip address ipv4-address subnet-mask
```

Note

The EIGRP router ID is not changed, unless the EIGRP process is removed with the **no router eigrp** command or if the router ID is manually configured with the **eigrp router-id** command. A change to the value of the router ID can also be implemented by restarting the EIGRP process using the **clear eigrp pid** global configuration command.

Verifying the EIGRP Process

The following shows the **show ip protocols** output for R1, including its router ID. The **show ip protocols** command displays the parameters and current state of any active routing protocol processes, including both EIGRP and OSPF. The **show ip protocols** command displays different types of output specific to each routing protocol.

```
R1# show ip protocols
*** IP Routing is NSF aware ***
Routing Protocol is "eigrp 1"
  Outgoing update filter list for all interfaces is not set
  Incoming update filter list for all interfaces is not set
  Default networks flagged in outgoing updates
```

```
Default networks accepted from incoming updates
EIGRP-IPv4 Protocol for AS(1)
  Metric weight K1=1, K2=0, K3=1, K4=0, K5=0
  NSF-aware route hold timer is 240
  Router-ID: 1.1.1.1
  Topology : 0 (base)
    Active Timer: 3 min
    Distance: internal 90 external 170
    Maximum path: 4
    Maximum hopcount 100
    Maximum metric variance 1
Automatic Summarization: disabled
Maximum path: 4
Routing for Networks:
Routing Information Sources:
  Gateway         Distance       Last Update
Distance: internal 90 external 170
R1#
```

Interactive Graphic

Activity 4.2.1.5: Configure the EIGRP Router ID

Go to the online course to use the Syntax Checker in the third graphic to configure and verify a router ID on router R3.

The Network Command (4.2.1.6)

EIGRP router configuration mode allows for the configuration of the EIGRP routing protocol. Figure 4-18 shows that R1, R2, and R3 all have networks that should be included within a single EIGRP routing domain. To enable EIGRP routing on an interface, use the **network** router configuration mode command and enter the classful network address for each directly connected network.

The **network** command has the same function as in all IGP routing protocols. The **network** command in EIGRP:

- Enables any interface on this router that matches the network address in the **network** router configuration mode command to send and receive EIGRP updates.

- The network of the interfaces is included in EIGRP routing updates.

```
Router(config-router)# network ipv4-network-address
```

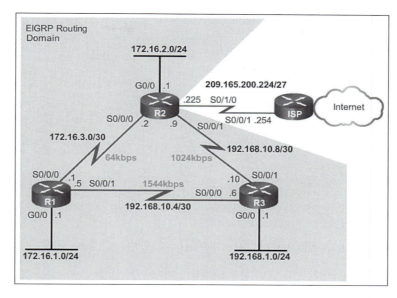

Figure 4-18   EIGRP for IPv4 Topology

The *ipv4-network-address* argument is the classful IPv4 network address for this
interface. Figure 4-19 shows the **network** commands configured for R1. In the figure,
a single classful **network** statement, **network 172.16.0.0**, is used on R1 to include
both interfaces in subnets 172.16.1.0/24 and 172.16.3.0/30. Notice that only the classful network address is used.

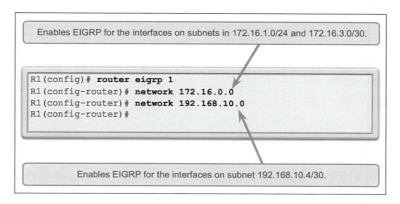

Figure 4-19   EIGRP Network Command for R1

The following shows the **network** command used to enable EIGRP on R2's interfaces
for subnets 172.16.1.0/24 and 172.16.2.0/24. When EIGRP is configured on R2's

S0/0/0 interface, DUAL sends a notification message to the console stating that a neighbor adjacency with another EIGRP router on that interface has been established. This new adjacency happens automatically because both R1 and R2 use the same **eigrp 1** autonomous system number, and both routers now send updates on their interfaces in the 172.16.0.0 network.

```
R2(config)# router eigrp 1
R2(config-router)# network 172.16.0.0
R2(config-router)#
*Feb 28 17:51:42.543: %DUAL-5-NBRCHANGE: EIGRP-IPv4 1: Neighbor 172.16.3.1
   (Serial0/0/0) is up: new adjacency
R2(config-router)#
```

By default, the **eigrp log-neighbor-changes** router configuration mode command is enabled. This command is used to:

- Display any changes in EIGRP neighbor adjacencies.

- Help verify neighbor adjacencies during configuration of EIGRP.

- Advise the network administrator when any EIGRP adjacencies have been removed.

The Network Command and Wildcard Mask (4.2.1.7)

By default, when using the **network** command and an IPv4 network address, such as 172.16.0.0, all interfaces on the router that belong to that classful network address are enabled for EIGRP. However, there may be times when the network administrator does not want to include all interfaces within a network when enabling EIGRP. For example, in Figure 4-20, assume that an administrator wants to enable EIGRP on R2, but only for the subnet 192.168.10.8 255.255.255.252, on the S0/0/1 interface.

To configure EIGRP to advertise specific subnets only, use the *wildcard-mask* option with the **network** command:

```
Router(config-router)# network network-address [ wildcard-mask ]
```

Think of a *wildcard mask* as the inverse of a subnet mask. In a wildcard mask, the network bits are represented by zeros and the host bits are represented by ones. The inverse of subnet mask 255.255.255.252 is 0.0.0.3. To calculate the inverse of the subnet mask, subtract the subnet mask from 255.255.255.255 as follows:

```
  255.255.255.255
- 255.255.255.252   Subtract the subnet mask
  ---------------
    0.  0.  0.  3   Wildcard mask
```

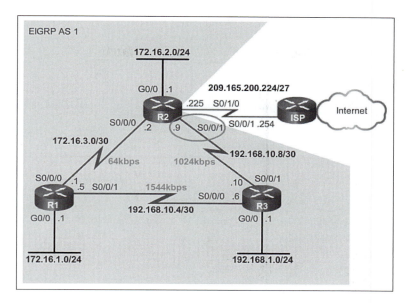

Figure 4-20   EIGRP for IPv4 Topology

Figure 4-21 continues the EIGRP network configuration of R2. The **network 192.168.10.8 0.0.0.3** command specifically enables EIGRP on the S0/0/1 interface, a member of the 192.168.10.8 255.255.255.252 subnet.

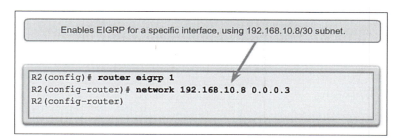

Figure 4-21   **network** Command with Wildcard Mask

Some IOS versions also let you enter the subnet mask instead of a wildcard mask. The following shows an example of configuring the same S0/0/1 interface on R2, but this time using a subnet mask in the **network** command. However, if the subnet mask is used, the IOS converts the command to the *wildcard-mask* format within the configuration. This is verified in the **show running-config** output.

```
R2(config)# router eigrp 1
R2(config-router)# network 192.168.10.8 255.255.255.252
R2(config-router)# end
R2# show running-config | section eigrp 1
router eigrp 1
```

```
network 172.16.0.0
network 192.168.10.8 0.0.0.3
eigrp router-id 2.2.2.2
R2#
```

Activity 4.2.1.7: Configuring the network **Command and Wildcard Mask**

Go to the online course to use the Syntax Checker in the fourth graphic to configure R3 to enable EIGRP on all interfaces.

Passive Interface (4.2.1.8)

As soon as a new interface is enabled within the EIGRP network, EIGRP attempts to form a neighbor adjacency with any neighboring routers to send and receive EIGRP updates.

At times it may be necessary, or advantageous, to include a directly connected network in the EIGRP routing update, but not allow any neighbor adjacencies off of that interface to form. The **passive-interface** command can be used to prevent the neighbor adjacencies. There are two primary reasons for enabling the **passive-interface** command:

- To suppress unnecessary update traffic, such as when an interface is a LAN interface, with no other routers connected

- To increase security controls, such as preventing unknown rogue routing devices from receiving EIGRP updates

Figure 4-22 shows R1, R2, and R3 do not have neighbors on their GigabitEthernet 0/0 interfaces.

The **passive-interface** router configuration mode command disables the transmission and receipt of EIGRP Hello packets on these interfaces:

```
Router(config)# router eigrp as-number
Router(config-router)# passive-interface interface-type interface-number
```

The following shows the **passive-interface** command configured to suppress Hello packets on the LANs for R1 and R3. R2 is configured using the Syntax Checker.

```
R1(config)# router eigrp 1
R1(config-router)# passive-interface gigabitethernet 0/0

R3(config)# router eigrp 1
R3(config-router)# passive-interface gigabitethernet 0/0
```

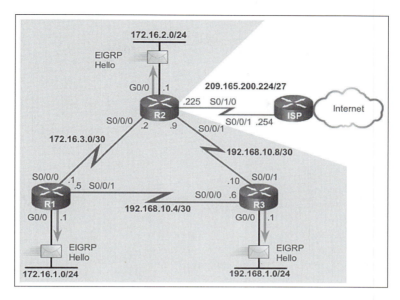

Figure 4-22   EIGRP for IPv4 Topology

Without a neighbor adjacency, EIGRP cannot exchange routes with a neighbor. Therefore, the **passive-interface** command prevents the exchange of routes on the interface. Although EIGRP does not send or receive routing updates on an interface configured with the **passive-interface** command, it still includes the address of the interface in routing updates sent out of other non-passive interfaces.

Note

To configure all interfaces as passive, use the **passive-interface default** command. To disable the interface as passive, use the **no passive-interface** command.

An example of using the passive interface to increase security controls is when a network must connect to a third-party organization, for which the local administrator has no control, such as when connecting to an ISP network. In this case, the local network administrator would need to advertise the interface link through their own network, but would not want the third-party organization to receive or send routing updates to the local routing device, as this is a security risk.

Verifying the Passive Interface

To verify whether any interface on a router is configured as passive, use the **show ip protocols** privileged EXEC mode command, as shown next. Notice that although R3's GigabitEthernet 0/0 interface is a passive interface, EIGRP still includes the interface's network address of 192.168.1.0 in its routing updates.

```
R3# show ip protocols
*** IP Routing is NSF aware ***
Routing Protocol is "eigrp 1"
<Output omitted>
Routing for Networks:
    192.168.1.0
    192.168.2.0
    192.168.3.0
    192.168.10.4/30
    192.168.10.8/30
Passive Interface(s):
    GigabitEthernet0/0
Routing Information Sources:
    Gateway         Distance      Last Update
    192.168.10.5         90       01:37:57
    192.168.10.9         90       01:37:57
Distance: internal 90 external 170
R3#
```

Activity 4.2.1.8: EIGRP Passive Interface

Go to the online course to use the Syntax Checker in the fourth graphic to configure R2 to suppress EIGRP Hello packets on the GigabitEthernet 0/0 interface while still advertising that network in EIGRP updates.

Verifying EIGRP with IPv4 (4.2.2)

This section discusses the importance of verifying that EIGRP was implemented correctly and the commands used to perform the verification of EIGRP for IPv4.

Verifying EIGRP: Examining Neighbors (4.2.2.1)

Before EIGRP can send or receive any updates, routers must establish adjacencies with their neighbors. EIGRP routers establish adjacencies with neighbor routers by exchanging EIGRP Hello packets.

Use the **show ip eigrp neighbors** command, as shown in Figure 4-23, to view the neighbor table and verify that EIGRP has established an adjacency with its neighbors. For each router, you should be able to see the IPv4 address of the adjacent router and the interface that this router uses to reach that EIGRP neighbor. Using this topology, each router has two neighbors listed in the neighbor table.

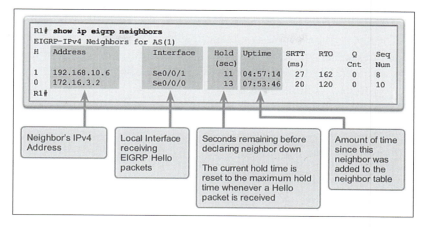

Figure 4-23   Verifying the Neighbor Adjacencies with EIGRP for IPv4

The **show ip eigrp neighbors** command output includes:

- **H column:** Lists the neighbors in the order that they were learned.

- **Address:** IPv4 address of the neighbor.

- **Interface:** Local interface on which this Hello packet was received.

- **Hold:** Current hold time. When a Hello packet is received, this value is reset to the maximum hold time for that interface, and then counts down to zero. If zero is reached, the neighbor is considered down.

- **Uptime:** Amount of time since this neighbor was added to the neighbor table.

- **Smooth Round Trip Timer (SRTT) and Retransmission Timeout (RTO):** Used by RTP to manage reliable EIGRP packets.

- **Queue Count:** Should always be zero. If more than zero, then EIGRP packets wait to be sent.

- **Sequence Number:** Used to track updates, queries, and reply packets.

The **show ip eigrp neighbors** command is very useful for verifying and troubleshooting EIGRP. If a neighbor is not listed after adjacencies have been established with a router's neighbors, check the local interface to ensure it is activated with the **show ip interface brief** command. If the interface is active, try pinging the IPv4 address of the neighbor. If the ping fails, it means that the neighbor interface is down and must be activated. If the ping is successful and EIGRP still does not see the router as a neighbor, examine the following configurations:

- Are both routers configured with the same EIGRP autonomous system number?

- Is the directly connected network included in the EIGRP **network** statements?

Verifying EIGRP: **show ip protocols** Command (4.2.2.2)

The **show ip protocols** command displays the parameters and other information about the current state of any active IPv4 routing protocol processes configured on the router. The **show ip protocols** command displays different types of output specific to each routing protocol.

The output in Figure 4-24 indicates several EIGRP parameters, including:

1. EIGRP is an active dynamic routing protocol on R1 configured with the autonomous system number 1.

2. The EIGRP router ID of R1 is 1.1.1.1.

3. The EIGRP administrative distances on R1 are internal AD of 90 and external AD of 170 (default values).

4. By default, EIGRP does not automatically summarize networks. Subnets are included in the routing updates.

Note

The entire output of the **show ip protocols** command in Figure 4-24 can be viewed in the online course on page 4.2.2.2 graphic number 1.

---

5. The EIGRP neighbor adjacencies with other routers used to receive EIGRP routing updates.

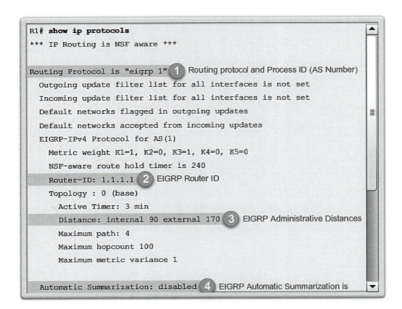

Figure 4-24   Verifying the Passive Interface with EIGRP for IPv4

> **Note**
>
> Prior to IOS 15, automatic summarization was enabled, by default, for EIGRP.

The output from the **show ip protocols** command is useful in debugging routing operations. Information in the Routing Information Sources field can help identify a router suspected of delivering bad routing information. The Routing Information Sources field lists all the EIGRP routing sources the Cisco IOS Software uses to build its IPv4 routing table. For each source, note the following:

- IPv4 address
- Administrative distance
- Time the last update was received from this source

As shown in Table 4-3, EIGRP has a default AD of 90 for internal routes and 170 for routes imported from an external source, such as default routes. When compared to other IGPs, EIGRP is the most preferred by the Cisco IOS, because it has the lowest administrative distance. EIGRP has a third AD value of 5, for summary routes.

Table 4-3   Default Administrative Distances

Route Source	Administrative Distance
Connected	0
Static	1
EIGRP summary route	5
External BGP	20
Internal EIGRP	90
IGRP	100
OSPF	110
IS-IS	115
RIP	120
External EIGRP	170
Internal BGP	200

Verifying EIGRP: Examine the IPv4 Routing Table (4.2.2.3)

Another way to verify that EIGRP and other functions of the router are configured properly is to examine the IPv4 routing tables with the **show ip route** command. As with any dynamic routing protocol, the network administrator must verify the information in the routing table to ensure that it is populated as expected, based on configurations entered. For this reason, it is important to have a good understanding of the routing protocol configuration commands, as well as the routing protocol operations and the processes used by the routing protocol to build the IP routing table.

Note

The outputs used throughout this course are from Cisco IOS 15. Prior to IOS 15, EIGRP automatic summarization was enabled by default. The state of automatic summarization can make a difference in the information displayed in the IPv4 routing table. If a previous version of the IOS is used, automatic summarization can be disabled using the **no auto-summary** router configuration mode command:

```
Router(config-router)# no auto-summary
```

Figure 4-25 shows the topology for R1, R2, and R3.

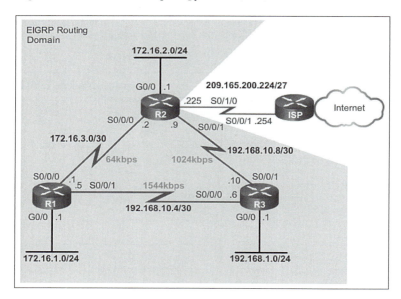

Figure 4-25   EIGRP for IPv4 Topology

In the following output, the IPv4 routing table is examined using the **show ip route** command. EIGRP routes are denoted in the routing table with a D. The letter D was used to represent EIGRP because the protocol is based upon the DUAL algorithm.

```
R1# show ip route
Codes: L - local, C - connected, S - static, R - RIP, M - mobile, B - BGP
       D - EIGRP, EX - EIGRP external, O - OSPF, IA - OSPF inter area
<Output omitted>
Gateway of last resort is not set
```

```
       172.16.0.0/16 is variably subnetted, 5 subnets, 3 masks
C          172.16.1.0/24 is directly connected, GigabitEthernet0/0
L          172.16.1.1/32 is directly connected, GigabitEthernet0/0
D          172.16.2.0/24 [90/2170112] via 172.16.3.2, 00:14:35, Serial0/0/0
C          172.16.3.0/30 is directly connected, Serial0/0/0
L          172.16.3.1/32 is directly connected, Serial0/0/0
D      192.168.1.0/24 [90/2170112] via 192.168.10.6, 00:13:57, Serial0/0/1
       192.168.10.0/24 is variably subnetted, 3 subnets, 2 masks
C          192.168.10.4/30 is directly connected, Serial0/0/1
L          192.168.10.5/32 is directly connected, Serial0/0/1
D          192.168.10.8/30 [90/2681856] via 192.168.10.6, 00:50:42, Serial0/0/1
                           [90/2681856] via 172.16.3.2, 00:50:42, Serial0/0/0
R1#
```

The **show ip route** command verifies that routes received by EIGRP neighbors are installed in the IPv4 routing table. The **show ip route** command displays the entire routing table, including remote networks learned dynamically, directly connected routes, and static routes. For this reason, it is normally the first command used to check for convergence. After routing is correctly configured on all routers, the **show ip route** command reflects that each router has a full routing table, with a route to each network in the topology.

Notice that R1 has installed routes to three IPv4 remote networks in its IPv4 routing table:

- 172.16.2.0/24 network via router R2 using its Serial0/0/0 interface

- 192.168.1.0/24 network via router R3 using its Serial0/0/1 interface

- 192.168.10.8/30 network via both R2 using its Serial0/0/0 interface and via R3 using its Serial0/0/1 interface

R1 has two paths to the 192.168.10.8/30 network, because its cost or metric to reach that network is the same or equal using both routers. These are known as equal cost routes. R1 uses both paths to reach this network, which is known as load balancing. The EIGRP metric is discussed later in this chapter.

The following output displays the routing table for R2. Notice similar results are displayed, including an equal cost route for the 192.168.10.4/30 network.

```
R2# show ip route
Codes: L - local, C - connected, S - static, R - RIP, M - mobile, B - BGP
        D - EIGRP, EX - EIGRP external, O - OSPF, IA - OSPF inter area
<Output omitted>
Gateway of last resort is not set
 172.16.0.0/16 is variably subnetted, 5 subnets, 3 masks
D          172.16.1.0/24 [90/2170112] via 172.16.3.1, 00:11:05, Serial0/0/0
C          172.16.2.0/24 is directly connected, GigabitEthernet0/0
```

```
L        172.16.2.1/32 is directly connected, GigabitEthernet0/0
C        172.16.3.0/30 is directly connected, Serial0/0/0
L        172.16.3.2/32 is directly connected, Serial0/0/0
D        192.168.1.0/24 [90/2170112] via 192.168.10.10, 00:15:16, Serial0/0/1
         192.168.10.0/24 is variably subnetted, 3 subnets, 2 masks
D           192.168.10.4/30 [90/2681856] via 192.168.10.10, 00:52:00, Serial0/0/1
                            [90/2681856] via 172.16.3.1, 00:52:00, Serial0/0/0
C           192.168.10.8/30 is directly connected, Serial0/0/1
L           192.168.10.9/32 is directly connected, Serial0/0/1
         209.165.200.0/24 is variably subnetted, 2 subnets, 2 masks
C           209.165.200.224/27 is directly connected, Loopback209
L           209.165.200.225/32 is directly connected, Loopback209
R2#
```

The following output displays the routing table for R3. Similar to the results for R1 and R2, remote networks are learned using EIGRP, including an equal cost route for the 172.16.3.0/30 network.

```
R3# show ip route
Codes: L - local, C - connected, S - static, R - RIP, M - mobile, B - BGP
       D - EIGRP, EX - EIGRP external, O - OSPF, IA - OSPF inter area
<Output omitted>
Gateway of last resort is not set
 172.16.0.0/16 is variably subnetted, 3 subnets, 2 masks
D        172.16.1.0/24 [90/2170112] via 192.168.10.5, 00:12:00, Serial0/0/0
D        172.16.2.0/24 [90/2170112] via 192.168.10.9, 00:16:49, Serial0/0/1
D        172.16.3.0/30 [90/2681856] via 192.168.10.9, 00:52:55, Serial0/0/1
                       [90/2681856] via 192.168.10.5, 00:52:55, Serial0/0/0
         192.168.1.0/24 is variably subnetted, 2 subnets, 2 masks
C        192.168.1.0/24 is directly connected, GigabitEthernet0/0
L        192.168.1.1/32 is directly connected, GigabitEthernet0/0
         192.168.10.0/24 is variably subnetted, 4 subnets, 2 masks
C        192.168.10.4/30 is directly connected, Serial0/0/0
L        192.168.10.6/32 is directly connected, Serial0/0/0
C        192.168.10.8/30 is directly connected, Serial0/0/1
L        192.168.10.10/32 is directly connected, Serial0/0/1
R3#
```

Packet Tracer Activity 4.2.2.4: Configuring Basic EIGRP for IPv4

In this activity, you will implement basic EIGRP configurations including network commands, passive interfaces, and disabling automatic summarization. You will then verify your EIGRP configuration using a variety of **show** commands and testing end-to-end connectivity.

Lab 4.2.2.5: Configuring Basic EIGRP for IPv4

In this lab, you will complete the following objectives:

- Part 1: Build the Network and Verify Connectivity
- Part 2: Configure EIGRP Routing
- Part 3: Verify EIGRP Routing
- Part 4: Configure Bandwidth and Passive Interfaces

Operation of EIGRP (4.3)

Understanding the operations of any routing protocol is critical to being able to properly implement, maintain, and troubleshoot the routing domain. Although the commands may seem fairly straightforward, the underlying protocols and processes can be more involved. These protocols and processes apply similarly to IPv4 and IPv6.

EIGRP Initial Route Discover (4.3.1)

This section discusses how EIGRP learns about remote network from EIGRP neighbors.

EIGRP Neighbor Adjacency (4.3.1.1)

The goal of any dynamic routing protocol is to learn about remote networks from other routers and to reach convergence in the routing domain. This section discusses how EIGRP routers form neighbor adjacencies and discover remote networks.

Before any EIGRP Update packets can be exchanged between routers, EIGRP must first discover its neighbors. EIGRP neighbors are other routers running EIGRP on directly connected networks.

EIGRP uses Hello packets to establish and maintain neighbor adjacencies. For two EIGRP routers to become neighbors, several parameters between the two routers must match. For example, two EIGRP routers must use the same EIGRP metric parameters and both must be configured using the same autonomous system number.

Each EIGRP router maintains a neighbor table, which contains a list of routers on shared links that have an EIGRP *adjacency* with this router. The neighbor table is used to track the status of these EIGRP neighbors.

Figure 4-26 shows two EIGRP routers exchanging initial EIGRP Hello packets. When an EIGRP-enabled router receives a Hello packet on an interface, it adds that router to its neighbor table.

1. A new router (R1) comes up on the link and sends an EIGRP Hello packet through all of its EIGRP-configured interfaces.

2. Router R2 receives the Hello packet on an EIGRP-enabled interface. R2 replies with an EIGRP Update packet that contains all the routes it has in its routing table, except those learned through that interface (split horizon). However, the neighbor adjacency is not established until R2 also sends an EIGRP Hello packet to R1.

3. After both routers have exchanged Hellos, the neighbor adjacency is established. R1 and R2 update their EIGRP neighbor tables adding the adjacent router as a neighbor.

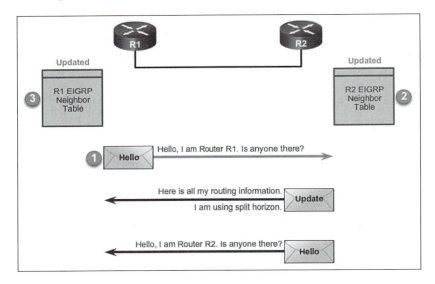

Figure 4-26   Discovering Neighbors

EIGRP Topology Table (4.3.1.2)

EIGRP updates contain networks that are reachable from the router sending the update. As EIGRP updates are exchanged between neighbors, the receiving router adds these entries to its EIGRP topology table.

Each EIGRP router maintains a topology table for each routed protocol configured, such as IPv4 and IPv6. The topology table includes route entries for every destination that the router learns from its directly connected EIGRP neighbors.

Figure 4-27 shows the continuation of the initial route discovery process from the previous page. It now shows the update of the topology table.

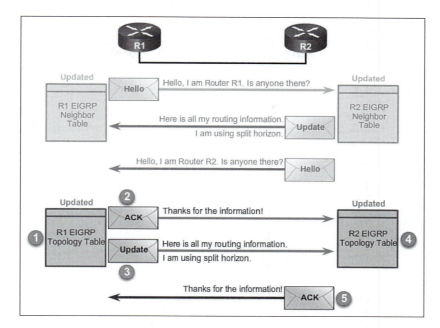

Figure 4-27 Exchanging Routing Updates

When a router receives an EIGRP routing update, it adds the routing information to its EIGRP topology table and replies with an EIGRP acknowledgment.

1. R1 receives the EIGRP update from neighbor R2 and includes information about the routes that the neighbor is advertising, including the metric to each destination. R1 adds all update entries to its topology table. The topology table includes all destinations advertised by neighboring (adjacent) routers and the cost (metric) to reach each network.

2. EIGRP Update packets use reliable delivery; therefore, R1 replies with an EIGRP acknowledgment packet informing R2 that it has received the update.

3. R1 sends an EIGRP update to R2 advertising the routes that it is aware of, except those learned from R2 (split horizon).

4. R2 receives the EIGRP update from neighbor R1 and adds this information to its own topology table.

5. R2 responds to the R1's EIGRP Update packet with an EIGRP acknowledgment.

EIGRP Convergence (4.3.1.3)

Figure 4-28 illustrates the final steps of the initial route discovery process.

1. After receiving the EIGRP Update packets from R2, using the information in the topology table, R1 updates its IP routing table with the best path to each destination, including the metric and the next-hop router.

2. Similar to R1, R2 updates its IP routing table with the best path routes to each network.

At this point, EIGRP on both routers is considered to be in the converged state.

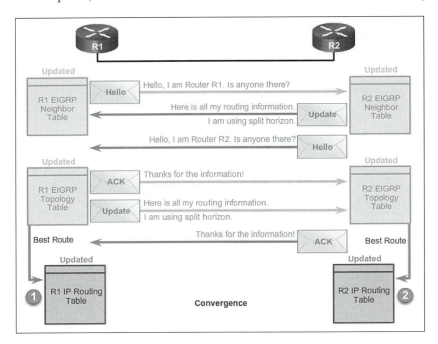

Figure 4-28   Updating the IPv4 Routing Table

Interactive Graphic

Activity 4.3.1.4: Identify the Steps in Establishing EIGRP Neighbor Adjacencies

Go to the online course to perform this practice activity.

Metrics (4.3.2)

This section examines the values used in the EIGRP metric and how EIGRP performs the calculation to arrive at the metric displayed in the routing table.

EIGRP Composite Metric (4.3.2.1)

By default, EIGRP uses the following values in its composite metric to calculate the preferred path to a network:

- **Bandwidth:** The slowest bandwidth among all of the outgoing interfaces, along the path from source to destination

- **Delay:** The cumulative (sum) of all interface delay along the path (in tens of microseconds)

The following values can be used, but are not recommended because they typically result in frequent recalculation of the topology table:

- **Reliability:** Represents the worst reliability between the source and destination, which is based on keepalives

- **Load:** Represents the worst load on a link between the source and destination, which is computed based on the packet rate and the configured bandwidth of the interface

Note

Although the MTU is included in the routing table updates, it is not a routing metric used by EIGRP.

The Composite Metric

Figure 4-29 shows the composite metric formula used by EIGRP. The formula consists of values K1 to K5, known as EIGRP metric weights. K1 and K3 represent bandwidth and delay, respectively. K2 represents load, and K4 and K5 represent reliability. By default, K1 and K3 are set to 1, and K2, K4, and K5 are set to 0. The result is that only the bandwidth and delay values are used in the computation of the default composite metric. EIGRP for IPv4 and EIGRP for IPv6 use the same formula for the composite metric.

The metric calculation method (*k* values) and the EIGRP autonomous system number must match between EIGRP neighbors. If they do not match, the routers do not form an adjacency.

The default *k* values can be changed with the **metric weights** router configuration mode command:

```
Router(config-router)# metric weights tos k1 k2 k3 k4 k5
```

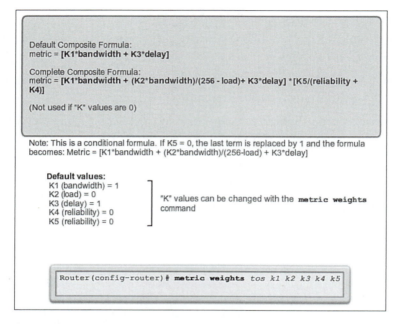

Figure 4-29   EIGRP Composite Metric

Modifying the **metric weights** value is generally not recommended, and is beyond the scope of this course. However, its relevance is important in establishing neighbor adjacencies. If one router has modified the metric weights and another router has not, an adjacency does not form.

Verifying the *k* Values

The **show ip protocols** command is used to verify the *k* values. The command output for R1 is shown next. Notice that the *k* values on R1 are set to the default.

```
R1# show ip protocols
*** IP Routing is NSF aware ***
Routing Protocol is "eigrp 1"
  Outgoing update filter list for all interfaces is not set
  Incoming update filter list for all interfaces is not set
  Default networks flagged in outgoing updates
  Default networks accepted from incoming updates
  EIGRP-IPv4 Protocol for AS(1)
    Metric weight K1=1, K2=0, K3=1, K4=0, K5=0
    NSF-aware route hold timer is 240
    Router-ID: 1.1.1.1
<Output omitted>
R1#
```

Examining Interface Values (4.3.2.2)

The interface parameters are used by EIGRP to calculate the EIGRP routing metric using the EIGRP composite metric.

Examining the Metric Values

The **show interface** command displays interface information, including the parameters used to compute the EIGRP metric. The following output shows the **show interface** command for the Serial 0/0/0 interface on R1:

- **BW:** Bandwidth of the interface (in kilobits per second).

- **DLY:** Delay of the interface (in microseconds).

- **Reliability:** Reliability of the interface as a fraction of 255 (255/255 is 100% reliability), calculated as an exponential average over five minutes. By default, EIGRP does not include its value in computing its metric.

- **Txload, rxload:** Transmit and receive load on the interface as a fraction of 255 (255/255 is completely saturated), calculated as an exponential average over five minutes. By default, EIGRP does not include its value in computing its metric.

```
R1# show interface serial 0/0/0
Serial0/0/0 is up, line protocol is up
  Hardware is WIC MBRD Serial
  Internet address is 172.16.3.1/30
  MTU 1500 bytes, BW 1544 Kbit/sec, DLY 20000 usec,
     reliability 255/255, txload 1/255, rxload 1/255
  Encapsulation HDLC, loopback not set
<Output omitted>
R1#
R1# show interface gigabitethernet 0/0
GigabitEthernet0/0 is up, line protocol is up
  Hardware is CN Gigabit Ethernet, address is fc99.4775.c3e0 (bia fc99.4775.c3e0)
  Internet address is 172.16.1.1/24
  MTU 1500 bytes, BW 100000 Kbit/sec, DLY 100 usec,
     reliability 255/255, txload 1/255, rxload 1/255
  Encapsulation ARPA, loopback not set
<Output omitted>
R1#
```

Note

Throughout this course, bandwidth is referenced as kb/s. However, router output displays bandwidth using the Kbit/sec abbreviation. Router output also displays delay as usec. In this course, delay is referenced as microseconds.

Bandwidth Metric (4.3.2.3)

The bandwidth metric is a static value used by some routing protocols, such as EIGRP and OSPF, to calculate their routing metric. The bandwidth is displayed in kilobits per second (kb/s). Most serial interfaces use the default bandwidth value of 1544 kb/s or 1,544,000 b/s (1.544 Mb/s). This is the bandwidth of a T1 connection. However, some serial interfaces use a different default bandwidth value. Figure 4-30 shows the topology used throughout this section. The types of serial interfaces and their associated bandwidths may not necessarily reflect the more common types of connections found in networks today.

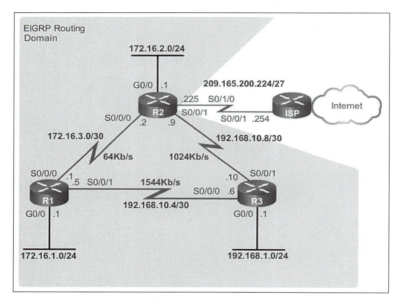

Figure 4-30   EIGRP for IPv4 Topology

Always verify bandwidth with the **show interfaces** command.

The default value of the bandwidth may or may not reflect the actual physical bandwidth of the interface. If actual bandwidth of the link differs from the default bandwidth value, the bandwidth value should be modified.

Configuring the Bandwidth Parameter

On most serial links, the bandwidth metric defaults to 1,544 kb/s. Because both EIGRP and OSPF use bandwidth in default metric calculations, a correct value for bandwidth is very important to the accuracy of routing information.

Use the following interface configuration mode command to modify the bandwidth metric:

```
Router(config-if)# bandwidth kilobits-bandwidth-value
```

Use the **no bandwidth** command to restore the default value.

In the following configurations, the link between R1 and R2 has a bandwidth of 64 kb/s, and the link between R2 and R3 has a bandwidth of 1,024 kb/s. The following shows the configurations used on all three routers to modify the bandwidth on the appropriate serial interfaces.

```
R1(config)# interface s 0/0/0
R1(config-if)# bandwidth 64


R2(config)# interface s 0/0/0
R2(config-if)# bandwidth 64
R2(config-if)# exit
R2(config)# interface s 0/0/1
R2(config-if)# bandwidth 1024


R3(config)# interface s 0/0/1
R3(config-if)# bandwidth 1024
```

Verifying the Bandwidth Parameter

Use the **show interfaces** command to verify the new bandwidth parameters, as shown in the following output. It is important to modify the bandwidth metric on both sides of the link to ensure proper routing in both directions.

```
R1# show interface s 0/0/0
Serial0/0/0 is up, line protocol is up
  Hardware is WIC MBRD Serial
  Internet address is 172.16.3.1/30
  MTU 1500 bytes, BW 64 Kbit/sec, DLY 20000 usec,
     reliability 255/255, txload 1/255, rxload 1/255
<Output omitted>
R1#


R2# show interface s 0/0/0
Serial0/0/0 is up, line protocol is up
  Hardware is WIC MBRD Serial
  Internet address is 172.16.3.2/30
  MTU 1500 bytes, BW 64 Kbit/sec, DLY 20000 usec,
     reliability 255/255, txload 1/255, rxload 1/255
<Output omitted>
R2#
```

Modifying the bandwidth value does not change the actual bandwidth of the link. The **bandwidth** command only modifies the bandwidth metric used by routing protocols, such as EIGRP and OSPF.

Delay Metric (4.3.2.4)

Delay is the measure of the time it takes for a packet to traverse a route. The delay (DLY) metric is a static value based on the type of link to which the interface is connected and is expressed in microseconds. Delay is not measured dynamically. In other words, the router does not actually track how long packets take to reach the destination. The delay value, much like the bandwidth value, is a default value that can be changed by the network administrator.

When used to determine the EIGRP metric, delay is the cumulative (sum) of all interface delays along the path (measured in tens of microseconds).

Table 4-4 shows the default delay values for various interfaces. Notice that the default value is 20,000 microseconds for serial interfaces and 10 microseconds for GigabitEthernet interfaces.

Table 4-4   Interface Delay Values

Media	Delay
Ethernet	1,000
Fast Ethernet	100
GigabitEthernet	10
16M Token Ring	630
FDDI	100
T1 (Serial Default)	20,000
DS0 (64kb/s)	20,000
1024 kb/s	20,000
56 kb/s	20,000

Use the **show interface** command to verify the delay value on an interface, as shown in the following output. Although an interface with various bandwidths can have the same delay value, by default, Cisco recommends not modifying the delay parameter, unless the network administrator has a specific reason to do so.

```
R1# show interface s 0/0/0
Serial0/0/0 is up, line protocol is up
  Hardware is WIC MBRD Serial
  Internet address is 172.16.3.1/30
  MTU 1500 bytes, BW 64 Kbit/sec, DLY 20000 usec,
     reliability 255/255, txload 1/255, rxload 1/255
<Output omitted>
R1#
R1# show interface g 0/0
GigabitEthernet0/0 is up, line protocol is up
  Hardware is CN Gigabit Ethernet, address is fc99.4775.c3e0 (bia fc99.4775.c3e0)
  Internet address is 172.16.1.1/24
  MTU 1500 bytes, BW 1000000 Kbit/sec, DLY 10 usec,
     reliability 255/255, txload 1/255, rxload 1/255
<Output omitted>
R1#
```

Calculating the EIGRP Metric (4.3.2.5)

Although EIGRP automatically calculates the routing table metric used to choose the best path, it is important that the network administrator understands how these metrics were determined.

Figure 4-31 shows the composite metric used by EIGRP. Using the default values for K1 and K3, the calculation can be simplified to the slowest bandwidth (or minimum bandwidth), plus the sum of all of the delays.

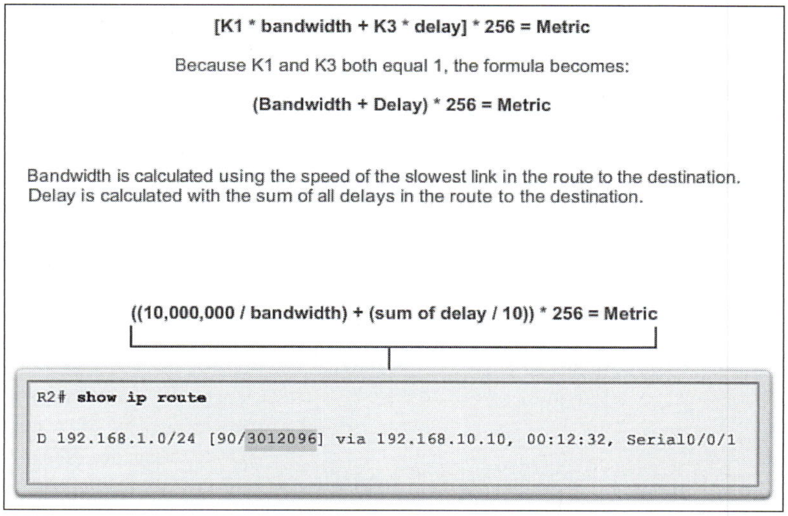

Figure 4-31   Default EIGRP Metric

In other words, by examining the bandwidth and delay values for all of the outgoing interfaces of the route, we can determine the EIGRP metric as follows:

Step 1.   Determine the link with the slowest bandwidth. Use that value to calculate bandwidth (10,000,000/bandwidth).

Step 2.   Determine the delay value for each outgoing interface on the way to the destination. Add the delay values and divide by 10 (sum of delay/10).

Step 3.   Add the computed values for bandwidth and delay, and multiply the sum by 256 to obtain the EIGRP metric.

The routing table output for R2 shows that the route to 192.168.1.0/24 has an EIGRP metric of 3,012,096.

Calculating the EIGRP Metric: Example (4.3.2.6)

Figure 4-32 displays the three router topology. This example illustrates how EIGRP determines the metric displayed in R2's routing table for the 192.168.1.0/24 network.

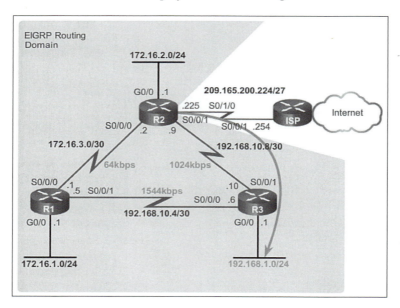

Figure 4-32   EIGRP for IPv4 Topology

Bandwidth

EIGRP uses the slowest bandwidth in its metric calculation. The slowest bandwidth can be determined by examining each interface between R2 and the destination network 192.168.1.0. The Serial 0/0/1 interface on R2 has a bandwidth of 1,024 kb/s. The

GigabitEthernet 0/0 interface on R3 has a bandwidth of 1,000,000 kb/s. Therefore, the slowest bandwidth is 1,024 kb/s and is used in the calculation of the metric.

EIGRP divides a *reference bandwidth* value of 10,000,000 by the interface bandwidth value in kb/s. This results in higher bandwidth values receiving a lower metric and lower bandwidth values receiving a higher metric. 10,000,000 is divided by 1,024. If the result is not a whole number, then the value is truncated. In this case, 10,000,000 divided by 1,024 equals 9,765.625. The .625 is dropped to yield 9,765 for the bandwidth portion of the composite metric, as shown in the following output:

```
R2# show interface s 0/0/1
Serial0/0/1 is up, line protocol is up
  Hardware is WIC MBRD Serial
  Internet address is 192.168.10.9/30
  MTU 1500 bytes, BW 1024 Kbit/sec, DLY 20000 usec,
    reliability 255/255, txload 1/255, rxload 1/255
<Output omitted>
R2#


R3# show interface g 0/0
GigabitEthernet0/0 is up, line protocol is up
  Hardware is CN Gigabit Ethernet, address is fc99.4771.7a20 (bia fc99.4771.7a20)
  Internet address is 192.168.1.1/24
  MTU 1500 bytes, BW 1000000 Kbit/sec, DLY 10 usec,
    reliability 255/255, txload 1/255, rxload 1/255
<Output omitted>
R3#
```

Calculate bandwidth using the slowest bandwidth to the destination: **1024**

(10,000,000 / **1024**)= 9,765

Note

9765.625 is rounded down to 9765.

Delay

The same outgoing interfaces are used to determine the delay value, as shown in the following output:

```
R2# show interface s 0/0/1
Serial0/0/1 is up, line protocol is up
  Hardware is WIC MBRD Serial
  Internet address is 192.168.10.9/30
  MTU 1500 bytes, BW 1024 Kbit/sec, DLY 20000 usec,
    reliability 255/255, txload 1/255, rxload 1/255
```

```
<Output omitted>
R2#


R3# show interface g 0/0
GigabitEthernet0/0 is up, line protocol is up
  Hardware is CN Gigabit Ethernet, address is fc99.4771.7a20 (bia fc99.4771.7a20)
  Internet address is 192.168.1.1/24
  MTU 1500 bytes, BW 1000000 Kbit/sec, DLY 10 usec,
     reliability 255/255, txload 1/255, rxload 1/255
<Output omitted>
R3#
```

Calculate delay using the sum of all delays to the destination: **20,000 + 10**

(20,000 + 10) / 10 = 2001

EIGRP uses the sum of all delays to the destination. The Serial 0/0/1 interface on R2 has a delay of 20,000 microseconds. The Gigabit 0/0 interface on R3 has a delay of 10 microseconds. The sum of these delays is divided by 10. In the example, (20,000+10)/10 results in a value of 2,001 for the delay portion of the composite metric.

Calculate Metric

Use the calculated values for bandwidth and delay in the metric formula. This results in a metric of 3,012,096, as shown in the following output. This value matches the value shown in the routing table for R2.

```
R2# show ip route
<Output omitted>
D    192.168.1.0/24 [90/3012096] via 192.168.10.10, 00:12:32, Serial0/0/1
```

Use the results in the default metric formula:

(Bandwidth + Delay) * 256 Metric

(9765 + 2001) * 256 = 3,012,096

Activity 4.3.2.7: Calculate the EIGRP Metric

Go to the online course to perform this practice activity.

DUAL and the Topology Table (4.3.3)

As stated in the section "Basic Features of EIGRP," the Diffusing Update Algorithm is the algorithm used by EIGRP. This section discusses how DUAL determines the best loop-free path and loop-free backup paths.

DUAL Concepts (4.3.3.1)

DUAL uses several terms, which are discussed in more detail throughout this section:

- Successor
- Feasible distance (FD)
- Feasible successor (FS)
- Reported distance (RD) or advertised distance (AD)
- Feasible condition or feasibility condition (FC)

These terms and concepts are at the center of the loop avoidance mechanism of DUAL.

Introduction to DUAL (4.3.3.2)

EIGRP uses convergence algorithm DUAL. Convergence is critical to a network to avoid routing loops.

Routing loops, even temporary ones, can be detrimental to network performance. Distance vector routing protocols, such as RIP, prevent routing loops with hold-down timers and split horizon. Although EIGRP uses both of these techniques, it uses them somewhat differently; the primary way that EIGRP prevents routing loops is with the DUAL algorithm.

Figures 4-33 through 4-36 demonstrate the sequence of EIGRP updates, queries, replies, and acknowledgments used by DUAL when there is a change in the topology:

1. A directly connected network on R2 goes down. R2 sends an EIGRP update message to its neighbors indicating the network is down (see Figure 4-33).

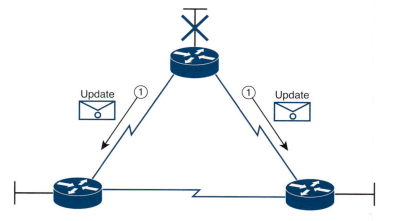

Figure 4-33   DUAL Operation: R2 Sends Update

2. R1 and R3 return an EIGRP acknowledgment indicating that they have received the update from R2 (see Figure 4-34).

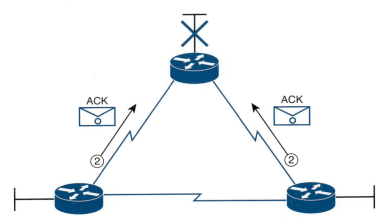

Figure 4-34   DUAL Operation: R1 and R3 Send Replies

3. R2 does not have an EIGRP backup route, known as a feasible successor. (This will be explained in the section "Feasible Successor, Feasibility Condition, and Reported Distance.") So, R2 sends an EIGRP query to its neighbors asking them whether they have a route to this downed network.

4. R1 and R3 return an EIGRP acknowledgment indicating that they have received the query from R2 (see Figure 4-35).

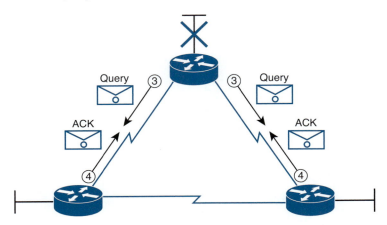

Figure 4-35   DUAL Operation: R2 Sends Queries; R1 and R3 Send Acknowledgments

5. R1 and R3 send an EIGRP reply message in response to the query sent by R2. In this case, the reply would state that the router does not have a route to this network.

6. R2 returns an acknowledgment indicating that it received the reply (see Figure 4-36).

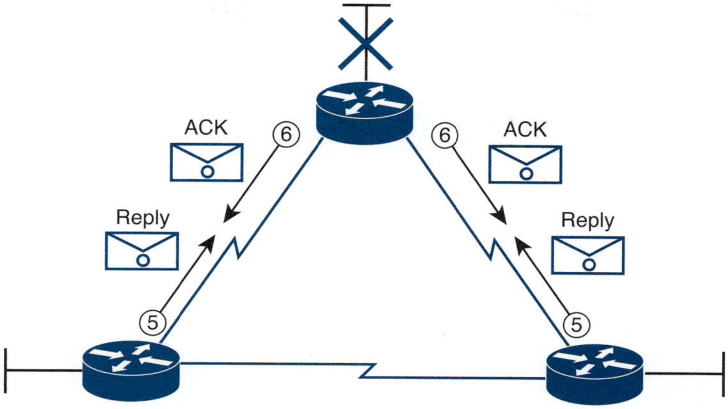

Figure 4-36   DUAL Operation: R1 and R3 Send Replies; R2 Sends Acknowledgment

The DUAL algorithm is used to obtain loop-freedom at every instance throughout a route computation. This allows all routers involved in a topology change to synchronize at the same time. Routers that are not affected by the topology changes are not involved in the recomputation. This method provides EIGRP with faster convergence times than other distance vector routing protocols.

The decision process for all route computations is done by the DUAL Finite State Machine (FSM). An FSM is a workflow model, similar to a flow chart, that is composed of the following:

- A finite number of stages (states)
- Transitions between those stages
- Operations

The DUAL FSM tracks all routes, uses EIGRP metrics to select efficient, loop-free paths, and identifies the routes with the least-cost path to be inserted into the routing table.

Recomputation of the DUAL algorithm can be processor-intensive. EIGRP avoids recomputation whenever possible by maintaining a list of backup routes that DUAL has already determined to be loop-free. If the primary route in the routing table fails, the best backup route is immediately added to the routing table.

Successor and Feasible Distance (4.3.3.3)

Figure 4-37 shows the topology for this topic. A *successor* is a neighboring router that is used for packet forwarding and is the least-cost route to the destination network. The IP address of a successor is shown in a routing table entry right after the word via.

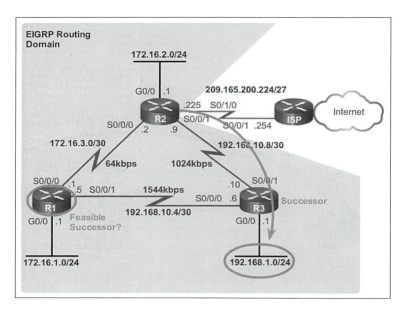

Figure 4-37 EIGRP for IPv4 Topology

Feasible distance (FD) is the lowest calculated metric to reach the destination network. FD is the metric listed in the routing table entry as the second number inside the brackets. As with other routing protocols, this is also known as the metric for the route.

Examining the routing table for R2 in Figure 4-38, notice that EIGRP's best path for the 192.168.1.0/24 network is through router R3, and that the feasible distance is 3,012,096. This is the metric that was calculated in the previous topic.

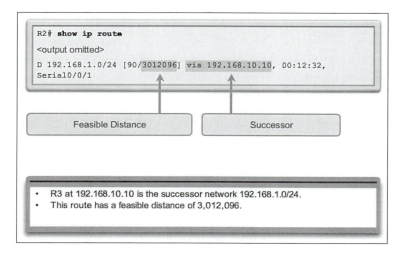

Figure 4-38 Feasible Distance and Successor

Feasible Successors, Feasibility Condition, and Reported Distance (4.3.3.4)

DUAL can converge quickly after a change in the topology because it can use backup paths to other networks without recomputing DUAL. These backup paths are known as feasible successors (FSs).

A *feasible successor* is a neighbor that has a loop-free backup path to the same network as the successor, and it satisfies the *feasibility condition* (FC). R2's successor for the 192.168.1.0/24 network is R3, providing the best path or lowest metric to the destination network. Notice in Figure 4-39 that R1 provides an alternative path, but is it an FS? Before R1 can be an FS for R2, R1 must first meet the FC.

The FC is met when a neighbor's reported distance (RD) to a network is less than the local router's feasible distance to the same destination network. If the reported distance is less, it represents a loop-free path. The *reported distance* is simply an EIGRP neighbor's feasible distance to the same destination network. The reported distance is the metric that a router reports to a neighbor about its own cost to that network.

In Figure 4-39, R1's feasible distance to 192.168.1.0/24 is 2,170,112.

- R1 reports to R2 that its FD to 192.168.1.0/24 is 2,170,112.

- From R2's perspective, 2,170,112 is R1's RD.

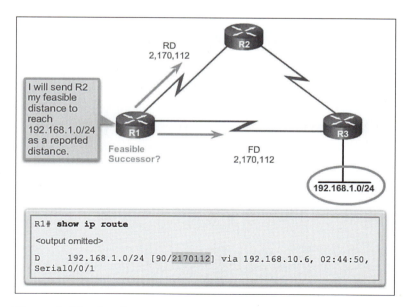

Figure 4-39   Sending the Reported Distance

R2 uses this information to determine if R1 meets the FC and, therefore, can be an FS.

As shown in Figure 4-40, because the RD of R1 (2,170,112) is less than R2's own FD (3,012,096), R1 meets the FC.

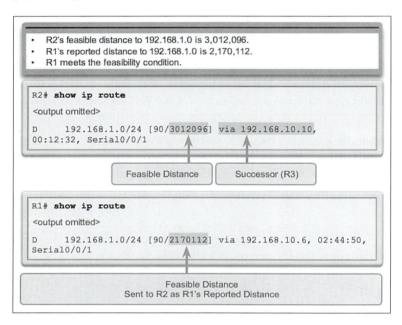

Figure 4-40   Does It Meet the Feasibility Condition?

R1 is now an FS for R2 to the 192.168.1.0/24 network.

If there is a failure in R2's path to 192.168.1.0/24 via R3 (successor), then R2 immediately installs the path via R1 (FS) in its routing table. R1 becomes the new successor for R2's path to this network, as shown in Figure 4-41.

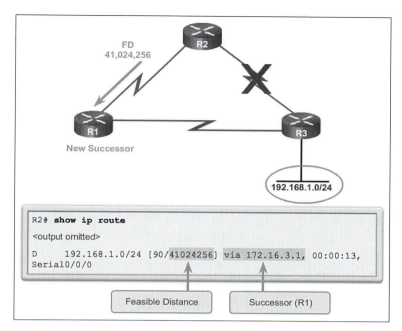

Figure 4-41   Using the Feasible Successor

Topology Table: **show ip eigrp topology** Command (4.3.3.5)

Figure 4-42 shows the topology.

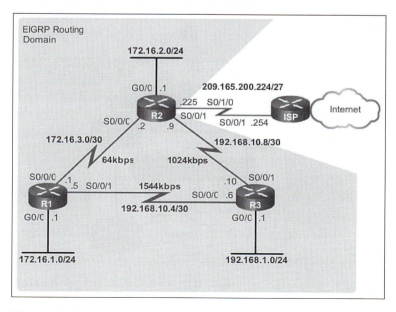

Figure 4-42   EIGRP for IPv4 Topology

The EIGRP topology table contains all of the routes that are known to each EIGRP neighbor. As an EIGRP router learns routes from its neighbors, those routes are installed in its EIGRP topology table.

As shown in Figure 4-43, use the **show ip eigrp topology** command to view the topology table. The *topology table* lists all successors and FSs that DUAL has calculated to destination networks. Only the successor is installed into the IP routing table.

```
R2# show ip eigrp topology
EIGRP-IPv4 Topology Table for AS(1)/ID(2.2.2.2)
Codes: P - Passive, A - Active, U - Update, Q - Query, R - Reply,
       r - reply Status, s - sia Status

P 172.16.2.0/24, 1 successors, FD is 2816
        via Connected, GigabitEthernet0/0
P 192.168.10.4/30, 1 successors, FD is 3523840
        via 192.168.10.10 (3523840/2169856), Serial0/0/1
        via 172.16.3.1 (41024000/2169856), Serial0/0/0
P 192.168.1.0/24, 1 successors, FD is 3012096
        via 192.168.10.10 (3012096/2816), Serial0/0/1
        via 172.16.3.1 (41024256/2170112), Serial0/0/0
P 172.16.3.0/30, 1 successors, FD is 40512000
        via Connected, Serial0/0/0
P 172.16.1.0/24, 1 successors, FD is 3524096
        via 192.168.10.10 (3524096/2170112), Serial0/0/1
        via 172.16.3.1 (40512256/2816), Serial0/0/0
P 192.168.10.8/30, 1 successors, FD is 3011840
        via Connected, Serial0/0/1

R2#
```

Figure 4-43   R2's Topology Table

As shown in Figure 4-44, the first line in the topology table displays:

- **P**: Route in the *passive state*. When DUAL is not performing its diffusing computations to determine a path for a network, the route is in a stable mode, known as the passive state. If DUAL recalculates or searches for a new path, the route is in an *active state* and displays an A. All routes in the topology table should be in the passive state for a stable routing domain.

- **192.168.1.0/24**: Destination network that is also found in the routing table.

- **1 successors**: Displays the number of successors for this network. If there are multiple equal cost paths to this network, there are multiple successors.

- **FD is 3012096**: FD, the EIGRP metric to reach the destination network. This is the metric displayed in the IP routing table.

As shown in Figure 4-45, the first subentry in the output shows the successor:

- **via 192.168.10.10**: Next-hop address of the successor, R3. This address is shown in the routing table.

- **3012096:** FD to 192.168.1.0/24. It is the metric shown in the IP routing table.

- **2816:** RD of the successor and is R3's cost to reach this network.

- **Serial0/0/1:** Outbound interface used to reach this network, also shown in the routing table.

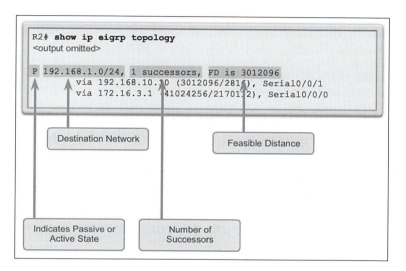

Figure 4-44   Examining an Entry in the Topology Table: Line 1

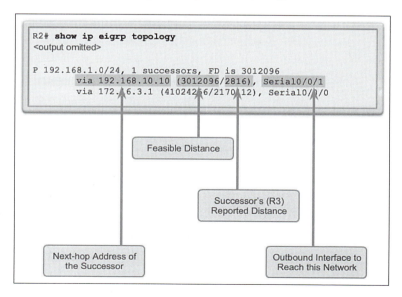

Figure 4-45   Examining an Entry in the Topology Table: Line 2

As shown in Figure 4-46, the second subentry shows the FS, R1 (if there is not a second entry, then there are no FSs):

- **via 172.16.3.1:** Next-hop address of the FS, R1.

- **41024256:** R2's new FD to 192.168.1.0/24, if R1 became the new successor and would be the new metric displayed in the IP routing table.

- **2170112:** RD of the FS, or R1's metric to reach this network. RD must be less than the current FD of 3,012,096 to meet the FC.

- **Serial0/0/0:** This is the outbound interface used to reach FS, if this router becomes the successor.

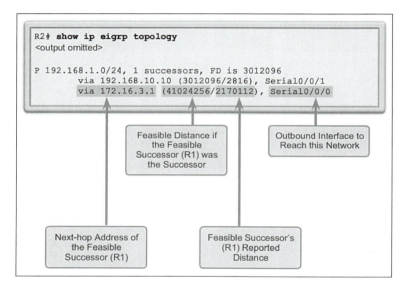

Figure 4-46   Examining an Entry in the Topology Table: Line 3

Topology Table: No Feasible Successor (4.3.3.7)

To see how DUAL uses successors and FSs, examine the router table of R1, assuming the network is converged, as shown in Figure 4-47.

Figure 4-47 displays a partial output from the **show ip route** command on R1. The route to 192.168.1.0/24 shows that the successor is R3 via 192.168.10.6 with an FD of 2,170,112.

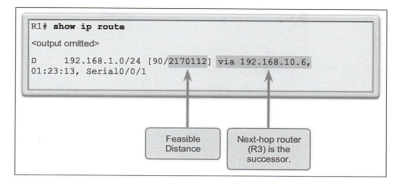

Figure 4-47   R1's Routing Table Entry for 192.168.1.0/24

The IP routing table only includes the best path, the successor. To see if there are any FSs, we must examine the EIGRP topology table. The topology table in Figure 4-48 only shows the successor 192.168.10.6, which is R3. There are no FSs. By looking at the actual physical topology or network diagram, it is obvious that there is a backup route to 192.168.1.0/24 through R2. R2 is not an FS because it does not meet the FC. Although, looking at the topology, it is obvious that R2 is a backup route, EIGRP does not have a map of the network topology. EIGRP is a distance vector routing protocol and only knows about remote network information through its neighbors.

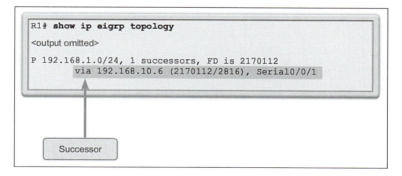

Figure 4-48   R1's Topology Table Entry for 192.168.1.0/24

DUAL does not store the route through R2 in the topology table. All links can be displayed using the **show ip eigrp topology all-links** command. This command displays links whether they satisfy the FC or not.

As shown in Figure 4-49, the **show ip eigrp topology all-links** command shows all possible paths to a network, including successors, FSs, and even those routes that are not FSs. R1's FD to 192.168.1.0/24 is 2,170,112 via the successor R3. For R2 to be considered an FS, it must meet the FC. R2's RD to R1 to reach 192.168.1.0/24 must be less than R1's current FD. Per the figure, R2's RD is 3,012,096, which is higher than R1's current FD of 2,170,112.

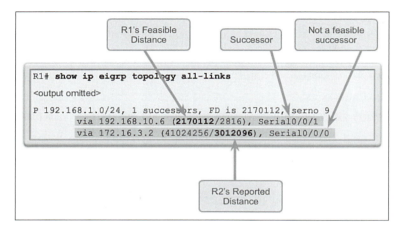

Figure 4-49   R1's All-links Topology Table Entry for 192.168.1.0/24

Even though R2 looks like a viable backup path to 192.168.1.0/24, R1 has no idea that the path is not a potential loop back through itself. EIGRP is a distance vector routing protocol, without the ability to see a complete, loop-free topological map of the network. DUAL's method of guaranteeing that a neighbor has a loop-free path is that the neighbor's metric must satisfy the FC. By ensuring that the RD of the neighbor is less than its own FD, the router can assume that this neighboring router is not part of its own advertised route; thus, always avoiding the potential for a loop.

R2 can be used as a successor if R3 fails; however, there is a longer delay before adding it to the routing table. Before R2 can be used as a successor, DUAL must do further processing.

Interactive Graphic

Activity 4.3.3.8: Determine the Feasible Successor

Go to the online course to perform this practice activity.

DUAL and Convergence (4.3.4)

Although EIGRP is an advanced distance vector routing protocol, unlike link-state routing protocols, it does not have a topological view of the routing domain. So, DUAL is the mechanism EIGRP neighbors use to guarantee loop-free primary and alternative paths to the destination network.

DUAL Finite State Machine (FSM) (4.3.4.1)

The centerpiece of EIGRP is DUAL and its EIGRP route-calculation engine. The actual name of this technology is ***DUAL Finite State Machine*** (FSM). This FSM contains all of the logic used to calculate and compare routes in an EIGRP network.

Figure 4-50 shows a simplified version of the DUAL FSM.

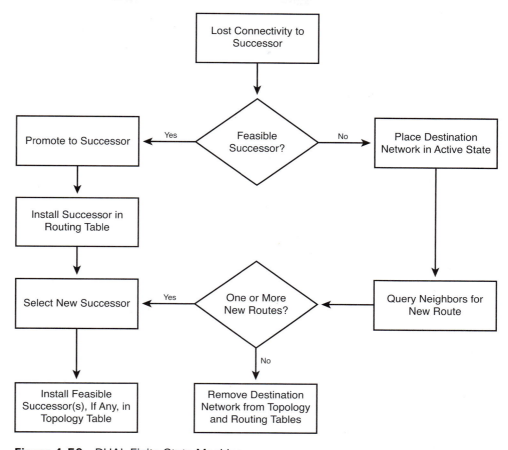

Figure 4-50   DUAL Finite State Machine

An FSM is an abstract machine, not a mechanical device with moving parts. FSMs define a set of possible states that something can go through, what events cause those states, and what events result from those states. Designers use FSMs to describe how a device, computer program, or routing algorithm reacts to a set of input events.

FSMs are beyond the scope of this course; however, the concept is used to examine some of the output from EIGRP's FSM using the **debug eigrp fsm** command. Use this command to examine what DUAL does when a route is removed from the routing table.

DUAL: Feasible Successor (4.3.4.2)

R2 is currently using R3 as the successor to 192.168.1.0/24. In addition, R2 currently lists R1 as an FS, as shown in Figure 4-51.

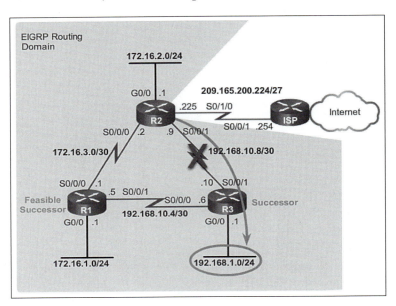

Figure 4-51   EIGRP for IPv4 Topology

The **show ip eigrp topology** output for R2 in Figure 4-52 verifies that R3 is the successor and R1 is the FS for the 192.168.1.0/24 network. To understand how DUAL can use an FS when the path using the successor is no longer available, a link failure is simulated between R2 and R3.

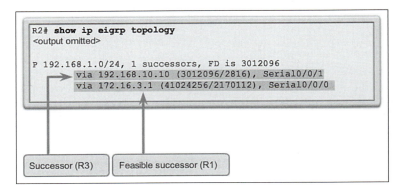

Figure 4-52   R2's Topology Table Entry for 192.168.1.0/24

Before simulating the failure, DUAL debugging must be enabled using the **debug eigrp fsm** command on R2, as shown next. A link failure is simulated using the **shutdown** command on the Serial 0/0/1 interface on R2.

```
R2# debug eigrp fsm
EIGRP Finite State Machine debugging is on
R2# conf t
Enter configuration commands, one per line.  End with CNTL/Z.
R2(config)# interface s 0/0/1
R2(config-if)# shutdown
<Output omitted>
EIGRP-IPv4(1):Find FS for dest 192.168.1.0/24. FD is 3012096, RD is 3012096 on tid 0
DUAL: AS(1) Removing dest 172.16.1.0/24, nexthop 192.168.10.10
DUAL: AS(1) RT installed 172.16.1.0/24 via 172.16.3.1
<Output omitted>
R2(config-if)# end
R2# undebug all
```

The **debug** output displays the activity generated by DUAL when a link goes down. R2 must inform all EIGRP neighbors of the lost link, as well as update its own routing and topology tables. This example only shows selected **debug** output. In particular, notice that the DUAL FSM searches for and finds an FS for the route in the EIGRP topology table.

The FS R1 now becomes the successor and is installed in the routing table as the new best path to 192.168.1.0/24, as shown in Figure 4-53. With an FS, this change in the routing table happens almost immediately.

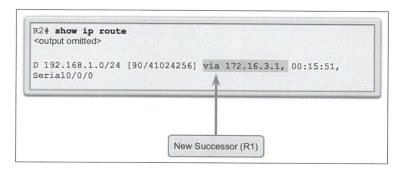

Figure 4-53   R2's Routing Table Entry for 192.168.1.0/24

As shown in Figure 4-54, the topology table for R2 now shows R1 as the successor and there are no new FSs. If the link between R2 and R3 is made active again, then R3 returns as the successor and R1 once again becomes the FS.

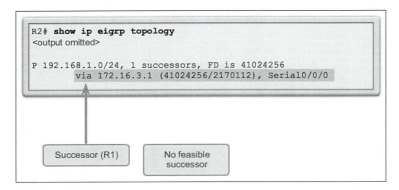

Figure 4-54   R2's Topology Table Entry for 192.168.1.0/24 without a Feasible Successor

DUAL: No Feasible Successor (4.3.4.3)

Occasionally, the path to the successor fails and there are not any FSs. In this instance, DUAL does not have a guaranteed loop-free backup path to the network, so the path is not in the topology table as an FS. If there are not any FSs in the topology table, DUAL puts the network into the active state. DUAL actively queries its neighbors for a new successor.

R1 is currently using R3 as the successor to 192.168.1.0/24, as shown in Figure 4-55. However, R1 does not have R2 listed as an FS, because R2 does not satisfy the FC. To understand how DUAL searches for a new successor when there is no FS, a link failure is simulated between R1 and R3.

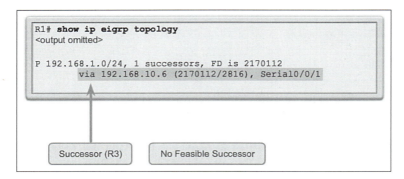

Figure 4-55   R1's Topology Table Entry for 192.168.1.0/24 with no Feasible Successor

Before the link failure is simulated, DUAL debugging is enabled with the **debug eigrp fsm** command on R1, as shown in the following output. A link failure is simulated using the **shutdown** command on the Serial 0/0/1 interface on R1.

```
R1# debug eigrp fsm
EIGRP Finite State Machine debugging is on
R1# conf t
```

```
Enter configuration commands, one per line.  End with CNTL/Z.
R1(config)# interface s 0/0/1
R1(config-if)# shutdown
<Output omitted>
EIGRP-IPv4(1): Find FS for dest 192.168.1.0/24. FD is 2170112, RD is 2170112
DUAL: AS(1) Dest 192.168.1.0/24 entering active state for tid 0.
EIGRP-IPv4(1): dest(192.168.1.0/24) active
EIGRP-IPv4(1): rcvreply: 192.168.1.0/24 via 172.16.3.2 metric 41024256/3012096 EIGRP-
    IPv4(1): reply count is 1
EIGRP-IPv4(1): Find FS for dest 192.168.1.0/24. FD is 72057594037927935, RD is
    72057594037927935
DUAL: AS(1) Removing dest 192.168.1.0/24, nexthop 192.168.10.6
DUAL: AS(1) RT installed 192.168.1.0/24 via 172.16.3.2
<Output omitted>
R1(config-if)# end
R1# undebug all
```

When the successor is no longer available and there is no feasible successor, DUAL puts the route into an active state. DUAL sends EIGRP queries asking other routers for a path to the network. Other routers return EIGRP replies, letting the sender of the EIGRP query know whether or not they have a path to the requested network. If none of the EIGRP replies have a path to this network, the sender of the query does not have a route to this network.

The selected debug output in Figure 4-56 shows the 192.168.1.0/24 network put into the active state and EIGRP queries sent to other neighbors. R2 replies with a path to this network, which becomes the new successor and is installed into the routing table.

If the sender of the EIGRP queries receives EIGRP replies that include a path to the requested network, the preferred path is added as the new successor and added to the routing table. This process takes longer than if DUAL had an FS in its topology table and was able to quickly add the new route to the routing table. In Figure 4-56, notice that R1 has a new route to the 192.168.1.0/24 network. The new EIGRP successor is router R2.

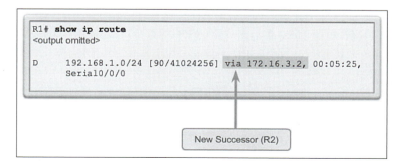

Figure 4-56   R1's Routing Table Entry for 192.168.1.0/24 with New Successor

Figure 4-57 shows that the topology table for R1 now has R2 as the successor with no new FSs. If the link between R1 and R3 is made active again, R3 returns as the successor. However, R2 is still not the FS, because it does not meet the FC.

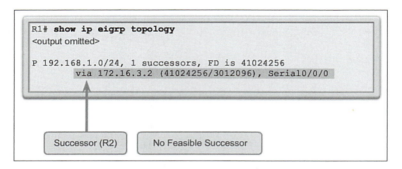

```
R1# show ip eigrp topology
<output omitted>

P 192.168.1.0/24, 1 successors, FD is 41024256
            via 172.16.3.2 (41024256/3012096), Serial0/0/0
```

Successor (R2)   No Feasible Successor

Figure 4-57   R1's Topology Table Entry for 192.168.1.0/24 with New Successor

Packet Tracer Activity 4.3.4.4: Investigating DUAL FSM

In this activity, you will modify the EIGRP metric formula to cause a change in the topology. This allows you to see how EIGRP reacts when a neighbor goes down due to unforeseen circumstances. You will then use the **debug** command to view topology changes and how the DUAL Finite State Machine determines successor and feasible successor paths to re-converge the network.

Configuring EIGRP for IPv6 (4.4)

The commands used to configure EIGRP for IPv6 are similar to the commands used to configure EIGRP for IPv4. DUAL and other operations are the same in both routing protocols, except for some variations such as the use of link-local addresses with IPv6.

EIGRP for IPv4 vs. IPv6 (4.4.1)

This section focuses on the similarities and differences between EIGRP for IPv4 and EIGRP for IPv6.

EIGRP for IPv6 (4.4.1.1)

Similar to its IPv4 counterpart, EIGRP for IPv6 exchanges routing information to populate the IPv6 routing table with remote prefixes. EIGRP for IPv6 was made available in Cisco IOS Release 12.4(6)T.

> **Note**
>
> In IPv6, the network address is referred to as the prefix and the subnet mask is called the prefix length.

EIGRP for IPv4 runs over the IPv4 network layer, communicating with other EIGRP IPv4 peers, and advertising only IPv4 routes. EIGRP for IPv6 has the same functionality as EIGRP for IPv4, but uses IPv6 as the network layer transport, communicating with EIGRP for IPv6 peers and advertising IPv6 routes.

EIGRP for IPv6 also uses DUAL as the computation engine to guarantee loop-free paths and backup paths throughout the routing domain.

As with all IPv6 routing protocols, EIGRP for IPv6 has separate processes from its IPv4 counterpart. The processes and operations are basically the same as in the IPv4 routing protocol; however, they run independently. EIGRP for IPv4 and EIGRP for IPv6 each have separate EIGRP neighbor tables, EIGRP topology tables, and IP routing tables, as shown in Figure 4-58. EIGRP for IPv6 is a separate protocol-dependent module (PDM).

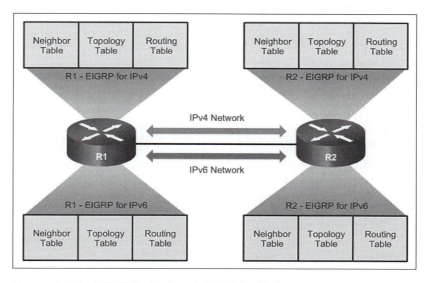

Figure 4-58   EIGRP for IPv4 and EIGRP for IPv6

The EIGRP for IPv6 configuration and verification commands are very similar to those used in EIGRP for IPv4. These commands are described later in this section.

Comparing EIGRP for IPv4 and IPv6 (4.4.1.2)

The following is a comparison of the main features of EIGRP for IPv4 and EIGRP for IPv6:

- **Advertised routes:** EIGRP for IPv4 advertises IPv4 networks, whereas EIGRP for IPv6 advertises IPv6 prefixes.

- **Distance vector:** Both EIGRP for IPv4 and EIGRP for IPv6 are advanced distance vector routing protocols. Both protocols use the same administrative distances.

- **Convergence technology:** EIGRP for IPv4 and EIGRP for IPv6 both use the DUAL algorithm. Both protocols use the same DUAL techniques and processes, including successor, FS, FD, and RD.

- **Metric:** Both EIGRP for IPv4 and EIGRP for IPv6 use bandwidth, delay, reliability, and load for their composite metric. Both routing protocols use the same composite metric and use only bandwidth and delay, by default.

- **Transport protocol:** The Reliable Transport Protocol (RTP) is responsible for guaranteed delivery of EIGRP packets to all neighbors for both protocols, EIGRP for IPv4 and EIGRP for IPv6.

- **Update messages:** Both EIGRP for IPv4 and EIGRP for IPv6 send incremental updates when the state of a destination changes. The terms *partial* and *bounded* are used when referring to updates for both protocols.

- **Neighbor discovery mechanism:** EIGRP for IPv4 and EIGRP for IPv6 use a simple Hello mechanism to learn about neighboring routers and form adjacencies.

- **Source and destination addresses:** EIGRP for IPv4 sends messages to the multicast address 224.0.0.10. These messages use the source IPv4 address of the outbound interface. EIGRP for IPv6 sends its messages to the multicast address FF02::A. EIGRP for IPv6 messages are sourced using the IPv6 link-local address of the exit interface.

- **Authentication:** EIGRP for IPv4 can use either plaintext authentication or Message Digest 5 (MD5) authentication. EIGRP for IPv6 uses MD5.

- **Router ID:** Both EIGRP for IPv4 and EIGRP for IPv6 use a 32-bit number for the EIGRP router ID. The 32-bit router ID is represented in dotted-decimal notation and is commonly referred to as an IPv4 address. If the EIGRP for IPv6 router has not been configured with an IPv4 address, the **eigrp router-id** command must be used to configure a 32-bit router ID. The process for determining the router ID is the same for both EIGRP for IPv4 and EIGRP for IPv6.

Table 4-5 summarizes the comparisons between EIGRP for IPv4 and EIGRP for IPv6.

Table 4-5   Comparing EIGRP for IPv4 and EIGRP for IPv6

	EIGRP for IPv4	**EIGRP for IPv6**
Advertised Routes	IPv4 networks	IPv6 prefixes
Distance Vector	Yes	Yes
Convergence Technology	DUAL	DUAL
Metric	Bandwidth and delay by default, reliability and load are optional	Bandwidth and delay by default, reliability and load are optional
Transport Protocol	RTP	RTP
Update Messages	Incremental, partial, and bounded updates	Incremental, partial, and bounded updates
Neighbor Discovery	Hello packets	Hello packets
Source and Destination Addresses	IPv4 source address and 224.0.0.10 IPv4 multicast destination address	IPv6 link-local source address and FF02::A IPv6 multicast destination address
Authentication	Plain text and MD5	MD5
Router ID	32-bit router ID	32-bit router ID

IPv6 Link-local Addresses (4.4.1.3)

Routers running a dynamic routing protocol, such as EIGRP, exchange messages between neighbors on the same subnet or link. Routers only need to send and receive routing protocol messages with their directly connected neighbors. These messages are always sent from the source IP address of the router that is doing the forwarding.

IPv6 link-local addresses are ideal for this purpose. An IPv6 *link-local address* enables a device to communicate with other IPv6-enabled devices on the same link and only on that link (subnet). Packets with a source or destination link-local address cannot be routed beyond the link from where the packet originated.

As shown in Figure 4-59, EIGRP for IPv6 messages are sent using:

- **Source IPv6 address:** This is the IPv6 link-local address of the exit interface.

- **Destination IPv6 address:** When the packet needs to be sent to a multicast address, it is sent to the IPv6 multicast address FF02::A, the all-EIGRP-routers with link-local scope. If the packet can be sent as a unicast address, it is sent to the link-local address of the neighboring router.

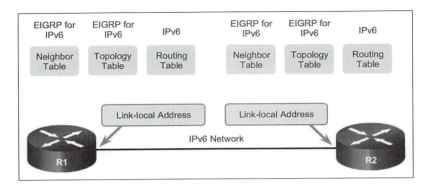

Figure 4-59   EIGRP for IPv6 and Link-local Addresses

Note

IPv6 link-local addresses are in the FE80::/10 range. The /10 indicates that the first 10 bits are 1111 1110 10xx xxxx, which results in the first hextet having a range of 1111 1110 1000 0000 (FE80) to 1111 1110 1011 1111 (FEBF).

Interactive Graphic

Activity 4.4.1.4: Compare EIGRPv4 and EIGRPv6

Go to the online course to perform this practice activity.

Configuring EIGRP for IPv6 (4.4.2)

The previous section introduced EIGRP for IPv6 and showed how it is similar to its EIGRP for IPv4 counterpart. This section demonstrates how configuring EIGRP for IPv6 is similar to configuring EIGRP for IPv4.

EIGRP for IPv6 Network Topology (4.4.2.1)

Figure 4-60 shows the network topology that is used for configuring EIGRP for IPv6. If the network is running dual-stack, using both IPv4 and IPv6 on all devices, EIGRP for both IPv4 and IPv6 can be configured on all the routers. However, in this section, the focus is solely on EIGRP for IPv6.

Only the IPv6 global unicast addresses have been configured on each router.

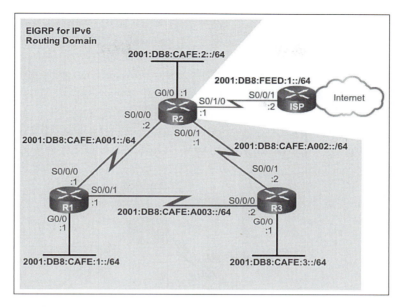

Figure 4-60   EIGRP for IPv6 Topology

The following output displays the starting interface configurations on each router. Notice the interface bandwidth values from the previous EIGRP for IPv4 configuration. Because EIGRP for IPv4 and EIGRP for IPv6 use the same metrics, modifying the bandwidth parameters influences both routing protocols.

```
R1# show running-config
<output omitted>>
!
interface GigabitEthernet0/0
 ipv6 address 2001:DB8:CAFE:1::1/64
!
interface Serial0/0/0
 ipv6 address 2001:DB8:CAFE:A001::1/64
 bandwidth 64
 clock rate 64000
!
interface Serial0/0/1
 ipv6 address 2001:DB8:CAFE:A003::1/64

R2# show running-config
<output omitted>>
!
interface GigabitEthernet0/0
 ipv6 address 2001:DB8:CAFE:2::1/64
!
```

```
interface Serial0/0/0
 ipv6 address 2001:DB8:CAFE:A001::2/64
 bandwidth 64

interface Serial0/0/1
 ipv6 address 2001:DB8:CAFE:A002::1/64
 bandwidth 1024
 clock rate 64000
!
interface Serial0/1/0
 ipv6 address 2001:DB8:FEED:1::1/64

R3# show running-config
<output omitted>>
!
interface GigabitEthernet0/0
 ipv6 address 2001:DB8:CAFE:3::1/64
!
interface Serial0/0/0
 ipv6 address 2001:DB8:CAFE:A003::2/64
 clock rate 64000
!
interface Serial0/0/1
 ipv6 address 2001:DB8:CAFE:A002::2/64
 bandwidth 1024
```

Configuring IPv6 Link-local Addresses (4.4.2.2)

Link-local addresses are automatically created when an IPv6 global unicast address is assigned to the interface. Global unicast addresses are not required on an interface; however, IPv6 link-local addresses are.

Unless configured manually, Cisco routers create the link-local address using the FE80::/10 prefix and the EUI-64 process. EUI-64 involves using the 48-bit Ethernet MAC address, inserting FFFE in the middle, and flipping the seventh bit. For serial interfaces, Cisco uses the MAC address of an Ethernet interface. A router with several serial interfaces can assign the same link-local address to each IPv6 interface, because link-local addresses only need to be local on the link.

Link-local addresses created using the EUI-64 format, or in some cases random interface IDs, make it difficult to recognize and remember those addresses. Because IPv6 routing protocols use IPv6 link-local addresses for unicast addressing and next-hop address information in the routing table, it is common practice to make it an easily recognizable address. Configuring the link-local address manually provides the ability to create an address that is recognizable and easier to remember.

Link-local addresses can be configured manually using the same interface configuration mode command used to create IPv6 global unicast addresses, but with different parameters:

```
Router(config-if)# ipv6 address link-local-address link-local
```

A link-local address has a prefix within the range FE80 to FEBF. When an address begins with this hextet (16-bit segment), the **link-local** keyword must follow the address.

The following shows the configuration of a link-local address using the **ipv6 address** interface configuration mode command. The link-local address FE80::1 is used to make it easily recognizable as belonging to router R1. The same IPv6 link-local address is configured on all of R1's interfaces. FE80::1 can be configured on each link because it only has to be unique on that link.

```
R1(config)# interface s 0/0/0
R1(config-if)# ipv6 address fe80::1 ?
  link-local  Use link-local address
R1(config-if)# ipv6 address fe80::1 link-local
R1(config-if)# exit
R1(config)# interface s 0/0/1
R1(config-if)# ipv6 address fe80::1 link-local
R1(config-if)# exit
R1(config)# interface g 0/0
R1(config-if)# ipv6 address fe80::1 link-local
R1(config-if)#
```

Similar to R1, as shown next, router R2 is configured with FE80::2 as the IPv6 link-local address on all of its interfaces:

```
R2(config)# interface s 0/0/0
R2(config-if)# ipv6 address fe80::2 link-local
R2(config-if)# exit
R2(config)# interface s 0/0/1
R2(config-if)# ipv6 address fe80::2 link-local
R2(config-if)# exit
R2(config)# interface s 0/1/0
R2(config-if)# ipv6 address fe80::2 link-local
R2(config-if)# exit
R2(config)# interface g 0/0
R2(config-if)# ipv6 address fe80::2 link-local
R2(config-if)#
```

Interactive Graphic

Activity 4.4.2.2: Configure IPv6 Link-local Addresses on Router R3

Go to the online course to use the Syntax Checker in the fourth graphic to configure R3's interfaces with the IPv6 link-local address FE80::3.

As shown in Figure 4-61, the **show ipv6 interface brief** command is used to verify the IPv6 link-local and global unicast addresses on all interfaces.

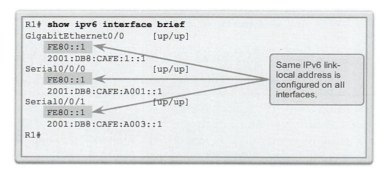

```
R1# show ipv6 interface brief
GigabitEthernet0/0      [up/up]
    FE80::1
    2001:DB8:CAFE:1::1
Serial0/0/0             [up/up]
    FE80::1
    2001:DB8:CAFE:A001::1
Serial0/0/1             [up/up]
    FE80::1
    2001:DB8:CAFE:A003::1
R1#
```

Same IPv6 link-local address is configured on all interfaces.

Figure 4-61   Verifying Link-local Addresses on R1

Configuring the EIGRP for IPv6 Routing Process (4.4.2.3)

The **ipv6 unicast-routing** global configuration mode command enables IPv6 routing on the router. This command is required before any IPv6 routing protocol can be configured. This command is not required to configure IPv6 addresses on the interfaces, but is necessary for the router to be enabled as an IPv6 router.

EIGRP for IPv6

The following global configuration mode command is used to enter router configuration mode for EIGRP for IPv6:

```
Router(config)# ipv6 router eigrp autonomous-system
```

Similar to EIGRP for IPv4, the *autonomous-system* value must be the same on all routers in the routing domain. The following shows that the EIGRP for IPv6 routing process could not be configured until IPv6 routing was enabled with the **ipv6 unicast-routing** global configuration mode command:

```
R1(config)# ipv6 router eigrp 2
% IPv6 routing not enabled
R1(config)# ipv6 unicast-routing
R1(config)# ipv6 router eigrp 2
R1(config-rtr)#
```

Router ID

The **eigrp router-id** command is used to configure the router ID, as shown next. EIGRP for IPv6 uses a 32-bit value for the router ID. To obtain that value, EIGRP for IPv6 uses the same process as EIGRP for IPv4. The **eigrp router-id** command takes precedence over any loopback or physical interface IPv4 addresses. If an EIGRP for IPv6 router does not have any active interfaces with an IPv4 address, then the **eigrp router-id** command is required.

```
R1(config)# ipv6 router eigrp 2
R1(config-rtr)# eigrp router-id 1.0.0.0
R1(config-rtr)#
```

The router ID should be a unique 32-bit number in the EIGRP for IP routing domain; otherwise, routing inconsistencies can occur.

Note

The **eigrp router-id** command is used to configure the router ID for EIGRP. Some versions of IOS will accept the command **router-id**, without first specifying **eigrp**. The running-config, however, will display **eigrp router-id** regardless of which command is used.

no shutdown Command

By default, the EIGRP for IPv6 process is in a shutdown state. The **no shutdown** command is required to activate the EIGRP for IPv6 process, as shown next. This command is not required for EIGRP for IPv4. Although EIGRP for IPv6 is enabled, neighbor adjacencies and routing updates cannot be sent and received until EIGRP is activated on the appropriate interfaces.

```
R1(config)# ipv6 router eigrp 2
R1(config-rtr)# eigrp router-id 1.0.0.0
R1(config-rtr)# no shutdown
R1(config-rtr)#
```

Both the **no shutdown** command and a router ID are required for the router to form neighbor adjacencies.

The following shows the complete EIGRP for IPv6 configuration for router R2:

```
R2(config)# ipv6 unicast-routing
R2(config)# ipv6 router eigrp 2
R2(config-rtr)# eigrp router-id 2.0.0.0
R2(config-rtr)# no shutdown
R2(config-rtr)#
```

Interactive Graphic

Activity 4.4.2.3: Enable EIGRP for IPv6 on Router R3

Go to the online course to use the Syntax Checker in the fifth graphic to enable EIGRP for IPv6 on R3.

ipv6 eigrp Interface Command (4.4.2.4)

EIGRP for IPv6 uses a different method to enable an interface for EIGRP. Instead of using the **network** router configuration mode command to specify matching interface addresses, EIGRP for IPv6 is configured directly on the interface.

Use the following interface configuration mode command to enable EIGRP for IPv6 on an interface:

```
Router(config-if)# ipv6 eigrp autonomous-system
```

The *autonomous-system* value must be the same as the autonomous system number used to enable the EIGRP routing process. Similar to the **network** command used in EIGRP for IPv4, the **ipv6 eigrp interface** command:

- Enables the interface to form adjacencies and send or receive EIGRP for IPv6 updates

- Includes the prefix (network) of this interface in EIGRP for IPv6 routing updates

The following shows the configuration to enable EIGRP for IPv6 on routers R1 and R2 interfaces. Notice the message following the Serial 0/0/0 interface in R2.

```
%DUAL-5-NBRCHANGE: EIGRP-IPv6 2: Neighbor FE80::1 (Serial0/0/0) is up: new adjacency
R1(config)# interface g0/0
R1(config-if)# ipv6 eigrp 2
R1(config-if)# exit
R1(config)# interface s 0/0/0
R1(config-if)# ipv6 eigrp 2
R1(config-if)# exit
R1(config)# interface s 0/0/1
R1(config-if)# ipv6 eigrp 2
R1(config-if)#


R2(config)# interface g 0/0
R2(config-if)# ipv6 eigrp 2
R2(config-if)# exit
R2(config)# interface s 0/0/0
R2(config-if)# ipv6 eigrp 2
R2(config-if)# exit
%DUAL-5-NBRCHANGE: EIGRP-IPv6 2: Neighbor FE80::1 (Serial0/0/0) is up: new adjacency
R2(config)# interface s 0/0/1
R2(config-if)# ipv6 eigrp 2
R2(config-if)#
```

This message indicates that R2 has now formed an EIGRP-IPv6 adjacency with the neighbor at link-local address FE80::1. Because static link-local addresses were configured on all three routers, it is easy to determine that this adjacency is with router R1 (FE80::1).

Interactive Graphic

Activity 4.4.2.4: Enable EIGRP for IPv6 on the Interface

Go to the online course to use the Syntax Checker in the second graphic to enable EIGRP for IPv6 on R3's interfaces.

Passive Interface with EIGRP for IPv6

The same **passive-interface** command used for IPv4 is used to configure an interface as passive with EIGRP for IPv6. As shown next, the **show ipv6 protocols** command is used to verify the configuration:

```
R1(config)# ipv6 router eigrp 2
R1(config-rtr)# passive-interface gigabitethernet 0/0
R1(config-rtr)# end

R1# show ipv6 protocols

IPv6 Routing Protocol is "eigrp 2"
EIGRP-IPv6 Protocol for AS(2)
<Output omitted>

  Interfaces:
    Serial0/0/0
    Serial0/0/1
    GigabitEthernet0/0 (passive)
  Redistribution:
    None
R1#
```

Verifying EIGRP for IPv6 (4.4.3)

Verifying EIGRP for IPv6 requires using similar commands to those used to verify EIGRP for IPv4.

Verifying EIGRP for IPv6: Examining Neighbors (4.4.3.1)

Similar to EIGRP for IPv4, before any EIGRP for IPv6 updates can be sent or received, routers must establish adjacencies with their neighbors, as shown in Figure 4-62.

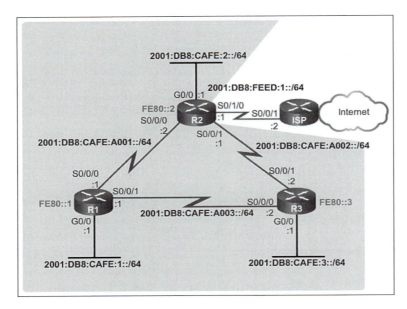

Figure 4-62   EIGRP for IPv6 Topology

Use the **show ipv6 eigrp neighbors** command to view the neighbor table and verify
that EIGRP for IPv6 has established an adjacency with its neighbors. The output shown
in Figure 4-63 displays the IPv6 link-local address of the adjacent neighbor and the
interface that this router uses to reach that EIGRP neighbor. Using meaningful link-local
addresses makes it easy to recognize the neighbors R2 at FE80::2 and R3 at FE80::3.

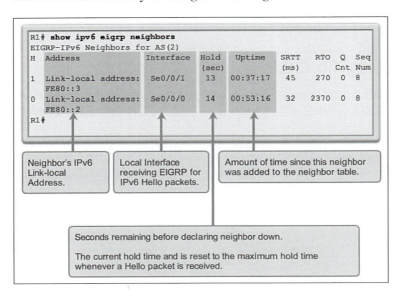

Figure 4-63   **show ipv6 eigrp neighbors** Command

The output from the **show ipv6 eigrp neighbors** command includes:

- **H column:** Lists the neighbors in the order they were learned.

- **Address:** IPv6 link-local address of the neighbor.

- **Interface:** Local interface on which this Hello packet was received.

- **Hold:** Current hold time. When a Hello packet is received, this value is reset to the maximum hold time for that interface and then counts down to zero. If zero is reached, the neighbor is considered down.

- **Uptime:** Amount of time since this neighbor was added to the neighbor table.

- **SRTT and RTO:** Used by RTP to manage reliable EIGRP packets.

- **Queue Count:** Should always be zero. If it is more than zero, then EIGRP packets are waiting to be sent.

- **Sequence Number:** Used to track updates, queries, and reply packets.

The **show ipv6 eigrp neighbors** command is useful for verifying and troubleshooting EIGRP for IPv6. If an expected neighbor is not listed, ensure that both ends of the link are up/up using the **show ipv6 interface brief** command. The same requirements exist for establishing neighbor adjacencies with EIGRP for IPv6 as it does with EIGRP for IPv4. If both sides of the link have active interfaces, check to see:

- Are both routers configured with the same EIGRP autonomous system number?

- Is the interface enabled for EIGRP for IPv6 with the correct autonomous system number?

Verifying EIGRP for IPv6: show ip protocols Command (4.4.3.2)

The **show ipv6 protocols** command displays the parameters and other information about the state of any active IPv6 routing protocol processes currently configured on the router. The **show ipv6 protocols** command displays different types of output specific to each IPv6 routing protocol.

The output in Figure 4-64 indicates several EIGRP for IPv6 parameters previously discussed, including:

1. EIGRP for IPv6 is an active dynamic routing protocol on R1 configured with the autonomous system number 2.

2. These are the k values used to calculate the EIGRP composite metric. K1 and K3 are 1, by default, and K2, K4, and K5 are 0, by default.

3. The EIGRP for IPv6 router ID of R1 is 1.0.0.0.

4. Same as EIGRP for IPv4, EIGRP for IPv6 administrative distances have internal AD of 90 and external AD of 170 (default values).

5. The interfaces enabled for EIGRP for IPv6.

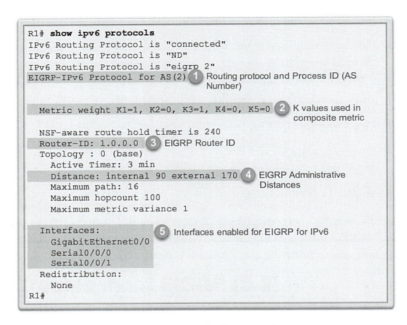

Figure 4-64   show ipv6 protocols Command

The output from the **show ipv6 protocols** command is useful in debugging routing operations. The Interfaces section shows on which interfaces EIGRP for IPv6 has been enabled. This is useful in verifying that EIGRP is enabled on all of the appropriate interfaces with the correct autonomous system number.

Verifying EIGRP for IPv6: Examine the IPv6 Routing Table (4.4.3.3)

As with any routing protocol, the goal is to populate the IP routing table with routes to remote networks and the best paths to reaching those networks. As with IPv4, it is important to examine the IPv6 routing table and determine whether it is populated with the correct routes.

The IPv6 routing table is examined using the **show ipv6 route** command. EIGRP for IPv6 routes are denoted in the routing table with a D, similar to its counterpart for IPv4.

The following output shows that R1 has installed three EIGRP routes to remote IPv6 networks in its IPv6 routing table:

- 2001:DB8:CAFE:2::/64 via R3 (FE80::3) using its Serial 0/0/1 interface

- 2001:DB8:CAFE:3::/64 via R3 (FE80::3) using its Serial 0/0/1 interface

- 2001:DB8:CAFE:A002::/64 via R3 (FE80::3) using its Serial 0/0/1 interface

```
R1# show ipv6 route
<Output omitted>
C    2001:DB8:CAFE:1::/64 [0/0]
     via GigabitEthernet0/0, directly connected
L    2001:DB8:CAFE:1::1/128 [0/0]
     via GigabitEthernet0/0, receive
D    2001:DB8:CAFE:2::/64 [90/3524096]
     via FE80::3, Serial0/0/1
D    2001:DB8:CAFE:3::/64 [90/2170112]
     via FE80::3, Serial0/0/1
C    2001:DB8:CAFE:A001::/64 [0/0]
     via Serial0/0/0, directly connected
L    2001:DB8:CAFE:A001::1/128 [0/0]
     via Serial0/0/0, receive
D    2001:DB8:CAFE:A002::/64 [90/3523840]
     via FE80::3, Serial0/0/1
C    2001:DB8:CAFE:A003::/64 [0/0]
     via Serial0/0/1, directly connected
L    2001:DB8:CAFE:A003::1/128 [0/0]
     via Serial0/0/1, receive
L    FF00::/8 [0/0]
     via Null0, receive
R1#
```

All three routes are using router R3 as the next-hop router (successor). Notice that the routing table uses the link-local address as the next-hop address. Because each router has had all its interfaces configured with a unique and distinguishable link-local address, it is easy to recognize that the next-hop router via FE80::3 is router R3.

The following output displays the IPv6 routing table for R2:

```
R2# show ipv6 route
<Output omitted>
D    2001:DB8:CAFE:1::/64 [90/3524096]
     via FE80::3, Serial0/0/1
C    2001:DB8:CAFE:2::/64 [0/0]
     via GigabitEthernet0/0, directly connected
L    2001:DB8:CAFE:2::1/128 [0/0]
     via GigabitEthernet0/0, receive
```

```
D    2001:DB8:CAFE:3::/64 [90/3012096]
     via FE80::3, Serial0/0/1
C    2001:DB8:CAFE:A001::/64 [0/0]
     via Serial0/0/0, directly connected
L    2001:DB8:CAFE:A001::2/128 [0/0]
     via Serial0/0/0, receive
C    2001:DB8:CAFE:A002::/64 [0/0]
     via Serial0/0/1, directly connected
L    2001:DB8:CAFE:A002::1/128 [0/0]
     via Serial0/0/1, receive
D    2001:DB8:CAFE:A003::/64 [90/3523840]
     via FE80::3, Serial0/0/1
C    2001:DB8:FEED:1::/64 [0/0]
     via Loopback6, directly connected
L    2001:DB8:FEED:1::1/128 [0/0]
     via Loopback6, receive
L    FF00::/8 [0/0]
     via Null0, receive
R2#
```

The following output displays the routing table for R3. Notice that R3 has two equal cost paths to the 2001:DB8:CAFE:A001::/64. One path is via R1 at FE80::1 and the other path is via R2 at FE80::2.

```
R3# show ipv6 route
<Output omitted>
D    2001:DB8:CAFE:1::/64 [90/2170112]
     via FE80::1, Serial0/0/0
D    2001:DB8:CAFE:2::/64 [90/3012096]
     via FE80::2, Serial0/0/1
C    2001:DB8:CAFE:3::/64 [0/0]
     via GigabitEthernet0/0, directly connected
L    2001:DB8:CAFE:3::1/128 [0/0]
     via GigabitEthernet0/0, receive
D    2001:DB8:CAFE:A001::/64 [90/41024000]
     via FE80::1, Serial0/0/0
     via FE80::2, Serial0/0/1
C    2001:DB8:CAFE:A002::/64 [0/0]
     via Serial0/0/1, directly connected
L    2001:DB8:CAFE:A002::2/128 [0/0]
     via Serial0/0/1, receive
C    2001:DB8:CAFE:A003::/64 [0/0]
     via Serial0/0/0, directly connected
L    2001:DB8:CAFE:A003::2/128 [0/0]
     via Serial0/0/0, receive
```

```
L    FF00::/8 [0/0]
        via Null0, receive
R3#
```

Packet Tracer Activity 4.4.3.4: Configuring Basic EIGRP for IPv6

In this activity, you will configure the network with EIGRP routing for IPv6. You will also assign router IDs, configure passive interfaces, verify the network is fully converged, and display routing information using **show** commands.

EIGRP for IPv6 has the same overall operation and features as EIGRP for IPv4. There are a few major differences between them:

- EIGRP for IPv6 is configured directly on the router interfaces.
- With EIGRP for IPv6, a router ID is required on each router or the routing process does not start.
- The EIGRP for IPv6 routing process uses a shutdown feature.

Lab 4.4.3.5: Configuring Basic EIGRP for IPv6

In this lab, you will complete the following objectives:

- Part 1: Build the Network and Verify Connectivity
- Part 2: Configure EIGRP for IPv6 Routing
- Part 3: Verify EIGRP for IPv6 Routing
- Part 4: Configure and Verify Passive Interfaces

Summary (4.5)

Class Activity 4.5.1.1: Portfolio RIP and EIGRP

Scenario

You are preparing a portfolio file for comparison of RIP and EIGRP routing protocols.

Think of a network with three interconnected routers with each router providing a LAN for PCs, printers, and other end devices.

In this modeling activity scenario, you will be creating, addressing, and configuring a topology, using verification commands, and comparing/contrasting RIP and EIGRP routing protocol outputs.

Complete the PDF reflection questions accompanying this activity. Save your work and be prepared to share your answers with the class. Also save a copy of your work for later use within this course or for portfolio reference.

EIGRP (Enhanced Interior Gateway Routing Protocol) is a classless, distance vector routing protocol. EIGRP is an enhancement of another Cisco routing protocol, IGRP (Interior Gateway Routing Protocol), which is now obsolete. EIGRP was initially released in 1992 as a Cisco proprietary protocol available only on Cisco devices. In 2013, Cisco released basic functionality of EIGRP as an open standard, to the IETF.

EIGRP uses the source code of "D" for DUAL in the routing table. EIGRP has a default administrative distance of 90 for internal routes and 170 for routes imported from an external source, such as default routes.

EIGRP is an advanced distance vector routing protocol that includes features not found in other distance vector routing protocols like RIP. These features include: Diffusing Update Algorithm (DUAL), establishing neighbor adjacencies, Reliable Transport Protocol (RTP), partial and bounded updates, and equal and unequal cost load balancing.

EIGRP uses PDMs (protocol-dependent modules), giving it the capability to support different Layer 3 protocols including IPv4 and IPv6. EIGRP uses RTP as the transport layer protocol for the delivery of EIGRP packets. EIGRP uses reliable delivery for EIGRP updates, queries, and replies, and uses unreliable delivery for EIGRP Hellos and acknowledgments. Reliable RTP means an EIGRP acknowledgment must be returned.

Before any EIGRP updates are sent, a router must first discover its neighbors. This is done with EIGRP Hello packets. The Hello and hold-down values do not need to match for two routers to become neighbors. The **show ip eigrp neighbors** command is used to view the neighbor table and verify that EIGRP for IPv4 has established an adjacency with its neighbors.

EIGRP does not send periodic updates like RIP. EIGRP sends partial or bounded updates, which includes only the route changes and only to those routers that are affected by the change. The EIGRP composite metric uses bandwidth, delay, reliability, and load to determine the best path. By default only bandwidth and delay are used.

At the center of EIGRP is DUAL (Diffusing Update Algorithm). The DUAL Finite State Machine is used to determine best path and potential backup paths to every destination network. The successor is a neighboring router that is used to forward the packet using the least-cost route to the destination network. Feasible distance (FD) is the lowest calculated metric to reach the destination network through the successor. A feasible successor (FS) is a neighbor who has a loop-free backup path to the same network as the successor, and also meets the feasibility condition. The feasibility condition (FC) is met when a neighbor's reported distance (RD) to a network is less than the local router's feasible distance to the same destination network. The reported distance is simply an EIGRP neighbor's feasible distance to the destination network.

EIGRP for IPv4 is configured with the **router eigrp** *autonomous-system* command. The autonomous-system value is actually a process ID and must be the same on all routers in the EIGRP routing domain. The EIGRP for IPv4 **network** command is similar to the same command used with RIP. The network is the classful network address of the directly connected interfaces on the router. A wildcard mask is an optional parameter that can be used to include only specific interfaces.

EIGRP for IPv6 is configured with the **ipv6 router eigrp** *autonomous-system* command. Instead of the **network** command, EIGRP for IPv6 is configured directly on the interface using the **ipv6 eigrp** *autonomous-system* command.

Practice

The following activities provide practice with the topics introduced in this chapter. The Labs and Class Activities are available in the companion *Routing Protocols Lab Manual* (978-1-58713-322-0). The Packet Tracer Activities PKA files are found in the online course.

Class Activities

Class Activity 4.0.1.2: Classless EIGRP

Class Activity 4.5.1.1: Portfolio RIP and EIGRP

Labs

Lab 4.2.2.5: Configuring Basic EIGRP for IPv4

Lab 4.4.3.5: Configuring Basic EIGRP for IPv6

Packet Tracer
☐ **Activity**

Packet Tracer Activities

Packet Tracer Activity 4.2.2.4: Configure Basic EIGRP for IPv4

Packet Tracer Activity 4.3.4.4: Investigating DUAL FSM

Packet Tracer Activity 4.4.3.4: Configuring Basic EIGRP for IPv6

Check Your Understanding Questions

Complete all the review questions listed here to test your understanding of the topics and concepts in this chapter. The appendix, "Answers to the 'Check Your Understanding' Questions," lists the answers.

1. What is the purpose of the EIGRP PDM?

    A. The PDM is the Layer 4 protocol EIGRP uses to share routing information.

    B. The PDM is the mechanism that EIGRP uses to ensure the availability of neighboring routers.

    C. The PDM is the algorithm engine used by EIGRP to create routing tables.

    D. The PDM provides modular support for Layer 3 protocols.

    E. The PDM is the distance to a destination as reported by a neighboring router.

2. Match the EIGRP terms and concepts with their correct descriptions.

    Terms and concepts:
        Neighbor table
        Topology table
        Routing table
        Successor
        Feasible successor router

    Descriptions:

    A. Contains the EIGRP routes to be used for packet forwarding

    B. The primary route to be used; selected by DUAL

    C. Important EIGRP data source; lists adjacent routers

    D. Backup path to a destination network

    E. Contains all learned routes to all destination networks

3. What type of EIGRP packet is used to discover, verify, and rediscover neighboring routers?

    A. Acknowledgment

    B. Hello

    C. Query

    D. Reply

4. If an EIGRP route goes down and a feasible successor is not found in the topology table, how does DUAL flag the route that has failed?

    A. Recomputed

    B. Passive

    C. Active

    D. Down

    E. Unreachable

    F. Successor

5. Which of the following tables does a router running EIGRP maintain? (Choose three.)

    A. DUAL table

    B. Feasible distance table

    C. Neighbor table

    D. OSPF table

    E. Routing table

    F. Topology table

6. What is the purpose of the EIGRP neighbor and topology tables?

  A. The neighbor and topology tables are used by DUAL to build the routing table.

  B. The neighbor table is sent to all neighboring routers, which use it to build topology tables.

  C. The topology table is sent to all routers listed in the neighbor table.

  D. The neighbor table is used by DUAL to create the topology table.

  E. The neighbor table is broadcast to neighbor routers, and the topology table is broadcast to all other routers.

7. Refer to the following output. What does the 255/255 value in the output represent?

```
R1# show interface serial 0/0/0
Serial0/0/0 is up, line protocol is up
   Hardware is GT96K Serial
   Description: Link to R2
   Internet address is 172.16.3.1/30
   MTU 1500 bytes, BW 1544 Kbit, DLY 20000 usec,
      Reliability 255/255, txload 1/255, rxload 1/255
   Encapsulation HDLC, loopback not set
```

  A. The number of times that the link was operational during 255 polls

  B. The link failure rate over 255 seconds

  C. The probability that the link will continue to be operational

  D. A static value representing the normal reliability of an interface type

8. Match the EIGRP term with its correct description.

Terms:
  Feasible successor
  Successor
  Feasible distance
  Routing table
  Topology table

Definitions:

  A. A viable backup path to a network

  B. A route that is used for packet forwarding and is the least-cost route

  C. The lowest calculated metric to reach the destination network

  D. A table that contains successors and feasible successors

  E. A table that contains only successors

9. A network administrator is troubleshooting an EIGRP for IPv4 routing issue. What command will show the administrator all possible paths to a destination?

   A. **show ip route**

   B. **show ip eigrp topology active**

   C. **show ip eigrp neighbors detail**

   D. **show ip eigrp topology all-links**

   E. **show ip eigrp topology summary**

10. Refer to the following output. What reported distance is the feasible successor to network 192.168.1.0 advertising?

```
R1# show ip eigrp topology

<output omitted>

P   192.168.10.0/24, 1 successors, FD is 3011840
          via Summary (3011840/0), Null0
          via 172.16.3.1 (41024000/2169856), Serial0/0/0
P   192.168.10.4/30, 1 successors, FD is 3523840
          via 192.168.10.10 (3253840/2169856), Serial0/0/1
P   192.168.1.0/24, 1 successors, FD is 3014400
          via 192.168.10.10 (3014400/28160), Serial0/0/1
          via 172.16.3.1 (41026560/2172416), Serial0/0/0
<output omitted>
```

   A. 28160

   B. 3014400

   C. 2172416

   D. 41026560

11. What routing algorithm does EIGRP use?

12. Does EIGRP send periodic updates? Explain your answer.

13. What command enables you to verify that EIGRP for IPv6 has established relationships with its directly connected neighbors?

14. What metrics does the EIGRP composite metric use? Which ones are used by default?

15. What is the feasibility condition?

16. Which set of commands are used to enable EIGRP AS 1 on the GigabitEthernet 0/0 interface with the IPv6 address 2001:DB8:ABCD:1::1/64?

   A. Router(config)# **ipv6 router eigrp 1**

       Router(config-rtr)# **network 2001:DB8:ABCD:1::1/64**

   B. Router(config)# **ipv6 router eigrp 1**

       Router(config-rtr)# **interface g 0/0**

   C. Router(config)# **interface g 0/0**

       Router(config-if)# **network 2001:DB8:ABCD:1::1/64**

   D. Router(config)# **interface g 0/0**

       Router(config-if)# **ipv6 eigrp 1**

17. When is it required to configure a router ID using the **eigrp router-id** command for EIGRP for IPv6?

   A. It is always required.

   B. Never; the router ID is not required for EIGRP for IPv6 or EIGRP for IPv4.

   C. It is required if the router does not have any active interfaces with an IPv4 address.

   D. It is not required because the router will use either an IPv6 loopback address or an IPv6 address on a physical interface.

CHAPTER 5

EIGRP Advanced Configurations and Troubleshooting

Objectives

Upon completion of this chapter, you will be able to answer the following questions:

- How is EIGRP configured for automatic summarization?

- How do you configure manual summarization?

- What are the commands to configure a router to propagate a default route in an EIGRP network?

- What are the commands used to modify EIGRP interface settings to improve network performance?

- How is EIGRP authentication configured to ensure secure routing updates?

- What processes and tools are used to troubleshoot an EIGRP network?

- How do you troubleshoot neighbor adjacency issues in an EIGRP network?

- What is the process to troubleshoot missing route entries in an EIGRP routing table?

Key Terms

This chapter uses the following key terms. You can find the definitions in the Glossary.

auto-summarization   *page 335*

border router   *page 337*

Null0 summary route   *page 345*

equal cost load balancing   *page 361*

Message Digest 5 (MD5) authentication
page 364

Introduction (5.0.1.1)

EIGRP is a versatile routing protocol that can be fine-tuned in many ways. Two of the most important tuning capabilities are the ability to summarize routes and the ability to implement load balancing. Other tuning capabilities include being able to propagate a default, fine-tune timers, and implement authentication between EIGRP neighbors to increase security.

This chapter discusses these additional tuning features and the configuration mode commands to implement these features for both IPv4 and IPv6.

Class Activity 5.0.1.2: EIGRP – Back to the Future

Scenario

This chapter teaches you how to maintain your EIGRP networks and to influence them to do what you want them to do. EIGRP concepts from this chapter include:

- Auto-summarization
- Load balancing
- Default routes
- Hold timers
- Authentication

With a partner, write 10 EIGRP review questions based on the previous chapter's curriculum content. Three of the questions must focus on these bulleted items. Ideally, Multiple Choice, True/False, or Fill in the Blank question types will be designed. As you design your questions, ensure that you record the curriculum section and page numbers of the supporting content in case you need to refer back for answer verification.

Save your work and then meet with another group, or the entire class, and quiz them using the questions you developed.

Advanced EIGRP Configurations (5.1)

This section discusses the commands used for EIGRP automatic route summarization, manual route summarization, propagating default routes, and EIGRP fine-tuning.

Auto-summarization (5.1.1)

EIGRP for IPv4 *auto-summarization* is the process of automatically summarizing networks at major classful boundaries. Auto-summarization is no longer the default, beginning with Cisco IOS Release 15.0(1)M and 12.2(33).

Network Topology (5.1.1.1)

To configure tuning features of EIGRP, it is necessary to start with a basic implementation of EIGRP.

Figure 5-1 shows the network topology used for this chapter.

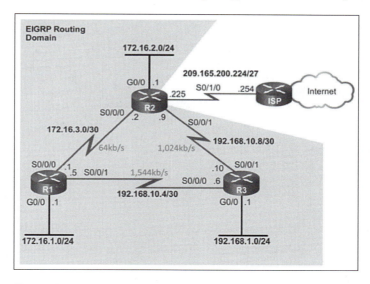

Figure 5-1   EIGRP for IPv4 Topology

The following output shows the IPv4 interface configurations and the EIGRP implementations on R1, R2, and R3, respectively.

```
R1# show running-config
<Output omitted>
version 15.2
!
interface GigabitEthernet0/0
 ip address 172.16.1.1 255.255.255.0
!
interface Serial0/0/0
 bandwidth 64
 ip address 172.16.3.1 255.255.255.252
 clock rate 64000
```

```
!
interface Serial0/0/1
 ip address 192.168.10.5 255.255.255.252
!
router eigrp 1
 network 172.16.0.0
 network 192.168.10.0
 eigrp router-id 1.1.1.1

R2# show running-config
<Output omitted>
version 15.2
!
interface GigabitEthernet0/0
 ip address 172.16.2.1 255.255.255.0
!
interface Serial0/0/0
 bandwidth 64
 ip address 172.16.3.2 255.255.255.252
!
interface Serial0/0/1
 bandwidth 1024
 ip address 192.168.10.9 255.255.255.252
 clock rate 64000
!
interface Serial0/1/0
 ip address 209.165.200.225 255.255.255.224
!
router eigrp 1
 network 172.16.0.0
 network 192.168.10.8 0.0.0.3
 eigrp router-id 2.2.2.2

R3# show running-config
<Output omitted>
version 15.2
!
interface GigabitEthernet0/0
 ip address 192.168.1.1 255.255.255.0
!
interface Serial0/0/0
 ip address 192.168.10.6 255.255.255.252
 clock rate 64000
!
interface Serial0/0/1
```

```
bandwidth 1024
 ip address 192.168.10.10 255.255.255.252
 !
router eigrp 1
 network 192.168.1.0
 network 192.168.10.4 0.0.0.3
 network 192.168.10.8 0.0.0.3
 eigrp router-id 3.3.3.3
```

The types of serial interfaces and their associated bandwidths may not necessarily reflect the more common types of connections found in networks today. The bandwidths of the serial links used in this topology help explain the calculation of the routing protocol metrics and the process of best path selection.

Notice that the **bandwidth** commands on the serial interfaces were used to modify the default bandwidth of 1,544 kb/s.

In this chapter, the ISP router is used as the routing domain's gateway to the Internet. All three routers are running Cisco IOS Release 15.2.

EIGRP Auto-summarization (5.1.1.2)

One of the most common tuning methods of EIGRP is enabling and disabling automatic route summarization. Route summarization allows a router to group networks together and advertise them as one large group using a single, summarized route. The ability to summarize routes is necessary due to the rapid growth of networks.

A *border router* is a router that sits at the edge of a network. This router must be able to advertise all of the known networks within its route table to a connecting network router or ISP router. This convergence can potentially result in very large route tables. Imagine if a single router had 10 different networks and had to advertise all 10 route entries to a connecting router. What if that connecting router also had 10 networks, and had to advertise all 20 routes to an ISP router? If every enterprise router followed this pattern, the routing table of the ISP router would be huge.

Summarization decreases the number of entries in routing updates and lowers the number of entries in local routing tables. It also reduces bandwidth utilization for routing updates and results in faster routing table lookups.

To limit the number of routing advertisements and the size of routing tables, routing protocols such as EIGRP use auto-summarization at classful boundaries. This means that EIGRP recognizes subnets as a single class A, B, or C network, and creates only one entry in the routing table for the summary route. As a result, all traffic destined for the subnets travels across that one path.

Figure 5-2 shows an example of how auto-summarization works. Routers R1 and R2 are both configured using EIGRP for IPv4 with auto-summarization. R1 has three subnets in its routing table: 172.16.1.0/24, 172.16.2.0/24, and 172.16.3.0/24. In the classful network addressing architecture, these subnets are all considered part of a larger class B network, 172.16.0.0/16. Because EIGRP on router R1 is configured for auto-summarization, when it sends its routing update to R2, it summarizes the three /24 subnets as a single network of 172.16.0.0/16, which reduces the number of routing updates sent and the number of entries in R2's IPv4 routing table.

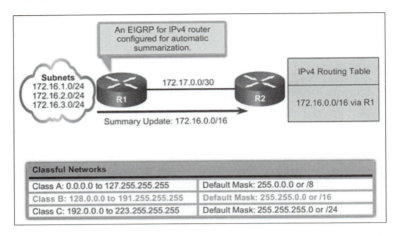

Figure 5-2   Automatic Summarization at Classful Network Boundary

All traffic destined for the three subnets travels across the one path. R2 does not maintain routes to individual subnets, and no subnet information is learned. In an enterprise network, the path chosen to reach the summary route may not be the best choice for the traffic that is trying to reach each individual subnet. The only way that all routers can find the best routes for each individual subnet is for neighbors to send subnet information. In this situation, auto-summarization should be disabled. When auto-summarization is disabled, updates include subnet information.

Configuring EIGRP Auto-summarization (5.1.1.3)

EIGRP for IPv4 auto-summarization is disabled by default beginning with Cisco IOS Release 15.0(1)M and 12.2(33). Prior to this, auto-summarization was enabled by default. This meant that EIGRP performed auto-summarization each time the EIGRP topology crossed a border between two different major class networks.

The following output from the **show ip protocols** command on R1 indicates that EIGRP auto-summarization is disabled. This router is running IOS 15.2; therefore, EIGRP auto-summarization is disabled by default.

```
R1# show ip protocols
*** IP Routing is NSF aware ***
Routing Protocol is "eigrp 1"
```

```
    Outgoing update filter list for all interfaces is not set
    Incoming update filter list for all interfaces is not set
    Default networks flagged in outgoing updates
    Default networks accepted from incoming updates
    EIGRP-IPv4 Protocol for AS(1)
      Metric weight K1=1, K2=0, K3=1, K4=0, K5=0
  <Output omitted>
    Automatic Summarization: disabled
    Maximum path: 4
    Routing for Networks:
      172.16.0.0
      192.168.10.0
  <Output omitted>
```

The following output shows the current routing table for R3. Notice that the IPv4 routing table for R3 contains all of the networks and subnets within the EIGRP routing domain.

```
R3# show ip route eigrp
<Output omitted>
  172.16.0.0/16 is variably subnetted, 3 subnets, 2 masks
D       172.16.1.0/24 [90/2170112] via 192.168.10.5, 02:21:10, Serial0/0/0
D       172.16.2.0/24 [90/3012096] via 192.168.10.9, 02:21:10, Serial0/0/1
D       172.16.3.0/30 [90/41024000] via 192.168.10.9, 02:21:10, Serial0/0/1
                      [90/41024000] via 192.168.10.5, 02:21:10, Serial0/0/0
R3#
```

To enable auto-summarization for EIGRP, use the **auto-summary** command in router configuration mode, as shown here:

```
R1(config)# router eigrp as-number
R1(config-router)# auto-summary
R1(config)# router eigrp 1
R1(config-router)# auto-summary
R1(config-router)#
*Mar  9 19:40:19.342: %DUAL-5-NBRCHANGE: EIGRP-IPv4 1: Neighbor 192.168.10.6
   (Serial0/0/1) is resync: summary configured
*Mar  9 19:40:19.342: %DUAL-5-NBRCHANGE: EIGRP-IPv4 1: Neighbor 192.168.10.6
   (Serial0/0/1) is resync: summary up, remove components
*Mar  9 19:41:03.630: %DUAL-5-NBRCHANGE: EIGRP-IPv4 1: Neighbor 192.168.10.6
   (Serial0/0/1) is resync: peer graceful-restart

R2(config)# router eigrp 1
R2(config-router)# auto-summary
R2(config-router)#
```

The **no** form of this command is used to disable auto-summarization.

Interactive Graphic

Activity 5.1.1.3: Configuring EIGRP Automatic Summarization on R3

Go to the online course to use the Syntax Checker in the fourth graphic to display the current EIGRP routing table on R3 prior to summarization.

Verifying Auto-Summary: **show ip protocols** (5.1.1.4)

In Figure 5-3, notice the EIGRP routing domain has three classful networks:

- 172.16.0.0/16 class B network consisting of 172.16.1.0/24, 172.16.2.0/24, and 172.16.3.0/30 subnets
- 192.168.10.0/24 class C network consisting of the 192.168.10.4/30 and 192.168.10.8/30 subnets
- 192.168.1.0/24 class C network, which is not subnetted

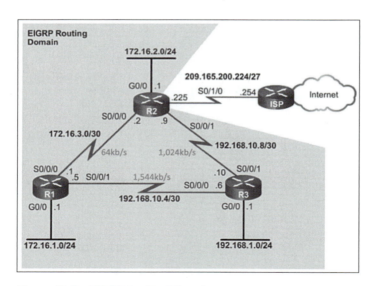

Figure 5-3   EIGRP for IPv4 Topology

The output from R1's **show ip protocols** command in Figure 5-4 shows that auto-summarization is now enabled. The output also indicates the networks that are summarized and on which interfaces. Notice that R1 summarizes two networks in its EIGRP routing updates:

- 192.168.10.0/24 sent out the GigabitEthernet 0/0 and Serial 0/0/0 interfaces
- 172.16.0.0/16 sent out the Serial 0/0/1 interface

```
R1# show ip protocols
*** IP Routing is NSF aware ***

Routing Protocol is "eigrp 1"
  Outgoing update filter list for all interfaces is not set
  Incoming update filter list for all interfaces is not set
  Default networks flagged in outgoing updates
  Default networks accepted from incoming updates
  EIGRP-IPv4 Protocol for AS(1)
    Metric weight K1=1, K2=0, K3=1, K4=0, K5=0
<output omitted>

Automatic Summarization: enabled
    192.168.10.0/24 for Gi0/0, Se0/0/0
      Summarizing 2 components with metric 2169856
    172.16.0.0/16 for Se0/0/1
      Summarizing 3 components with metric 2816
<output omitted>
```

Figure 5-4   Verifying Automatic Summarization Is Enabled

R1 has the subnets 192.168.10.4/30 and 192.168.10.8/30 in its IPv4 routing table.

As indicated in Figure 5-5, R1 summarizes the 192.168.10.4/30 and 192.168.10.8/30 subnets. It forwards the summarized address of 192.168.10.0/24 to its neighbors on its Serial 0/0/0 and GigabitEthernet 0/0 interfaces. Because R1 does not have any EIGRP neighbors on its GigabitEthernet 0/0 interface, the summarized routing update is only received by R2.

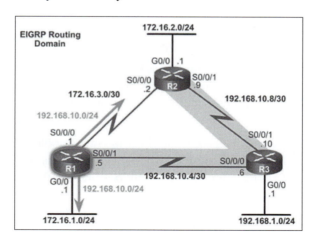

Figure 5-5   R1's 192.168.10.0/24 Summary

As indicated in Figure 5-6, R1 also has the 172.16.1.0/24, 172.16.2.0/24, and 172.16.3.0/30 subnets in its IPv4 routing table. R3 selects R1 as the successor to 172.16.0.0/16 because it has a lower feasible distance. The R3 S0/0/0 interface connecting to R1 uses a default bandwidth of 1,544 kb/s. The R3 link to R2 has a higher feasible distance because the R3 S0/0/1 interface has been configured with a lower bandwidth of 1,024 kb/s.

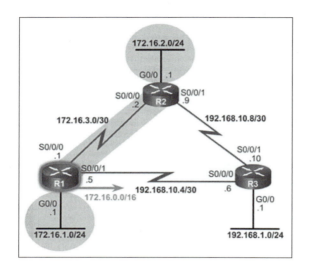

Figure 5-6   R1's 172.16.0.0/16 Summary

Notice that the 172.16.0.0/16 summarized update is not sent out R1's GigabitEthernet 0/0 and Serial 0/0/0 interfaces. This is because these two interfaces are members of the same 172.16.0.0/16 class B network. The 172.16.1.0/24 non-summarized routing update is sent by R1 to R2. Summarized updates are only sent out interfaces on different major classful networks.

Verifying Auto-Summary: Topology Table (5.1.1.5)

In Figure 5-7, routers R1 and R2 will send R3 a summarized EIGRP routing update of 172.16.0.0/16. Routing tables for R1 and R2 contain subnets of the 172.16.0.0/16 network; therefore, both routers send the summary advertisement across a different major network to R3.

The following shows the output from the **show ip eigrp topology all-links** command used to view R3's complete EIGRP topology table. This verifies that R3 has received the 172.16.0.0/16 summary route from both R1 at 192.168.10.5 and R2 at 192.168.10.9. The first entry via 192.168.10.5 is the successor and the second entry via 192.168.10.9 is the feasible successor. R1 is the successor because its 1,544 kb/s link with R3 gives R3 a better EIGRP cost to 172.16.0.0/16 than R2, which is using a slower 1,024 kb/s link.

```
R3# show ip eigrp topology all-links
P 172.16.0.0/16, 1 successors, FD is 2170112, serno 9
        via 192.168.10.5 (2170112/2816), Serial0/0/0
        via 192.168.10.9 (3012096/2816), Serial0/0/1
<Output omitted>
```

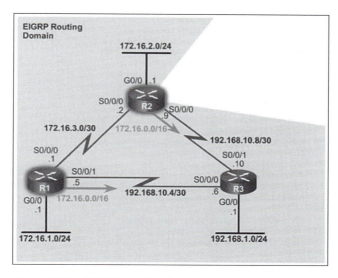

EIGRP Routing Domain

172.16.2.0/24

G0/0 .1

S0/0/0 .2   R2   S0/0/0 .9

172.16.3.0/30   172.16.0.0/16

192.168.10.8/30

S0/0/0 .1

S0/0/1 .10

S0/0/1 .5

S0/0/0 .6   R3

R1   172.16.0.0/16   192.168.10.4/30

G0/0 .1

G0/0 .1

172.16.1.0/24   192.168.1.0/24

Figure 5-7   EIGRP for IPv4 Topology

The **all-links** option shows all received updates, whether the route qualifies as a feasible successor (FS) or not. In this instance, R2 does qualify as an FS. R2 is considered an FS because its reported distance (RD) of 2,816 is less than the feasible distance (FD) of 2,170,112 via R1.

Verifying Auto-Summary: Routing Table (5.1.1.6)

Examine the routing table to verify that the summarized route was received.

The following listings show R3's routing table prior to auto-summarization, and then with auto-summarization enabled using the **auto-summary** command. Notice that with auto-summarization enabled, R3's routing table now only contains the single class B network address 172.16.0.0/16. The successor or next-hop router is R1 via 192.168.10.5.

Automatic Summarization Disabled:

```
R3# show ip route eigrp
<Output omitted>
   172.16.0.0/16 is variably subnetted, 3 subnets, 2 masks
D        172.16.1.0/24 [90/2170112] via 192.168.10.5, 02:21:10, Serial0/0/0
D        172.16.2.0/24 [90/3012096] via 192.168.10.9, 02:21:10, Serial0/0/1
D        172.16.3.0/30 [90/41024000] via 192.168.10.9, 02:21:10, Serial0/0/1
                       [90/41024000] via 192.168.10.5, 02:21:10, Serial0/0/0
R3#
```

Automatic Summarization Enabled:

```
R3# show ip route eigrp
<Output omitted>
D        172.16.0.0/16 [90/2170112] via 192.168.10.5, 00:12:05, Serial0/0/0
         192.168.10.0/24 is variably subnetted, 5 subnets, 3 masks
D           192.168.10.0/24 is a summary, 00:11:43, Null0
R3#
```

Note

Auto-summarization is only an option with EIGRP for IPv4. Classful addressing does not exist in IPv6; therefore, there is no need for auto-summarization with EIGRP for IPv6.

When enabling auto-summarization, it is also necessary to understand the Null interface. The following output shows the routing table for R1. Notice the two entries highlighted are using an exit interface of Null0. EIGRP has automatically included a summary route to Null0 for two classful networks 192.168.10.0/24 and 172.16.0.0/16.

```
R1# show ip route
         172.16.0.0/16 is variably subnetted, 6 subnets, 4 masks
D        172.16.0.0/16 is a summary, 00:03:06, Null0
C        172.16.1.0/24 is directly connected, GigabitEthernet0/0
L        172.16.1.1/32 is directly connected, GigabitEthernet0/0
D        172.16.2.0/24 [90/40512256] via 172.16.3.2, 00:02:52, Serial0/0/0
C        172.16.3.0/30 is directly connected, Serial0/0/0
L        172.16.3.1/32 is directly connected, Serial0/0/0
D     192.168.1.0/24 [90/2170112] via 192.168.10.6, 00:02:51, Serial0/0/1
      192.168.10.0/24 is variably subnetted, 4 subnets, 3 masks
D        192.168.10.0/24 is a summary, 00:02:52, Null0
C        192.168.10.4/30 is directly connected, Serial0/0/1
L        192.168.10.5/32 is directly connected, Serial0/0/1
D        192.168.10.8/30 [90/3523840] via 192.168.10.6, 00:02:59, Serial0/0/1
R1#
```

The Null0 interface is a virtual IOS interface that is a route to nowhere, commonly known as "the bit bucket." Packets that match a route with a Null0 exit interface are discarded.

EIGRP for IPv4 automatically includes a Null0 summary route whenever the following conditions exist:

■ There is at least one subnet that was learned via EIGRP.

■ There are two or more **network** EIGRP router configuration mode commands.

■ Auto-summarization is enabled.

The purpose of the *Null0 summary route* is to prevent routing loops for destinations that are included in the summary but do not actually exist in the routing table.

Summary Route (5.1.1.7, 5.1.1.8)

Figure 5-8 illustrates a scenario where a routing loop could occur:

1. R1 has a default route, 0.0.0.0/0 via the ISP router.

2. R1 sends a routing update to R2 containing the default route.

3. R2 installs the default route from R1 in its IPv4 routing table.

4. R2's routing table contains the 172.16.1.0/24, 172.16.2.0/24, and 172.16.3.0/24 subnets in its routing table.

5. R2 sends a summarized update to R1 for the 172.16.0.0/16 network.

6. R1 installs the summarized route for 172.16.0.0/16 via R2.

7. R1 receives a packet for 172.16.4.10. Because R1 has a route for 172.16.0.0/16 via R2, it forwards the packet to R2.

8. R2 receives the packet with the destination address 172.16.4.10 from R1. The packet does not match any specific route, so R2, using the default route in its routing table, forwards the packet to R1.

9. The packet for 172.16.4.10 is looped between R1 and R2 until the TTL expires and the packet is dropped.

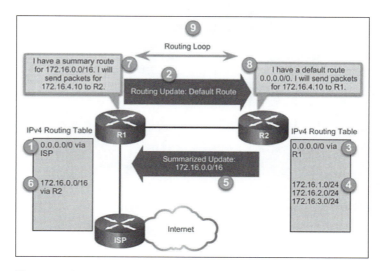

Figure 5-8   Example of a Routing Loop

EIGRP uses the Null0 interface to prevent these types of routing loops. Figure 5-9 illustrates a scenario where a Null0 route prevents the routing loop illustrated in the previous example:

1. R1 has a default route, 0.0.0.0/0 via the ISP router.

2. R1 sends a routing update to R2 containing the default route.

3. R2 installs the default route from R1 in its IPv4 routing table.

4. R2's routing table contains the 172.16.1.0/24, 172.16.2.0/24, and 172.16.3.0/24 subnets in its routing table.

5. R2 installs the 172.16.0.0/16 summary route to Null0 in its routing table.

6. R2 sends a summarized update to R1 for the 172.16.0.0/16 network.

7. R1 installs the summarized route for 172.16.0.0/16 via R2.

8. R1 receives a packet for 172.16.4.10. Because R1 has a route for 172.16.0.0/16 via R2, it forwards the packet to R2.

9. R2 receives the packet with the destination address 172.16.4.10 from R1. The packet does not match any specific subnet of 172.16.0.0 but does match the 172.16.0.0/16 summary route to Null0. Using the Null0 route, the packet is discarded.

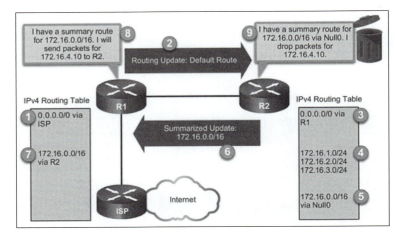

Figure 5-9   Null0 Route Is Used for Loop Prevention

A summary route on R2 for 172.16.0.0/16 to the Null0 interface discards any packets that begin with 172.16.x.x but do not have a longer match with any of the subnets: 172.16.1.0/24, 172.16.2.0/24, or 172.16.3.0/24.

Even if R2 has a default route of 0.0.0.0/0 in its routing table, the Null0 route is a longer match.

> **Note**
>
> The Null0 summary route is removed when auto-summary is disabled using the **no auto-summary** router configuration mode command.

Interactive Graphic

Activity 5.1.1.9: Determine the Classful Summarization

Go to the online course to perform this practice activity.

Interactive Graphic

Activity 5.1.1.10: Determine the Exit Interface for a Given Packet

Go to the online course to perform this practice activity.

Manual Summarization (5.1.2)

Manual summarization gives the network administrator more control over where to summarize routing updates and which networks to summarize. This section discusses the configuration and verification of manually summarizing routes using EIGRP.

Manual Summary Routes (5.1.2.1)

EIGRP can be configured to summarize routes, whether or not auto-summarization (**auto-summary**) is enabled. Because EIGRP is a classless routing protocol and includes the subnet mask in the routing updates, manual summarization can include supernet routes. Remember, a supernet is an aggregation of multiple major classful network addresses.

In Figure 5-10, two more networks are added to router R3 using loopback interfaces: 192.168.2.0/24 and 192.168.3.0/24. Although the loopback interfaces are virtual interfaces, they are used to represent physical networks for this example.

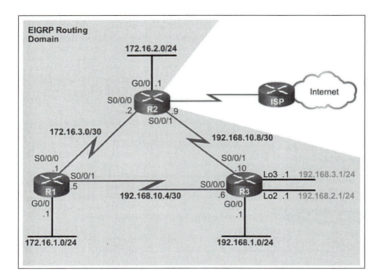

Figure 5-10   EIGRP for IPv4 Topology

The following shows the commands on R3 to configure the two loopback interfaces and the configuration to enable both interfaces for EIGRP:

```
R3(config)# interface loopback 2
R3(config-if)# ip add 192.168.2.1 255.255.255.0
R3(config-if)# exit
R3(config)# interface loopback 3
R3(config-if)# ip add 192.168.2.1 255.255.255.0
R3(config-if)# ip add 192.168.3.1 255.255.255.0
R3(config-if)# exit
R3(config)# router eigrp 1
R3(config-router)# network 192.168.2.0
R3(config-router)# network 192.168.3.0
R3(config-router)#
```

To verify that R3 sent EIGRP update packets to R1 and R2, the routing tables are examined on both routers.

The following shows only the pertinent routes. R1 and R2 routing tables show these additional networks in their routing tables: 192.168.2.0/24 and 192.168.3.0/24. Instead of sending three separate networks, R3 can summarize the 192.168.1.0/24, 192.168.2.0/24, and 192.168.3.0/24 networks as a single route.

```
R1# show ip route
<Output omitted>
D    192.168.1.0/24 [90/2170112] via 192.168.10.6, 00:47:39, Serial0/0/1
D    192.168.2.0/24 [90/2297856] via 192.168.10.6, 00:08:09, Serial0/0/1
D    192.168.3.0/24 [90/2297856] via 192.168.10.6, 00:08:04, Serial0/0/1
R1#
```

```
R2# show ip route
<Output omitted>
D    192.168.1.0/24 [90/3012096] via 192.168.10.10, 00:47:58, Serial0/0/1
D    192.168.2.0/24 [90/3139840] via 192.168.10.10, 00:08:28, Serial0/0/1
D    192.168.3.0/24 [90/3139840] via 192.168.10.10, 00:08:23, Serial0/0/1
R2#
```

Configuring EIGRP Manual Summary Routes (5.1.2.2)

Manual summary routes can be configured on any EIGRP router and are sent between EIGRP neighbors.

Determining the Summary EIGRP Route

Figure 5-11 shows the two manual summary routes that are configured on R3. These summary routes are sent out of the Serial 0/0/0 and Serial 0/0/1 interfaces to R3's EIGRP neighbors.

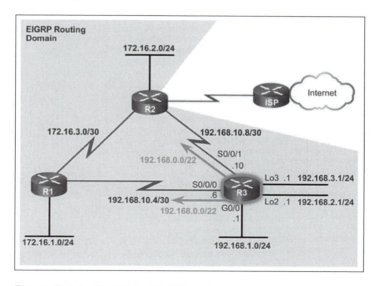

Figure 5-11   EIGRP for IPv4 Topology

To determine the summary of these three networks, the same method is used to determine summary static routes, as shown in Figure 5-12:

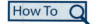

Step 1.   Write out the networks to be summarized in binary.

Step 2.   To find the subnet mask for summarization, start with the far left bit.

Step 3.   Working from left to right, find all the bits that match consecutively.

Step 4. When there is a column of bits that do not match, stop. This is the summary boundary.

Step 5. Count the number of far left matching bits, which in this example is 22. This number is used to determine the subnet mask for the summarized route: /22 or 255.255.252.0.

Step 6. To find the network address for summarization, copy the matching 22 bits and add all 0 bits to the end to make 32 bits.

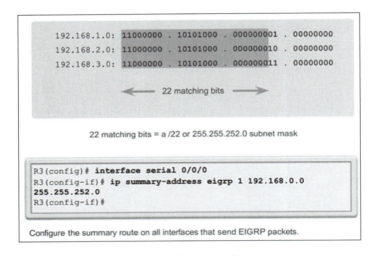

Figure 5-12   Calculating a Summary Route

The result is the summary network address and mask for 192.168.0.0/22.

Configure EIGRP Manual Summarization

To establish EIGRP manual summarization on a specific EIGRP interface, use the following interface configuration mode command:

```
Router(config-if)# ip summary-address eigrp as-number network-address subnet-mask
```

Figure 5-12 shows the configuration to propagate a manual summary route on R3's Serial 0/0/0 interface. Because R3 has two EIGRP neighbors, the EIGRP manual summarization must be configured on both Serial 0/0/0 and Serial 0/0/1.

Activity 5.1.2.2: Configuring a Manual Summary Route on R3

Go to the online course to use the Syntax Checker in the third graphic to configure an EIGRP summary route to summarize the networks on R3's Serial 0/0/0 interface for EIGRP AS 1.

Verifying Manual Summary Routes (5.1.2.3)

The following output illustrates that, after the summary route is configured,
the routing tables of R1 and R2 no longer include the individual 192.168.1.0/24,
192.168.2.0/24, and 192.168.3.0/24 networks. Instead, they show a single summary
route of 192.168.0.0/22. Summary routes reduce the number of total routes in routing
tables, which makes the routing table lookup process more efficient. Summary routes
also require less bandwidth utilization for the routing updates, because a single route
can be sent instead of multiple individual routes.

```
R1# show ip route
<Output omitted>
D     192.168.0.0/22 [90/2170112] via 192.168.10.6, 01:53:19, Serial0/0/1
R1#


R2# show ip route
<Output omitted>
D     192.168.0.0/22 [90/3012096] via 192.168.10.10, 01:53:33, Serial0/0/1
R2#
```

EIGRP for IPv6: Manual Summary Routes (5.1.2.4)

While auto-summarization is not available for EIGRP IPv6 networks, it is possible to
enable manual summarization for EIGRP IPv6.

Figure 5-13 shows an EIGRP IPv6 topology with four loopback addresses configured
on R3. These virtual addresses are used to represent physical networks in R3's IPv6
routing table. These networks can be manually summarized in EIGRP for IPv6.

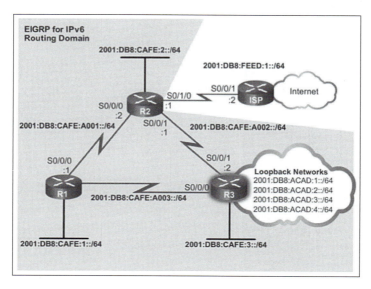

Figure 5-13   EIGRP for IPv6 Topology

The following shows the configuration of the IPv6 loopback addresses on R3. Only four loopback addresses are shown in the topology and configured on R3; however, for this example it is assumed that all 2001:DB8:ACAD::/48 subnets can be reachable via R3.

```
R3(config)# interface loopback 11
R3(config-if)# ipv6 address 2001:db8:acad:1::1/64
R3(config-if)# ipv6 eigrp 2
R3(config-if)# exit
R3(config)# interface loopback 12
R3(config-if)# ipv6 address 2001:db8:acad:2::1/64
R3(config-if)# ipv6 eigrp 2
R3(config-if)# exit
R3(config)# interface loopback 13
R3(config-if)# ipv6 address 2001:db8:acad:3::1/64
R3(config-if)# ipv6 eigrp 2
R3(config-if)# exit
R3(config)# interface loopback 14
R3(config-if)# ipv6 address 2001:db8:acad:4::1/64
R3(config-if)# ipv6 eigrp 2
```

To configure EIGRP for IPv6 manual summarization on a specific EIGRP interface, use the following interface configuration mode command:

```
Router(config-if)# ipv6 summary-address eigrp as-number prefix/prefix-length
```

The following shows the configuration to propagate an EIGRP for IPv6 manual summary route to R1 and R2 for the 2001:DB8:ACAD::/48 prefix. Similar to EIGRP for IPv4, R3 includes a summary route to Null0 as a loop prevention mechanism.

```
R3(config)# interface serial 0/0/0
R3(config-if)# ipv6 summary-address eigrp 2 2001:db8:acad::/48
R3(config-if)# exit
R3(config)# interface serial 0/0/1
R3(config-if)# ipv6 summary-address eigrp 2 2001:db8:acad::/48
R3(config-if)# end
R3# show ipv6 route
D   2001:DB8:ACAD::/48 [5/128256]
     via Null0, directly connected
<Output omitted>
```

The reception of the manual summary route can be verified by examining the routing table of the other routers in the routing domain. The following output shows the 2001:DB8:ACAD::/48 route in the IPv6 routing table of R1:

```
R1#  show ipv6 route | include 2001:DB8:ACAD:
D   2001:DB8:ACAD::/48 [90/2297856]
R1#
```

Packet Tracer Activity 5.1.2.5: Configuring EIGRP Manual Summary Routes for IPv4 and IPv6

In this activity, you will calculate and configure summary routes for the IPv4 and IPv6 networks. EIGRP is already configured; however, you are required to configure IPv4 and IPv6 summary routes on the specified interfaces. EIGRP will replace the current routes with a more specific summary route, thereby reducing the size of the routing tables.

Default Route Propagation (5.1.3)

Routing protocols such as EIGRP often need to propagate a default route from an edge router to other routers within the routing domain. The edge router or gateway router is typically an ISP-facing router that connects the routing domain to the Internet.

Propagating a Default Static Route (5.1.3.1)

Using a static route to 0.0.0.0/0 as a default route is not routing protocol–dependent. The "quad zero" static default route can be used with any currently supported routing protocols. The static default route is usually configured on the router that has a connection to a network outside the EIGRP routing domain; for example, to an ISP.

In Figure 5-14, R2 is the gateway router connecting the EIGRP routing domain with the Internet. When the static default route is configured, it is necessary to propagate that route throughout the EIGRP domain, as shown in Figure 5-15.

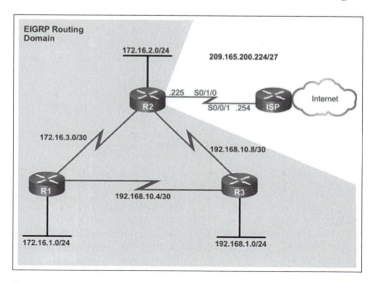

Figure 5-14   Propagating a Default Route

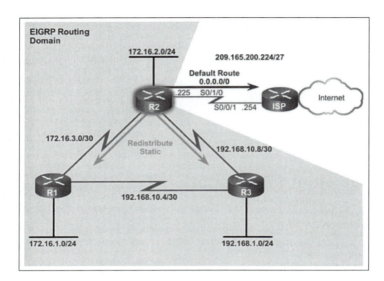

Figure 5-15   EIGRP for IPv4 Topology

One method of propagating a static default route within the EIGRP routing domain is by using the **redistribute static** command. The **redistribute static** command tells EIGRP to include static routes in its EIGRP updates to other routers. The following shows the configuration of the static default route and the **redistribute static** command on router R2:

```
R2(config)# ip route 0.0.0.0 0.0.0.0 serial 0/1/0
R2(config)# router eigrp 1
R2(config-router)# redistribute static
```

The following output verifies that the default route has been received by router R2 and installed in its IPv4 routing table:

```
R2# show ip route | include 0.0.0.0
Gateway of last resort is 0.0.0.0 to network 0.0.0.0
S*    0.0.0.0/0 is directly connected, Serial0/1/0
R2#
```

The following output of the **show ip protocols** command verifies that R2 is redistributing static routes within the EIGRP routing domain:

```
R2# show ip protocols
*** IP Routing is NSF aware ***
Routing Protocol is "eigrp 1"
  Outgoing update filter list for all interfaces is not set
  Incoming update filter list for all interfaces is not set
```

```
    Default networks flagged in outgoing updates
    Default networks accepted from incoming updates
    Redistributing: static
    EIGRP-IPv4 Protocol for AS(1)
<Output omitted>
```

Verifying the Propagated Default Route (5.1.3.2)

The following output displays a portion of the IPv4 routing tables for R1 and R3:

```
R1# show ip route | include 0.0.0.0
Gateway of last resort is 192.168.10.6 to network 0.0.0.0
D*EX  0.0.0.0/0 [170/3651840] via 192.168.10.6, 00:25:23, Serial0/0/1
R1#


R3# show ip route | include 0.0.0.0
Gateway of last resort is 192.168.10.9 to network 0.0.0.0
D*EX  0.0.0.0/0 [170/3139840] via 192.168.10.9, 00:27:17, Serial0/0/1
R3#
```

In the routing tables for R1 and R3, notice the routing source and administrative distance for the new default route learned using EIGRP. The entry for the EIGRP learned default route is identified by the following:

- **D:** This route was learned from an EIGRP routing update.

- ***:** The route is a candidate for a default route.

- **EX:** The route is an external EIGRP route, in this case a static route outside of the EIGRP routing domain.

- **170:** This is the administrative distance of an external EIGRP route.

Notice that R1 selects R3 as the successor to the default route because it has a lower feasible distance. Default routes provide a default path to outside the routing domain and, like summary routes, minimize the number of entries in the routing table.

EIGRP for IPv6: Default Route (5.1.3.3)

Recall that EIGRP maintains separate tables for IPv4 and IPv6; therefore, an IPv6 default route must be propagated separately, as shown in Figure 5-16.

Similar to EIGRP for IPv4, a default static route is configured on the gateway router (R2), as shown here:

```
R2(config)# ipv6 route ::/0 serial 0/1/0
R2(config)# ipv6 router eigrp 2
R2(config-router)# redistribute static
```

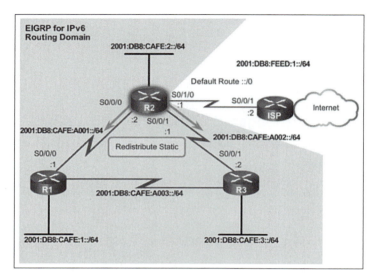

Figure 5-16   EIGRP for IPv6 Topology

The ::/0 prefix and prefix-length is equivalent to the 0.0.0.0 0.0.0.0 address and subnet mask used in IPv4. Both are all-zero addresses with a /0 prefix-length.

The IPv6 default static route is redistributed into the EIGRP for IPv6 domain using the same **redistribute static** command used in EIGRP for IPv4.

Note

Some IOS versions may require that the **redistribute static** command include the EIGRP metric parameters before the static route can be redistributed.

Verifying Propagation of Default Route

The propagation of the IPv6 static default route can be verified by examining R1's IPv6 routing table using the **show ipv6 route** command, as shown in the following output. Notice that the successor or next-hop address is not R2, but R3. This is because R3 provides a better path to R2, at a lower cost metric than R1.

```
R1# show ipv6 route
IPv6 Routing Table - default - 12 entries
Codes: C - Connected, L - Local, S - Static, U - Per-user Static route
       B - BGP, R - RIP, I1 - ISIS L1, I2 - ISIS L2
       IA - ISIS interarea, IS - ISIS summary, D - EIGRP, EX - EIGRP external
       ND - ND Default, NDp - ND Prefix, DCE - Destination, NDr - Redirect
       O - OSPF Intra, OI - OSPF Inter, OE1 - OSPF ext 1, OE2 - OSPF ext 2
       ON1 - OSPF NSSA ext 1, ON2 - OSPF NSSA ext 2
```

```
EX  ::/0 [170/3523840]
       via FE80::3, Serial0/0/1
```

Packet Tracer Activity 5.1.3.4: Propagating a Default Route in EIGRP for IPv4 and IPv6

In this activity, you will configure and propagate a default route in EIGRP for IPv4 and IPv6 networks. EIGRP is already configured. However, you are required to configure an IPv4 and an IPv6 default route. Then, you will configure the EIGRP routing process to propagate the default route to downstream EIGRP neighbors. Finally, you will verify the default routes by pinging hosts outside the EIGRP routing domain.

Fine-tuning EIGRP Interfaces (5.1.4)

There are several ways to fine-tune the EIGRP routing process. This section discusses three of these methods: EIGRP bandwidth utilization, modifying the default Hello and Hold Time values, and equal cost load balancing.

EIGRP Bandwidth Utilization (5.1.4.1)

The primary benefit of controlling EIGRP's bandwidth usage is to avoid losing EIGRP packets, which could occur when EIGRP generates data faster than the interface line can absorb it. This is of particular benefit on Frame Relay networks, where the access interface bandwidth and the PVC (permanent virtual circuit) capacity may be very different. A secondary benefit is to allow the network administrator to ensure that some bandwidth remains for passing user data, even when EIGRP is very busy.

Note

Frame Relay is discussed in the CCNA Connecting Networks course.

EIGRP Bandwidth for IPv4

By default, EIGRP uses only up to 50 percent of an interface's bandwidth for EIGRP information. This prevents the EIGRP process from over-utilizing a link and not allowing enough bandwidth for the routing of normal traffic.

Use the **ip bandwidth-percent eigrp** command to configure the percentage of bandwidth that can be used by EIGRP on an interface:

```
Router(config-if)# ip bandwidth-percent eigrp as-number percent
```

In Figure 5-17, R1 and R2 share a very slow 64 kb/s link. The configuration to limit how much bandwidth EIGRP uses is shown, along with the **bandwidth** command.

The **ip bandwidth-percent eigrp** command uses the amount of configured bandwidth (or the default bandwidth) when calculating the percent that EIGRP can use. In this example, EIGRP is limited to no more than 50 percent of the link's bandwidth, as shown in the subsequent listing. Therefore, EIGRP never uses more than 32 kb/s of the link's bandwidth for EIGRP packet traffic.

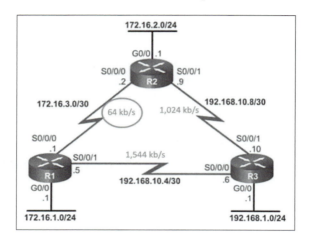

Figure 5-17 EIGRP for IPv4 Topology

```
R1(config)# interface serial 0/0/0
R1(config-if)# bandwidth 64
R1(config-if)# ip bandwidth-percent eigrp 1 50
R1(config-if)#


R2(config)# interface serial 0/0/0
R2(config-if)# bandwidth 64
R2(config-if)# ip bandwidth-percent eigrp 1 50
R2(config-if)#
```

To restore the default value, use the **no** form of this command.

Interactive Graphic

Activity 5.1.4.1: Configure EIGRP Bandwidth Utilization

Go to the online course to use the Syntax Checker in the third graphic to configure the interfaces between R2 and R3 to limit the EIGRP AS 1 traffic to no more than 75 percent of the link's bandwidth.

EIGRP Bandwidth for IPv6

To configure the percentage of bandwidth that can be used by EIGRP for IPv6 on an interface, use the **ipv6 bandwidth-percent eigrp** command in interface configuration mode. To restore the default value, use the **no** form of this command.

```
Router(config-if)# ipv6 bandwidth-percent eigrp as-number percent
```

The following shows the configuration of the interfaces between R1 and R2 to limit the bandwidth used by EIGRP for IPv6:

```
R1(config)# interface serial 0/0/0
R1(config-if)# ipv6 bandwidth-percent eigrp 2 50
R1(config-if)#

R2(config)# interface serial 0/0/0
R2(config-if)# ipv6 bandwidth-percent eigrp 2 50
R2(config-if)#
```

Hello and Hold Timers (5.1.4.2)

Hello intervals and other timers vary among different routing protocols. For example, EIGRP does not require neighbors to have matching Hello times, whereas OSPF does. This is due to the differences in the operational requirements and functionality of the two protocols.

Hello Intervals and Hold Times with EIGRP for IPv4

EIGRP uses a lightweight Hello protocol to establish and monitor the connection status of its neighbor. The Hold time tells the router the maximum time that the router should wait to receive the next Hello before declaring that neighbor as unreachable.

Hello intervals and Hold times are configurable on a per-interface basis and do not have to match with other EIGRP routers to establish or maintain adjacencies. The command to configure a different Hello interval is:

```
Router(config-if)# ip hello-interval eigrp as-number seconds
```

If the Hello interval is changed, ensure that the Hold time value is equal to, or greater than, the Hello interval. Otherwise, neighbor adjacency goes down after the Hold time expires and before the next Hello interval. Use the following command to configure a different Hold time:

```
Router(config-if)# ip hold-time eigrp as-number seconds
```

The *seconds* value for both Hello and Hold time intervals can range from 1 to 65,535.

The following shows the configuration of R1 to use a 60-second Hello interval and 180-second Hold time. The default Hello intervals and Hold times for EIGRP are provided in Table 5-1. The **no** form can be used on both of these commands to restore the default values.

```
R1(config)# interface serial 0/0/0
R1(config-if)# ip hello-interval eigrp 1 60
R1(config-if)# ip hold-time eigrp 1 180
```

Table 5-1   Default Hello Intervals and Hold Times for EIGRP

Bandwidth	Example Link	Default Hello Interval	Default Hold Time
1.544 Mb/s	Multipoint Frame Relay	60 seconds	180 seconds
Greater than 1.544 Mb/s	Ethernet	5 seconds	15 seconds

The Hello interval time and Hold time do not need to match for two routers to form an EIGRP adjacency.

Interactive Graphic

Activity 5.1.4.2: Configuring Timers on R2

Go to the online course to use the Syntax Checker in the second graphic to configure R2's Serial 0/0/0 interface to use a Hello interval of 60 seconds and a hold time of 180 seconds for AS 1.

Hello Intervals and Hold Times with EIGRP for IPv6

EIGRP for IPv6 uses the same Hello interval and Hold time as EIGRP for IPv4. The interface configuration mode commands are similar to those for IPv4:

```
Router(config-if)# ipv6 hello-interval eigrp as-number seconds
Router(config-if)# ipv6 hold-time eigrp as-number seconds
```

The following shows the Hello interval and Hold time configurations for R1 and R2 with EIGRP for IPv6:

```
R1(config)# inter serial 0/0/0
R1(config-if)# ipv6 hello-interval eigrp 2 60
R1(config-if)# ipv6 hold-time eigrp 2 180

R2(config)# inter serial 0/0/0
R2(config-if)# ipv6 hello-interval eigrp 2 60
R2(config-if)# ipv6 hold-time eigrp 2 180
```

Load Balancing IPv4 (5.1.4.3)

Equal cost load balancing is the ability of a router to distribute outbound traffic using all interfaces that have the same metric from the destination address. Load balancing uses network segments and bandwidth more efficiently. For IP, Cisco IOS Software applies load balancing using up to four equal cost paths by default.

Figure 5-18 shows the EIGRP for IPv4 network topology. In this topology, R3 has two EIGRP equal cost routes for the network between R1 and R2, 172.16.3.0/30. One route is via R1 at 192.168.10.4/30 and the other route is via R2 at 192.168.10.8/30.

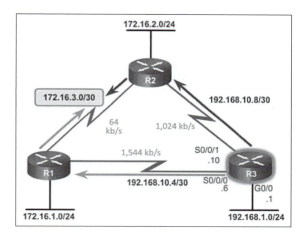

Figure 5-18   EIGRP for IPv4 Topology

The **show ip protocols** command can be used to verify the number of equal cost paths currently configured on the router. The following output shows that R3 is using the default of four equal cost paths:

```
R3# show ip protocols
*** IP Routing is NSF aware ***
Routing Protocol is "eigrp 1"
  Outgoing update filter list for all interfaces is not set
  Incoming update filter list for all interfaces is not set
  Default networks flagged in outgoing updates
  Default networks accepted from incoming updates
  EIGRP-IPv4 Protocol for AS(1)
    Metric weight K1=1, K2=0, K3=1, K4=0, K5=0
    NSF-aware route hold timer is 240
    Router-ID: 3.3.3.3
    Topology : 0 (base)
      Active Timer: 3 min
      Distance: internal 90 external 170
      Maximum path: 4
```

```
      Maximum hopcount 100
      Maximum metric variance 1
  Automatic Summarization: disabled
  Address Summarization:
    192.168.0.0/22 for Se0/0/0, Se0/0/1
      Summarizing 3 components with metric 2816
  Maximum path: 4
<Output omitted>
```

The routing table maintains both routes. The following output shows that R3 has two EIGRP equal cost routes for the 172.16.3.0/30 network. One route is via R1 at 192.168.10.5 and the other route is via R2 at 192.168.10.9. Looking at the topology in Figure 5-18, it may seem as if the path via R1 is the better route because there is a 1,544 kb/s link between R3 and R1, whereas the link to R2 is only a 1,024 kb/s link. However, EIGRP only uses the slowest bandwidth in its composite metric, which is the 64 kb/s link between R1 and R2. Both paths have the same 64 kb/s link as the slowest bandwidth, which results in both paths being equal. All the serial links in the topology have the same delay value, so both paths have the same cumulative delay.

```
R3# show ip route eigrp
<Output omitted>
Gateway of last resort is 192.168.10.9 to network 0.0.0.0
D*EX  0.0.0.0/0 [170/3139840] via 192.168.10.9, 00:14:24, Serial0/0/1
      172.16.0.0/16 is variably subnetted, 3 subnets, 2 masks
D        172.16.1.0/24 [90/2170112] via 192.168.10.5, 00:14:28, Serial0/0/0
D        172.16.2.0/24 [90/3012096] via 192.168.10.9, 00:14:24, Serial0/0/1
D        172.16.3.0/30 [90/41024000] via 192.168.10.9, 00:14:24, Serial0/0/1
                       [90/41024000] via 192.168.10.5, 00:14:24, Serial0/0/0
D     192.168.0.0/22 is a summary, 00:14:40, Null0
R3#
```

When a packet is process-switched, load balancing over equal cost paths occurs on a per-packet basis. When packets are fast-switched, load balancing over equal cost paths occurs on a per-destination basis. Cisco Express Forwarding (CEF) can perform both per-packet and per-destination load balancing.

Cisco IOS, by default, allows load balancing using up to four equal cost paths; however, this can be modified. Using the **maximum-paths** router configuration mode command, up to 32 equal cost routes can be kept in the routing table:

```
Router(config-router)# maximum-paths value
```

The *value* argument refers to the number of paths that should be maintained for load balancing. If the value is set to **1**, load balancing is disabled.

Load Balancing IPv6 (5.1.4.4)

Figure 5-19 shows the EIGRP for IPv6 network topology. The serial links in the topology have the same bandwidth that is used in the EIGRP for IPv4 topology.

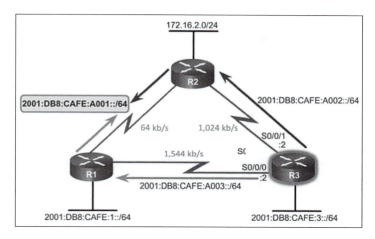

Figure 5-19   EIGRP for IPv6 Topology

Similar to the previous scenario for IPv4, R3 has two EIGRP equal cost routes for the network between R1 and R2, 2001:DB8:CAFE:A001::/64. One route is via R1 at FE80::1 and the other route is via R2 at FE80::2.

The following output shows that the EIGRP metrics are the same in the IPv6 routing table and in the IPv4 routing table for the 2001:DB8:CAFE:A001::/64 and 172.16.3.0/30 networks. This is because the EIGRP composite metric is the same for both EIGRP for IPv6 and EIGRP for IPv4.

```
R3# show ipv6 route eigrp
<Output omitted>
EX   ::/0 [170/3011840]
       via FE80::2, Serial0/0/1
D    2001:DB8:ACAD::/48 [5/128256]
       via Null0, directly connected
D    2001:DB8:CAFE:1::/64 [90/2170112]
       via FE80::1, Serial0/0/0
D    2001:DB8:CAFE:2::/64 [90/3012096]
       via FE80::2, Serial0/0/1
D    2001:DB8:CAFE:A001::/64 [90/41024000]
       via FE80::2, Serial0/0/1
       via FE80::1, Serial0/0/0
R3#
```

> **Note**
>
> EIGRP for IPv4 and EIGRP for IPv6 can also balance traffic across multiple routes that have different metrics. This type of balancing is called unequal cost load balancing.

Interactive Graphic

Activity 5.1.4.5: Determine the EIGRP Fine Tuning Commands

Go to the online course to perform this practice activity.

Secure EIGRP (5.1.5)

Securing routing protocol messages helps to prevent malicious attacks on the network and prevent routing information propagating from rogue or nonproduction routers joining the network.

Routing Protocol Authentication Overview (5.1.5.1)

Network administrators must be aware that routers are at risk from attack just as much as end-user devices. Anyone with a packet sniffer, such as Wireshark, can read information propagating between routers. In general, routing systems can be attacked through the disruption of peer devices or the falsification of routing information.

Disruption of peers is the less critical of the two attacks because routing protocols heal themselves, making the disruption last only slightly longer than the attack itself.

The falsification of routing information is a more subtle class of attack that targets the information carried within the routing protocol. The consequences of falsifying routing information are as follows:

- Redirect traffic to create routing loops
- Redirect traffic to monitor on an insecure line
- Redirect traffic to discard it

A method to protect routing information on the network is to authenticate routing protocol packets using the *Message Digest 5 (MD5) algorithm*. MD5 allows the routers to compare signatures that should all be the same, confirming that the routing information is from a credible source.

The three components of such a system include:

- Encryption algorithm, which is generally public knowledge
- Key used in the encryption algorithm, which is a secret shared by the routers authenticating their packets
- Contents of the packet itself

Figure 5-20 shows how each router authenticates the routing information. Generally, the originator of the routing information produces a signature using the key and routing data it is about to send as inputs to the encryption algorithm. The router receiving the routing data can then repeat the process using the same key and the same routing data it has received. If the signature the receiver computes is the same as the signature, the sender accepts the update as authenticated and considered reliable.

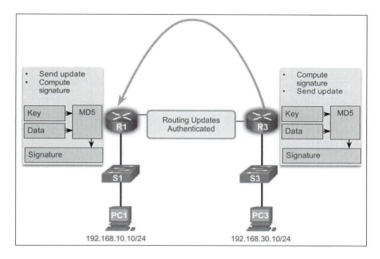

Figure 5-20   Authentication Using MD5

Routing protocols such as RIPv2, EIGRP, OSPF, IS-IS, and BGP all support various forms of MD5 authentication.

Configuring EIGRP with MD5 Authentication (5.1.5.2)

EIGRP message authentication ensures that routers only accept routing messages from other routers that know the same pre-shared key. Without authentication configured, if an unauthorized person introduces another router with different or conflicting route information on the network, the routing tables on the legitimate routers can become corrupt and a DoS attack may ensue. Thus, when authentication is added to the EIGRP messages sent between routers, it prevents someone from purposely, or accidentally, adding another router to the network and causing a problem.

EIGRP supports routing protocol authentication using MD5. As shown in the following steps, the configuration of EIGRP message authentication consists of two steps: the creation of a key chain and key, and the configuration of EIGRP authentication to use that key chain and key.

Step 1. **Create a key chain and key.** Routing authentication requires a key on a key chain to function. Before authentication can be enabled, create a key chain and at least one key.

    a. In global configuration mode, create the key chain. Although multiple keys can be configured, this section focuses on the use of a single key.

```
Router(config)# key chain name-of-chain
```

    b. Specify the key ID. The key ID is the number used to identify an authentication key within a key chain. The range of keys is from 0 to 2,147,483,647. It is recommended that the key number be the same on all routers in the configuration.

```
Router(config-keychain)# key key-id
```

    c. Specify the key string for the key. The key string is similar to a password. Routers exchanging authentication keys must be configured using the same key string.

```
Router(config-keychain-key )# key-string key-string-text
```

Step 2. **Configure EIGRP authentication using key chain and key.** Configure EIGRP to perform message authentication with the previously defined key. Complete this configuration on all interfaces enabled for EIGRP.

    a. In global configuration mode, specify the interface on which to configure EIGRP message authentication.

```
Router(config)# interface type number
```

    b. Enable EIGRP message authentication. The **md5** keyword indicates that the MD5 hash is to be used for authentication.

```
Router(config-if)# ip authentication mode eigrp as-number md5
```

    c. Specify the key chain that should be used for authentication. The *name-of-chain* argument specifies the key chain that was created in Step 1.

```
Router(config-if)# ip authentication key-chain eigrp as-number name-of-chain
```

Each key has its own key ID, which is stored locally. The combination of the key ID and the interface associated with the message uniquely identifies the authentication algorithm and MD5 authentication key in use. The key chain and the routing update are processed using the MD5 algorithm to produce a unique signature.

EIGRP Authentication Example (5.1.5.3)

To authenticate routing updates, all EIGRP-enabled interfaces must be configured to support authentication. Figure 5-21 shows the IPv4 topology and which interfaces are configured with authentication.

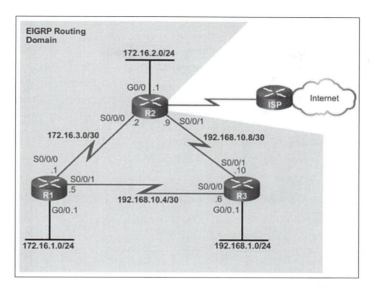

Figure 5-21   EIGRP for IPv4 Topology

The following shows the configuration for router R1 using the **EIGRP_KEY** key chain and the **cisco123** key string. After R1 is configured, the other routers receive authenticated routing updates. Adjacencies are lost until the neighbors are configured with routing protocol authentication.

```
R1(config)# key chain EIGRP_KEY
R1(config-keychain)# key 1
R1(config-keychain-key)# key-string cisco123
R1(config-keychain-key)# exit
R1(config-keychain)# exit
R1(config)# interface serial 0/0/0
R1(config-if)# ip authentication mode eigrp 1 md5
R1(config-if)# ip authentication key-chain eigrp 1 D
R1(config-if)# exit
R1(config)# interface serial 0/0/1
R1(config-if)# ip authentication mode eigrp 1 md5
R1(config-if)# ip authentication key-chain eigrp 1 EIGRP_KEY
R1(config-if)# end
R1#
```

The following shows a similar configuration for router R2. Notice that the same key string, **cisco123**, is used to authenticate information with R1 and ultimately R3.

```
R2(config)# key chain EIGRP_KEY
R2(config-keychain)# key 1
R2(config-keychain-key)# key-string cisco123
R2(config-keychain-key)# exit
```

```
R2(config-keychain)# exit
R2(config)# interface serial 0/0/0
R2(config-if)# ip authentication mode eigrp 1 md5
R2(config-if)# ip authentication key-chain eigrp 1 EIGRP_KEY
R2(config-if)# exit
R2(config)# interface serial 0/0/1
R2(config-if)# ip authentication mode eigrp 1 md5
R2(config-if)# ip authentication key-chain eigrp 1 EIGRP_KEY
R2(config-if)# end
R2#
```

Interactive Graphic

Activity 5.1.5.3: Configure EIGRP Authentication on R3

Go to the online course to use the Syntax Checker in the fourth graphic to configure R3's serial interfaces for EIGRP authentication.

Configuring EIGRP for IPv6 Authentication

The algorithms and the configuration to authenticate EIGRP for IPv6 messages are the same as those for EIGRP for IPv4. The only difference is the interface configuration mode commands use **ipv6** instead of **ip**.

```
Router(config-if)# ipv6 authentication mode eigrp as-number md5
Router(config-if)# ipv6 authentication key-chain eigrp as-number name-of-chain
```

The following shows the commands to configure EIGRP for IPv6 authentication on router R1 using the **EIGRP_IPV6_KEY** key chain and the **cisco123** key string. Similar configurations would be entered on R2 and R3.

```
R1(config)# key chain EIGRP_IPV6_KEY
R1(config-keychain)# key 1
R1(config-keychain-key)# key-string cisco123
R1(config-keychain-key)# exit
R1(config-keychain)# exit
R1(config)# interface serial 0/0/0
R1(config-if)# ipv6 authentication mode eigrp 2 md5
R1(config-if)# ipv6 authentication key-chain eigrp 2 EIGRP_IPV6_KEY
R1(config-if)# exit
R1(config)# interface serial 0/0/1
R1(config-if)# ipv6 authentication mode eigrp 2 md5
R1(config-if)# ipv6 authentication key-chain eigrp 2 EIGRP_IPV6_KEY
R1(config-if)#
```

Verify Authentication (5.1.5.4)

After EIGRP message authentication is configured on one router, any adjacent neighbors that have not yet been configured for authentication are no longer EIGRP neighbors. For example, when R1's Serial 0/0/0 interface was configured for MD5 authentication, but R2 had not yet been configured, the following IOS message appeared on R1:

```
%DUAL-5-NBRCHANGE: EIGRP-IPv4 1: Neighbor 172.16.3.2 (Serial0/0/0) is down:
authentication mode changed
```

When the adjacent Serial 0/0/0 interface on R2 is configured, the adjacency is re-established and the following IOS message is displayed on R1:

```
%DUAL-5-NBRCHANGE: EIGRP-IPv4 1: Neighbor 172.16.3.2 (Serial0/0/0) is up:
new adjacency
```

Similar messages are also displayed on R2.

Adjacencies are only formed when both connecting devices have authentication configured. To verify that the correct EIGRP adjacencies were formed after being configured for authentication, use the **show ip eigrp neighbors** command on each router. The following output shows that all three routers have re-established neighbor adjacencies after being configured for EIGRP authentication.

To verify the neighbor adjacencies with EIGRP for IPv6, use the **show ipv6 eigrp neighbors** command.

```
R1# show ip eigrp neighbors
EIGRP-IPv4 Neighbors for AS(1)
H   Address          Interface    Hold Uptime    SRTT   RTO  Q   Seq
                                  (sec)          (ms)        Cnt Num
1   172.16.3.2       Se0/0/0       140 03:28:12    96   2340  0   23
0   192.168.10.6     Se0/0/1        14 03:28:27    49    294  0   24
R1#


R2# show ip eigrp neighbors
EIGRP-IPv4 Neighbors for AS(1)
H   Address          Interface    Hold Uptime    SRTT   RTO  Q   Seq
                                  (sec)          (ms)        Cnt Num
1   172.16.3.1       Se0/0/0       136 00:22:50  1046   5000  0   32
0   192.168.10.10    Se0/0/1        10 07:51:37    62    372  0   35
R2#
```

```
R3# show ip eigrp neighbors
EIGRP-IPv4 Neighbors for AS(1)
H   Address                 Interface      Hold Uptime    SRTT    RTO   Q   Seq
                                           (sec)          (ms)          Cnt Num
0   192.168.10.5            Se0/0/0         14 00:21:26 1297    5000    0   33
1   192.168.10.9            Se0/0/1         14 07:51:50   43     258    0   36
R3#
```

 Lab 5.1.5.5: Configuring Advanced EIGRP for IPv4 Features

In this lab, you will complete the following objectives:

- Part 1: Build the Network and Configure Basic Device Settings
- Part 2: Configure EIGRP and Verify Connectivity
- Part 3: Configure Summarization for EIGRP
- Part 4: Propagate a Default Route
- Part 5: Fine-Tune EIGRP
- Part 6: Configure EIGRP Authentication

Troubleshoot EIGRP (5.2)

Troubleshooting a routing protocol is an important skill set for any network administrator to have. It is usually during troubleshooting that the skills and knowledge about the routing protocol are tested.

Components of Troubleshooting EIGRP (5.2.1)

This section examines the components of troubleshooting EIGRP and the commands used to solve common EIGRP problems.

Basic EIGRP Troubleshooting Commands (5.2.1.1)

EIGRP is commonly used in large enterprise networks. Troubleshooting problems related to the exchange of routing information is an essential skill for a network administrator. This is particularly true for administrators who are involved in the implementation and maintenance of large, routed enterprise networks that use EIGRP as the IGP. There are several commands that are useful when troubleshooting an EIGRP network.

The **show ip eigrp neighbors** command verifies that the router recognizes its neighbors. The following output indicates two successful EIGRP neighbor adjacencies on R1:

```
R1# show ip eigrp neighbors
EIGRP-IPv4 Neighbors for AS(1)
 H   Address          Interface    Hold Uptime     SRTT   RTO  Q  Seq
                                   (sec)           (ms)       Cnt Num
 1   172.16.3.2       Se0/0/0      140 03:28:12     96  2340   0  23
 0   192.168.10.6     Se0/0/1       14 03:28:27     49   294   0  24
R1#
```

In the following output, the **show ip route** command verifies that the router learned the route to a remote network through EIGRP. The output shows that R1 has learned about four remote networks through EIGRP.

```
R1# show ip route eigrp
Gateway of last resort is 192.168.10.6 to network 0.0.0.0
D*EX  0.0.0.0/0 [170/3651840] via 192.168.10.6, 05:32:02, Serial0/0/1
       172.16.0.0/16 is variably subnetted, 5 subnets, 3 masks
D          172.16.2.0/24 [90/3524096] via 192.168.10.6, 05:32:02, Serial0/0/1
D        192.168.0.0/22 [90/2170112] via 192.168.10.6, 05:32:02, Serial0/0/1
       192.168.10.0/24 is variably subnetted, 3 subnets, 2 masks
D          192.168.10.8/30 [90/3523840] via 192.168.10.6, 05:32:02, Serial0/0/1
R1#
```

The following shows the output from the **show ip protocols** command. This command verifies that EIGRP displays the currently configured values for various properties of any enabled routing protocols.

```
R1# show ip protocols
*** IP Routing is NSF aware ***
Routing Protocol is "eigrp 1"
  Outgoing update filter list for all interfaces is not set
  Incoming update filter list for all interfaces is not set
  Default networks flagged in outgoing updates
  Default networks accepted from incoming updates
  EIGRP-IPv4 Protocol for AS(1)
    Metric weight K1=1, K2=0, K3=1, K4=0, K5=0
    NSF-aware route hold timer is 240
    Router-ID: 1.1.1.1
    Topology : 0 (base)
      Active Timer: 3 min
      Distance: internal 90 external 170
      Maximum path: 4
      Maximum hopcount 100
      Maximum metric variance 1
```

```
Automatic Summarization: disabled
Maximum path: 4
Routing for Networks:
  172.16.0.0
  192.168.10.0
Passive Interface(s):
  GigabitEthernet0/0
Routing Information Sources:
  Gateway          Distance        Last Update
  192.168.10.6           90        05:43:44
  172.16.3.2             90        05:43:44
Distance: internal 90 external 170
R1#
```

EIGRP for IPv6

Similar commands and troubleshooting criteria also apply to EIGRP for IPv6.

The following are the equivalent commands used with EIGRP for IPv6:

- Router# **show ipv6 eigrp neighbors**
- Router# **show ipv6 route**
- Router# **show ipv6 protocols**

Components (5.2.1.2)

Figure 5-22 shows a flowchart for diagnosing EIGRP connectivity issues.

After configuring EIGRP, the first step is to test connectivity to the remote network. If the ping fails, confirm the EIGRP neighbor adjacencies. Neighbor adjacency might not be formed for a number of reasons, including the following:

- The interface between the devices is down.
- The two routers have mismatching EIGRP autonomous system numbers (process IDs).
- Proper interfaces are not enabled for the EIGRP process.
- An interface is configured as passive.

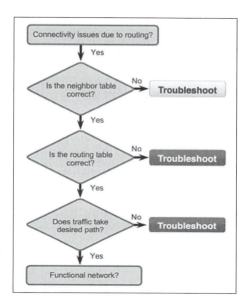

Figure 5-22   Diagnosing EIGRP Connectivity Issues

Some of the commands used to troubleshoot these issues include:

- Router# **show ip eigrp neighbors**

- Router# **show ip interfaces brief**

- Router# **show ip eigrp interface**

Aside from these issues, there are a number of other, more advanced issues that can cause neighbor adjacencies to not be formed. Two examples are misconfigured EIGRP authentication or mismatched k values, which EIGRP uses to calculate its metric.

If the EIGRP neighbor adjacency is formed between the two routers, but there is still a connection issue, there may be a routing problem. Some issues that may cause a connectivity problem for EIGRP include:

- Proper networks are not being advertised on remote routers.

- An incorrectly configured passive interface, or an ACL, is blocking advertisements of remote networks.

- Auto-summarization is causing inconsistent routing in a discontiguous network.

Some of the commands used to troubleshoot these issues include:

- Router# **show ip protocols**

- Router# **show ip route eigrp**

If all of the required routes are in the routing table, but the path that traffic takes is not correct, verify the interface bandwidth values using the **show ip eigrp interface** command.

Interactive Graphic

Activity 5.2.1.3: Identify the Troubleshooting Command

Go to the online course to perform this practice activity.

Troubleshoot EIGRP Neighbor Issues (5.2.2)

Before EIGRP neighbors can exchange routing updates, the routers must first form an EIGRP adjacency. Neighbor adjacency is typically one of the first things to verify when troubleshooting most routing protocols.

Layer 3 Connectivity (5.2.2.1)

A prerequisite for a neighbor adjacency to form between two directly connected routers is Layer 3 connectivity. By examining the output of the **show ip interface brief** command, a network administrator can verify that the status and protocol of connecting interfaces are up. A ping from one router to another, directly connected router should confirm IPv4 connectivity between the devices. The following displays the **show ip interface brief** command output for R1. R1 shows connectivity to R2, and pings are successful.

```
R1# show ip interface brief
Interface            IP-Address       OK? Method Status              Protocol
GigabitEthernet0/0   172.16.1.1       YES manual up                  up
Serial0/0/0          172.16.3.1       YES manual up                  up
Serial0/0/1          192.168.10.5     YES manual up                  up
R1# ping 172.16.3.2
Type escape sequence to abort.
Sending 5, 100-byte ICMP Echos to 172.16.3.2, timeout is 2 seconds:
!!!!!
Success rate is 100 percent (5/5), round-trip min/avg/max = 28/28/28 ms
R1#
```

If the ping is unsuccessful, check the cabling and verify that the interfaces on connected devices are on a common subnet. A log message that states that EIGRP neighbors are "not on common subnet" indicates that there is an incorrect IPv4 address on one of the two EIGRP neighbor interfaces.

EIGRP for IPv6

Similar commands and troubleshooting criteria also apply to EIGRP for IPv6. The equivalent command used with EIGRP for IPv6 is **show ipv6 interface brief**.

EIGRP Parameters (5.2.2.2)

When troubleshooting an EIGRP network, one of the first things to verify is that all routers that are participating in the EIGRP network are configured with the same autonomous system number. The **router eigrp** *as-number* command starts the EIGRP process and is followed by a number that is the autonomous system number. The value of the *as-number* argument must be the same in all routers that are in the EIGRP routing domain.

Figure 5-23 shows that all routers should be participating in autonomous system number 1. In the subsequent listing, the **show ip protocols** command verifies that R1, R2, and R3 all use the same autonomous system number.

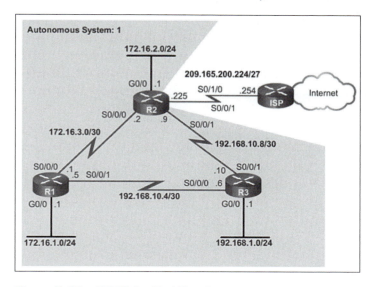

Figure 5-23   EIGRP for IPv4 Topology

```
R1# show ip protocols
*** IP Routing is NSF aware ***
Routing Protocol is "eigrp 1"
<Output omitted>
R2# show ip protocols
*** IP Routing is NSF aware ***
Routing Protocol is "eigrp 1"
<Output omitted>
R3# show ip protocols
```

```
*** IP Routing is NSF aware ***
Routing Protocol is "eigrp 1"
<Output omitted>
```

EIGRP for IPv6

Similar commands and troubleshooting criteria also apply to EIGRP for IPv6.

The following are the equivalent commands used with EIGRP for IPv6:

- Router(config)# **ipv6 router eigrp** *as-number*

- Router# **show ipv6 protocols**

> **Note**
>
> At the top of the output, "IP Routing is NSF aware" refers to Nonstop Forwarding (NSF). This capability allows the EIGRP peers of a failing router to retain the routing information that it has advertised, and to continue using this information until the failed router resumes normal operation and is able to exchange routing information. For more information refer to: http:// www.cisco.com/en/US/docs/ios-xml/ios/iproute_eigrp/configuration/15-mt/eigrp-nsf-awa. html

EIGRP Interfaces (5.2.2.3)

In addition to verifying the autonomous system number, it is necessary to verify that all interfaces are participating in the EIGRP network. The **network** command that is configured under the EIGRP routing process indicates which router interfaces participate in EIGRP. This command is applied to the classful network address of the interface or to a subnet when the wildcard mask is included.

In Figure 5-24, the **show ip eigrp interfaces** command displays which interfaces are enabled for EIGRP on R1. If connected interfaces are not enabled for EIGRP, then neighbors do not form an adjacency.

> **Note**
>
> The entire output of R1 in Figure 5-24 can be viewed in the online course on page 5.2.2.3 graphic number 1.

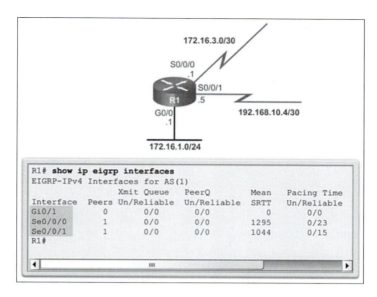

Figure 5-24 IPv4 EIGRP Interfaces

In the following output, the "Routing for Networks" section of the **show ip protocols** command indicates which networks have been configured; any interfaces in those networks participate in EIGRP.

```
R1# show ip protocols
*** IP Routing is NSF aware ***
Routing Protocol is "eigrp 1"
<Output omitted>
Routing for Networks:
    172.16.0.0
    192.168.10.0
  Passive Interface(s):
    GigabitEthernet0/0
  Routing Information Sources:
    Gateway         Distance      Last Update
    192.168.10.6          90      00:42:31
    172.16.3.2            90      00:42:31
  Distance: internal 90 external 170
R1#
```

If the network is not present in this section, use **show running-config** to ensure that the proper **network** command was configured.

The following output from the **show running-config** command confirms that any interfaces with these addresses, or a subnet of these addresses, are enabled for EIGRP:

```
R1# show running-config | section eigrp 1
router eigrp 1
 network 172.16.0.0
 network 192.168.10.0
 passive-interface GigabitEthernet0/0
 eigrp router-id 1.1.1.1
R1#
```

EIGRP for IPv6

Similar commands and troubleshooting criteria also apply to EIGRP for IPv6.

The following are the equivalent commands used with EIGRP for IPv6:

- Router# **show ipv6 protocols**
- Router# **show ipv6 eigrp interfaces**

Interactive Graphic

Activity 5.2.2.4: Troubleshoot EIGRP Neighbor Issues

Go to the online course to perform this practice activity.

Troubleshooting EIGRP Routing Table Issues (5.2.3)

Although EIGRP routers may form an adjacency, due to other issues, we may not see the routes we expect to see in the routing table. Troubleshooting EIGRP routing table issues is another key component in troubleshooting EIGRP.

Passive Interface (5.2.3.1)

One reason that route tables may not reflect the correct routes is due to the **passive-interface** command. With EIGRP running on a network, the **passive-interface** command stops both outgoing and incoming routing updates. For this reason, routers do not become neighbors.

To verify whether any interface on a router is configured as passive, use the **show ip protocols** command in privileged EXEC mode. The following output shows that R2's GigabitEthernet 0/0 interface is configured as a passive interface, because there are no neighbors on that link:

```
R2# show ip protocols
*** IP Routing is NSF aware ***
```

```
Routing Protocol is "eigrp 1"
<Output omitted>
Routing for Networks:
     172.16.0.0
     192.168.10.8/30
  Passive Interface(s):
     GigabitEthernet0/0
  Routing Information Sources:
     Gateway          Distance        Last Update
     192.168.10.10           90        00:08:59
     172.16.3.1              90        00:08:59
  Distance: internal 90 external 170
R2#
```

In addition to being configured on interfaces that have no neighbors, a passive interface can be enabled on interfaces for security purposes. In Figure 5-25, notice that
the shading for the EIGRP routing domain is different from previous topologies. The
209.165.200.224/27 network is now included in R2's EIGRP updates. However, for
security reasons, the network administrator does not want R2 to form an EIGRP
neighbor adjacency with the ISP router.

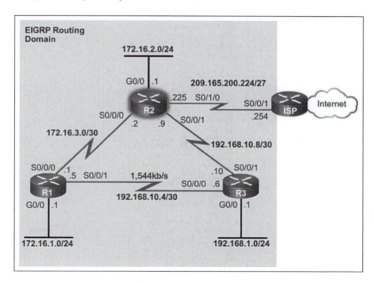

Figure 5-25   EIGRP for IPv4 Topology

The following shows the addition of the 209.165.200.224/27 **network** command
on R2. R2 now advertises this network to the other routers in the EIGRP routing
domain.

```
R2(config)# router eigrp 1
R2(config-router)# network 209.165.200.0
```

```
R2(config-router)# passive-interface serial 0/1/0
R2(config-router)# end
R2# show ip eigrp neighbors
EIGRP-IPv4 Neighbors for AS(1)
H   Address         Interface       Hold Uptime    SRTT  RTO  Q   Seq
                                    (sec)          (ms)       Cnt Num
1   172.16.3.1      Se0/0/0          175 01:09:18    80 2340  0   16
0   192.168.10.10   Se0/0/1           11 01:09:33  1037 5000  0   17
R2#
```

The **passive-interface** router configuration mode command is configured on Serial 0/1/0 to prevent R2's EIGRP updates from being sent to the ISP router. The **show ip eigrp neighbors** command on R2 verifies that R2 has not established a neighbor adjacency with the ISP router. The previous output displays both of these changes.

The following output shows that R1 has an EIGRP route to the 209.165.200.224/27 network in its IPv4 routing table (R3 will also have an EIGRP route to that network in its IPv4 routing table). However, R2 does not have a neighbor adjacency with the ISP router.

```
R1# show ip route | include 209.165.200.224
D    209.165.200.224 [90/3651840] via 192.168.10.6, 00:06:02, Serial0/0/1
R1#
```

EIGRP for IPv6

Similar commands and troubleshooting criteria also apply to EIGRP for IPv6.

The following are the equivalent commands used with EIGRP for IPv6:

- Router# **show ipv6 protocols**
- Router(config-router)# **passive-interface** *type number*

Missing Network Statement (5.2.3.2)

Figure 5-26 shows that R1's GigabitEthernet 0/1 interface has now been configured with the 10.10.10.1/24 address and is active.

R1 and R3 still have their neighbor adjacency, but a ping test from the R3 router to R1's G0/1 interface of 10.10.10.1 is unsuccessful. The following output shows a failed connectivity test from R3 to the destination network of 10.10.10.0/24:

```
R3# ping 10.10.10.1
Type escape sequence to abort.
Sending 5, 100-byte ICMP Echos to 10.10.10.1, timeout is 2 seconds:
.....
Success rate is 0 percent (0/5)
R3#
```

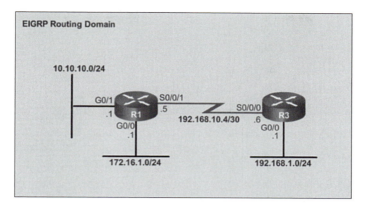

Figure 5-26   EIGRP for IPv4 Topology

The following output, using the **show ip protocols** command on the R1 router, shows that the network 10.10.10.0/24 is not advertised to EIGRP neighbors:

```
R1# show ip protocols | begin Routing for Networks
  Routing for Networks:
    172.16.0.0
    192.168.10.0
  Passive Interface(s):
    GigabitEthernet0/0
  Routing Information Sources:
    Gateway           Distance       Last Update
    192.168.10.6            90        01:34:19
    172.16.3.2             90        01:34:19
  Distance: internal 90 external 170
R1#
```

As shown next, R1's EIGRP process is configured to include the advertisement of the 10.10.10.0/24 network:

```
R1(config)# router eigrp 1
R1(config-router)# network 10.0.0.0
```

The following shows that there is now a route in R3's routing table for the 10.10.10.0/24 network and reachability is verified by pinging R1's GigabitEthernet 0/1 interface:

```
R3# show ip route | include 10.10.10.0
D        10.10.10.0 [90/2172416] via 192.168.10.5, 00:04:14, Serial0/0/0
R3#
R3# ping 10.10.10.1
Type escape sequence to abort.
Sending 5, 100-byte ICMP Echos to 10.10.10.1, timeout is 2 seconds:
```

```
!!!!!
Success rate is 100 percent (5/5), round-trip min/avg/max = 24/27/28 ms
R3#
```

EIGRP for IPv6

Similar commands and troubleshooting criteria also apply to EIGRP for IPv6.

The following are the equivalent commands used with EIGRP for IPv6:

- Router# **show ipv6 protocols**

- Router# **show ipv6 route**

- Router(config-if)# ipv6 eigrp *autonomous-system-number*

Note

Another form of missing route may result from the router filtering inbound or outbound routing updates. ACLs provide filtering for different protocols, and these ACLs may affect the exchange of the routing protocol messages that cause routes to be absent from the routing table. The **show ip protocols** command shows whether there are any ACLs that are applied to EIGRP.

Auto-summarization (5.2.3.3)

Another issue that may create problems for the network administrator is EIGRP auto-summarization.

Figure 5-27 shows a different network topology than what has been used throughout this chapter. There is no connection between R1 and R3. R1's LAN has the network address 10.10.10.0/24, while R3's LAN is 10.20.20.0/24. The serial connections between both routers and R2 have the same bandwidth of 1,024 kb/s.

R1 and R3 have their LAN and serial interfaces enabled for EIGRP, as shown next. Both routers perform EIGRP auto-summarization.

```
R1(config)# router eigrp 1
R1(config-router)# network 10.0.0.0
R1(config-router)# network 172.16.0.0
R1(config-router)# auto-summary

R3(config)# router eigrp 1
R3(config-router)# network 10.0.0.0
R3(config-router)# network 192.168.10.0
R3(config-router)# auto-summary
```

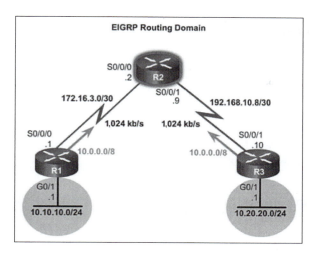

Figure 5-27   EIGRP for IPv4 Topology

EIGRP for IPv4 can be configured to automatically summarize routes at classful boundaries. If there are discontiguous networks, auto-summarization causes inconsistent routing.

In the following output, R2's routing table shows that it does not receive individual routes for the 10.10.10.0/24 and 10.20.20.0/24 subnets. Both R1 and R3 automatically summarized those subnets to the 10.0.0.0/8 classful boundary when sending EIGRP update packets to R2. The result is that R2 has two equal cost routes to 10.0.0.0/8 in the routing table, which can result in inaccurate routing and packet loss. Depending upon whether per-packet, per-destination, or CEF load balancing is being used, packets may or may not be forwarded out the proper interface.

```
R2# show ip route
<Output omitted>
        10.0.0.0/8 is subnetted, 1 subnets
D          10.0.0.0 [90/3014400] via 192.168.10.10, 00:02:06, Serial0/0/1
                    [90/3014400] via 172.16.3.1, 00:02:06, Serial0/0/0
```

The following **show ip protocols** command output verifies that auto-summarization is performed on both R1 and R3. Notice that both routers summarize the 10.0.0.0/8 network using the same metric.

```
R1# show ip protocols
*** IP Routing is NSF aware ***
Routing Protocol is "eigrp 1"

  Automatic Summarization: enabled
    10.0.0.0/8 for Se0/0/0
```

```
            Summarizing 1 component with metric 28160
<Output omitted>


R3# show ip protocols
*** IP Routing is NSF aware ***
Routing Protocol is "eigrp 1"

  Automatic Summarization: enabled
    10.0.0.0/8 for Se0/0/1
      Summarizing 1 component with metric 28160
<Output omitted>
```

The **auto-summary** command is disabled by default on Cisco IOS Software versions of 15 and newer versions of 12.2(33). By default, older software has auto-summarization enabled. To disable auto-summarization, enter the **no auto-summary** command in **router EIGRP** configuration mode.

To correct this problem, R1 and R3 have auto-summarization disabled:

```
R1(config)# router eigrp 1
R1(config-router)# no auto-summary


R3(config)# router eigrp 1
R3(config-router)# no auto-summary
```

After auto-summarization has been disabled on R1 and R3, R2's routing table now indicates that it receives the individual 10.10.10.0/24 and 10.20.20.0/24 subnets from R1 and R3, respectively, as shown in the following output. Accurate routing and connectivity to both subnets is now restored.

```
R2# show ip route
<Output omitted>
 10.0.0.0/24 is subnetted, 2 subnets
D       10.10.10.0 [90/3014400] via 172.16.3.1, 00:00:27, Serial0/0/0
D       10.20.20.0 [90/3014400] via 192.168.10.10, 00:00:11, Serial0/0/1
```

EIGRP for IPv6

Classful networks do not exist in IPv6; therefore EIGRP for IPv6 does not support auto-summarization. All summarization must be accomplished using EIGRP manual summary routes.

Interactive Graphic

Activity 5.2.3.4: Troubleshoot EIGRP Routing Table Issues

Go to the online course to perform this practice activity.

Packet Tracer Activity 5.2.3.5: Troubleshooting EIGRP for IPv4

In this activity, you will troubleshoot EIGRP neighbor issues. Use **show** commands to identify errors in the network configuration. Then, you will document the errors you discover and implement an appropriate solution. Finally, you will verify full end-to-end connectivity is restored.

Lab 5.2.3.6: Troubleshooting Basic EIGRP for IPv4 and IPv6

In this lab, you will complete the following objectives:

- Part 1: Build the Network and Load Device Configurations
- Part 2: Troubleshoot Layer 3 Connectivity
- Part 3: Troubleshoot EIGRP for IPv4
- Part 4: Troubleshoot EIGRP for IPv6

Lab 5.2.3.7: Troubleshooting Advanced EIGRP

In this lab, you will complete the following objectives:

- Part 1: Build the Network and Load Device Configurations
- Part 2: Troubleshoot EIGRP

Summary (5.3)

Class Activity 5.3.1.1: Tweaking EIGRP

Go to the online course to perform this practice activity.

Scenario

The purpose of this activity is to review EIGRP routing protocol fine-tuning concepts.

You will work with a partner to design one EIGRP topology. This topology is the basis for two parts of the activity. The first uses default settings for all configurations, and the second incorporates at least three of the following fine-tuning EIGRP options:

- Manual summary route
- Default routes
- Default routes propagation
- Hello interval timer settings

Refer to the labs, Packet Tracer activities, and interactive activities to help you as you progress through this modeling activity.

Directions are listed on the PDF file for this activity. Share your completed work with another group. You may want to save a copy of this activity to a portfolio.

Packet Tracer Activity 5.3.1.2: Skills Integration Challenge

In this activity, you are tasked with implementing EIGRP for IPv4 and IPv6 on two separate networks. Your task includes enabling EIGRP, assigning router IDs, changing the Hello timers, configuring EIGRP summary routes, and limiting EIGRP advertisements.

EIGRP is one of the routing protocols commonly used in large enterprise networks. Modifying EIGRP features and troubleshooting problems is one of the most essential skills for a network engineer involved in the implementation and maintenance of large routed enterprise networks that use EIGRP.

Summarization decreases the number of entries in routing updates and lowers the number of entries in local routing tables. It also reduces bandwidth utilization for routing updates and results in faster routing table lookups. EIGRP for IPv4 auto-summarization is disabled by default beginning with Cisco IOS Release 15.0(1)M and

12.2(33). Prior to this, auto-summarization was enabled by default. To enable auto-summarization for EIGRP, use the **auto-summary** command in router configuration mode. Use the **show ip protocols** command to verify the status of auto-summarization. Examine the routing table to verify that auto-summarization is working.

EIGRP automatically includes summary routes to Null0 to prevent routing loops that are included in the summary but do not actually exist in the routing table. The Null0 interface is a virtual IOS interface that is a route to nowhere, commonly known as "the bit bucket." Packets that match a route with a Null0 exit interface are discarded.

To establish EIGRP manual summarization on a specific EIGRP interface, use the following interface configuration mode command:

```
Router(config-if)# ip summary-address eigrp as-number network-address subnet-mask
```

To configure EIGRP for IPv6 manual summarization on a specific EIGRP interface, use the following interface configuration mode command:

```
Router(config-if)# ipv6 summary-address eigrp as-number prefix/prefix-length
```

One method of propagating a default route within the EIGRP routing domain is to use the **redistribute static** command. This command tells EIGRP to include this static route in its EIGRP updates to other routers. The **show ip protocols** command verifies that static routes within the EIGRP routing domain are being redistributed.

Use the **ip bandwidth-percent eigrp** *as-number percent* interface configuration mode command to configure the percentage of bandwidth that can be used by EIGRP on an interface.

To configure the percentage of bandwidth that can be used by EIGRP for IPv6 on an interface, use the **ipv6 bandwidth-percent eigrp** command in interface configuration mode. To restore the default value, use the **no** form of this command.

Hello intervals and Hold times are configurable on a per-interface basis in EIGRP and do not have to match with other EIGRP routers to establish or maintain adjacencies.

For IP in EIGRP, Cisco IOS Software applies load balancing using up to four equal cost paths by default. With the **maximum-paths** router configuration mode command, up to 32 equal cost routes can be kept in the routing table.

EIGRP supports routing protocol authentication using MD5. The algorithms and the configuration to authenticate EIGRP for IPv4 messages are the same as those for EIGRP for IPv6. The only difference is that the interface configuration mode commands use **ip** instead of **ipv6**.

```
Router(config-if)# ipv6 authentication mode eigrp as-number md5
Router(config-if)# ipv6 authentication key-chain eigrp as-number name-of-chain
```

To verify that the correct EIGRP adjacencies were formed after being configured for authentication, use the **show ip eigrp neighbors** command on each router.

The **show ip route** command verifies that the router learned EIGRP routes. The **show ip protocols** command is used to verify that EIGRP displays the currently configured values.

Practice

The following activities provide practice with the topics introduced in this chapter. The Labs and Class Activities are available in the companion *Routing Protocols Lab Manual* (978-1-58713-322-0). The Packet Tracer Activities PKA files are found in the online course.

Class Activities

Class Activity 5.0.1.2: EIGRP – Back to the Future

Class Activity 5.3.1.1: Tweaking EIGRP

Labs

Lab 5.1.5.5: Configuring Advanced EIGRP for IPv4 Features

Lab 5.2.3.6: Troubleshooting Basic EIGRP for IPv4 and IPv6

Lab 5.2.3.7: Troubleshooting Advanced EIGRP

Packet Tracer
Activity

Packet Tracer Activities

Packet Tracer Activity 5.1.2.5: Configuring EIGRP Manual Summary Routes for IPv4 and IPv6

Packet Tracer Activity 5.1.3.4: Propagating a Default Route in EIGRP for IPv4 and IPv6

Packet Tracer Activity 5.2.3.5: Troubleshooting EIGRP for IPv4

Check Your Understanding Questions

Complete all the review questions listed here to test your understanding of the topics and concepts in this chapter. The appendix, "Answers to the 'Check Your Understanding' Questions," lists the answers.

1. Which EIGRP router command will enable auto-summarization for a router running IOS 15.0(1)?

   A. **autosummary**

   B. **auto-summary**

   C. **ip eigrp auto-summary**

   D. There is no command needed. EIGRP auto-summarization is enabled by default when using IOS 15.0(1).

2. True/False: The **show ip protocols** command will verify that EIGRP auto-summarization is enabled or disabled.

3. Which set of commands would configure an EIGRP AS 1 summary route for 172.16.0.0/16 on the Serial 0/0/1 interface?

   A. Router(config)# **interface serial 0/0/1**

   Router(config-if)# **ip summary-address eigrp 1 172.16.0.0 255.255.0.0**

   B. Router(config)# **interface serial 0/0/1**

   Router(config-if)# **ip summary-address eigrp 1 172.16.0.0 0.0.255.255**

   C. Router(config)# **router eigrp 1**

   Router(config-router)# **summary-address 172.16.0.0 255.255.0.0 serial 0/0/1**

   D. Router(config)# **router eigrp 1**

   Router(config-router)# **network 172.16.0.0 255.255.0.0 serial 0/0/1**

4. What is the effect of the interface command **ip bandwidth-percent eigrp 1 25**?

   A. This command will limit the EIGRP process to using no more than 25% of the bandwidth on the link for Hello packets.

   B. This command will limit the EIGRP process to using no more than 25% of the bandwidth on the link for routing updates during initial convergence.

   C. This command will reserve 25% of the link's bandwidth for EIGRP messages, reducing the overall link bandwidth to 75% for other packets.

   D. This command will limit the EIGRP process to using no more than 25% of the bandwidth on the link.

5. What is the effect of the EIGRP **passive-interface** command? (Choose two.)

   A. Stops outgoing routing updates from being sent on the interface

   B. Does not accept incoming routing updates on the interface

   C. No longer advertises the network address for that interface even if that network is included in an EIGRP network statement

   D. Allows routers to still become neighbors on the interface

6. With automatic summarization enabled, EIGRP includes a Null0 summary route whenever which of the following exists? (Choose two.)

   A. There are one or more subnets in the routing table learned via EIGRP.

   B. There are one or more subnets in the routing table learned via a static route.

   C. There are one or more subnets in the routing table learned via a directly connected interface.

   D. There is at least one **network** EIGRP command.

   E. There are two or more **network** EIGRP router configuration commands.

7. Automatic summarization for EIGRP for IPv6:

   A. Is enabled using the **ipv6 auto-summary router configuration** command

   B. Is enabled using the **ipv6 auto-summary interface** command

   C. Is enabled automatically

   D. Cannot be enabled

8. An IPv4 default route is propagated in EIGRP for IPv4 using which of the following commands?

   A. Router(config-router)# **redistribute static**

   B. Router(config-router)# **default-information originate**

   C. Router(config)# **ip eigrp redistribute static**

   D. Router(config-if)# **ip eigrp redistribute static**

9. What is the purpose of the EIGRP **maximum-paths** router configuration command?

   A. Determines how many EIGRP routes can be in the routing table

   B. Modifies the number of equal cost paths for load balancing

   C. Determines the maximum number of EIGRP neighbors a router can have

   D. Determines the maximum number of interfaces that can be enabled for EIGRP

10. Which command(s) would be used to configure EIGRP authentication on an interface using the key chain configured below?

```
Router(config)# key chain SECRET_KEY
Router(config-keychain)# key 1
Router(config-keychain-key)# key-string mypassword
```

A. **ip authentication mode eigrp 1 md5**

   ip authentication key-chain eigrp 1 mypassword

B. **ip authentication key-chain eigrp 1 SECRET-KEY**

C. **ip authentication mode eigrp 1 SECRET-KEY**

D. **ip authentication mode eigrp 1 md5**

   ip authentication key-chain eigrp 1 SECRET-KEY

CHAPTER 6

Single-Area OSPF

Objectives

Upon completion of this chapter, you will be able to answer the following questions:

- What is the process by which link-state routers learn about other networks?

- How do you describe the types of packets used by Cisco IOS routers to establish and maintain an OSPF network?

- How do you explain how Cisco IOS routers achieve convergence in an OSPF network?

- How do you configure an OSPF router ID?

- How do you configure single-area OSPFv2 in a small, routed IPv4 network?

- How does OSPF use cost to determine the best path?

- How do you verify single-area OSPFv2 in a small, routed network?

- How do you describe the characteristics and operations of OSPFv2 and OSPFv3?

- How do you configure single-area OSPFv3 in a small, routed IPv6 network?

- How do you verify single-area OSPFv3 in a small, routed network?

Key Terms

This chapter uses the following key terms. You can find the definitions in the Glossary.

Introduction (6.0.1.1)

Open Shortest Path First (OSPF) is a link-state routing protocol that was developed as a replacement for the distance vector routing protocol, RIP. RIP was an acceptable routing protocol in the early days of networking and the Internet. However, RIP's reliance on hop count as the only metric for determining best route quickly became problematic. Using hop count does not scale well in larger networks with multiple paths of varying speeds. OSPF has significant advantages over RIP in that it offers faster convergence and scales to much larger network implementations.

OSPF is a classless routing protocol that uses the concept of areas for scalability. This chapter covers basic, single-area OSPF implementations and configurations.

Class Activity 6.0.1.2: Can Submarines Swim?

Edsger Wybe Dijkstra was a famous computer programmer and theoretical physicist. One of his most famous quotes was: "The question of whether computers can think is like the question of whether submarines can swim." Dijkstra's work has been applied, among other things, to routing protocols. He created the Shortest Path First (SPF) algorithm for network routing.

Now, open the PDF provided with this activity and answer the reflection questions. Save your work.

Get together with two of your classmates to compare your answers.

After completing this activity, do you have an idea as to how the OSPF protocol may work?

Characteristics of OSPF (6.1)

OSPF is a commonly implemented classless routing protocol that converges quickly and scales to large enterprise networks using areas. In this section, you will learn the basic operation of OSPF.

Evolution of OSPF (6.1.1.1)

As shown in Table 6-1, OSPF version 2 (OSPFv2) is available for IPv4 while OSPF version 3 (OSPFv3) is available for IPv6.

The initial development of OSPF began in 1987 by the Internet Engineering Task Force (IETF) OSPF Working Group. At that time, the Internet was largely an academic and research network funded by the U.S. government.

In 1989, the specification for OSPFv1 was published in RFC 1131. Two implementations were written. One implementation was developed to run on routers and the other to run on UNIX workstations. The latter implementation became a widespread UNIX process known as GATED. OSPFv1 was an experimental routing protocol and was never deployed.

In 1991, OSPFv2 was introduced in RFC 1247 by John Moy. OSPFv2 offered significant technical improvements over OSPFv1. It is classless by design; therefore, it supports VLSM and CIDR.

At the same time OSPF was introduced, ISO was working on a link-state routing protocol of their own, Intermediate System-to-Intermediate System (IS-IS). IETF chose OSPF as their recommended Interior Gateway Protocol (IGP).

Table 6-1   Interior and Exterior Gateway Routing Protocols

	Interior Gateway Protocols				Exterior Gateway Protocols
	Distance Vector		Link-State		Path Vector
IPv4	RIPv2	EIGRP	OSPFv2	IS-IS	BGP-4
IPv6	RIPng	EIGRP for IPv6	OSPFv3	IS-IS for IPv6	MP-BGP

In 1998, the OSPFv2 specification was updated in RFC 2328, which remains the current RFC for OSPF.

In 1999, OSPFv3 for IPv6 was published in RFC 2740. OSPF for IPv6, created by John Moy, Rob Coltun, and Dennis Ferguson, is not only a new protocol implementation for IPv6, but also a major rewrite of the operation of the protocol.

In 2008, OSPFv3 was updated in RFC 5340 as OSPF for IPv6.

Note

In this chapter, unless explicitly identified as OSPFv2 or OSPFv3, the term OSPF is used to indicate concepts that are shared by both.

Features of OSPF (6.1.1.2)

OSPF features include:

- *Classless*: It is classless by design; therefore, it supports VLSM and CIDR.

- **Efficient**: Routing changes trigger routing updates (no periodic updates). It uses the SPF algorithm to choose the best path.

- **Fast convergence**: It quickly propagates network changes.

- **Scalable:** It works well in small and large network sizes. Routers can be grouped into areas to support a hierarchical system.

- **Secure:** It supports Message Digest 5 (MD5) authentication. When enabled, OSPF routers only accept encrypted routing updates from peers with the same pre-shared password.

Administrative distance (AD) is the trustworthiness (or preference) of the route source. OSPF has a default administrative distance of 110. As shown in Table 6-2, OSPF is preferred over IS-IS and RIP.

Table 6-2   OSPF Administrative Distance

Route Source	Administrative Distance
Connected	0
Static	1
EIGRP summary route	5
External BGP	20
Internal EIGRP	90
IGRP	100
OSPF	110
IS-IS	115
RIP	120
External EIGRP	170
Internal BGP	200

Components of OSPF (6.1.1.3)

All routing protocols share similar components. They all use routing protocol messages to exchange route information. The messages help build data structures, which are then processed using a routing algorithm.

The three main components of the OSPF routing protocol include:

- Data structures
- Routing protocol messages
- Algorithm

Data Structures

As shown in Table 6-3, OSPF creates and maintains three databases.

Table 6-3   OSPF Data Structures

Database	Table	Description
Adjacency database	*Neighbor table*	■ List of all neighbor routers to which a router has established bidirectional communication. ■ This table is unique for each router. ■ Can be viewed using the **show ip ospf neighbor** command.
Link-state database *(LSDB)*	Topology table	■ List of information about all other routers in the network. ■ The database shows the network topology. ■ All routers within an area have identical link-state databases. ■ Can be viewed using the **show ip ospf database** command
Forwarding database	Routing table	■ List of routes generated when an algorithm is run on the link-state database. ■ Each router's routing table is unique and contains information on how and where to send packets to other routers. ■ Can be viewed using the **show ip route command**.

These tables contain a list of neighboring routers to exchange routing information with and are kept and maintained in RAM.

Routing Protocol Messages

OSPF exchanges messages to convey routing information using the following five types of packets:

- Hello packet

- Database Description (DBD) packet

- Link-State Request (LSR) packet

- Link-State Update (LSU) packet

- Link-State Acknowledgment (LSAck) packet

These packets are used to discover neighboring routers and also to exchange routing information to maintain accurate information about the network.

Algorithm

The CPU processes the neighbor and topology tables using Dijkstra's SPF algorithm. The SPF algorithm is based on the cumulative cost to reach a destination.

The SPF algorithm creates an SPF tree by placing each router at the root of the tree and calculating the shortest path to each node. The SPF tree is then used to calculate the best routes. OSPF places the best routes into the forwarding database, which is used to make the routing table.

Link-State Operation (6.1.1.4)

To maintain routing information, OSPF routers complete the following generic link-state routing process to reach a state of convergence:

1. Establish neighbor adjacencies. OSPF-enabled routers must recognize each other on the network before they can share information. An OSPF-enabled router sends Hello packets out all OSPF-enabled interfaces to determine if neighbors are present on those links. If a neighbor is present, the OSPF-enabled router attempts to establish a neighbor adjacency with that neighbor.

2. Exchange link-state advertisements. After adjacencies are established, routers then exchange *link-state advertisements (LSAs)*. LSAs contain the state and cost of each directly connected link. Routers flood their LSAs to adjacent neighbors. Adjacent neighbors receiving the LSA immediately flood the LSA to other directly connected neighbors, until all routers in the area have all LSAs.

3. Build the topology table. As shown in Figure 6-1, after LSAs are received, OSPF-enabled routers build the topology table (LSDB) based on the received LSAs. This database eventually holds all the information about the topology of the network.

4. Execute the SPF algorithm. Routers then execute the SPF algorithm. The gears in Figure 6-1 are used to indicate the execution of the SPF algorithm. The SPF algorithm creates the SPF tree shown in the figure.

The content of the R1 SPF tree is displayed in Figure 6-2.

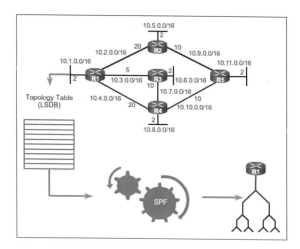

Figure 6-1   R1 Creates the SPF Tree

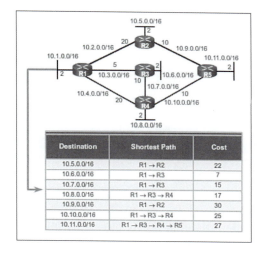

Destination	Shortest Path	Cost
10.5.0.0/16	R1 → R2	22
10.6.0.0/16	R1 → R3	7
10.7.0.0/16	R1 → R3	15
10.8.0.0/16	R1 → R3 → R4	17
10.9.0.0/16	R1 → R2	30
10.10.0.0/16	R1 → R3 → R4	25
10.11.0.0/16	R1 → R3 → R4 → R5	27

Figure 6-2   Content of the R1 SPF Tree

From the SPF tree, the best paths are inserted into the routing table. Routing decisions are made based on the entries in the routing table.

Single-Area and Multiarea OSPF (6.1.1.5)

To make OSPF more efficient and scalable, OSPF supports hierarchical routing using areas. An OSPF area is a group of routers that share the same link-state information in their LSDBs.

OSPF can be implemented in one of two ways:

- *Single-area OSPF*: In Figure 6-3, all routers are in one area called the backbone area (area 0). Single-area OSPF is useful in smaller networks with fewer routers.

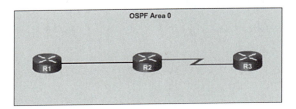

Figure 6-3   Single-Area OSPF

- *Multiarea OSPF*: In Figure 6-4, OSPF is implemented using a two-layer area hierarchy as all areas must connect to the backbone area (area 0). A router that interconnects two different areas is referred to as an *Area Border Router (ABR)*. Multiarea OSPF is useful in large network deployments to reduce processing and memory overload.

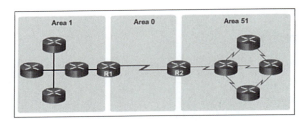

Figure 6-4   Multiarea OSPF

With multiarea OSPF, OSPF can divide one large autonomous system (AS) into smaller areas, to support hierarchical routing. With hierarchical routing, routing still occurs between the areas (inter-area routing), while many of the processor-intensive routing operations, such as recalculating the database, are kept within an area.

For instance, any time a router receives new information about a topology change within the area (including the addition, deletion, or modification of a link), the router must rerun the SPF algorithm, create a new SPF tree, and update the routing table. The SPF algorithm is CPU-intensive and the time it takes for calculation depends on the size of the area.

Note

Topology changes are distributed to routers in other areas in a distance vector format. In other words, these routers only update their routing tables and do not need to rerun the SPF algorithm.

Too many routers in one area would make the LSDBs very large and increase the load on the CPU. Therefore, arranging routers into areas effectively partitions a potentially large database into smaller and more manageable databases.

The hierarchical-topology possibilities of multiarea OSPF have these advantages:

- **Smaller routing tables:** Fewer routing table entries because network addresses can be summarized between areas. Route summarization is not enabled by default.

- **Reduced link-state update overhead:** Minimizes processing and memory requirements.

- **Reduced frequency of SPF calculations:** Localizes the impact of a topology change within an area. For instance, it minimizes routing update impact because LSA flooding stops at the area boundary as shown in Figure 6-5.

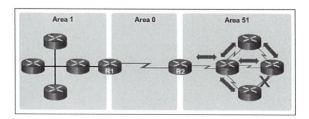

Figure 6-5   Link Change Impacts Local Area Only

For example, in Figure 6-5, R2 is an ABR for area 51. As an ABR, it would summarize the area 51 routes into area 0. When one of the summarized links fails, LSAs are exchanged within area 51 only. Routers in area 51 must rerun the SPF algorithm to identify the best routes. However, the routers in area 0 and area 1 do not receive any updates; therefore, they do not execute the SPF algorithm.

The focus of this chapter is on single-area OSPF.

Interactive Graphic

Activity 6.1.1.6: Identify OSPF Features and Terminology

Go to the online course to perform this practice activity.

OSPF Messages (6.1.2)

There are five types of OSPF messages that OSPF-enabled routers use to achieve convergence. This section describes the contents of these encapsulated OSPF messages and the five packet types.

Encapsulating OSPF Messages (6.1.2.1)

OSPF messages transmitted over an Ethernet link contain the following information:

- **Data Link Ethernet Frame Header:** Identifies the destination multicast MAC address 01-00-5E-00-00-05 or 01-00-5E-00-00-06.

- **IP Packet Header:** Identifies the IPv4 protocol field 89, which indicates that this is an OSPF packet. It also identifies one of two OSPF multicast addresses, 224.0.0.5 or 224.0.0.6.

- **OSPF Packet Header:** Identifies the OSPF packet type, the router ID, and the area ID.

- **OSPF Packet Type–Specific Data:** Contains the OSPF packet type information. The content differs depending on the packet type. In this case, it is an IPv4 Header.

Figure 6-6 displays the OSPFv2 field headers and summarizes the content of each header.

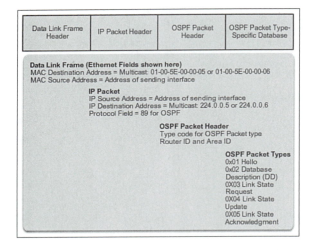

Figure 6-6   OSPF IPv4 Header Fields

Types of OSPF Packets (6.1.2.2)

OSPF uses link-state packets (LSPs) to establish and maintain neighbor adjacencies and exchange routing updates.

There are five different types of LSPs used by OSPF. Each packet serves a specific purpose in the OSPF routing process:

- **Type 1:** *Hello packet*: Used to discover, establish, and maintain adjacency with other OSPF routers.

- **Type 2:** *Database Description (DBD) packet*: Contains an abbreviated list of the sending router's LSDB and is used by receiving routers to check against the local LSDB. The LSDB must be identical on all link-state routers within an area to construct an accurate SPF tree.

- **Type 3:** *Link-State Request (LSR) packet*: Receiving routers can then request more information about any entry in the DBD by sending an LSR.

- **Type 4:** *Link-State Update (LSU) packet*: Used to reply to LSRs and to announce new information. LSUs contain seven different types of LSAs.

- **Type 5:** *Link-State Acknowledgment (LSAck) packet*: When an LSU is received, the router sends an LSAck to confirm receipt of the LSU. The LSAck data field is empty.

Hello Packet (6.1.2.3)

The OSPF Type 1 packet is the Hello packet. Hello packets are used to:

- Discover OSPF neighbors and establish neighbor adjacencies.

- Advertise parameters on which two routers must agree to become neighbors.

- Elect the Designated Router (DR) and Backup Designated Router (BDR) on multi-access networks like Ethernet and Frame Relay. Point-to-point links do not require DR or BDR.

Figure 6-7 displays the fields contained in the Type 1 Hello packet.

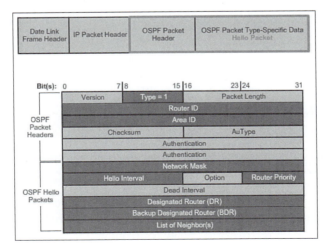

Figure 6-7   OSPF Hello Packet Content

Important fields shown in the figure include:

- **Type:** Identifies the type of packet. A one (1) indicates a Hello packet. A value of 2 identifies a DBD packet, 3 an LSR packet, 4 an LSU packet, and 5 an LSAck packet.

- **Router ID:** A 32-bit value expressed in dotted-decimal notation (an IPv4 address) used to uniquely identify the originating router.

- **Area ID:** Area from which the packet originated.

- **Network Mask:** Subnet mask associated with the sending interface.

- **Hello Interval:** Specifies the frequency, in seconds, at which a router sends Hello packets. The default Hello interval on multi-access and point-to-point networks is 10 seconds. This timer must be the same on neighboring routers; otherwise, an adjacency is not established.

- **Router Priority:** Used in a DR/BDR election. The default priority for all OSPF routers is 1, but can be manually altered from 0 to 255. The higher the value, the more likely the router becomes the DR on the link.

- **Dead Interval:** Is the time, in seconds, that a router waits to hear from a neighbor before declaring the neighboring router out of service. By default, the router Dead Interval is four times the Hello interval. This timer must be the same on neighboring routers; otherwise, an adjacency is not established.

- **Designated Router (DR):** Router ID of the DR.

- **Backup Designated Router (BDR):** Router ID of the BDR.

- **List of Neighbors:** List that identifies the router IDs of all adjacent routers.

Hello Packet Intervals (6.1.2.4)

OSPF Hello packets are transmitted to multicast address 224.0.0.5 in IPv4 and FF02::5 in IPv6 (all OSPF routers) every:

- 10 seconds (default on multi-access and point-to-point networks)

- 30 seconds (default on *nonbroadcast multi-access [NBMA]* networks; for example, Frame Relay)

The Dead Interval is the period that the router waits to receive a Hello packet before declaring the neighbor down. If the Dead Interval expires before the routers receive a Hello packet, OSPF removes that neighbor from its LSDB. The router floods the LSDB with information about the down neighbor out all OSPF-enabled interfaces.

Cisco uses a default of four times the Hello interval:

- 40 seconds (default on multi-access and point-to-point networks)
- 120 seconds (default on NBMA networks; for example, Frame Relay)

Link-State Updates (6.1.2.5)

Routers initially exchange Type 2 DBD packets, which is an abbreviated list of the sending router's LSDB and is used by receiving routers to check against the local LSDB.

A Type 3 LSR packet is used by the receiving routers to request more information about an entry in the DBD.

The Type 4 LSU packet is used to reply to an LSR packet.

LSUs are also used to forward OSPF routing updates, such as link changes. Specifically, an LSU packet can contain 11 different types of OSPFv2 LSAs, as shown in Figure 6-8. OSPFv3 renamed several of these LSAs and also contains two additional LSAs.

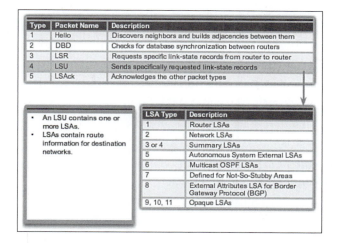

Type	Packet Name	Description
1	Hello	Discovers neighbors and builds adjacencies between them
2	DBD	Checks for database synchronization between routers
3	LSR	Requests specific link-state records from router to router
4	LSU	Sends specifically requested link-state records
5	LSAck	Acknowledges the other packet types

- An LSU contains one or more LSAs.
- LSAs contain route information for destination networks.

LSA Type	Description
1	Router LSAs
2	Network LSAs
3 or 4	Summary LSAs
5	Autonomous System External LSAs
6	Multicast OSPF LSAs
7	Defined for Not-So-Stubby Areas
8	External Attributes LSA for Border Gateway Protocol (BGP)
9, 10, 11	Opaque LSAs

Figure 6-8   LSUs Contain LSAs

Note

The difference between the LSU and LSA terms can sometimes be confusing because these terms are often used interchangeably. However, an LSU contains one or more LSAs.

Interactive Graphic

Activity 6.1.2.6: Identify the OSPF Packet Types

Go to the online course to perform this practice activity.

OSPF Operation (6.1.3)

OSPF routers must first become neighbors, exchange routing information, and achieve convergence. This section describes how OSPF neighbors transition between several states to achieve this convergence.

OSPF Operational States (6.1.3.1)

When an OSPF router is initially connected to a network, it attempts to:

- Create adjacencies with neighbors
- Exchange routing information
- Calculate the best routes
- Reach convergence

OSPF progresses through several states while attempting to reach convergence. The first three states are used to establish neighbor adjacencies:

- **Down state:** This is when there are no Hello packets exchanged. When a router sends and receives Hello packets, OSPF transitions to the Init state.

- **Init state:** This state starts when a router receives a Hello packet that contains the sender's router ID.

- **Two-Way state:** On Ethernet links, routers elect a *Designated Router (DR)* and *Backup Designated Router (BDR)*.

Once adjacencies are established, the routers proceed to the following states to synchronize their OSPF databases:

- **ExStart state:** Routers negotiate a master/slave relationship and the master initiates the DBD exchange.

- **Exchange state:** Each router forwards its DBD.

- **Loading state:** If additional information is required, the routers use LSRs and LSUs to gain additional router information. Routers are processed using the SPF algorithm.

- **Full state:** This state is achieved only when the routers have converged.

Establish Neighbor Adjacencies (6.1.3.2)

When OSPF is enabled on an interface, the router must determine if there is another OSPF neighbor on the link. To accomplish this, the router forwards a Hello packet that contains its router ID out all OSPF-enabled interfaces. The OSPF router ID is used by the OSPF process to uniquely identify each router in the OSPF area. A router ID is an IP address assigned to identify a specific router among OSPF peers.

When a neighboring OSPF-enabled router receives a Hello packet with a router ID that is not within its neighbor list, the receiving router attempts to establish an adjacency with the initiating router.

Refer to R1 in Figure 6-9. When OSPF is enabled, the enabled GigabitEthernet 0/0 interface transitions from the Down state to the Init state. R1 starts sending Hello packets out all OSPF-enabled interfaces to discover OSPF neighbors to develop adjacencies with.

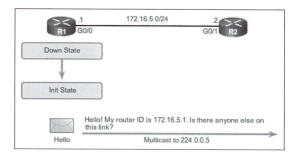

Figure 6-9   Down to Init States

In Figure 6-10, R2 receives the Hello packet from R1 and adds the R1 router ID to its neighbor list. R2 then sends a Hello packet to R1. The packet contains the R2 router ID and the R1 router ID in its list of neighbors on the same interface.

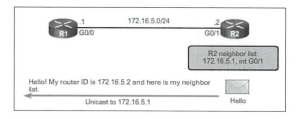

Figure 6-10   Init State

When R1 receives the Hello, it adds the R2 router ID to its list of OSPF neighbors. It also notices its own router ID in the Hello packet's list of neighbors. When a router receives a Hello packet with its router ID listed in the list of neighbors, the router transitions from the Init state to the Two-Way state.

The action performed in Two-Way state depends on the type of inter-connection between the adjacent routers:

- If the two adjacent neighbors are interconnected over a point-to-point link, then they immediately transition from the Two-Way state to the database synchronization phase.

- If the routers are interconnected over a common Ethernet network, then a Designated Router DR and a BDR must be elected.

Because R1 and R2 are interconnected over an Ethernet network, a DR and BDR election takes place. As shown in Figure 6-11, R2 becomes the DR and R1 is the BDR. This process only occurs on multiaccess networks such as Ethernet LANs.

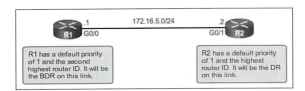

Figure 6-11   Elect the DR and BDR

Note

Hello packets will continue to be exchanged to maintain neighbor adjacencies.

OSPF DR and BDR (6.1.3.3)

Why is a DR and BDR election necessary?

Multi-access networks can create two challenges for OSPF regarding the flooding of LSAs:

- **Creation of multiple adjacencies:** Ethernet networks could potentially interconnect many OSPF routers over a common link. Creating adjacencies with every router is unnecessary and undesirable. It would lead to an excessive number of LSAs exchanged between routers on the same network.

- **Extensive flooding of LSAs:** Link-state routers flood their LSAs any time OSPF is initialized, or when there is a change in the topology. This flooding can become excessive.

To understand the problem with multiple adjacencies, we must study a formula.

For any number of routers (designated as n) on a multi-access network, there are $n (n - 1) / 2$ adjacencies.

Figure 6-12 shows a simple topology of five routers, all of which are attached to the same multi-access Ethernet network.

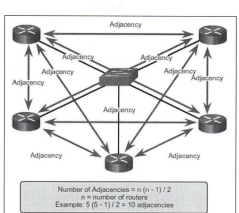

Figure 6-12   Creating Adjacencies with Every Neighbor

Without some type of mechanism to reduce the number of adjacencies, collectively these routers would form 10 adjacencies:

5 (5 − 1) / 2 = 10

This may not seem like much, but as routers are added to the network, the number of adjacencies increases dramatically, as shown in Table 6-4.

Table 6-4   More Routers = More Adjacencies

Routers	Adjacencies
N	*n (n − 1) / 2*
5	10
10	45
20	190
100	4,950

To understand the problem of extensive flooding of LSAs, refer to Figure 6-13. In the example, R2 is advertising a new route and therefore sends individual LSAs to each of its OSPF neighbors.

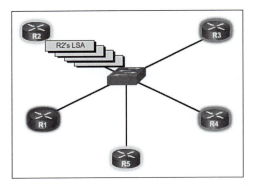

Figure 6-13   R2 Sends an LSA to Each Neighbor

This event triggers every neighbor router to also send out an LSA, as illustrated in Figure 6-14. Not shown in the figure are the required acknowledgments sent for every LSA received. If every router in a multi-access network had to flood and acknowledge all received LSAs to all other routers on that same multi-access network, the network traffic would become quite chaotic.

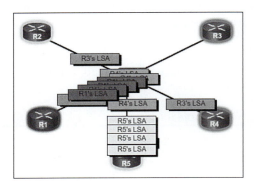

Figure 6-14   Flooding LSAs

Video

Video 6.1.3.3-A: Flooding LSAs

Go to the online course and play the animation in the third graphic to see how exchanging LSAs without a DR generates a flood of LSAs to be exchanged.

The solution to managing the number of adjacencies and the flooding of LSAs on a multi-access network is the DR. On multi-access networks, OSPF elects a DR to be the collection and distribution point for LSAs sent and received. A BDR is also elected in case the DR fails. All other routers become DROTHERs. A ***DROTHER*** is a router that is neither the DR nor the BDR.

In Figure 6-15, R2 has been elected the DR and R3 is the BDR. When a route change occurs on R1, it sends an LSA to the DR and BDR only using the multicast address of 224.0.0.6 (All Designated Routers).

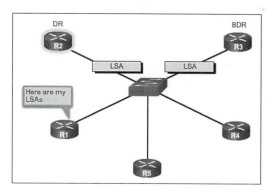

Figure 6-15   R1 Sends LSAs to the DR and BDR

As shown in Figure 6-16, the DR then sends LSAs to all of its OSPF adjacencies on behalf of R1 using the multicast address of 224.0.0.5 (All OSPF Routers).

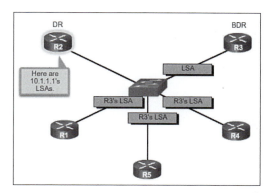

Figure 6-16   DR Sends LSAs to Adjacent Routers

Video 6.1.3.3-B: LSAs and DR

Go to the online course and play the animation in the fourth graphic to see how the number of LSAs is reduced when using the services of a DR.

Synchronizing OSPF Databases (6.1.3.4)

After the Two-Way state, routers transition to database synchronization states. While the Hello packet was used to establish neighbor adjacencies, the other four types of OSPF packets are used during the process of exchanging and synchronizing LSDBs.

In the ExStart state, a master and slave relationship is created between each router and its adjacent DR and BDR. The router with the higher router ID acts as the master for the Exchange state. In Figure 6-17, R2 becomes the master.

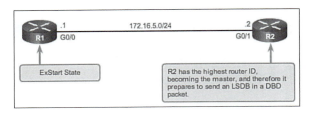

Figure 6-17   Routers Decide Who Initiates the First DBD

In the Exchange state, the master and slave routers exchange one or more DBD packets. A DBD packet includes information about the LSA entry header that appears in the router's LSDB. The entries can be about a link or about a network. Each LSA entry header includes information about the link-state type, the address of the advertising router, the link's cost, and the sequence number. The router uses the sequence number to determine the newness of the received link-state information.

In Figure 6-18, R2 sends a DBD packet to R1.

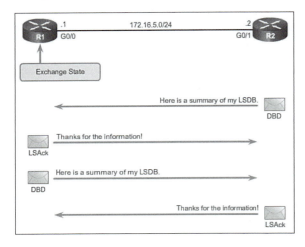

Figure 6-18   Exchange DBD Packets

When R1 receives the DBD packet, the following actions occur:

1. R1 acknowledges the receipt of the DBD using the LSAck packet.

2. R1 then sends DBD packets to R2.

3. R2 acknowledges R1.

R1 compares the information received with the information it has in its own LSDB. If the DBD packet has a more current link-state entry, the router transitions to the Loading state.

For example, in Figure 6-19, R1 sends an LSR regarding network 172.16.6.0 to R2. R2 responds with the complete information about 172.16.6.0 in an LSU packet. Again, when R1 receives an LSU, it sends an LSAck. R1 then adds the new link-state entries into its LSDB.

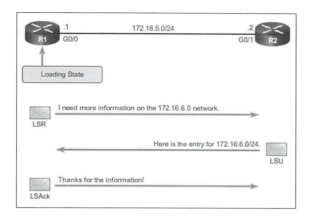

Figure 6-19   Getting Additional Route Information

After all LSRs have been satisfied for a given router, the adjacent routers are considered synchronized and in a Full state.

As long as the neighboring routers continue receiving Hello packets, the network in the transmitted LSAs remain in the topology database. After the topological databases are synchronized, updates (LSUs) are sent only to neighbors when:

- A change is perceived (incremental updates)
- Every 30 minutes

Interactive Graphic

Activity 6.1.3.5: Identify the OSPF States for Establishing Adjacency

Go to the online course to perform this practice activity.

Video

Video 6.1.3.6: Observing OSPF Protocol Communications

Go to the online course and play the animation to see how to configure OSPFv2 and then observe the neighbor adjacencies.

Configuring Single-Area OSPFv2 (6.2)

This section discusses the commands used for basic OSPF configuration. As you will see, the commands used are not much different from the commands you have already used in other routing protocols.

OSPF Network Topology (6.2.1.1)

Figure 6-20 shows the topology used for configuring OSPFv2 in this section. The types of serial interfaces and their associated bandwidths may not necessarily reflect the more common types of connections found in networks today. The bandwidths of the serial links used in this topology were chosen to help explain the calculation of the routing protocol metrics and the process of best path selection.

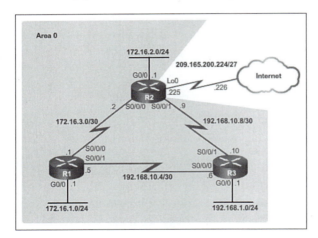

Figure 6-20   OSPF Basic Reference Topology

The routers in the topology have a starting configuration, including interface addresses. There is currently no static routing or dynamic routing configured on any of the routers. All interfaces on routers R1, R2, and R3 (except the loopback on R2) are within the OSPF backbone area. The loopback interface on R2 is used as the routing domain's gateway to the Internet.

Note

In this topology the loopback interface is used to simulate the WAN link to the Internet.

Router OSPF Configuration Mode (6.2.1.2)

OSPFv2 is enabled using the **router ospf** *process-id* global configuration mode command. The *process-id* value represents a number between 1 and 65,535 and is selected by the network administrator. The *process-id* value is locally significant, which means that it does not have to be the same value on the other OSPF routers to establish adjacencies with those neighbors.

Figure 6-21 provides an example of entering router OSPF configuration mode on R1 and displaying some of the OSPF router commands.

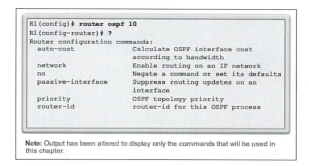

```
R1(config)# router ospf 10
R1(config-router)# ?
Router configuration commands:
   auto-cost              Calculate OSPF interface cost
                          according to bandwidth
   network                Enable routing on an IP network
   no                     Negate a command or set its defaults
   passive-interface      Suppress routing updates on an
                          interface
   priority               OSPF topology priority
   router-id              router-id for this OSPF process
```

Note: Output has been altered to display only the commands that will be used in this chapter.

Figure 6-21   OSPF Router Configuration Mode

> **Note**
>
> The list of commands has been altered to display only the commands that are used in this chapter.

Activity 6.2.1.2: Entering Router OSPF Configuration Mode on R2

Go to the online course to use the Syntax Checker in the third graphic to enter OSPF router configuration mode on R2 and list the commands available at the prompt.

Router IDs (6.2.1.3)

Every router requires a router ID to participate in an OSPF domain. The router ID can be defined by an administrator or automatically assigned by the router. The router ID is used by the OSPF-enabled router to:

- **Uniquely identify the router:** The router ID is used by other routers to uniquely identify each router within the OSPF domain and all packets that originate from them.

■ **Participate in the election of the DR:** In a multi-access LAN environment, the election of the DR occurs during initial establishment of the OSPF network. When OSPF links become active, the routing device configured with the highest priority is elected the DR. Assuming there is no priority configured, or there is a tie, then the router with the highest router ID is elected the DR. The routing device with the second highest router ID is elected the BDR.

But how does the router determine the router ID? As illustrated in Figure 6-22, Cisco routers derive the router ID based on one of three criteria, in the following preferential order:

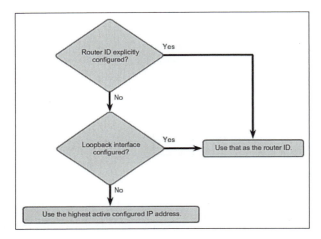

Figure 6-22 Router ID Order of Precedence

■ The router ID is explicitly configured using the OSPF **router-id** *rid* router configuration mode command. The *rid* value is any 32-bit value expressed as an IPv4 address. This is the recommended method to assign a router ID.

■ If the router ID is not explicitly configured, the router chooses the highest IPv4 address of any of the configured loopback interfaces. This is the next best alternative to assigning a router ID.

■ If no loopback interfaces are configured, then the router chooses the highest active IPv4 address of any of its physical interfaces. This is the least recommended method because it makes it more difficult for administrators to distinguish between specific routers.

If the router uses the highest IPv4 address for the router ID, the interface does not need to be OSPF-enabled. This means that the interface address does not need to be included in one of the OSPF **network** commands for the router to use that IP address as the router ID. The only requirement is that the interface is active and in the up state.

Note

The router ID looks like an IP address, but it is not routable and, therefore, is not included in the routing table, unless the OSPF routing process chooses an interface (physical or loopback) that is appropriately defined by a **network** command.

Configuring an OSPF Router ID (6.2.1.4)

Use the **router-id** *rid* router configuration mode command to manually assign a 32-bit value expressed as an IPv4 address to a router. An OSPF router identifies itself to other routers using this router ID.

As shown in Figure 6-23, R1 should be assigned the router ID of 1.1.1.1, R2 the router ID of 2.2.2.2, and R3 the router ID of 3.3.3.3.

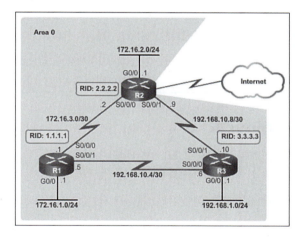

Figure 6-23   Router IDs

In Figure 6-24, the router ID 1.1.1.1 is assigned to R1. Use the **show ip protocols** command to verify the router ID.

Note

R1 had never been configured with an OSPF router ID. If it had, then the router ID would have to be modified.

If the router ID is the same on two neighboring routers, the router displays an error message similar to the one below:

```
%OSPF-4-DUP_RTRID1: Detected router with duplicate router ID.
```

To correct this problem, configure all routers so that they have unique OSPF router IDs.

```
R1(config)# router ospf 10
R1(config-router)# router-id 1.1.1.1
R1(config-router)# end
R1#
*Mar 25 19:50:36.595: %SYS-5-CONFIG_I: Configured from
console by console
R1#
R1# show ip protocols
*** IP Routing is NSF aware ***

Routing Protocol is "ospf 10"
  Outgoing update filter list for all interfaces is not set
  Incoming update filter list for all interfaces is not set
  Router ID 1.1.1.1
  Number of areas in this router is 0. 0 normal 0 stub 0
nssa
  Maximum path: 4
  Routing for Networks:
  Routing Information Sources:
    Gateway         Distance      Last Update
  Distance: (default is 110)

R1#
```

Figure 6-24   Assigning a Router ID to R1

Interactive Graphic

Activity 6.2.1.4: Assigning the Router ID on R2 and R3

Go to the online course to use the Syntax Checker in the third graphic to assign the router ID on R2 and R3.

Modifying a Router ID (6.2.1.5)

Sometimes a router ID needs to be changed, for example, when a network administrator establishes a new router ID scheme for the network. However, after a router selects a router ID, an active OSPF router does not allow the router ID to be changed until the router is reloaded or the OSPF process is cleared.

In Figure 6-25, notice that the current router ID is 192.168.10.5. The router ID should be 1.1.1.1.

```
R1# show ip protocols
*** IP Routing is NSF aware ***

Routing Protocol is "ospf 10"
  Outgoing update filter list for all interfaces is not set
  Incoming update filter list for all interfaces is not set
  Router ID 192.168.10.5
  Number of areas in this router is 1. 1 normal 0 stub 0
nssa
  Maximum path: 4
  Routing for Networks:
    172.16.1.0 0.0.0.255 area 0
    172.16.3.0 0.0.0.3 area 0
    192.168.10.4 0.0.0.3 area 0
  Routing Information Sources:
    Gateway         Distance      Last Update
    209.165.200.225      110       00:07:02
    192.168.10.10        110       00:07:02
  Distance: (default is 110)

R1#
```

Figure 6-25   Verifying the Router ID

In the following listing, the router ID 1.1.1.1 is being assigned to R1. Notice in the output how an informational message appears stating that the OSPF process must be cleared or that the router must be reloaded. The reason is because R1 already has adjacencies with other neighbors using the router ID 192.168.10.5. Those adjacencies must be renegotiated using the new router IP 1.1.1.1.

```
R1(config)# router ospf 10
R1(config-router)# router-id 1.1.1.1
% OSPF: Reload or use "clear ip ospf process" command, for this to take effect
R1(config-router)# end
R1#
*Mar 25 19:46:09.711: %SYS-5-CONFIG_I: Configured from console by console
```

Clearing the OSPF process is the preferred method to reset the router ID.

In Figure 6-26, the OSPF routing process is cleared using the **clear ip ospf process** privileged EXEC mode command. This forces OSPF on R1 to transition to the Down and Init states. Notice the adjacency messages change from Full to Down and then from Loading to Full. The **show ip protocols** command verifies that the router ID has changed.

```
R1# clear ip ospf process
Reset ALL OSPF processes? [no]: y
R1#
*Mar 25 19:46:22.423: %OSPF-5-ADJCHG: Process 10, Nbr
3.3.3.3 on Serial0/0/1 from FULL to DOWN, Neighbor Down:
Interface down or detached
*Mar 25 19:46:22.423: %OSPF-5-ADJCHG: Process 10, Nbr
2.2.2.2 on Serial0/0/0 from FULL to DOWN, Neighbor Down:
Interface down or detached
*Mar 25 19:46:22.475: %OSPF-5-ADJCHG: Process 10, Nbr
3.3.3.3 on Serial0/0/1 from LOADING to FULL, Loading Done
*Mar 25 19:46:22.475: %OSPF-5-ADJCHG: Process 10, Nbr
2.2.2.2 on Serial0/0/0 from LOADING to FULL, Loading Done
R1#
R1# show ip protocols | section Router ID
   Router ID 1.1.1.1
R1#
```

Figure 6-26   Clearing the OSPF Process

Interactive Graphic

Activity 6.2.1.5: Modifying the Router ID

Go to the online course to use the Syntax Checker in the fourth graphic to modify the router ID for R1.

Using a Loopback Interface as the Router ID (6.2.1.6)

A router ID can also be assigned using a loopback interface.

The IPv4 address of the loopback interface should be configured using a 32-bit subnet mask (255.255.255.255). This effectively creates a host route. A 32-bit host route does not get advertised as a route to other OSPF routers.

The following displays how to configure a loopback interface with a host route on R1. R1 uses the host route as its router ID, assuming there is no router ID explicitly configured or previously learned.

```
R1(config)# interface loopback 0
R1(config-if)# ip address 1.1.1.1 255.255.255.255
R1(config-if)# end
R1#
```

Note

Some older versions of the IOS do not recognize the **router-id** command; therefore, the best way to set the router ID on those routers is by using a loopback interface.

Configure Single-Area OSPFv2 (6.2.2)

This section discusses the commands used for configuring basic single-area OSPFv2.

Enabling OSPF on Interfaces (6.2.2.1)

The **network** command determines which interfaces participate in the routing process for an OSPF area. Any interfaces on a router that match the network address in the **network** command are enabled to send and receive OSPF packets. As a result, the network (or subnet) address for the interface is included in OSPF routing updates.

The basic command syntax is **network** *network-address wildcard-mask* **area** *area-id*.

The **area** *area-id* syntax refers to the OSPF area. When configuring single-area OSPF, the **network** command must be configured with the same *area-id* value on all routers. Although any area ID can be used, it is good practice to use an area ID of 0 with single-area OSPF. This convention makes it easier if the network is later altered to support multiarea OSPF.

Wildcard Mask (6.2.2.2)

OSPFv2 uses the argument combination of *network-address wildcard-mask* to enable OSPF on interfaces. OSPF is classless by design; therefore, the wildcard mask is always required. When identifying interfaces that are participating in a routing process, the wildcard mask is typically the inverse of the subnet mask configured on that interface.

A wildcard mask is a string of 32 binary digits used by the router to determine which bits of the address to examine for a match. In a subnet mask, binary 1 is equal to a match and binary 0 is not a match. In a wildcard mask, the reverse is true:

- **Wildcard mask bit 0:** Matches the corresponding bit value in the address

- **Wildcard mask bit 1:** Ignores the corresponding bit value in the address

The easiest method for calculating a wildcard mask is to subtract the network subnet mask from 255.255.255.255.

The example in Figure 6-27 calculates the wildcard mask from the network address of 192.168.10.0/24. To do so, the subnet mask 255.255.255.0 is subtracted from 255.255.255.255, providing a result of 0.0.0.255. Therefore, 192.168.10.0/24 is 192.168.10.0 with a wildcard mask of 0.0.0.255.

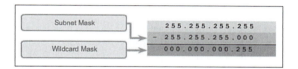

Figure 6-27   Calculating a Wildcard Mask for /24

The example in Figure 6-28 calculates the wildcard mask from the network address of 192.168.10.64/26. Again, the subnet mask 255.255.255.192 is subtracted from 255.255.255.255, providing a result of 0.0.0.63. Therefore, 192.168.10.0/26 is 192.168.10.0 with a wildcard mask of 0.0.0.63.

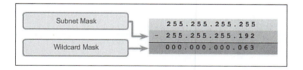

Figure 6-28   Calculating a Wildcard Mask for /26

The network Command (6.2.2.3)

There are several ways to identify the interfaces that will participate in the OSPFv2 routing process.

The following displays the required commands to determine which interfaces on R1 participate in the OSPFv2 routing process for an area. Notice the use of wildcard masks to identify the respective interfaces based on their network addresses. Because this is a single-area OSPF network, all area IDs are set to 0.

```
R1(config)# router ospf 10
R1(config-router)# network 172.16.1.0 0.0.0.255 area 0
R1(config-router)# network 172.16.3.0 0.0.0.3 area 0
R1(config-router)# network 192.168.10.4 0.0.0.3 area 0
R1(config-router)#
```

As an alternative, OSPFv2 can be enabled using the **network** *intf-ip-address* **0.0.0.0** *area area-id* router configuration mode command.

The following is an example of specifying the interface IPv4 address with a quad 0 wildcard mask. Entering **network 172.16.3.1 0.0.0.0 area 0** on R1 tells the router to enable interface Serial l0/0/0 for the routing process. As a result, the OSPFv2 process will advertise the network that is on this interface (172.16.3.0/30).

```
R1(config)# router ospf 10
R1(config-router)# network 172.16.1.1 0.0.0.0 area 0
R1(config-router)# network 172.16.3.1 0.0.0.0 area 0
R1(config-router)# network 192.168.10.5 0.0.0.0 area 0
R1(config-router)#
```

The advantage of specifying the interface is that the wildcard mask calculation is not necessary. OSPFv2 uses the interface address and subnet mask to determine the network to advertise.

Some IOS versions allow the subnet mask to be entered instead of the wildcard mask. The IOS then converts the subnet mask to the wildcard mask format.

Interactive Graphic

Activity 6.2.2.3: Advertising Networks in OSPF

Go to the online course to use the Syntax Checker in the third graphic to advertise the networks connected to R2.

Note

While completing the Syntax Checker, observe the informational messages describing the adjacency between R1 (1.1.1.1) and R2 (2.2.2.2). The IPv4 addressing scheme used for the router ID makes it easy to identify the neighbor.

Passive Interface (6.2.2.4)

By default, OSPF messages are forwarded out all OSPF-enabled interfaces. However, these messages really only need to be sent out interfaces connecting to other OSPF-enabled routers.

Refer to the topology in Figure 6-23. OSPF messages are forwarded out of all three routers' G0/0 interface even though no OSPF neighbor exists on that LAN. Sending out unneeded messages on a LAN affects the network in three ways:

- **Inefficient use of bandwidth:** Available bandwidth is consumed transporting unnecessary messages. Messages are multicasted; therefore, switches are also forwarding the messages out all ports.

- **Inefficient use of resources:** All devices on the LAN must process the message and eventually discard the message.

- **Increased security risk:** Advertising updates on a broadcast network is a security risk. OSPF messages can be intercepted with packet sniffing software. Routing updates can be modified and sent back to the router, corrupting the routing table with false metrics that misdirect traffic.

Configuring Passive Interfaces (6.2.2.5)

Use the **passive-interface** router configuration mode command to prevent the transmission of routing messages through a router interface but still allow that network to be advertised to other routers, as shown next for router R1. Specifically, the command stops routing messages from being sent out the specified interface. However, the network that the specified interface belongs to is still advertised in routing messages that are sent out other interfaces.

```
R1(config)# router ospf 10
R1(config-router)# passive-interface GigabitEthernet 0/0
R1(config-router)# end
R1#
```

For instance, there is no need for R1, R2, and R3 to forward OSPF messages out of their LAN interfaces. The configuration identifies the R1 G0/0 interface as passive.

It is important to know that a neighbor adjacency cannot be formed over a passive interface. This is because link-state packets cannot be sent or acknowledged.

The **show ip protocols** command is then used to verify that the Gigabit Ethernet interface was passive, as shown in Figure 6-29. Notice that the G0/0 interface is now listed under the Passive Interface(s) section. The network 172.16.1.0 is still listed under Routing for Networks, which means that this network is still included as a route entry in OSPF updates that are sent to R2 and R3.

Note

OSPFv2 and OSPFv3 both support the **passive-interface** command.

```
R1# show ip protocols
*** IP Routing is NSF aware ***

Routing Protocol is "ospf 10"
  Outgoing update filter list for all interfaces is not set
  Incoming update filter list for all interfaces is not set
  Router ID 1.1.1.1
  Number of areas in this router is 1. 1 normal 0 stub 0 nssa
  Maximum path: 4
  Routing for Networks:
    172.16.1.1 0.0.0.0 area 0
    172.16.3.1 0.0.0.0 area 0
    192.168.10.5 0.0.0.0 area 0
  Passive Interface(s):
    GigabitEthernet0/0
  Routing Information Sources:
    Gateway         Distance      Last Update
    3.3.3.3             110       00:08:35
    2.2.2.2             110       00:08:35
  Distance: (default is 110)

R1#
```

Figure 6-29   Verifying Passive Interfaces on R1

As an alternative, all interfaces can be made passive using the **passive-interface default** command. Interfaces that should not be passive can be re-enabled using the **no passive-interface** command.

Activity 6.2.2.5: Configuring Passive Interfaces

Go to the online course to use the Syntax Checker in the third graphic to configure the LAN interfaces as passive interfaces on R2 and R3.

Note

While completing the Syntax Checker, notice the OSPF informational state messages as the interfaces are all rendered passive and then the two serial interfaces are made non-passive.

Activity 6.2.2.6: Calculate the Subnet and Wildcard Masks

Go to the online course to perform this practice activity.

Packet Tracer Activity 6.2.2.7: Configuring OSPFv2 in a Single-Area

In this activity, the IP addressing is already configured. You are responsible for configuring the three-router topology with basic single-area OSPFv2, and then verifying connectivity between end devices.

OSPF Cost (6.2.3)

The OSPF metric is called *cost*. In this topic you will learn how Cisco IOS Software uses the cumulative bandwidths of the outgoing interfaces from the router to the destination network as the cost value.

OSPF Metric = Cost (6.2.3.1)

Recall that a routing protocol uses a metric to determine the best path of a packet across a network. A metric gives indication of the overhead that is required to send packets across a certain interface. OSPF uses cost as a metric. A lower cost indicates a better path than a higher cost.

The cost of an interface is inversely proportional to the bandwidth of the interface. Therefore, a higher bandwidth indicates a lower cost. More overhead and time delays equal a higher cost. Therefore, a 10-Mb/s Ethernet line has a higher cost than a 100-Mb/s Ethernet line.

The formula used to calculate the OSPF cost is:

Cost = *reference bandwidth / interface bandwidth*

The default reference bandwidth is 10^8 (100,000,000); therefore, the formula is:

Cost = *100,000,000 b/s / interface bandwidth in b/s*

Refer to Figure 6-30 for a breakdown of the cost calculation. Notice that Fast Ethernet, Gigabit Ethernet, and 10-Gigabit Ethernet interfaces share the same cost, because the OSPF cost value must be an integer. Consequently, because the default reference bandwidth is set to 100 Mb/s, all links that are faster than Fast Ethernet also have a cost of 1.

Interface Type	Reference Bandwidth in bps	Default Bandwidth in bps	Cost	
10 Gigabit Ethernet 10 Gb/s	100,000,000 ÷	10,000,000,000	1	
Gigabit Ethernet 1 Gb/s	100,000,000 ÷	1,000,000,000	1	Same Cost due to reference bandwidth
Fast Ethernet 100 Mb/s	100,000,000 ÷	100,000,000	1	
Ethernet 10 Mb/s	100,000,000 ÷	10,000,000	10	
Serial 1.544 Mb/s	100,000,000 ÷	1,544,000	64	
Serial 128 kb/s	100,000,000 ÷	128,000	781	
Serial 64 kb/s	100,000,000 ÷	64,000	1562	

Figure 6-30   Default Cisco OSPF Cost Values

OSPF Accumulates Costs (6.2.3.2)

The cost of an OSPF route is the accumulated value from one router to the destination network.

For example, in Figure 6-31, the cost to reach the R2 LAN 172.16.2.0/24 from R1 should be as follows:

- Serial link from R1 to R2 cost = 64

- Gigabit Ethernet link on R2 cost = 1

- Total cost to reach 172.16.2.0/24 = 65

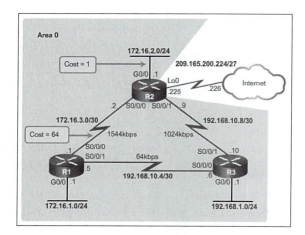

Figure 6-31   OSPF Reference Topology

The routing table of R1 in Figure 6-32 confirms that the metric to reach the R2 LAN is a cost of 65.

```
R1# show ip route | include 172.16.2.0
O        172.16.2.0/24 [110/65] via 172.16.3.2, 03:39:07,
         Serial0/0/0
R1#
R1# show ip route 172.16.2.0
Routing entry for 172.16.2.0/24
  Known via "ospf 10", distance 110, metric 65, type intra
  area
  Last update from 172.16.3.2 on Serial0/0/0, 03:39:15 ago
  Routing Descriptor Blocks:
  * 172.16.3.2, from 2.2.2.2, 03:39:15 ago, via Serial0/0/0
      Route metric is 65, traffic share count is 1
R1#
```

Figure 6-32   Verifying the Cost to the R2 LAN

Adjusting the Reference Bandwidth (6.2.3.3)

OSPF uses a reference bandwidth of 100 Mb/s for any links that are equal to or faster than a Fast Ethernet connection. Therefore, the cost assigned to a Fast Ethernet interface with an interface bandwidth of 100 Mb/s would equal 1:

```
Cost = 100,000,000 b/s / 100,000,000 = 1
```

While this calculation works for Fast Ethernet interfaces, it is problematic for links that are faster than 100 Mb/s, because the OSPF metric only uses integers as its final cost of a link. If something less than an integer is calculated, OSPF rounds up to the nearest integer. For this reason, from the OSPF perspective, an interface with an interface bandwidth of 100 Mb/s (a cost of 1) has the same cost as an interface with a bandwidth of 100 Gb/s (a cost of 1).

To assist OSPF in making the correct path determination, the reference bandwidth must be changed to a higher value to accommodate networks with links faster than 100 Mb/s.

Adjusting the Reference Bandwidth

Changing the reference bandwidth does not actually affect the bandwidth capacity on the link; rather, it simply affects the calculation used to determine the metric. To adjust the reference bandwidth, use the **auto-cost reference-bandwidth** *Mb/s* router configuration command. This command must be configured on every router in the OSPF domain. Notice that the value is expressed in Mb/s; therefore, to adjust the costs for:

- **Gigabit Ethernet:** Use the **auto-cost reference-bandwidth 1000** command
- **10-Gigabit Ethernet:** Use **auto-cost reference-bandwidth 10000** command

To return to the default reference bandwidth, use the **auto-cost reference-bandwidth 100** command.

Note

The reference bandwidth should be adjusted any time there are links faster than Fast Ethernet (100 Mb/s).

Table 6-5 displays the OSPF cost if the reference bandwidth is set to Gigabit Ethernet. Although the metric values increase, OSPF makes better choices because it can now distinguish between Fast Ethernet and Gigabit Ethernet links.

Table 6-5   Costs when Configured with **auto-cost reference-bandwidth 1000**

Interface Type	Reference Bandwidth in b/s		Default Bandwidth in b/s	Cost
10-Gigabit Ethernet 10 Gb/s	1,000,000,000	÷	10,000,000,000	1
Gigabit Ethernet 1 Gb/s	1,000,000,000	÷	1,000,000,000	1
Fast Ethernet 100 Mb/s	1,000,000,000	÷	100,000,000	10
Ethernet 10 Mb/s	1,000,000,000	÷	10,000,000	100
Serial 1.544 Mb/s	1,000,000,000	÷	1,544,000	647
Serial 128 kb/s	1,000,000,000	÷	128,000	7812
Serial 64 kb/s	1,000,000,000	÷	64,000	15625

Table 6-6 displays the OSPF cost if the reference bandwidth is adjusted to accommodate 10-Gigabit Ethernet links.

Table 6-6   Costs when Configured with **auto-cost reference-bandwidth 10000**

Interface Type	Reference Bandwidth in b/s		Default Bandwidth in b/s	Cost
10-Gigabit Ethernet 10 Gb/s	10,000,000,000	÷	10,000,000,000	1
Gigabit Ethernet 1 Gb/s	10,000,000,000	÷	1,000,000,000	10
Fast Ethernet 100 Mb/s	10,000,000,000	÷	100,000,000	100

Interface Type	Reference Bandwidth in b/s		Default Bandwidth in b/s	Cost
Ethernet 10 Mb/s	10,000,000,000	÷	10,000,000	1000
Serial 1.544 Mb/s	10,000,000,000	÷	1,544,000	6477
Serial 128 kb/s	10,000,000,000	÷	128,000	78125
Serial 64 kb/s	10,000,000,000	÷	64,000	156250

Note

The costs represent whole numbers that have been rounded down.

In Figure 6-33, all routers have been configured to accommodate the Gigabit Ethernet link with the **auto-cost reference-bandwidth 1000 router** configuration command. The following is the new accumulated cost to reach the R2 LAN 172.16.2.0/24 from R1:

- Serial link from R1 to R2 cost = 647

- Gigabit Ethernet link on R2 cost = 1

- Total cost to reach 172.16.2.0/24 = **648**

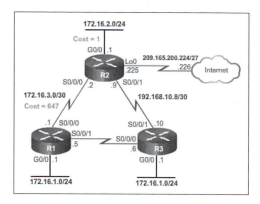

Figure 6-33   OSPF Reference Topology

Use the **show ip ospf interface s0/0/0** command to verify the current OSPF cost assigned to the R1 Serial 0/0/0 interface, as shown in Figure 6-34. Notice how it displays a cost of 647.

```
R1# show ip ospf interface serial 0/0/0
Serial0/0/0 is up, line protocol is up
  Internet Address 172.16.3.1/30,Area 0,Attached via Network Statement
  Process ID 10,Router ID 1.1.1.1,Network Type POINT_TO_POINT,Cost:647
  Topology-MTID    Cost    Disabled    Shutdown       Topology Name
        0           647       no          no              Base
  Transmit Delay is 1 sec, State POINT_TO_POINT
  Timer intervals configured, Hello 10, Dead 40, Wait 40, Retransmit 5
    oob-resync timeout 40
    Hello due in 00:00:01
  Supports Link-local Signaling (LLS)
  Cisco NSF helper support enabled
  IETF NSF helper support enabled
  Index 3/3, flood queue length 0
  Next 0x0(0)/0x0(0)
  Last flood scan length is 1, maximum is 1
  Last flood scan time is 0 msec, maximum is 0 msec
  Neighbor Count is 1, Adjacent neighbor count is 1
    Adjacent with neighbor 2.2.2.2
  Suppress hello for 0 neighbor(s)
R1#
```

Figure 6-34   Verifying the S0/0/0 Link Cost

The routing table of R1 in Figure 6-35 confirms that the metric to reach the R2 LAN is a cost of 648.

```
R1# show ip route | include 172.16.2.0
O       172.16.2.0/24 [110/648] via 172.16.3.2, 00:06:03, Serial0/0/0
R1#
R1# show ip route 172.16.2.0
Routing entry for 172.16.2.0/24
  Known via "ospf 10", distance 110, metric 648, type intra area
  Last update from 172.16.3.2 on Serial0/0/0, 00:06:17 ago
  Routing Descriptor Blocks:
  * 172.16.3.2, from 2.2.2.2, 00:06:17 ago, via Serial0/0/0
      Route metric is 648, traffic share count is 1
R1#
```

Figure 6-35   Verifying the Metric to the R2 LAN

Default Interface Bandwidths (6.2.3.4)

All interfaces have default bandwidth values assigned to them. As with reference bandwidth, interface bandwidth values do not actually affect the speed or capacity of the link. Instead, they are used by OSPF to compute the routing metric. Therefore, it is important that the bandwidth value reflect the actual speed of the link so that the routing table has accurate best path information.

Although the bandwidth values of Ethernet interfaces usually match the link speed, some other interfaces may not. For instance, the actual speed of serial interfaces is often different than the default bandwidth. On Cisco routers, the default bandwidth on most serial interfaces is set to 1.544 Mb/s.

Note

Older serial interfaces may default to 128 kb/s.

Refer to the example in Figure 6-36. Notice that the link between:

- R1 and R2 should be set to 1,544 kb/s (default value)

- R2 and R3 should be set to 1,024 kb/s

- R1 and R3 should be set to 64 kb/s

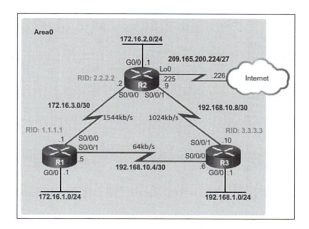

Figure 6-36 OSPF Reference Topology

Use the **show interfaces** command to view the interface bandwidth setting. Figure 6-37 displays the serial 0/0/0 interface settings for R1. The bandwidth setting is accurate and therefore the serial interface does not have to be adjusted.

Note

The entire output in Figure 6-37 can be viewed in the online course on page 6.2.3.4 graphic number 2.

```
R1# show interfaces serial 0/0/0
Serial0/0/0 is up, line protocol is up
  Hardware is WIC MBRD Serial
  Description: Link to R2
  Internet address is 172.16.3.1/30
  MTU 1500 bytes, BW 1544 Kbit/sec, DLY 20000 usec,
     reliability 255/255, txload 1/255, rxload 1/255
  Encapsulation HDLC, loopback not set
  Keepalive set (10 sec)
  Last input 00:00:05, output 00:00:03, output hang never
  Last clearing of "show interface" counters never
  Input queue: 0/75/0/0 (size/max/drops/flushes); Total
output drops: 0
  Queueing strategy: fifo
  Output queue: 0/40 (size/max)
  5 minute input rate 0 bits/sec, 0 packets/sec
  5 minute output rate 0 bits/sec, 0 packets/sec
     215 packets input, 17786 bytes, 0 no buffer
     Received 109 broadcasts (0 IP multicasts)
     0 runts, 0 giants, 0 throttles
     0 input errors, 0 CRC, 0 frame, 0 overrun, 0 ignored,
0 abort
     216 packets output, 17712 bytes, 0 underruns
     0 output errors, 0 collisions, 5 interface resets
```

Figure 6-37   Verifying the Default Bandwidth Settings of R1 Serial 0/0/0

The following output displays the serial 0/0/1 interface settings for R1. It also confirms that the interface is using the default interface bandwidth of 1,544 kb/s.

```
R1# show interfaces serial 0/0/1 | include BW
  MTU 1500 bytes, BW 1544 Kbit/sec, DLY 20000 usec,
R1#
```

According to the reference topology, this should be set to 64 kb/s. Therefore, the R1 Serial 0/0/1 interface must be adjusted.

Figure 6-38 displays the resulting cost metric of 647, which is based on the reference bandwidth set to 1,000,000,000 b/s and the default interface bandwidth of 1,544 kb/s (1,000,000,000 / 1,544,000).

```
R1# show ip ospf interface serial 0/0/1
Serial0/0/1 is up, line protocol is up
  Internet Address 192.168.10.5/30, Area 0, Attached via
  Network Statement
  Process ID 10, Router ID 1.1.1.1, Network Type
  POINT_TO_POINT, Cost: 647
  Topology-MTID    Cost    Disabled    Shutdown    Topology Name
        0          647        no          no          Base
  Transmit Delay is 1 sec, State POINT_TO_POINT
  Timer intervals configured, Hello 10, Dead 40, Wait 40,
  Retransmit 5
    oob-resync timeout 40
    Hello due in 00:00:04
  Supports Link-local Signaling (LLS)
  Cisco NSF helper support enabled
  IETF NSF helper support enabled
  Index 3/3, flood queue length 0
  Next 0x0(0)/0x0(0)
  Last flood scan length is 1, maximum is 1
  Last flood scan time is 0 msec, maximum is 0 msec
  Neighbor Count is 1, Adjacent neighbor count is 1
    Adjacent with neighbor 3.3.3.3
  Suppress hello for 0 neighbor(s)
R1#
```

Figure 6-38   R1 Serial 0/0/1 Settings

Note

The entire output in Figure 6-38 can be viewed in the online course on page 6.2.3.4 graphic number 4.

Adjusting the Interface Bandwidths (6.2.3.5)

To adjust the interface bandwidth, use the **bandwidth** *kilobits* interface configuration command. Use the **no bandwidth** command to restore the default value.

The example in Figure 6-39 adjusts the R1 Serial 0/0/1 interface bandwidth to 64 kb/s. A quick verification confirms that the interface bandwidth setting is now 64 kb/s.

The bandwidth must be adjusted at each end of the serial links, therefore:

- R2 requires its S0/0/1 interface to be adjusted to 1,024 kb/s.

- R3 requires its Serial 0/0/0 interface to be adjusted to 64 kb/s and its Serial 0/0/1 interface to be adjusted to 1,024 kb/s.

```
R1(config)# int s0/0/1
R1(config-if)# bandwidth 64
R1(config-if)# end
R1#
*Mar 27 10:10:07.735: %SYS-5-CONFIG_I: Configured from console by c
R1#
R1# show interfaces serial 0/0/1 | include BW
  MTU 1500 bytes, BW 64 Kbit/sec, DLY 20000 usec,
R1#
R1# show ip ospf interface serial 0/0/1 | include Cost:
  Process ID 10, Router ID 1.1.1.1, Network Type
  POINT_TO_POINT, Cost: 15625
R1#
```

Figure 6-39   Adjusting the Bandwidth of the R1 Serial 0/0/1 Interface

Interactive Graphic

Activity 6.2.3.5: Adjusting Interface Bandwidths

Go to the online course to use the Syntax Checker in the second graphic to adjust the serial interface of R2 and R3.

Note

A common misconception for students who are new to networking and the Cisco IOS is to assume that the **bandwidth** command changes the physical bandwidth of the link. The command only modifies the bandwidth metric used by EIGRP and OSPF. The command does not modify the actual bandwidth on the link.

Manually Setting the OSPF Cost (6.2.3.6)

As an alternative to setting the default interface bandwidth, the cost can be manually configured on an interface using the **ip ospf cost** *value* interface configuration command.

An advantage of configuring a cost over setting the interface bandwidth is that the router does not have to calculate the metric when the cost is manually configured. In contrast, when the interface bandwidth is configured, the router must calculate the OSPF cost based on the bandwidth. The **ip ospf cost** command is useful in multivendor environments where non-Cisco routers may use a metric other than bandwidth to calculate the OSPF costs.

Both the **bandwidth** interface command and the **ip ospf cost** interface command achieve the same result, which is to provide an accurate value for use by OSPF in determining the best route.

For instance, in the example in Figure 6-40, the interface bandwidth of Serial 0/0/1 is reset to the default value and the OSPF cost is manually set to 15,625. Although the interface bandwidth is reset to the default value, the OSPF cost is set as if the bandwidth was still calculated.

```
R1(config)# int s0/0/1
R1(config-if)# no bandwidth 64
R1(config-if)# ip ospf cost 15625
R1(config-if)# end
R1#
R1# show interface serial 0/0/1 | include BW
    MTU 1500 bytes, BW 1544 Kbit/sec, DLY 20000 usec,
R1#
R1# show ip ospf interface serial 0/0/1 | include Cost:
    Process ID 10, Router ID 1.1.1.1, Network Type POINT_TO_POINT,
    Cost: 15625
R1#
```

Figure 6-40   Adjusting the Cost of the R1 Serial 0/0/1 Interface

Figure 6-41 shows the two alternatives that can be used in modifying the costs of the serial links in the topology. The right side of the figure shows the **ip ospf cost** command equivalents of the **bandwidth** commands on the left.

Adjusting the Interface Bandwidth	=	Manually Setting the OSPF Cost
R1(config)# interface S0/0/1 R1(config-if)# bandwidth 64	=	R1(config)# interface S0/0/1 R1(config-if)# ip ospf cost 15625
R2(config)# interface S0/0/1 R2(config-if)# bandwidth 1024	=	R2(config)# interface S0/0/1 R2(config-if)# bandwidth 976
R3(config)# interface S0/0/0 R3(config-if)# bandwidth 64	=	R3(config)# interface S0/0/0 R3(config-if)# ip ospf cost 15625
R3(config)# interface S0/0/1 R3(config-if)# bandwidth 1024	=	R3(config)# interface S0/0/1 R3(config-if)# ip ospf cost 976

Figure 6-41   Bandwidth and IP OSPF Cost

Verify OSPF (6.2.4)

This section discusses the commands used for basic verification and troubleshooting of OSPFv2.

Verify OSPF Neighbors (6.2.4.1)

Use the **show ip ospf neighbor** command to verify that the router has formed an adjacency with its neighboring routers. If the router ID of the neighboring router is not displayed, or if it does not show as being in a state of FULL, the two routers have not formed an OSPF adjacency.

If two routers do not establish adjacency, link-state information is not exchanged. Incomplete LSDBs can cause inaccurate SPF trees and routing tables. Routes to destination networks may not exist, or may not be the optimum path.

Figure 6-42 displays the neighbor adjacency of R1.

```
R1# show ip ospf neighbor

Neighbor ID  Pri  State   Dead Time  Address       Interface
3.3.3.3       0   FULL/-  00:00:37   192.168.10.6  Serial0/0/1
2.2.2.2       0   FULL/-  00:00:30   172.16.3.2    Serial0/0/0
R1#
```

Figure 6-42   Verifying R1's OSPF Neighbors

For each neighbor, this command displays the following output:

- **Neighbor ID:** The router ID of the neighboring router.

- **Pri:** The OSPF priority of the interface. This value is used in the DR and BDR election.

- **State:** The OSPF state of the interface. FULL state means that the router and its neighbor have identical OSPF LSDBs. On multi-access networks, such as Ethernet, two routers that are adjacent may have their states displayed as 2WAY. The dash indicates that no DR or BDR is required because of the network type.

- **Dead Time:** The amount of time remaining that the router waits to receive an OSPF Hello packet from the neighbor before declaring the neighbor down. This value is reset when the interface receives a Hello packet.

- **Address:** The IPv4 address of the neighbor's interface to which this router is directly connected.

- **Interface:** The interface on which this router has formed adjacency with the neighbor.

<table>
<tr><td>Interactive
Graphic</td><td>

Activity 6.2.4.1: Verifying OSPF Neighbors

Go to the online course to use the Syntax Checker in the third graphic to verify the R2 and R3 neighbors using the **show ip ospf neighbor** command.

</td></tr>
</table>

Two routers may not form an OSPF adjacency if:

- The subnet masks do not match, causing the routers to be on separate networks.

- OSPF Hello or Dead Timers do not match.

- OSPF network types do not match.

- There is a missing or incorrect OSPF **network** command.

Verify OSPF Protocol Settings (6.2.4.2)

As shown in Figure 6-43, the **show ip protocols** command is a quick way to verify vital OSPF configuration information. This includes the OSPF process ID, the router ID, networks the router is advertising, the neighbors the router is receiving updates from, and the default administrative distance, which is 110 for OSPF.

```
R1# show ip protocols
*** IP Routing is NSF aware ***

Routing Protocol is "ospf 10"
  Outgoing update filter list for all interfaces is not
  set
  Incoming update filter list for all interfaces is not
  set
  Router ID 1.1.1.1
  Number of areas in this router is 1. 1 normal 0 stub 0
  nssa
  Maximum path: 4
  Routing for Networks:
    172.16.1.0 0.0.0.255 area 0
    172.16.3.0 0.0.0.3 area 0
    192.168.10.4 0.0.0.3 area 0
  Routing Information Sources:
    Gateway         Distance      Last Update
    2.2.2.2            110         00:17:18
    3.3.3.3            110         00:14:49
  Distance: (default is 110)

R1#
```

Figure 6-43 Verifying R1's OSPF Protocol Settings

Activity 6.2.4.2: Verifying OSPF Protocol Settings

Go to the online course to use the Syntax Checker in the second graphic to verify the OSPF protocol settings of R2 and R3 using the **show ip protocols** command.

Verify OSPF Process Information (6.2.4.3)

The **show ip ospf** command can also be used to examine the OSPF process ID and router ID, as shown in Figure 6-44. This command displays the OSPF area information and the last time the SPF algorithm was calculated.

```
R1# show ip ospf
Routing Process "ospf 10" with ID 1.1.1.1
Start time: 01:37:15.156, Time elapsed: 01:32:57.776
Supports only single TOS(TOS0) routes
Supports opaque LSA
Supports Link-local Signaling (LLS)
Supports area transit capability
Supports NSSA (compatible with RFC 3101)
Event-log enabled, Maximum number of events: 1000, Mode:
cyclic
Router is not originating router-LSAs with maximum metric
Initial SPF schedule delay 5000 msecs
Minimum hold time between two consecutive SPFs 10000 msecs
Maximum wait time between two consecutive SPFs 10000 msecs
Incremental-SPF disabled
Minimum LSA interval 5 secs
Minimum LSA arrival 1000 msecs
LSA group pacing timer 240 secs
Interface flood pacing timer 33 msecs
Retransmission pacing timer 66 msecs
Number of external LSA 0. Checksum Sum 0x000000
Number of opaque AS LSA 0. Checksum Sum 0x000000
Number of DCbitless external and opaque AS LSA 0
Number of DoNotAge external and opaque AS LSA 0
```

Figure 6-44 Verifying R1's OSPF Process

> **Note**
>
> The entire output in Figure 6-44 can be viewed in the online course on page 6.2.4.3 graphic number 2.

Activity 6.2.4.3: Verifying OSPF Process Information

Go to the online course to use the Syntax Checker in the second graphic to verify the OSPF process of R2 and R3 using the **show ip ospf** command.

Verify OSPF Interface Settings (6.2.4.4)

The quickest way to verify OSPF interface settings is to use the **show ip ospf interface** command. This command provides a detailed list for every OSPF-enabled interface. The command is useful to determine whether the **network** statements were correctly composed.

To get a summary of OSPF-enabled interfaces, use the **show ip ospf interface brief** command, as shown in Figure 6-45.

```
R1# show ip ospf interface brief
Interface  PID  Area  IP Address/Mask   Cost   State  Nbrs F/C
Se0/0/1    10   0     192.168.10.5/30   15625  P2P    1/1
Se0/0/0    10   0     172.16.3.1/30     647    P2P    1/1
Gi0/0      10   0     172.16.1.1/24     1      DR     0/0
R1#
```

Figure 6-45   Verifying R1's OSPF Interfaces

Activity 6.2.4.4: Verifying OSPF Interface Settings

Go to the online course to use the Syntax Checker in the second graphic to retrieve and view a summary of OSPF-enabled interfaces on R2 and R3 using the **show ip ospf interface brief** command and the **show ip ospf interface serial 0/0/1** command.

Lab 6.2.4.5: Configuring Basic Single-Area OSPFv2

In this lab, you will complete the following objectives:

- Part 1: Build the Network and Configure Basic Device Settings
- Part 2: Configure and Verify OSPF Routing
- Part 3: Change Router ID Assignments
- Part 4: Configure OSPF Passive Interfaces
- Part 5: Change OSPF Metrics

Configure Single-Area OSPFv3 (6.3)

OSPFv3 is operationally similar to OSPFv2. They both have the same data structures and operational features. However, OSPFv3 is configured differently than OSPFv2. This topic discusses similarities and differences between OSPFv2 and OSPFv3.

OSPFv3 (6.3.1.1)

OSPFv3 is the OSPFv2 equivalent for exchanging IPv6 prefixes. Recall that in IPv6, the network address is referred to as the prefix and the subnet mask is called the prefix-length.

Similar to its IPv4 counterpart, OSPFv3 exchanges routing information to populate the IPv6 routing table with remote prefixes, as shown in Figure 6-46.

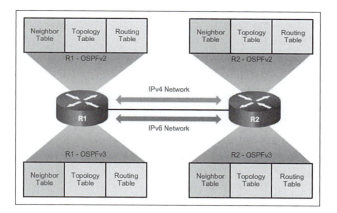

Figure 6-46   OSPFv2 and OSPFv3 Data Structures

> **Note**
>
> With the OSPFv3 Address Families feature, OSPFv3 includes support for both IPv4 and IPv6.

OSPFv2 runs over the IPv4 network layer, communicating with other OSPF IPv4 peers, and advertising only IPv4 routes.

OSPFv3 has the same functionality as OSPFv2, but uses IPv6 as the network layer transport, communicating with OSPFv3 peers and advertising IPv6 routes. OSPFv3 also uses the SPF algorithm as the computation engine to determine the best paths throughout the routing domain.

As with all IPv6 routing protocols, OSPFv3 has separate processes from its IPv4 counterpart. The processes and operations are basically the same as in the IPv4 routing protocol, but run independently. OSPFv2 and OSPFv3 each have separate adjacency tables, OSPF topology tables, and IP routing tables, as shown in Figure 6-46.

The OSPFv3 configuration and verification commands are similar to those used in OSPFv2.

Similarities Between OSPFv2 and OSPFv3 (6.3.1.2)

The following are similarities between OSPFv2 and OSPFv3:

- **Link-state:** OSPFv2 and OSPFv3 are both classless link-state routing protocols.

- **Routing algorithm:** OSPFv2 and OSPFv3 use the SPF algorithm to make routing decisions.

- **Metric:** The RFCs for both OSPFv2 and OSPFv3 define the metric as the cost of sending packets out the interface. OSPFv2 and OSPFv3 can be modified using the **auto-cost reference-bandwidth** *ref-bw* router configuration mode command. The command only influences the OSPF metric where it was configured. For example, if this command was entered for OSPFv3, it does not affect the OSPFv2 routing metrics.

- **Areas:** The concept of multiple areas in OSPFv3 is the same as in OSPFv2. Multiareas minimize link-state flooding and provide better stability with the OSPF domain.

- **OSPF packet types:** OSPFv3 uses the same five basic packet types as OSPFv2 (Hello, DBD, LSR, LSU, and LSAck).

- **Neighbor discovery mechanism:** The neighbor state machine, including the list of OSPF neighbor states and events, remains unchanged. OSPFv2 and OSPFv3 use the Hello mechanism to learn about neighboring routers and form adjacencies. However, in OSPFv3, there is no requirement for matching subnets to form neighbor adjacencies. This is because neighbor adjacencies are formed using link-local addresses, not global unicast addresses.

- **DR/BDR election process:** The DR/BDR election process remains unchanged in OSPFv3.

- **Router ID:** Both OSPFv2 and OSPFv3 use a 32-bit number for the router ID represented in dotted-decimal notation. Typically this is an IPv4 address. The OSPF **router-id** command must be used to configure the router ID. The process in determining the 32-bit router ID is the same in both protocols. Use an explicitly configured router ID; otherwise, the highest loopback IPv4 address becomes the router ID.

Differences Between OSPFv2 and OSPFv3 (6.3.1.3)

OSPFv2 and OSPFv3 differ in the following manner:

- **Advertises:** OSPFv2 advertises IPv4 routes, whereas OSPFv3 advertises routes for IPv6.

- **Source address:** OSPFv2 messages are sourced from the IPv4 address of the exit interface. In OSPFv3, OSPF messages are sourced using the link-local address of the exit interface.

- **All OSPF Routers multicast address:** OSPFv2 uses 224.0.0.5, whereas OSPFv3 uses FF02::5.

- **DR/BDR multicast address:** OSPFv2 uses 224.0.0.6, whereas OSPFv3 uses FF02::6.

- **Advertise networks:** OSPFv2 advertises networks using the **network** router configuration command, whereas OSPFv3 uses the **ipv6 ospf** *process-id* **area** *area-id* interface configuration command.

- **IP unicast routing:** Enabled, by default, in IPv4, whereas the **ipv6 unicast-routing** global configuration command must be configured.

- **Authentication:** OSPFv2 uses either plaintext authentication or MD5 authentication. OSPFv3 uses IPv6 authentication.

Table 6-7 highlights the differences between OSPFv2 and OSPFv3

Table 6-7   Differences Between OSPFv2 and OSPFv3

	OSPFv2	**OSPFv3**
Advertises	IPv4 networks	IPv6 prefixes
Source address	IPv4 source address	IPv6 link-local address
Destination address	Either the: - Neighbor IPv4 unicast address - 224.0.0.5 All-OSPF-Routers multicast address - 224.0.0.6 DR/BDR multicast address	Either the: - Neighbor IPv6 link-local address - FF02::5 All-OSPFv3-Routers multicast address - FF02::6 DR/BDR multicast address
Advertise networks	Configured using the network router configuration command	Configured using the **ipv6 ospf process-id area area-id** interface configuration command

	OSPFv2	OSPFv3
IP unicast routing	IPv4 unicast routing is enabled by default.	IPv6 unicast forwarding is not enabled by default. The **ipv6 unicast-routing** global configuration command must be configured.
Authentication	Plain text and MD5	IPv6 authentication

Link-Local Addresses (6.3.1.4)

Routers running a dynamic routing protocol, such as OSPF, exchange messages between neighbors on the same subnet or link. Routers only need to send and receive routing protocol messages with their directly connected neighbors. These messages are always sent from the source IPv4 address of the router doing the forwarding.

IPv6 link-local addresses are ideal for this purpose. An IPv6 link-local address enables a device to communicate with other IPv6-enabled devices on the same link, and only on that link (subnet). Packets with a source or destination link-local address cannot be routed beyond the link from where the packet originated.

As shown in Figure 6-47, OSPFv3 messages are sent using:

- **Source IPv6 address:** This is the IPv6 link-local address of the exit interface.

- **Destination IPv6 address:** OSPFv3 packets can be sent to a unicast address using the neighbor IPv6 link-local address. They can also be sent using a multicast address. The FF02::5 address is the All OSPF Routers address, while FF02::6 is the DR/BDR multicast address.

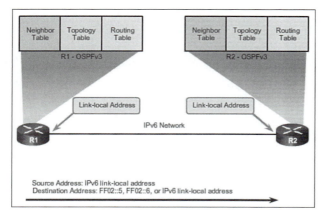

Figure 6-47   OSPFv3 Packet Destination

Activity 6.3.1.5: Compare and Contrast OSPFv2 and OSPFv3

Go to the online course to perform this practice activity.

Configuring OSPFv3 (6.3.2)

This section discusses the commands used for configuring basic single-area OSPFv3.

OSPFv3 Network Topology (6.3.2.1)

Figure 6-48 displays the network topology that is used to configure OSPFv3.

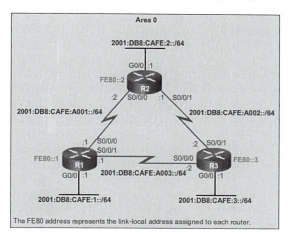

Figure 6-48 OSPFv3 Topology

The following shows the configuration of IPv6 unicast routing and the configuration of the *global unicast address* for the Gigabit Ethernet 0/0 and Serial 0/0/0 interfaces of R1, as identified in Figure 6-48. Assume that the interfaces of R2 and R3 have also been configured with their global unicast addresses, as identified in the referenced topology.

```
R1(config)# ipv6 unicast-routing
R1(config)#
R1(config)# interface GigabitEthernet 0/0
R1(config-if)# description R1 LAN
R1(config-if)# ipv6 address 2001:DB8:CAFE:1::1/64
R1(config-if)# no shut
R1(config-if)#
R1(config-if)# interface Serial0/0/0
R1(config-if)# description Link to R2
```

```
R1(config-if)# ipv6 address 2001:DB8:CAFE:A001::1/64
R1(config-if)# clock rate 128000
R1(config-if)# no shut
R1(config-if)#
R1(config-if)# interface Serial0/0/1
R1(config-if)# description Link to R3
R1(config-if)# ipv6 address 2001:DB8:CAFE:A003::1/64
R1(config-if)# no shut
R1(config-if)# end
R1#
```

In this topology, none of the routers have IPv4 addresses configured. A network with router interfaces configured with IPv4 and IPv6 addresses is referred to as dual-stacked. A dual-stacked network can have OSPFv2 and OSPFv3 simultaneously enabled.

The steps to configure basic OSPFv3 in a single area are:

Step 1.   Enable IPv6 unicast routing: **ipv6 unicast-routing**

Step 2.   (Optional) Configure link-local addresses.

Step 3.   Configure a 32-bit router ID in OSPFv3 router configuration mode using the **router-id** *rid* command.

Step 4.   Configure optional routing specifics such as adjusting the reference bandwidth.

Step 5.   Configure optional OSPFv3 interface-specific settings.

Step 6.   Adjust the interface bandwidth.

Step 7.   Enable IPv6 on the interface using the **ipv6 ospf area** interface configuration command.

Link-Local Addresses (6.3.2.2)

In Figure 6-49, the output of the **show ipv6 interface brief** command confirms that the correct global IPv6 addresses have been successfully configured and that the interfaces are enabled. Also, notice that each interface automatically generated a link-local address, as highlighted in the figure.

Link-local addresses are automatically created when an IPv6 global unicast address is assigned to the interface. Global unicast addresses are not required on an interface; however, IPv6 link-local addresses are.

```
R1# show ipv6 interface brief
Em0/0                  [administratively down/down]
   unassigned
GigabitEthernet0/0     [up/up]
      FE80::32F7:DFF:FEA3:DA0
      2001:DB8:CAFE:1::1
GigabitEthernet0/1     [administratively down/down]
   unassigned
Serial0/0/0            [up/up]
      FE80::32F7:DFF:FEA3:DA0
      2001:DB8:CAFE:A001::1
Serial0/0/1            [up/up]
      FE80::32F7:DFF:FEA3:DA0
      2001:DB8:CAFE:A003::1
R1#
```

Figure 6-49   Verifying the IPv6-Enabled Interfaces on R1

Unless configured manually, Cisco routers create the link-local address using the FE80::/10 prefix and the EUI-64 process. EUI-64 involves using the 48-bit Ethernet MAC address, inserting FFFE in the middle, and flipping the seventh bit. For serial interfaces, Cisco uses the MAC address of an Ethernet interface. Notice in Figure 6-49 that all three interfaces are using the same link-local address.

Assigning Link-Local Addresses (6.3.2.3)

Link-local addresses created using the EUI-64 format or, in some cases, random interface IDs, make it difficult to recognize and remember those addresses. Because IPv6 routing protocols use IPv6 link-local addresses for unicast addressing and next-hop address information in the routing table, it is common practice to make the link-local address an easily recognizable address.

Configuring the link-local address manually provides the ability to create an address that is recognizable and easier to remember. As well, a router with several interfaces can assign the same link-local address to each IPv6 interface. This is because the link-local address is only required for local communications.

Link-local addresses can be configured manually by using the same **interface** command used to create IPv6 global unicast addresses, but appending the **link-local** keyword to the **ipv6 address** command.

A link-local address has a prefix within the range FE80 to FEBF. When an address begins with this hextet (16-bit segment), the **link-local** keyword must follow the address.

The following example configures the same link-local address FE80::1 on the three R1 interfaces. FE80::1 was chosen to make it easy to remember the link-local addresses of R1.

```
R1(config)# interface GigabitEthernet 0/0
R1(config-if)# ipv6 address fe80::1 link-local
R1(config-if)# exit
R1(config)# interface Serial0/0/0
```

```
R1(config-if)# ipv6 address fe80::1 link-local
R1(config-if)# exit
R1(config)# interface Serial0/0/1
R1(config-if)# ipv6 address fe80::1 link-local
R1(config-if)#
```

A quick look at the interfaces as shown in Figure 6-50 confirms that the R1 interface link-local addresses have been changed to FE80::1.

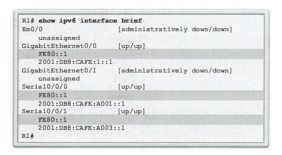

Figure 6-50   Verifying Link-Local Addresses on R1

Activity 6.3.2.3: Configuring Link-Local Addresses

Go to the online course to use the Syntax Checker in the third graphic to configure and verify link-local address FE80::2 on R2 and link-local address FE80::3 on R3.

Configuring the OSPFv3 Router ID (6.3.2.4)

Use the **ipv6 router ospf** *process-id* global configuration mode command to enter router configuration mode. The IPv6 router configuration mode prompt is different than the IPv4 router configuration mode prompt. Use the IPv6 router confirmation mode to configure global OSPFv3 parameters, such as assigning a 32-bit OSPF router ID and reference bandwidth.

IPv6 routing protocols are enabled on an interface, and not from router configuration mode, like their IPv4 counterparts. The **network** IPv4 router configuration mode command does not exist in IPv6.

Like OSPFv2, the *process-id* value is a number between 1 and 65,535 and is chosen by the network administrator. The *process-id* value is locally significant, which means that it does not have to match other OSPF routers to establish adjacencies with those neighbors.

OSPFv3 requires a 32-bit router ID to be assigned before OSPF can be enabled on an interface. The logic diagram in Figure 6-51 displays how a router ID is chosen. Like OSPFv2, OSPFv3 uses:

- An explicitly configured router ID first.

- If none are configured, then the router uses the highest configured IPv4 address of a loopback interface.

- If none are configured, then the router uses the highest configured IPv4 address of an active interface.

- If there are no sources of IPv4 addresses on a router, then the router displays a console message to configure the router ID manually.

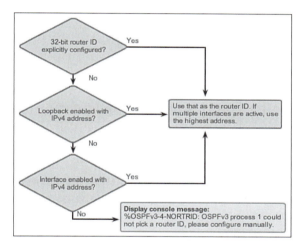

Figure 6-51   Router ID Order of Precedence

Note

For consistency, all three routers use the process ID of 10.

As shown in the topology in Figure 6-52, routers R1, R2, and R3 are to be assigned the router IDs indicated. The **router-id** *rid* command used to assign a router ID in OSPFv2 is the same command used in OSPFv3.

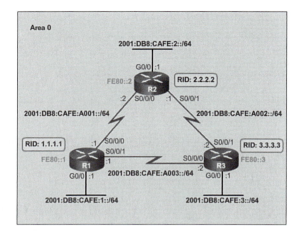

Figure 6-52   OSPF Topology with Router-IDs

The example in Figure 6-53:

- Enters the router OSPFv3 configuration mode. Notice how the router prompt is different than the default IPv4 routing protocol mode router prompt. Also notice how an informational console message appeared when the OSPFv3 router configuration mode was accessed.

- Assigns the router ID 1.1.1.1.

- Adjusts the reference bandwidth to 1,000,000,000 b/s (1 Gb/s), because there are Gigabit Ethernet links in the network. Notice the information console message that this command must be configured on all routers in the routing domain.

- The **show ipv6 protocols** command is used to verify that the OSPFv3 process ID 10 is using the router ID 1.1.1.1.

```
R1(config)# ipv6 router ospf 10
R1(config-rtr)#
*Mar 29 11:21:53.739: %OSPFv3-4-NORTRID: Process OSPFv3-1-
IPv6 could not pick a router-id, please configure manually
R1(config-rtr)#
R1(config-rtr)# router-id 1.1.1.1
R1(config-rtr)#
R1(config-rtr)# auto-cost reference-bandwidth 1000
% OSPFv3-1-IPv6: Reference bandwidth is changed. Please
ensure reference bandwidth is consistent across all routers.
R1(config-rtr)#
R1(config-rtr)# end
R1#
R1# show ipv6 protocols
IPv6 Routing Protocol is "connected"
IPv6 Routing Protocol is "ND"
IPv6 Routing Protocol is "ospf 10"
  Router ID 1.1.1.1
  Number of areas: 0 normal, 0 stub, 0 nssa
  Redistribution:
    None
R1#
```

Figure 6-53   Assigning a Router ID to R1

Activity 6.3.2.4: Assigning a Router ID

Go to the online course to use the Syntax Checker in the fourth graphic to configure global OSPFv3 settings on R2 and R3.

Modifying an OSPFv3 Router ID (6.3.2.5)

Router IDs sometimes must be changed, for example, if the network administrator has established a new router ID identification scheme. However, after an OSPFv3 router establishes a router ID, that router ID cannot be changed until the router is reloaded or the OSPF process is cleared.

In the following output, notice that the current router ID is 10.1.1.1. The OSPFv3 router ID should be 1.1.1.1.

```
R1# show ipv6 protocols
IPv6 Routing Protocol is "connected"
IPv6 Routing Protocol is "ND"
IPv6 Routing Protocol is "ospf 10"
  Router ID 10.1.1.1
  Number of areas: 0 normal, 0 stub, 0 nssa
  Redistribution:
    None
R1#
```

The following assigns the router ID 1.1.1.1 to R1:

```
R1(config)# ipv6 router ospf 10
R1(config-rtr)# router-id 1.1.1.1
R1(config-rtr)# end
R1#
```

Note

Clearing the OSPF process is the preferred method to reset the router ID.

The following clears the OSPF routing process using the **clear ipv6 ospf process** privileged EXEC mode command. Doing this forces OSPF on R1 to renegotiate neighbor adjacencies using the new router ID.

```
R1# clear ipv6 ospf process
Reset selected OSPFv3 processes? [no]: y
R1#
R1# show ipv6 protocols
IPv6 Routing Protocol is "connected"
IPv6 Routing Protocol is "ND"
IPv6 Routing Protocol is "ospf 10"
```

```
Router ID 1.1.1.1
Number of areas: 0 normal, 0 stub, 0 nssa
Redistribution:
  None
R1#
```

The **show ipv6 protocols** command verifies that the router ID has changed.

Activity 6.3.2.5: Modifying the Router ID

Go to the online course to use the Syntax Checker in the fourth graphic to modify the router ID for R1.

Enabling OSPFv3 on Interfaces (6.3.2.6)

OSPFv3 uses a different method to enable an interface for OSPF. Instead of using the **network** router configuration mode command to specify matching interface addresses, OSPFv3 is configured directly on the interface.

To enable OSPFv3 on an interface, use the **ipv6 ospf** *process-id* **area** *area-id* interface configuration mode command.

The *process-id* value identifies the specific routing process and must be the same as the process ID used to create the routing process in the **ipv6 router ospf** *process-id* command.

The *area-id* value is the area to be associated with the OSPFv3 interface. Although any value could have been configured for the area, 0 was selected because area 0 is the backbone area to which all other areas must attach, as shown in Figure 6-54. This helps in the migration to multiarea OSPF, if the need arises.

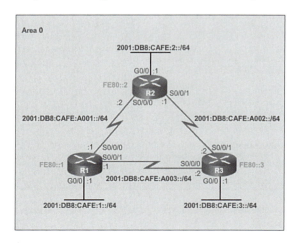

Figure 6-54   OSPFv3 Topology in Area 0

In Figure 6-55, OSPFv3 is enabled on the R1 interfaces using the **ipv6 ospf 10 area 0** command. The **show ipv6 ospf interface brief** command displays the active OSPFv3 interfaces.

```
R1(config)# interface GigabitEthernet 0/0
R1(config-if)# ipv6 ospf 10 area 0
R1(config-if)#
R1(config-if)# interface Serial0/0/0
R1(config-if)# ipv6 ospf 10 area 0
R1(config-if)#
R1(config-if)# interface Serial0/0/1
R1(config-if)# ipv6 ospf 10 area 0
R1(config-if)#
R1(config-if)# end
R1#
R1# show ipv6 ospf interfaces brief
Interface  PID  Area      Intf ID  Cost   State  Nbra F/C
Se0/0/1    10   0         7        15625  P2P    0/0
Se0/0/0    10   0         6        647    P2P    0/0
Gi0/0      10   0         3        1      WAIT   0/0
R1#
```

Figure 6-55   Enable OSPFv3 on the R1 Interfaces

Interactive Graphic

Activity 6.3.2.6: Enable OSPFv3 on the R2 and R3 Interfaces

Go to the online course to use the Syntax Checker in the third graphic to enable OSPFv3 on the R2 and R3 interfaces.

Verify OSPFv3 (6.3.3)

This section discusses the commands used for basic verification and troubleshooting of OSPFv3.

Verify OSPFv3 Neighbors (6.3.3.1)

Use the **show ipv6 ospf neighbor** command to verify that the router has formed an adjacency with its neighboring routers. If the router ID of the neighboring router is not displayed, or if it does not show as being in a state of FULL, the two routers have not formed an OSPF adjacency.

If two routers do not establish a neighbor adjacency, link-state information is not exchanged. Incomplete LSDBs can cause inaccurate SPF trees and routing tables. Routes to destination networks may not exist or may not be the optimum path.

Figure 6-56 displays the neighbor adjacency of R1. For each neighbor, this command displays the following output:

- **Neighbor ID:** The router ID of the neighboring router.

- **Pri:** The OSPF priority of the interface. Value is used in the DR and BDR election.

- **State:** The OSPF state of the interface. FULL state means that the router and its neighbor have identical OSPF LSDBs. On multi-access networks such as Ethernet, two routers that are adjacent may have their states displayed as 2WAY. The dash indicates that no DR or BDR is required because of the network type.

- **Dead Time:** The amount of time remaining that the router waits to receive an OSPF Hello packet from the neighbor before declaring the neighbor down. This value is reset when the interface receives a Hello packet.

- **Interface ID:** The interface ID or link ID.

- **Interface:** The interface on which this router has formed adjacency with the neighbor.

```
R1# show ipv6 ospf neighbor

OSPFv3 Router with ID (1.1.1.1) (Process ID 10)

Neighbor ID  Pri  State     Dead Time  Interface ID  Interface
3.3.3.3        0  FULL/  -  00:00:39   6             Serial0/0/1
2.2.2.2        0  FULL/  -  00:00:36   6             Serial0/0/0
R1#
```

Figure 6-56   Verifying OSPFv3 Neighbors for R1

Interactive Graphic

Activity 6.3.3.1: Verifying OSPFv3 Neighbors for R2 and R3

Go to the online course to use the Syntax Checker in the second graphic to verify the R2 and R3 neighbors using the **show ipv6 ospf neighbor** command.

Verify OSPFv3 Protocol Settings (6.3.3.2)

As shown in the following output, the **show ipv6 protocols** command is a quick way to verify vital OSPFv3 configuration information, including the OSPF process ID, the router ID, and the interfaces enabled for OSPFv3:

```
R1# show ipv6 protocols
IPv6 Routing Protocol is "connected"
IPv6 Routing Protocol is "ND"
IPv6 Routing Protocol is "ospf 10"
  Router ID 1.1.1.1
  Number of areas: 1 normal, 0 stub, 0 nssa
  Interfaces (Area 0):
    Serial0/0/1
    Serial0/0/0
    GigabitEthernet0/0
```

```
      Redistribution:
        None
R1#
```

Activity 6.3.3.2: Verifying OSPFv3 Protocol Settings on R2 and R3

Go to the online course to use the Syntax Checker in the second graphic to verify the OSPF protocol settings of R2 and R3 using the **show ipv6 protocols** command.

Use the **show ipv6 ospf** command to also examine the OSPFv3 process ID and router ID. This command displays the OSPF area information and the last time the SPF algorithm was calculated.

Verify OSPFv3 Interfaces (6.3.3.3)

The quickest way to verify OSPF interface settings is to use the **show ipv6 ospf interface** command. This command provides a detailed list for every OSPF-enabled interface.

To retrieve and view a summary of OSPFv3-enabled interfaces on R1, use the **show ipv6 ospf interface brief** command, as shown in Figure 6-57.

```
R1# show ipv6 ospf interface brief
Interface   PID  Area        Intf ID   Cost  State Nbrs F/C
Se0/0/1     10   0           7         15625 P2P   1/1
Se0/0/0     10   0           6         647   P2P   1/1
Gi0/0       10   0           3         1     DR    0/0
R1#
```

Figure 6-57   Verifying R1's OSPFv3 Interfaces

Activity 6.3.3.3: Verifying OSPFv3 Interfaces on R2 and R3

Go to the online course to use the Syntax Checker in the second graphic to view a summary of OSPF-enabled interfaces on R2 and R3 using the **show ipv6 ospf interface brief** command. Notice that specifying the interface name as done in the **show ipv6 ospf interface serial** command provides detailed OSPF information.

Verify the IPv6 Routing Table (6.3.3.4)

In Figure 6-58, the **show ipv6 route ospf** command provides specifics about OSPF routes in the routing table.

```
R1# show ipv6 route ospf
IPv6 Routing Table - default - 10 entries
Codes: C - Connected, L - Local, S - Static, U - Per-user
Static route
       B - BGP, R - RIP, H - NHRP, I1 - ISIS L1
       I2 - ISIS L2, IA - ISIS interarea, IS - ISIS
summary, D - EIGRP
       EX - EIGRP external, ND - ND Default, NDp - ND
Prefix, DCE - Destination
       NDr - Redirect, O - OSPF Intra, OI - OSPF Inter,
OE1 - OSPF ext 1
       OE2 - OSPF ext 2, ON1 - OSPF NSSA ext 1, ON2 - OSPF
NSSA ext 2
O   2001:DB8:CAFE:2::/64 [110/657]
      via FE80::2, Serial0/0/0
O   2001:DB8:CAFE:3::/64 [110/1304]
      via FE80::2, Serial0/0/0
O   2001:DB8:CAFE:A002::/64 [110/1294]
      via FE80::2, Serial0/0/0
R1#
```

Figure 6-58   Verifying the IPv6 Routing Table

Activity 6.3.3.4: Verifying the IPv6 Routing Table of R2 and R3

Go to the online course to use the Syntax Checker in the second graphic to verify the OSPFv3 routing table of R2 and R3, by using the **show ipv6 route ospf** command.

Packet Tracer Activity 6.3.3.5: Configuring Basic OSPFv3

In this activity, the IPv6 addressing is already configured. You are responsible for configuring the three-router topology with a basic single-area OSPFv3, and then verifying connectivity between end devices.

Lab 6.3.3.6: Configuring Basic Single-Area OSPFv3

In this lab, you will complete the following objectives:

- Part 1: Build the Network and Configure Basic Device Settings
- Part 2: Configure OSPFv3 Routing
- Part 3: Configure OSPFv3 Passive Interfaces

Summary (6.4)

Class Activity 6.4.1.1: Stepping Through OSPFv3

This class activity is designed for groups of three students. The objective is to review the Shortest Path First (SPF) routing process.

You will design and address a network, communicate the network address scheme and operation of network links to your group members, and compute the SPF.

Complete the steps as shown on the PDF for this class activity.

If you have time, share your network design and Open Shortest Path First (OSPF) process with another group.

Packet Tracer Activity 6.4.1.2: Skills Integration Challenge

In this Skills Integration Challenge, your focus is OSPFv2 and OSPFv3 configurations. You will configure IP addressing for all devices. Then you will configure OSPFv2 routing for the IPv4 portion of the network and OSPFv3 routing for the IPv6 portion of the network. One router will be configured with both IPv4 and IPv6 configurations. Finally, you will verify your configurations and test connectivity between end devices.

The current version of OSPF for IPv4 is OSPFv2, introduced in RFC 1247 and updated in RFC 2328 by John Moy. In 1999, OSPFv3 for IPv6 was published in RFC 2740.

OSPF is a classless, link-state routing protocol with a default administrative distance of 110, and is denoted in the routing table with a route source code of O.

OSPF is enabled with the **router ospf** *process-id* global configuration mode command. The *process-id* value is locally significant, which means that it does not need to match other OSPF routers to establish adjacencies with those neighbors.

The **network** command used with OSPF has the same function as when used with other IGP routing protocols, but with slightly different syntax. The *wildcard-mask* value is the inverse of the subnet mask, and the *area-id* value should be set to **0** for single-area OSPF.

By default, OSPF Hello packets are sent every 10 seconds on multi-access and point-to-point segments and every 30 seconds on NBMA segments (Frame Relay, X.25, ATM), and are used by OSPF to establish neighbor adjacencies. The Dead interval is four times the Hello interval, by default.

For routers to become adjacent, their Hello Interval, Dead interval, network types, and subnet masks must match. Use the **show ip ospf neighbors** command to verify OSPF adjacencies.

OSPF elects a DR to act as the collection and distribution point for LSAs sent and received in the multi-access network. A BDR is elected to assume the role of the DR should the DR fail. All other routers are known as DROTHERs. All routers send their LSAs to the DR, which then floods the LSA to all other routers in the multi-access network.

The **show ip protocols** command is used to verify important OSPF configuration information, including the OSPF process ID, the router ID, and the networks the router is advertising.

OSPFv3 is enabled on an interface and not under router configuration mode. OSPFv3 needs link-local addresses to be configured. IPv6 unicast routing must be enabled for OSPFv3. A 32-bit router ID is required before an interface can be enabled for OSPFv3.

Practice

The following activities provide practice with the topics introduced in this chapter. The Labs and Class Activities are available in the companion *Routing Protocols Lab Manual* (978-1-58713-322-0). The Packet Tracer Activities PKA files are found in the online course.

Class Activities

Class Activity 6.0.1.2: Can Submarines Swim?

Class Activity 6.4.1.1: Stepping Through OSPFv3

Labs

Lab 6.2.4.5: Configuring Basic Single-Area OSPFv2

Lab 6.3.3.6: Configuring Basic Single-Area OSPFv3

Packet Tracer
☐ Activity

Packet Tracer Activities

Packet Tracer Activity 6.2.2.7: Configuring OSPFv2 in a Single-Area

Packet Tracer Activity 6.3.3.5: Configuring Basic OSPFv3

Packet Tracer Activity 6.4.1.2: Skills Integration Challenge

Check Your Understanding Questions

Complete all the review questions listed here to test your understanding of the topics and concepts in this chapter. The appendix, "Answers to the 'Check Your Understanding' Questions," lists the answers.

1. Which of the following statements are true regarding routing protocols that use the link-state routing algorithm? (Choose three.)

   A. They are known collectively as link-state routing protocols.

   B. They learn routes and send them to directly connected neighbors.

   C. They maintain a database of the network topology.

   D. They are based on the Dijkstra algorithm.

   E. They are considered a good choice for small networks with low-end routers.

2. What reasons would a network administrator have for using loopback interfaces when configuring OSPF? (Choose two.)

   A. Loopbacks are logical interfaces and do not go down.

   B. Only loopback addresses can be used for an OSPF router ID.

   C. Loopback interfaces are used to set the OSPF metric.

   D. The loopback address will be used as the router ID, overriding the physical IP address values.

   E. OSPF error checking is enabled by loopback addresses.

   F. The loopback address will override the configured router priority value.

3. In which of the following types of networks will OSPF Designated Routers not be elected? (Choose two.)

   A. Point to point

   B. Point to multipoint

   C. Broadcast multi-access

   D. Nonbroadcast multiaccess

4. After routers have converged, which OSPF component is identical on all OSPF routers in an area?

   A. Adjacency database

   B. Link-state database

   C. Routing table

   D. SPF tree

5. A network administrator enters the **router ospf 100** command. What is the function of the number 100 in this command?

   A. Autonomous system number

   B. Metric

   C. Process ID

   D. Administrative distance

6. On a router running OSPF, what is the purpose of entering the **bandwidth 56** command on a serial interface?

   A. Changes the cost value

   B. Functions only as a description

   C. Changes the throughput of the interface to 56 kb/s

   D. Is necessary for the DUAL algorithm

7. What factor does the Cisco implementation of OSPF use to pick the best route?

   A. Uptime

   B. Reliability

   C. Bandwidth

   D. Load

   E. Shortest number of hops

8. Which wildcard mask would be used to advertise the 192.168.1.64/27 network as part of an OSPF configuration?

   A. 0.0.0.15

   B. 0.0.0.16

   C. 0.0.0.31

   D. 0.0.0.32

   E. 255.255.255.192

   F. 255.255.255.224

9. During an OSPF DR/BDR election, what is used to determine the DR or BDR when participating OSPF routers have identical interface priorities?

   A. The highest OSPF process ID

   B. The lowest interface IP address

   C. The lowest interface cost

   D. The highest router ID

10. Which packet type is invalid for OSPF?

    A. Hello

    B. LRU

    C. LSR

    D. LSAck

    E. DBD

11. How do OSPFv2 and OSPFv3 differ?

    A. Their metric calculation is different.

    B. The Hello mechanism is different.

    C. OSPFv3 has different packet types.

    D. OSPFv3 authenticates differently.

    E. The DR/BDR election works differently.

12. Which command is used to verify specific OSPFv3 routes in the IPv6 routing table?

13. In the **router ospf** command, does the process ID need to match on all routers?

14. Given the following configuration, what is the OSPF router ID of RouterA?

```
RouterA(config)# interface serial 0/0/0
RouterA(config-if)# ip add 192.168.2.1 255.255.255.252
RouterA(config-if)# interface loopback 0
RouterA(config-if)# ip add 10.1.1.1 255.255.255.255
RouterA(config-if)# router ospf 1
RouterA(config-router)# network 192.168.2.0 0.0.0.3 area 0
```

15. What command enables you to verify or determine the bandwidth value of an interface used by the OSPF metric?

16. What command enables you to modify the OSPF cost of an interface without modifying the bandwidth value of that interface?

17. What is the default Hello interval on Ethernet networks and serial point-to-point networks? What is the default Hello interval on NBMA networks?

18. What values must match before two routers will form an OSPF adjacency?

19. What problems does electing a DR and BDR solve?

20. How are the DR and BDR elected?

CHAPTER 7

Adjust and Troubleshoot Single-Area OSPF

Objectives

Upon completion of this chapter, you will be able to answer the following questions:

- How do you modify the OSPF interface priority to influence the DR/BDR election?

- How do you configure a router to propagate a default route in an OSPF network?

- How do you modify the interface settings to improve network performance?

- How do you configure OSPF authentication to ensure secure routing updates?

- How do you explain the process and tools used to troubleshoot a single-area OSPF network?

- Can you troubleshoot missing route entries in a single-area OSPFv2 route table?

- Can you troubleshoot missing route entries in a single-area OSPFv3 route table?

Key Terms

This chapter uses the following key terms. You can find the definitions in the Glossary.

Introduction (7.0.1.1)

OSPF is a popular link-state routing protocol that can be fine-tuned in many ways. Some of the most common methods of fine-tuning include manipulating the Designated Router/Backup Designated Router (DR/BDR) election process, propagating default routes, fine-tuning the OSPFv2 and OSPFv3 interfaces, and configuring authentication.

This chapter on OSPF describes these tuning features, the configuration mode commands to implement these features for both IPv4 and IPv6, and the components and commands used to troubleshoot OSPFv2 and OSPFv3.

Class Activity 7.0.1.2: DR and BDR Election

You are trying to decide how to influence the selection of the designated router and backup designated router for your OSPF network. This activity simulates that process.

Three separate Designated Router election scenarios will be presented. The focus is on electing a DR and BDR for your group. Refer to the PDF for this activity for the remaining instructions.

If additional time is available, two groups can be combined to simulate DR and BDR elections.

Advanced Single-Area OSPF Configurations (7.1)

In this section you will learn how to configure advanced single-area OSPF features, including selecting a DR, propagating a default route, securing routing updates, and fine-tuning OSPF interfaces.

OSPF Network Types (7.1.1.1)

To configure OSPF adjustments, start with a basic implementation of the OSPF routing protocol.

OSPF defines five network types, as shown in Figures 7-1 to 7-5:

- **Point-to-point:** As shown in Figure 7-1, two routers are interconnected over a common link. No other routers are on the link. This is often the configuration in WAN links.

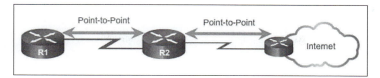

Figure 7-1   OSPF Point-to-Point Network

■ **Broadcast multiaccess:** As shown in Figure 7-2, multiple routers are interconnected over an Ethernet network.

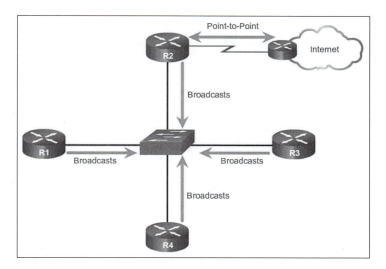

Figure 7-2   OSPF Multiaccess Network

■ **Nonbroadcast multiaccess (NBMA):** As shown in Figure 7-3, multiple routers are interconnected over an NBMA network such as Frame Relay. In this scenario, R1, R2, and R3 are interconnected over a Frame Relay network. Frame Relay is an NBMA network and therefore does not forward broadcasts. For this reason, OSPF must be configured accordingly to create neighbor adjacencies.

■ **Point-to-multipoint:** As shown in Figure 7-4, multiple routers are interconnected in a hub-and-spoke topology over an NBMA network. In this scenario, R1, R2, and R3 are interconnected over an NBMA Frame Relay network and therefore OSPF must be configured accordingly to create neighbor adjacencies. Point-to-multipoint is often used to connect branch sites (spokes) to a central site (hub).

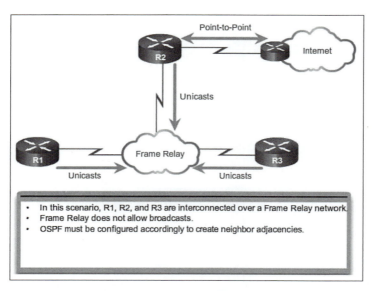

Figure 7-3   OSPF Nonbroadcast Multiaccess Network

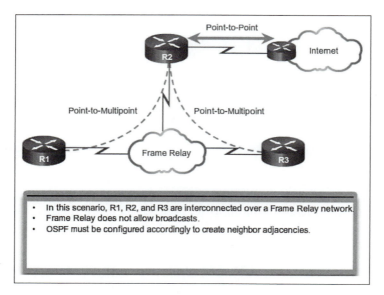

Figure 7-4   OSPF Point-to-Multipoint Network

■ **Virtual links:** As shown in Figure 7-5, virtual links are used to interconnect distant OSPF areas to the backbone area. In this scenario, area 51 cannot connect directly to area 0. Therefore, area 1 must be configured as a virtual link to connect area 51 to area 0.

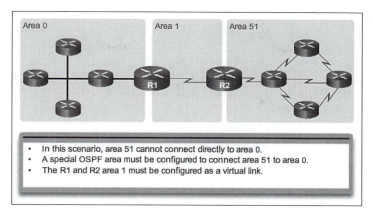

Area 0   Area 1   Area 51

- In this scenario, area 51 cannot connect directly to area 0.
- A special OSPF area must be configured to connect area 51 to area 0.
- The R1 and R2 area 1 must be configured as a virtual link.

Figure 7-5   OSPF Virtual Link Network

A *multiaccess network* is a network with multiple devices on the same shared media, which are sharing communications. Ethernet LANs are the most common example of broadcast multiaccess networks. In broadcast networks, all devices on the network see all broadcast and multicast frames. They are multiaccess networks because there may be numerous hosts, printers, routers, and other devices that are all members of the same network.

Challenges in Multiaccess Networks (7.1.1.2)

Multiaccess networks can create two challenges for OSPF regarding the flooding of LSAs:

- **Creation of multiple adjacencies:** Ethernet networks could potentially interconnect many OSPF routers over a common link. Creating adjacencies with every router is unnecessary and undesirable. This would lead to an excessive number of LSAs exchanged between routers on the same network.

- **Extensive flooding of LSAs:** Link-state routers flood their link-state packets when OSPF is initialized, or when there is a change in the topology. This flooding can become excessive.

The following formula can be used to calculate the number of required adjacencies. The number of adjacencies required for any number of routers (designated as *n*) on a multiaccess network is:

$n (n - 1) / 2$

Figure 7-6 shows a simple topology of four routers, all of which are attached to the same multiaccess Ethernet network.

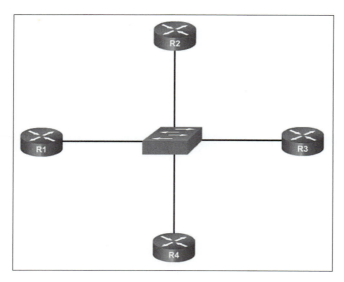

Figure 7-6   Simple OSPF Multiaccess Network

Without some type of mechanism to reduce the number of adjacencies, collectively these routers would form six adjacencies: 4 (4 − 1) / 2 = 6, as shown in Figure 7-7.

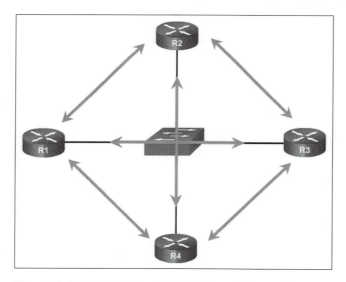

Figure 7-7   Establishing Six Neighbor Adjacencies

Table 7-1 shows that as routers are added to the network, the number of adjacencies increases dramatically.

Table 7-1   More Routers = More Adjacencies

Routers	Adjacencies
N	$n(n-1)/2$
4	6
5	10
10	45
20	190
50	1225

OSPF Designated Router (7.1.1.3)

The solution to managing the number of adjacencies and the flooding of LSAs on a multiaccess network is the designated router (DR). On multiaccess networks, OSPF elects a DR to be the collection and distribution point for LSAs sent and received. A BDR is also elected in case the DR fails. The BDR listens passively to this exchange and maintains a relationship with all the routers. If the DR stops producing Hello packets, the BDR promotes itself and assumes the role of DR.

All routers other than the DR and BDR become DROTHER (a router that is neither the DR nor the BDR).

In Figure 7-8, R1 has been elected as the designated router for the Ethernet LAN interconnecting R2, R3, and R4. Notice how the number of adjacencies has been reduced to three. Without this method it would require six adjacencies.

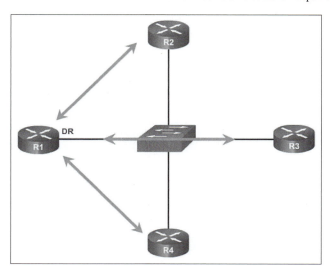

Figure 7-8   Establishing Adjacencies

Routers on a multiaccess network elect a DR and BDR. DROTHERs only form full adjacencies with the DR and BDR in the network. Instead of flooding LSAs to all routers in the network, DROTHERs only send their LSAs to the DR and BDR using the multicast address 224.0.0.6 (All Designated Routers).

In Figure 7-9, R2 has been elected the DR and R3 is the BDR. When a route change occurs on R1, R1 sends LSAs to the DR and BDR only.

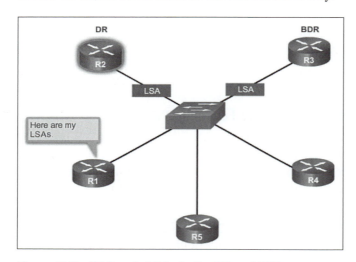

Figure 7-9   R1 Sends LSAs to the DR and BDR

As shown in Figure 7-10, the DR then sends LSAs to all of its OSPF adjacencies on behalf of R1. The DR is responsible for forwarding the LSAs from R1 to all other routers. The DR uses the multicast address 224.0.0.5 (All-OSPF-Routers). The end result is that there is only one router doing all of the flooding of all LSAs in the multiaccess network.

Video

Video 7.1.1.3: Role of the DR

Go to the online course and play the animation in the second graphic to see how a DR reduces the number of LSAs being redistributed.

Note

DR/BDR elections only occur in multiaccess networks and do not occur in point-to-point networks.

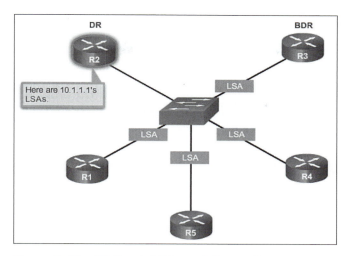

Figure 7-10 DR Sends LSAs to Adjacent Routers

Verifying DR/BDR Roles (7.1.1.4)

In the multiaccess topology shown in Figure 7-11, there are three routers interconnected over a common Ethernet multiaccess network, 192.168.1.0/28. Each router is configured with the indicated IP address on the GigabitEthernet 0/0 interface.

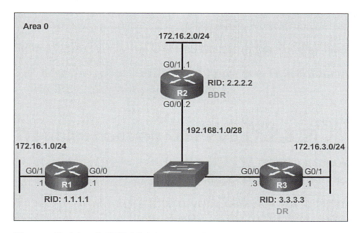

Figure 7-11 OSPF Multiaccess Broadcast Reference Topology

Because the routers are connected over a common multiaccess broadcast network, OSPF has automatically elected a DR and BDR. In this example, R3 has been elected as the DR because its router ID is 3.3.3.3, which is the highest in this network. R2 is the BDR because it has the second highest router ID in the network.

To verify the roles of the router, use the **show ip ospf interface** command.

For example, the output generated by R1, shown in Figure 7-12, confirms that:

- R1 is not the DR or BDR, but is a DROTHER with a default priority of 1. (1)

- The DR is R3 with router ID 3.3.3.3 at IP address 192.168.1.3, while the BDR is R2 with router ID 2.2.2.2 at IP address 192.168.1.2. (2)

- R1 has two adjacencies: one with the BDR and one with the DR. (3)

The output generated by R2, shown in Figure 7-13, confirms that:

- R2 is the BDR with a default priority of 1. (1)

- The DR is R3 with router ID 3.3.3.3 at IP address 192.168.1.3, while the BDR is R2 with router ID 2.2.2.2 at IP address 192.168.1.2. (2)

- R2 has two adjacencies: one with a neighbor with router ID 1.1.1.1 (R1) and the other with the DR. (3)

```
R1# show ip ospf interface GigabitEthernet 0/0
GigabitEthernet0/0 is up, line protocol is up
  Internet Address 192.168.1.1/28,Area 0,Attached via Network Statement
  Process ID 10, Router ID 1.1.1.1, Network Type BROADCAST, Cost: 1
  Topology-MTID    Cost    Disabled    Shutdown      Topology Name
        0           1         no          no            Base
 ① Transmit Delay is 1 sec, State DROTHER, Priority 1
    Designated Router (ID) 3.3.3.3, Interface address 192.168.1.3
 ② Backup Designated router (ID) 2.2.2.2, Interface address 192.168.1.2
  Timer intervals configured, Hello 10, Dead 40, Wait 40, Retransmit 5
    oob-resync timeout 40
    Hello due in 00:00:06
  Supports Link-local Signaling (LLS)
  Cisco NSF helper support enabled
  IETF NSF helper support enabled
  Index 2/2, flood queue length 0
  Next 0x0(0)/0x0(0)
  Last flood scan length is 1, maximum is 2
  Last flood scan time is 0 msec, maximum is 0 msec
  Neighbor Count is 2, Adjacent neighbor count is 2
 ③  Adjacent with neighbor 2.2.2.2  (Backup Designated Router)
    Adjacent with neighbor 3.3.3.3  (Designated Router)
  Suppress hello for 0 neighbor(s)
R1#
```

Figure 7-12   Verifying the Role of R1

```
R2# show ip ospf interface GigabitEthernet 0/0
GigabitEthernet0/0 is up, line protocol is up
  Internet Address 192.168.1.2/28,Area 0,Attached via Network Statement
  Process ID 10, Router ID 2.2.2.2, Network Type BROADCAST, Cost: 1
  Topology-MTID    Cost    Disabled    Shutdown      Topology Name
        0           1         no          no            Base
  Transmit Delay is 1 sec, State BDR, Priority 1
  Designated Router (ID) 3.3.3.3, Interface address 192.168.1.3
  Backup Designated router (ID) 2.2.2.2, Interface address 192.168.1.2
  Timer intervals configured, Hello 10, Dead 40, Wait 40, Retransmit 5
    oob-resync timeout 40
    Hello due in 00:00:06
  Supports Link-local Signaling (LLS)
  Cisco NSF helper support enabled
  IETF NSF helper support enabled
  Index 2/2, flood queue length 0
  Next 0x0(0)/0x0(0)
  Last flood scan length is 1, maximum is 2
  Last flood scan time is 0 msec, maximum is 0 msec
  Neighbor Count is 2, Adjacent neighbor count is 2
    Adjacent with neighbor 1.1.1.1
    Adjacent with neighbor 3.3.3.3   (Designated Router)
  Suppress hello for 0 neighbor(s)
R2#
```

Figure 7-13   Verifying the Role of R2

The output generated by R3, shown in Figure 7-14, confirms that:

- R3 is the DR with a default priority of 1. (1)

- The DR is R3 with router ID 3.3.3.3 at IP address 192.168.1.3, while the BDR is R2 with router ID 2.2.2.2 at IP address 192.168.1.2. (2)

- R3 has two adjacencies: one with a neighbor with router ID 1.1.1.1 (R1) and the other with the BDR. (3)

```
R3# show ip ospf interface GigabitEthernet 0/0
GigabitEthernet0/0 is up, line protocol is up
  Internet Address 192.168.1.3/28,Area 0,Attached via Network Statement
  Process ID 10, Router ID 3.3.3.3, Network Type BROADCAST, Cost: 1
  Topology-MTID    Cost    Disabled    Shutdown      Topology Name
        0           1         no          no            Base
  Transmit Delay is 1 sec, State DR, Priority 1
  Designated Router (ID) 3.3.3.3, Interface address 192.168.1.3
  Backup Designated router (ID) 2.2.2.2, Interface address 192.168.1.2
  Timer intervals configured, Hello 10, Dead 40, Wait 40, Retransmit 5
    oob-resync timeout 40
    Hello due in 00:00:02
  Supports Link-local Signaling (LLS)
  Cisco NSF helper support enabled
  IETF NSF helper support enabled
  Index 2/2, flood queue length 0
  Next 0x0(0)/0x0(0)
  Last flood scan length is 3, maximum is 3
  Last flood scan time is 0 msec, maximum is 0 msec
  Neighbor Count is 2, Adjacent neighbor count is 2
    Adjacent with neighbor 1.1.1.1
    Adjacent with neighbor 2.2.2.2   (Backup Designated Router)
  Suppress hello for 0 neighbor(s)
R3#
```

Figure 7-14   Verifying the Role of R3

Verifying DR/BDR Adjacencies (7.1.1.5)

To verify the OSPF adjacencies, use the **show ip ospf neighbor** command as shown in Figure 7-15.

Unlike serial links that only display a state of FULL/-, the state of neighbors in multi-access networks can be:

- *FULL/DROTHER*: This is a DR or BDR router that is fully adjacent with a router that is neither the DR nor the BDR. These two neighbors can exchange Hello packets, updates, queries, replies, and acknowledgments.

- *FULL/DR*: The router is fully adjacent with the indicated DR neighbor. These two neighbors can exchange Hello packets, updates, queries, replies, and acknowledgments.

Figure 7-15   Verifying the Neighbor Adjacencies of R1

- *FULL/BDR*: The router is fully adjacent with the indicated BDR neighbor. These two neighbors can exchange Hello packets, updates, queries, replies, and acknowledgments.

- *2-WAY/DROTHER*: The DROTHER has a neighbor relationship with another DROTHER. These two neighbors exchange Hello packets.

The normal state for an OSPF router is usually FULL. If a router is stuck in another state, it is an indication that there are problems in forming adjacencies. The only exception to this is the 2-WAY state, which is normal in a multiaccess broadcast network.

In multiaccess networks, DROTHERs only form FULL adjacencies with the DR and BDR. However, DROTHERs will still form a 2-WAY neighbor adjacency with any DROTHERs that join the network. This means that all DROTHER routers in the multiaccess network still receive Hello packets from all other DROTHER routers. In this way, they are aware of all routers in the network. When two DROTHER routers form a neighbor adjacency, the neighbor state displays as 2-WAY/DROTHER.

The output generated by R1, shown in Figure 7-15, confirms that R1 has adjacencies with routers R2 and R3 and that they have the following status and role:

- R2 with router ID 2.2.2.2 is in a Full state and the role of R2 is BDR. (1)

- R3 with router ID 3.3.3.3 is in a Full state and the role of R3 is DR. (2)

The output generated by R2, shown in Figure 7-16, confirms that R2 has adjacencies with routers R2 and R3 and that they have the following status and role:

- R1 with router ID 1.1.1.1 is in a Full state and is neither the DR nor the BDR. (1)

- R3 with router ID 3.3.3.3 is in a Full state and the role of R3 is DR. (2)

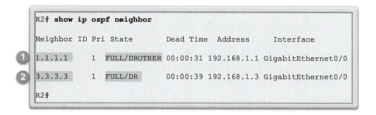

Figure 7-16   Verifying the Neighbor Adjacencies of R2

The output generated by R3, shown in Figure 7-17, confirms that R3 has adjacencies with routers R2 and R3 and that they have the following status and role:

- R1 with router ID 1.1.1.1 is in a Full state and is neither the DR nor the BDR. (1)

- R2 with router ID 2.2.2.2 is in a Full state and the role of R2 is BDR. (2)

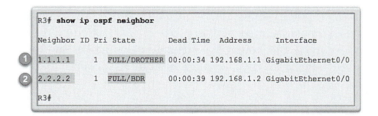

Figure 7-17   Verifying the Neighbor Adjacencies of R3

Default DR/BDR Election Process (7.1.1.6)

How do the DR and BDR get elected? The OSPF DR and BDR election decision is based on the following criteria, in sequential order:

1. The routers in the network elect the router with the highest interface priority as the DR. The router with the second highest interface priority is elected as the BDR. The priority can be configured to be any number between 0 and 255. The higher the priority, the likelier the router will be selected as the DR. If the priority is set to 0, the router is not capable of becoming the DR. The default priority of multiaccess broadcast interfaces is 1. Therefore, unless otherwise configured, all routers have an equal priority value and must rely on another tie-breaking method during the DR/BDR election.

2. If the interface priorities are equal, then the router with the highest router ID is elected the DR. The router with the second highest router ID is the BDR.

Recall that the router ID is determined in one of three ways:

- The router ID can be manually configured.

- If no router IDs are configured, the router ID is determined by the highest loopback IP address.

- If no loopback interfaces are configured, the router ID is determined by the highest active IPv4 address.

Note

In an IPv6 network, if there are no IPv4 addresses configured on the router, then the router ID must be manually configured with the **router-id** *rid* command; otherwise, OSPFv3 does not start.

Refer to the topology shown in Figure 7-11 earlier in the chapter. All Ethernet router interfaces have a default priority of 1. As a result, based on the selection criteria listed above, the OSPF router ID is used to elect the DR and BDR. R3, with the highest router ID, becomes the DR; and R2, with the second highest router ID, becomes the BDR.

Note

Serial interfaces have default priorities set to 0; therefore, they do not elect DRs and BDRs.

The DR and BDR election process takes place as soon as the first router with an OSPF-enabled interface is active on the multiaccess network. This can happen when the routers are powered on, or when the OSPF **network** command for that interface is configured. The election process only takes a few seconds. If all of the routers on the multiaccess network have not finished booting, it is possible that a router with a lower router ID becomes the DR. (This can be a lower-end router that takes less time to boot.)

DR/BDR Election Process (7.1.1.7)

OSPF DR and BDR elections are not preemptive. If a new router with a higher priority or higher router ID is added to the network after the DR and BDR election, the newly added router does not take over the DR role or the BDR role. This is because those roles have already been assigned. The addition of a new router does not initiate a new election process.

After the DR is elected, it remains the DR until one of the following events occurs:

- The DR fails
- The OSPF process on the DR fails or is stopped
- The multiaccess interface on the DR fails or is shut down

If the DR fails, the BDR is automatically promoted to DR. This is the case even if another DROTHER with a higher priority or router ID is added to the network after the initial DR/BDR election. However, after a BDR is promoted to DR, a new BDR election occurs and the DROTHER with the higher priority or router ID is elected as the new BDR.

Figures 7-18 through 7-21 illustrate various scenarios relating to the DR and BDR election process.

In Figure 7-18, the current DR (R3) fails; therefore, the pre-elected BDR (R2) assumes the role of DR. Subsequently, an election is held to choose a new BDR. Because R1 is the only DROTHER, it is elected as the BDR.

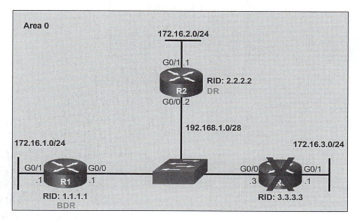

Figure 7-18   R3 Fails

In Figure 7-19, R3 has rejoined the network after several minutes of being unavailable. Because the DR and BDR already exist, R3 does not take over either role; instead, it becomes a DROTHER.

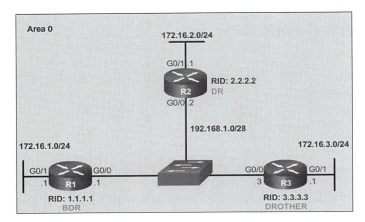

Figure 7-19   R3 Rejoins the Network

In Figure 7-20, a new router (R4) with a higher router ID is added to the network. The DR (R2) and BDR (R1) retain the DR and BDR roles. R4 automatically becomes a DROTHER.

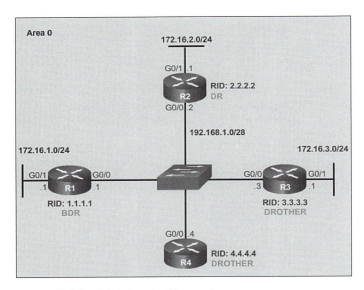

Figure 7-20   R4 Joins the Network

In Figure 7-21, R2 has failed. The BDR (R1) automatically becomes the DR and an election process selects R4 as the BDR because it has the higher router ID.

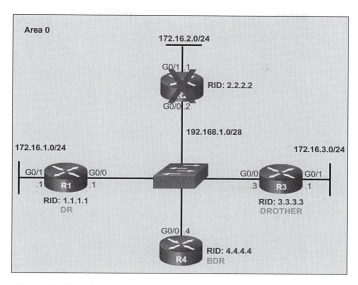

Figure 7-21 R2 Fails

The OSPF Priority (7.1.1.8)

The DR becomes the focal point for the collection and distribution of LSAs; therefore, this router must have sufficient CPU and memory capacity to handle the workload. It is possible to influence the DR/BDR election process through configurations.

If the interface priorities are equal on all routers, the router with the highest router ID is elected the DR. It is possible to configure the router ID to manipulate the DR/BDR election. However, this process only works if there is a stringent plan for setting the router ID on all routers. In large networks, this can be cumbersome.

Instead of relying on the router ID, it is better to control the election by setting interface priorities. Priorities are an interface-specific value, which means setting priorities provides better control on a multiaccess network. This also allows a router to be the DR in one network and a DROTHER in another.

To set the priority of an interface, use the following commands:

- **ip ospf priority** *value*: OSPFv2 interface command
- **ipv6 ospf priority** *value*: OSPFv3 interface command

The *value* can be:

- **0**: Does not become a DR or BDR.
- **1–255**: The higher the priority value, the more likely the router becomes the DR or BDR on the interface.

Refer to Figure 7-11 earlier in the chapter. In the figure, all routers have an equal OSPF priority because the priority value defaults to 1 for all router interfaces. Therefore, the router ID is used to determine the DR (R3) and BDR (R2). Changing the priority value on an interface from 1 to a higher value would enable the router to become a DR or BDR router during the next election.

If the interface priority is configured after OSPF is enabled, the administrator must shut down the OSPF process on all routers, and then re-enable the OSPF process, to force a new DR/BDR election.

Changing the OSPF Priority (7.1.1.9)

In the topology in Figure 7-11, R3 is the DR and R2 is the BDR. It has been decided that:

- R1 should be the DR and will be configured with a priority of 255.

- R2 should be the BDR and will be left with the default priority of 1.

- R3 should never be a DR or BDR and will be configured with a priority of 0.

The following changes the R1 interface GigabitEthernet 0/0 priority from 1 to 255:

```
R1(config)# interface GigabitEthernet 0/0
R1(config-if)# ip ospf priority 255
R1(config-if)# end
R1#
```

The following changes the R3 interface GigabitEthernet 0/0 priority from 1 to 0:

```
R3(config)# interface GigabitEthernet 0/0
R3(config-if)# ip ospf priority 0
R3(config-if)# end
R3#
```

The changes do not automatically take effect because the DR and BDR are already elected. Therefore, the OSPF election must be negotiated using one of the following methods:

- Shut down the router interfaces and then re-enable them starting with the DR, then the BDR, and then all other routers.

- Reset the OSPF process using the **clear ip ospf process** privileged EXEC mode command on all routers.

The following displays how to clear the OSPF process on R1:

```
R1# clear ip ospf process
Reset ALL OSPF processes? [no]: yes
R1#
*Apr  6 16:00:44.282: %OSPF-5-ADJCHG: Process 10, Nbr 2.2.2.2 on GigabitEthernet0/0
   from FULL to DOWN, Neighbor Down: Interface down or detached
```

```
*Apr  6 16:00:44.282: %OSPF-5-ADJCHG: Process 10, Nbr 3.3.3.3 on GigabitEthernet0/0
   from FULL to DOWN, Neighbor Down: Interface down or detached
R1#
```

Assume that the **clear ip ospf process** privileged EXEC mode command has also been configured on R2 and R3. Notice the OSPF state information generated.

The output displayed in Figure 7-22 confirms that R1 is now the DR with a priority of 255 and identifies the new neighbor adjacencies of R1.

```
R1# show ip ospf interface GigabitEthernet 0/0
GigabitEthernet0/0 is up, line protocol is up
  Internet Address 192.168.1.1/28, Area 0, Attached via Network Statement
  Process ID 10, Router ID 1.1.1.1, Network Type BROADCAST, Cost: 1
  Topology-MTID    Cost    Disabled    Shutdown      Topology Name
       0            1         no          no             Base
  Transmit Delay is 1 sec, State DR, Priority 255
  Designated Router (ID) 1.1.1.1, Interface address 192.168.1.1
  Backup Designated router (ID) 2.2.2.2, Interface address 192.168.1.2
  Timer intervals configured, Hello 10, Dead 40, Wait 40, Retransmit 5
    oob-resync timeout 40
    Hello due in 00:00:05
  Supports Link-local Signaling (LLS)
  Cisco NSF helper support enabled
  IETF NSF helper support enabled
  Index 2/2, flood queue length 0
  Next 0x0(0)/0x0(0)
  Last flood scan length is 1, maximum is 2
  Last flood scan time is 0 msec, maximum is 0 msec
  Neighbor Count is 2, Adjacent neighbor count is 2
    Adjacent with neighbor 2.2.2.2  (Backup Designated Router)
    Adjacent with neighbor 3.3.3.3
  Suppress hello for 0 neighbor(s)
R1#
R1# show ip ospf neighbor

Neighbor ID  Pri   State        Dead Time Address     Interface
2.2.2.2       1    FULL/BDR     00:00:30  192.168.1.2 GigabitEthernet0/0
3.3.3.3       0    FULL/DROTHER 00:00:38  192.168.1.3 GigabitEthernet0/0
R1#
```

Figure 7-22   Verifying the Role and Adjacencies of R1

Interactive Graphic

Activity 7.1.1.9: Verify the Role and Adjacencies

Go to the online course to use the Syntax Checker in the sixth graphic to verify the role and adjacencies of R2 and R3.

Interactive Graphic

Activity 7.1.1.10: Identify OSPF Network Type Terminology

Go to the online course to perform this practice activity.

Interactive Graphic

Activity 7.1.1.11: Select the Designated Router

Go to the online course to perform this practice activity

Packet Tracer Activity 7.1.1.12: Determining the DR and BDR

In this activity, you will examine DR and BDR roles and watch the roles change when there is a change in the network. You will then modify the priority to control the roles and force a new election. Finally, you will verify routers are filling the desired roles.

Lab 7.1.1.13: Configuring OSPFv2 on a Multiaccess Network

In this lab, you will complete the following objectives:

- Part 1: Build the Network and Configure Basic Device Settings
- Part 2: Configure and Verify OSPFv2 on the DR, BDR, and DROTHER
- Part 3: Configure OSPFv2 Interface Priority to Determine the DR and BDR

Default Route Propagation (7.1.2)

This section discusses how to propagate a default route throughout the single-area OSPF network.

Propagating a Default Static Route in OSPFv2 (7.1.2.1)

As with EIGRP, the router connected to the Internet is used to propagate a default route to other routers in the OSPF routing domain. This router is sometimes called the edge, entrance, or gateway router. However, in OSPF terminology, the router located between an OSPF routing domain and a non-OSPF network is also called the autonomous system boundary router (ASBR).

In Figure 7-23, R2 is single-homed to a service provider. Therefore, all that is required for R2 to reach the Internet is a default static route to the service provider.

Note

In this example, a loopback interface with IP address 209.165.200.225 is used to simulate the connection to the service provider.

To propagate a default route, the edge router (R2) must be configured with:

- A default static route using the **ip route 0.0.0.0 0.0.0.0** {*ip-address | exit-intf*} command.
- The **default-information originate** router configuration mode command. This instructs R2 to be the source of the default route information and propagate the default static route in OSPF updates.

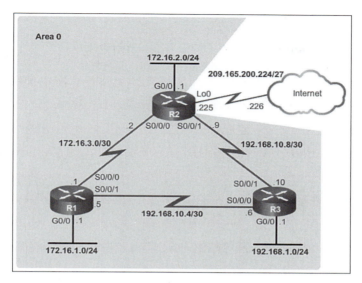

Figure 7-23   Propagating a Default Route

The following shows how to configure a fully specified default static route to the service provider:

```
R2(config)# ip route 0.0.0.0 0.0.0.0 lo0 209.165.200.226
R2(config)#
R2(config)# router ospf 10
R2(config-router)# default-information originate
R2(config-router)# end
R2#
```

Verifying the Propagated Default Route (7.1.2.2)

Verify the default route settings on R2 using the **show ip route** command, as shown in Figure 7-24.

When verifying that the default route was propagated to another router, the route source will indicate an entry of O*E2. This signifies that the default route was learned using OSPF. The asterisk identifies this as a good candidate for the default route. The E2 designation identifies that it is an external route.

```
R2# show ip route | begin Gateway

Gateway of last resort is 209.165.200.226 to network 0.0.0.0

S*  0.0.0.0/0 [1/0] via 209.165.200.226, Loopback0
     172.16.0.0/16 is variably subnetted, 5 subnets, 3 masks
O    172.16.1.0/24 [110/65] via 172.16.3.1, 00:01:44,
     Serial0/0/0
C    172.16.2.0/24 is directly connected, GigabitEthernet0/0
L    172.16.2.1/32 is directly connected, GigabitEthernet0/0
C    172.16.3.0/30 is directly connected, Serial0/0/0
L    172.16.3.2/32 is directly connected, Serial0/0/0
O    192.168.1.0/24 [110/65] via 192.168.10.10, 00:01:12,
     Serial0/0/1
     192.168.10.0/24 is variably subnetted, 3 subnets, 2
      masks
O    192.168.10.4/30 [110/128] via 192.168.10.10, 00:01:12,
     Serial0/0/1
             [110/128] via 172.16.3.1, 00:01:12, Serial0/0/0
C    192.168.10.8/30 is directly connected, Serial0/0/1
L    192.168.10.9/32 is directly connected, Serial0/0/1
     209.165.200.0/24 is variably subnetted, 2 subnets, 2
      masks
C    209.165.200.224/30 is directly connected, Loopback0
L    209.165.200.225/32 is directly connected, Loopback0
R2#
```

Figure 7-24   Verifying a Default Route on R2

Activity 7.1.2.2: Verify a Propagated Default Route on R1 and R3

Go to the online course to use the Syntax Checker in the second graphic to verify that the default route has been propagated to R1 and R3.

External routes are either external type 1 (E1) or external type 2 (E2). The difference between the two is in the way the cost (metric) of the route is being calculated. The cost of a type 2 route is always the external cost, regardless of the interior cost to reach that route. A type 1 cost is the addition of the external cost and the internal cost used to reach that route. A type 1 route is always preferred over a type 2 route for the same destination.

Propagating a Default Static Route in OSPFv3 (7.1.2.3)

The process of propagating a default static route in OSPFv3 is almost identical to OSPFv2.

In Figure 7-25, R2 is single-homed to a service provider. Therefore, all that is required for R2 to reach the Internet is a default static route to the service provider.

Note

In this example, a loopback interface with the IP address of 2001:DB8:FEED:1::1/64 is used to simulate the connection to the service provider.

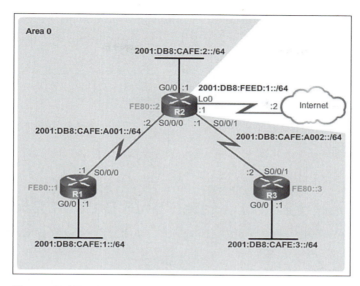

Figure 7-25 OSPFv3 Topology

Figure 7-26 displays the current IPv6 routing table of R1. Notice that it has no knowledge of the route to the Internet.

To propagate a default route, the edge router (R2) must be configured with:

- A default static route using the **ipv6 route ::/0** {*ipv6-address* | *exit-intf*} command.

- The **default-information originate** router configuration mode command. This instructs R2 to be the source of the default route information and propagate the default static route in OSPF updates.

```
R1# show ipv6 route ospf
IPv6 Routing Table - default - 8 entries
Codes:
  C - Connected, L - Local, S - Static, U - Per-user Static route
  B - BGP, R - RIP, H - NHRP, I1 - ISIS L1
  I2 - ISIS L2, IA - ISIS interarea, IS - ISIS summary, D - EIGRP
  EX - EIGRP external, ND - ND Default, NDp - ND Prefix, DCE -
  Destination
  NDr - Redirect, O - OSPF Intra, OI - OSPF Inter, OE1 - OSPF ext 1
  OE2 - OSPF ext 2, ON1 - OSPF NSSA ext 1, ON2 - OSPF NSSA ext 2
O    2001:DB8:CAFE:2::/64 [110/648]
     via FE80::2, Serial0/0/0
O    2001:DB8:CAFE:3::/64 [110/648]
     via FE80::2, Serial0/0/0
O    2001:DB8:CAFE:A002::/64 [110/1294]
     via FE80::2, Serial0/0/0
R1#
```

Figure 7-26 Verify the IPv6 Routing Table on R1

The following example configures a fully specified default static route to the service provider:

```
R2(config)# ipv6 route 0::/0 lo0 2001:DB8:FEED:1::2
R2(config)#
R2(config)# ipv6 router ospf 10
R2(config-rtr)# default-information originate
R2(config-rtr)# end
R2#
*Apr 10 11:36:21.995: %SYS-5-CONFIG_I: Configured from console by console
R2#
```

Verifying the Propagated IPv6 Default Route (7.1.2.4)

Verify the default static route setting on R2 using the **show ipv6 route** command, as follows:

```
R2# show ipv6 route static
IPv6 Routing Table - default - 12 entries
Codes: C - Connected, L - Local, S - Static, U - Per-user Static route
       B - BGP, R - RIP, H - NHRP, I1 - ISIS L1
       I2 - ISIS L2, IA - ISIS interarea, IS - ISIS summary, D - EIGRP
       EX - EIGRP external, ND - ND Default, NDp - ND Prefix,
       DCE - Destination, NDr - Redirect, O - OSPF Intra, OI - OSPF Inter,
       OE1 - OSPF ext 1, OE2 - OSPF ext 2, ON1 - OSPF NSSA ext 1,
       ON2 - OSPF NSSA ext 2
S    ::/0 [1/0]
     via 2001:DB8:FEED:1::2, Loopback0
R2#
```

When verifying that the default route was propagated to another router, the route source will indicate an entry of OE2. Similar to O*E2 in OSPFv2, this signifies that the default route was learned using OSPFv3. The E2 designation identifies that it is an external route.

Interactive Graphic

Activity 7.1.2.4: Verify an IPv6 Default Route on R1 and R3

Go to the online course to use the Syntax Checker in the second graphic to verify that the default route has been propagated to R1 and R3.

Unlike the IPv4 routing table, IPv6 does not use the asterisk to signify that the route is a good candidate for the default route.

Packet Tracer Activity 7.1.2.5: Propagating a Default Route in OSPFv2

In this activity, you will configure an IPv4 default route to the Internet and propagate that default route to other OSPF routers. You will then verify the default route is in downstream routing tables and that hosts can now access a web server on the Internet.

Fine-tuning OSPF Interfaces (7.1.3)

This section discusses how to adjust OSPF Hello and Dead intervals on specific interfaces.

OSPF Hello and Dead Intervals (7.1.3.1)

Like EIGRP, the *OSPF Hello and Dead intervals* are configurable on a per-interface basis. Unlike EIGRP, the OSPF intervals must match or a neighbor adjacency does not occur.

To verify the currently configured interface intervals, use the **show ip ospf interface** command, as shown in Figure 7-27. The Serial 0/0/0 Hello and Dead intervals are set to the default 10 seconds and 40 seconds respectively.

```
R1# show ip ospf interface serial 0/0/0
Serial0/0/0 is up, line protocol is up
  Internet Address 172.16.3.1/30, Area 0, Attached via
Network Statement
  Process ID 10, Router ID 1.1.1.1, Network Type
POINT_TO_POINT, Cost: 64
  Topology-MTID  Cost  Disabled    Shutdown      Topology Name
       0          64      no          no            Base
  Transmit Delay is 1 sec, State POINT_TO_POINT
  Timer intervals configured, Hello 10, Dead 40, Wait 40,
Retransmit 5
    oob-resync timeout 40
    Hello due in 00:00:03
  Supports Link-local Signaling (LLS)
  Cisco NSF helper support enabled
  IETF NSF helper support enabled
  Index 2/2, flood queue length 0
  Next 0x0(0)/0x0(0)
  Last flood scan length is 1, maximum is 1
  Last flood scan time is 0 msec, maximum is 0 msec
  Neighbor Count is 1, Adjacent neighbor count is 1
    Adjacent with neighbor 2.2.2.2
  Suppress hello for 0 neighbor(s)
R1#
```

Figure 7-27   Verifying the OSPF Intervals on R1

The following is an example of using a filtering technique to display the OSPF intervals for the OSPF-enabled interface Serial 0/0/0 on R1:

```
R1# show ip ospf interface | include Timer
   Timer intervals configured, Hello 10, Dead 40, Wait 40,
Retransmit 5
   Timer intervals configured, Hello 10, Dead 40, Wait 40,
Retransmit 5
   Timer intervals configured, Hello 10, Dead 40, Wait 40,
Retransmit 5
R1#
```

In the following example, the **show ip ospf neighbor** command is used on R1 to verify that R1 is adjacent to R2 and R3. Notice in the output that the Dead Time is counting down from 40 seconds. By default, this value is refreshed every 10 seconds when R1 receives a Hello from the neighbor.

```
R1# show ip ospf neighbor
Neighbor ID    Pri    State    Dead Time    Address        Interface
3.3.3.3        0      FULL/-   00:00:35     192.168.10.6   Serial0/0/1
2.2.2.2        0      FULL/-   00:00:33     172.16.3.2     Serial0/0/0
R1#
```

Modifying OSPFv2 Intervals (7.1.3.2)

It may be desirable to change the OSPF timers so that routers detect network failures in less time. Doing this increases traffic, but sometimes the need for quick convergence is more important than the extra traffic it creates.

> **Note**
>
> The default Hello and Dead intervals are based on best practices and should only be altered in rare situations.

OSPF Hello and Dead intervals can be modified manually using the following interface configuration mode commands:

- **ip ospf hello-interval** *seconds*
- **ip ospf dead-interval** *seconds*

Use the **no ip ospf hello-interval** and **no ip ospf dead-interval** commands to reset the intervals to their default.

The following example modifies the Hello interval to 5 seconds:

```
R1(config)# interface Serial 0/0/0
R1(config-if)# ip ospf hello-interval 5
R1(config-if)# ip ospf dead-interval 20
R1(config-if)# end
R1#
R1#
*Apr  7 17:28:21.529: %OSPF-5-ADJCHG: Process 10, Nbr 2.2.2.2 on Serial0/0/0 from
   FULL to DOWN, Neighbor Down: Dead timer expired
R1#
```

Immediately after changing the Hello interval, the Cisco IOS automatically modifies the Dead interval to four times the Hello interval. However, it is always good practice to explicitly modify the timer instead of relying on an automatic IOS feature so that modifications are documented in the configuration. Therefore, the Dead interval is also manually set to 20 seconds on the R1 Serial 0/0/0 interface.

As displayed by the highlighted OSPFv2 adjacency message in the preceding output, when the Dead Timer on R1 expires, R1 and R2 lose adjacency. The reason is because the values have only been altered on one side of the serial link between R1 and R2. Recall that the OSPF Hello and Dead intervals must match between neighbors.

Use the **show ip ospf neighbor** command on R1 to verify the neighbor adjacencies, as shown in the following example:

```
R1# show ip ospf neighbor

Neighbor ID     Pri   State        Dead Time   Address         Interface
3.3.3.3           0   FULL/   -    00:00:37    192.168.10.6    Serial0/0/1
R1#
```

Notice that the only neighbor listed is the 3.3.3.3 (R3) router and that R1 is no longer adjacent with the 2.2.2.2 (R2) neighbor. The timers set on Serial 0/0/0 do not affect the neighbor adjacency with R3.

To restore adjacency between R1 and R2, the R2 Serial 0/0/0 interface Hello interval is set to **5** seconds, as shown in the following output. Almost immediately, the IOS displays a message that adjacency has been established with a state of FULL.

```
R2(config)# interface serial 0/0/0
R2(config-if)# ip ospf hello-interval 5
R2(config-if)#
*Apr  7 17:41:49.001: %OSPF-5-ADJCHG: Process 10, Nbr 1.1.1.1 on Serial0/0/0 from
   LOADING to FULL, Loading Done
R2(config-if)# end
R2#
```

Verify the interface intervals using the **show ip ospf interface** command, as follows:

```
R2# show ip ospf interface s0/0/0 | include Timer
   Timer intervals configured, Hello 5, Dead 20, Wait 20, Retransmit 5
R2#
R2# show ip ospf neighbor
Neighbor ID     Pri   State        Dead Time   Address        Interface
3.3.3.3          0    FULL/  -     00:00:35    192.168.10.10  Serial0/0/1
1.1.1.1          0    FULL/  -     00:00:17    172.16.3.1     Serial0/0/0
R2#
```

Notice that the Hello Time is 5 seconds and that the Dead Time was automatically set to 20 seconds instead of the default 40 seconds. Remember that OSPF automatically sets the Dead interval to four times the Hello interval.

Modifying OSPFv3 Intervals (7.1.3.3)

Like OSPFv2, OSPFv3 intervals can also be adjusted.

OSPFv3 Hello and Dead intervals can be modified manually using the following interface configuration mode commands:

- **ipv6 ospf hello-interval** *seconds*
- **ipv6 ospf dead-interval** *seconds*

> **Note**
>
> Use the **no ipv6 ospf hello-interval** and **no ipv6 ospf dead-interval** commands to reset the intervals to their default.

Refer back to the IPv6 topology shown in Figure 7-25. Assume that the network has converged using OSPFv3.

The following example modifies the OSPFv3 Hello interval to 5 seconds:

```
R1(config)# interface Serial 0/0/0
R1(config-if)# ipv6 ospf hello-interval 5
R1(config-if)# ipv6 ospf dead-interval 20
R1(config-if)# end
R1#
*Apr 10 15:03:51.175: %OSPFv3-5-ADJCHG: Process 10, Nbr 2.2.2.2 on Serial0/0/0 from
    FULL to DOWN, Neighbor Down: Dead timer expired
R1#
```

Immediately after changing the Hello interval, the Cisco IOS automatically modifies the Dead interval to four times the Hello interval. However, as with OSPFv2, it is always good practice to explicitly modify the timer instead of relying on an automatic IOS feature so that modifications are documented in the configuration. Therefore, the Dead interval is also manually set to 20 seconds on the R1 Serial 0/0/0 interface.

Once the Dead Timer on R1 expires, R1 and R2 lose adjacency, as displayed by the highlighted OSPFv3 adjacency message in the previous example, because the values have only been altered on one side of the serial link between R1 and R2. Recall that the OSPFv3 Hello and Dead intervals must be equivalent between neighbors.

Use the **show ipv6 ospf neighbor** command on R1 to verify the neighbor adjacencies as shown here. Notice that R1 is no longer adjacent with the 2.2.2.2 (R2) neighbor.

```
R1# show ipv6 ospf neighbor
R1#
```

To restore adjacency between R1 and R2, the R2 Serial 0/0/0 interface Hello interval is set to 5 seconds as shown. Almost immediately, the IOS displays a message that adjacency has been established with a state of FULL.

Verify the interface intervals using the **show ipv6 ospf interface** command as shown in Figure 7-28. Notice that the Hello Time is 5 seconds and that the Dead Time was automatically set to 20 seconds instead of the default 40 seconds. Remember that OSPF automatically sets the Dead interval to four times the Hello interval.

```
R2# show ip ospf interface s0/0/0 | include Timer
   Timer intervals configured, Hello 5, Dead 20, Wait 20,
Retransmit 5
R2#
R2# show ip ospf neighbor

Neighbor ID    Pri   State    Dead Time   Address        Interface
3.3.3.3        0     FULL/-   00:00:35    192.168.10.10  Serial0/0/1
1.1.1.1        0     FULL/-   00:00:17    172.16.3.1     Serial0/0/0
R2#
```

Figure 7-28   Verifying the OSPFv3 Neighbor Adjacencies on R2

Secure OSPF (7.1.4)

This section discusses how to secure OSPF routing updates between neighbors.

Routers Are Targets (7.1.4.1)

The role of routers in a network is so crucial that they are often the targets of network attacks. Network administrators must be aware that routers are at risk from attack just as much as end-user systems.

In general, routing systems can be attacked by disrupting the routing peers or by falsifying the information carried within the routing protocol. Falsified routing information may generally be used to cause systems to misinform (lie to) each other, cause a denial-of-service (DoS) attack, or cause traffic to follow a path it would not normally follow. The consequences of falsifying routing information are:

- Redirecting traffic to create routing loops

- Redirecting traffic so it can be monitored on an insecure link

- Redirecting traffic to discard it

Refer to Figures 7-29 to 7-32 for an example of an attack that creates a routing loop. In Figure 7-29, an attacker has been able to connect directly to the link between routers R1 and R2. The attacker injects false routing information destined to router R1 only, indicating that R3 is the preferred destination to the 192.168.10.10/32 host route. Although R1 has a routing table entry to the directly connected 192.168.10.0/24 network, it adds the injected route 192.168.10.10/32 to its routing table because of the longer /32 subnet mask of the false route. A route with a longer matching subnet mask is considered to be superior to a route with a shorter subnet mask. Consequently, when a router receives a packet, it selects the longer subnet mask, because it is a more precise route to the destination.

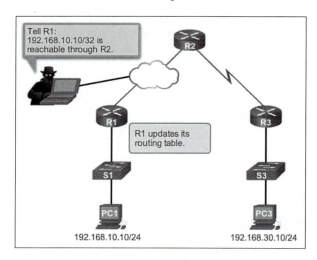

Figure 7-29   Attacker Injects False Route

In Figure 7-30, PC3 sends a packet to PC1 (192.168.10.10). R1 should forward the packet to PC1.

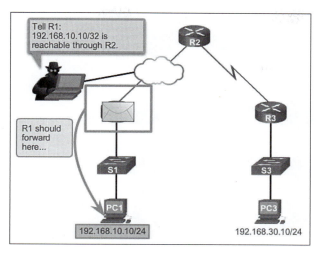

Figure 7-30   R1 Should Forward Packet to PC1

However, R1 does not forward the packet to the PC1 host, as shown in Figure 7-31. Because of the false route injected by the attacker, R1 now forwards the packet back to R2.

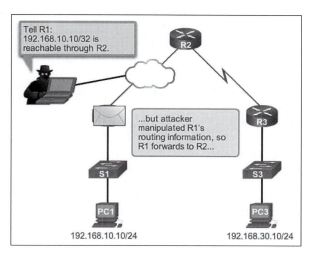

Figure 7-31   R1 Incorrectly Forwards the Packet to R2

When R2 gets the packet, it looks in its routing table and forwards the packet back to R1 as shown in Figure 7-32. Inevitably, this creates the loop.

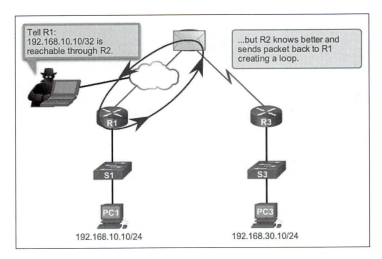

Figure 7-32   A Routing Loop Is Created

Video 7.1.1.3: Role of the DR

Go to the online course and play the animation to see how an attacker can create a routing loop.

To mitigate against routing protocol attacks, configure OSPF authentication.

Secure Routing Updates (7.1.4.2)

When neighbor authentication has been configured on a router, the router authenticates the source of each routing update packet that it receives. This is accomplished by the exchange of an authenticating key (sometimes referred to as a password) that is known to both the sending and the receiving router.

To exchange routing update information in a secure manner, enable OSPF authentication. *OSPF authentication* can either be none (or null), simple, or Message Digest 5 (MD5).

OSPF supports three types of authentication:

- **Null:** This is the default method and means that no authentication is used for OSPF.

- **Simple password authentication:** This is also referred to as plaintext authentication because the password in the update is sent in plaintext over the network. This is considered to be a legacy method of OSPF authentication.

- **MD5 authentication:** This is the most secure and recommended method of authentication. MD5 authentication provides higher security because the password is never exchanged between peers. Instead it is calculated using the MD5 algorithm. Matching results authenticate the sender.

Refer to Figures 7-33 to 7-35 for a simple example of how OSPF MD5 authentication is used to authenticate neighboring peer messages. In Figure 7-33, R3 wants to send a routing update to R1. Before sending the update, R3 generates a unique signature using the MD5 algorithm on the routing update data and a pre-shared secret key. This signature is attached to the routing update and sent to R1.

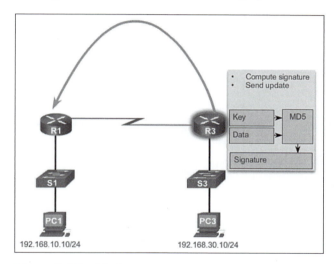

Figure 7-33 R3 Generates a Unique Signature to a Routing Update

In Figure 7-34, R1 receives the update. Next, R1 generates a unique signature using the MD5 algorithm on the routing update data and a pre-shared secret key.

If the signature that R1 generates matches the signature attached to the routing update from R3, then the update is accepted and the peer has been authenticated, as shown in Figure 7-35. If the signatures do not match, then the update is discarded.

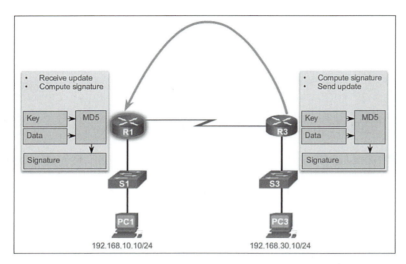

Figure 7-34   R1 Generates a Signature

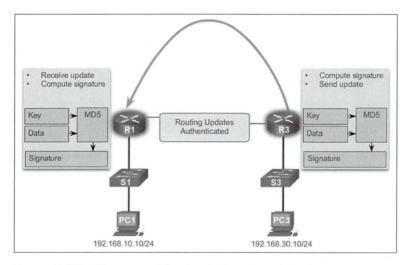

Figure 7-35   Signatures Match = Authenticated Updated

Video 7.1.4.3: OSPF MD5 Authentication

Go to the online course and play the animation to see an example of how two OSPF routers use authentication to exchange routing updates securely.

Note

RIPv2, EIGRP, OSPF, IS-IS, and BGP all support various forms of MD5 authentication.

MD5 Authentication (7.1.4.3)

The following example illustrates how MD5 authentication is used to authenticate two neighboring OSPF routers.

In Figure 7-36, R1 combines the routing message with the pre-shared secret key and calculates the signature using the MD5 algorithm. The signature is also known as a hash value.

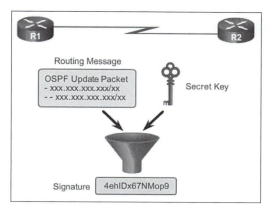

Figure 7-36   R1 Generates the Signature

In Figure 7-37, R1 adds the signature to the routing message and sends it to R2. It is important to note that MD5 does not encrypt the message. An intercepted routing update could be easily read. MD5 is used to authenticate the sender of the message.

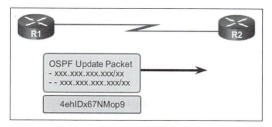

Figure 7-37   R1 Sends the MD5 Authenticated Routing Message

In Figure 7-38, R2 opens the packet, combines the routing message with the pre-shared secret key, and calculates the signature using the MD5 algorithm.

- If the signatures match, then R2 accepts the routing update.

- If the signatures do not match, then R2 discards the update.

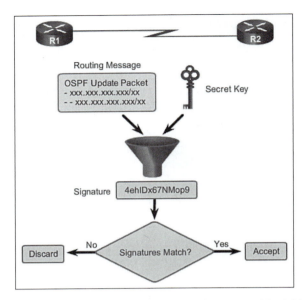

Figure 7-38   R2 Calculates and Compares Hash Values

OSPFv3 (OSPF for IPv6) does not include any authentication capabilities of its own. Instead it relies entirely on IPsec to secure communications between neighbors using the **ipv6 ospf authentication ipsec spi** interface configuration mode command. This is beneficial in simplifying the OSPFv3 protocol and standardizing its authentication mechanism.

Configuring OSPF MD5 Authentication (7.1.4.4)

OSPF supports routing protocol authentication using MD5. MD5 authentication can be enabled globally for all interfaces or on a per-interface basis.

To enable OSPF MD5 authentication globally, configure:

- **area** *area-id* **authentication message-digest** router configuration mode command

- **ip ospf message-digest-key** *key* **md5** *password* interface configuration mode command

This method forces authentication on all OSPF-enabled interfaces. If an interface is not configured with the **ip ospf message-digest-key** command, it will not be able to form adjacencies with other OSPF neighbors.

To provide more flexibility, authentication is now supported on a per-interface basis. To enable MD5 authentication on a per-interface basis, configure:

- **ip ospf message-digest-key** *key* **md5** *password* interface configuration mode command

- **ip ospf authentication message-digest** interface configuration mode command

Global and per-interface OSPF MD5 authentication can be used on the same router. However, the interface setting overrides the global setting. MD5 authentication passwords do not have to be the same throughout an area; however, they do need to be the same between neighbors.

OSPF MD5 Authentication Example (7.1.4.5)

For this example, refer to Figure 7-39.

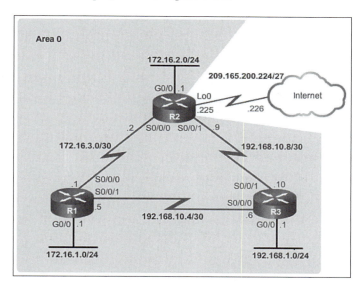

Figure 7-39   *OSPF Authentication Reference Topology*

Assume that all routers in the figure have converged using OSPF and routing is functioning properly. OSPF authentication will be implemented on all routers.

The example in Figure 7-40 configures R1 to enable OSPF MD5 authentication on all interfaces. Notice the informational messages stating that the OSPF neighbor adjacencies with R2 and R3 have changed to the Down state, because R2 and R3 have not yet been configured to support MD5 authentication.

```
R1(config)# router ospf 10
R1(config-router)# area 0 authentication message-digest
R1(config-router)# exit
R1(config)#
*Apr  8 09:58:09.899: %OSPF-5-ADJCHG: Process 10, Nbr 2.2.2.2
on Serial0/0/0 from FULL to DOWN, Neighbor Down: Dead timer
expired
R1(config)#
*Apr  8 09:58:28.627: %OSPF-5-ADJCHG: Process 10, Nbr 3.3.3.3
on Serial0/0/1 from FULL to DOWN, Neighbor Down: Dead timer
expired
R1(config)#
R1(config)# interface GigabitEthernet 0/0
R1(config-if)# ip ospf message-digest-key 1 md5 CISCO-123
R1(config-if)# exit
R1(config)#
R1(config)# interface Serial 0/0/0
R1(config-if)# ip ospf message-digest-key 1 md5 CISCO-123
R1(config-if)# exit
R1(config)#
R1(config)# interface Serial 0/0/1
R1(config-if)# ip ospf message-digest-key 1 md5 CISCO-123
R1(config-if)#
```

Figure 7-40   Enabling OSPF MD5 Authentication Globally on R1

As an alternative to globally enabling MD5 authentication, the example in Figure 7-41 demonstrates how to configure R1 to enable OSPF MD5 authentication on a per-interface basis. Again, notice how the OSPF neighbor adjacencies have changed to the Down state.

```
R1(config)# interface GigabitEthernet 0/0
R1(config-if)# ip ospf message-digest-key 1 md5 CISCO-123
R1(config-if)# ip ospf authentication message-digest
R1(config-if)# exit
R1(config)#
R1(config)# interface Serial 0/0/0
R1(config-if)# ip ospf message-digest-key 1 md5 CISCO-123
R1(config-if)# ip ospf authentication message-digest
R1(config-if)# exit
R1(config)#
R1(config)# interface Serial 0/0/1
R1(config-if)# ip ospf message-digest-key 1 md5 CISCO-123
R1(config-if)# ip ospf authentication message-digest
R1(config-if)# exit
R1(config)#
*Apr  8 10:20:10.647: %OSPF-5-ADJCHG: Process 10, Nbr 2.2.2.2
on Serial0/0/0 from FULL to DOWN, Neighbor Down: Dead timer
expired
R1(config)#
*Apr  8 10:20:50.007: %OSPF-5-ADJCHG: Process 10, Nbr 3.3.3.3
on Serial0/0/1 from FULL to DOWN, Neighbor Down: Dead timer
expired
R1(config)#
```

Figure 7-41   Enabling OSPF MD5 Authentication on the R1 Interfaces

Interactive
Graphic

Activity 7.1.4.5: Enabling OSPF MD5 Authentication

Go to the online course to use the Syntax Checker in the third graphic to enable OSPF MD5 authentication globally on R2 and R3.

Again, informational messages appear. The first message is because the neighbor adjacency with R1 has been re-established. However, the adjacency with R3 has transitioned to the Down state, because R3 is still not configured

After R3 is configured, all neighbor adjacencies have been re-established.

Verifying OSPF MD5 Authentication (7.1.4.6)

To verify that OSPF MD5 authentication is enabled, use the **show ip ospf interface** privileged EXEC mode command. By verifying that the routing table is complete, successful authentication can be confirmed.

Figure 7-42 verifies the OSPF MD5 authentication on the Serial 0/0/0 interface on R1.

```
R1# show ip ospf interface serial 0/0/0
Serial0/0/0 is up, line protocol is up
  Internet Address 172.16.3.1/30, Area 0, Attached via
Network Statement
  Process ID 10, Router ID 1.1.1.1, Network Type
POINT_TO_POINT, Cost: 64
Topology-MTID   Cost  Disabled  Shutdown      Topology Name
      0           64      no        no             Base
  Transmit Delay is 1 sec, State POINT_TO_POINT
  Timer intervals configured, Hello 5, Dead 20, Wait 20,
Retransmit 5
    oob-resync timeout 40
    Hello due in 00:00:02
  Supports Link-local Signaling (LLS)
  Cisco NSF helper support enabled
  IETF NSF helper support enabled
  Index 2/2, flood queue length 0
  Next 0x0(0)/0x0(0)
  Last flood scan length is 1, maximum is 1
  Last flood scan time is 0 msec, maximum is 0 msec
  Neighbor Count is 1, Adjacent neighbor count is 1
    Adjacent with neighbor 2.2.2.2
  Suppress hello for 0 neighbor(s)
  Message digest authentication enabled
```

Figure 7-42   Verify the OSPF MD5 Authentication Settings of R1

Figure 7-43 confirms that the authentication is successful.

```
R1# show ip route ospf
Codes: L - local, C - connected, S - static, R - RIP,
       M - mobile, B - BGP, D - EIGRP,
       EX - EIGRP external, O - OSPF, IA - OSPF inter area
       N1 - OSPF NSSA external type 1,
       N2 - OSPF NSSA external type 2
       E1 - OSPF external type 1
       E2 - OSPF external type 2
       i - IS-IS, su - IS-IS summary, L1 - IS-IS level-1,
       L2 - IS-IS level-2, ia - IS-IS inter area,
       * - candidate default, U - per-user static route
       o - ODR, P - periodic downloaded static route
       H - NHRP, l - LISP
       + - replicated route, % - next hop override

Gateway of last resort is 172.16.3.2 to network 0.0.0.0

O*E2 0.0.0.0/0 [110/1] via 172.16.3.2, 00:33:17, Serial0/0/0
       172.16.0.0/16 is variably subnetted, 5 subnets, 3 masks
O         172.16.2.0/24 [110/65] via 172.16.3.2, 00:33:17, Serial0/0/0
O      192.168.1.0/24 [110/65] via 192.168.10.6, 00:30:43, Serial0/0/1
       192.168.10.0/24 is variably subnetted, 3 subnets, 2 masks
O         192.168.10.8/30 [110/128] via 192.168.10.6, 00:30:43, Serial0/0/1
                          [110/128] via 172.16.3.2, 00:33:17, Serial0/0/0
R1#
```

Figure 7-43   Verify the Routing Table on R1

Note

The entire output in Figure 7-43 can be viewed in the online course on page 7.1.4.6 graphic number 1.

Activity 7.1.4.6: Verify the OSPF MD5 Authentication on R2

Go to the online course to use the Syntax Checker in the third graphic to verify the OSPF MD5 authentication on R2 and R3.

Packet Tracer Activity 7.1.4.7: Configuring OSPFv2 Advance Features

In this activity, OSPF is already configured and all end devices currently have full connectivity. You will modify the default OSPF routing configuration by changing the Hello and Dead Timers, adjusting the bandwidth of a link, and enabling OSPF authentication. Then you will verify that full connectivity is restored for all end devices.

Lab 7.1.4.8: Configuring OSPFv2 Advance Features

In this lab, you will complete the following objectives:

- Part 1: Build the Network and Configure Basic Device Settings
- Part 2: Configure and Verify OSPF Routing
- Part 3: Change OSPF Metrics
- Part 4: Configure and Propagate a Static Default Route
- Part 5: Configure OSPF Authentication

Troubleshooting Single-Area OSPF Implementations (7.2)

OSPF is a popularly implemented routing protocol used in large enterprise networks. Troubleshooting problems related to the exchange of routing information is one of the most essential skills for a network professional that is involved in the implementation and maintenance of large, routed enterprise networks that use OSPF as the IGP.

Issues with forming OSPF adjacencies include:

- The interfaces are not on the same network.
- OSPF network types do not match.
- OSPF Hello or Dead Timers do not match.
- Interface to neighbor is incorrectly configured as passive.
- There is a missing or incorrect OSPF **network** command.
- Authentication is misconfigured.

OSPF States (7.2.1.2)

To troubleshoot OSPF, it is important to understand how OSPF routers traverse different OSPF states when adjacencies are being established.

Figure 7-44 lists the *OSPF states*. When troubleshooting OSPF neighbors, be aware that the Full and Two-Way states are normal. All other states are transitory; that is, the router should not remain in those states for extended periods of time.

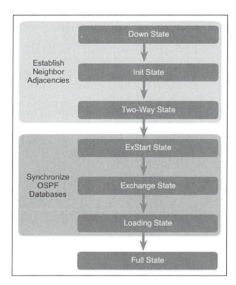

Figure 7-44   Transitioning Through the OSPF States

OSPF Troubleshooting Commands (7.2.1.3)

There are many different OSPF commands that can be used to help in the trouble-shooting process. The following summarizes the most common of these commands:

- **show ip protocols** (Figure 7-45): Used to verify vital OSPF configuration information, including the OSPF process ID, the router ID, networks the router is advertising, the neighbors the router is receiving updates from, and the default administrative distance, which is 110 for OSPF.

- **show ip ospf neighbor** (Figure 7-46): Used to verify that the router has formed an adjacency with its neighboring routers. Displays the neighbor router ID, neighbor priority, OSPF state, Dead Timer, neighbor interface IP address, and interface that the neighbor is accessible through. If the router ID of the neighboring router is not displayed, or if it does not show as a state of FULL or 2WAY, the two routers have not formed an OSPF adjacency. If two routers do not establish adjacency, link-state information will not be exchanged. Incomplete link-state databases can cause inaccurate SPF trees and routing tables. Routes to destination networks may not exist or may not be the most optimum path.

```
R1# show ip protocols
*** IP Routing is NSF aware ***

Routing Protocol is "ospf 10"
  Outgoing update filter list for all interfaces is not set
  Incoming update filter list for all interfaces is not set
  Router ID 1.1.1.1
  Number of areas in this router is 1. 1 normal 0 stub 0 nssa
  Maximum path: 4
  Routing for Networks:
    172.16.1.1 0.0.0.0 area 0
    172.16.3.1 0.0.0.0 area 0
    192.168.10.5 0.0.0.0 area 0
  Passive Interface(s):
    GigabitEthernet0/0
  Routing Information Sources:
    Gateway         Distance      Last Update
    3.3.3.3              110      00:08:35
    2.2.2.2              110      00:08:35
  Distance: (default is 110)

R1#
```

Figure 7-45   Verify the OSPF Settings on R1

```
R1# show ip ospf neighbor

Neighbor ID Pri State        Dead Time Address      Interface
2.2.2.2       1 FULL/BDR     00:00:30  192.168.1.2  GigabitEthernet0/0
3.3.3.3       0 FULL/DROTHER 00:00:38  192.168.1.3  GigabitEthernet0/0
R1#
```

Figure 7-46   Verify the OSPF Neighbor Adjacencies on R1

■ **show ip ospf interface** (Figure 7-47): Used to display the OSPF parameters configured on an interface, such as the OSPF process ID that the interface is assigned to, the area that the interfaces are in, the cost of the interface, and the Hello and Dead intervals. Adding the interface name and number to the command displays output for a specific interface.

■ **show ip ospf** (Figure 7-48): Used to examine the OSPF process ID and router ID. Additionally, this command displays the OSPF area information, as well as the last time the SPF algorithm was calculated.

```
R1# show ip ospf interface Serial 0/0/0
Serial0/0/0 is up, line protocol is up
  Internet Address 172.16.3.1/30, Area 0, Attached via Network
Statement
  Process ID 10, Router ID 1.1.1.1, Network Type POINT_TO_POINT,
Cost: 64
  Topology-MTID   Cost   Disabled   Shutdown    Topology Name
        0          64       no         no           Base
  Transmit Delay is 1 sec, State POINT_TO_POINT
  Timer intervals configured, Hello 5, Dead 20, Wait 20, Retransmit 5
    oob-resync timeout 40
    Hello due in 00:00:02
  Supports Link-local Signaling (LLS)
  Cisco NSF helper support enabled
  IETF NSF helper support enabled
  Index 2/2, flood queue length 0
  Next 0x0(0)/0x0(0)
  Last flood scan length is 1, maximum is 1
  Last flood scan time is 0 msec, maximum is 0 msec
  Neighbor Count is 1, Adjacent neighbor count is 1
    Adjacent with neighbor 2.2.2.2
  Suppress hello for 0 neighbor(s)
  Message digest authentication enabled
    Youngest key id is 1
R1#
```

Figure 7-47   Verify the OSPF Interface Settings of Serial 0/0/0 on R1

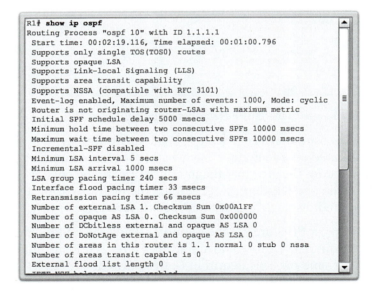

Figure 7-48   Display OSPF Parameters

Note

The entire output in Figure 7-48 can be viewed in the online course on page 7.2.1.3 graphic number 4.

- **show ip route ospf** (Figure 7-49): Used to display only the OSPF learned routes in the routing table. The output shows that R1 has learned about four remote networks through OSPF.

```
R1# show ip route ospf
Codes:L - local,C - connected,S - static,R - RIP,M - mobile,B - BGP
      D - EIGRP, EX - EIGRP external, O - OSPF, IA - OSPF inter area
      N1 - OSPF NSSA external type 1, N2 - OSPF NSSA external type 2
      E1 - OSPF external type 1, E2 - OSPF external type 2
      i - IS-IS,su - IS-IS summary,L1 - IS-IS level-1,L2-IS-IS level-2
      ia - IS-IS inter area,*-candidate default,U-per-user static route
      o - ODR, P - periodic downloaded static route, H - NHRP, l - LISP
      + - replicated route, % - next hop override

Gateway of last resort is 172.16.3.2 to network 0.0.0.0

O*E2  0.0.0.0/0 [110/1] via 172.16.3.2, 00:33:17, Serial0/0/0
      172.16.0.0/16 is variably subnetted, 5 subnets, 3 masks
O        172.16.2.0/24 [110/65] via 172.16.3.2, 00:33:17,Serial0/0/0
O     192.168.1.0/24 [110/65] via 192.168.10.6, 00:30:43, Serial0/0/1
      192.168.10.0/24 is variably subnetted, 3 subnets, 2 masks
O        192.168.10.8/30[110/128] via 192.168.10.6,00:30:43,Serial0/0/1
                        [110/128] via 172.16.3.2,00:33:17,Serial0/0/0
R1#
```

Figure 7-49 Verify the OSPF Routes in the Routing Table on R1

- **clear ip ospf** [*process-id*] **process:** Used to reset the OSPFv2 neighbor adjacencies.

Components of Troubleshooting OSPF (7.2.1.4)

OSPF problems usually relate to:

- Neighbor adjacencies
- Missing routes
- Path selection

When troubleshooting neighbor issues, verify if the router has established adjacencies with neighboring routers using the **show ip ospf neighbors** command. Figure 7-50 provides a graphical view for troubleshooting neighbor issues. If there is no adjacency, then the routers cannot exchange routes. Verify if interfaces are operational and enabled for OSPF using the **show ip interface brief** and **show ip ospf interface** commands. If the interfaces are operational and enabled for OSPF, ensure that interfaces on both routers are configured for the same OSPF area and the interfaces are not configured as passive interfaces.

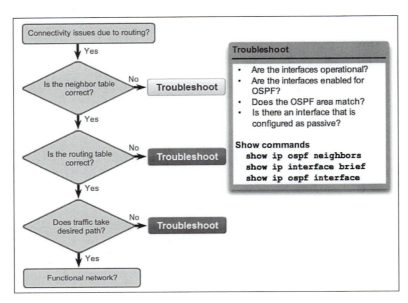

Figure 7-50   Troubleshooting Neighbor Issues

If adjacency between two routers is established, verify that there are OSPF routes in the routing table using the **show ip route ospf** command. Figure 7-51 provides a graphical view for troubleshooting routing table issues. If there are no OSPF routes, verify that there are no other routing protocols with lower administrative distances running in the network. Verify if all of the required networks are advertised into OSPF. Also verify if an access list is configured on a router that would filter either incoming or outgoing routing updates.

If all of the required routes are in the routing table, but the path that traffic takes is not correct, verify the OSPF cost on interfaces on the path. Figure 7-52 provides a graphical view for troubleshooting data path issues. Also be careful in cases where the interfaces are faster than 100 Mb/s, because all interfaces above this bandwidth have the same OSPF cost, by default.

Interactive Graphic

Activity 7.2.1.5: Identify the Troubleshooting Command

Go to the online course to perform this practice activity.

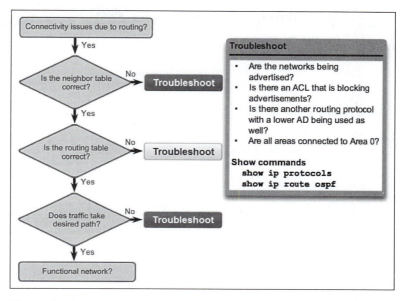

Figure 7-51   Troubleshooting Routing Table Issues

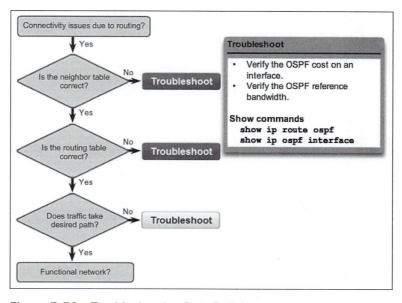

Figure 7-52   Troubleshooting Data Path Issues

Troubleshoot Single-Area OSPFv2 Routing Issues (7.2.2)

The example in this section highlights how to troubleshoot neighbor problems.

Troubleshooting Neighbor Issues (7.2.2.1)

Refer back to the topology in Figure 7-39. Assume all of the routers have been configured to support OSPF routing.

A quick look at the R1 routing table, as shown in Figure 7-53, reveals that R1 is not adding any OSPF routes. There are multiple reasons why this could be. However, a prerequisite for the neighbor relationship to form between two routers is OSI Layer 3 connectivity.

```
R1# show ip route
Codes: L -  local, C - connected, S - static, R - RIP, M -
            mobile, B - BGP
       D -  EIGRP, EX - EIGRP external, O - OSPF, IA - OSPF
            inter area
       N1 - OSPF NSSA external type 1, N2 - OSPF NSSA
            external type 2
       E1 - OSPF external type 1, E2 - OSPF external type 2
       i -  IS-IS, su - IS-IS summary, L1 - IS-IS level-1,
            L2 - IS-IS level-2
       ia - IS-IS inter area, * - candidate default, U -
            per-user static route
       o -  ODR, P - periodic downloaded static route, H -
            NHRP, l - LISP
       + -  replicated route, % - next hop override

Gateway of last resort is not set

   172.16.0.0/16 is variably subnetted, 4 subnets, 3 masks
C     172.16.1.0/24 is directly connected, GigabitEthernet0/0
L     172.16.1.1/32 is directly connected, GigabitEthernet0/0
C     172.16.3.0/30 is directly connected, Serial0/0/0
L     172.16.3.1/32 is directly connected, Serial0/0/0
R1#
```

Figure 7-53   Investigating Missing OSPF Routes in the Routing Table of R1

The output in Figure 7-54 confirms that the S0/0/0 interface is up and active. The successful ping also confirms that the R2 serial interface is active. A successful ping does not mean an adjacency will form, because it is possible to have overlapping subnets. You still have to verify that interfaces on the connected devices share the same subnet. If the ping was not successful, check the cabling and verify that interfaces on connected devices are configured correctly and operational.

Note

The entire output in Figure 7-54 can be viewed in the online course on page 7.2.2.1 graphic number 3.

```
R1# show ip interface brief
Interface                    IP-Address      OK?  Method  Status
Embedded-Service-Engine0/0   unassigned      YES  unset   administr
GigabitEthernet0/0           172.16.1.1      YES  manual  up
GigabitEthernet0/1           unassigned      YES  unset   administr
Serial0/0/0                  172.16.3.1      YES  manual  up
Serial0/0/1                  unassigned      YES  TFTP    up
R1#
R1# ping 172.16.3.2
Type escape sequence to abort.
Sending 5, 100-byte ICMP Echos to 172.16.3.2, timeout is 2 seco
!!!!!
Success rate is 100 percent (5/5), round-trip min/avg/max = 12/
R1#
```

Figure 7-54 Verify Layer 3 Connectivity to R2

For an interface to be enabled for OSPF, a matching **network** command must be configured under the OSPF routing process. Active OSPF interfaces can be verified using the **show ip ospf interface** command. The output in Figure 7-55 verifies that the Serial 0/0/0 interface is enabled for OSPF. If connected interfaces on two routers are not enabled for OSPF, the neighbors will not form an adjacency.

Verify the OSPF settings using the **show ip protocols** command. The output displayed in Figure 7-56 verifies that OSPF is enabled and also lists the networks being advertised as enabled by the **network** command. If an IP address on an interface falls within a network that has been enabled for OSPF, the interface will be enabled for OSPF.

```
R1# show ip ospf interface serial 0/0/0
Serial0/0/0 is up, line protocol is up
  Internet Address 172.16.3.1/30, Area 0, Attached via
  Network Statement
  Process ID 10, Router ID 1.1.1.1, Network Type
  POINT_TO_POINT, Cost: 64
  Topology-MTID    Cost  Disabled  Shutdown   Topology Name
       0            64    no        no         Base
  Transmit Delay is 1 sec, State POINT_TO_POINT
  Timer intervals configured, Hello 5, Dead 20, Wait 20,
  Retransmit 5
    oob-resync timeout 40
    No Hellos (Passive interface)
  Supports Link-local Signaling (LLS)
  Cisco NSF helper support enabled
  IETF NSF helper support enabled
  Index 2/2, flood queue length 0
  Next 0x0(0)/0x0(0)
  Last flood scan length is 1, maximum is 1
  Last flood scan time is 0 msec, maximum is 0 msec
  Neighbor Count is 0, Adjacent neighbor count is 0
  Suppress hello for 0 neighbor(s)
  Message digest authentication enabled
    Youngest key id is 1
```

Figure 7-55 Verify If OSPF Is Enabled on the R1 Serial 0/0/0 Interface

However, notice that the Serial 0/0/0 interface is listed as passive. Recall that the **passive-interface** command stops both outgoing and incoming routing updates because the effect of the command causes the router to stop sending and receiving Hello packets over an interface. For this reason, the routers will not become neighbors.

```
R1# show ip protocols
*** IP Routing is NSF aware ***

Routing Protocol is "ospf 10"
  Outgoing update filter list for all interfaces is not set
  Incoming update filter list for all interfaces is not set
  Router ID 1.1.1.1
  Number of areas in this router is 1. 1 normal 0 stub 0 nssa
  Maximum path: 4
  Routing for Networks:
    172.16.1.1 0.0.0.0 area 0
    172.16.3.1 0.0.0.0 area 0
  Passive Interface(s):
    GigabitEthernet0/0
    Serial0/0/0
  Routing Information Sources:
    Gateway         Distance      Last Update
    3.3.3.3             110       00:50:03
    2.2.2.2             110       04:27:25
  Distance: (default is 110)

R1#
```

Figure 7-56   Verify OSPF Settings on R1

To disable the interface as passive, use the **no passive-interface** router configuration mode command as shown next. After you disable the passive interface, the routers become adjacent, as indicated by an automatically generated information message.

```
R1(config)# router ospf 10
R1(config-router)# no passive-interface s0/0/0
R1(config-router)#
*Apr  9 13:14:15.454: %OSPF-5-ADJCHG: Process 10, Nbr 2.2.2.2 on Serial0/0/0 from
   LOADING to FULL, Loading Done
R1(config-router)# end
R1#
```

A quick verification of the routing table as shown in Figure 7-57 confirms that OSPF is now exchanging routing information.

Note

The entire output in Figure 7-57 can be viewed in the online course on page 7.2.2.1 graphic number 7.

```
                external type 2
       E1 - OSPF external type 1, E2 - OSPF external type 2
       i -  IS-IS, su - IS-IS summary, L1 - IS-IS level-1,
            L2 -IS-IS level-2
       ia - IS-IS inter area, * - candidate default, U -
            per-user static route
       o -  ODR, P - periodic downloaded static route, H -
            NHRP, l - LISP
       + -  replicated route, % - next hop override

Gateway of last resort is 172.16.3.2 to network 0.0.0.0

O*E2  0.0.0.0/0 [110/1] via 172.16.3.2, 00:00:18,
Serial0/0/0
        172.16.0.0/16 is variably subnetted, 5 subnets, 3
masks
O       172.16.2.0/24 [110/65] via 172.16.3.2, 00:00:18,
          Serial0/0/0
O       192.168.1.0/24 [110/129] via 172.16.3.2, 00:00:18,
          Serial0/0/0
        192.168.10.0/30 is subnetted, 1 subnets
O         192.168.10.8 [110/128] via 172.16.3.2, 00:00:18,
          Serial0/0/0
R1#
```

Figure 7-57   Verify OSPF Neighbor Routes in the Routing Table of R1

Another problem that may arise is when two neighboring routers have mismatched MTU sizes on their connecting interfaces. The MTU size is the largest network layer packet that the router will forward out each interface. Routers default to an MTU size of 1,500 bytes. However, this value can be changed for IPv4 packets using the **ip mtu** *size* interface configuration command and changed for IPv6 packets using the **ipv6 mtu** *size* interface command. If two connecting routers had mismatched MTU values, they would still attempt to form an adjacency, but they would not exchange their LSDBs and the neighbor relationship would fail.

Troubleshooting OSPF Routing Table Issues (7.2.2.2)

Refer back to the topology in Figure 7-39. Assume all of the routers have been configured to support OSPF routing.

A quick look at the R1 routing table, shown in Figure 7-58, reveals that it receives default route information, the R2 LAN (172.16.2.0/24), and the link between R2 and R3 (192.168.10.8/30). However, it does not receive the R3 LAN OSPF route.

```
   ia   IS-IS inter area,     candidate default, U
        per-user static route
   o -  ODR, P - periodic downloaded static route, H -
        NHRP, l - LISP
   + -  replicated route, % - next hop override

Gateway of last resort is 172.16.3.2 to network 0.0.0.0

O*E2  0.0.0.0/0 [110/1] via 172.16.3.2, 00:05:26,
      Serial0/0/0
      172.16.0.0/16 is variably subnetted, 5 subnets, 3
      masks
C        172.16.1.0/24 is directly connected,
         GigabitEthernet0/0
L        172.16.1.1/32 is directly connected,
         GigabitEthernet0/0
O        172.16.2.0/24 [110/65] via 172.16.3.2, 00:05:26,
         Serial0/0/0
C        172.16.3.0/30 is directly connected, Serial0/0/0
L        172.16.3.1/32 is directly connected, Serial0/0/0
      192.168.10.0/30 is subnetted, 1 subnets
O        192.168.10.8 [110/128] via 172.16.3.2, 00:05:26,
         Serial0/0/0
R1#
```

Figure 7-58 Verify OSPF Routes in the Routing Table of R1

The output in Figure 7-59 verifies the OSPF settings on R3. Notice that R3 only advertises the link between R3 and R2. It does not advertise the R3 LAN (192.168.1.0/24).

```
R3# show ip protocols
*** IP Routing is NSF aware ***
Routing Protocol is "ospf 10"
  Outgoing update filter list for all interfaces is not set
  Incoming update filter list for all interfaces is not set
  Router ID 3.3.3.3
  Number of areas in this router is 1. 1 normal 0 stub 0
  nssa
  Maximum path: 4
  Routing for Networks:
    192.168.10.8 0.0.0.3 area 0
  Passive Interface(s):
    Embedded-Service-Engine0/0
    GigabitEthernet0/0
    GigabitEthernet0/1
    GigabitEthernet0/3
    RG-AR-IF-INPUT1
  Routing Information Sources:
    Gateway         Distance       Last Update
    1.1.1.1              110       00:02:48
    2.2.2.2              110       00:02:48
  Distance: (default is 110)

R3#
```

Figure 7-59   Verify OSPF Settings on R3

For an interface to be enabled for OSPF, a matching **network** command must be configured under the OSPF routing process. The following output confirms that the R3 LAN is not advertised in OSPF:

```
R3# show running-config | section router ospf
router ospf 10
 router-id 3.3.3.3
 passive-interface default
 no passive-interface Serial0/0/1
 network 192.168.10.8 0.0.0.3 area 0
R3#
```

The following example adds a **network** command for the R3 LAN. R3 should now advertise the R3 LAN to its OSPF neighbors.

```
R3# conf t
Enter configuration commands, one per line.  End with CNTL/Z.
R3(config)# router ospf 10
R3(config-router)# network 192.168.1.0 0.0.0.255 area 0
R3(config-router)# end
R3#
*Apr 10 11:03:11.115: %SYS-5-CONFIG_I: Configured from console by console
R3#
```

The output in Figure 7-60 verifies that the R3 LAN is now in the routing table of R1.

```
         E1 - OSPF external type 1, E2 - OSPF external type 2
         i - IS-IS, su - IS-IS summary, L1 - IS-IS level-1,
             L2 - IS-IS level-2
         ia - IS-IS inter area, * - candidate default, U -
             per-user static route
         o - ODR, P - periodic downloaded static route, H -
             NHRP, l - LISP
         + - replicated route, % - next hop override

Gateway of last resort is 172.16.3.2 to network 0.0.0.0

O*E2  0.0.0.0/0 [110/1] via 172.16.3.2, 00:08:38,
         Serial0/0/0
         172.16.0.0/16 is variably subnetted, 5 subnets, 3
         masks
O        172.16.2.0/24 [110/65] via 172.16.3.2, 00:08:38,
             Serial0/0/0
O        192.168.1.0/24 [110/129] via 172.16.3.2, 00:00:37,
             Serial0/0/0
         192.168.10.0/30 is subnetted, 1 subnets
O            192.168.10.8 [110/128] via 172.16.3.2, 00:08:38,
             Serial0/0/0
R1#
```

Figure 7-60   Verify the R3 LAN OSPF Route in the Routing Table of R1

Packet Tracer Activity 7.2.2.3: Troubleshooting Single-Area OSPFv2

In this activity, you will troubleshoot OSPF routing issues using **ping** and **show** commands to identify errors in the network configuration. Then, you will document the errors you discover and implement an appropriate solution. Finally, you will verify end-to-end connectivity is restored.

Troubleshoot Single-Area OSPFv3 Routing Issues (7.2.3)

Troubleshooting OSPFv3 is almost identical to troubleshooting OSPFv2. In this section, you will learn the commands to troubleshoot a single-area OSPFv3 implementation.

OSPFv3 Troubleshooting Commands (7.2.3.1)

For this example, refer to the topology shown in Figure 7-61.

Troubleshooting OSPFv3 is almost identical to troubleshooting OSPFv2; therefore, many OSPFv3 commands and troubleshooting criteria also apply to OSPFv3.

For example, the following are the equivalent commands used with OSPFv3:

- **show ipv6 protocols:** As shown in the following output, this command is used to verify vital OSPFv3 configuration information, including the OSPFv3 process ID, the router ID, networks the router is advertising, and the neighbors the router is receiving updates from.

```
R1# show ipv6 protocols
IPv6 Routing Protocol is "connected"
IPv6 Routing Protocol is "ND"
IPv6 Routing Protocol is "ospf 10"
  Router ID 1.1.1.1
  Number of areas: 1 normal, 0 stub, 0 nssa
  Interfaces (Area 0):
    Serial0/0/0
    GigabitEthernet0/0
  Redistribution:
    None
R1#
```

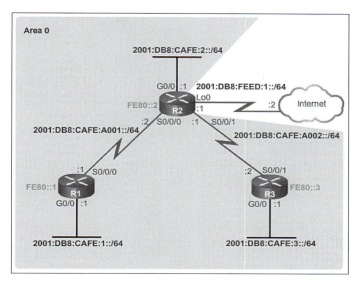

Figure 7-61   OSPFv3 Troubleshooting Topology

- **show ipv6 ospf neighbor:** As shown in the following output, this command is used to verify that the router has formed an adjacency with its neighboring routers. This output displays the neighbor router ID, the neighbor priority, OSPFv3 state, Dead Timer, neighbor interface ID, and the interface that the neighbor is accessible through. If the router ID of the neighboring router is not displayed, or if it does not show as a state of FULL or 2WAY, the two routers have not formed an OSPFv3 adjacency. If two routers do not establish adjacency, link-state information will not be exchanged. Incomplete link-state databases can cause inaccurate SPF trees and routing tables. Routes to destination networks may not exist, or they may not be the most optimum paths.

```
R1# show ipv6 ospf neighbor

Neighbor ID    Pri    State    Dead Time    Interface ID    Interface
2.2.2.2        0      FULL/-   00:00:33     7               Serial0/0/0
R1#
```

- **show ipv6 ospf interface** (Figure 7-62): This command is used to display the OSPFv3 parameters configured on an interface, such as the OSPFv3 process ID that the interface is assigned to, the area that the interfaces are in, the cost of the interface, and the Hello and Dead intervals. Adding the interface name and number to the command displays output for a specific interface.

```
R1# show ipv6 ospf interface s0/0/0
Serial0/0/0 is up, line protocol is up
  Link Local Address FE80::1, Interface ID 6
  Area 0, Process ID 10, Instance ID 0, Router ID 1.1.1.1
  Network Type POINT_TO_POINT, Cost: 647
  Transmit Delay is 1 sec, State POINT_TO_POINT
  Timer intervals configured, Hello 10, Dead 40, Wait 40,
Retransmit 5
    Hello due in 00:00:08
  Graceful restart helper support enabled
  Index 1/2/2, flood queue length 0
  Next 0x0(0)/0x0(0)/0x0(0)
  Last flood scan length is 2, maximum is 6
  Last flood scan time is 0 msec, maximum is 0 msec
  Neighbor Count is 1, Adjacent neighbor count is 1
    Adjacent with neighbor 2.2.2.2
  Suppress hello for 0 neighbor(s)
R1#
```

Figure 7-62   Display the OSPFv3 Parameters

- **show ipv6 ospf** (Figure 7-63): This command is used to examine the OSPF process ID and router ID, as well as information about the LSA transmissions.

```
R1# show ipv6 ospf
 Routing Process "ospfv3 10" with ID 1.1.1.1
 Event-log enabled, Maximum number of events: 1000, Mode:
cyclic
 Router is not originating router-LSAs with maximum metric
 Initial SPF schedule delay 5000 msecs
 Minimum hold time between two consecutive SPFs 10000 msecs
 Maximum wait time between two consecutive SPFs 10000 msecs
 Minimum LSA interval 5 secs
 Minimum LSA arrival 1000 msecs
 LSA group pacing timer 240 secs
 Interface flood pacing timer 33 msecs
 Retransmission pacing timer 66 msecs
 Number of external LSA 1. Checksum Sum 0x0017E9
 Number of areas in this router is 1. 1 normal 0 stub 0 nssa
 Graceful restart helper support enabled
 Reference bandwidth unit is 1000 mbps
 RFC1583 compatibility enabled
    Area BACKBONE(0)
Number of interfaces in this area is 2
SPF algorithm executed 8 times
Number of LSA 13. Checksum Sum 0x063D5D
Number of DCbitless LSA 0
Number of indication LSA 0
```

Figure 7-63   Verify the OSPFv3 Interface Settings of S0/0/0 on R1

Note

The entire output in Figure 7-63 can be viewed in the online course on page 7.2.3.1 graphic number 5.

- **show ipv6 route ospf** (Figure 7-64): This command is used to display only the OSPFv3 learned routes in the routing table. The output shows that R1 has learned about four remote networks through OSPFv3.

```
R1# show ipv6 route ospf
IPv6 Routing Table - default - 9 entries
Codes: C - Connected, L - Local, S - Static, U - Per-user
Static route
       B -   BGP, R - RIP, H - NHRP, I1 - ISIS L1
       I2 -  ISIS L2, IA - ISIS interarea, IS - ISIS
             summary, D - EIGRP
       EX -  EIGRP external, ND - ND Default, NDp - ND
             Prefix, DCE - Destination
       NDr - Redirect, O - OSPF Intra, OI - OSPF Inter, OE1
             - OSPF ext 1
       OE2 - OSPF ext 2, ON1 - OSPF NSSA ext 1, ON2 - OSPF
             NSSA ext 2
OE2 ::/0 [110/1], tag 10
    via FE80::2, Serial0/0/0
O   2001:DB8:CAFE:2::/64 [110/648]
    via FE80::2, Serial0/0/0
O   2001:DB8:CAFE:3::/64 [110/648]
    via FE80::2, Serial0/0/0
O   2001:DB8:CAFE:A002::/64 [110/1294]
    via FE80::2, Serial0/0/0
R1#
```

Figure 7-64   Verify the OSPFv3 Routes in the Routing Table on R1

- **clear ipv6 ospf** [*process-id*] **process:** This command is used to reset the OSPFv3 neighbor adjacencies.

Troubleshooting OSPFv3 (7.2.3.2)

Refer back to Figure 7-61 for the OSPFv3 reference topology. Assume that all of the routers have been configured to support OSPFv3 routing.

A quick look at the R1 IPv6 routing table, shown in Figure 7-65, reveals that it receives the default route, the R2 LAN (2001:DB8:CAFE:2::/64), and the link between R2 and R3 (2001:DB8:CAFE:A002::/64). However, it does not receive the R3 LAN OSPFv3 route (2001:DB8:CAFE:3::/64).

```
R1# show ipv6 route ospf
IPv6 Routing Table - default - 8 entries
Codes: C - Connected, L - Local, S - Static, U - Per-user
          Static route
        B -    BGP, R - RIP, H - NHRP, I1 - ISIS L1
        I2 -   ISIS L2, IA - ISIS interarea, IS - ISIS summary,
               D - EIGRP
        EX -   EIGRP external, ND - ND Default, NDp - ND
               Prefix, DCE - Destination
        NDr -  Redirect, O - OSPF Intra, OI - OSPF Inter, OE1
               - OSPF ext 1
        OE2 -  OSPF ext 2, ON1 - OSPF NSSA ext 1, ON2 - OSPF
               NSSA ext 2
OE2 ::/0 [110/1], tag 10
     via FE80::2, Serial0/0/0
O    2001:DB8:CAFE:2::/64 [110/648]
     via FE80::2, Serial0/0/0
O    2001:DB8:CAFE:A002::/64 [110/1294]
     via FE80::2, Serial0/0/0
R1#
```

Figure 7-65   Verify OSPFv3 Routes in the Routing Table of R1

The following output verifies the OSPFv3 settings on R3. Notice that R3 is only enabled on the Serial 0/0/1 interface. It appears that it is not enabled on the G0/0 R3 interface.

```
R3# show ipv6 protocols
IPv6 Routing Protocol is "connected"
IPv6 Routing Protocol is "ND"
IPv6 Routing Protocol is "ospf 10"
  Router ID 3.3.3.3
  Number of areas: 1 normal, 0 stub, 0 nssa
  Interfaces (Area 0):
    Serial0/0/1
  Redistribution:
    None
R3#
```

Unlike OSPFv2, OSPFV3 does not use the **network** command. Instead OSPFv3 is enabled directly on the interface. The following output confirms that the R3 interface is not enabled for OSPFv3:

```
R3# show running-config interface g0/0
Building configuration...

Current configuration : 196 bytes
!
interface GigabitEthernet0/0
 description R3 LAN
 no ip address
```

```
 duplex auto
 speed auto
 ipv6 address FE80::3 link-local
 ipv6 address 2001:DB8:CAFE:3::1/64
end


R3#
```

The following example enables OSPFv3 on the R3 GigabitEthernet 0/0 interface. R3 should now advertise the R3 LAN to its OSPFv3 neighbors.

```
R3# conf t
Enter configuration commands, one per line.  End with CNTL/Z.
R3(config)# interface g0/0
R3(config-if)# ipv6 ospf 10 area 0
R3(config-if)# end
R3#
```

The output in Figure 7-66 verifies that the R3 LAN is now in the routing table of R1.

```
R1# show ipv6 route ospf
IPv6 Routing Table - default - 9 entries
Codes: C - Connected, L - Local, S - Static, U - Per-user
Static route
       B -  BGP, R - RIP, H - NHRP, I1 - ISIS L1
       I2 - ISIS L2, IA - ISIS interarea, IS - ISIS summary, D
            - EIGRP
       EX -  EIGRP external, ND - ND Default, NDp - ND Prefix,
            DCE - Destination
       NDr - Redirect, O - OSPF Intra, OI - OSPF Inter, OE1 -
            OSPF ext 1
       OE2 - OSPF ext 2, ON1 - OSPF NSSA ext 1, ON2 - OSPF
            NSSA ext 2
OE2 ::/0 [110/1], tag 10
     via FE80::2, Serial0/0/0
O    2001:DB8:CAFE:2::/64 [110/648]
     via FE80::2, Serial0/0/0
O    2001:DB8:CAFE:3::/64 [110/1295]
     via FE80::2, Serial0/0/0
O    2001:DB8:CAFE:A002::/64 [110/1294]
     via FE80::2, Serial0/0/0
R1#
```

Figure 7-66   Verify the R3 LAN OSPFv3 Route in the Routing Table of R1

Lab 7.2.3.3: Troubleshooting Basic Single-Area OSPFv2 and OSPFv3

In this lab, you will complete the following objectives:

- Part 1: Build the Network and Load Device Configurations
- Part 2: Troubleshoot Layer 3 Connectivity
- Part 3: Troubleshoot OSPFv2
- Part 4: Troubleshoot OSPFv3

Lab 7.2.3.4: Troubleshooting Advanced Single-Area OSPFv2

In this lab, you will complete the following objectives:

- Part 1: Build the Network and Load Device Configurations
- Part 2: Troubleshoot OSPF

Summary (7.3)

Class Activity 7.3.1.1: OSPF Troubleshooting Mastery

You have decided to change your routing protocol from RIPv2 to OSPFv2. Your small- to medium-sized business network topology will not change from its original physical settings. Use the diagram on the PDF for this activity as your company's small- to medium-sized business network design.

Your addressing design is complete and you then configure your routers with IPv4 and VLSM. OSPF has been applied as the routing protocol. However, some routers are sharing routing information with each other and some are not.

Open the PDF file that accompanies this modeling activity and follow the directions to complete the activity.

When the steps in the directions are complete, regroup as a class and compare recorded activity correction times. The group taking the shortest time to find and fix the configuration error will be declared the winner only after successfully explaining how they found the error, fixed it, and proved that the topology is now working.

Packet Tracer Activity 7.3.1.2: Skills Integration Challenge

In this Skills Integration Challenge, your focus is OSPFv2 advanced configurations. IP addressing has been configured for all devices. You will configure OSPFv2 routing with passive interfaces and default route propagation. You will modify the OSPFv2 configuration by adjusting timers and establishing MD5 authentication. Finally, you will verify your configurations and test connectivity between end devices.

OSPF defines five network types: point-to-point, broadcast multiaccess, nonbroadcast multiaccess, point-to-multipoint, and virtual links.

Multiaccess networks can create two challenges for OSPF regarding the flooding of LSAs: creation of multiple adjacencies and extensive flooding of LSAs. The solution to managing the number of adjacencies and the flooding of LSAs on a multiaccess network is the DR and BDR. If the DR stops producing Hellos, the BDR promotes itself and assumes the role of DR.

The routers in the network elect the router with the highest interface priority as DR. The router with the second highest interface priority is elected the BDR. The higher the priority, the likelier the router will be selected as the DR. If set to 0, the router is not capable of becoming the DR. The default priority of multiaccess broadcast interfaces is 1. Therefore, unless otherwise configured, all routers have an equal priority value and must rely on another tie-breaking method during the DR/BDR election. If the interface priorities are equal, then the router with the highest router ID is elected the DR. The router with the second highest router ID is the BDR. The addition of a new router does not initiate a new election process.

To propagate a default route in OSPF, the router must be configured with a default static route and the **default-information originate** command must be added to the configuration. Verify routes with the **show ip route** or **show ipv6 route** command.

To assist OSPF in making the correct path determination, the reference bandwidth must be changed to a higher value to accommodate networks with links faster than 100 Mb/s. To adjust the reference bandwidth, use the **auto-cost reference-bandwidth** *Mb/s* router configuration mode command. To adjust the interface bandwidth, use the **bandwidth** *kilobits* interface configuration mode command. The cost can be manually configured on an interface using the **ip ospf cost** *value* interface configuration mode command.

The OSPF Hello and Dead intervals must match or a neighbor adjacency does not occur. To modify these intervals, use the following interface commands:

- **ip ospf hello-interval** *seconds*
- **ip ospf dead-interval** *seconds*
- **ipv6 ospf hello-interval** *seconds*
- **ipv6 ospf dead-interval** *seconds*

OSPF supports three types of authentication: null, simple password authentication, and MD5 authentication. OSPF MD5 authentication can be configured globally or per interface. To verify OSPF MD5 implementation is enabled, use the **show ip ospf interface** privileged EXEC mode command.

When troubleshooting OSPF neighbors, be aware that the FULL or 2WAY states are normal. The following commands summarize IPv4 OSPF troubleshooting:

- **show ip protocols**
- **show ip ospf neighbor**
- **show ip ospf interface**
- **show ip ospf**
- **show ip route ospf**
- **clear ip ospf** [*process-id*] **process**

Troubleshooting OSPFv3 is similar to troubleshooting OSPFv2. The following commands are the equivalent commands used with OSPFv3: **show ipv6 protocols**, **show ipv6 ospf neighbor**, **show ipv6 ospf interface**, **show ipv6 ospf**, **show ipv6 route ospf**, and **clear ipv6 ospf** [*process-id*] **process**.

Practice

The following activities provide practice with the topics introduced in this chapter. The Labs and Class Activities are available in the companion *Routing Protocols Lab Manual* (978-1-58713-322-0). The Packet Tracer Activities PKA files are found in the online course.

Class Activities

Class Activity 7.0.1.2: DR and BDR Election

Class Activity 7.3.1.1: OSPF Troubleshooting Mastery

Labs

Lab 7.1.1.13: Configuring OSPFv2 on a Multiaccess Network

Lab 7.1.4.8: Configuring OSPFv2 Advance Features

Lab 7.2.3.3: Troubleshooting Basic Single-Area OSPFv2 and OSPFv3

Lab 7.2.3.4: Troubleshooting Advanced Single-Area OSPFv2

Packet Tracer Activities

Packet Tracer Activity 7.1.1.12: Determining the DR and BDR

Packet Tracer Activity 7.1.2.5: Propagating a Default Route in OSPFv2

Packet Tracer Activity 7.1.4.7: Configuring OSPFv2 Advance Features

Packet Tracer Activity 7.2.2.3: Troubleshooting Single-Area OSPFv2

Packet Tracer Activity 7.3.1.2: Skills Integration Challenge

Check Your Understanding Questions

Complete all the review questions listed here to test your understanding of the topics and concepts in this chapter. The appendix, "Answers to the 'Check Your Understanding' Questions," lists the answers.

1. In which of the following types of networks will OSPF designated routers be elected? (Choose two.)

   A. Point-to-point

   B. Point-to-multipoint

   C. Broadcast multiaccess

   D. Nonbroadcast multiaccess

2. Which command allows a router to advertise default static routes via OSPF?

   A. **redistribute static**

   B. **network 0.0.0.0 0.0.0.0 area 0**

   C. **default-information originate**

   D. Default routes are local only and cannot be advertised using OSPF.

3. During an OSPF DR/BDR election, what is used to determine the DR or BDR when participating OSPF routers have identical interface priorities?

   A. The highest OSPF process ID

   B. The lowest interface IP address

   C. The lowest interface cost

   D. The highest router ID

4. Which two pieces of information are used by the OSPF MD5 algorithm to generate a signature? (Choose two.)

   A. Interface IP address

   B. OSPF message

   C. OSPF router ID

   D. Router hostname

   E. Secret key

5. What is the default Hello interval on Ethernet networks and serial point-to-point networks? What is the default Hello interval on NBMA networks?

6. What values must match before two routers will form an OSPF adjacency?

7. What problems does electing a DR and BDR solve?

8. How are the DR and BDR elected?

9. What does the **clear ip ospf process** command do and when should it be used?

10. Which command will a network engineer issue to verify the configured Hello and Dead Timer intervals between two routers that are running OSPFv2?

11. How is the MD5 authentication more secure?

CHAPTER 8

Multiarea OSPF

Objectives

Upon completion of this chapter, you will be able to answer the following questions:

- How do you explain why multiarea OSPF is used?

- How do you explain how multiarea OSPF uses link-state advertisements in order to maintain routing tables?

- How do you explain how OSPF established neighbor adjacencies in a multiarea OSPF implementation?

- How do you configure multiarea OSPFv2 and OSPFv3 in a routed network?

- How do you configure multiarea OSPF route summarization in a routed network?

- How do you verify multiarea OSPFv2 and OSPFv3 operations?

Key Terms

This chapter uses the following key terms. You can find the definitions in the Glossary.

Introduction (8.0.1.1)

Multiarea OSPF is used to divide a large OSPF network. Too many routers in one area increase the load on the CPU and create a large link-state database. In this chapter, directions are provided to effectively partition a large single area into multiple areas. Area 0 used in a single-area OSPF is known as the backbone area.

Discussion is focused on the LSAs exchanged between areas. In addition, activities for configuring OSPFv2 and OSPFv3 are provided. The chapter concludes with the **show** commands used to verify OSPF configurations.

Class Activity 8.0.1.2: Leaving on a Jet Plane

You and a classmate are starting a new airline to serve your continent.

In addition to your core area or headquarters airport, you will locate and map four intra-continental airport service areas and one transcontinental airport service area that can be used for additional source and destination travel.

Use the blank world map provided to design your airport locations. Additional instructions for completing this activity can be found in the accompanying PDF.

Multiarea OSPF Operation (8.1)

In smaller networks with simple routing requirements, OSPF can be deployed in a single area with all routers in area 0. However, OSPF can scale to support the routing needs of large organizations by using a hierarchical, multiarea deployment. This section compares single-area and multiarea OSPF deployments and operation.

Single-Area OSPF (8.1.1.1)

Single-area OSPF is useful in smaller networks where the web of router links is not complex, and paths to individual destinations are easily deduced.

However, if an area becomes too big, the issues illustrated in Figure 8-1 must be addressed:

- **Large routing table:** OSPF does not perform route summarization by default. If the routes are not summarized, the routing table can become very large, depending on the size of the network.

  - **Large link-state database (LSDB) :** Because the LSDB covers the topology of the entire network, each router must maintain an entry for every network in the area, even if not every route is selected for the routing table.

- **Frequent SPF algorithm calculations:** In a large network, changes are inevitable, so the routers spend many CPU cycles recalculating the SPF algorithm and updating the routing table.

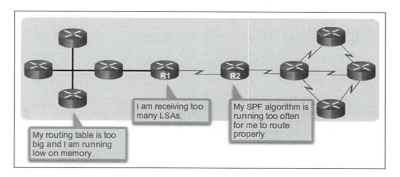

Figure 8-1   Issues in a Large OSPF Single Area

To make OSPF more efficient and scalable, OSPF supports hierarchical routing using areas. An OSPF area is a group of routers that share the same link-state information in their link-state databases.

Multiarea OSPF (8.1.1.2)

When a large OSPF area is divided into smaller areas, this is called multiarea OSPF. Multiarea OSPF is useful in larger network deployments to reduce processing and memory overhead.

For instance, any time a router receives new information about the topology, as with additions, deletions, or modifications of a link, the router must rerun the SPF algorithm, create a new SPF tree, and update the routing table. The SPF algorithm is CPU-intensive and the time it takes for calculation depends on the size of the area. Too many routers in one area make the LSDB larger and increase the load on the CPU. Therefore, arranging routers into areas effectively partitions one potentially large database into smaller and more manageable databases.

Multiarea OSPF requires a hierarchical network design. The main area is called the backbone area (area 0) and all other areas must connect to the backbone area. With hierarchical routing, routing still occurs between the areas (interarea routing), while many of the tedious routing operations, such as recalculating the database, are kept within an area.

As illustrated in Figure 8-2, the hierarchical-topology possibilities of multiarea OSPF have these advantages:

- **Smaller routing tables:** There are fewer routing table entries, as network addresses can be summarized between areas. For example, R1 summarizes the routes from area 1 to area 0, and R2 summarizes the routes from area 51 to area 0. R1 and R2 also propagate a default static route to area 1 and area 51.

- **Reduced link-state update overhead:** Minimizes processing and memory requirements, because there are fewer routers exchanging LSAs.

- **Reduced frequency of SPF calculations:** Localizes impact of a topology change within an area. For instance, it minimizes routing update impact, because LSA flooding stops at the area boundary.

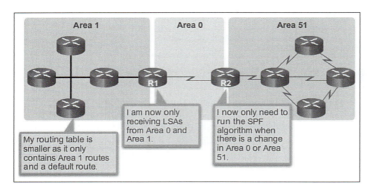

Figure 8-2   Multiarea OSPF Advantages

In Figure 8-3, the link between two internal routers fails in area 51. Notice that only the routers in area 51 exchange LSAs and rerun the SPF algorithm for this event. R1 does not receive LSAs from area 51 and does not recalculate the SPF algorithm.

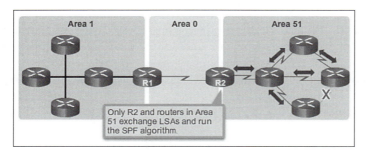

Figure 8-3   Reduced OSPF Calculations

OSPF Two-Layer Area Hierarchy (8.1.1.3)

Multiarea OSPF is implemented in a two-layer area hierarchy:

- ***Backbone (transit) area***: The backbone area is an OSPF area whose primary function is the fast and efficient movement of IP packets. As shown in Figure 8-4, backbone areas interconnect with other OSPF areas. Generally, end users are not found within a backbone area. The backbone area is also called OSPF area 0. Hierarchical networking defines area 0 as the core to which all other areas directly connect.

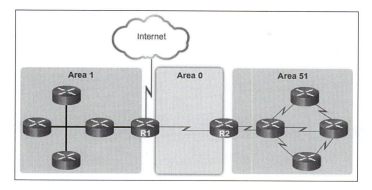

Figure 8-4   Backbone (Transit) Area

- *Regular (non-backbone) area*: Regular areas are interconnected through the backbone area as shown in Figure 8-5. Regular areas connect users and resources. Regular areas are usually set up along functional or geographical groupings. By default, a regular area does not allow traffic from another area to use its links to reach other areas. All traffic from other areas must cross a transit area.

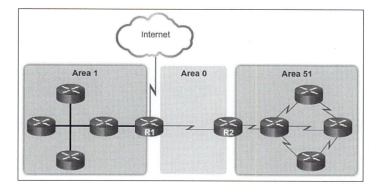

Figure 8-5   Regular (Non-backbone) Area

OSPF enforces this rigid two-layer area hierarchy. The underlying physical connectivity of the network must map to the two-layer area structure, with all non-backbone areas attaching directly to area 0. All traffic moving from one area to another area must traverse the backbone area. This traffic is referred to as interarea traffic.

The optimal number of routers per area varies based on factors such as network stability, but Cisco recommends the following guidelines:

- An area should have no more than 50 routers.

- A router should not be in more than three areas.

- Any single router should not have more than 60 neighbors.

Types of OSPF Routers (8.1.1.4)

OSPF routers of different types control the traffic that goes in and out of areas. The OSPF routers are categorized based on the function they perform in the routing domain.

There are four different types of OSPF routers:

- *Internal router*: As shown in Figure 8-6, internal routers have all of their interfaces in the same area. All internal routers in an area have identical LSDBs.

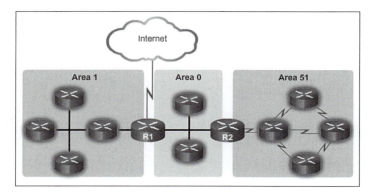

Figure 8-6   Internal Routers

- *Backbone router*: As shown in Figure 8-7, backbone routers have at least one interface in area 0.

- **Area Border Router (ABR):** As shown in Figure 8-8, an ABR has interfaces attached to multiple areas. It must maintain separate LSDBs for each area it is connected to, and can route between areas. ABRs are exit points for the area, which means that routing information destined for another area can get there only via the ABR of the local area. ABRs can be configured to summarize the routing information from the LSDBs of their attached areas. ABRs distribute the routing information into the backbone. The backbone routers then forward the information to the other ABRs. In a multiarea network, an area can have one or more ABRs.

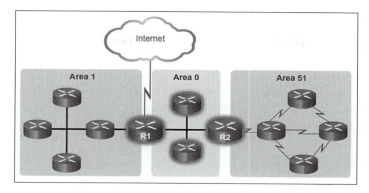

Figure 8-7   Backbone Routers

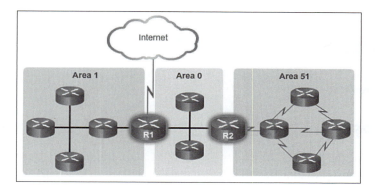

Figure 8-8   Area Border Routers (ABRs)

- *Autonomous System Boundary Router (ASBR)*: As shown in Figure 8-9, an ASBR has at least one interface attached to an external internetwork (another autonomous system), such as a non-OSPF network. An ASBR can import non-OSPF network information to the OSPF network, and vice versa, using a process called route redistribution.

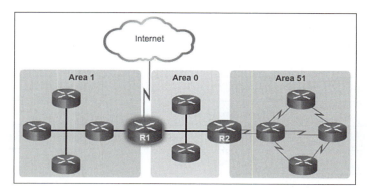

Figure 8-9   Autonomous System Boundary Router (ASBR)

Redistribution in multiarea OSPF occurs when an ASBR connects different routing domains (e.g., EIGRP and OSPF) and configures them to exchange and advertise routing information between those routing domains.

A router can be classified as more than one router type. For example, if a router connects to area 0 and area 1 and in addition maintains routing information for another, non-OSPF network, it falls under three different classifications: a backbone router, an ABR, and an ASBR.

Activity 8.1.1.5: Identify the Multiarea OSPF Terminology

Go to the online course to perform this practice activity.

Multiarea OSPF LSA Operation (8.1.2)

In this section, you will learn how multiarea OSPF exchanges special LSAs to provide interarea information.

OSPF LSA Types (8.1.2.1)

LSAs are the building blocks of the OSPF LSDB. Individually, they act as database records and provide specific OSPF network details. In combination, they describe the entire topology of an OSPF network or area.

The RFCs for OSPF currently specify up to 11 different LSA types, as listed and described in Table 8-1. However, any implementation of multiarea OSPF must support the first five LSAs: LSA 1 to LSA 5. The focus of this section is on these first five LSAs.

Table 8-1   LSA Types and Descriptions

LSA Type	Description
1	Router LSA
2	Network LSA
3 and 4	Summary LSAs
5	AS external LSA
6	Multicast OSPF LSA (This is not implemented by Cisco.)
7	Defined for NSSAs

LSA Type	Description
8	External attributes LSA for Border Gateway Protocol (BGP) (This is not implemented by Cisco.)
9, 10, or 11	Opaque LSAs

Each router link is defined as an LSA type. The LSA includes a link ID field that identifies, by network number and mask, the object to which the link connects. Depending on the type, the link ID has different meanings. LSAs differ on how they are generated and propagated within the routing domain.

Note

OSPFv3 includes additional LSA types.

OSPF LSA Type 1 (8.1.2.2)

As shown in Figure 8-10, all routers advertise their directly connected OSPF-enabled links in a *type 1 router LSA* and forward their network information to OSPF neighbors. The LSA contains a list of the directly connected interfaces, link types, and link states.

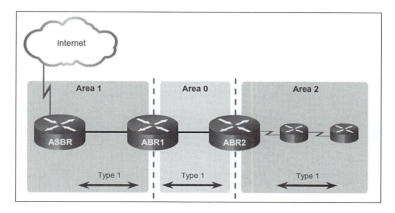

Figure 8-10   Type 1 LSA Message Propagation

Type 1 LSAs are also referred to as router link entries. They include a list of directly connected network prefixes and link types. All routers generate type 1 LSAs.

Type 1 LSAs are flooded only within the area in which they originate and do not propagate beyond an ABR. ABRs subsequently advertise the networks learned from the type 1 LSAs to other areas as type 3 LSAs.

The type 1 LSA link ID is identified by the router ID of the originating router.

OSPF LSA Type 2 (8.1.2.3)

A type 2 network LSA only exists for multiaccess and nonbroadcast multiaccess (NBMA) networks where there is a DR elected and at least two routers on the multiaccess segment. The *type 2 network LSA* contains the router ID and IP address of the DR, along with the router ID of all other routers on the multiaccess segment. A type 2 LSA is created for every multiaccess network in the area.

Type 2 LSAs are also referred to as network link entries. The purpose of a type 2 LSA is to give other routers information about multiaccess networks within the same area. Type 2 LSAs identify the routers and the network addresses of the multiaccess links.

Only a DR generates a type 2 LSA. The DR floods type 2 LSAs only within the area in which they originated. Type 2 LSAs are not forwarded outside of an area. The link-state ID for a network LSA is the IP interface address of the DR that advertises it.

As shown in Figure 8-11, ABR1 is the DR for the Ethernet network in area 1. It generates the type 2 LSA and forwards it into area 1. ABR2 is the DR for the multiaccess network in area 0. There are no multiaccess networks in area 2 and, therefore, no type 2 LSAs are ever propagated in that area.

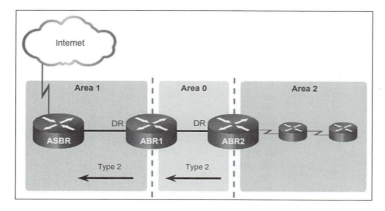

Figure 8-11   Type 2 LSA Message Propagation

OSPF LSA Type 3 (8.1.2.4)

*Type 3 summary LSA*s are used by ABRs to advertise networks from other areas. ABRs collect type 1 LSAs in the LSDB. After an OSPF area has converged, the ABR creates a type 3 LSA for each of its learned OSPF networks. Therefore, an ABR with many OSPF routes must create type 3 LSAs for each network.

As shown in Figure 8-12, ABR1 and ABR2 flood type 3 LSAs from one area to other areas. The ABRs propagate the type 3 LSAs into other areas.

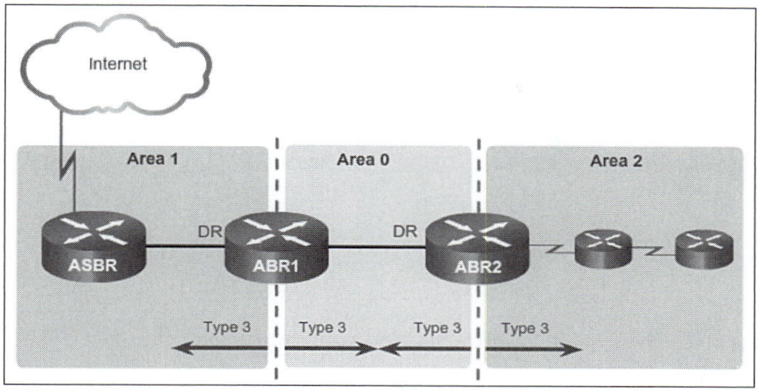

Figure 8-12   Type 3 LSA Message Propagation

By default, routes are not summarized. In a large OSPF deployment with many networks, propagating type 3 LSAs can cause significant flooding problems. For this reason, it is strongly recommended that manual route summarization be configured on the ABR.

ABRs flood type 3 LSAs to other areas and are regenerated by other ABRs. A type 3 LSA link-state ID is identified by the network address.

Receiving a type 3 LSA into its area does not cause a router to run the SPF algorithm. The routes being advertised in the type 3 LSAs are appropriately added to or deleted from the router's routing table, but a full SPF calculation is not necessary.

OSPF LSA Type 4 (8.1.2.5)

Type 4 and type 5 LSAs are used collectively to identify an ASBR and advertise external networks into an OSPF routing domain.

A *type 4 summary LSA* is generated by an ABR only when an ASBR exists within an area. Type 4 LSAs are used to advertise an ASBR to other areas and provide a route to the ASBR. All traffic destined to an external autonomous system requires routing table knowledge of the ASBR that originated the external routes. A type 4 LSA is generated by the originating ABR and is regenerated by other ABRs.

As shown in Figure 8-13, the ASBR sends a type 1 LSA, identifying itself as an ASBR. The LSA includes a special bit known as the external bit (e bit) that is used to identify the router as an ASBR. When ABR1 receives the type 1 LSA, it notices the e bit, builds a type 4 LSA, and then floods the type 4 LSA to the backbone (area 0). Subsequent ABRs flood the type 4 LSA into other areas.

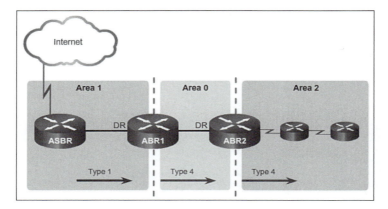

Figure 8-13   Type 4 LSA Message Propagation

The link-state ID is set to the ASBR router ID.

OSPF LSA Type 5 (8.1.2.6)

*Type 5 external LSA*s describe routes to networks outside the OSPF autonomous system. Type 5 LSAs are originated by the ASBR and are flooded to the entire autonomous system and regenerated by other ABRs. A type 5 LSA link-state ID is the external network address.

Type 5 LSAs are also referred to as autonomous system external LSA entries.

In Figure 8-14, the ASBR generates type 5 LSAs for each of its external routes and floods them into the area. Subsequent ABRs also flood the type 5 LSA into other areas. Routers in other areas use the information from the type 4 LSA to reach the external routes.

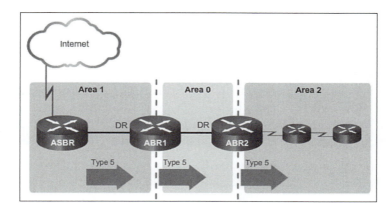

Figure 8-14   Type 5 LSA Message Propagation

By default, external routes are not summarized. In a large OSPF deployment with many networks, propagating multiple type 5 LSAs can cause significant flooding problems. For this reason, it is strongly recommended that manual route summarization be configured on the ASBR.

Activity 8.1.2.7: Identify the OSPF LSA Type

Go to the online course to perform this practice activity.

OSPF Routing Table and Types of Routes (8.1.3)

Multiarea OSPF uses special route descriptors to indicate routes learned from other areas. In this section, you will learn about these descriptors and their meaning.

OSPF Routing Table Entries (8.1.3.1)

Figure 8-15 provides a sample routing table for a multiarea OSPF topology with a link to an external non-OSPF network.

```
R1# show ip route
Codes:L - local, C-connected, S-static, R-RIP, M-mobile, B-BGP
        D - EIGRP, EX - EIGRP external, O - OSPF, IA - OSPF inter area
        N1 - OSPF NSSA external type 1, N2 - OSPF NSSA external type 2
        E1 - OSPF external type 1, E2 - OSPF external type 2
        i - IS-IS, su-IS-IS summary, L1-IS-IS level-1, L2-IS-IS level-2
        ia - IS-IS inter area,*-candidate default,U-per-user static route
        o - ODR, P-periodic downloaded static route, H-NHRP, l-LISP
        + - replicated route, % - next hop override

Gateway of last resort is 192.168.10.2 to network 0.0.0.0

O*E2 0.0.0.0/0 [110/1] via 192.168.10.2, 00:00:19, Serial0/0/0
        10.0.0.0/8 is variably subnetted, 5 subnets, 2 masks
C       10.1.1.0/24 is directly connected, GigabitEthernet0/0
L       10.1.1.1/32 is directly connected, GigabitEthernet0/0
C       10.1.2.0/24 is directly connected, GigabitEthernet0/1
L       10.1.2.1/32 is directly connected, GigabitEthernet0/1
O       10.2.1.0/24 [110/648] via 192.168.10.2, 00:04:34, Serial0/0/0
O IA 192.168.1.0/24 [110/1295] via 192.168.10.2, 00:01:48,Serial0/0/0
O IA 192.168.2.0/24 [110/1295] via 192.168.10.2, 00:01:48,Serial0/0/0
        192.168.10.0/24 is variably subnetted, 3 subnets, 2 masks
C       192.168.10.0/30 is directly connected, Serial0/0/0
L       192.168.10.1/32 is directly connected, Serial0/0/0
O       192.168.10.4/30 [110/1294] via 192.168.10.2, 00:01:55,Serial0/0/0
R1#
```

Figure 8-15   Router and Network Routing Table Entries

OSPF routes in an IPv4 routing table are identified using the following descriptors:

- **O:** Router (type 1) and network (type 2) LSAs describe the details within an area. The routing table reflects this link-state information with a designation of O, meaning that the route is intra-area.

- **O IA:** When an ABR receives summary LSAs, it adds them to its LSDB and regenerates them into the local area. The internal routers then assimilate the information into their databases. Summary LSAs appear in the routing table as IA (interarea) routes.

- **O E1** or **O E2:** When an ABR receives external LSAs, it adds them to its LSDB and floods them into the area. External LSAs appear in the routing table marked as external type 1 (E1) or external type 2 (E2) routes.

Figure 8-16 displays an IPv6 routing table with OSPF router, interarea, and external routing table entries.

```
R1# show ipv6 route
IPv6 Routing Table - default - 9 entries
Codes:C - Connected, L - Local, S - Static, U-Per-user Static route
      B - BGP, R - RIP, H - NHRP, I1 - ISIS L1
      I2 - ISIS L2, IA - ISIS interarea, IS - ISIS summary, D - EIGRP
      EX - EIGRP external, ND-ND Default,NDp-ND Prefix,DCE-Destination
      NDr - Redirect, O-OSPF Intra, OI-OSPF Inter, OE1-OSPF ext 1
      OE2 - OSPF ext 2, ON1 - OSPF NSSA ext 1, ON2 - OSPF NSSA ext 2
OE2 ::/0 [110/1], tag 10
     via FE80::2, Serial0/0/0
C    2001:DB8:CAFE:1::/64 [0/0]
     via GigabitEthernet0/0, directly connected
L    2001:DB8:CAFE:1::1/128 [0/0]
     via GigabitEthernet0/0, receive
O    2001:DB8:CAFE:2::/64 [110/648]
     via FE80::2, Serial0/0/0
OI   2001:DB8:CAFE:3::/64 [110/1295]
     via FE80::2, Serial0/0/0
C    2001:DB8:CAFE:A001::/64 [0/0]
     via Serial0/0/0, directly connected
L    2001:DB8:CAFE:A001::1/128 [0/0]
     via Serial0/0/0, receive
O    2001:DB8:CAFE:A002::/64 [110/1294]
     via FE80::2, Serial0/0/0
L    FF00::/8 [0/0]
     via Null0, receive
R1#
```

Figure 8-16   OSPFv3 Routing Table Entries

OSPF Route Calculation (8.1.3.2)

Each router uses the SPF algorithm against the LSDB to build the SPF tree. The SPF tree is used to determine the best paths.

As shown in Figure 8-17, the order in which the best paths are calculated is as follows:

1. All routers calculate the best paths to destinations within their area (intra-area) and add these entries to the routing table. These are the type 1 and type 2 LSAs, which are noted in the routing table with a routing designator of O. (1)

2. All routers calculate the best paths to the other areas within the internetwork. These best paths are the interarea route entries, or type 3 and type 4 LSAs, and are noted with a routing designator of O IA. (2)

3. All routers (except those that are in a form of stub area) calculate the best paths to the external autonomous system (type 5) destinations. These are noted with either an O E1 or an O E2 route designator, depending on the configuration. (3)

```
R1# show ip route | begin Gateway
Gateway of last resort is 192.168.10.2 to network 0.0.0.0
O*E2 0.0.0.0/0 [110/1] via 192.168.10.2, 00:00:19, Serial0/0/0
      10.0.0.0/8 is variably subnetted, 5 subnets, 2 masks
C        10.1.1.0/24 is directly connected, GigabitEthernet0/0
L        10.1.1.1/32 is directly connected, GigabitEthernet0/0
C        10.1.2.0/24 is directly connected, GigabitEthernet0/1
L        10.1.2.1/32 is directly connected, GigabitEthernet0/1
O        10.2.1.0/24 [110/648] via 192.168.10.2, 00:04:34, Serial0/0/0
O IA  192.168.1.0/24 [110/1295] via 192.168.10.2, 00:01:48, Serial0/0/0
O IA  192.168.2.0/24 [110/1295] via 192.168.10.2, 00:01:48, Serial0/0/0
      192.168.10.0/24 is variably subnetted, 3 subnets, 2 masks
C        192.168.10.0/30 is directly connected, Serial0/0/0
L        192.168.10.1/32 is directly connected, Serial0/0/0
O        192.168.10.4/30 [110/1294] via 192.168.10.2, 00:01:55, Serial0/0/0
R1#
```

Figure 8-17   Steps to OSPF Convergence

When converged, a router can communicate with any network within or outside the OSPF autonomous system.

Interactive Graphic

Activity 8.1.3.3: Order the Steps for OSPF Best Path Calculations

Go to the online course to perform this practice activity.

Configuring Multiarea OSPF (8.2)

Configuring multiarea OSPF is similar to configuring single-area OSPF. In this section, you will learn how to configure multiarea OSPF.

Implementing Multiarea OSPF (8.2.1.1)

OSPF can be implemented as single-area or multiarea. The type of OSPF implementation to choose depends on the specific requirements and existing topology.

There are four steps to implementing multiarea OSPF. Steps 1 and 2 are part of the planning process.

How To Q

The steps to implement multiarea OSPF are:

Step 1.   Gather the network requirements and parameters. This includes determining the number of host and network devices, the IP addressing scheme (if already implemented), the size of the routing domain, the size of the routing tables, the risk of topology changes, and other network characteristics.

Step 2.   Define the OSPF parameters. Based on information gathered during Step 1, the network administrator must determine if single-area or multiarea OSPF is the preferred implementation. If multiarea OSPF is selected, there are several considerations the network administrator must take into account while determining the OSPF parameters, to include:

- **IP addressing plan:** This governs how OSPF can be deployed and how well the OSPF deployment might scale. A detailed IP addressing plan, along with the IP subnetting information, must be created. A good IP addressing plan should enable the usage of OSPF multiarea design and summarization. This plan more easily scales the network, as well as optimizes OSPF behavior and the propagation of LSAs.

- **OSPF areas:** Dividing an OSPF network into areas decreases the LSDB size and limits the propagation of link-state updates when the topology changes. The routers that are to be ABRs and ASBRs must be identified, as those are to perform any summarization or redistribution.

- **Network topology:** This consists of links that connect the network equipment and belong to different OSPF areas in a multiarea OSPF design. Network topology is important to determine primary and backup links. Primary and backup links are defined by the changing OSPF cost on interfaces. A detailed network topology plan should also be used to determine the different OSPF areas, ABR, and ASBR as well as summarization and redistribution points, if multiarea OSPF is used.

Step 3.   Configure the multiarea OSPF implementation based on the parameters.

Step 4.   Verify the multiarea OSPF implementation based on the parameters.

Configuring Multiarea OSPF (8.2.1.2)

Figure 8-18 displays the reference OSPFv2 multiarea topology.

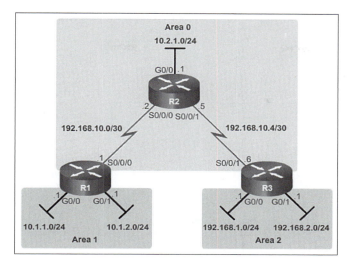

Figure 8-18   OSPFv2 Multiarea Topology

In this example:

- R1 is an ABR because it has interfaces in area 1 and an interface in area 0.

- R2 is an internal backbone router because all of its interfaces are in area 0.

- R3 is an ABR because it has interfaces in area 2 and an interface in area 0.

There are no special commands required to implement this multiarea OSPF network. A router simply becomes an ABR when it has two network statements in different areas.

As shown in the following example, R1 is assigned the router ID 1.1.1.1. This example enables OSPF on the two LAN interfaces in area 1. The serial interface is configured as part of OSPF area 0. Because R1 has interfaces connected to two different areas, it is an ABR.

```
R1(config)# router ospf 10
R1(config-router)# router-id 1.1.1.1
R1(config-router)# network 10.1.1.1 0.0.0.0 area 1
R1(config-router)# network 10.1.2.1 0.0.0.0 area 1
R1(config-router)# network 192.168.10.1 0.0.0.0 area 0
R1(config-router)# end
R1#
```

Interactive Graphic

Activity 8.2.1.2: Configuring Multiarea OSPF on R2 and R3

Go to the online course to use the Syntax Checker in the third graphic to configure multiarea OSPF on R2 and R3. In this Syntax Checker, on R2, use the wildcard mask of the interface network address. On R3, use the 0.0.0.0 wildcard mask for all networks.

Configuring Multiarea OSPFv3 (8.2.1.3)

Figure 8-19 displays the reference OSPFv3 multiarea topology.

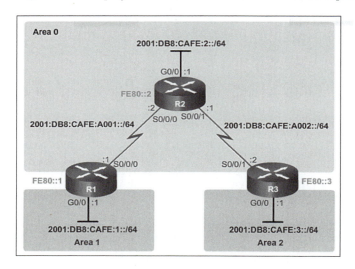

Figure 8-19 OSPFv3 Multiarea Topology

As with OSPFv2, implementing the multiarea OSPFv3 topology shown in Figure 8-19 is simple. There are no special commands required. A router simply becomes an ABR when it has two interfaces in different areas.

In the following example, R1 is assigned the router ID 1.1.1.1. The example also enables OSPF on the LAN interface in area 1 and the serial interface in area 0. Because R1 has interfaces connected to two different areas, it becomes an ABR.

```
R1(config)# ipv6 router ospf 10
R1(config-rtr)# router-id 1.1.1.1
R1(config-rtr)# exit
R1(config)#
R1(config)# interface GigabitEthernet 0/0
R1(config-if)# ipv6 ospf 10 area 1
R1(config-if)#
R1(config-if)# interface Serial0/0/0
R1(config-if)# ipv6 ospf 10 area 0
```

```
R1(config-if)# end
R1#
```

Activity 8.2.1.3: Configuring Multiarea OSPFv3 on R2 and R3

Go to the online course to use the Syntax Checker in the third graphic to configure multiarea OSPFv3 on R2 and on R3.

OSPF Route Summarization (8.2.2.1)

Summarization helps keep routing tables small. It involves consolidating multiple routes into a single advertisement, which can then be propagated into the backbone area.

Normally, type 1 and type 2 LSAs are generated inside each area, translated into type 3 LSAs, and sent to other areas. If area 1 had 30 networks to advertise, then 30 type 3 LSAs would be forwarded into the backbone. With route summarization, the ABR consolidates the 30 networks into one or two advertisements.

In Figure 8-20, R1 consolidates all of the network advertisements into one summary LSA. Instead of forwarding individual LSAs for each route in area 1, R1 forwards a summary LSA to the core router C1. C1, in turn, forwards the summary LSA to R2 and R3. R2 and R3 then forward it to their respective internal routers.

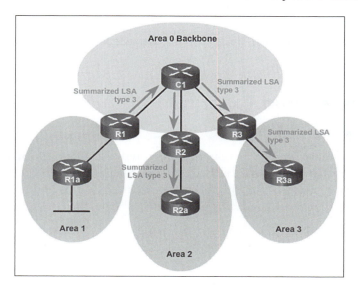

Figure 8-20 Propagating a Summary Route

Summarization also helps increase the network's stability, because it reduces unnecessary LSA flooding. This directly affects the amount of bandwidth, CPU, and memory resources consumed by the OSPF routing process. Without route summarization, every specific-link LSA is propagated into the OSPF backbone and beyond, causing unnecessary network traffic and router overhead.

In Figure 8-21, a network link on R1a fails. R1a sends an LSA to R1. However, R1 does not propagate the update, because it has a summary route configured. Specific-link LSA flooding outside the area does not occur.

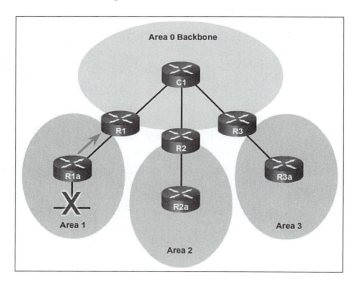

Figure 8-21   Suppressing Updates with Summarization

Interarea and External Route Summarization (8.2.2.2)

In OSPF, summarization can only be configured on ABRs or ASBRs. Instead of advertising many specific networks, the ABR routers and ASBR routers can advertise a summary route. ABR routers can summarize type 3 LSAs and ASBR routers can summarize type 5 LSAs.

By default, summary LSAs (type 3 LSAs) and external LSAs (type 5 LSAs) do not contain summarized (aggregated) routes; that is, by default, summary LSAs are not summarized.

Route summarization can be configured as follows:

- *Interarea route summarization*: As shown in Figure 8-22, interarea route summarization occurs on ABRs and applies to routes from within each area. It does not apply to external routes injected into OSPF via redistribution. To perform effective interarea route summarization, network addresses within areas should be assigned contiguously so that these addresses can be summarized into a minimal number of summary addresses.

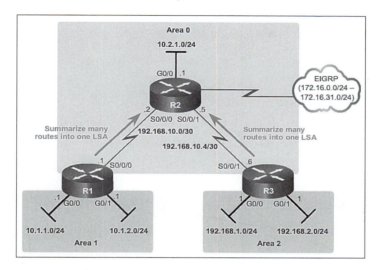

Figure 8-22   Summarizing Interarea Routes on ABRs

Note

Interarea route summarization is configured on ABRs using the `area area-id range address mask` router configuration mode **command**.

- *External route summarization*: External route summarization is specific to external routes that are injected into OSPF via route redistribution. Again, it is important to ensure the contiguity of the external address ranges that are being summarized. Generally, only ASBRs summarize external routes. As shown in Figure 8-23, EIGRP external routes are summarized by ASBR R2 in a single LSA and sent to R1 and R3.

Note

External route summarization is configured on ASBRs using the **summary-address** *address mask* router configuration mode command.

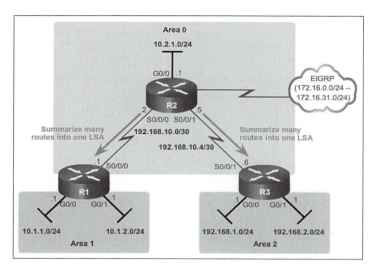

Figure 8-23 Summarizing External Routes on an ASBR

Interarea Route Summarization (8.2.2.3)

OSPF does not perform auto-summarization. Interarea summarization must be manually configured on ABRs.

Summarization of internal routes can only be done by ABRs. When summarization is enabled on an ABR, it injects into the backbone a single type 3 LSA describing the summary route. Multiple routes inside the area are summarized by the one LSA.

A summary route is generated if at least one subnet within the area falls in the summary address range. The summarized route metric is equal to the lowest cost of all subnets within the summary address range.

Note

An ABR can only summarize routes that are within the areas connected to the ABR.

Figure 8-24 shows a multiarea OSPF topology.

The routing tables of R1 and R3 are examined to see the effect of the summarization. Figure 8-25 displays the R1 routing table before summarization is configured.

Figure 8-26 displays the R3 routing table. Notice how R3 currently has two interarea entries to the R1 area 1 networks.

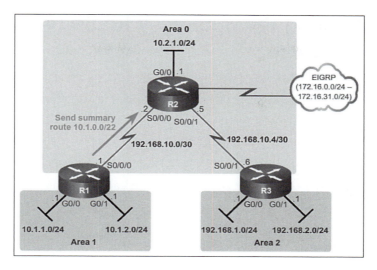

Figure 8-24   Summarizing Interarea Routes on ABRs

```
R1# show ip route ospf | begin Gateway
Gateway of last resort is not set

        10.0.0.0/8 is variably subnetted, 5 subnets, 2 masks
O          10.2.1.0/24 [110/648] via 192.168.10.2, 00:00:49,
           Serial0/0/0
O IA    192.168.1.0/24 [110/1295] via 192.168.10.2, 00:00:49,
           Serial0/0/0
O IA    192.168.2.0/24 [110/1295] via 192.168.10.2, 00:00:49,
           Serial0/0/0
        192.168.10.0/24 is variably subnetted, 3 subnets, 2
        masks
O          192.168.10.4/30 [110/1294] via 192.168.10.2,
           00:00:49, Serial0/0/0
R1#
```

Figure 8-25   Verify the R1 Routing Table Before Summarization

```
R3# show ip route ospf | begin Gateway
Gateway of last resort is not set

        10.0.0.0/24 is subnetted, 3 subnets
O IA      10.1.1.0 [110/1295] via 192.168.10.5, 00:27:14, Serial0/0/1
O IA      10.1.2.0 [110/1295] via 192.168.10.5, 00:27:14, Serial0/0/1
O         10.2.1.0 [110/648] via 192.168.10.5, 00:27:57,  Serial0/0/1
        192.168.10.0/24 is variably subnetted, 3 subnets, 2 masks
O          192.168.10.0/30 [110/1294] via 192.168.10.5, 00:27:57,
           Serial0/0/1
R3#
```

Figure 8-26   Verify the R3 Routing Table Before Summarization

Calculating the Summary Route (8.2.2.4)

Summarizing networks into a single address and mask can be done in three steps:

Step 1.   List the networks in binary format.

Step 2.   Count the number of far left matching bits to determine the mask for the summary route.

Step 3.   Copy the matching bits and then add zero bits to determine the summarized network address.

Refer to Figure 8-27 for an example on how to calculate a summary route.

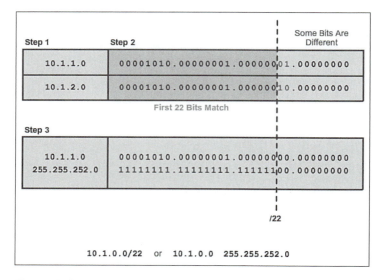

Figure 8-27   Calculating Summary Routes on R1

In the example, the two R1 area 1 networks 10.1.1.0/24 and 10.1.2.0/24 are listed in binary format. As highlighted, the first 22 far left matching bits match. This results in the prefix /22 or subnet mask 255.255.252.0. The matching bits with zeros at the end result in a network address of 10.1.0.0/22. This summary address summarizes four networks: 10.1.0.0/24, 10.1.1.0/24, 10.1.2.0/24, and 10.1.3.0/24. In the example the summary address matches four networks although only two networks exist.

Configuring Interarea Route Summarization (8.2.2.5)

To manually configure interarea route summarization on an ABR, use the **area** *area-id* **range** *address mask* router configuration mode command. This instructs the ABR to summarize routes for a specific area before injecting them into a different area, via the backbone as type 3 summary LSAs.

Note

In OSPFv3, the command is identical except for the IPv6 network address. The command syntax for OSPFv3 is **area** *area-id* **range** *prefix/prefix-length*.

The following summarizes the two internal area 1 routes on R1 into one OSPF interarea summary route. The summarized route 10.1.0.0/22 actually summarizes four network addresses, 10.1.0.0/24 to 10.1.3.0/24.

```
R1(config)# router ospf 10
R1(config-router)# area 1 range 10.1.0.0 255.255.252.0
R1(config-router)#
```

Figure 8-28 displays the IPv4 routing table of R1. Notice how a new entry has appeared with a Null0 exit interface. The Cisco IOS automatically creates a summary route to the Null0 interface when manual summarization is configured to prevent routing loops. A packet sent to a null interface is dropped.

```
R1# show ip route ospf | begin Gateway
Gateway of last resort is not set

      10.0.0.0/8 is variably subnetted, 6 subnets, 3 masks
O        10.1.0.0/22 is a summary, 00:00:09, Null0
O        10.2.1.0/24 [110/648] via 192.168.10.2, 00:00:09, Serial0/0/0
O IA  192.168.1.0/24 [110/1295] via 192.168.10.2, 00:00:09, Serial0/0/0
O IA  192.168.2.0/24 [110/1295] via 192.168.10.2, 00:00:09, Serial0/0/0
      192.168.10.0/24 is variably subnetted, 3 subnets, 2 masks
O        192.168.10.4/30 [110/1294] via 192.168.10.2, 00:00:09, Serial0/0/0
R1#
```

Figure 8-28   Verify the R1 Routing Table After Summarization

For example, assume R1 received a packet destined for 10.1.0.10. Although it would match the R1 summary route, R1 does not have a valid route in area 1. Therefore, R1 would refer to the routing table for the next longest match, which would be the Null0 entry. The packet would get forwarded to the Null0 interface and dropped. This prevents the router from forwarding the packet to a default route and possibly creating a routing loop.

Figure 8-29 displays the updated R3 routing table. Notice how there is now only one interarea entry going to the summary route 10.1.0.0/22. Although this example only reduced the routing table by one entry, summarization could be implemented to summarize many networks. This would reduce the size of routing tables.

```
R3# show ip route ospf | begin Gateway
Gateway of last resort is not set

     10.0.0.0/8 is variably subnetted, 2 subnets, 2 masks
O IA    10.1.0.0/22 [110/1295] via 192.168.10.5, 00:00:06, Serial0/0/1
O       10.2.1.0/24 [110/648] via 192.168.10.5, 00:29:23, Serial0/0/1
     192.168.10.0/24 is variably subnetted, 3 subnets, 2 masks
O       192.168.10.0/30 [110/1294] via 192.168.10.5, 00:29:23,
Serial0/0/1
R3#
```

Figure 8-29   Verify the R3 Routing Table After Summarization

Activity 8.2.2.5: Summarizing Area 2 Routes

Go to the online course to use the Syntax Checker in the fifth graphic to summarize the area 2 routes on R3.

Verifying Multiarea OSPF (8.2.3.1)

The same verification commands used to verify single-area OSPF also can be used to verify multiarea OSPF:

- **show ip ospf neighbor**
- **show ip ospf**
- **show ip ospf interface**

Commands that verify specific multiarea information include:

- **show ip protocols**
- **show ip ospf interface brief**
- **show ip route ospf**
- **show ip ospf database**

Note

For the equivalent OSPFv3 command, simply substitute **ip** with **ipv6**.

Verify General Multiarea OSPF Settings (8.2.3.2)

Use the **show ip protocols** command to verify the OSPF status. The output of the command reveals which routing protocols are configured on a router. It also includes routing protocol specifics such as the router ID, number of areas in the router, and networks included within the routing protocol configuration.

Figure 8-30 displays the OSPF settings of R1. Notice that the command shows that there are two areas. The "Routing for Networks" section of the output identifies the networks and their respective areas.

```
R1# show ip protocols
*** IP Routing is NSF aware ***

Routing Protocol is "ospf 10"
  Outgoing update filter list for all interfaces is not set
  Incoming update filter list for all interfaces is not set
  Router ID 1.1.1.1
  It is an area border router
  Number of areas in this router is 2. 2 normal 0 stub 0 nssa
  Maximum path: 4
  Routing for Networks:
    10.1.1.1 0.0.0.0 area 1
    10.1.2.1 0.0.0.0 area 1
    192.168.10.1 0.0.0.0 area 0
  Routing Information Sources:
    Gateway         Distance      Last Update
    3.3.3.3              110       02:20:36
    2.2.2.2              110       02:20:39
  Distance: (default is 110)

R1#
```

Figure 8-30   Verifying Multiarea OSPF Status on R1

Use the **show ip ospf interface brief** command to display concise OSPF-related information of OSPF-enabled interfaces. This command reveals useful information, such as the OSPF process ID that the interface is assigned to, the area that the interfaces are in, and the cost of the interface.

Figure 8-31 verifies the OSPF-enabled interfaces and the areas to which they belong.

```
R1# show ip ospf interface brief
Interface  PID  Area  IP Address/Mask   Cost  State  Nbrs F/C
Se0/0/0    10   0     192.168.10.1/30   64    P2P    1/1
Gi0/1      10   1     10.1.2.1/24       1     DR     0/0
Gi0/0      10   1     10.1.1.1/24       1     DR     0/0
R1#
```

Figure 8-31   Verifying OSPF-Enabled Interfaces on R1

Interactive Graphic

Activity 8.2.3.2: Verifying Multiarea OSPF Status

Go to the online course to use the Syntax Checker in the third graphic to verify general settings on R2 and R3.

Verify the OSPF Routes (8.2.3.3)

The most common command used to verify a multiarea OSPF configuration is the **show ip route** command. Add the **ospf** parameter to display only OSPF-related information.

Figure 8-32 displays the routing table of R1.

```
R1# show ip route ospf | begin Gateway
Gateway of last resort is not set

     10.0.0.0/8 is variably subnetted, 5 subnets, 2 masks
O     10.2.1.0/24 [110/648] via 192.168.10.2, 00:26:03,
                                             Serial0/0/0
O IA 192.168.1.0/24 [110/1295] via 192.168.10.2, 00:26:03,
                                             Serial0/0/0
O IA 192.168.2.0/24 [110/1295] via 192.168.10.2, 00:26:03,
                                             Serial0/0/0
     192.168.10.0/24 is variably subnetted,3 subnets,2 masks
O     192.168.10.4/30 [110/1294] via 192.168.10.2, 00:26:03,
                                             Serial0/0/0
R1#
```

Figure 8-32 Verifying Multiarea OSPF Routes on R1

Notice how the O IA entries in the routing table identify networks learned from other areas. Specifically, O represents OSPF intra-area routes, and IA represents interarea, which means that the route originated from another area. Recall that R1 is in area 0, and the 192.168.1.0 and 192.168.2.0 subnets are connected to R3 in area 2. The [110/1295] entry in the routing table represents the administrative distance that is assigned to OSPF (110) and the total cost of the routes (cost of 1295).

Interactive Graphic

Activity 8.2.3.3: Verifying Multiarea OSPF Routes on R2 and R3

Go to the online course to use the Syntax Checker in the second graphic to verify the routing table of R2 and R3 using the **show ip route ospf** command.

Verify the Multiarea OSPF LSDB (8.2.3.4)

Use the show **ip ospf database** command to verify the contents of the LSDB.

There are many command options available with the **show ip ospf database** command.

For example, Figure 8-33 displays the content of the LSDB of R1.

```
R1# show ip ospf database
             OSPF Router with ID (1.1.1.1) (Process ID 10)

             Router Link States (Area 0)
Link ID       ADV Router    Age   Seq#        Checksum Link count
1.1.1.1       1.1.1.1       725   0x80000005  0x00F9B0 2
2.2.2.2       2.2.2.2       695   0x80000007  0x003DB1 5
3.3.3.3       3.3.3.3       681   0x80000005  0x00FF91 2
             Summary Net Link States (Area 0)
Link ID       ADV Router    Age   Seq#        Checksum
10.1.1.0      1.1.1.1       725   0x80000006  0x00D155
10.1.2.0      1.1.1.1       725   0x80000005  0x00C85E
192.168.1.0   3.3.3.3       681   0x80000006  0x00724E
192.168.2.0   3.3.3.3       681   0x80000005  0x006957

             Router Link States (Area 1)
Link ID       ADV Router    Age   Seq#        Checksum Link count
1.1.1.1       1.1.1.1       725   0x80000006  0x007D7C 2
             Summary Net Link States (Area 1)
Link ID       ADV Router    Age   Seq#        Checksum
10.2.1.0      1.1.1.1       725   0x80000005  0x004A9C
192.168.1.0   1.1.1.1       725   0x80000005  0x00B593
192.168.2.0   1.1.1.1       725   0x80000005  0x00AA9D
192.168.10.0  1.1.1.1       725   0x80000005  0x00B3D0
192.168.10.4  1.1.1.1       725   0x80000005  0x000E32
R1#
```

Figure 8-33   Verifying the OSPF LSDB on R1

Notice R1 has entries for area 0 and area 1, because ABRs must maintain a separate LSDB for each area to which they belong. In the output, "Router Link States" in area 0 identifies three routers. The "Summary Net Link States" section identifies networks learned from other areas and which neighbor advertised the network.

Interactive Graphic

Activity 8.2.3.4: Verify the OSPF LSDB on R2 and R3

Go to the online course to use the Syntax Checker in the second graphic to verify the LSDB of R2 and R3 using the **show ip ospf database** command. R2 only has interfaces in area 0; therefore, only one LSDB is required. Like R1, R3 contains two LSDBs.

Verify Multiarea OSPFv3 (8.2.3.5)

Like OSPFv2, OSPFv3 provides similar OSPFv3 verification commands. Refer to the reference OSPFv3 topology in Figure 8-34.

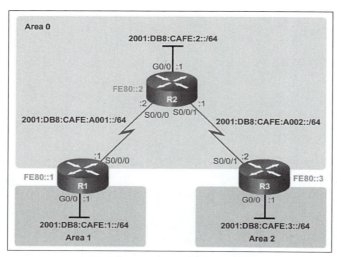

Figure 8-34   *Verifying the Multiarea OSPFv3 Topology*

The following output displays the OSPFv3 settings of R1. Notice that the command confirms that there are now two areas. It also identifies each interface enabled for the respective area.

```
R1# show ipv6 protocols
IPv6 Routing Protocol is "connected"
IPv6 Routing Protocol is "ND"
IPv6 Routing Protocol is "ospf 10"
  Router ID 1.1.1.1
  Area border router
  Number of areas: 2 normal, 0 stub, 0 nssa
  Interfaces (Area 0):
    Serial0/0/0
  Interfaces (Area 1):
    GigabitEthernet0/0
  Redistribution:
    None
R1#
```

Figure 8-35 verifies the OSPFv3-enabled interfaces and the area to which they belong.

```
R1# show ipv6 ospf interface brief
Interface      PID   Area         Intf ID    Cost  State Nbrs F/C
Se0/0/0        10    0            6          647   P2P   1/1
Gi0/0          10    1            3          1     DR    0/0
R1#
```

Figure 8-35 Verifying OSPFv3-Enabled Interfaces on R1

Figure 8-36 displays the routing table of R1. Notice how the IPv6 routing table displays OI entries in the routing table to identify networks learned from other areas. Specifically, O represents OSPF intra-area routes, and I represents interarea, which means that the route originated from another area. Recall that R1 is in area 0, and the 2001:DB8:CAFE3::/64 subnet is connected to R3 in area 2. The [110/1295] entry in the routing table represents the administrative distance that is assigned to OSPF (110) and the total cost of the routes (cost of 1295).

```
R1# show ipv6 route ospf
IPv6 Routing Table - default - 8 entries
Codes: C - Connected, L - Local, S - Static, U - Per-user Static
route
       B - BGP, R - RIP, H - NHRP, I1 - ISIS L1
       I2 - ISIS L2, IA - ISIS interarea, IS - ISIS summary, D -
       EIGRP
       EX - EIGRP external, ND - ND Default, NDp - ND Prefix, DCE -
Destination
       NDr - Redirect, O - OSPF Intra, OI - OSPF Inter, OE1 - OSPF
       ext 1
       OE2 - OSPF ext 2, ON1 - OSPF NSSA ext 1, ON2 - OSPF NSSA ext 2
O   2001:DB8:CAFE:2::/64 [110/648]
     via FE80::2, Serial0/0/0
OI  2001:DB8:CAFE:3::/64 [110/1295]
     via FE80::2, Serial0/0/0
O   2001:DB8:CAFE:A002::/64 [110/1294]
     via FE80::2, Serial0/0/0
R1#
```

Figure 8-36 Verifying Multiarea Routes on R1

Figure 8-37 displays the content of the LSDB of R1. The command offers similar information to its OSPFv2 counterpart. However, the OSPFv3 LSDB contains additional LSA types not available in OSPFv2.

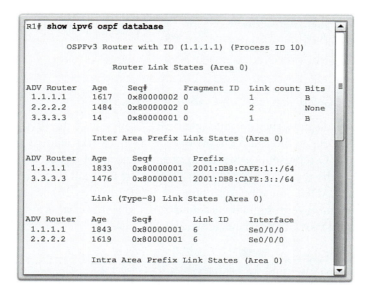

```
R1# show ipv6 ospf database

            OSPFv3 Router with ID (1.1.1.1) (Process ID 10)

                 Router Link States (Area 0)

ADV Router    Age     Seq#          Fragment ID  Link count Bits
  1.1.1.1     1617    0x80000002 0                   1      B
  2.2.2.2     1484    0x80000002 0                   2      None
  3.3.3.3     14      0x80000001 0                   1      B

            Inter Area Prefix Link States (Area 0)

ADV Router    Age     Seq#          Prefix
  1.1.1.1     1833    0x80000001    2001:DB8:CAFE:1::/64
  3.3.3.3     1476    0x80000001    2001:DB8:CAFE:3::/64

            Link (Type-8) Link States (Area 0)

ADV Router    Age     Seq#        Link ID    Interface
  1.1.1.1     1843    0x80000001  6          Se0/0/0
  2.2.2.2     1619    0x80000001  6          Se0/0/0

            Intra Area Prefix Link States (Area 0)
```

Figure 8-37   Verifying the OSPFv3 LSDB on R1

Note

The entire output in Figure 8-37 can be viewed in the online course on page 8.2.3.5 graphic number 5.

Packet Tracer Activity 8.2.3.6: Configuring Multiarea OSPFv2

In this activity, you will configure multiarea OSPFv2. The network is already connected and interfaces are configured with IPv4 addressing. Your job is to enable multiarea OSPFv2, verify connectivity, and examine the operation of multiarea OSPFv2.

Packet Tracer Activity 8.2.3.7: Configuring Multiarea OSPFv3

In this activity, you will configure multiarea OSPFv3. The network is already connected and interfaces are configured with IPv6 addressing. Your job is to enable multiarea OSPFv3, verify connectivity, and examine the operation of multiarea OSPFv3

Lab 8.2.3.8: Configuring Multiarea OSPFv2

In this lab, you will complete the following objectives:

- Part 1: Build the Network and Configure Basic Device Settings
- Part 2: Configure a Multiarea OSPFv2 Network
- Part 3: Configure Interarea Summary Routes

Lab 8.2.3.9: Configuring Multiarea OSPFv3

In this lab, you will complete the following objectives:

- Part 1: Build the Network and Configure Basic Device Settings
- Part 2: Configure a Multiarea OSPFv3 Network
- Part 3: Configure Interarea Route Summarization

Lab 8.2.3.10: Troubleshooting Multiarea OSPF

In this lab, you will complete the following objectives:

Part 1: Build the Network and Load Device Configurations

Part 2: Troubleshoot Layer 3 Connectivity

Part 3: Troubleshoot OSPFv2

Part 4: Troubleshoot OSPFv3

Summary (8.3)

Class Activity 8.3.1.1: Digital Trolleys

Your city has an aging digital trolley system based on a one-area design. All communications within this one area are taking longer to process as trolleys are being added to routes serving the population of your growing city. Trolley departures and arrivals are also taking a little longer, because each trolley must check large routing tables to determine where to pick up and deliver residents from their source and destination streets.

A concerned citizen has come up with the idea of dividing the city into different areas for a more efficient way to determine trolley routing information. It is thought that if the trolley maps are smaller, the system might be improved because of faster and smaller updates to the routing tables.

Your city board approves and implements the new area-based, digital trolley system. But to ensure the new area routes are more efficient, the city board needs data to show the results at the next open board meeting.

Complete the directions found in the PDF for this activity. Share your answers with your class.

Single-area OSPF is useful in smaller networks but in larger networks multiarea OSPF is a better choice. Multiarea OSPF solves the issues of large routing table, large link-state database, and frequent SPF algorithm calculations.

The main area is called the backbone area (area 0) and all other areas must connect to the backbone area. Routing still occurs between the areas while many of the routing operations, such as recalculating the database, are kept within an area.

There are four different types of OSPF routers: internal router, backbone router, Area Border Router (ABR), and Autonomous System Boundary Router (ASBR). A router can be classified as more than one router type.

Link-state advertisements (LSAs) are the building blocks of OSPF. This chapter concentrated on LSA type 1 to LSA type 5. Type 1 LSAs are referred to as the router link entries. Type 2 LSAs are referred to as the network link entries and are flooded by a DR. Type 3 LSAs are referred to as the summary link entries and are created and propagated by ABRs. A type 4 summary LSA is generated by an ABR only when an ASBR exists within an area. Type 5 external LSAs describe routes to networks outside the OSPF autonomous system. Type 5 LSAs are originated by the ASBR and are flooded to the entire autonomous system.

OSPF routes in an IPv4 routing table are identified using the following descriptors: O, O IA, O E1, or O E2. Each router uses the SPF algorithm against the LSDB to build the SPF tree. The SPF tree is used to determine the best paths.

There are no special commands required to implement a multiarea OSPF network. A router simply becomes an ABR when it has two **network** statements in different areas.

An example of multiarea OSPF configuration:

```
R1(config)# router ospf 10
R1(config-router)# router-id 1.1.1.1
R1(config-router)# network 10.1.1.1 0.0.0.0 area 1
R1(config-router)# network 10.1.2.1 0.0.0.0 area 1
R1(config-router)# network 192.168.10.1 0.0.0.0 area 0
```

OSPF does not perform auto-summarization. In OSPF, summarization can only be configured on ABRs or ASBRs. Interarea route summarization must be manually configured and occurs on ABRs and applies to routes from within each area. To manually configure interarea route summarization on an ABR, use the **area** *area-id* **range** *address mask* router configuration mode command.

External route summarization is specific to external routes that are injected into OSPF via route redistribution. Generally, only ASBRs summarize external routes. External route summarization is configured on ASBRs using the **summary-address** *address mask* router configuration mode command.

Commands that are used to verify OSPF configuration consist of the following:

- **show ip ospf neighbor**
- **show ip ospf**
- **show ip ospf interface**
- **show ip protocols**
- **show ip ospf interface brief**
- **show ip route ospf**
- **show ip ospf database**

Practice

The following activities provide practice with the topics introduced in this chapter. The Labs and Class Activities are available in the companion *Routing Protocols Lab Manual* (978-1-58713-322-0). The Packet Tracer Activities PKA files are found in the online course.

Class Activities

Class Activity 8.0.1.2: Leaving on a Jet Plane

Class Activity 8.3.1.1: Digital Trolleys

Labs

Lab 8.2.3.8: Configuring Multiarea OSPFv2

Lab 8.2.3.9: Configuring Multiarea OSPFv3

Lab 8.2.3.10: Troubleshooting Multiarea OSPF

Packet Tracer
☐ Activity

Packet Tracer Activities

Packet Tracer Activity 8.2.3.6: Configuring Multiarea OSPFv2

Packet Tracer Activity 8.2.3.7: Configuring Multiarea OSPFv3

Check Your Understanding Questions

Complete all the review questions listed here to test your understanding of the topics and concepts in this chapter. The appendix, "Answers to the 'Check Your Understanding' Questions," lists the answers.

1. Which statement describes a multiarea OSPF network?

   A. Consists of multiple network areas that are daisy-chained together.

   B. It has a core backbone area with other areas connected to the backbone area.

   C. It has multiple routers that run multiple routing protocols simultaneously, and each protocol consists of an area.

   D. It requires a three-layer hierarchical network design approach.

2. What is one advantage of using multiarea OSPF?

   A. It allows OSPFv2 and OSPFv3 to exchange routing updates.

   B. It enables multiple routing protocols to be running in a large network.

   C. It improves the routing efficiency by reducing the routing table and link-state update overhead.

   D. It increases the routing performance by dividing the neighbor table into separate smaller ones.

3. Which characteristic describes ABRs and ASBRs implemented in a multiarea OSPF network?

   A. They are required to perform any summarization or redistribution tasks.

   B. They are required to reload frequently and quickly in order to update the LSDB.

   C. They both run multiple routing protocols simultaneously.

   D. They usually have many local networks attached.

4. An ABR in a multiarea OSPF network receives LSAs from its neighbor that identify the neighbor as an ASBR with learned external networks from the Internet. Which LSA type would the ABR send to other areas to identify the ASBR, so that internal traffic that is destined for the Internet will be sent through the ASBR??

   A. LSA type 1

   B. LSA type 2

   C. LSA type 3

   D. LSA type 4

   E. LSA type 5

5. Which two statements correctly describe OSPF type 3 LSAs? (Choose two.)

   A. Type 3 LSAs are generated without requiring a full SPF calculation.

   B. Type 3 LSAs are known as autonomous system external LSA entries.

   C. Type 3 LSAs are known as router link entries.

   D. Type 3 LSAs are used for routes to networks outside the OSPF autonomous system.

   E. Type 3 LSAs are used to update routes between OSPF areas.

6. What can be concluded about a routing table entry with a route source of "O"?

   A. The route entry was learned from an ABR.

   B. The route entry was learned from an ASBR.

   C. The route entry was learned from an internal router in another area.

   D. The route entry was learned from an internal router in the same area.

7. What can be concluded about a routing table entry with a route source of "O IA"?

   A. The route entry was learned from an ABR.

   B. The route entry was learned from an ASBR.

   C. The route entry was learned from an internal router in another area.

   D. The route entry was learned from an internal router in the same area.

8. What can be concluded about a routing table entry with a route source of "O*E2"?

   A. The route entry was learned from an ABR.

   B. The route entry was learned from an ASBR.

   C. The route entry was learned from an internal router in another area.

   D. The route entry was learned from an internal router in the same area.

9. Which statement is true regarding an ABR?

   A. It can also be an internal router.

   B. It is a router with all of its interfaces in the same area.

   C. It is a router with at least one interface attached in a non-OSPF network.

   D. It is a router with interfaces attached to multiple areas.

10. Which statement is true regarding an ASBR?

   A. It can also be an internal router.

   B. It is a router in the backbone area.

   C. It is a router with all of its interfaces in the same area.

   D. It is a router with at least one interface attached in a non-OSPF network.

   E. It is a router with interfaces attached to multiple areas.

CHAPTER 9

Access Control Lists

Objectives

Upon completion of this chapter, you will be able to answer the following questions:

- How are ACLs used to filter traffic?

- What is the difference between standard and extended IPv4 ACLs?

- How are wildcard masks used with ACLs?

- What are the guidelines for creating ACLs?

- What are the guidelines for placing ACLs?

- How are standard IPv4 ACLs used to filter traffic according to network requirements?

- How do you modify a standard IPv4 ACL using sequencing numbers?

- How do you configure a standard ACL to secure VTY access?

- What is the structure of an extended access control entry (ACE)?

- How do you configure extended IPv4 ACLs to filter traffic according to network requirements?

- How do you configure an ACL to limit debug output?

- How does a router process packets when an ACL is applied?

- How do you troubleshoot common ACL errors using CLI commands?

- What are the differences between creating IPv4 ACLs and IPv6 ACLs?

- How do you configure IPv6 ACLs to filter traffic according to network requirements?

Key Terms

This chapter uses the following key terms. You can find the definitions in the Glossary.

Introduction (9.0.1.1)

Network security is a huge subject, and much of it is far beyond the scope of this course. However, one of the most important skills a network administrator needs is mastery of access control lists (ACLs).

Network designers use firewalls to protect networks from unauthorized use. Firewalls are hardware or software solutions that enforce network security policies. Consider a lock on a door to a room inside a building. The lock allows only authorized users with a key or access card to pass through the door. Similarly, a firewall filters unauthorized or potentially dangerous packets from entering the network. On a Cisco router, you can configure a simple firewall that provides basic traffic filtering capabilities using ACLs. Administrators use ACLs to stop traffic or permit only specified traffic on their networks.

An *access control list (ACL)* is a sequential list of permit or deny statements that apply to addresses or upper-layer protocols. ACLs provide a powerful way to control traffic into and out of a network. ACLs can be configured for all routed network protocols.

The most important reason to configure ACLs is to provide security for a network. This chapter explains how to use standard and extended ACLs on a Cisco router as part of a security solution. Included are tips, considerations, recommendations, and general guidelines on how to use ACLs.

This chapter includes an opportunity to develop your mastery of ACLs with a series of lessons, activities, and lab exercises.

Class Activity 9.0.1.2: Permit Me to Assist You

Scenario

Each individual in the class will record five questions they would ask a candidate who is applying for a security clearance for a network assistant position within a small- to medium-sized business. The list of questions should be listed in order of importance to selecting a good candidate for the job. The preferred answers will also be recorded.

Two interviewers from the class will be selected. The interview process will begin. Candidates will be allowed or denied the opportunity to move to the next level of questions based upon their answers to the interviewer's questions.

Refer to the accompanying PDF for further instructions for this activity.

The entire class will then get together and discuss their observations regarding the process to permit or deny them the opportunity to continue on to the next level of interviews.

IP ACL Operation (9.1)

ACLs enable you to control traffic into and out of your network. This control can be as simple as permitting or denying network hosts or addresses. This section discusses the purpose, operation, and types of ACLs.

Purpose of ACLs (9.1.1)

The primary purpose of IP ACLs is to filter network traffic. However, IP ACLs are also used to define traffic to Network Address Translation (NAT) or encryption.

What Is an ACL? (9.1.1.1)

An ACL is a series of IOS commands that control whether a router forwards or drops packets based on information found in the packet header. ACLs are among the most commonly used features of Cisco IOS Software.

When configured, ACLs perform the following tasks:

- **Limit network traffic to increase network performance:** For example, if corporate policy does not allow video traffic on the network, ACLs that block video traffic could be configured and applied. This would greatly reduce the network load and increase network performance.

- **Provide traffic flow control:** ACLs can restrict the delivery of routing updates. If updates are not required because of network conditions, bandwidth is preserved.

- **Provide a basic level of security for network access:** ACLs can allow one host to access a part of the network and prevent another host from accessing the same area. For example, access to the Human Resources network can be restricted to authorized users.

- **Filter traffic based on traffic type:** For example, an ACL can permit email traffic but block all Telnet traffic.

- **Screen hosts to permit or deny access to network services:** ACLs can permit or deny a user to access file types, such as FTP or HTTP.

By default, a router does not have ACLs configured; therefore, by default a router does not filter traffic. Traffic that enters the router is routed solely based on information within the routing table. However, when an ACL is applied to an interface, the router performs the additional task of evaluating all network packets as they pass through the interface to determine if the packets can be forwarded.

In addition to either permitting or denying traffic, ACLs can be used for selecting types of traffic to be analyzed, forwarded, or processed in other ways. For example,

ACLs can be used to classify traffic to enable priority processing. This capability is similar to having a VIP pass at a concert or sporting event. The VIP pass gives selected guests privileges not offered to general admission ticket holders, such as priority entry or being able to enter a restricted area.

Figure 9-1 shows a sample topology with ACLs applied.

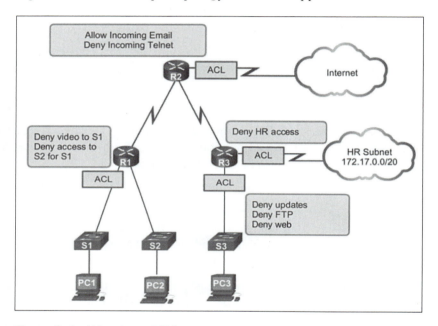

Figure 9-1   What Is an ACL?

A TCP Conversation (9.1.1.2)

ACLs enable administrators to control traffic into and out of a network. This control can be as simple as permitting or denying traffic based on network addresses or as complex as controlling network traffic based on the TCP port being requested. It is easier to understand how an ACL filters traffic by examining the dialogue that occurs during a TCP conversation, such as when requesting a webpage.

TCP Communication

When a client requests data from a web server, IP (Layer 3) manages the communication between the PC (source) and the server (destination). TCP (Layer 4) manages the communication between the web browser (application) and the network server software.

When you send an email, look at a webpage, or download a file, TCP is responsible for breaking data down into segments for IP before they are sent. TCP also manages assembling the data from the segments when they arrive. The TCP process is very much like a conversation in which two nodes on a network agree to pass data between one another.

TCP provides a connection-oriented, reliable, byte stream service. Connection-oriented means that the two applications must establish a TCP connection prior to exchanging data. TCP is a full-duplex protocol, meaning that each TCP connection supports a pair of byte streams, each stream flowing in one direction. TCP includes a flow-control mechanism for each byte stream that allows the receiver to limit how much data the sender can transmit. TCP also implements a congestion-control mechanism.

Figure 9-2 illustrates how a TCP/IP conversation takes place. TCP segments are marked with flags that denote their purpose: a SYN starts (synchronizes) the session, an ACK is an acknowledgment that an expected segment was received, and a FIN finishes the session. A SYN/ACK acknowledges that the transfer is synchronized. TCP data segments include the higher level protocol needed to direct the application data to the correct application.

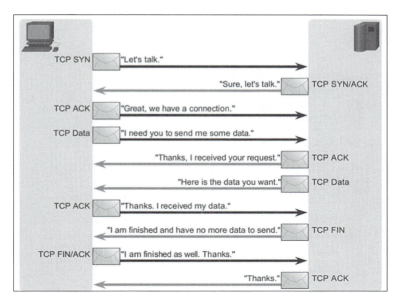

Figure 9-2   A TCP Conversation

The TCP data segment also identifies the port which matches the requested service. For example, HTTP is port 80, SMTP is port 25, and FTP is port 20 and port 21. Table 9-1 shows ranges of UDP and TCP ports.

Table 9-1   Port Numbers

Port Number Range	Port Group
0 to 1023	Well Known Ports
1024 to 49151	Registered Ports
49152 to 65535	Private and/or Dynamic Ports

Figures 9-3 through 9-5 explore TCP/UDP ports.

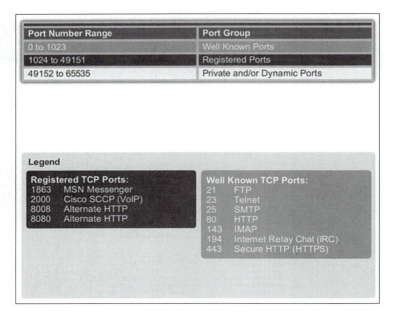

Figure 9-3   TCP Ports

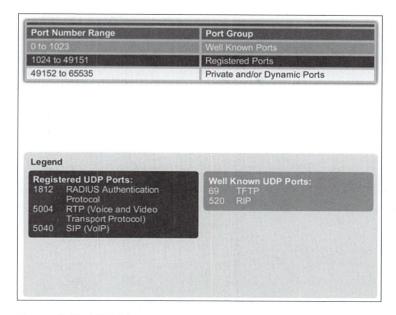

Figure 9-4   UDP Ports

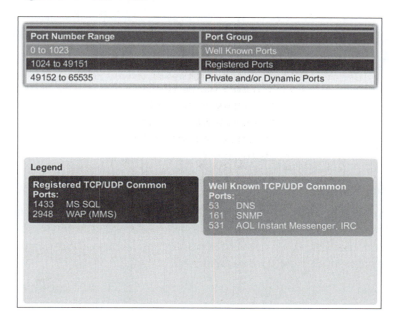

Figure 9-5   TCP/UDP Common Ports

Packet Filtering (9.1.1.3)

So how does an ACL use the information passed during a TCP/IP conversation to filter traffic?

Packet filtering, sometimes called static packet filtering, controls access to a network by analyzing the incoming and outgoing packets and passing or dropping them based on given criteria, such as the source IP address, destination IP addresses, and the protocol carried within the packet.

A router acts as a packet filter when it forwards or denies packets according to filtering rules. When a packet arrives at the packet-filtering router, the router extracts certain information from the packet header. Using this information, the router makes decisions, based on configured filter rules, as to whether the packet can pass through or be discarded. As shown in Figure 9-6, packet filtering can work at different layers of the OSI model, or at the Internet layer of TCP/IP.

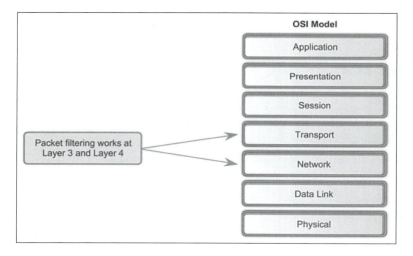

Figure 9-6   Packet Filtering

A packet-filtering router uses rules to determine whether to permit or deny traffic. A router can also perform packet filtering at Layer 4, the transport layer. The router can filter packets based on the source port and destination port of the TCP or UDP segment. These rules are defined using ACLs.

An ACL is a sequential list of permit or deny statements, known as access control entries (ACEs). ACEs are also commonly called ACL statements. ACEs can be created to filter traffic based on certain criteria such as: the source address, destination address, the protocol, and port numbers. When network traffic passes through an interface configured with an ACL, the router compares the information within the packet against each ACE, in sequential order, to determine if the packet matches one of the statements. If a match is found, the packet is processed accordingly. In this way, ACLs can be configured to control access to a network or subnet.

To evaluate network traffic, the ACL extracts the following information from the Layer 3 packet header:

- Source IP address
- Destination IP address
- ICMP message type

The ACL can also extract upper layer information from the Layer 4 header, including:

- TCP/UDP source port
- TCP/UDP destination port

Packet Filtering Example (9.1.1.4)

To understand the concept of how a router uses packet filtering, imagine that a guard has been posted at a locked door. The guard's instructions are to allow only people whose names appear on a list to pass through the door. The guard is filtering people based on the criterion of having their names on the authorized list. An ACL works in a similar manner, making decisions based on set criteria.

For example, an ACL could be configured to logically, "Permit web access to users from network A but deny all other services to network A users. Deny HTTP access to users from network B, but permit network B users to have all other access." Refer to Figure 9-7 to examine the decision path the packet filter uses to accomplish this task.

For this scenario, the packet filter looks at each packet as follows:

- If the packet is a TCP SYN from Network A using Port 80, it is allowed to pass. All other access is denied to those users.
- If the packet is a TCP SYN from Network B using Port 80, it is blocked. However, all other access is permitted.

This is just a simple example. Multiple rules can be configured to further permit or deny services to specific users.

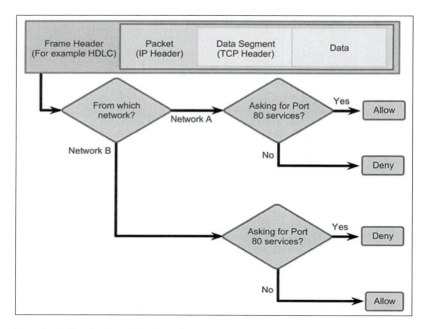

Figure 9-7   Packet Filtering Example

ACL Operation (9.1.1.5)

ACLs define the set of rules that give added control for packets that enter inbound interfaces, packets that relay through the router, and packets that exit outbound interfaces of the router. ACLs do not act on packets that originate from the router itself.

ACLs are configured to apply to inbound traffic or to apply to outbound traffic (as shown in Figure 9-8):

- **Inbound ACLs:** Incoming packets are processed before they are routed to the outbound interface. An inbound ACL is efficient because it saves the overhead of routing lookups if the packet is discarded. If the packet is permitted by the tests, it is then processed for routing. Inbound ACLs are best used to filter packets when the network attached to an inbound interface is the only source of the packets that need to be examined.

- **Outbound ACLs:** Incoming packets are routed to the outbound interface, and then they are processed through the outbound ACL. Outbound ACLs are best used when the same filter will be applied to packets coming from multiple inbound interfaces before exiting the same outbound interface.

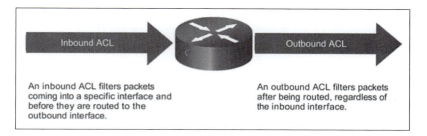

Figure 9-8 Inbound and Outbound ACLs

The last statement of an ACL is always an implicit deny. This statement is automatically inserted at the end of each ACL even though it is not physically present. The implicit deny blocks all traffic. Because of this implicit deny, an ACL that does not have at least one permit statement will block all traffic.

Packet Tracer Activity 9.1.1.6: ACL Demonstration

In this activity, you will observe how an access control list (ACL) can be used to prevent a ping from reaching hosts on remote networks. After removing the ACL from the configuration, the pings will be successful.

Standard Versus Extended IPv4 ACLs (9.1.2)

Network administrators use a variety of tools to create a secure and efficient network infrastructure. IP ACLs are often used to provide security by performing traffic filtering.

Types of Cisco IPv4 ACLs (9.1.2.1)

The two types of Cisco IPv4 ACLs are standard and extended.

Note

Cisco IPv6 ACLs are similar to IPv4 extended ACLs and are discussed in a later section.

Standard ACLs

Standard ACLs can be used to permit or deny traffic only from source IPv4 addresses. The destination of the packet and the ports involved are not evaluated. The following example allows all traffic from the 192.168.30.0/24 network. Because of the implied "deny any" at the end, all other traffic is blocked with this ACL. Standard ACLs are created in global configuration mode.

```
access-list 10 permit 192.168.30.0.0.0.0.255
```

Standard ACLs filter IP packets based on the source address only

Extended ACLs

Extended ACLs filter IPv4 packets based on several attributes:

- Protocol type
- Source IPv4 address
- Destination IPv4 address
- Source TCP or UDP ports
- Destination TCP or UDP ports
- Optional protocol type information for finer control

In the following example, ACL 103 permits traffic originating from any address on the 192.168.30.0/24 network to any IPv4 network if the destination host port is 80 (HTTP). Extended ACLs are created in global configuration mode.

```
access-list 103 permit 192.168.30.0.0.0.0.255 any eq 80
```

The commands for ACLs are explained in the next few topics.

> **Note**
>
> Standard and extended ACLs are discussed in more detail later in this chapter.

Numbering and Naming ACLs (9.1.2.2)

Standard and extended ACLs can be created using either a number or a name to identify the ACL and its list of statements.

Using numbered ACLs is an effective method for determining the ACL type on smaller networks with more homogeneously defined traffic. However, a number does not provide information about the purpose of the ACL. For this reason, starting with Cisco IOS Release 11.2, a name can be used to identify a Cisco ACL.

The following lists summarize the rules to follow to designate numbered ACLs and named ACLs.

Numbered ACL

Assign a number based on the protocol to be filtered:

- "1 to 99" and "1300 and 1999": Standard IP ACL

- "100 to 199" and "2000 to 2699": Extended IP ACL

Numbers 200 to 1299 are skipped because those numbers are used by other protocols, many of which are legacy or obsolete. This course focuses only on IP ACLs. Examples of legacy ACL protocol numbers are 600 to 699 used by AppleTalk, and numbers 800 to 899 used by IPX.

Named ACL

Assign a name to identify the ACL:

- Names can contain alphanumeric characters.

- It is suggested that the name be written in CAPITAL LETTERS.

- Names cannot contain spaces or punctuation.

- Entries can be added or deleted within the ACL.

Wildcard Masks in ACLs (9.1.3)

Wildcard masks are used with the **network** command used in IPv4 routing protocols such as EIGRP and OSPF to identify a specific network or networks.

Introducing ACL Wildcard Masking (9.1.3.1)

Wildcard masks have a similar role when used with IPv4 ACEs.

Wildcard Masking

IPv4 ACEs include the use of wildcard masks. Wildcard masks are used in ACLs to match specific bits within the address. A wildcard mask is a string of 32 binary digits used by the router to determine which bits of the address to examine for a match.

> **Note**
>
> Unlike IPv4 ACLs, IPv6 ACLs do not use wildcard masks. Instead, the prefix-length is used to indicate how much of an IPv6 source or destination address should be matched. IPv6 ACLs are discussed later in this chapter.

As with subnet masks, the numbers 1 and 0 in the wildcard mask identify how to treat the corresponding IP address bits. However, in a wildcard mask, these bits are used for different purposes and follow different rules.

Subnet masks use binary 1s and 0s to identify the network, subnet, and host portion of an IP address. Wildcard masks use binary 1s and 0s to filter individual IP addresses or groups of IP addresses to permit or deny access to resources.

Wildcard masks and subnet masks differ in the way they match binary 1s and 0s. Wildcard masks use the following rules to match binary 1s and 0s:

- **Wildcard mask bit 0**: Match the corresponding bit value in the address.

- **Wildcard mask bit 1**: Ignore the corresponding bit value in the address.

Figure 9-9 shows how different wildcard masks filter IP addresses. In the example, remember that binary 0 signifies a bit that must match, and binary 1 signifies a bit that can be ignored.

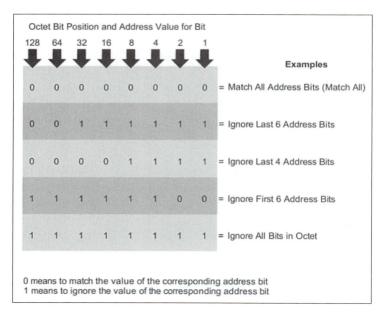

Figure 9-9 Wildcard Masking

Note

Wildcard masks are often referred to as an inverse mask. The reason is that, unlike a subnet mask in which binary 1 is equal to a match and binary 0 is not a match, in a wildcard mask the reverse is true.

Using a Wildcard Mask

Table 9-2 shows the results of applying a 0.0.255.255 wildcard mask to a 32-bit IPv4 address. Remember that a binary 0 indicates a value that is matched.

Table 9-2   Wildcard Mask Example

	Decimal Address	Binary Address
IP Address to be Processed	192.168.10.0	11000000.10101000.00001010.00000000
Wildcard Mask	0.0.255.255	00000000.00000000.11111111.11111111
Resulting IP Address	192.168.0.0	11000000.10101000.00000000.00000000

Wildcard masks are also used when configuring some IPv4 routing protocols, such as OSPF, to enable the protocol on specific interfaces.

Wildcard Mask Examples (9.1.3.2)

The best way to understand wildcard masks is to see some examples.

Wildcard Masks to Match IPv4 Subnets

Calculating the wildcard mask can take some practice. Tables 9-3 through 9-5 provide three examples of wildcard masks. In Table 9-3, the wildcard mask stipulates that every bit in the IPv4 192.168.1.1 must match exactly.

Table 9-3   Wildcard Masks to Match IPv4 Hosts and Subnets: Example 1

	Decimal	Binary
IP Address	192.168.1.1	11000000.10101000.00000001.00000001
Wildcard Mask	0.0.0.0	00000000.00000000.00000000.00000000
Result	192.168.1.1	11000000.10101000.00000001.00000001

In Table 9-4, the wildcard mask stipulates that anything will match.

Table 9-4   Wildcard Masks to Match IPv4 Hosts and Subnets: Example 2

	Decimal	Binary
IP Address	192.168.1.1	11000000.10101000.00000001.00000001
Wildcard Mask	255.255.255.255	11111111.11111111.11111111.11111111
Result	0.0.0.0	00000000.00000000.00000000.00000000

In Table 9-5, the wildcard mask stipulates that any host within the 192.168.1.0/24 network will match.

Table 9-5   Wildcard Masks to Match IPv4 Hosts and Subnets: Example 3

	Decimal	Binary
IP Address	192.168.1.1	11000000.10101000.00000001.00000001
Wildcard Mask	0.0.0.255	00000000.00000000.00000000.11111111
Result	192.168.1.0	11000000.10101000.00000001.00000000

These examples were fairly simple and straightforward. However, the calculation of wildcard masks can be more complex.

Wildcard Masks to Match Ranges

The two examples in Tables 9-6 and 9-7 are more complex. In Table 9-6, the first two octets and first four bits of the third octet must match exactly. The last four bits in the third octet and the last octet can be any valid number. This results in a mask that checks for the range of networks 192.168.16.0 to 192.168.31.0.

Table 9-6   Wildcard Masks to Match Ranges: Example 1

	Decimal	Binary
IP Address	192.168.16.0	11000000.10101000.00010000.00000001
Wildcard Mask	0.0.15.255	00000000.00000000.00001111.11111111
Result Range	192.168.16.0 to 192.168.31.255	11000000.10101000.00010000.00000000 to 11000000.10101000.00011111.11111111

Table 9-7 shows a wildcard mask that matches the first two octets, and the least significant bit in the third octet. The last octet and the first seven bits in the third octet can be any valid number. The result is a mask that would permit or deny all hosts from odd subnets from the 192.168.0.0 major network.

Table 9-7   Wildcard Masks to Match Ranges: Example 2

	Decimal	Binary
IP Address	192.168.1.0	11000000.10101000.00000001.00000000
Wildcard Mask	0.0.254.255	00000000.00000000.11111110.11111111

	Decimal	Binary
Result Range	192.168.1.0, 192.168.3.0, continue with odd third octet to 192.168.255.0	11000000.10101000.00000001.00000000
	All odd numbered subnets in the 192.168.0.0 major network	

Calculating the Wildcard Mask (9.1.3.3)

Calculating wildcard masks can be challenging. One shortcut method is to subtract the subnet mask from 255.255.255.255.

Wildcard Mask Calculation: Example 1

In the first example in Figure 9-10, assume you wanted to permit access to all users in the 192.168.3.0 network. Because the subnet mask is 255.255.255.0, you could take the 255.255.255.255 and subtract the subnet mask 255.255.255.0 as is indicated in the figure. The solution produces the wildcard mask 0.0.0.255.

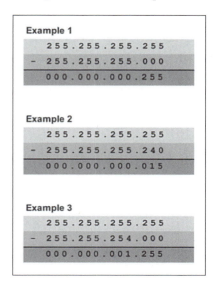

Figure 9-10 Wildcard Mask Calculation

Wildcard Mask Calculation: Example 2

In the second example in Figure 9-10, assume you wanted to permit network access for the 14 users in the subnet 192.168.3.32/28. The subnet mask for the IP subnet is 255.255.255.240, therefore take 255.255.255.255 and subtract the subnet mask 255.255.255.240. The solution this time produces the wildcard mask 0.0.0.15.

Wildcard Mask Calculation: Example 3

In the third example in Figure 9-10, assume you wanted to match only networks 192.168.10.0 and 192.168.11.0. Again, you take the 255.255.255.255 and subtract the regular subnet mask, which in this case would be 255.255.254.0. The result is 0.0.1.255.

You could accomplish the same result with statements like these two:

```
R1(config)# access-list 10 permit 192.168.10.0
R1(config)# access-list 10 permit 192.168.11.0
```

It is far more efficient to configure the wildcard mask in the following way:

```
R1(config)# access-list 10 permit 192.168.10.0 0.0.1.255
```

Consider the following configuration to match networks in the range between 192.168.16.0 to 192.168.31.0:

```
R1(config)# access-list 10 permit 192.168.16.0
R1(config)# access-list 10 permit 192.168.17.0
R1(config)# access-list 10 permit 192.168.18.0
R1(config)# access-list 10 permit 192.168.19.0
R1(config)# access-list 10 permit 192.168.20.0
R1(config)# access-list 10 permit 192.168.21.0
R1(config)# access-list 10 permit 192.168.22.0
R1(config)# access-list 10 permit 192.168.23.0
R1(config)# access-list 10 permit 192.168.24.0
R1(config)# access-list 10 permit 192.168.25.0
R1(config)# access-list 10 permit 192.168.26.0
R1(config)# access-list 10 permit 192.168.27.0
R1(config)# access-list 10 permit 192.168.28.0
R1(config)# access-list 10 permit 192.168.29.0
R1(config)# access-list 10 permit 192.168.30.0
R1(config)# access-list 10 permit 192.168.31.0
```

The previous 16 configuration statements can be reduced to a single statement using the correct wildcard mask as shown below:

```
R1(config)# access-list 10 permit 192.168.16.0 0.0.15.255
```

Wildcard Mask Keywords (9.1.3.4)

Wildcard mask keywords are used to help make some uses of the wildcard mask more understandable.

Wildcard Bit Mask Keywords

Working with decimal representations of binary wildcard mask bits can be tedious. To simplify this task, the keywords **host** and **any** help identify the most common uses of wildcard masking. These keywords eliminate entering wildcard masks when identifying a specific host or an entire network. These keywords also make it easier to read an ACL by providing visual clues as to the source or destination of the criteria.

The **host** keyword substitutes for the 0.0.0.0 mask. This mask states that all IPv4 address bits must match or only one host is matched.

The **any** option substitutes for the IP address and 255.255.255.255 mask. This mask says to ignore the entire IPv4 address or to accept any addresses.

Example 1: Wildcard Masking Process with a Single IP Address

In Example 1 in Figure 9-11, instead of entering **192.168.10.10 0.0.0.0**, you can use **host 192.168.10.10**.

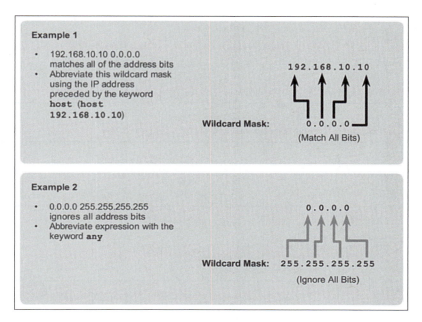

Figure 9-11   Wildcard Bit Mask Abbreviations

Example 2: Wildcard Masking Process with a Match Any IP Address

In Example 2 in Figure 9-11, instead of entering **0.0.0.0 255.255.255.255**, you can use the keyword **any** by itself.

Note

The keywords **host** and **any** can also be used when configuring an IPv6 ACL.

Examples Wildcard Mask Keywords (9.1.3.5)

The **any** and **host** keywords are used to help simplify the configuration and readability of IP ACEs.

The **any** and **host** Keywords

Example 9-1 shows how to use the **any** keyword to substitute for the IPv4 address 0.0.0.0 with a wildcard mask of 255.255.255.255.

Example 9-1   The **any** Keyword

```
R1 (config)# access-list 1 permit 0.0.0.0 255.255.255.255
R1 (config)# access-list 1 permit any
```

Example 9-2 shows how to use the **host** keyword to substitute for the wildcard mask when identifying a single host.

Example 9-2   The **host** Keyword

```
R1 (config)# access-list 1 permit 192.168.10.10 0.0.0.0
R1 (config)# access-list 1 permit host 192.168.10.10
```

Activity 9.1.3.6: Determine the Correct Wildcard Mask

Go to the online course to perform this practice activity.

Activity 9.1.3.7: Determine the Permit or Deny

Go to the online course to perform this practice activity.

Guidelines for ACL Creation (9.1.4)

There are several guidelines for creating IP ACLs to help ensure the ACL is placed where it can have the most effect with minimal configuration.

General Guidelines for Creating ACLs (9.1.4.1)

Writing ACLs can be a complex task. For every interface there may be multiple policies needed to manage the type of traffic allowed to enter or exit that interface. The router in Figure 9-12 has two interfaces configured for IPv4 and IPv6. If we needed ACLs for both protocols, on both interfaces, and in both directions, this would require eight separate ACLs. Each interface would have four ACLs: two ACLs for IPv4 and two ACLs for IPv6. For each protocol, one ACL is for inbound traffic and one is for outbound traffic.

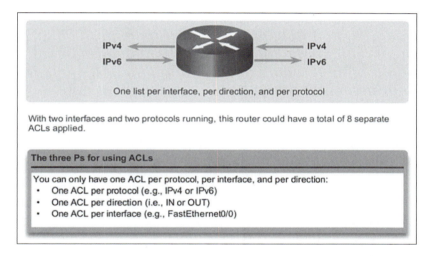

One list per interface, per direction, and per protocol

With two interfaces and two protocols running, this router could have a total of 8 separate ACLs applied.

The three Ps for using ACLs

You can only have one ACL per protocol, per interface, and per direction:
- One ACL per protocol (e.g., IPv4 or IPv6)
- One ACL per direction (i.e., IN or OUT)
- One ACL per interface (e.g., FastEthernet0/0)

Figure 9-12   ACL Traffic Filtering on a Router

Note

ACLs do not have to be configured in both directions. The number of ACLs and their direction applied to the interface will depend on the requirements being implemented.

Here are some guidelines for using ACLs:

- Use ACLs in firewall routers positioned between your internal network and an external network such as the Internet.

- Use ACLs on a router positioned between two parts of your network to control traffic entering or exiting a specific part of your internal network.

- Configure ACLs on border routers, that is, routers situated at the edges of your networks. This provides a very basic buffer from the outside network, or between a less controlled area of your own network and a more sensitive area of your network.

- Configure ACLs for each network protocol configured on the border router interfaces.

The Three Ps

A general rule for applying ACLs on a router can be recalled by remembering the three Ps. You can configure one ACL per protocol, per direction, per interface:

- **One ACL per protocol:** To control traffic flow on an interface, an ACL must be defined for each protocol enabled on the interface.

- **One ACL per direction:** ACLs control traffic in one direction at a time on an interface. Two separate ACLs must be created to control inbound and outbound traffic.

- **One ACL per interface:** ACLs control traffic for an interface, for example, GigabitEthernet 0/0.

ACL Best Practices (9.1.4.2)

Using ACLs requires attention to detail and great care. Mistakes can be costly in terms of downtime, troubleshooting efforts, and poor network service. Before configuring an ACL, basic planning is required. Table 9-8 presents guidelines that form the basis of an ACL best practices list.

Table 9-8   ACL Best Practices

Guideline	Benefit
Base your ACLs on the security policy of the organization.	This will ensure you implement organizational security guidelines.
Prepare a description of what you want your ACLs to do.	This will help you avoid inadvertently creating potential access problems.
Use a text editor to create, edit, and save ACLs.	This will help you create a library of reusable ACLs.
Test your ACLs on a development network before implementing them on a production network.	This will help you avoid costly errors.

Activity 9.1.4.3: ACL Operation

Go to the online course to perform this practice activity.

Guidelines for ACL Placement (9.1.5)

This section examines the guidelines for the placement of ACLs.

Where to Place ACLs (9.1.5.1)

The proper placement of an ACL can make the network operate more efficiently. An ACL can be placed to reduce unnecessary traffic. For example, traffic that will be denied at a remote destination should not be forwarded using network resources along the route to that destination.

Every ACL should be placed where it has the greatest impact on efficiency. As shown in Figure 9-13, the basic rules are:

- **Extended ACLs:** Locate extended ACLs as close as possible to the source of the traffic to be filtered. This way, undesirable traffic is denied close to the source network without crossing the network infrastructure.

- **Standard ACLs:** Because standard ACLs do not specify destination addresses, place them as close to the destination as possible. Placing a standard ACL at the source of the traffic will effectively prevent that traffic from reaching any other networks through the interface where the ACL is applied.

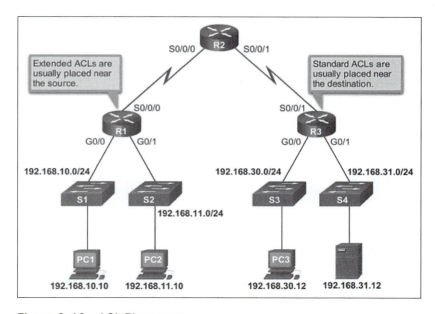

Figure 9-13 ACL Placement

Placement of the ACL and therefore the type of ACL used may also depend on:

- **The extent of the network administrator's control:** Placement of the ACL can depend on whether or not the network administrator has control of both the source and destination networks.

- **Bandwidth of the networks involved:** Filtering unwanted traffic at the source prevents transmission of the traffic before it consumes bandwidth on the path to a destination. This is especially important in low bandwidth networks.

- **Ease of configuration:** If a network administrator wants to deny traffic coming from several networks, one option is to use a single standard ACL on the router closest to the destination. The disadvantage is that traffic from these networks will use bandwidth unnecessarily. An extended ACL could be used on each router where the traffic originated. This will save bandwidth by filtering the traffic at the source but requires creating extended ACLs on multiple routers.

Note

For CCNA certification the general rule is that extended ACLs are placed as close as possible to the source and standard ACLs are placed as close as possible to the destination.

Standard ACL Placement (9.1.5.2)

A standard ACL can only filter traffic based on a source address. The basic rule for placement of a standard ACL is to place the ACL as close as possible to the destination network. This allows the traffic to reach all other networks except the network where the packets will be filtered.

In Figure 9-14, the administrator wants to prevent traffic originating in the 192.168.10.0/24 network from reaching the 192.168.30.0/24 network.

If the standard ACL is placed on the outbound interface of R1, this would prevent traffic on the 192.168.10.0/24 network from reaching any networks reachable through the Serial 0/0/0 interface of R1.

Following the basic placement guidelines of placing the standard ACL close to the destination, Figure 9-14 shows two possible interfaces on R3 to apply the standard ACL:

- **R3 S0/0/1 interface:** Applying a standard ACL to prevent traffic from 192.168.10.0/24 from entering the S0/0/1 interface will prevent this traffic from reaching 192.168.30.0/24 and all other networks reachable by R3. This includes the 192.168.31.0/24 network. Because the intent of the ACL is to filter traffic destined only for 192.168.30.0/24, a standard ACL should not be applied to this interface.

- **R3 G0/0 interface:** Applying the standard ACL to traffic exiting the G0/0 interface will filter packets from 192.168.10.0/24 to 192.168.30.0/24. This will not affect other networks reachable by R3. Packets from 192.16810.0/24 will still be able to reach 192.168.31.0/24.

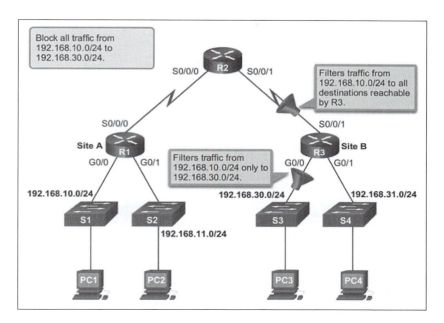

Figure 9-14   Standard ACL Placement

Extended ACL Placement (9.1.5.3)

Like a standard ACL, an extended ACL can filter traffic based on the source address. However, an extended ACL can also filter traffic based on the destination address, protocol, and port number. This allows network administrators more flexibility in the type of traffic that can be filtered and where to place the ACL. The basic rule for placing an extended ACL is to place it as close to the source as possible. This prevents unwanted traffic from being sent across multiple networks only to be denied when it reaches its destination.

Network administrators can only place ACLs on devices that they control. Therefore, placement must be determined in the context of where the control of the network administrator extends. In Figure 9-15, the administrator of Company A, which includes the 192.168.10.0/24 and 192.168.11.0/24 networks (referred to as .10 and .11 in this example), wants to control traffic to Company B. Specifically, the administrator wants to deny Telnet and FTP traffic from the .11 network to Company B's 192.168.30.0/24 (.30, in this example) network. At the same time, all other traffic from the .11 network must be permitted to leave Company A without restriction.

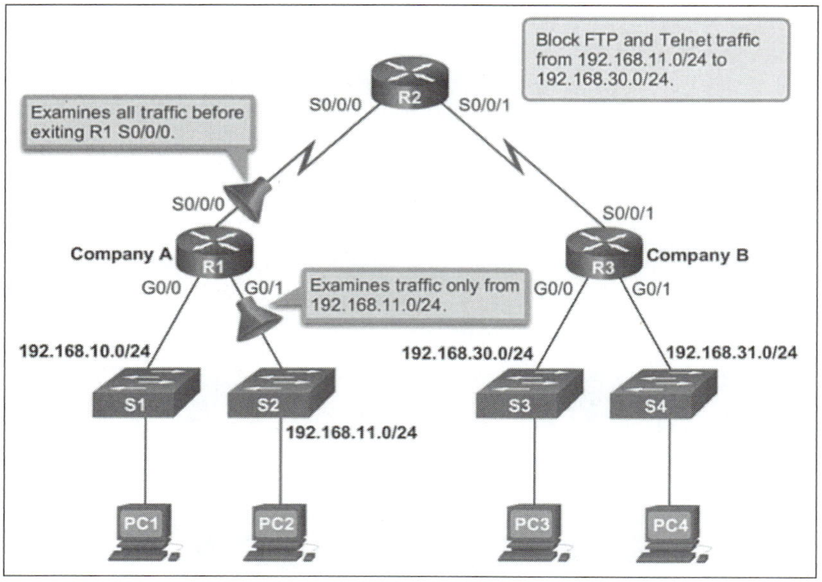

Figure 9-15   Extended ACL Placement

There are several ways to accomplish these goals. An extended ACL on R3 that blocks Telnet and FTP from the .11 network would accomplish the task, but the administrator does not control R3. In addition, this solution also allows unwanted traffic to cross the entire network, only to be blocked at the destination. This affects overall network efficiency.

A better solution is to place an extended ACL on R1 that specifies both source and destination addresses (.11 network and .30 network, respectively) and enforces the rule, "Telnet and FTP traffic from the .11 network is not allowed to go to the .30 network." Figure 9-15 shows two possible interfaces on R1 to apply the extended ACL:

- **R1 S0/0/0 interface (outbound):** One possibility is to apply an extended ACL outbound on the S0/0/0 interface. Because the extended ACL can examine both source and destination addresses, only FTP and Telnet packets from 192.168.11.0/24 will be denied. Other traffic from 192.168.11.0/24 and other networks will be forwarded by R1. The disadvantage of placing the extended ACL on this interface is that all traffic exiting S0/0/0 must be processed by the ACL, including packets from 192.168.10.0/24.

- **R1 G0/1 interface (inbound):** Applying an extended ACL to traffic entering the G0/1 interface means that only packets from the 192.168.11.0/24 network are subject to ACL processing on R1. Because the filter is to be limited to only those packets leaving the 192.168.11.0/24 network, applying the extended ACL to G0/1 is the best solution.

Interactive Graphic

Activity 9.1.5.3: Placing Standard and Extended ACLs

Go to the online course to perform this practice activity.

Standard IPv4 ACLs (9.2)

There are two types of IPv4 ACLs: standard ACLs and extended ACLs. This part of the chapter examines configuration and verification of standard ACLs. Both standard numbered ACLs and standard named ACLs are discussed.

Configure Standard IPv4 ACLs (9.2.1)

This section examines how to configure standard ACLs.

Entering Criteria Statements (9.2.1.1)

When traffic enters the router, the traffic is compared to all ACEs in the order that the entries occur in the ACL. The router continues to process the ACEs until it finds a match. The router will process the packet based on the first match found and no other ACEs will be examined.

If no matches are found when the router reaches the end of the list, the traffic is denied. This is because, by default, there is an implied deny at the end of all ACLs for traffic that was not matched to a configured entry. A single-entry ACL with only one deny entry has the effect of denying all traffic. At least one permit ACE must be configured in an ACL or all traffic is blocked.

For the network in Figure 9-16, applying either ACL 1 or ACL 2 to the S0/0/0 interface of R1 in the outbound direction will have the same effect. Network 192.168.10.0 will be permitted to access the networks reachable through S0/0/0 while 192.168.11.0 will not be allowed to access those networks.

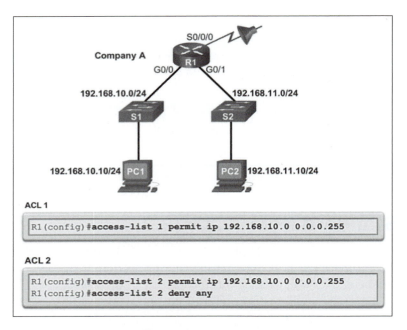

Figure 9-16   Entering Criteria Statements

Standard ACL Logic (9.2.1.2)

In Figure 9-17, packets that enter the router through interface G0/0 are checked for their source addresses based on the following entries:

```
access-list 2 deny 192.168.10.10
access-list 2 permit 192.168.10.0 0.0.0.255
access-list 2 deny 192.168.0.0 0.0.255.255
access-list 2 permit 192.0.0.0 0.255.255.255
```

Note

An ACE without the use of a wildcard mask defaults to a 0.0.0.0 wildcard mask. This has the same effect as using the **host** keyword.

If packets are permitted, they are routed through the router to an output interface. If packets are denied, they are dropped at the incoming interface.

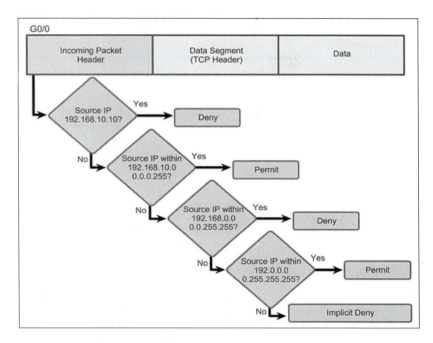

Figure 9-17   Standard ACL Logic

Configuring a Standard ACL (9.2.1.3)

To use numbered standard ACLs on a Cisco router, you must first create the standard ACL and then activate the ACL on an interface.

The **access-list** global configuration command defines a standard ACL with a number in the range of 1 through 99. Cisco IOS Software Release 12.0.1 extended these numbers by allowing 1300 to 1999 to be used for standard ACLs. This allows for a maximum of 798 possible standard ACLs. These additional numbers are referred to as expanded IP ACLs.

The full syntax of the standard ACL command is as follows:

```
Router(config)# access-list access-list-number { deny | permit | remark } source [
source-wildcard ] [ log ]
```

Table 9-9 provides a detailed explanation of the syntax for a standard ACL.

Table 9-9   Standard **access-list** Command Syntax

Parameter	Description
access-list-number	Number of an access list. This is a decimal number from 1 to 99 or from 1300 to 1999.
deny	Denies access if the conditions are matched.
permit	Permits access if the conditions are matched.
remark	Add a remark about entries in an IP access list to make the list easier to understand.
source	Number of the network or host from which the packet is being sent. There are two alternative ways to specify the source: ■ Use a 32-bit quantity in four-part, dotted-decimal format. ■ Use the **any** keyword as an abbreviation for a source and source-wildcard of 0.0.0.0 255.255.255.255.
source-wildcard	(Optional) Wildcard bits to be applied to the source. There are two alternative ways to specify the source wildcard: ■ Use a 32-bit quantity in four-part, dotted-decimal format. Place 1s in the bit positions you want to ignore. ■ Use the **any** keyword as an abbreviation for a source and source-wildcard of 0.0.0.0 255.255.255.255.
log	(Optional) Causes an informational logging message about the packet that matches the entry to be sent to the console. (The level of messages logged to the console is controlled by the **logging console** command.) The message includes the access list number, whether the packet was permitted or denied, the source address, and the number of packets. The message is generated for the first packet that matches, and then at 5-minute intervals, including the number of packets permitted or denied in the prior 5-minute interval.

ACEs can deny or permit an individual host or a range of host addresses. To create a host statement in numbered ACL 10 that permits a specific host with the IP address 192.168.10.0, you would enter:

```
R1(config)# access-list 10 permit host 192.168.10.10
```

As shown in the following example, to create a statement that will permit a range of IPv4 addresses in a numbered ACL 10 that permits all IPv4 addresses in the network 192.168.10.0/24, you would enter:

```
R1(config)# access-list 10 permit 192.168.10.0 0.0.0.255
R1(config)# exit
R1# show access-lists
```

```
Standard IP access list 10
    10 permit 192.168.10.0, wildcard bits 0.0.0.255
R1# conf t
Enter configuration commands, one per line.  End with CNTL/Z.
R1(config)# no access-list 10
R1(config)# exit
R1# show access-lists
R1#
```

To remove the ACL, the global configuration **no access-list** command is used. Issuing the **show access-list** command confirms that access list 10 has been removed.

Typically, when an administrator creates an ACL, the purpose of each statement is known and understood. However, to ensure that the administrator and others recall the purpose of a statement, remarks should be included. The **remark** keyword is used for documentation and makes access lists a great deal easier to understand. Each remark is limited to 100 characters. The following ACL, although fairly simple, is used to provide an example. When reviewing the ACL in the configuration using the **show running-config** command, the remark is also displayed.

```
R1(config)# access-list 10 remark Permit hosts from the 192.168.10.0 LAN
R1(config)# access-list 10 permit 192.168.10.0 0.0.0.255
R1(config)# exit
R1# show running-config | include access-list 10
access-list 10 remark Permit hosts from the 192.168.10.0 LAN
access-list 10 permit 192.168.10.0 0.0.0.255
R1#
```

Internal Logic (9.2.1.4)

Cisco IOS applies an internal logic when accepting and processing standard ACEs. As discussed previously, ACEs are processed sequentially. Therefore, the order in which ACEs are entered is important.

In the following example, ACL 3 contains two ACEs. The first ACE uses a wildcard mask to deny a range of addresses, which includes all hosts in the 192.168.10.0/24 network. The second ACE is a host statement that examines a specific host: 192.168.10.10. This is a host within the range of hosts that was configured in the previous statement. In other words, 192.168.10.10 is a host in the 192.168.10.0/24 network. The IOS internal logic for standard access lists rejects the second statement and returns an error message because it is a subset of the previous statement. Notice that the router automatically assigns sequence num 10 as the sequence number assigned to the first statement entered in this example. The router output includes the message that the rule is "part of the existing rule at sequence num 10" and does not accept the statement.

```
R1(config)# access-list 3 deny 192.168.10.0 0.0.0.255
R1(config)# access-list 3 permit host 192.168.10.10
% Access rule can't be configured at higher sequence num as it is part of the
    existing rule at sequence num 10
R1(config)#
```

Note

Currently, extended ACLs do not produce a similar error.

The following configuration of ACL 4 has the same two statements but in reverse order. This is a valid sequence of statements because the first statement refers to a specific host, not a range of hosts.

```
R1(config)# access-list 4 permit host 192.168.10.10
R1(config)# access-list 4 deny 192.168.10.0 0.0.0.255
R1(config)#
```

Note

A host statement can always be configured before range statements.

In the following example, ACL 5 shows that a host statement can be configured after a statement that denotes a range of hosts. The host must not be within the range covered by a previous statement. The 192.168.11.10 host address is not a member of the 192.168.10.0/24 network so this is a valid statement.

```
R1(config)# access-list 5 deny 192.168.10.0 0.0.0.255
R1(config)# access-list 5 permit host 192.168.11.10
R1(config)#
```

Note

The order in which standard ACEs are entered may not be the order that they are stored, displayed, or processed by the router. This will be discussed in a later section.

Applying Standard ACLs to Interfaces: Permit a Specific Subnet (9.2.1.5)

After a standard ACL is configured, it is linked to an interface using the **ip access-group** command in interface configuration mode:

```
Router(config-if)# ip access-group { access-list-number | access-list-name }
{ in | out }
```

To remove an ACL from an interface, first enter the **no ip access-group** command on the interface, and then enter the global **no access-list** command to remove the entire ACL.

The following lists the steps and syntax to configure and apply a numbered standard ACL on a router:

How To

Step 1.   Use the **access-list** global configuration command to create an entry in a standard IPv4 ACL:

```
R1(config)# access-list 1 permit 192.168.10.0 0.0.0.255
```

The example statement matches any address that starts with 192.168.10.x. Use the **remark** option to add a description to your ACL.

Step 2.   Use the interface **configuration** command to select an interface to which to apply the ACL:

```
R1(config)# interface serial 0/0/0
```

Step 3.   Use the **ip access-group** interface configuration command to activate the existing ACL on an interface:

```
R1(config-if)# ip access-group 1 out
```

This example activates the standard IPv4 ACL 1 on the interface as an outbound filter.

Figure 9-18 shows an example of an ACL to permit a single network.

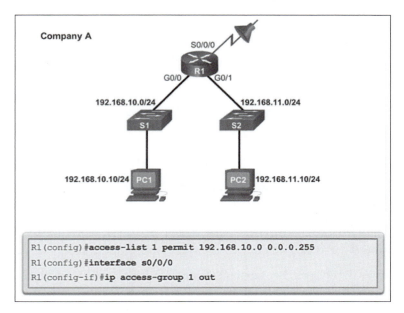

Figure 9-18   Permit a Specific Subnet

This ACL allows only traffic from source network 192.168.10.0 to be forwarded out of interface S0/0/0. Traffic from networks other than 192.168.10.0 is blocked.

The first line identifies the ACL as access list 1. It permits traffic that matches the selected parameters. In this case, the IPv4 address and wildcard mask identifying the source network is 192.168.10.0 0.0.0.255. Recall that there is an implicit deny all statement that is equivalent to adding the line **access-list 1 deny 0.0.0.0 255.255.255.255**.

The **ip access-group 1 out** interface configuration command links and ties ACL 1 to the Serial 0/0/0 interface as an outbound filter.

Therefore, ACL 1 only permits hosts from the 192.168.10.0/24 network to exit router R1. It denies any other network, including the 192.168.11.0 network.

Applying Standard ACLs to Interfaces: Deny a Specific Host (9.2.1.6)

Figure 9-19 shows an example of an ACL that permits a specific subnet except for a specific host on that subnet.

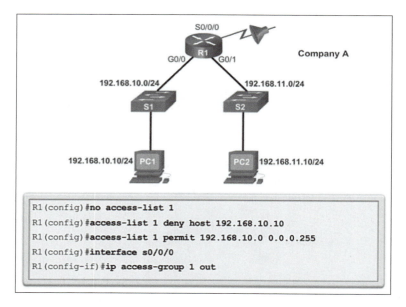

Figure 9-19 Deny a Specific Host and Permit a Specific Subnet

This ACL replaces the previous example, but also blocks traffic from a specific address. The first command deletes the previous version of ACL 1. The next ACL statement denies the PC1 host located at 192.168.10.10. Every other host on the

192.168.10.0/24 network is permitted. Again, the implicit deny statement matches every other network.

The ACL is reapplied to interface S0/0/0 in an outbound direction.

Figure 9-20 shows an example of an ACL that denies a specific host. This ACL replaces the previous example. This example still blocks traffic from host PC1 but permits all other traffic.

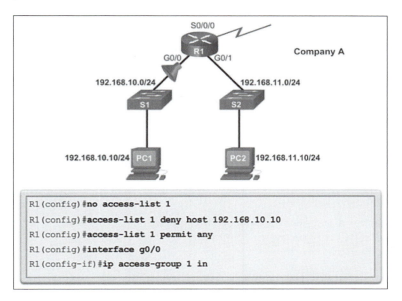

Figure 9-20   Deny a Specific Host

The first two commands are the same as the previous example. The first command deletes the previous version of ACL 1 and the next ACL statement denies the PC1 host that is located at 192.168.10.10.

The third line is new and permits all other hosts. This means that all hosts from the 192.168.10.0/24 network will be permitted except for PC1, which was denied in the previous statement.

This ACL is applied to interface G0/0 in the inbound direction. Because the filter only affects the 192.168.10.0/24 LAN on G0/0, it is more efficient to apply the ACL to the inbound interface. The ACL could be applied to S0/0/0 in the outbound direction but then R1 would have to examine packets from all networks, including 192.168.11.0/24.

Creating Named Standard ACLs (9.2.1.7)

Naming an ACL makes it easier to understand its function. For example, an ACL configured to deny FTP could be called NO_FTP. When you identify your ACL with a name instead of with a number, the configuration mode and command syntax are slightly different.

The following shows the steps required to create a standard named ACL.

Step 1. Starting from the global configuration mode, use the **ip access-list** command to create a named ACL. ACL names are alphanumeric, case sensitive, and must be unique. The command **ip access-list standard** *name* is used to create a standard named ACL, whereas the command **ip access-list extended** *name* is used for an extended access list. After entering the command, the router is in named standard ACL configuration mode as indicated by the prompt.

```
Router(config)# ip access-list {standard | extended} name
```

Alphanumeric name string must be unique and cannot begin with a number.

Note

Numbered ACLs use the global configuration command **access-list**, whereas named IPv4 ACLs use the **ip access-list** command.

Step 2. From the named ACL configuration mode, use **permit** or **deny** statements to specify one or more conditions for determining whether a packet is forwarded or dropped.

```
Router(config-std-nacl)# [permit | deny | remark] {source [source-wildcard]}
[log]
```

Step 3. Apply the ACL to an interface using the **ip access-group** command. Specify if the ACL should be applied to packets as they enter into the interface (**in**) or applied to packets as they exit the interface (**out**).

```
Router(config-if)# ip access-group name [in | out]
```

Activates the named IP ACL on an interface.

Figure 9-21 shows the commands used to configure a standard named ACL on router R1, interface G0/0 that denies host 192.168.11.10 access to the 192.168.10.0 network. The ACL is named NO_ACCESS.

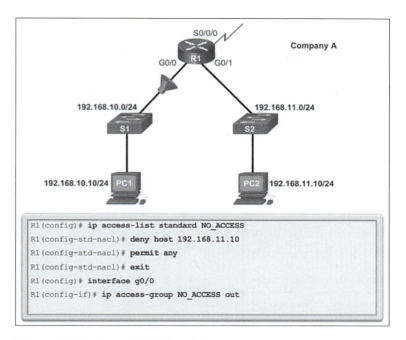

```
R1(config)# ip access-list standard NO_ACCESS
R1(config-std-nacl)# deny host 192.168.11.10
R1(config-std-nacl)# permit any
R1(config-std-nacl)# exit
R1(config)# interface g0/0
R1(config-if)# ip access-group NO_ACCESS out
```

Figure 9-21   Named ACL Example

Capitalizing ACL names is not required, but makes them stand out when viewing the running-config output. It also makes it less likely that you will accidentally create two different ACLs with the same name but with different uses of capitalization.

Commenting ACLs (9.2.1.8)

You can use the **remark** keyword to include comments (remarks) about entries in any IP standard or extended ACL. The remarks make the ACL easier for you to understand and scan. Each remark line is limited to 100 characters.

The remark can go before or after a **permit** or **deny** statement. You should be consistent about where you put the remark so that it is clear which remark describes which **permit** or **deny** statement. For example, it would be confusing to have some remarks before the associated **permit** or **deny** statements and some remarks after the statements.

To include a comment for IPv4 numbered standard or extended ACLs, use the **access-list** *access-list_number* **remark** *remark* global configuration command. To remove the remark, use the **no** form of this command.

In Example 9-3, the numbered ACL denies the 192.168.10.10 guest workstation from exiting S0/0/0 but permits all other devices from 192.168.0.0/16.

Example 9-3   Commenting a Numbered ACL

```
R1(config)# access-list 1 remark Do not allow Guest workstation through
R1(config)# access-list 1 deny host 192.168.10.10
R1(config)# access-list 1 remark Allow devices from all other 192.168.x.x subnets
R1(config)# access-list 1 permit 192.168.0.0 0.0.255.255
R1(config)# interface s0/0/0
R1(config-if)# ip access-group 1 out
R1(config-if)#
```

For an entry in a named standard or extended ACL, use the **remark** access-list configuration command. To remove the remark, use the **no** form of this command. Example 9-4 shows a standard named ACL. In this example, the remark statements indicate that the lab workstation with the host address 192.168.11.10 is denied but devices from all other networks are permitted.

Example 9-4   Commenting a Named ACL

```
R1(config)# ip access-list standard NO_ACCESS
R1(config-std-nacl)# remark Do not allow access from Lab workstation
R1(config-std-nacl)# deny host 192.168.11.10
R1(config-std-nacl)# remark Allow access from all other networks
R1(config-std-nacl)# permit any
R1(config-std-nacl)# interface G0/0
R1(config-if)# ip access-group NO_ACCESS out
R1(config-if)#
```

Activity 9.2.1.9: Configuring Standard ACLs

Go to the online course to perform this practice activity.

Packet Tracer Activity 9.2.1.10: Configuring Standard ACLs

Standard access control lists (ACLs) are router configuration scripts that control whether a router permits or denies packets based on the source address. This activity focuses on defining filtering criteria, configuring standard ACLs, applying ACLs to router interfaces, and verifying and testing the ACL implementation. The routers are already configured, including IP addresses and EIGRP routing.

Packet Tracer Activity 9.2.1.11: Configuring Named Standard ACLs

The senior network administrator has tasked you to create a standard named ACL to prevent access to a file server. All clients from one network and one specific workstation from a different network should be denied access.

Modifying IPv4 ACLs (9.2.2)

This section discusses how to modify standard and named ACLs. A standard numbered ACL can be edited either by using a text editor or by using sequence numbers.

Editing Standard Numbered ACLs: Using a Text Editor (9.2.2.1)

When configuring a standard ACL, the statements are added to the running-config. However, there is no built-in editing feature that allows you to edit a change in an ACL.

After you are familiar with creating and editing ACLs, it may be easier to construct the ACL using a text editor such as Microsoft Notepad. This allows you to create or edit the ACL and then paste it into the router. For an existing ACL, you can use the **show running-config** command to display the ACL, copy and paste it into the text editor, make the necessary changes, and paste it back in.

For example, assume that the following host IPv4 address was incorrectly entered:

```
R1(config)# access-list 1 deny host 192.168.10.99
R1(config)# access-list 1 permit 192.168.0.0 0.0.255.255
```

Instead of the 192.168.10.99 host, it should have been the 192.168.10.10 host. Here are the steps to edit and correct ACL 1:

Step 1.   Display the ACL using the **show running-config** command. The following uses the **include** keyword to display only the ACEs:

```
R1# show running-config ⊠ include access-list 1
access-list 1 deny host 192.168.10.99
access-list 1 permit 192.168.0.0 0.0.255.255
```

Step 2.   Highlight the ACL, copy it, and then paste it into Microsoft Notepad. Edit the list as required, as shown next. After the ACL is correctly displayed in Microsoft Notepad, highlight it and copy it.

```
<Text editor>
access-list 1 deny host 192.168.10.10
access-list permit 192.168.0.0 0.0.255.255
```

Step 3.   In global configuration mode, remove the access list using the **no access-list 1** command. Otherwise, the new statements would be appended to the existing ACL. Then paste the new ACL into the configuration of the router.

```
R1# config t
Enter configuration commands, one per line. End with CNTL/Z.
R1(config)# no access-list 1
R1(config)# access-list 1 deny host 192.168.10.10
R1(config)# access-list 1 permit 192.168.0.0 0.0.255.255
```

Step 4.   Using the **show running-config** command, verify the changes:

```
R1# show running-config ⊠ include access-list 1
access-list 1 deny host 192.168.10.10
access-list 1 permit 192.168.0.0 0.0.255.255
```

It should be mentioned that when using the **no access-list** command, different IOS software releases act differently. If the ACL that has been deleted is still applied to an interface, some IOS versions act as if no ACL is protecting your network while others deny all traffic. For this reason it is good practice to remove the reference to the access list from the interface before modifying the access list. Also, be aware that if there is an error in the new list, you need to disable it and troubleshoot the problem. In that instance, again, the network has no ACL during the correction process.

Editing Standard Numbered ACLs: Using the Sequence Number (9.2.2.2)

As shown next, the initial configuration of ACL 1 included a host statement for host 192.168.10.99:

```
R1(config)# access-list 1 deny host 192.168.10.99
R1(config)# access-list 1 permit 192.168.0.0 0.0.255.255
```

This was in error. The host should have been configured as 192.168.10.10. To edit the ACL using sequence numbers, follow these steps:

How To

Step 1.   Display the current ACL using the **show access-lists 1** command. The output from this command will be discussed in more detail later in this section. The sequence number is displayed at the beginning of each statement. The sequence number was automatically assigned when the access list statement was entered. Notice that the misconfigured statement has the sequence number 10.

```
R1# show access-lists 1
Standard IP access list 1
    10 deny   192.168.10.99
    20 permit 192.168.0.0, wildcard bits 0.0.255.255
R1#
```

Step 2. Enter the **ip access-lists standard** command that is used to configure named ACLs. The ACL number, 1, is used as the name. First, the misconfigured statement needs to be deleted using the **no 10** command, with 10 referring to the sequence number. Next, a new sequence number 10 statement is added using the command **10 deny host 192.168.10.10**. Complete the changes by using the **end** command.

```
R1# conf t
R1(config)# ip access-list standard 1
R1(config-std-nacl)# no 10
R1(config-std-nacl)# 10 deny host 192.168.10.10
R1(config-std-nacl)# end
R1#
```

> **Note**
>
> Statements cannot be overwritten using the same sequence number as an existing statement. The current statement must be deleted first, and then the new one can be added.

Step 3. Verify the changes using the **show access-lists** command:

```
R1# show access-lists
Standard IP access list 1
    10 deny   192.168.10.10
    20 permit 192.168.0.0, wildcard bits 0.0.255.255
R1#
```

As discussed previously, Cisco IOS implements an internal logic to standard access lists. The order in which standard ACEs are entered may not be the order in which they are stored, displayed, or processed by the router. The **show access-lists** command displays the ACEs with their sequence numbers.

Editing Standard Named ACLs (9.2.2.3)

In the example in the previous section, sequence numbers were used to edit a standard numbered ACL. By referring to the statement sequence numbers, individual statements can easily be inserted or deleted. This method can also be used to edit standard named ACLs.

The output shows an example of inserting a line into a named ACL.

```
R1# show access-lists
Standard IP access list NO_ACCESS
    10 deny   192.168.11.10
    20 permit 192.168.11.0, wildcard bits 0.0.0.255
R1# conf t
Enter configuration commands, one per line.  End with CNTL/Z.
```

```
R1(config)# ip access-list standard NO_ACCESS
R1(config-std-nacl)# 15 deny host 192.168.11.11
R1(config-std-nacl)# end
R1# show access-lists
Standard IP access list NO_ACCESS
    10 deny    192.168.11.10
    15 deny    192.168.11.11
    20 permit 192.168.11.0, wildcard bits 0.0.0.255
R1#
```

- In the first **show** command output, you can see that the ACL named NO_ACCESS has two numbered lines indicating access rules for a workstation with the IPv4 address 192.168.11.10.

- The **ip access-list standard** command is used to configure named ACLs. From named access list configuration mode, statements can be inserted or removed. The **no** *sequence-number* command is used to delete individual statements.

- To add a statement to deny another workstation requires inserting a numbered line. In the example, the workstation with the IPv4 address 192.168.11.11 is being added using a new sequence number of 15. Complete the changes by using the **end** command.

- The final **show** command output verifies that the new workstation is now denied access.

Verifying ACLs (9.2.2.4)

As shown in the following example, the **show ip interface** command is used to verify the ACL on the interface. The output from this command includes the number or name of the access list and the direction in which the ACL was applied. The output shows router R1 has the access list 1 applied to its S0/0/0 outbound interface and the access list NO_ACCESS applied to its g0/0 interface, also in the outbound direction.

```
R1# show ip interface s0/0/0
Serial0/0/0 is up, line protocol is up
  Internet address is 10.1.1.1/30
  <output omitted>
  Outgoing access list is 1
  Inbound  access list is not set
 <output omitted>
R1# show ip interface g0/0
GigabitEthernet0/0 is up, line protocol is up
  Internet address is 192.168.10.1/24
  <output omitted>
  Outgoing access list is NO_ACCESS
  Inbound  access list is not set
  <output omitted>
```

The following example shows the result of issuing the **show access-lists** command on router R1. To view an individual access list, use the **show access-lists** command followed by the access list number or name. The NO_ACCESS statements may look strange. Notice that sequence number 15 is displayed prior to sequence number 10. This is a result of the router internal process.

```
R1# show access-lists
Standard IP access list 1
    10 deny   192.168.10.10
    20 permit 192.168.0.0, wildcard bits 0.0.255.255
Standard IP access list NO_ACCESS
    15 deny   192.168.11.11
    10 deny   192.168.11.10
    20 permit 192.168.11.0, wildcard bits 0.0.0.255
R1#
```

ACL Statistics (9.2.2.5)

Once the ACL has been applied to an interface and some testing has occurred, the **show access-lists** command will show statistics for each statement that has been matched. In the output in Figure 9-22, note that some of the statements have been matched. When traffic is generated that should match an ACL statement, the matches shown in the **show access-lists** command output should increase. For instance in this example, if a ping is issued from PC1 to PC3 or PC4, the output will show an increase in the matches for the deny statement of ACL 1.

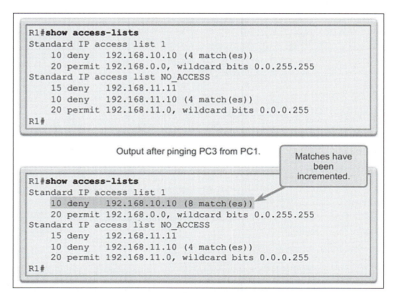

Figure 9-22 Viewing ACL Statistics

Both permit and deny statements will track statistics for matches; however, recall that every ACL has an implied deny any as the last statement. This statement will not appear in the **show access-lists** command, therefore, statistics for that statement will not appear. To view statistics for the implied deny any statement, the statement can be configured manually and will appear in the output. Extreme caution should be taken when manually configuring the deny any statement, as it will match all traffic. If this statement is not configured as the last statement in the ACL, it could cause unexpected results.

During testing of an ACL, the counters can be cleared using the **clear access-list counters** command. This command can be used alone or with the number or name of a specific ACL. As shown in Figure 9-23 this command clears the statistic counters for an ACL.

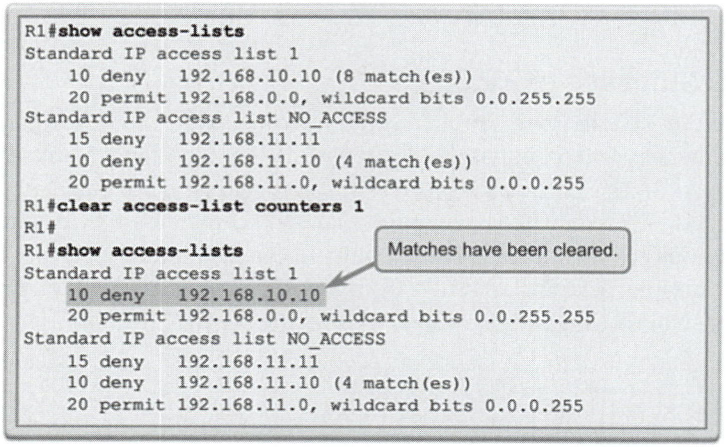

```
R1#show access-lists
Standard IP access list 1
    10 deny    192.168.10.10 (8 match(es))
    20 permit 192.168.0.0, wildcard bits 0.0.255.255
Standard IP access list NO_ACCESS
    15 deny    192.168.11.11
    10 deny    192.168.11.10 (4 match(es))
    20 permit 192.168.11.0, wildcard bits 0.0.0.255
R1#clear access-list counters 1
R1#
R1#show access-lists                    ┌─────────────────────────────┐
Standard IP access list 1               │ Matches have been cleared.  │
    10 deny    192.168.10.10             └─────────────────────────────┘
    20 permit 192.168.0.0, wildcard bits 0.0.255.255
Standard IP access list NO_ACCESS
    15 deny    192.168.11.11
    10 deny    192.168.11.10 (4 match(es))
    20 permit 192.168.11.0, wildcard bits 0.0.0.255
```

Figure 9-23   Clearing ACL Statistics

Standard ACL Sequence Numbers (9.2.2.6)

Cisco IOS implements an internal logic to standard ACLs. As discussed previously, part of this logic prevents host statements from being configured after a range statement if the host is a member of that range, as shown in the following output:

```
R1(config)# access-list 3 deny 192.168.10.0 0.0.0.255
R1(config)# access-list 3 permit host 192.168.10.10
Access rule can't be configured at higher sequence num as it is part of the existing
    rule at sequence num 10
R1(config)#
```

Another part of the IOS internal logic involves the internal sequencing of standard ACEs. Figure 9-24 shows the configuration of a standard access list. Range statements that deny three networks are configured first followed by five host statements.

The host statements are all valid statements because their host IP addresses are not part of the previously entered range statements.

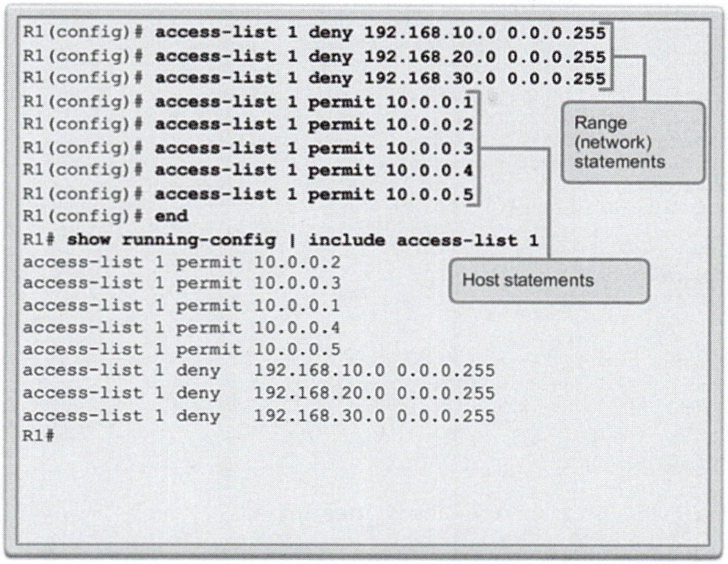

```
R1(config)# access-list 1 deny 192.168.10.0 0.0.0.255
R1(config)# access-list 1 deny 192.168.20.0 0.0.0.255
R1(config)# access-list 1 deny 192.168.30.0 0.0.0.255
R1(config)# access-list 1 permit 10.0.0.1
R1(config)# access-list 1 permit 10.0.0.2
R1(config)# access-list 1 permit 10.0.0.3
R1(config)# access-list 1 permit 10.0.0.4
R1(config)# access-list 1 permit 10.0.0.5
R1(config)# end
R1# show running-config | include access-list 1
access-list 1 permit 10.0.0.2
access-list 1 permit 10.0.0.3
access-list 1 permit 10.0.0.1
access-list 1 permit 10.0.0.4
access-list 1 permit 10.0.0.5
access-list 1 deny    192.168.10.0 0.0.0.255
access-list 1 deny    192.168.20.0 0.0.0.255
access-list 1 deny    192.168.30.0 0.0.0.255
R1#
```

Range (network) statements

Host statements

Figure 9-24   Sequencing Considerations During Configuration

The **show running-config** command is used to verify the ACL configuration. Notice that the statements are listed in a different order than they were entered. We will use the **show access-lists** command to understand the logic behind this.

As shown in Figure 9-25, the **show access-lists** command displays ACEs along with their sequence numbers. We might expect the order of the statements in the output to reflect the order in which they were entered. However, the **show access-lists** output shows that this is not the case.

The order in which the standard ACEs are listed is the sequence used by the IOS to process the list. Notice that the statements are grouped into two sections, host statements followed by range statements. The sequence number indicates the order in which the statement was entered, not the order in which the statement will be processed.

The host statements are listed first but not necessarily in the order in which they were entered. The IOS puts host statements in an order using a special hashing function. The resulting order optimizes the search for a host ACL entry.

```
R1# show access-lists 1
Standard IP access list 1
  50 permit 10.0.0.2
  60 permit 10.0.0.3
  40 permit 10.0.0.1          Host statements are listed first, in an order to be
  70 permit 10.0.0.4          efficiently processed by the IOS.
  80 permit 10.0.0.5
  10 deny    192.168.10.0, wildcard bits 0.0.0.255
  20 deny    192.168.20.0, wildcard bits 0.0.0.255
  30 deny    192.168.30.0, wildcard bits 0.0.0.255
R1# copy running-config startup-config
R1# reload
R1# show access-lists 1              Range statements are listed after host
Standard IP access list 1           statements, in the order they were entered.
  10 permit 10.0.0.2
  20 permit 10.0.0.3
  30 permit 10.0.0.1
  40 permit 10.0.0.4
  50 permit 10.0.0.5
  60 deny    192.168.10.0, wildcard bits 0.0.0.255
  70 deny    192.168.20.0, wildcard bits 0.0.0.255
  80 deny    192.168.30.0, wildcard bits 0.0.0.255
R1#
```

Figure 9-25   Sequence Numbers After Reload

The range statements are displayed after the host statements. These statements are listed in the order in which they were entered.

Recall that standard and numbered ACLs can be edited using sequence numbers. The sequence number shown in the **show access-lists** command output is the number used when deleting an individual statement from the list. When inserting a new ACL statement, the sequence number will only affect the location of a range statement in the list. Host statements will always be put in order using the hashing function.

Continuing with the example, after saving the running-configuration, the router is reloaded (rebooted). As shown in Figure 9-25, the **show access-lists** command displays the ACL in the same order, but the statements have been renumbered. The sequence numbers are now in numerical order.

Note

The hashing function is only applied to host statements in an IPv4 standard access list. The algorithm is not used for IPv4 extended ACLs or IPv6 ACLs. This is because extended and IPv6 ACLs filter on more than just a single source address. The details of the hashing function are beyond the scope of this course.

Lab 9.2.2.7: Configuring and Verifying Standard ACLs

In this lab, you will complete the following objectives:

- Part 1: Set Up the Topology and Initialize Devices
- Part 2: Configure Devices and Verify Connectivity
- Part 3: Configure and Verify Standard Numbered and Named ACLs
- Part 4: Modify a Standard ACL

Securing VTY Ports with a Standard IPv4 ACL (9.2.3)

This section describes the use of IP ACLs to help secure Telnet connections.

Configuring a Standard ACL to Secure a VTY Port (9.2.3.1)

IP ACLs can be used to help restrict Telnet connectivity when SSH is not available.

Using an ACL to Control VTY Access

Cisco recommends using SSH for administrative connections to routers and switches. If the Cisco IOS Software image on your router does not support SSH, you can improve the security of administrative lines by restricting VTY access. This technique can also be used with SSH to further improve administrative access security.

Restricting VTY access is a technique that allows you to define which IP addresses are allowed Telnet or SSH access to the router EXEC process. You can control which administrative workstation or network manages your router with an ACL and an **access-class** statement configured on your VTY lines.

The **access-class** command configured in line configuration mode restricts incoming and outgoing connections between a particular VTY (into a Cisco device) and the addresses in an access list.

Standard and extended access lists apply to packets that travel through a router. They are not designed to block packets that originate within the router. An outbound Telnet extended ACL does not prevent router-initiated Telnet sessions, by default.

Filtering Telnet or SSH traffic is typically considered an extended IP ACL function because it filters a higher level protocol. However, because the **access-class** command is used to filter incoming or outgoing Telnet/SSH sessions by source address, a standard ACL can be used.

The command syntax of the **access-class** command is:

```
Router(config-line)# access-class access-list-number { in [ vrf-also ] | out }
```

The parameter **in** restricts incoming connections between the addresses in the access list and the Cisco device, while the parameter **out** restricts outgoing connections between a particular Cisco device and the addresses in the access list.

An example allowing a range of addresses to access VTY lines 0 to 4 is shown in Figure 9-26. The ACL in the figure is configured to permit network 192.168.10.0 to access VTY lines 0–4 but deny all other networks.

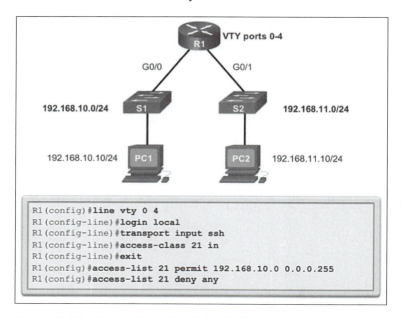

Figure 9-26   Permit Only 192.168.10.0/24 Access to VTY Lines

The following should be considered when configuring access lists on VTYs:

- Only numbered access lists can be applied to VTYs.

- Identical restrictions should be set on all the VTYs, because a user can attempt to connect to any of them.

Activity 9.2.3.1: Securing VTY Access

Go to the online course to use the Syntax Checker in the second graphic to practice securing VTY access.

Verifying a Standard ACL Used to Secure a VTY Port (9.2.3.2)

After the ACL to restrict access to the VTY lines is configured, it is important to verify that it is working as expected. Figure 9-27 shows two devices attempting to connect to R1 using SSH. Access list 21 has been configured on the VTY lines on R1. PC1 is successful while PC2 fails to establish an SSH connection. This is the expected behavior, as the configured access list permits VTY access from the 192.168.10.0/24 network while denying all other devices.

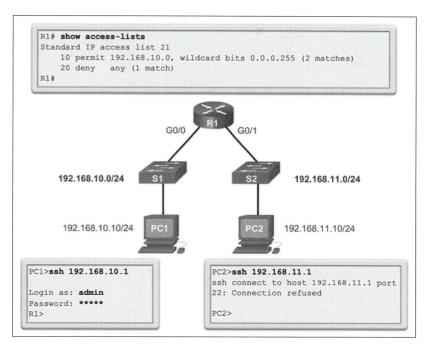

Figure 9-27   Verifying a Standard ACL Securing a VTY Port

The output for R1 shows the result of issuing the **show access-lists** command after the SSH attempts by PC1 and PC2. The match in the permit line of the output is a result of a successful SSH connection by PC1. The match in the deny statement is due to the failed attempt to create an SSH connection by PC2, a device on the 192.168.11.0/24 network.

Packet Tracer Activity 9.2.3.3: Configuring an ACL on VTY Lines

As administrator of a network, you need to have remote access to your router. This access should not be available to other users of the network. Therefore, you will configure and apply an ACL that allows PC access to the Telnet lines, but denies all other source IP addresses.

Lab 9.2.3.4: Configuring and Verifying VTY Restrictions

In this lab, you will complete the following objectives:

- Part 1: Configure Basic Device Settings
- Part 2: Configure and Apply the Access Control List on R1
- Part 3: Verify the Access Control List Using Telnet
- Part 4: Challenge - Configure and Apply the Access Control List on S1

Extended IPv4 ACLs (9.3)

Standard IPv4 ACLs only filter on source IPv4 addresses. Extended IPv4 ACLs can filter on the source IPv4 addresses along with other information.

Structure of an Extended IPv4 ACL (9.3.1)

The structure of an extended IPv4 is similar to that of a standard IPv4 ACL, but, as the name suggests, it offers some additional options to be used to filter network traffic.

Extended ACLs: Testing Packets (9.3.1.1)

For more precise traffic-filtering control, you can use extended ACLs numbered 100 to 199 and 2000 to 2699, providing a total of 798 possible extended ACLs. Extended ACLs can also be named.

Extended ACLs are used more often than standard ACLs because they provide a greater degree of control. As shown in Figure 9-28, like standard ACLs, extended ACLs check source addresses of packets, but they also check the destination addresses, protocols, and port numbers (or services). This provides a greater range of criteria on which to base the ACL. For example, an extended ACL can simultaneously allow email traffic from a network to a specific destination while denying file transfers and web browsing.

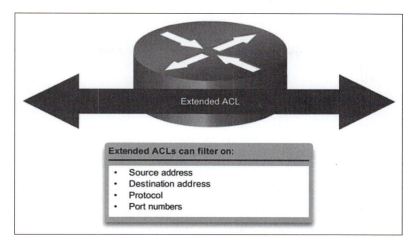

Figure 9-28   Extended ACLs

Extended ACLs: Testing Ports and Services (9.3.1.2)

The ability to filter on protocol and port number allows network administrators to build very specific extended ACLs. An application can be specified by configuring either the port number or the name of a well-known port.

The following are some examples of how an administrator specifies a TCP or UDP port number by placing the port number at the end of the extended ACL statement. Logical operations can be used, such as equal (**eq**), not equal (**neq**), greater than (**gt**), and less than (**lt**).

Using port numbers:

```
access-list 114 permit tcp 192.168.20.0 0.0.0.255 any eq 23
access-list 114 permit tcp 192.168.20.0 0.0.0.255 any eq 21
access-list 114 permit tcp 192.168.20.0 0.0.0.255 any eq 20
```

Using keywords:

```
access-list 114 permit tcp 192.168.20.0 0.0.0.255 any eq telnet
access-list 114 permit tcp 192.168.20.0 0.0.0.255 any eq ftp
access-list 114 permit tcp 192.168.20.0 0.0.0.255 any eq ftp-data
```

The following shows how to display a list of port numbers and keywords that can be used when building an ACL:

```
R1(config)# access-list 101 permit tcp any any eq ?
  <0-65535>            Port number
  bgp                 Border Gateway Protocol (179)
  chargen             Character generator (19)
  cmd                 Remote commands (rcmd, 514)
  connectedapps-plain ConnectedApps Cleartext (15001)
```

connectedapps-tls	ConnectedApps TLS (15002)
daytime	Daytime (13)
discard	Discard (9)
domain	Domain Name Service (53)
echo	Echo (7)
exec	Exec (rsh, 512)
finger	Finger (79)
ftp	File Transfer Protocol (21)
ftp-data	FTP data connections (20)
gopher	Gopher (70)
hostname	NIC hostname server (101)
ident	Ident Protocol (113)
irc	Internet Relay Chat (194)
klogin	Kerberos login (543)
kshell	Kerberos shell (544)
login	Login (rlogin, 513)
lpd	Printer service (515)
msrpc	MS Remote Procedure Call (135)
nntp	Network News Transport Protocol (119)
pim-auto-rp	PIM Auto-RP (496)
pop2	Post Office Protocol v2 (109)
pop3	Post Office Protocol v3 (110)
smtp	Simple Mail Transport Protocol (25)
sunrpc	Sun Remote Procedure Call (111)
syslog	Syslog (514)
tacacs	TAC Access Control System (49)
talk	Talk (517)
telnet	Telnet (23)
time	Time (37)
uucp	Unix-to-Unix Copy Program (540)
whois	Nicname (43)
www	World Wide Web (HTTP, 80)

```
R1(config)# access-list 101 permit tcp any any eq
```

Configure Extended IPv4 ACLs (9.3.2)

This section describes the configuration of extended IPv4 ACLs.

Configuring Extended ACLs (9.3.2.1)

The procedural steps for configuring extended ACLs are the same as for standard ACLs. The extended ACL is first configured, and then it is activated on an interface. However, the command syntax and parameters are more complex to support the additional features provided by extended ACLs.

Note

The internal logic applied to the ordering of standard ACL statements does not apply to extended ACLs. The order in which the statements are entered during configuration is the order in which they are displayed and processed.

The following shows the common command syntax for extended IPv4 ACLs. Note that there are many keywords and parameters for extended ACLs. It is not necessary to use all of the keywords and parameters when configuring an extended ACL. Recall that the ? can be used to get help when entering complex commands.

```
access-list access-list-number {deny | permit | remark} protocol source source-wild-
card [operator operand [port port-number or name]] destination destination-wildcard
[operator operand [port port-number or name]] [established]
```

The parameters and their descriptions are as follows:

- *access-list-number*: Number of an access list. This is a decimal number from 100 to 199 or from 2000 to 2699.

- **deny:** Denies access if the conditions are matched.

- **permit:** Permits access if the conditions are matched.

- **remark:** Used to enter a remark or comment.

- *protocol*: Name or number of an Internet protocol. It can be one of the keywords **eigrp**, **icmp**, **ip**, **ospf**, **tcp**, or **udp**, or an integer in the range from 0 to 255 representing an Internet protocol number. To match any Internet protocol (including ICMP, TCP, and UDP), use the **ip** keyword.

- *source*: Number of the network or host from which the packet is being sent.

- *source-wildcard*: Wildcard bits to be applied to source.

- *destination*: Number of the network or host to which the packet is being sent.

- *destination-wildcard*: Wildcard bits to be applied to the destination.

- *operator*: (Optional) Compares source or destination ports. Possible operands include **lt** (less than), **gt** (greater than), **eq** (equal), **neq** (not equal), and **range** (inclusive range).

- *port*: (Optional) The decimal number or name of a TCP or UDP port.

- **established:** (Optional) For the TCP protocol only. Indicates an established connection. A match occurs if the TCP datagram has the ACK or RST control bits set. The nonmatching case is that of the initial TCP datagram to form a connection.

Figure 9-29 shows an example of an extended ACL. In this example, the network administrator has configured ACLs to restrict network access to allow website browsing only from the LAN attached to interface G0/0 to any external network. ACL 103 allows traffic coming from any address on the 192.168.10.0 network to go to any destination, subject to the limitation that the traffic is using ports 80 (HTTP) and 443 (HTTPS) only.

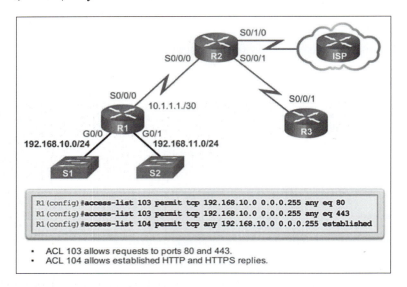

Figure 9-29   Example of Configuring Extended ACLs

The nature of HTTP requires that traffic flow back into the network from websites accessed from internal clients. The network administrator wants to restrict that return traffic to HTTP exchanges from requested websites, while denying all other traffic. ACL 104 does that by blocking all incoming traffic, except for previously established connections. The permit statement in ACL 104 allows inbound traffic using the **established** parameter.

The **established** parameter allows only responses to traffic that originates from the 192.168.10.0/24 network to return to that network. A match occurs if the returning TCP segment has the ACK or reset (RST) bits set, which indicates that the packet belongs to an existing connection. Without the **established** parameter in the ACL statement, clients could send traffic to a web server, but not receive traffic returning from the web server.

Applying Extended ACLs to Interfaces (9.3.2.2)

In the previous example, the network administrator configured an ACL to allow users from the 192.168.10.0/24 network to browse both insecure and secure websites. Even though it has been configured, the ACL will not filter traffic until it is applied to an interface. To apply an ACL to an interface, first consider whether the traffic to be filtered is going in or out. When a user on the internal LAN accesses a website on the

Internet, traffic is going out to the Internet. When an internal user receives an email from the Internet, traffic is coming into the local router. However, when applying an ACL to an interface, in and out take on different meanings. From an ACL consideration, in and out are in reference to the router interface.

In the topology in Figure 9-30, R1 has three interfaces. It has a serial interface, S0/0/0, and two Gigabit Ethernet interfaces, G0/0 and G0/1. Recall that an extended ACL should typically be applied close to the source. In this topology the interface closest to the source of the target traffic is the G0/0 interface.

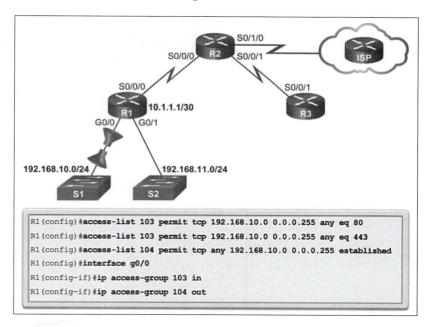

Figure 9-30   Applying an ACL to an Interface

Web request traffic from users on the 192.168.10.0/24 LAN is inbound to the G0/0 interface. Return traffic from established connections to users on the LAN is outbound from the G0/0 interface. The example applies the ACL to the G0/0 interface in both directions. The inbound ACL, 103, checks for the type of traffic. The outbound ACL, 104, checks for return traffic from established connections. This will restrict 192.168.10.0 Internet access to allow only website browsing.

Note

The access lists could have been applied to the S0/0/0 interface, but in that case, the router's ACL process would have to examine all packets entering the router, not only traffic to and from 192.168.11.0. This would cause unnecessary processing by the router.

Filtering Traffic with Extended ACLs (9.3.2.3)

The example shown in Figure 9-31 denies FTP traffic from subnet 192.168.11.0 that is going to subnet 192.168.10.0, but permits all other traffic. Note the use of wildcard masks and the explicit deny any statement. Remember that FTP uses TCP ports 20 and 21; therefore the ACL requires both port name keywords **ftp** and **ftp-data** or **eq 20** and **eq 21** to deny FTP.

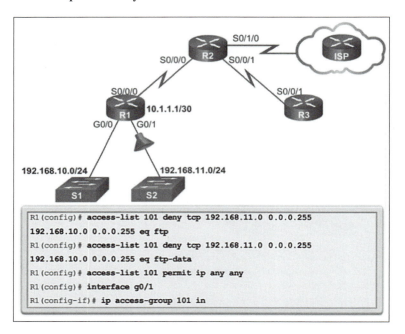

Figure 9-31   Extended ACL to Deny FTP

If using port numbers instead of port names, the commands would be written as:

```
access-list 101 permit tcp 192.168.11.0 0.0.0.255 192.168.10.0 0.0.0.255 eq 20
access-list 101 permit tcp 192.168.11.0 0.0.0.255 192.168.10.0 0.0.0.255 eq 21
```

To prevent the implied deny any statement at the end of the ACL from blocking all traffic, the permit ip any any statement is added. Without at least one permit statement in an ACL, all traffic on the interface where that ACL was applied would be dropped. The ACL should be applied inbound on the G0/1 interface so that traffic from the 192.168.11.0/24 LAN is filtered as it enters the router interface.

The example shown in Figure 9-32 denies Telnet traffic from any source to the 192.168.11.0/24 LAN, but allows all other IP traffic. Because traffic destined for the 192.168.11.0/24 LAN is outbound on interface G0/1, the ACL would be applied to G0/1 using the **out** keyword. Note the use of the **any** keywords in the permit statement. This permit statement is added to ensure that no other traffic is blocked.

Note

The examples in Figures 9-31 and 9-32 both use the permit ip any any statement at the end of the ACL. For greater security the **permit 192.168.11.0 0.0.0.255 any** command may be used.

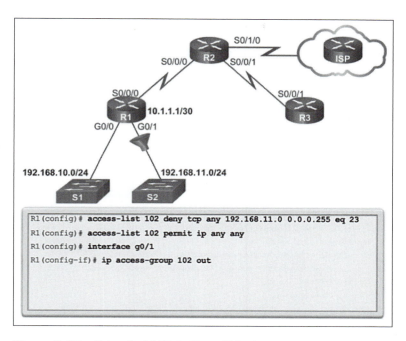

Figure 9-32   Extended ACL to Deny Telnet

Creating Named Extended ACLs (9.3.2.4)

Named extended ACLs are created in essentially the same way that named standard ACLs are created. Follow these steps to create an extended ACL, using names:

Step 1.   From global configuration mode, use the **ip access-list extended** *name* command to define a name for the extended ACL.

Step 2.   In named ACL configuration mode, specify the conditions to **permit** or **deny**.

Step 3.   Return to privileged EXEC mode and verify the ACL with the **show access-lists** *name* command.

Step 4.   Save the entries in the configuration file with the **copy running-config startup-config** command.

To remove a named extended ACL, use the **no ip access-list extended** *name* global configuration command.

Figure 9-33 shows the named versions of the ACLs created in the previous examples. The named ACL, SURFING, permits the users on the 192.168.10.0/24 LAN to access websites. The named ACL, BROWSING, allows the return traffic from established connections. Using the ACL names, the rules are applied inbound and outbound on the G0/0 interface.

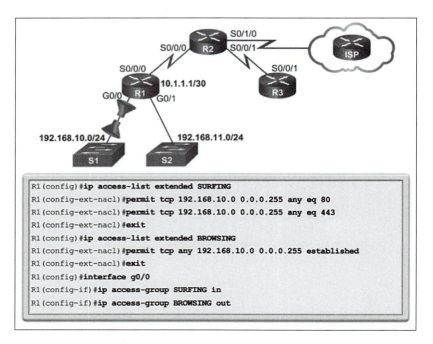

```
R1(config)#ip access-list extended SURFING
R1(config-ext-nacl)#permit tcp 192.168.10.0 0.0.0.255 any eq 80
R1(config-ext-nacl)#permit tcp 192.168.10.0 0.0.0.255 any eq 443
R1(config-ext-nacl)#exit
R1(config)#ip access-list extended BROWSING
R1(config-ext-nacl)#permit tcp any 192.168.10.0 0.0.0.255 established
R1(config-ext-nacl)#exit
R1(config)#interface g0/0
R1(config-if)#ip access-group SURFING in
R1(config-if)#ip access-group BROWSING out
```

Figure 9-33 Creating Named Extended ACLs

Verifying Extended ACLs (9.3.2.5)

After an ACL has been configured and applied to an interface, use Cisco IOS **show** commands to verify the configuration. The top example below shows the Cisco IOS command used to display the contents of all ACLs. The bottom example shows the result of issuing the **show ip interface g0/0** command on router R1.

```
R1# show access-lists
Extended IP access list BROWSING
    10 permit tcp any 192.168.10.0 0.0.0.255 established
Extended IP access list SURFING
    10 permit tcp 192.168.10.0 0.0.0.255 any eq www
    20 permit tcp 192.168.10.0 0.0.0.255 any eq 443
R1#
R1# show ip interface g0/0
GigabitEthernet0/0 is up, line protocol is up
  Internet address is 192.168.10.1/24
```

```
<output omitted for brevity>
Outgoing access list is BROWSING
Inbound  access list is SURFING
<Output omitted for brevity>
```

Unlike standard ACLs, extended ACLs do not implement the same internal logic and hashing function. The output and sequence numbers displayed in the **show access-lists** command output is the order in which the statements were entered. Host entries are not automatically listed prior to range entries.

The **show ip interface** command is used to verify the ACL on the interface and the direction in which it was applied. The output from this command includes the number or name of the access list and the direction in which the ACL was applied. The capitalized ACL names BROWSING and SURFING stand out in the screen output.

After an ACL configuration has been verified, the next step is to confirm that the ACLs work as planned, blocking and permitting traffic as expected.

The guidelines discussed earlier in this section suggest that ACLs should be configured on a test network and then implemented on the production network.

Editing Extended ACLs (9.3.2.6)

Editing an extended ACL can be accomplished using the same process as editing a standard ACL, as discussed earlier in the chapter. An extended ACL can be modified using:

- **Text editor (Method 1):** Using this method, the ACL is copied and pasted into the text editor where the changes are made. The current access list is removed using the **no access-list** command. The modified ACL is then pasted back into the configuration.

- **Sequence numbers (Method 2):** Sequence numbers can be used to delete or insert an ACL statement. The **ip access-list extended** *name* command is used to enter named-ACL configuration mode. If the ACL is numbered instead of named, the ACL number is used in the *name* parameter. ACEs can be inserted or removed.

In Figure 9-34 the administrator needs to edit the ACL named SURFING to correct a typo in the source network statement. To view the current sequence numbers, the **show access-lists** command is used. The statement to be edited is identified as statement 10. The original statement is removed with the **no** *sequence_#* command. The corrected statement is added, replacing the original statement.

```
R1# show access-lists
Extended IP access list BROWSING
    10 permit tcp any 192.168.10.0 0.0.0.255 established
Extended IP access list SURFING
    10 permit tcp 192.168.11.0 0.0.0.255 any eq www          Should be
    20 permit tcp 192.168.10.0 0.0.0.255 any eq 443          192.168.10.0
R1#
R1# configure terminal
R1(config)# ip access-list extended SURFING
R1(config-ext-nacl)# no 10
R1(config-ext-nacl)# 10 permit tcp 192.168.10.0 0.0.0.255 any eq
www
R1(config-ext-nacl)# end
R1#
R1# show access-lists
Extended IP access list BROWSING
    10 permit tcp any 192.168.10.0 0.0.0.255 established
Extended IP access list SURFING
    10 permit tcp 192.168.10.0 0.0.0.255 any eq www
    20 permit tcp 192.168.10.0 0.0.0.255 any eq 443
```

Figure 9-34   Editing Extended ACLs

Activity 9.3.2.7: Creating an Extended ACL Statement

Go to the online course to perform this practice activity.

Activity 9.3.2.8: Evaluating Extended ACEs

Go to the online course to perform this practice activity.

Activity 9.3.2.9: ACL Testlet

Go to the online course to perform this practice activity.

Packet Tracer Activity 9.3.2.10: Configuring Extended ACLs - Scenario 1

Two employees need access to services provided by the server. PC1 only needs FTP access while PC2 only needs web access. Both computers will be able to ping the server, but not each other.

Packet Tracer Activity 9.3.2.11: Configuring Extended ACLs - Scenario 2

In this scenario, devices on one LAN are allowed to remotely access devices in another LAN using the Telnet protocol. Besides ICMP, all traffic from other networks is denied.

Packet Tracer Activity 9.3.2.12: Configuring Extended ACLs - Scenario 3

In this scenario, specific devices on the LAN are allowed to access various services on servers located on the Internet.

Lab 9.3.2.13: Configuring and Verifying Extended ACLs

In this lab, you will complete the following objectives:

- Part 1: Set Up the Topology and Initialize Devices
- Part 2: Configure Devices and Verify Connectivity
- Part 3: Configure and Verify Extended Numbered and Named ACLs
- Part 4: Modify and Verify Extended ACLs

Troubleshoot ACLs (9.4)

Using the **show** commands described earlier in the chapter reveals most of the more common ACL errors before they cause problems in your network. Hopefully, you are using a good test procedure to protect your network from errors during the development stage of your ACL implementation.

When you look at an ACL, check it against the rules you learned about how to build ACLs correctly. Most errors occur because these basic rules are ignored. In fact, the most common errors are entering ACL statements in the wrong order and not applying adequate criteria to your rules.

Processing Packets with ACLs (9.4.1)

To properly configure and troubleshoot ACLs, it is necessary to understand the ACL logic and decision process.

Inbound and Outbound ACL Logic (9.4.1.1)

This section describes the logic associated with inbound and outbound ACLs.

Inbound ACL Logic

Figure 9-35 shows the logic for an inbound ACL. If the information in a packet header and an ACL statement match, the rest of the statements in the list are skipped, and the packet is permitted or denied as specified by the matched statement. If a packet header does not match an ACL statement, the packet is tested against the next statement in the list. This matching process continues until the end of the list is reached.

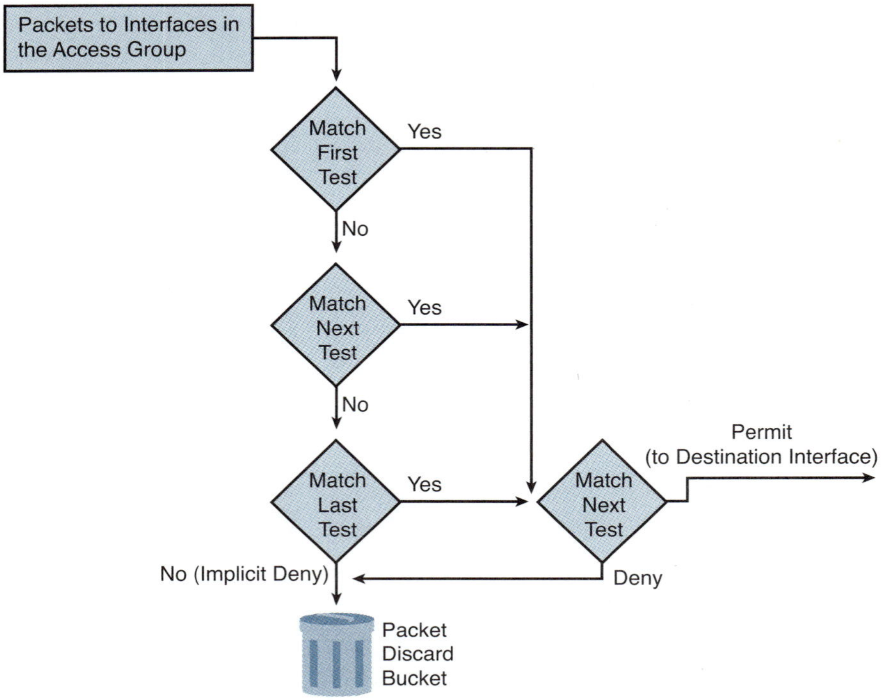

Figure 9-35   ACL Logic for an Inbound ACL

At the end of every ACL is an implicit deny any statement. This statement is not shown in output. This final implied statement is applied to all packets for which conditions did not test true. This final test condition matches all other packets and results in a "deny" action. Instead of proceeding into or out of an interface, the router drops all of these remaining packets. This final statement is often referred to as the "implicit deny any" statement or the "deny all traffic" statement. Because of this statement, an ACL should have at least one permit statement in it; otherwise, the ACL blocks all traffic.

Outbound ACL Logic

Figure 9-36 shows the logic for an outbound ACL. Before a packet is forwarded to an outbound interface, the router checks the routing table to see if the packet is routable. If the packet is not routable, it is dropped and is not tested against the ACEs. Next, the router checks to see whether the outbound interface is grouped to an ACL. If the outbound interface is not grouped to an ACL, the packet can be sent to the output buffer. Examples of outbound ACL operation are as follows:

- **No ACL applied to the interface:** If the outbound interface is not grouped to an outbound ACL, the packet is sent directly to the outbound interface.

■ **ACL applied to the interface:** If the outbound interface is grouped to an outbound ACL, the packet is not sent out on the outbound interface until it is tested by the combination of ACEs that are associated with that interface. Based on the ACL tests, the packet is permitted or denied.

For outbound lists, "permit" means to send the packet to the output buffer, and "deny" means to discard the packet.

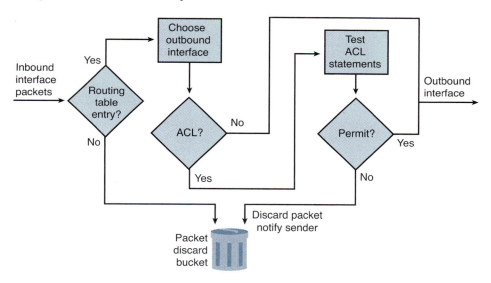

Figure 9-36 ACL Logic for an Outbound ACL

ACL Logic Operations (9.4.1.2)

Figure 9-37 shows the logic of routing and ACL processes. When a packet arrives at a router interface, the router process is the same, whether ACLs are used or not. As a frame enters an interface, the router checks to see whether the destination Layer 2 address matches its interface Layer 2 address, or whether the frame is a broadcast frame.

If the frame address is accepted, the frame information is stripped off and the router checks for an ACL on the inbound interface. If an ACL exists, the packet is tested against the statements in the list.

If the packet matches a statement, the packet is either permitted or denied. If the packet is accepted, it is then checked against routing table entries to determine the destination interface. If a routing table entry exists for the destination, the packet is then switched to the outgoing interface, otherwise the packet is dropped.

Next, the router checks whether the outgoing interface has an ACL. If an ACL exists, the packet is tested against the statements in the list.

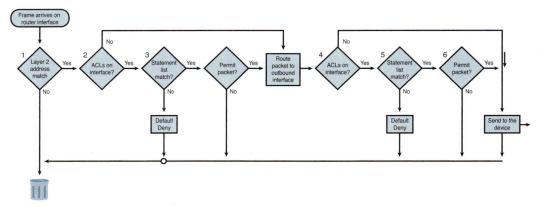

Figure 9-37 ACL and Routing Processes in a Router

If the packet matches a statement, it is either permitted or denied.

If there is no ACL or the packet is permitted, the packet is encapsulated in the new Layer 2 protocol and forwarded out the interface to the next device.

Standard ACL Decision Process (9.4.1.3)

Standard ACLs only examine the source IPv4 address. The destination of the packet and the ports involved are not considered.

The decision process for a standard ACL is mapped in Figure 9-38. Cisco IOS software tests addresses against the conditions in the ACL one by one. The first match determines whether the software accepts or rejects the address. Because the software stops testing conditions after the first match, the order of the conditions is critical. If no conditions match, the address is rejected.

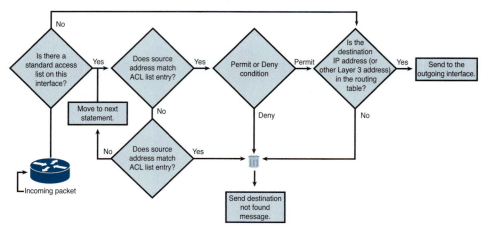

Figure 9-38 How a Standard ACL Works

Extended ACL Decision Process (9.4.1.4)

Figure 9-39 shows the logical decision path used by an extended ACL built to filter on source and destination addresses, and protocol and port numbers. In this example, the ACL first filters on the source address, then on the port and protocol of the source. It then filters on the destination address, then on the port and protocol of the destination, and makes a final permit or deny decision.

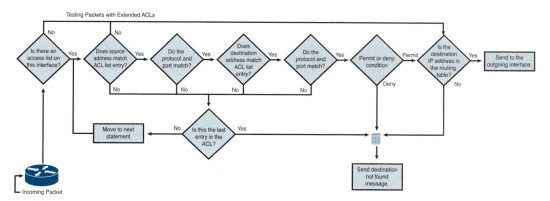

Figure 9-39 Testing Packets with Extended ACLs

Recall that entries in ACLs are processed one after the other, so a No decision does not necessarily equal a Deny. As you go through the logical decision path, note that a No means go to the next entry until a condition is matched.

Activity 9.4.1.5: Place in Order the Steps of the ACL Decision Making Process

Go to the online course to perform this practice activity.

Common ACL Errors (9.4.2)

Configuring ACLs for the first time can sometimes be a challenge and lead to mistakes. This section describes common ACL errors and solutions.

Troubleshooting Common ACL Errors - Example 1 (9.4.2.1)

Using the **show** commands described earlier reveals most of the more common ACL errors. The most common errors are entering ACEs in the wrong order and not applying adequate criteria to the ACL rules.

In Figure 9-40, host 192.168.10.10 has no Telnet connectivity with 192.168.30.12. When viewing the output of the **show access-lists** command, matches are shown for the first deny statement. This is an indicator that this statement has been matched by traffic.

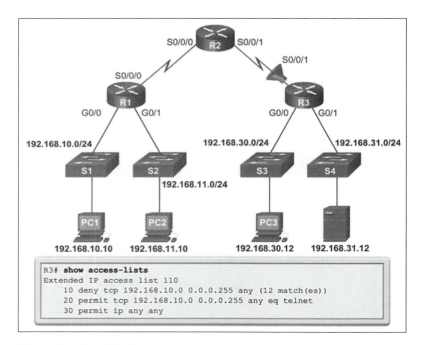

```
R3# show access-lists
Extended IP access list 110
    10 deny tcp 192.168.10.0 0.0.0.255 any (12 match(es))
    20 permit tcp 192.168.10.0 0.0.0.255 any eq telnet
    30 permit ip any any
```

Figure 9-40 ACL Error Example 1

Solution

Look at the order of the ACEs. Host 192.168.10.10 has no connectivity with 192.168.30.12 because of the order of rule 10 in the access list. Because the router processes ACLs from the top down, statement 10 denies host 192.168.10.10, so statement 20 can never be matched. Statements 10 and 20 should be reversed. The last line allows all other non-TCP traffic that falls under IP (ICMP, UDP, etc.).

Troubleshooting Common ACL Errors - Example 2 (9.4.2.2)

In Figure 9-41, the 192.168.10.0/24 network cannot use TFTP to connect to the 192.168.30.0/24 network.

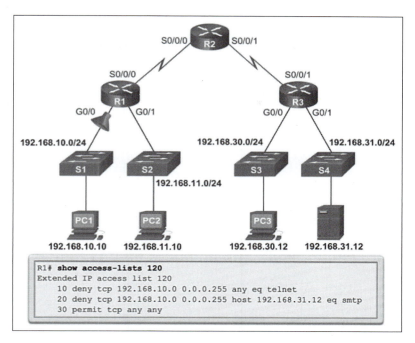

```
R1# show access-lists 120
Extended IP access list 120
    10 deny tcp 192.168.10.0 0.0.0.255 any eq telnet
    20 deny tcp 192.168.10.0 0.0.0.255 host 192.168.31.12 eq smtp
    30 permit tcp any any
```

Figure 9-41   ACL Error Example 2

Solution

The 192.168.10.0/24 network cannot use TFTP to connect to the 192.168.30.0/24 network because TFTP uses the transport protocol UDP. Statement 30 in access list 120 allows all other TCP traffic. However, because TFTP uses UDP instead of TCP, it is implicitly denied. Recall that the implied deny any statement does not appear in **show access-lists** output and therefore matches are not shown.

Statement 30 should be **permit ip any any**.

This ACL works whether it is applied to G0/0 of R1, or S0/0/1 of R3, or S0/0/0 of R2 in the incoming direction. However, based on the rule about placing extended ACLs closest to the source, the best option is to place it inbound on G0/0 of R1 because it allows undesirable traffic to be filtered without crossing the network infrastructure.

Troubleshooting Common ACL Errors - Example 3 (9.4.2.3)

In Figure 9-42, the 192.168.11.0/24 network can use Telnet to connect to 192.168.30.0/24, but according to company policy, this connection should not be allowed. The results of the **show access-lists 130** command indicate that the permit statement has been matched.

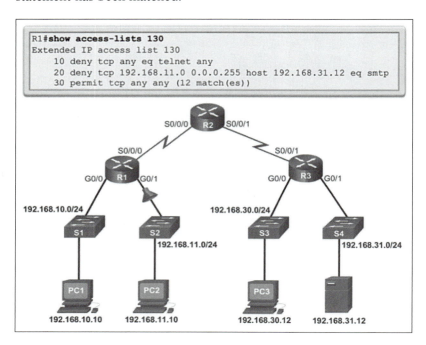

```
R1#show access-lists 130
Extended IP access list 130
    10 deny tcp any eq telnet any
    20 deny tcp 192.168.11.0 0.0.0.255 host 192.168.31.12 eq smtp
    30 permit tcp any any (12 match(es))
```

Figure 9-42   ACL Error Example 3

Solution

The 192.168.11.0/24 network can use Telnet to connect to the 192.168.30.0/24 network because the Telnet port number in statement 10 of access list 130 is listed in the wrong position in the ACL statement. Statement 10 currently denies any source packet with a port number that is equal to Telnet. To deny Telnet traffic inbound on G0/1, deny the destination port number that is equal to Telnet, for example, **deny tcp any any eq telnet**.

Troubleshooting Common ACL Errors - Example 4 (9.4.2.4)

In Figure 9-43, host 192.168.30.12 is able to use Telnet to connect to 192.168.31.12, but company policy states that this connection should not be allowed. Output from the **show access-lists 140** command indicates that the permit statement has been matched.

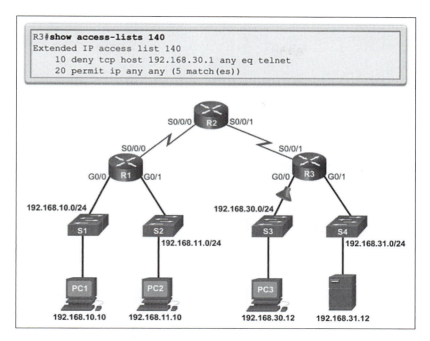

```
R3#show access-lists 140
Extended IP access list 140
    10 deny tcp host 192.168.30.1 any eq telnet
    20 permit ip any any (5 match(es))
```

Figure 9-43   ACL Error Example 4

Solution

Host 192.168.30.12 can use Telnet to connect to 192.168.31.12 because there are no rules that deny host 192.168.30.12 or its network as the source. Statement 10 of access list 140 denies the router interface on which traffic enters the router. The host IPv4 address in statement 10 should be 192.168.30.12.

Troubleshooting Common ACL Errors - Example 5 (9.4.2.5)

In Figure 9-44, host 192.168.30.12 can use Telnet to connect to 192.168.31.12, but according to the security policy, this connection should not be allowed. Output from the **show access-lists 150** command indicates that no matches have occurred for the deny statement as expected.

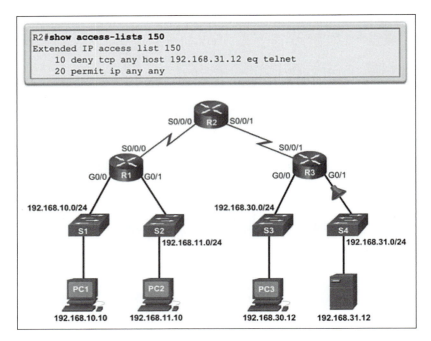

```
R2#show access-lists 150
Extended IP access list 150
    10 deny tcp any host 192.168.31.12 eq telnet
    20 permit ip any any
```

Figure 9-44   ACL Error Example 5

Solution

Host 192.168.30.12 can use Telnet to connect to 192.168.31.12 because of the direction in which access list 150 is applied to the G0/1 interface. Statement 10 denies any source address to connect to host 192.168.31.12 using Telnet. However, this filter should be applied outbound on G0/1 to filter correctly.

Packet Tracer
☐ Activity

Packet Tracer Activity 9.4.2.6: Troubleshooting ACLs

Scenario

Create a network that has the following three policies implemented:

- Hosts from the 192.168.0.0/24 network are unable to access any TCP service of Server3.
- Hosts from the 10.0.0.0/8 network are unable to access the HTTP service of Server1.
- Hosts from the 172.16.0.0/16 network are unable to access the FTP service of Server2.

Lab 9.4.2.7: Troubleshooting ACL Configuration and Placement

In this lab, you will complete the following objectives:

- Part 1: Build the Network and Configure Basic Device Settings
- Part 2: Troubleshoot Internal Access
- Part 3: Troubleshoot Remote Access

Packet Tracer Activity 9.4.2.8: Skills Integration Challenge

In this challenge activity, you will finish the addressing scheme, configure routing, and implement named access control lists.

IPv6 ACLs (9.5)

This section discusses IPv6 ACLs.

IPv6 ACL Creation (9.5.1)

This section describes the configuration and verification of IPv6 ACLs.

Type of IPv6 ACLs (9.5.1.1)

IPv6 ACLs are very similar to IPv4 ACLs in both operation and configuration. Being familiar with IPv4 access lists makes IPv6 ACLs easy to understand and configure.

In IPv4 there are two types of ACLs, standard and extended. Both types of ACLs can be either numbered or named ACLs.

With IPv6, there is only one type of ACL, which is equivalent to an IPv4 extended named ACL. There are no numbered ACLs in IPv6. As summarized in Figure 9-45, IPv6 ACLs are:

- Named ACLs only
- Equivalent to the functionality of an IPv4 extended ACL

An IPv4 ACL and an IPv6 ACL cannot share the same name.

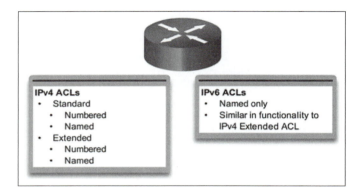

Figure 9-45   IPv6 ACLs

Comparing IPv4 and IPv6 ACLs (9.5.1.2)

Although IPv4 and IPv6 ACLs are very similar, there are three significant differences between them.

Applying an IPv6 ACL

The first difference is the command used to apply an IPv6 ACL to an interface. IPv4 uses the command **ip access-group** to apply an IPv4 ACL to an IPv4 interface. IPv6 uses the **ipv6 traffic-filter** command to perform the same function for IPv6 interfaces.

No Wildcard Masks

Unlike IPv4 ACLs, IPv6 ACLs do not use wildcard masks. Instead, the prefix-length is used to indicate how much of an IPv6 source or destination address should be matched.

Additional Default Statements

The last major difference is the addition of two implicit **permit** statements at the end of each IPv6 access list. At the end of every IPv4 standard or extended ACL is an implicit **deny any** or **deny any any**. IPv6 includes a similar **deny ipv6 any any** statement at the end of each IPv6 ACL. The difference is IPv6 also includes two other implicit statements by default:

```
permit icmp any any nd-na
permit icmp any any nd-ns
```

These two statements allow the router to participate in the IPv6 equivalent of ARP for IPv4. Recall that ARP is used in IPv4 to resolve Layer 3 addresses to Layer 2 MAC addresses. As shown in Figure 9-46, IPv6 uses ICMP Neighbor Discovery (ND) messages to accomplish the same thing. ND uses Neighbor Solicitation (NS) and Neighbor Advertisement (NA) messages.

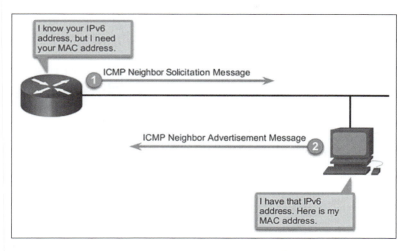

Figure 9-46   IPv6 Neighbor Discovery

ND messages are encapsulated in IPv6 packets and require the services of the IPv6 network layer, while ARP for IPv4 does not use Layer 3. Because IPv6 uses the Layer 3 service for neighbor discovery, IPv6 ACLs need to implicitly permit ND packets to be sent and received on an interface. Specifically, both Neighbor Discovery–Neighbor Advertisement (**nd-na**) and Neighbor Discovery–Neighbor Solicitation (**nd-ns**) messages are permitted.

Configuring IPv6 ACLs (9.5.2)

Configuring IPv6 ACLs is similar to configuring IPv4 ACLs.

Configuring IPv6 Topology (9.5.2.1)

Figure 9-47 shows the topology that will be used for configuring IPv6 ACLs. The topology is similar to the previous IPv4 topology except for the IPv6 addressing scheme. There are three 2001:DB8:CAFE::/64 subnets: 2001:DB8:CAFE:10::/64, 2001:DB8:CAFE:11::/64, and 2001:DB8:CAFE:30::/64. Two serial networks connect the three routers: 2001:DB8:FEED:1::/64 and 2001:DB8:FEED:2::/64.

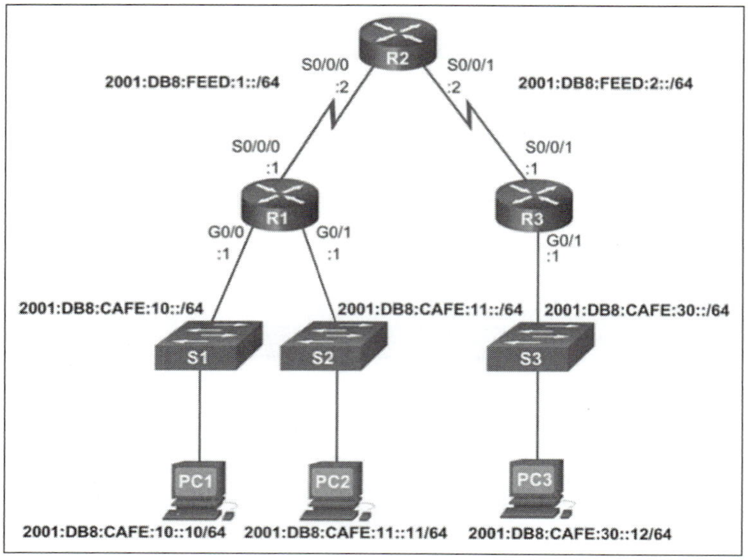

Figure 9-47   IPv6 Topology

The following three outputs show the IPv6 address configuration for each router. The **show ipv6 interface brief** command is used to verify the address and the state of the interface.

```
R1(config)# interface g0/0
R1(config-if)# ipv6 address 2001:db8:cafe:10::1/64
R1(config-if)# exit
R1(config)# interface s0/0/0
R1(config-if)# ipv6 address 2001:db8:feed:1::1/64
R1(config-if)# exit
R1(config)# interface g0/1
R1(config-if)# ipv6 address 2001:db8:cafe:11::1/64
R1(config-if)# end
R1# show ipv6 interface brief
GigabitEthernet0/0      [up/up]
    FE80::FE99:47FF:FE75:C3E0
    2001:DB8:CAFE:10::1
GigabitEthernet0/1      [up/up]
    FE80::FE99:47FF:FE75:C3E1
    2001:DB8:CAFE:11::1
Serial0/0/0             [up/up]
    FE80::FE99:47FF:FE75:C3E0
    2001:DB8:FEED:1::1
<Output omitted for brevity>
R1#
R2(config)# interface s0/0/0
```

```
R2(config-if)# ipv6 address 2001:db8:feed:1::2/64
R2(config-if)# exit
R2(config)# interface s0/0/1
R2(config-if)# ipv6 address 2001:db8:feed:2::2/64
R2(config-if)# end
R2# show ipv6 interface brief
Serial0/0/0              [up/up]
    FE80::FE99:47FF:FE71:78A0
    2001:DB8:FEED:1::2
Serial0/0/1             [up/up]
    FE80::FE99:47FF:FE71:78A0
    2001:DB8:FEED:2::2
<Output omitted for brevity>
R2#
R3(config)# interface s0/0/1
R3(config-if)# ipv6 address 2001:db8:feed:2::1/64
R3(config-if)# exit
R3(config)# interface g0/0
R3(config-if)# ipv6 address 2001:db8:cafe:30::1/64
R3(config-if)# end
R3# show ipv6 interface brief
GigabitEthernet0/0      [up/up]
    FE80::FE99:47FF:FE71:7A20
    2001:DB8:CAFE:30::1
Serial0/0/1            [up/up]
    FE80::FE99:47FF:FE71:7A20
    2001:DB8:FEED:2::1
R3#
```

Note

The **no shutdown** command and the **clock rate** command are not shown.

Syntax for Configuring IPv6 ACLs (9.5.2.2)

In IPv6 there are only named ACLs. The configuration is similar to that of an IPv4 extended named ACL.

The following shows the command syntax for IPv6 ACLs, which is described in Table 9-10. The syntax is similar to the syntax used for an IPv4 extended ACL. One significant difference is the use of the IPv6 prefix-length instead of an IPv4 wildcard mask.

```
R1(config-ipv6-acl)# deny | permit protocol {source-ipv6-prefix/prefix-length | any
| host source-ipv6-address} [operator [port-number]] {destination-ipv6-prefix/prefix-
length | any | host destination-ipv6-address} [operator [port-number]]
```

Table 9-10   IPv6

Parameter	Description
deny | permit	Specifies whether to deny or permit the packet.
protocol	Enter the name or number of an Internet protocol, or an integer representing an IPv6 protocol number.
source-ipv6-prefix/ prefix-length *destination-ipv6- address/prefix-length*	The source or destination IPv6 network or class of networks for which to set deny or permit conditions.
any	Enter **any** as an abbreviation for the IPv6 prefix ::/0. This matches all addresses.
host	For **host** *source-ipv6-address* or *destination-ipv6-address*, enter the source or destination IPv6 host address for which to set deny or permit conditions.
operator	(Optional) An operand that compares the source or destination ports of the specified protocol. Operands are **lt** (less than), **gt** (greater than), **eq** (equal), **neq** (not equal), and **range**.
port-number	(Optional) A decimal number or the name of a TCP or UDP port for filtering TCP or UDP, respectively.

How To

There are three basic steps to configure an IPv6 ACL:

Step 1.   From global configuration mode, use the **ipv6 access-list** *name* command to create an IPv6 ACL. Like IPv4 named ACLs, IPv6 names are alphanumeric, case sensitive, and must be unique. Unlike IPv4, there is no need for a standard or extended option.

Step 2.   From the named ACL configuration mode, use the permit or deny statements to specify one or more conditions to determine if a packet is forwarded or dropped.

Step 3.   Return to privileged EXEC mode with the **end** command.

The following demonstrates the steps to create an IPv6 ACL with a simple example based on the previous topology. The first statement names the IPv6 access list NO-R3-LAN-ACCESS. Similar to IPv4 named ACLs, capitalizing IPv6 ACL names is not required, but makes them stand out when viewing the running-config output.

```
R1(config)# ipv6 access-list NO-R3-LAN-ACCESS
R1(config-ipv6-acl)# deny ipv6 2001:db8:cafe:30::/64 any
R1(config-ipv6-acl)# permit ipv6 any any
R1(config-ipv6-acl)# end
R1#
```

The second statement denies all IPv6 packets from the 2001:DB8:CAFE:30::/64 destined for any IPv6 network. The third statement allows all other IPv6 packets.

Applying an IPv6 ACL to an Interface (9.5.2.3)

After an IPv6 ACL is configured, it is linked to an interface using the **ipv6 traffic-filter** command:

```
Router(config-if)# ipv6 traffic-filter access-list-name { in | out }
```

Figure 9-48 shows the NO-R3-LAN-ACCESS ACL configured previously and the commands used to apply the IPv6 ACL inbound to the S0/0/0 interface. Applying the ACL to the inbound S0/0/0 interface will deny packets from 2001:DB8:CAFE:30::/64 to both of the LANs on R1.

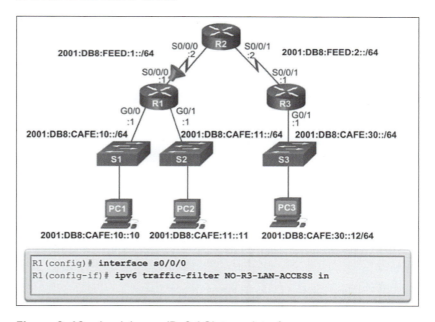

```
R1(config)# interface s0/0/0
R1(config-if)# ipv6 traffic-filter NO-R3-LAN-ACCESS in
```

Figure 9-48   Applying an IPv6 ACL to an Interface

To remove an ACL from an interface, first enter the **no ipv6 traffic-filter** command on the interface, and then enter the global **no ipv6 access-list** command to remove the access list.

Note

IPv4 and IPv6 both use the **ip access-class** command to apply an access list to VTY ports.

IPv6 ACL Examples (9.5.2.4)

This section presents two IPv6 ACL examples and shows how they are applied to an interface. The topology for the examples is shown in Figure 9-49.

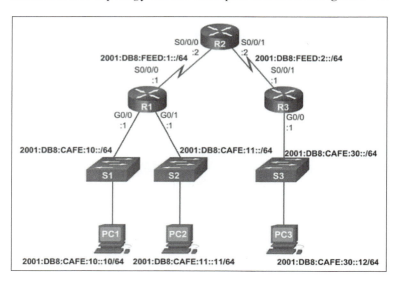

Figure 9-49   IPv6 Topology

Deny FTP

In the first example, shown next, router R1 is configured with an IPv6 access list to deny FTP traffic to 2001:DB8:CAFE:11::/64. Ports for both FTP data (port 20) and FTP control (port 21) need to be blocked. Because the filter is applied inbound on the G0/0 interface on R1, only traffic from the 2001:DB8:CAFE:10::/64 network will be denied.

```
R1(config)# ipv6 access-list NO-FTP-TO-11
R1(config-ipv6-acl)# deny tcp any 2001:db8:cafe:11::/64 eq ftp
R1(config-ipv6-acl)# deny tcp any 2001:db8:cafe:11::/64 eq ftp-data
R1(config-ipv6-acl)# permit ipv6 any any
R1(config-ipv6-acl)# exit
R1(config)# interface g0/0
R1(config-if)# ipv6 traffic-filter NO-FTP-TO-11 in
R1(config-if)#
```

Restricted Access

The second example, shown in Figure 9-50, identifies the IPv6 ACL commands used to give the LAN on R3 limited access to the LANs on R1. Comments are added in the configuration to document the ACL.

The IPv6 ACL on R3 is configured using the command:

```
R3(config)# ipv6 access-list RESTRICTED-ACCESS
```

The following features have been labeled in the ACL:

1. The first two permit statements allow access from any device to the web server at 2001:DB8:CAFE:10::10.

2. All other devices are denied access to the 2001:DB8:CAFE:10::/64 network.

3. PC3 at 2001:DB8:CAFE:30::12 is permitted Telnet access to PC2, which has the IPv6 address 2001:DB8:CAFE:11::11.

4. All other devices are denied Telnet access to PC2.

5. All other IPv6 traffic is permitted to all other destinations.

6. The IPv6 access list is applied to interface G0/0 in the inbound direction, so only the 2001:DB8:CAFE:30::/64 network is affected, using these commands:

```
R3(config)# interface g0/0
R3(config-if)# ipv6 traffic-filter RESTRICTED-ACCESS in
```

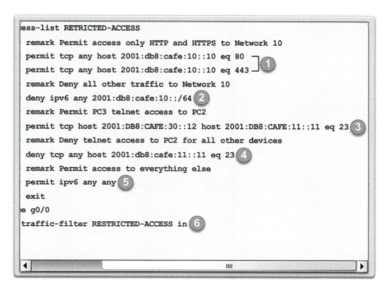

Figure 9-50   Restrict Access

Verifying IPv6 ACLs (9.5.2.5)

The commands used to verify an IPv6 access list are similar to those used for IPv4 ACLs. Using these commands, the IPv6 access list RESTRICTED-ACCESS that was configured previously can be verified. The following output shows the output of the

show ipv6 interface command. The output confirms that the RESTRICTED-ACCESS ACL is configured inbound on the G0/0 interface.

```
R3# show ipv6 interface g0/0
GigabitEthernet0/0 is up, line protocol is up
  Global unicast address(es):
    2001:DB8:CAFE:30::1, subnet is 2001:DB8:CAFE:30::/64
  Input features: Access List
  Inbound access list RESTRICTED-ACCESS
<Output omitted for brevity>
```

As shown in the following output, the **show access-lists** command displays all access lists on the router including both IPv4 and IPv6 ACLs. Notice that with IPv6 ACLs the sequence numbers occur at the end of the statement and not the beginning as with IPv4 access lists. Although the statements appear in the order they were entered, they are not always incremented by 10. This is because the remark statements that were entered use a sequence number but are not displayed in the output of the **show access-lists** command.

```
R3# show access-lists
IPv6 access list RESTRICTED-ACCESS
    permit tcp any host 2001:DB8:CAFE:10::10 eq www sequence 20
    permit tcp any host 2001:DB8:CAFE:10::10 eq 443 sequence 30
    deny ipv6 any 2001:DB8:CAFE:10::/64 sequence 50
    permit tcp host 2001:DB8:CAFE:30::12 host 2001:DB8:CAFE:11::11 eq telnet sequence
70
    deny tcp any host 2001:DB8:CAFE:11::11 eq telnet sequence 90
    permit ipv6 any any sequence 110
R3#
```

Similar to extended ACLs for IPv4, IPv6 access lists are displayed and processed in the order the statements are entered. Remember, IPv4 standard ACLs use an internal logic which changes their order and processing sequence.

As shown in the following output, the **show running-config** command includes all of the ACEs and remark statements. Remark statements can come before or after permit or deny statements but should be consistent in their placement.

```
R3# show running-config
<Output omitted>
ipv6 access-list RESTRICTED-ACCESS
 remark Permit access only HTTP and HTTPS to Network 10
 permit tcp any host 2001:DB8:CAFE:10::10 eq www
 permit tcp any host 2001:DB8:CAFE:10::10 eq 443
 remark Deny all other traffic to Network 10
 deny ipv6 any 2001:DB8:CAFE:10::/64
 remark Permit PC3 telnet access to PC2
 permit tcp host 2001:DB8:CAFE:30::12 host 2001:DB8:CAFE:11::11 eq telnet
```

```
remark Deny telnet access to PC2 for all other devices
deny tcp any host 2001:DB8:CAFE:11::11 eq telnet
remark Permit access to everything else
permit ipv6 any any
```

Packet Tracer Activity 9.5.2.6: Configuring IPv6 ACLs

Objectives

- Part 1: Configure, Apply, and Verify an IPv6 ACL
- Part 2: Configure, Apply, and Verify a Second IPv6 ACL

Lab 9.5.2.7: Configuring and Verifying IPv6 ACLs

In this lab, you will complete the following objectives:

- Part 1: Set Up the Topology and Initialize Devices
- Part 2: Configure Devices and Verify Connectivity
- Part 3: Configure and Verify IPv6 ACLs
- Part 4: Edit IPv6 ACLs

Summary (9.6)

Class Activity 9.6.1.1: FTP Denied

Go to the online course to perform this practice activity.

Scenario

It was recently reported that viruses are on the rise within your small- to medium-sized business network. Your network administrator has been tracking network performance and has determined that one particular host is constantly downloading files from a remote FTP server. This host just may be the virus source perpetuating throughout the network!

Use Packet Tracer to complete this activity. Write a named ACL to deny the host access to the FTP server. Apply the ACL to the most effective interface on the router.

To complete the physical topology, you must use:

- One PC host station
- Two switches
- One Cisco 1941 series Integrated Services Router
- One server

Using the Packet Tracer text tool, record the ACL you prepared. Validate that the ACL works to deny access to the FTP server by trying to access the FTP server's address. Observe what happens while in simulation mode.

Save your file and be prepared to share it with another student, or with the entire class.

By default a router does not filter traffic. Traffic that enters the router is routed solely based on information within the routing table.

Packet filtering controls access to a network by analyzing the incoming and outgoing packets and passing or dropping them based on criteria such as the source IP address, destination IP addresses, and the protocol carried within the packet. A packet-filtering router uses rules to determine whether to permit or deny traffic. A router can also perform packet filtering at Layer 4, the transport layer.

An ACL is a sequential list of permit or deny statements. The last statement of an ACL is always an implicit deny which blocks all traffic. To prevent the implied deny any statement at the end of the ACL from blocking all traffic, the permit ip any statement can be added.

When network traffic passes through an interface configured with an ACL, the router compares the information within the packet against each entry, in sequential order, to determine if the packet matches one of the statements. If a match is found, the packet is processed accordingly.

ACLs are configured to apply to inbound traffic or to apply to outbound traffic.

Standard ACLs can be used to permit or deny traffic only from a source IPv4 address. The destination of the packet and the ports involved are not evaluated. The basic rule for placing a standard ACL is to place it close to the destination.

Extended ACLs filter packets based on several attributes: protocol type, source or destination IPv4 address, and source or destination ports. The basic rule for placing an extended ACL is to place it as close to the source as possible.

The **access-list** global configuration command defines a standard ACL with a number in the range of 1 to 99 and 1300 to 1999 or an extended ACL with a number in the range of 100 to 199 and 2000 to 2699. Both standard and extended ACLs can also be named. The command **ip access-list standard** *name* is used to create a standard named ACL, whereas the command **ip access-list extended** *name* is used for an extended access list. IPv4 ACEs include the use of wildcard masks.

After an ACL is configured, it is linked to an interface using the **ip access-group** command in interface configuration mode. Remember the three Ps: one ACL per protocol, per direction, per interface.

To remove an ACL from an interface, first enter the **no ip access-group** command on the interface, and then enter the global **no access-list** command to remove the entire ACL.

The **show running-config** and **show access-lists** commands are used to verify ACL configuration. The **show ip interface** command is used to verify the ACL on the interface and the direction in which it is applied.

The **access-class** command configured in line configuration mode restricts incoming and outgoing connections between a particular VTY and the addresses in an access list.

Like IPv4 named ACLs, IPv6 names are alphanumeric, case sensitive, and must be unique. Unlike IPv4, there is no need for a standard or extended option.

From global configuration mode, use the **ipv6 access-list** *name* command to create an IPv6 ACL. Unlike IPv4 ACLs, IPv6 ACLs do not use wildcard masks. Instead, the prefix-length is used to indicate how much of an IPv6 source or destination address should be matched.

After an IPv6 ACL is configured, it is linked to an interface using the **ipv6 traffic-filter** command.

Practice

The following activities provide practice with the topics introduced in this chapter. The Labs and Class Activities are available in the companion *Routing Protocols Lab Manual* (978-1-58713-322-0). The Packet Tracer Activities PKA files are found in the online course.

Class Activities

Class Activity 9.0.1.2: Permit Me to Assist You

Class Activity 9.6.1.1: FTP Denied

Labs

Lab 9.2.2.7: Configuring and Verifying Standard ACLs

Lab 9.2.3.4: Configuring and Verifying VTY Restrictions

Lab 9.3.2.13: Configuring and Verifying Extended ACLs

Lab 9.4.2.7: Troubleshooting ACL Configuration and Placement

Lab 9.5.2.7: Configuring and Verifying IPv6 ACLs

Packet Tracer Activities

Packet Tracer Activity 9.1.1.6: ACL Demonstration

Packet Tracer Activity 9.2.1.10: Configuring Standard ACLs

Packet Tracer Activity 9.2.1.11: Configuring Named Standard ACLs

Packet Tracer Activity 9.2.3.3: Configuring an ACL on VTY Lines

Packet Tracer Activity 9.3.2.10: Configuring Extended ACLs – Scenario 1

Packet Tracer Activity 9.3.2.11: Configuring Extended ACLs – Scenario 2

Packet Tracer Activity 9.3.2.12: Configuring Extended ACLs – Scenario 3

Packet Tracer Activity 9.4.2.6: Troubleshooting ACLs

Packet Tracer Activity 9.4.2.8: Skills Integration Challenge

Packet Tracer Activity 9.5.2.6: Configuring IPv6 ACLs

Check Your Understanding Questions

Complete all the review questions listed here to test your understanding of the topics and concepts in this chapter. The appendix, "Answers to the 'Check Your Understanding' Questions," lists the answers.

1. Which statements correctly describe Cisco access control lists? (Choose two.)

    A. Extended ACLs are created in interface configuration mode.

    B. Extended ACLs filter traffic based on source and destination IP, port number, and protocol.

    C. Standard IP ACLs are numbered 1 to 99 and 1300 to 1999, and extended ACLs are numbered 100 to 199 and 1300 to 1999.

    D. Standard ACLs permit or deny traffic to specific IP addresses.

    E. Standard ACLs do not permit the use of wildcard masks.

2. Which statement is true about applying an access list to an interface?

    A. Access lists are applied in global configuration mode.

    B. Named access lists are applied using the **ip access-name** command.

    C. Standard access lists should be applied to an interface as close as possible to the destination.

    D. The command for applying access list 101 inbound is **ip access-list 101**.

3. Which statement is a guideline to be followed when designing access control lists?

    A. Because ACL tests are executed in order, they should be organized from the most general condition to the most specific.

    B. Because ACL tests are executed in order, they should be organized from the most specific condition to the most general.

    C. Because all statements in an ACL are evaluated before they are executed, an explicit deny any statement must be written for an ACL to function properly.

    D. Because all statements in an ACL are evaluated before they are executed, an explicit permit any statement must be written for an ACL to function properly.

4. What occurs if the network administrator applies an IP access control list that has no permit statement outbound on an interface? (Choose two.)

    A. All traffic outbound is denied.

    B. All traffic outbound is allowed.

    C. Only traffic originating from the router is allowed outbound.

    D. The ACL restricts all incoming traffic and filters outgoing traffic.

5. Which solutions can be implemented with ACLs? (Choose two.)

   A. Segment the network to increase available bandwidth.

   B. Create a firewall on a router to filter inbound traffic from an external network.

   C. Control traffic entering or exiting different areas of a local network.

   D. Distribute DHCP traffic to allow easier network availability.

   E. Allow or deny traffic into the network based on the MAC address.

6. Match each command with its description:

   ```
   any
   show running-config
   show access-list
   host
   show ip interface
   ```

   A. Substitutes for the 0.0.0.0 mask.

   B. Indicates whether any ACLs are set on an interface.

   C. Displays the contents of all ACLs on the router.

   D. Represents an IP address and mask pair of 0.0.0.0 255.255.255.255.

   E. Reveals the ACLs and interface assignments on a router.

7. Which IPv4 address and wildcard mask test for hosts from an entire subnet of network 192.168.12.0 using a 29-bit mask?

   A. 192.168.12.56 0.0.0.15

   B. 192.168.12.56 0.0.0.8

   C. 192.168.12.56 0.0.0.31

   D. 192.168.12.84 0.0.0.7

   E. 192.168.12.84 0.0.0.3

   F. 192.168.12.84 0.0.0.255

8. What kind of access list is created with the command **ip access-list standard fastaccess?**

   A. Turbo ACL

   B. Reflexive ACL

   C. Named ACL

   D. Dynamic ACL

9. Categorize the following descriptions as belonging to either a standard IP ACL or an extended IP ACL:

   A. Checks only the source address _____

   B. Access list numbers 100 to 199 _____

   C. Checks protocol and port numbers _____

   D. Permits/denies entire protocol suite based on network address _____

   E. Access list numbers 1 to 99 _____

   F. Checks source and destination address _____

10. Refer to the following configuration. Assuming that this ACL is correctly applied to a router interface, which statements describe traffic on the network? (Choose two.)

    ```
    access-list 199 deny tcp 178.15.0.0 0.0.255.255 any eq 23
    access-list 199 permit ip any any
    ```

    A. All FTP traffic from network 178.15.0.0 will be permitted.

    B. All Telnet traffic destined for network 178.15.0.0 will be denied.

    C. Telnet and FTP traffic will be permitted from all hosts on network 178.15.0.0 to any destination.

    D. Telnet traffic will not be permitted from any hosts on network 178.15.0.0 to any destination.

    E. Telnet traffic will not be permitted to any host on network 178.15.0.0 from any destination.

11. What is the difference between IPv4 ACLs and IPv6 ACLs? (Choose three.)

    A. IPv6 ACLs use prefix-lengths instead of wildcard masks.

    B. IPv6 ACLs do not include an explicit **deny any**.

    C. IPv4 ACLs do not include an explicit **deny any**.

    D. IPv6 ACLs use the **ipv6 traffic-filter** command to apply an IPv6 ACL to an interface.

    E. IPv6 ACLs include two implicit permit statements for ICMPv6 Neighbor Solicitation and Neighbor Advertisement messages.

12. Describe the "three Ps" rule associated with access control lists.

13. Describe the two basic rules associated with the placement of standard and extended ACLs.

CHAPTER 10

IOS Images and Licensing

Objectives

Upon completion of this chapter, you will be able to answer the following questions:

- What are the IOS image naming conventions implemented by Cisco?

- How do you calculate the memory requirements needed when upgrading an IOS system image?

- What is the licensing process for IOS software in a small- to medium-sized network?

- How do you configure a router to install an IOS software image license?

Key Terms

This chapter uses the following key terms. You can find the definitions in the Glossary.

mainline train   page 656

technology train   page 656

extended maintenance release (EM release)   page 660

standard maintenance release (T release)   page 660

Product Activation Key (PAK)   page 663

Unique Device Identifier (UDI)   page 676

Evaluation Right-To-Use (RTU) licenses   page 680

Introduction (10.0.1.1)

Cisco IOS (originally Internetwork Operating System) is software used on most Cisco routers and switches. IOS is a package of routing, switching, security, and other internetworking technologies integrated into a single multitasking operating system.

The Cisco IOS portfolio supports a broad range of technologies and features. Customers choose an IOS based on a set of protocols and features supported by a particular image. Understanding the Cisco portfolio of feature sets is helpful in selecting the proper IOS to meet the needs of an organization.

Cisco made significant changes in the packaging and licensing of its IOS when transitioning from IOS 12.4 to 15.0. This chapter explains the naming conventions and packaging of IOS 12.4 and 15. Beginning with IOS 15, Cisco also implemented a new packaging format and licensing process for IOS. This chapter discusses the process of obtaining, installing, and managing Cisco IOS 15 software licenses.

Note

The release of IOS after 12.4 is 15.0. There is no IOS software release 13.0 or 14.0.

Class Activity 10.0.1.2: IOS Detection

Scenario

Your school or university has just received a donation of Cisco routers and switches. You transport them from your shipping and receiving department to your Cisco networking lab and start sorting them into switch and router groups.

Refer to the accompanying PDF for directions on how to proceed with this modeling activity. Save your work and share the data you found with another group or the entire class.

Managing IOS System Files (10.1)

Cisco IOS is a sophisticated operating system optimized for internetworking. Cisco IOS can be thought of as an internetworking brain, a highly intelligent administrator that manages and controls complex, distributed network resources and functions.

Naming Conventions (10.1.1)

It is important to understand the naming conventions of Cisco IOS so you can implement the correct set of features and technologies on your router or switch.

Cisco IOS Software Release Families and Trains (10.1.1.1)

Cisco IOS Software has evolved from a single platform operating system for routing, to a sophisticated operating system that supports a large array of features and technologies such as VoIP, NetFlow, and IPsec. To better meet the requirements of the different market segments, the software is organized into software release families and software trains.

A software release family is comprised of multiple IOS software release versions that:

- Share a code base
- Apply to related hardware platforms
- Overlap in support coverage (as one OS comes to end-of-life, another OS is introduced and supported)

Examples of IOS software releases, within a software release family, include 12.3, 12.4, 15.0, and 15.1.

Along with each software release, there are new versions of the software created to implement bug fixes and new features. IOS refers to these versions as trains.

A Cisco IOS train is used to deliver releases with a common code base to a specific set of platforms and features. A train may contain several releases, each release being a snapshot of the code base of the train at the moment of the release. Because different software release families can apply to different platforms or market segments, several trains can be current at any point in time.

This chapter examines the trains of both IOS 12.4 and 15.

Cisco IOS 12.4 Mainline and T Trains (10.1.1.2)

IOS 12.4 was the final software release before transitioning to the new packaging format and licensing process with IOS 15. There are also significant changes in how IOS 15 handles maintenance and minor releases compared to previous versions such as IOS 12.4. This section explains the numbering and system image packaging of IOS 12.4.

12.4 Trains

Figure 10-1 shows the migration from software release 12.3 to 12.4. Within a software release family there may be two or more closely related and active trains. For example, the Cisco IOS Software 12.4 release family has two trains, the 12.4 mainline train and the 12.4T train.

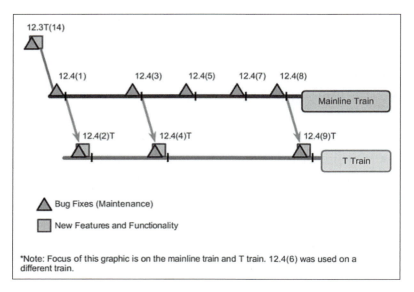

Figure 10-1   Cisco IOS Software 12.4 Release Family

The Cisco IOS Software 12.4 train is considered the mainline train. The *mainline train* receives mostly software (bug) fixes with the goal of increasing software quality. The mainline train releases are also designated as Maintenance Deployment (MD) releases.

A mainline train is always associated with a *technology train* (T train). A T train, such as 12.4T, receives the same software bug fixes as the mainline train. The T train also receives new software and hardware support features. Releases in the Cisco IOS Software 12.4T train are considered Early Deployment (ED) releases.

There may be other trains, depending on the software release family. For example, another train available is the service provider train (S train). An S train will contain specific features designed to meet service provider requirements.

All child trains of the mainline train (T, S, etc.) typically contain an uppercase letter designating the train type.

Mainline train = 12.4

T train = 12.4T (12.4 + new software and hardware support features)

Up to and including the Cisco IOS Software 12.4 release family, the mainline and T trains were separated. In other words, from the mainline train, a T train would branch out and become a separate code base that received new features and hardware support. Eventually, a new mainline train would evolve from an established T train and the cycle would start again. This use of multiple trains was changed with the software release Cisco IOS 15.

Figure 10-1 illustrates the relationships between the release of the Cisco IOS Software 12.4 mainline train and the 12.4T train.

Cisco IOS 12.4 Mainline and T Numbering (10.1.1.3)

The IOS release numbering convention is used to identify the release of the IOS software, including any bug fixes and new software features. An example of the numbering scheme is shown in Figure 10-2 for both the mainline and T trains:

- The software release numbering scheme for a mainline train is composed of a train number, a maintenance identifier, and a rebuild identifier. For example, the Cisco IOS Software Release 12.4(21a) is a mainline train. The release for a T train is composed of a train number, a maintenance identifier, a train identifier, and a rebuild identifier. For example, Cisco IOS Software Release 12.4(20)T1 belongs to the Cisco IOS Software 12.4T train.

- Each maintenance identifier of Cisco IOS Software 12.4 mainline, such as 12.4(7), includes additional software and maintenance fixes. This change is indicated with the number within the parentheses. Each maintenance release of Cisco IOS Software 12.4T, such as 12.4(20)T, includes these same software fixes, along with additional software features, and hardware support.

- Cisco uses rebuilds of an individual release to integrate fixes for significant issues. This reduces the possible impact on customers who have already deployed and certified an individual release. A rebuild typically includes fixes to a limited number of software defects, which are known as caveats. It is indicated by a lowercase letter inside the parentheses of mainline trains, or by a final number in other trains. For example, Cisco IOS Software Release 12.4(21) received a few caveat fixes and the resulting rebuild was named 12.4(21a). Similarly, 12.4(15)T8 is the eighth rebuild of 12.4(15)T. Each new rebuild increments the rebuild identifier and delivers additional software fixes on an accelerated schedule, prior to the next planned individual release. The criteria for making changes in a rebuild are strict.

A single set of individual release numbers is used for all Cisco IOS Software 12.4 trains. Cisco IOS Software Maintenance Release 12.4 and Cisco IOS Software Release 12.4T use a pool of individual release numbers that is shared across the entire Cisco IOS Software 12.4 release family. Cisco IOS Software Release 12.4(6)T was followed by 12.4(7)T and 12.4(8)T. This permits the administrator to track changes introduced in the code.

Note

Any caveat that is fixed in a T train release should be implemented in the next mainline release.

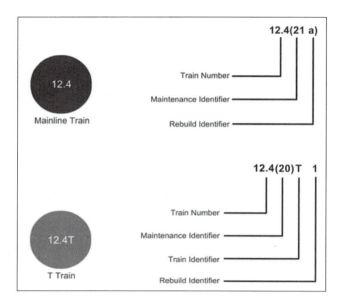

Figure 10-2   Cisco IOS 12 Software Mainline and T Trains Numbering

Cisco IOS 12.4 System Image Packaging (10.1.1.4)

Pre Cisco IOS Software Release 15.0, Cisco IOS Software packaging consisted of eight packages for Cisco routers, as shown in Figure 10-3. This packaging scheme was introduced with the Cisco IOS Software 12.3 mainline train and was later used in other trains. The image packaging consists of eight IOS images, three of which are considered premium packages.

The five non-premium packages are:

- **IP Base:** The entry-level Cisco IOS Software image

- **IP Voice:** Converged voice and data, VoIP, VoFR, and IP Telephony

- **Advanced Security:** Security and VPN features including Cisco IOS Firewall, IDS/IPS, IPsec, 3DES, and VPN

- **SP (Service Provider) Services:** Adds SSH/SSL, ATM, VoATM, and MPLS to IP Voice

- **Enterprise Base:** Enterprise protocols: AppleTalk, IPX, and IBM support

Note

Starting with the Cisco IOS Software 12.4 release family, SSH is available in all images.

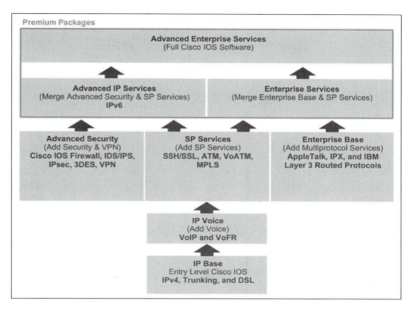

Figure 10-3 Cisco System Image Packaging

Three other premium packages offer additional IOS software feature combinations that address more complex network requirements. All features merge in the Advanced Enterprise Services package. This package integrates support for all routing protocols with Voice, Security, and VPN capabilities:

- **Advanced Enterprise Services:** Full Cisco IOS Software features

- **Enterprise Services:** Enterprise Base and Service Provider Services

- **Advanced IP Services:** Advanced Security, Service Provider Services, and support for IPv6

> **Note**
>
> The Cisco Feature Navigator is a tool used to find the right Cisco operating system depending on the features and technologies needed.

Cisco IOS 15.0 M and T Trains (10.1.1.5)

Following the Cisco IOS 12.4(24)T release, the next release of Cisco IOS Software was 15.0.

IOS 15.0 provides several enhancements to the operating system including:

- New feature and hardware support

- Broadened feature consistency with other major IOS releases

- More predictable new feature release and rebuild schedules

- Proactive individual release support policies

- Simplified release numbering

- Clearer software deployment and migration guidelines

As shown in Figure 10-4, Cisco IOS 15 uses a different release model from the traditional separate mainline and T trains of 12.4. Instead of diverging into separate trains, Cisco IOS Software 15 mainline and T will have *extended maintenance release (EM release)* and *standard maintenance release (T release)*. With the new IOS release model, Cisco IOS 15 mainline releases are referred to as M trains.

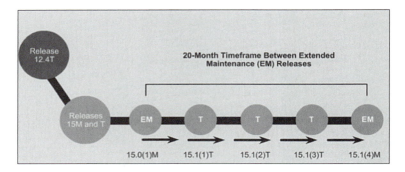

Figure 10-4   Cisco IOS Software 15 Release Family

Beginning with 15.0, new releases in the form of a T train are available approximately two to three times per year. EM releases are available approximately every 16 to 20 months. T releases enable faster Cisco feature delivery before the next EM release becomes available.

An EM release incorporates the features and hardware support of all the previous T releases. This makes newer EM releases available that contain the full functionality of the train at the time of release.

In summary, the benefits of the new Cisco IOS release model include:

- Feature inheritance from Cisco IOS Software Releases 12.4T and 12.4 mainline

- New feature releases approximately two to three times a year delivered sequentially from a single train

- EM releases approximately every 16 to 20 months and include new features

- T releases for the very latest features and hardware support before next EM release becomes available on Cisco.com

- Maintenance rebuilds of M and T releases contain bug fixes only

Cisco IOS 15 Train Numbering (10.1.1.6)

The release numbering convention for IOS 15 identifies the specific IOS release, including bug fixes and new software features, similar to previous IOS release families. Figure 10-5 shows examples of this convention for both the EM release and T release.

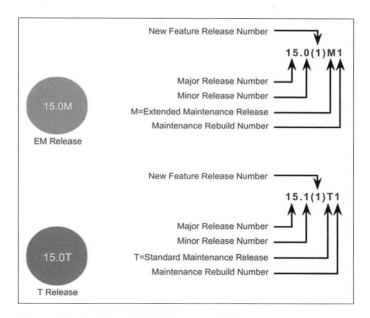

Figure 10-5   Cisco IOS Software 15 Train Numbering

Extended Maintenance Release

The EM release is ideal for long-term maintenance, enabling customers to qualify, deploy, and remain on the release for an extended period. The mainline train incorporates features delivered in previous releases plus incremental new feature enhancements and hardware support.

The first maintenance rebuild (for bug fixes only, not new features or new hardware support) of Release 15.0(1)M is numbered 15.0(1)M1. Subsequent maintenance releases are defined by an increment of the maintenance rebuild number (i.e., M2, M3, etc.).

Standard Maintenance Release

The T release is used for short deployment releases ideal for the latest new features and hardware support before the next EM release becomes available. The T release provides regular bug fix maintenance rebuilds, plus critical fix support for network affecting bugs such as Product Security Incident Report Team (PSIRT) issues.

The first planned 15 T new feature release is numbered Release 15.1(1)T. The first maintenance rebuild (for bug fixes only, not new features or new hardware support) of Release 15.1(1)T will be numbered 15.1(1)T1. Subsequent releases are defined by an increment of the maintenance rebuild number (i.e., T2, T3, etc.).

IOS 15 System Image Packaging (10.1.1.7)

Cisco Integrated Services Routers Generation Two (ISR G2) 1900, 2900, and 3900 Series support services on demand through the use of software licensing. The Services on Demand process enables customers to realize operational savings through ease of software ordering and management. When an order is placed for a new ISR G2 platform, the router is shipped with a single universal Cisco IOS Software image and a license is used to enable the specific feature set packages, as shown in Figure 10-6.

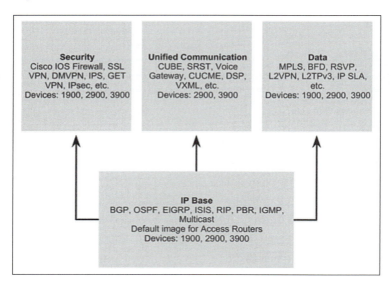

Figure 10-6   IOS Packaging Model for ISR G2 Routers

There are two types of universal images supported in ISR G2:

- **Universal images with the "universalk9" designation in the image name:** This universal image offers all of the Cisco IOS Software features, including strong payload cryptography features, such as IPsec VPN, SSL VPN, and Secure Unified Communications.

- **Universal images with the "universalk9_npe" designation in the image name:**
  The strong enforcement of encryption capabilities provided by Cisco IOS
  Software Activation satisfies requirements for the export of encryption capabilities. However, some countries have import requirements that require that the
  platform does not support any strong cryptography functionality, such as payload cryptography. To satisfy the import requirements of those countries, the
  npe universal image does not support any strong payload encryption.

With Cisco IOS Software Release 15.0, the cross-platform feature sets simplify the
image selection process by providing similar functions across platform boundaries.
Each device ships with the universal image. The technology packages IP Base, Data,
UC (Unified Communications), and SEC (Security) are enabled in the universal image
using Cisco IOS Software Activation licensing keys. Each licensing key is unique to a
particular device and is obtained from Cisco by providing the product ID and serial
number of the router and a *Product Activation Key (PAK)*. The PAK is provided by
Cisco at the time of software purchase. The IP Base is installed by default.

Table 10-1 shows the suggested migration for the next generation ISRs from the IOS
12 (IOS Reformation Packaging) to IOS 15 (Simplified Packaging).

Table 10-1   Suggested Transition from IOS 12 to 15

Reformation Packaging	Suggested Transition to Simplified Packaging
IP Base	IP Base
IP Voice	Unified Communications
Enterprise Base	Data
Enterprise Services	Data + Unified Communications
SP Services	Data + Unified Communications (for feature parity and Enterprise features)
Advanced Security	Security
Advanced IP Services	Security + Unified Communications + Data (for feature parity and Enterprise features)

IOS Image Filenames (10.1.1.8)

When selecting or upgrading a Cisco IOS router, it is important to choose the proper
IOS image with the correct feature set and version. The Cisco IOS image file is based
on a special naming convention. The name for the Cisco IOS image file contains multiple parts, each with a specific meaning. It is important to understand this naming
convention when upgrading and selecting a Cisco IOS Software image.

As shown in the following output, the **show flash** command displays the files stored in flash memory, including the system image files:

```
R1# show flash0:
-# - --length-- -----date/time------ path
<Output omitted>
8   68831808   Apr 2 2013 21:29:58 +00:00 c1900-universalk9-mz.SPA.152-4.M3.bin
182394880 bytes available (74092544 bytes used)
R1#
```

An example of an IOS 12.4 software image name is shown in Figure 10-7 and described here:

- **Image name (c2800nm):** Identifies the platform on which the image runs. In this example, the platform is a Cisco 2800 router with a network module.

- **advipservicesk9:** Specifies the feature set. In this example, advipservicesk9 refers to the Advanced IP Services feature set, which includes both the Advanced Security and Service Provider Services packages, along with IPv6 support.

- **mz:** Indicates where the image runs and if the file is compressed. In this example, mz indicates that the file runs from RAM and is compressed.

- **124-6.T:** The filename format for image 12.4(6)T. This is the train number, maintenance release number, and the train identifier.

- **bin:** The file extension. This extension indicates that this file is a binary executable file.

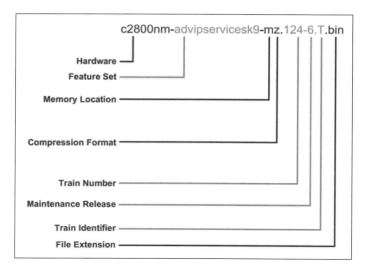

Figure 10-7 Example of a Cisco IOS 12.4 Software Image Name

Figure 10-8 illustrates the different parts of an IOS 15 system image file displayed with the **show flash** command:

- **Image name (c1900):** Identifies the platform on which the image runs. In this example, the platform is a Cisco 1900 router.

- **universalk9:** Specifies the feature set. In this case, universal refers to the universal, single image set, which includes IP Base, Security, Unified Communications, and Data feature sets. Each router is activated for the IP Base feature set. However, for other feature sets, IOS software activation is needed.

- **mz:** Indicates where the image runs and if the file is compressed. In this example, mz indicates that the file runs from RAM and is compressed.

- **SPA:** Designates that the file is digitally signed by Cisco.

- **152-4.M3:** Specifies the filename format for the image 15.2(4)M3. This is the version of IOS, which includes the major release, minor release, maintenance release, and maintenance rebuild numbers. The M indicates this is an extended maintenance release.

- **bin:** The file extension. This extension indicates that this file is a binary executable file.

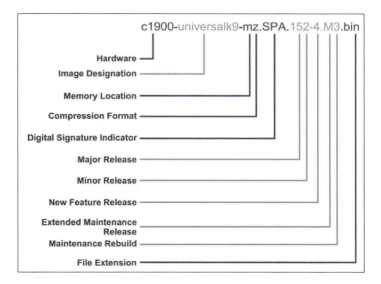

Figure 10-8   Example of a Cisco IOS 15.2 Software Image Name on an ISR G2 Device

The most common designation for memory location and compression format is mz. The first letter indicates the location where the image is executed on the router. The locations can include:

- **f:** Flash

- **m:** RAM

- **r:** ROM

- **l:** Relocatable

The compression format can be either z for zip or x for mzip. Zipping is a method Cisco uses to compress some run-from-RAM images that is effective in reducing the size of the image. It is self-unzipping, so when the image is loaded into RAM for execution, the first action is to unzip.

Note

The Cisco IOS Software naming conventions, field meaning, image content, and other details are subject to change.

Memory Requirements

On most Cisco routers, including the Integrated Services Routers (ISR), the IOS is stored in CompactFlash as a compressed image and loaded into DRAM during boot-up. The Cisco IOS Software Release 15.0 feature sets available for the Cisco 1900 and 2900 ISR require 256MB of flash and 512MB of RAM. The 3900 ISR requires 256MB of flash and 1GB of RAM. This does not include additional management tools such as Cisco Configuration Professional (Cisco CP). For complete details, refer to the product data sheet for the specific router.

Packet Tracer Activity 10.1.1.9: Decode IOS Image Names

As a network technician, it is important that you are familiar with the IOS image naming convention so that you can, at a glance, determine important information about operating systems currently running on a device. In this scenario, Company A has merged with Company B. Company A has inherited network equipment from Company B. You have been assigned to document the features for the IOS images on these devices.

Managing Cisco IOS Images (10.1.2)

It is import for network administrators to know how to manage their Cisco IOS images, including how to back up the image.

TFTP Servers as a Backup Location (10.1.2.1)

As a network grows, Cisco IOS Software images and configuration files can be stored on a central TFTP server, as shown in Figure 10-9. This helps to control the number of IOS images and the revisions to those IOS images, as well as the configuration files that must be maintained.

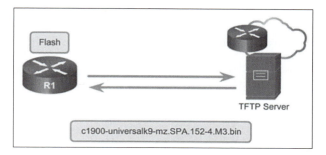

Figure 10-9   Central TFTP Server Used as Backup Location

Production internetworks usually span wide areas and contain multiple routers. For any network, it is good practice to keep a backup copy of the Cisco IOS Software image in case the system image in the router becomes corrupted or accidentally erased.

Widely distributed routers need a source or backup location for Cisco IOS Software images. Using a network TFTP server allows image and configuration uploads and downloads over the network. The network TFTP server can be another router, a workstation, or a host system.

Creating Cisco IOS Image Backup (10.1.2.2)

To maintain network operations with minimum down time, it is necessary to have procedures in place for backing up Cisco IOS images. This allows the network administrator to quickly copy an image back to a router in case of a corrupted or erased image.

In Figure 10-10, the network administrator wants to create a backup of the current image file on the router (c1900-universalk9-mz.SPA.152-4.M3.bin) to the TFTP server at 172.16.1.100.

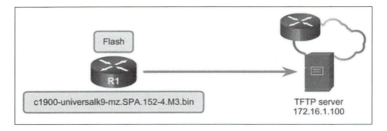

Figure 10-10   Creating Cisco IOS Image Backup

To create a backup of the Cisco IOS image to a TFTP server, perform the following three steps:

Step 1. Ensure that there is access to the network TFTP server. Ping the TFTP server to test connectivity, as shown in the following outputs.

Verify connectivity to the server:

```
R1# ping 172.16.1.100
Type escape sequence to abort.
Sending 5, 100-byte ICMP Echos to 172.16.1.100, timeout is 2 seconds:
!!!!!
Success rate is 100 percent (5/5), round-trip min/avg/max = 56/56/56 ms
```

Verify the image size:

```
R1# show flash0:
-# - --length-- -----date/time------ path
8   68831808   Apr 2 2013 21:29:58  +00:00 c1900-universalk9-mz.SPA.152-4.
M3.bin
<Output omitted>
```

Step 2. Verify that the TFTP server has sufficient disk space to accommodate the Cisco IOS Software image. Use the **show flash0:** command on the router to determine the size of the Cisco IOS image file. The file in the example is 68831808 bytes long, as shown in the previous output.

Step 3. Copy the image to the TFTP server using the **copy** *source-url destination-url* command:

```
R1# copy flash0: tftp:
Source filename []? c1900-universalk9-mz.SPA.152-4.M3.bin
Address or name of remote host []? 172.16.1.100
Destination filename []? c1900-universalk9-mz.SPA.152-4.M3.bin
!!!!!!!!!!!!!!!!!!!
<output omitted>
68831808 bytes copied in 363.468 secs (269058 bytes/sec)
```

After issuing the command using the specified source and destination URLs, the user is prompted for the source file name, IP address of the remote host, and destination file name. The transfer will then begin.

Activity 10.1.2.2: Backing Up Cisco IOS to TFTP Server

Go to the online course to use the Syntax Checker in the fourth graphic to practice copying the IOS to a TFTP server.

Copying a Cisco IOS Image (10.1.2.3)

Cisco consistently releases new Cisco IOS Software versions to resolve caveats and provide new features. This example uses IPv6 for the transfer to show that TFTP can also be used across IPv6 networks.

Figure 10-11 illustrates copying a Cisco IOS router image from a TFTP server. A new image file (c1900-universalk9-mz.SPA.152-4.M3.bin) will be copied from the TFTP server at 2001:DB8:CAFE:100::99 to the router.

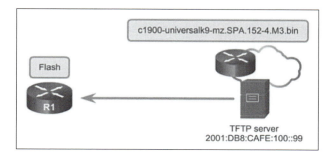

Figure 10-11   Copying Cisco IOS

Follow these steps to upgrade the software on the Cisco router:

How To

Step 1.   Select a Cisco IOS image file that meets the requirements in terms of platform, features, and software. Download the file from Cisco.com and transfer it to the TFTP server.

Step 2.   Verify connectivity to the TFTP server. Ping the TFTP server from the router. The following output shows the TFTP server is accessible from the router.

```
R1# ping 2001:DB8:CAFE:100::99
Type escape sequence to abort.
Sending 5, 100-byte ICMP Echos to 2001:DB8:CAFE:100::99, timeout is 2
seconds:
!!!!!
Success rate is 100 percent (5/5), round-trip min/avg/max = 56/56/56 ms
```

Step 3. Ensure that there is sufficient flash space on the router that is being upgraded. The amount of free flash can be verified using the **show flash0:** command. Compare the free flash space with the new image file size. The **show flash0:** command in the following example is used to verify free flash size. Free flash space in the example is 182,394,880 bytes.

```
R1# show flash0:
-# - --length-- -----date/time------ path
<Output omitted>
182394880 bytes available (74092544 bytes used)
R1#
```

Step 4. Copy the IOS image file from the TFTP server to the router using the **copy** command, as shown next. After issuing this command with specified source and destination URLs, the user will be prompted for the IP address of the remote host, source file name, and destination file name. The transfer of the file will begin.

```
R1# copy tftp: flash0:
Address or name of remote host []? 2001:DB8:CAFE:100::99
Source filename []? c1900-universalk9-mz.SPA.152-4.M3.bin
Destination filename []? c1900-universalk9-mz.SPA.152-4.M3.bin
Accessing tftp://2001:DB8:CAFE:100::99/c1900-universalk9-mz.SPA.152-4.
M3.bin...
Loading c1900-universalk9-mz.SPA.152-4.M3.bin from 2001:DB8:CAFE:100::99
(via
GigabitEthernet0/0): !!!!!!!!!!!!!!!!!!!!!
<Output omitted>
[OK - 68831808 bytes]
68831808 bytes copied in 368.128 secs (265652 bytes/sec)
```

Boot System (10.1.2.4)

To upgrade to the copied IOS image after that image is saved on the router's flash memory, configure the router to load the new image during bootup using the **boot system** command. Save the configuration. Reload the router to boot the router with the new image. After the router has booted, to verify the new image has loaded, use the **show version** command.

During startup, the bootstrap code parses the startup configuration file in NVRAM for the **boot system** commands that specify the name and location of the Cisco IOS Software image to load. Several **boot system** commands can be entered in sequence to provide a fault-tolerant boot plan.

The **boot system** command is a global configuration command that allows the user to specify the source for the Cisco IOS Software image to load. Set the image to boot and reload the system:

```
R1# configure terminal
R1(config)# boot system flash0://c1900-universalk9-mz.SPA.152-4.M3.bin
R1(config)# exit
R1# copy running-config startup-config
R1# reload
```

Some of the syntax options available include:

- Specify the flash device as the source of the Cisco IOS image:

  ```
  Router(config)# boot system flash0://c1900-universalk9-mz.SPA.152-4.M3.bin
  ```

- Specify the TFTP server as a source of the Cisco IOS image, with ROMmon as backup:

  ```
  Router(config)# boot system tftp://c1900-universalk9-mz.SPA.152-4.M3.bin
  Router(config)# boot system rom
  ```

If there are no **boot system** commands in the configuration, the router defaults to loading the first valid Cisco IOS image in flash memory and running it.

As shown in the following output, the **show version** command can be used to verify the software image file:

```
R1# show version
Cisco IOS Software, C1900 Software (C1900-UNIVERSALK9-M), Version 15.2(4)M3, RELEASE
    SOFTWARE (fc2)
Technical Support: http://www.cisco.com/techsupport
Copyright (c) 1986-2013 by Cisco Systems, Inc.
Compiled Tue 26-Feb-13 02:11 by prod_rel_team
ROM: System Bootstrap, Version 15.0(1r)M15, RELEASE SOFTWARE (fc1)
R1 uptime is 1 hour, 2 minutes
System returned to ROM by power-on
System image file is "flash0:c1900-universalk9-mz.SPA.152-4.M3.bin"
```

Packet Tracer Activity 10.1.2.5: Using a TFTP Server to Upgrade a Cisco IOS Image

A TFTP server can help manage the storage of IOS images and revisions to IOS images. For any network, it is good practice to keep a backup copy of the Cisco IOS Software image in case the system image in the router becomes corrupted or accidentally erased. A TFTP server can also be used to store new upgrades to the IOS and then deploy the upgrades throughout the network where they are needed. In this activity, you will upgrade the IOS images on Cisco devices by using a TFTP server. You will also back up an IOS image with the use of a TFTP server.

Video

Video Demonstration 10.1.2.6: Managing Cisco IOS Images

Go to the online course to view the video, Managing Cisco IOS Images. This video is also available on YouTube.com: http://www.youtube.com/watch?feature=player_embedded&v=aqSPf5Mcn54

IOS Licensing (10.2)

This section discusses the process of obtaining, installing, verifying, backing up, and uninstalling an IOS license.

Software Licensing (10.2.1)

Upgrading the IOS requires understanding and using the licensing process to install the software package. This section provides an overview of IOS licensing procedures and how to install specific software packages and features.

Licensing Overview (10.2.1.1)

Beginning with Cisco IOS Software Release 15.0, Cisco modified the process to enable new technologies within the IOS feature sets. Cisco IOS Software Release 15.0 incorporates cross-platform feature sets to simplify the image selection process. It does this by providing similar functions across platform boundaries. Each device ships with the same universal image. Technology packages are enabled in the universal image via Cisco IOS Software Activation licensing keys. The Cisco IOS Software Activation feature allows the user to enable licensed features and register licenses. The Cisco IOS Software Activation feature is a collection of processes and components used to activate Cisco IOS Software feature sets by obtaining and validating Cisco software licenses.

Figure 10-12 shows the technology packages that are available:

- IP Base
- Data
- Unified Communications (UC)
- Security (SEC)

Note

The IP Base license is a prerequisite for installing the Data, Security, and Unified Communications licenses. For earlier router platforms that can support Cisco IOS Software Release 15.0, a universal image is not available. It is necessary to download a separate image that contains the desired features.

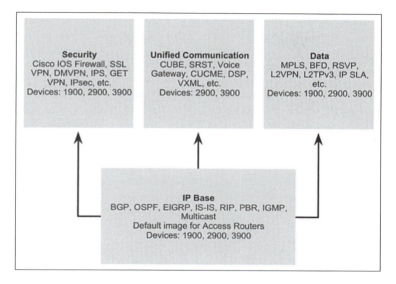

Figure 10-12 IOS Packaging Model for ISR G2 Routers

Technology Package Licenses

Technology package licenses are supported on Cisco ISR G2 platforms (Cisco 1900, 2900, and 3900 Series routers). The Cisco IOS universal image contains all packages and features in one image. Each package is a grouping of technology-specific features. Multiple technology package licenses can be activated on the Cisco 1900, 2900, and 3900 Series ISR platforms.

The details of each technology package license are as follows:

- **IP Base:** Offers features found in IPBase IOS image on ISR 1900, 2900, and 3900 + Flexible NetFlow + IPV6 parity for IPV4 features present in IPBase. Some of the key feature are AAA, BGP, OSPF, EIGRP, ISIS, RIP, PBR, IGMP, Multicast, DHCP, HSRP, GLBP, NHRP, HTTP, HQF, QoS, ACL, NBAR, GRE, CDP, ARP, NTP, PPP, PPPoA, PPPoE, RADIUS, TACACS, SCTP, SMDS, SNMP, STP, VLAN, DTP, IGMP, Snooping, SPAN, WCCP, ISDN, ADSL over ISDN, NAT-Basic X.25, RSVP, NTP, Flexible NetFlow, etc.

- **Data:** Data features found in SP Services and Enterprise Services IOS image on ISR 1900, 2900, and 3900; e.g., MPLS, BFD, RSVP, L2VPN, L2TPv3, Layer 2 Local Switching, Mobile IP, Multicast Authentication, FHRP-GLBP, IP SLAs, PfR, DECnet, RSRB, BIP, DLSw+, FRAS, Token Ring, ISL, IPX, STUN, SNTP, SDLC, QLLC, etc.

- **Unified Communications:** Offers the UC features found in IPVoice IOS image on ISR 1900, 2900, and 3900; e.g., TDM/PSTN Gateway, Video Gateway[H320/324], Voice Conferencing, Codec Transcoding, RSVP Agent (voice), FAX T.37/38, CAC/QOS, Hoot-n-Holler, etc.

- **Security:** Offers the security features found in Advanced Security IOS image on ISR 1900, 2900, and 3900; e.g., IKEv1/IPsec/PKI, IPsec/GRE, Easy VPN w/ DVTI, DMVPN, Static VTI, Firewall, Network Foundation Protection, GETVPN, etc.

Note

Use the **show license feature** command to view the technology package licenses and feature licenses supported on the router.

Licensing Process (10.2.1.2)

When a new router is shipped, it comes preinstalled with the software image and the corresponding permanent licenses for the customer-specified packages and features.

The router also comes with the evaluation license, known as a temporary license, for most packages and features supported on the specified router. This allows customers to try a new software package or feature by activating a specific evaluation license. If customers want to permanently activate a software package or feature on the router, they must get a new software license.

Figure 10-13 shows the three steps to permanently activate a new software package or feature on the router.

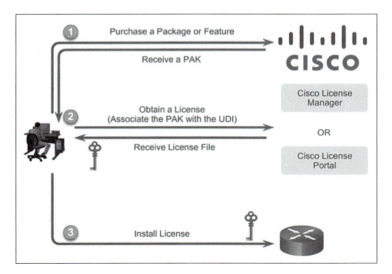

Figure 10-13   Licensing Overview

Step 1. Purchase the Software Package or Feature to Install (10.2.1.3)

The first step is to purchase the software package or feature needed. This may be the IP Base license for a specific software release or adding a package to IP Base, such as Security.

Software Claim Certificates are used for licenses that require IOS software activation. The claim certificate provides the Product Activation Key (PAK) for the license and important information regarding the Cisco End User License Agreement (EULA). In most instances, Cisco or the Cisco channel partner will have already activated the licenses ordered at the time of purchase and no Software Claim Certificate is provided.

In either instance, customers receive a PAK with their purchase. The PAK serves as a receipt and is used to obtain a license. A PAK is an 11-digit alphanumeric key created by Cisco manufacturing. It defines the Feature Set associated with the PAK. A PAK is not tied to a specific device until the license is created. A PAK can be purchased that generates any specified number of licenses. As shown in Figure 10-14, a separate license is required for each package: IP Base, Data, UC, and SEC.

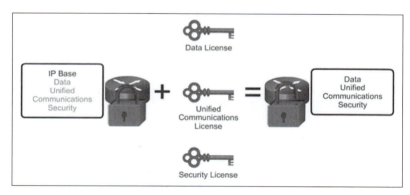

Figure 10-14   Purchasing a License for a Feature

Step 2. Obtain a License (10.2.1.4)

The next step is to obtain the license, which is actually a license file. A license file, also known as an IOS Software Activation License, is obtained using one of the following options:

- **Cisco License Manager (CLM):** This is a free software application available at http://www.cisco.com/go/clm. Cisco License Manager is a standalone application from Cisco that helps network administrators rapidly deploy multiple Cisco software licenses across their networks. Cisco License Manager can discover network devices, view their license information, and acquire and deploy licenses from

Cisco. The application provides a GUI that simplifies installation and helps automate license acquisition, as well as perform multiple licensing tasks from a central location. CLM is free of charge and can be downloaded from Cisco.com.

- **Cisco License Registration Portal:** This is the web-based portal for getting and registering individual software licenses, available at http://www.cisco.com/go/license.

Both of these processes require a PAK number and a *Unique Device Identifier (UDI)*.

The PAK is received during purchase.

The UDI is a combination of the Product ID (PID), the Serial Number (SN), and the hardware version. The SN is an 11-digit number which uniquely identifies a device. The PID identifies the type of device. Only the PID and SN are used for license creation. This UDI can be displayed using the **show license udi** command, as shown in the following output. This information is also available on a pull-out label tray found on the device. Figure 10-15 shows an example of the pull-out label on a Cisco 1941 router.

```
R1# show license udi
Device#     PID              SN              UDI
-------------------------------------------------------------------------
*0          CISCO1941/K9     FTX1636848Z     CISCO1941/K9:FTX1636848Z
R1#
```

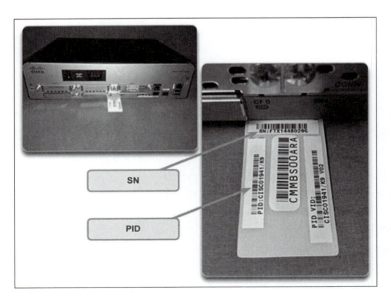

Figure 10-15   Displaying the UDI (PID/SN) on a Pull-out Label

After entering the appropriate information, the customer receives an email containing the license information to install the license file. The license file is an XML text file with a .lic extension.

Interactive Graphic

Activity 10.2.1.4: Displaying the UDI on Router R2

Go to the online course to use the Syntax Checker in the third graphic to practice displaying the UDI on a router.

Step 3. Install the License (10.2.1.5)

After the license has been purchased, the customer receives a license file, which is an XML text file with a .lic extension.

How To

Installing a permanent license requires two steps:

1. Use the **license install** *stored-location-url* privileged EXEC mode command to install a license file.

2. Reload the router using the privileged EXEC mode command **reload**. A reload is not required if an evaluation license is active.

The following output shows the configuration for installing the permanent license for the Security package on the router:

```
R1# license install flash0:seck9-C1900-SPE150_K9-FHH12250057.xml
Installing licenses from "seck9-c1900-SPE150_K9-FHH12250057.xml"
Installing...Feature:seck9...Successful:Supported
1/1 licenses were successfully installed
0/1 licenses were existing licenses
0/1 licenses were failed to install
R1#
*Jul 7 17:24:57.391: %LICENSE-6-INSTALL: Feature seck9 1.0 was installed in this
  device.
UDI=1900-SPE150/K9:FHH12250057; StoreIndex=15:Primary License Storage
*Jul 7 17:24:57.615: %IOS_LICENSE_IMAGE_APPLICATION-6-LICENSE_LEVEL: Module name =
  c1900
Next reboot level = seck9 and License = seck9
R1# reload
```

Note

Unified Communications is not supported on 1941 routers.

A permanent license is a license that never expires. After a permanent license is installed on a router, it is good for that particular feature set for the life of the router, even across IOS versions. For example, when a UC, SEC, or Data license is installed on a router, the subsequent features for that license are activated even if the router is upgraded to a new IOS release. A permanent license is the most common license type used when a feature set is purchased for a device.

> **Note**
>
> Cisco manufacturing preinstalls the appropriate permanent license on the ordered device for the purchased feature set. No customer interaction with the Cisco IOS Software Activation processes is required to enable that license on new hardware.

Interactive Graphic

Activity 10.2.1.5: Installing the Security on Router R2

Go to the online course to use the Syntax Checker in the second graphic to install a permanent license file on router R2.

License Verification and Management (10.2.2)

This section discusses how to verify, activate, back up, and uninstall a Cisco IOS license.

License Verification (10.2.2.1)

After a new license has been installed, the router must be rebooted using the **reload** command. As shown in the following example, the **show version** command is used after the router is reloaded to verify that the license has been installed:

```
R1# show version
<Output omitted>
License Info:
License UDI:
-------------------------------------------------
Device#    PID                   SN
-------------------------------------------------
*0         CISCO1941/K9          FTX1636848Z
Technology Package License Information for Module:'c1900'
-----------------------------------------------------------------
Technology    Technology-package              Technology-package
              Current       Type              Next reboot
-----------------------------------------------------------------
ipbase        ipbasek9      Permanent         ipbasek9
security      seck9         Permanent         seck9
```

```
uc             None          None          None
data           None          None          None
```

The **show license** command in the following example is used to display additional information about Cisco IOS Software licenses. This command displays license information used to help with troubleshooting issues related to Cisco IOS Software licenses. This command displays all the licenses installed in the system. In this example, both the IP Base and Security licenses have been installed. This command also displays the features that are available but not licensed to execute, such as the Data feature set. Output is grouped according to how the features are stored in license storage.

```
R1# show license
Index 1 Feature: ipbasek9
         Period left: Life time
         License Type: Permanent
         License State: Active, In Use
         License Count: Non-Counted
         License Priority: Medium
Index 2 Feature: securityk9
         Period left: Life time
         License Type: Permanent
         License State: Active, In Use
         License Count: Non-Counted
         License Priority: Medium
Index 3 Feature: datak9
         Period left: Not Activated
         Period Used: 0  minute  0   second
         License Type: EvalRightToUse
         License State: Not in Use, EULA not accepted
         License Count: Non-Counted
         License Priority: None
<Output omitted>
```

The following is a brief description of the output:

- **Feature:** Name of the feature.

- **License Type:** Type of license, such as Permanent or EvalRightToUse.

- **License State:** Status of the license, such as Active, In Use or Not in Use, EULA not accepted.

- **License Count:** Number of licenses available and in use, if counted. If Non-Counted is indicated, the license is unrestricted.

- **License Priority:** Priority of the license, such as high, medium, low, or none.

Note

Refer to the Cisco IOS IOS Software Activation Command Reference for complete details on the information displayed in the **show license** command.

Activate an Evaluation Right-To-Use License (10.2.2.2)

The Evaluation license process has gone through three revisions on the ISR G2 devices. The latest revision, starting with Cisco IOS Releases 15.0(1)M6, 15.1(1)T4, 15.1(2)T4, 15.1(3)T2, and 15.1(4)M Evaluation licenses, are replaced with *Evaluation Right-To-Use (RTU) licenses* after 60 days. An Evaluation license is good for a 60-day evaluation period. After the 60 days, this license automatically transitions into an RTU license. These licenses are available on the honor system and require the customer's acceptance of the EULA. The EULA is automatically applied to all Cisco IOS Software licenses.

The **license accept end user agreement** global configuration mode command is used to configure a one-time acceptance of the EULA for all Cisco IOS Software packages and features. After the command is issued and the EULA is accepted, the EULA is automatically applied to all Cisco IOS Software licenses and the user is not prompted to accept the EULA during license installation.

The following shows how to configure a one-time acceptance of the EULA:

```
R1(config)# license accept end user agreement
R1(config)# license boot module c1900 technology-package datak9
% use 'write' command to make license boot config take effect on next boot
R1(config)#
*Apr 25 23:15:01.874: %IOS_LICENSE_IMAGE_APPLICATION-6-LICENSE_LEVEL: Module name =
    c1900 Next reboot level = datak9 and License = datak9
*Apr 25 23:15:02.502: %LICENSE-6-EULA_ACCEPTED: EULA for feature datak9 1.0 has been
    accepted. UDI=CISCO1941/K9:FTX1636848Z; StoreIndex=1:Built-In License Storage
R1(config)#
```

As indicated in the second line, the following command syntax is used to activate an Evaluation RTU license:

```
Router# license boot module module-name technology-package package-name
```

Use the **?** command in place of the arguments to determine which module names and supported software packages are available on the router. Technology package names for Cisco ISR G2 platforms are:

- **ipbasek9**: IP Base technology package
- **securityk9**: Security technology package

- **datak9**: Data technology package
- **uck9**: Unified Communications package (not available on 1900 Series)

Evaluation licenses are temporary, and are used to evaluate a feature set on new hardware. Temporary licenses are limited to a specific usage period (for example, 60 days).

Reload the router after a license is successfully installed using the **reload** command. The **show license** command verifies that the license has been installed:

```
R1# show license
Index 1 Feature: ipbasek9
        Period left: Life time
        License Type: Permanent
        License State: Active, In Use
        License Count: Non-Counted
        License Priority: Medium
 Index 2 Feature: securityk9
        Period left: Life time
        License Type: Permanent
        License State: Active, In Use
        License Count: Non-Counted
        License Priority: Medium
 Index 3 Feature: datak9
        Period left: 8  weeks 4  days
        Period Used: 0  minute  0  second
        License Type: EvalRightToUse
        License State: Active, Not in Use, EULA accepted
        License Count: Non-Counted
        License Priority: Low
<Output omitted>
```

Activity 10.2.2.2: Activate an Evaluation Right-To-Use License

Go to the online course to use the Syntax Checker in the third graphic to save all license files on router R2 to accept the EULA and activate an Evaluation RTU data package license on the 1900 router.

Back Up the License (10.2.2.3)

The **license save** command is used to copy all licenses in a device and store them in a format required by the specified storage location. Saved licenses are restored by using the **license install** command.

The command to back up a copy of the licenses on a device is:

```
Router# license save file-sys://lic-location
```

Use the **show flash0:** command to verify that the licenses have been saved, as shown in Figure 10-16.

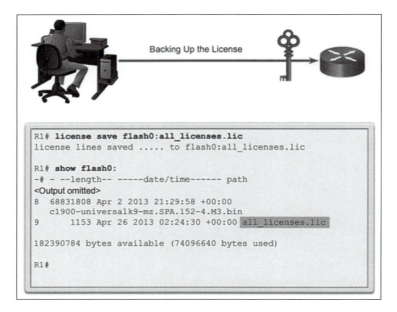

```
R1# license save flash0:all_licenses.lic
license lines saved ..... to flash0:all_licenses.lic

R1# show flash0:
-# - --length-- -----date/time------ path
<Output omitted>
8   68831808 Apr 2 2013 21:29:58 +00:00
    c1900-universalk9-mz.SPA.152-4.M3.bin
9       1153 Apr 26 2013 02:24:30 +00:00 all_licenses.lic

182390784 bytes available (74096640 bytes used)

R1#
```

Figure 10-16   Backing Up the License

The license storage location can be a directory or a URL that points to a file system. Use the **?** command to see the storage locations supported by a device.

Interactive Graphic

Activity 10.2.2.3: Saving the License Files to Flash

Go to the online course to use the Syntax Checker in the second graphic to save all license files on router R2.

Uninstall the License (10.2.2.4)

To clear an active permanent license from the Cisco 1900 Series, 2900 Series, and 3900 Series routers, perform the following steps:

Step 1.   Disable the technology package.

Disable the active license with the command:

```
Router(config)# license boot module module-name technology-package package-
name disable
```

Reload the router using the **reload** command. A reload is required to make the software package inactive.

Step 2.   Clear the license.

Clear the technology package license from license storage:

```
Router# license clear feature-name
```

Clear the **license boot module** *module-name* **technology-package** *package-name* **disable** command used for disabling the active license:

```
Router(config)# no license boot module module-name technology-package
package-name disable
```

Note

Some licenses, such as built-in licenses, cannot be cleared. Only licenses that have been added by using the **license install** command are removed. Evaluation licenses are not removed.

Figure 10-17 shows an example of clearing an active license.

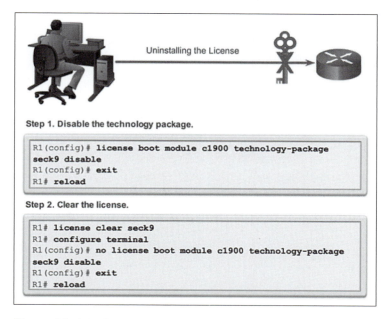

Figure 10-17   Clearing an Active and Permanent License

Interactive Graphic

Activity 10.2.2.4: Uninstalling the License on R2

Go to the online course to use the Syntax Checker in the second graphic to uninstall the security license on router R2.

Video

Video Demonstration 10.2.2.5: Working with IOS 15 Image Licenses on an ISR-G2 Device

Go to the online course to view the video, Working with IOS 15 Image Licenses on an ISR-G2 Device. This video is also available on YouTube.com: http://www.youtube.com/watch?feature=player_embedded&v=ojCFW92tY_E

Summary (10.3)

Class Activity 10.3.1.1: Powerful Protocols

Go to the online course to perform this practice activity.

Scenario

At the end of this course, you are asked to complete two Capstone Projects where you will create, configure, and verify two network topologies using the two main routing protocols taught in this course, EIGRP and OSPF.

To make things easier, you decide to create a chart of configuration and verification commands to use for these two design projects. To help devise the protocol charts, ask another student in the class to help you.

Refer to the PDF for this chapter for directions on how to create a design for this modeling project. When complete, share your work with another group or with the class. You may also want to save the files created for this project in a network portfolio for future reference.

Interactive Graphic

Packet Tracer Activity 10.3.1.2: EIGRP Capstone

In this Capstone Project activity, you will demonstrate your ability to:

- Design, configure, verify, and secure EIGRP, IPv4, or IPv6 on a network
- Design a VLSM addressing scheme for the devices connected to the LANs
- Present your design using network documentation from your Capstone Project network

Packet Tracer ☐ Activity

Packet Tracer Activity 10.3.1.3: OSPF Capstone

In this Capstone Project activity, you will demonstrate your ability to:

- Configure basic OSPFv2 to enable internetwork communications in a small- to medium-sized IPv4 business network
- Implement advanced OSPF features to enhance operation in a small- to medium-sized business network
- Implement multiarea OSPF for IPv4 to enable internetwork communications in a small- to medium-sized business network
- Configure basic OSPFv3 to enable internetwork communications in a small- to medium-sized IPv6 business network

Packet Tracer
☐ Activity

Packet Tracer Activity 10.3.1.4: Skills Integration Challenge

As a network technician familiar with IPv4 addressing, routing, and network security, you are now ready to apply your knowledge and skills to a network infrastructure. Your task is to finish designing the VLSM IPv4 addressing scheme, implement multi-area OSPF, and secure access to the VTY lines using access control lists.

Examples of Cisco IOS Software releases include 12.3, 12.4, 15.0, and 15.1. Along with each software release there are new versions of the software used to implement bug fixes and new features.

Cisco IOS Software 12.4 incorporates new software features and hardware support that was introduced in the Cisco IOS Software 12.3T train and additional software fixes. Mainline releases (also called maintenance releases) contain no uppercase letter in their release designation and inherit new Cisco IOS Software functionality and hardware from lower numbered T releases. Prior to and including 12.4, the mainline "M" train received bug fixes only. The technology "T" train includes fixes as well as new features and platforms. The 12.4T train provides Cisco IOS Software functionality and hardware adoption that introduces new technology, functionality, and hardware advances that are not available in the Cisco IOS Software 12.4 mainline train.

In the Cisco IOS Software 15.0 release family, a new strategy is in place. The Cisco IOS 15.0 release family does not diverge into separate M and T trains but into M and T releases in the same train. For example, the first release in the Cisco IOS Software 15.0 release family is 15.0(1)M, where M indicates it is an extended maintenance release. An extended maintenance release is ideal for long-term maintenance. Not all releases in the Cisco IOS Software 15.0 release family will be extended maintenance releases; there will also be standard maintenance releases that receive the latest features and hardware support. The standard maintenance releases will have an uppercase T in their designation.

When selecting or upgrading a Cisco IOS router, it is important to choose the proper IOS image with the correct feature set and version. The Cisco IOS image file is based on a special naming convention. The name for the Cisco IOS image file contains multiple parts, each with a specific meaning (example: c1900-universalk9-mz.SPA.152-4. M3.bin).

Commands are available for upgrading and verification of IOS in flash. The **show flash** command displays the files stored in flash memory, including the system image files. This command can also be used to verify free flash size. The **boot system** command is a global configuration command which allows the user to specify the source for the Cisco IOS.

Using a network TFTP server allows image and configuration uploads and downloads over the network. The network TFTP server can be another router, a workstation, or a host system.

Beginning with Cisco IOS Software Release 15.0, Cisco modified the process to enable new technologies within the IOS feature sets. Each device ships with the same universal image. Technology packages such as IP Base, Data, UC (Unified Communications), and SEC are enabled in the universal image via Cisco IOS Software Activation licensing keys. Each licensing key is unique to a particular device and is obtained from Cisco by providing the product ID and serial number of the router and a Product Activation Key (PAK).

License activation is not necessary for factory ordered preconfigured licenses prior to use. IP Base comes shipped as a permanent license on all ISR-G2 devices. The other three technology packages, Data, Security, and Unified Communications, come with the option of activating an Evaluation license, but a permanent license may be purchased.

A permanent license is a license that never expires. For example, once a UC, Security, or Data license is installed on a router, the subsequent features for that license will be activated even if the router is upgraded to a new IOS release.

Installing a License

Prerequisites:

- Obtain the necessary PAK, which is an 11-digit ID that can be delivered by mail or electronically

- Need to have a valid Cisco username/password

- Retrieve serial number and PID with the **show license udi** command or from the router label tray

The **show version** command is used after the router is reloaded to verify that the license has been installed.

The **show license** command is used to display additional information about Cisco IOS Software licenses.

The **license accept end user agreement** global configuration command is used to configure a one-time acceptance of the EULA for all Cisco IOS Software packages and features.

Use the Cisco.com website to research other benefits and information on IOS 15.

Practice

The following activities provide practice with the topics introduced in this chapter. The Labs and Class Activities are available in the companion *Routing Protocols Lab Manual* (978-1-58713-322-0). The Packet Tracer Activities PKA files are found in the online course.

Class Activities

Class Activity 10.0.1.2: IOS Detection

Class Activity 10.3.1.1: Powerful Protocols

Packet Tracer Activities

Packet Tracer Activity 10.1.1.9: Decoding IOS Image Names

Packet Tracer Activity 10.1.2.5: Using a TFTP Server to Upgrade a Cisco IOS Image

Packet Tracer Activity 10.3.1.2: EIGRP Capstone

Packet Tracer Activity 10.3.1.3: OSPF Capstone

Packet Tracer Activity 10.3.1.4: Skills Integration Challenge

Check Your Understanding Questions

Complete all the review questions listed here to test your understanding of the topics and concepts in this chapter. The appendix, "Answers to the 'Check Your Understanding' Questions," lists the answers.

1. Which IOS 12.4 software package will integrate security features such as Cisco IOS Firewall and IDS/IPS? (Choose three.)

   A. IP Base

   B. IP Voice

   C. Advanced Security

   D. SP Services

   E. Enterprise Base

   F. Advanced IP Services

   G. Enterprise Services

   H. Advanced Enterprise Services

2. What is the minor release number in the IOS image name c1900-universalk9-mz.
   SPA.152-4.M3.bin?

   A. 1

   B. 15

   C. 5

   D. 2

   E. 3

   F. 9

3. Using the following output, which licenses are currently installed on this router?
   (Choose all that apply.)

   ```
   Router# show license
   Index 1 Feature: ipbasek9
           Period left: Life time
           License Type: Permanent
           License State: Active, In Use
           License Count: Non-Counted
           License Priority: Medium
   Index 2 Feature: securityk9
           Period left: Not Activated
           Period Used: 0  minute  0  second
           License Type: Evaluation
           License State: Not in Use, EULA not accepted
           License Count: Non-Counted
           License Priority: None
   Index 3 Feature: uck9
           Period left: Not Activated
           Period Used: 0  minute  0  second
           License Type: Evaluation
           License State: Not in Use, EULA not accepted
           License Count: Non-Counted
           License Priority: None
   Index 4 Feature: datak9
           Period left: 625 weeks 0  day
           Period Used: 0  minute  0  second
           License Type: Evaluation
           License State: Active, Not in Use, EULA accepted
           License Count: Non-Counted
           License Priority: Low
   ```

   A. IP Base

   B. Security

   C. Unified Communications

   D. Data

4. What does the "mz" indicate in the IOS image name c1900-universalk9-mz. SPA.152-3.T.bin?

A. The file is compressed.

B. The file is digitally signed by Cisco.

C. The file is loaded in DRAM during boot-up.

D. The image is an extended maintenance release 1.

5. What command is used on a 2900 Series ISR G2 to verify the name of the IOS images in flash?

A. **show version**

B. **show flash0:**

C. **show memory**

D. **show running-config**

6. Which Cisco IOS 15.0 software image and license enables Cisco IOS Firewall on a 2900 Series ISR G2?

A. IP Base

B. Security

C. Unified Communications

D. Data

7. Which Cisco IOS 15.0 software image and license enables EIGRP for IPv6 on a 2900 Series ISR G2?

A. IP Base

B. Security

C. Unified Communications

D. Data

8. How long is the evaluation period for the Cisco IOS 15 Unified Communications software package?

A. 1 day

B. 7 days

C. 30 days

D. 60 days

E. 180 days

9. What is the PAK used for? (Choose two.)

   A. Serves as a receipt for the purchase

   B. Contains important information regarding the end user agreement

   C. Contains the 11-digit alphanumeric serial number

   D. Used to obtain a license

10. What command will display the UDI (Unique Device Identifier) on a Cisco ISR Series router running IOS 15?

   A. show udi

   B. show license udi

   C. show version

   D. show license

11. What command is used to configure a one-time acceptance of the Cisco End User License agreement for all Cisco IOS Software packages and features?

   A. license eula accept

   B. license accept end user agreement

   C. license install

   D. license save end user agreement

   E. license boot module

12. What command is used to activate an Evaluation RTU license?

   A. license eula accept

   B. license accept end user agreement

   C. license install

   D. license save end user agreement

   E. license boot module

Answers to the "Check Your Understanding" Questions

Chapter 1

1. D. Explanation: RAM stores the running IOS, running configuration file, IP routing and ARP tables, and memory buffers for various packets. ROM on the other hand stores the bootstrap instructions, basic diagnostic software, and a limited version of the IOS. NVRAM stores the start-up configuration file, and Flash is used to store the IOS and other system-related files.

2. D. Explanation: The **show ip interface brief** command is very useful, as it displays a summary status of all configured interfaces. Specifically, it displays the IP address and Layer 1 statuses. The three other choices are not valid commands.

3. A. Explanation: The **enable secret quiz** command configures and encrypts the privileged EXEC password "quiz". Option B is not a valid command. Option C would create a privileged EXEC password, but it would not be encrypted and would actually be "secret quiz". Finally, option D is not correct because the resulting password would be "password quiz".

4. C. Explanation: To determine the best path, the router searches its routing table for a network address that matches the destination IP address of the packet.

5. B and D. Explanation: One task that routing protocols are responsible for is discovering networks and adding those networks to the routing table. After those routes are added to the routing table, the routing protocol is responsible for updating and maintaining the routes in the routing table. Routing protocols are not responsible for discovering hosts, propagating a default gateway for hosts, or assigning IP addresses.

6. C. Explanation: At this point, only the router's directly connected networks are in the routing table. Remote networks can be added only by configuring static routes or by using a dynamic routing protocol.

7. B and D. Explanation: All packets that are forwarded by the router must be resolved to an exit interface in the routing table. If a route only has a next-hop IP address, that next-hop address must eventually be resolved to another route in the routing table that does include an exit interface, such as a directly connected network.

8. D. Explanation: The **link-local** parameter tells the router to use this address as a link-local address rather than the automatically derived link-local address. The **eui-64** parameter in the **ipv6 address** command specifies that the router should combine the configured network prefix with an automatically generated interface identifier. Using the command **ipv6 enable** instructs the router to use router advertisements to automatically determine both the network prefix and the interface identifier.

9. A. Explanation: A metric is used by routing protocols as a quantitative value to measure the distance to a remote network.

10. B. Explanation: The only correct option is B.

11. C. Explanation: By default, Cisco routers can load balance up to four equal cost paths. The maximum number of equal cost paths depends on the routing protocol and IOS version.

12. A and C. Explanation: Options A and C are correct.

13. A. Explanation: As a packet travels across Layer 3 devices, the Layer 2 addresses must change at every hop. The Layer 3 devices must remove the existing source and destination Layer 2 addresses and replace them with the appropriate ones for the next network segment.

14. Explanation:

Central processing unit (CPU): Executes operating system instructions, such as system initialization, routing functions, and network interface control.

Random Access Memory (RAM): Stores the routing table and other data structures that the router needs when forwarding packets.

Read-Only Memory (ROM): Holds basic diagnostic software used when the router is powered on.

Non-Volatile RAM (NVRAM): Stores the startup configuration, including IP addresses, routing protocol, and other related information. NVRAM is a portion of the boot ROM chip.

Flash memory: Stores the operating system (Cisco IOS) and other files.

15. Explanation:

Test the router hardware:

Perform POST.

Execute bootstrap loader.

Locate and load the Cisco IOS Software:

Locate the IOS.

Load the IOS.

Locate and load the startup configuration file or enter setup mode:

Locate the configuration file.

Execute the configuration file.

Enter setup mode if there is not startup configuration available.

16. Explanation: A router connects multiple IP networks and determines the best path to send packets.

17. Explanation: The steps to configure the basic settings on a router are:

Step 1. Name the device.

Step 2. Secure management access.

Step 3. Configure a banner.

Step 4. Save the configuration.

18. Explanation: A routing table provides the router with the necessary information to carry out its primary function—forwarding packets toward the destination network.

19. Explanation: A router learns about networks in the following ways:

Connected routes

Static routes

Dynamic routes

20. B, E, and F. Explanation: Options B, E, and F are correct.

21. Explanation: By default, all router interfaces are shut down. The **no shutdown** command must be configured on the interface.

22. Explanation: All IPv6-enabled interfaces must have a link-local IPv6 address. This address can be statically configured or dynamically configured.

23. Explanation: An ARP request is used to determine any unknown MAC address when the destination IP address is known. In an IPv4-based network, this request is sent as a Layer 2 broadcast.

Chapter 2

1. A and D. Explanation: The **ip route 10.0.0.0 255.0.0.0 172.16.40.2** command is used by Router A to reach Router B's remote network. The **ip route 192.168.1.0 255.255.255.0 172.16.40.1** command is used by Router B to reach Router A's remote network. Both commands use the IPv4 address of the next-hop router.

2. C and D. Explanation: All routes in the routing table must be resolved to an exit interface in the routing table. If a route only has a next-hop address, that next-hop address must eventually be resolved to another route in the routing table that does include an exit interface, such as a directly connected network. When a router is enabled with CEF, the FIB and adjacency tables work together to determine the exit interface. Therefore, a recursive lookup is not required.

3. A and E. Explanation: Configuring a static route does not ensure that a path is always available. If the exit interface or next-hop address is not available, then the static route will not be included in the routing table. Dynamic routing protocols are used to dynamically determine the best path to a destination network. Dynamic routing protocols are typically a better option on large networks and most networks that are not stub networks.

4. D. Explanation: The correct command is **ip route 0.0.0.0 0.0.0.0 10.0.0.1**. When configuring IPv4 static routes, the **ip** command is used. The subnet mask in dotted decimal notation must be included.

5. C. Explanation: The correct command is **ipv6 route ::/0 2001:DB8:ACAD:1::1**. When configuring IPv6 static routes, the **ipv6** command is used. The :: represents the all-zeros address, followed by a /0 prefix length with no spaces.

6. False. Explanation: By default, all static routes have an administrative distance of 1. Only a directly connected network can have an administrative distance of 0. Static routes can be configured with an administrative distance greater than 1, commonly used to configure a floating static route.

7. C. Explanation: The summary address would be 10.0.12.0 255.255.252.0. The first step is to list all four addresses in binary format. The second step is to count the number of matching bits to determine the subnet mask or prefix length. The number of matching bits is 14 or /14 prefix length. A /14 prefix length is equivalent to a 255.255.252.0 subnet mask. The last step is to add all zeros to the rest of the address to determine the network address.

8. A. Explanation: A default route is used when there is not a more specific match in the routing table for the destination IP address of the packet. A summary route is used to replace multiple static routes using the same next-hop router, with a single static route. There is no such route formally known as a backup static route.

9. True. Explanation: It is common that a static route, such as a default static route, is configured on the router connected to the upstream provider, such as an ISP. The static route can be propagated by the dynamic routing protocol to other routers in the routing domain if desired.

10. C. Explanation: The **show ipv6 route** command is used to display the IPv6 routing table. The **show ipv6 route static** command will only display static routes in the IPv6 routing table.

Chapter 3

1. B and D. Explanation: Static routes are considered more secure because they are not propagated between routers and therefore are not susceptible to snooping or malicious attacks. Dynamic routes can be secured using authentication. Static routes require no computing overhead because they are not propagated between routers. Note: There is some computing overhead with static routes, but it is minimal.

2. Explanation:

   A. Path vector exterior routing protocol: BGP

   B. Cisco advanced interior routing protocol: EIGRP

   C. Link-state interior routing protocol: OSPF

   D. Distance vector interior routing protocol: RIP

   E. Cisco distance vector interior routing protocol: IGRP

3. B. Explanation: Convergence is the time required by routers to have complete and accurate information about the network.

4. C and E. Explanation: Dynamic routing protocols perform network discovery and update and maintain routing tables.

5. A and C. Explanation: Hop count is used by RIP. Bandwidth is used by IGRP, EIGRP, and OSPF. The other choices are not valid routing protocol metrics.

6. A. Explanation: Given these choices, EIGRP internal routes are the most trustworthy, with the lowest administrative distance of 90. IS-IS has an administrative distance of 115, OSPF has an administrative distance of 110, and RIP, which includes both versions 1 and 2, has an administrative distance of 120.

7. B. Explanation: The **show ip route** command displays route entry information, including the administrative distance. The administrative distance is the first number in brackets, followed by the metric. For example, [120/2] shows an administrative distance of 120 (RIP) and a metric of 2 (hop count).

8. D. Explanation: A directly connected network will appear in the routing table when it is addressed and operational at Layer 3—in other words, when it has been configured with an IP address and subnet mask, and the interface and line protocol are both in the up state.

9. A. Explanation: Router R1 will choose the path with the lowest metric. If two paths share the same metric, then R1 will load balance across each link (up to four equal cost links by default).

10. A and C. Explanation: An LSP (link-state packet) is sent during initial startup of the routing protocol process on a router; and whenever there is a change in the topology, including a link going down or coming up, or a neighbor adjacency being established or broken. Data traffic congestion does not directly influence routing protocol behavior. LSPs are not flooded periodically, and update timers are not relevant to LSPs.

11. C. Explanation: If the best match is a level 1 ultimate route, then the router will forward the packet to that network. A level 1 parent route is a route that contains subnets and is not used to forward packets. Level 1 child routes and level 2 supernet routes are not valid routing table entries.

12. A. Explanation: Routers running IOS release 15 have link-local routing table entries for both IPv4 and IPv6. The selection of both IPv6 routes and IPv4 routes is based on the longest matching prefix. The routing tables of both IPv6 and IPv4 use directly connected interfaces, static routes, and dynamically learned routes.

13. Explanation:

   A. eBGP: 20

   B. EIGRP (Internal): 90

   C. EIGRP (External): 170

   D. IS-IS: 115

   E. OSPF: 110

   F. RIP: 120

14. Explanation:

   A. Does not support discontiguous networks: classful routing protocol

   B. EIGRP, OSPF, and BGP: classless routing protocol

   C. Sends subnet mask information in routing updates: classless routing protocol

   D. Supports discontiguous networks: classless routing protocol

    E.   RIP version 1 and IGRP: classful routing protocol

    F.   Does not send subnet mask in its routing updates: classful routing protocol

    G.   Allows for use of both 172.16.1.0/26 and 172.16.1.128/27 subnets in the same topology: classless routing protocol

15. Explanation: Static routing is more secure, uses less router computational power, and is easier to understand. It is more secure because routers do not advertise routing information to other routers. It uses less router resources than dynamic routing, which requires the implementation of algorithms and the processing of update packets. It is often easier to understand than some of the more complex routing protocols.

16. Explanation: Dynamic routing protocols can be classified as either interior or exterior, distance vector or link-state, classful or classless, and by speed of convergence.

17. Explanation: Hop count, bandwidth, delay, and cost.

18. Explanation: Administrative distance is a measure of the trustworthiness of a route source. It is used when a router has learned routes to the same destination from two different route sources. It is important because not all route sources are equal. For example, you certainly would not want a router sending traffic to another router if the destination is a directly connected network! Administrative distance ensures that this does not happen because directly connected routes are trusted over all other route sources.

19. Explanation: A passive interface allows a router to receive routing updates on an interface but not send updates via that interface.

Chapter 4

1. D. Explanation: The PDM, or protocol-dependent module, gives EIGRP the capability to support different Layer 3 protocols such as IPv4, IPX, and AppleTalk.

2.

    C

    E

    A

    B

    D

3. B. Explanation: EIGRP uses Hello packets to discover neighbors and to form adjacencies with those neighbors. EIGRP Hello packets are multicasts and use unreliable delivery. An EIGRP router assumes that as long as it is receiving Hello packets from a neighbor, the neighbor and its routes remain viable.

4. C. Explanation: When a route has failed and there is not a feasible successor in the topology table, DUAL puts the route into active state as it queries its neighbors looking for a new successor.

5. C, E, and F. Explanation: Besides the IP routing table, EIGRP maintains a separate neighbor table and topology table.

6. A. Explanation: Before EIGRP exchanges any routing updates with other routers, it must first discover its neighbors. These neighbors are added to the neighbor table. EIGRP also maintains a topology table with the successors and feasible successors. Only the successors are entered into the routing table.

7. C. Explanation: The value of 255/255 represents a link that is 100 percent reliable. Reliability is a measurement of the probability that the link will fail or how often the link has experienced errors.

8. A

   B

   C

   E

   D

9. D. Explanation: The command **show ip eigrp topology all-links** will show successors, feasible successors, and next-hop routers that do not meet the feasibility condition.

10. C. Explanation: The feasible successor is the second entry, via 172.16.3.1, because its feasible distance is higher than the via 192.168.10.10 entry. The first value, 41026560, would be the feasible distance to 192.168.1.0/24 should Router1 use this path as the successor. The second value, 2172416, is the reported distance. The reported distance or advertised distance is simply an EIGRP neighbor's feasible distance to the same destination network. The reported distance is the metric that a router reports to a neighbor about its own cost to that network.

11. Explanation: DUAL (Diffusing Update Algorithm)

12. Explanation: No, EIGRP sends nonperiodic bounded updates, only the routing information that is needed and only to those routers that need it. *Nonperiodic* means that the updates are not sent at regular intervals, and are only sent when there is a metric change.

13. Explanation: **show ipv6 eigrp neighbors**

14. Explanation: Bandwidth, delay, reliability, and load. Only bandwidth and delay are used by default.

15. Explanation: When the neighbor's reported distance (RD) to a network is less than this router's feasible distance (FD) to the same destination network.

16. D. Explanation: EIGRP for IPv6 uses a different method to enable an interface for EIGRP. Instead of using the **network** router configuration mode command to specify matching interface addresses, EIGRP for IPv6 is configured directly on the interface using the interface command **ipv6 eigrp** *autonomous-system*.

17. C. Explanation: EIGRP for IPv6 uses a 32-bit router ID, similar to EIGRP for IPv4. If an EIGRP for IPv6 router does not have any active interfaces with an IPv4 address, then the **eigrp router-id** command is required.

Chapter 5

1. B. Explanation: The EIGRP router command **auto-summary** is used. Beginning with IOS 15.0(1) and 12.2(33), auto-summarization is disabled by default.

2. True. Explanation: The **show ip protocols** command will display the status of EIGRP auto-summarization as either "enabled" or "disabled."

3. A. Explanation: Manual EIGRP auto-summarization is enabled on the interface using the **ip summary-address eigrp** *as-number network-address subnet-mask* command.

4. D. Explanation: This command will limit the EIGRP process to using no more than 25% of the link's bandwidth.

5. A and B. Explanation: The EIGRP **passive-interface** command prevents both outgoing and incoming routing updates. The router will not form a neighbor adjacency with any other routers on that interface. EIGRP will still advertise the interface's network address as long as it is included in a network statement.

6. A. Explanation: When EIGRP automatic summarization is enable, an EIGRP summary Null0 route is created when there is at least one subnet that was learned via EIGRP and there are two or more network EIGRP router configuration commands. The purpose of the Null0 summary route is to prevent routing loops.

7. D. Explanation: EIGRP for IPv6 does not use automatic summarization because there are no classful networks in IPv6 addressing.

8. A. Explanation: An IPv4 default static route is configured using the **ip route** global configuration command. This route can be propagated using the **redistribute static** EIGRP router configuration command. There are other methods that can be used to distribute a default route in EIGRP depending on the topology and the requirements of the network.

9. B. Explanation: By default, Cisco IOS allows load balancing of up to four equal cost paths. The EIGRP **maximum-paths** command is used to modify the number of equal cost routes, up to 32.

10. D. Explanation: EIGRP authentication using MD5 requires two steps: the creation of a key chain and key, and the configuration of EIGRP authentication to use that key chain and key. There are two interface commands required to apply the MD5 authentication using the key: **ip authentication mode eigrp** *as-number* **md5** and **ip authentication key-chain eigrp** *as-number name-of-key*.

Chapter 6

1. A, C, and D. Explanation: Link-state routing protocols use a link-state routing algorithm, as compared to distance vector routing protocols, which use some form of the Bellman-Ford algorithm. Link-state routing protocols base their algorithm on Dijkstra's algorithm. This algorithm uses a database of link-state information to determine the shortest path to each network.

2. A and D. Explanation: Loopback addresses are commonly used to configure the router ID in OSPF. One of their main benefits is that these interfaces cannot go down, which creates a stable and predictable OSPF router ID.

3. A and B. Explanation: The DR and BDR are only elected on multi-access networks such as Ethernet.

4. B. Explanation: Each OSPF router builds adjacencies based on its own position in the topology. Each routing table in the area is developed individually through the application of the SPF algorithm. The link-state database for an area, however, must reflect the same information for all routers.

5. C. Explanation: The number 100 represents the OSPF process ID. This value has local significance only and does not need to match the process ID on other routers in the OSPF routing domain.

6. A. Explanation: The **bandwidth** command is used to modify the value of the interface used in determining the OSPF routing metric. It does not have an effect on the actual speed of the link. The bandwidth value should reflect the actual speed of the link; otherwise, the routing tables might not reflect the best paths to networks.

7. C. Explanation: The RFC for OSPF states that cost of an interface is used for the routing metric. However, the RFC does not specify how to determine that cost. Cisco IOS Software uses the cumulative bandwidths of the outgoing interfaces from the router to the destination network to calculate the cost value.

8. C. Explanation: The wildcard mask can be found by subtracting the subnet mask from 255.255.255.255.

9. D. Explanation: If OSPF interface priorities are equal, which they are by default with a value of 1, the router with the highest router ID becomes the DR, and the router with the second highest router ID becomes the BDR.

10. B. Explanation: Hello, LSR (link-state request), LSAck (LSA acknowledgment), and DBD (database description) are all valid OSPF packets. LRU is not a valid OSPF packet, but LSU (link-state update) would be.

11. D. Explanation: Both versions of OSPF use the same five basic packet types, the cost metric, and the DR/BDR election process. Hello packets are used in both versions to build adjacencies. OSPFv3, however, uses advanced encryption and authentication features that are provided by IPsec, while OSPFv2 uses either plain text or MD5 authentication.

12. Explanation: The **show ipv6 route ospf** command.

13. Explanation: No, unlike EIGRP, the OSPF process ID is locally significant and does not need to match other OSPF routers.

14. Explanation: The OSPF router ID is 10.1.1.1, the highest loopback address in the absence of the OSPF **router-id** command.

15. Explanation: The **show interfaces** command.

16. Explanation: The **ip ospf cost** interface command.

17. Explanation: By default, OSPF Hello packets are sent every 10 seconds on multi-access and point-to-point segments and every 30 seconds on NBMA segments (Frame Relay, X.25, ATM).

18. Explanation: Hello interval, Dead interval, network type, and subnet masks.

19. Explanation: Creation of multiple adjacencies, one adjacency for every pair of routers in a multi-access network. Extensive flooding of LSAs (link state advertisements) due to the high number of adjacencies.

20. Explanation: The DR is the router with the highest OSPF interface priority, and the BDR has the second highest OSPF interface priority. If the OSPF interface priorities are equal, the highest router ID is used to break the tie.

Chapter 7

1. C and D. Explanation: DR and BDR election happens in broadcast multiaccess and NBMA networks.

2. C. Explanation: Similar to RIP, OSPF uses the **default-information originate** command to propagate a default route within the OSPF routing domain.

3. D. Explanation: If OSPF interface priorities are equal, which they are by default with a value of 1, the router with the highest router ID becomes the DR, and the router with the second highest router ID becomes the BDR.

4. B and E. Explanation: OSPF MD5 authentication takes the contents of each OSPF message and the configured secret key as input to the MD5 hashing algorithm. The algorithm uses this information to create a signature that is sent with the OSPF message so that the neighbor can verify its authenticity.

5. Explanation: By default, OSPF Hello packets are sent every 10 seconds on multiaccess and point-to-point segments and every 30 seconds on NBMA segments (Frame Relay, X.25, ATM).

6. Explanation: The Hello interval, Dead interval, network type, and subnet masks must match.

7. Explanation: Creation of multiple adjacencies, one adjacency for every pair of routers. Extensive flooding of LSAs (link-state advertisements).

8. Explanation: The DR is the router with the highest OSPF interface priority, and the BDR has the second highest OSPF interface priority. If the OSPF interface priorities are equal, the highest router ID is used to break the tie.

9. Explanation: It forces the router to delete the current router adjacencies and re-transition through the OSPF states. It should be issued when a router ID has changed on a working router for the new router ID to take effect.

10. Explanation: The **show ip ospf interface** command will display the configured Hello and Dead Timer intervals between two OSPFv2 routers, while the **show ipv6 ospf interface** command will display the timer intervals between two OSPFv3 routers. The **show ip ospf neighbor** command will display the Dead interval elapsed time since the last Hello message was received, but does not show the configured value of the timer.

11. Explanation: MD5 does not send the configured password across the network. MD5 generates a special hash, or signature, that is attached to the messages and sent to the neighbor. This signature is used to validate the neighbor instead of the password. MD5 does not use a username and does not enforce a minimum length on the password. While IPsec tunnels can be used to keep updates secure, they are not used specifically by MD5.

Chapter 8

1. B. Explanation: A multiarea OSPF network requires hierarchical network design (two levels). The main area is called the backbone area, and all other areas must connect to the main area.

2. C. Explanation: A multiarea OSPF network improves routing performance and efficiency in a large network. As the network is divided into smaller areas, each router maintains a smaller routing table because routes between areas can be summarized. Also, fewer updated routes means fewer LSAs are exchanged, thus reducing the need for CPU resources. Running multiple routing protocols simultaneously and implementing both IPv4 and IPv6 do not provide reasons for a multiarea OSPF network.

3. A. Explanation: ABRs and ASBRs need to perform any summarization or redistribution among multiple areas, and thus demand more router resources than a regular router in an OSPF area.

4. D. Explanation: An OSPF type 4 summary LSA is generated by an ABR only when an ASBR exists within an area. A type 4 LSA identifies the ASBR and provides a route to it so the routing table will have an entry for traffic that is destined for the external autonomous network.

5. A and E. Explanation: Type 3 LSAs can be generated without requiring a full SPF calculation. Type 3 LSAs are used to carry routes between OSPF areas.

6. D. Explanation: In a routing table, a route with the label O indicates a network that is advertised by another router in the same area.

7. A. Explanation: In a routing table, a route with the designation O IA means the entry was learned from an interarea LSA that was generated from an ABR.

8. B. Explanation: In a routing table, a route with the designation O*E2 indicates an external network.

9. D. Explanation: An ABR has two or more interfaces in different areas.

10. D. Explanation: ASBRs have at least one interface that is connected to a non-OSPF network.

Chapter 9

1. B and C. Explanation: Standard ACLs filter packets based solely on the source IP addresses and are numbered 1 to 99 and 1300 to 1999. Extended ACLs filter IP packets based on several attributes, such as protocol type, source and IP address, destination IP address, source TCP or UDP ports, destination TCP or UDP ports, and optional protocol type information. Extended ACLs are numbered 100 to 199 and 1300 to 1999.

2. C. Explanation: Because standard ACLs do not specify destination addresses, they should be placed as close to the destination as possible so that they filter traffic only to the destination network.

3. B. Explanation: An ACL is executed in order of the statements. The most specific condition must be examined before the more general conditions. Otherwise, the packet might pass the test condition of the general condition and never be examined by the more specific condition.

4. A and C. Explanation: At the end of every ACL is an "implicit deny any" statement or the "deny all traffic" statement. Without any permit statements, all traffic would be denied or dropped on the outbound interface. Traffic originating from the router would be permitted, because access lists do not apply to traffic that originates from the router.

5. B and C. Explanation: ACLs can be used to help create a firewall by filtering inbound and outbound traffic. This includes controlling the traffic entering and exiting LANs. ACLs don't distribute DHCP traffic.

6. D

   E

   C

   A

   B

7. D. Explanation: The wildcard mask can be derived by subtracting the 29-bit mask, 255.255.255.248, from 255.255.255.255. This results in the wildcard mask 0.0.0.7. 192.168.12.84 is a subnet of 192.168.12.0/29.

8. C. Explanation: A standard named access list is created with the global configuration command **ip access-list standard** *name*.

9. Standard IP ACL

   Extended IP ACL

   Extended IP ACL

   Standard IP ACL

   Standard IP ACL

   Extended IP ACL

10. A and D. Explanation: The first line of the ACL denies Telnet traffic originating from the 178.15.0.0/16 network to any destination network. The second line permits all other IP traffic, including FTP.

11. A, D, and E. Explanation: IPv6 ACLs use prefix-lengths instead of a wildcard mask. IPv6 ACLs do not use the **ip access-group** command to apply an ACL to an interface but instead use the **ipv6 traffic-filter** command. IPv6 ACLs include two implicit permit statements to resolve Layer 3 addresses to Layer 2 MAC addresses: **permit icmp any any nd-na** and **permit icmp any any nd-ns**. This permits both ICMPv6 Neighbor Discovery–Neighbor Advertisement (nd-na) messages and Neighbor Discovery–Neighbor Solicitation (nd-ns) messages.

12. One ACL per protocol: To control traffic flow on an interface, an ACL must be defined for each protocol enabled on the interface.

   One ACL per direction: ACLs control traffic in one direction at a time on an interface. Two separate ACLs must be created to control inbound and outbound traffic.

   One ACL per interface: ACLs control traffic for an interface, such as FastEthernet 0/0.

13. Standard ACLs: Because standard ACLs do not specify destination addresses, place them as close to the destination as possible.

   Extended ACLs: Locate extended ACLs as close as possible to the source of the traffic denied. This way, undesirable traffic is filtered without crossing the network infrastructure.

Chapter 10

1. C, F, and H. Explanation: The Advanced Security, Advanced IP Services, and Advanced Enterprise Services packages will all integrate support for security features such as IDS/IPS.

2. D. Explanation: The part of the image name 152-4 indicates that the major release is 15, the minor release is 2, and the new feature release is 4.

3. A and D. Explanation: The IP Base license is installed permanently. The Data software package is also installed as an Evaluation Right-To-Use license.

4. A. Explanation: The "mz" indicates the file is compressed. The z indicates "zip." The file is self-unzipping, so when the image is loaded into RAM for execution, the first action is to unzip.

5. B. Explanation: The **show flash0:** command will display the files contained in flash along with the total amount of flash memory and how much flash is currently available.

6. B. Explanation: The Security image and license contains the Cisco IOS Firewall feature.

7. A. Explanation: All routing protocols are part of the IP Base package, including EIGRP for IPv4 and IPv6. A router must still be enabled as an IPv6 router using the global configuration command **ipv6 unicast-routing**.

8. D. Explanation: The evaluation period is 60 days for any Cisco IOS Software package.

9. A and D. Explanation: The PAK (Product Activation Key) serves as a receipt for the purchase and is used to obtain a license for the specific software package.

10. B. Explanation: The **show license udi** command will display the UDI (Unique Device Identifier), the PID (Product ID), and the SN (Serial Number). The UDI can also be viewed in the pull-out label tray on the device.

11. B. Explanation: The **license accept end user agreement** global configuration command is used to configure a one-time acceptance of the End User License Agreement (EULA) for all Cisco IOS Software packages and features.

12. E. Explanation: The **license boot module** global configuration command is used to activate the Evaluation RTU license. The router must be rebooted for the software package to be activated.

Glossary

2-WAY/DROTHER   A DROTHER is a router that is neither the DR nor the BDR but has a neighbor relationship with another DROTHER. These two neighbors exchange Hello packets.

2-way state   Designates that bidirectional communication has been established between two routers in OSPF. The term is also referred to as Two-Way state and occurs after the Init state. Bidirectional means that each router has seen the other's Hello packet.

A

access control entry (ACE)   A single line in an ACL. Also known as an ACL statement.

access control list (ACL)   A series of ACEs that controls whether a router forwards or drops packets based on information found in the packet header.

active state   In EIGRP, a state in which there is no feasible successor in the topology table. The router enters active state and queries its neighbors for routing information.

addressing table   A table that captures device names, interfaces, IPv4 addresses, subnet masks, and default gateway addresses.

adjacency   A relationship formed between selected neighboring routers and end nodes for the purpose of exchanging routing information. Adjacency is based on the use of a common media segment.

adjacency database   Also called the neighbor table, an OSPF database that contains a list of all neighbors' routers to which a router has established bidirectional communication. This table is unique for each router and can be viewed using the **show ip ospf neighbor** command.

administrative distance (AD)   The feature that routers use to select the best path when there are two or more different routes to the same destination from two different routing protocols. The AD represents the "trustworthiness" or reliability of the route.

Advanced Research Projects Agency Network (ARPANET)   One of the world's first operational packet switching networks. It was also the first network to implement TCP/IP, and the precursor to the global Internet.

algorithm   Well-defined rule or process for arriving at a solution to a problem. In networking, algorithms are commonly used to determine the best route for traffic from a particular source to a particular destination.

Area Border Router (ABR)   A router interconnecting the areas in a multiarea OSPF network.

autonomous system (AS)   A collection of routers under a common administration such as a company or an organization.

Autonomous System Boundary Router (ASBR)   The OSPF router located between an OSPF autonomous system network and a non-OSPF network. ASBRs run both OSPF and another routing protocol, such as RIP. ASBRs must reside in a nonstub OSPF area.

auto-summarization   Feature that consolidates networks and advertises them in classful network advertisements.

availability   A measure of the probability that the network is available for use when it is required.

B

backbone (transit) area   Also known as area 0. In any OSPF network design, there must be at least one area. Traditionally this area is numbered 0 and is known as the backbone area. In single-area OSPF, the lone area is area 0. In multiarea OSPF, area 0 forms the core of the network, as all other areas attach to the backbone area to facilitate interarea communication.

backbone router   An OSPF router that has at least one interface in area 0.

backup designated router (BDR)   A router that becomes the designated router if the current designated router fails. The BDR is the OSPF router with the second-highest priority at the time of the last DR election.

best path   The path with the lowest metric to a destination network.

Border Gateway Protocol (BGP)   The only Exterior Gateway Protocol (EGP) designed to exchange routing and reachability information between autonomous systems on the Internet.

border router   A router that sits on the edge of two discontiguous classful networks. A border router can also be known as a router that sits on the edge of two different networks that have different routing protocols. Sometime the word boundary router is loosely used when discussing OSPF and Autonomous System Boundary Routers (ASBRs).

bounded triggered update   Updates are sent immediately upon being discovered, without waiting for a timer to expire. Also known as a *flash update*.

C

child route   A route that is a subnet of a classful network address. Also known as a level 2 route.

Cisco Express Forwarding (CEF)   An advanced, Layer 3 switching technology inside a router. CEF defines the fastest method by which a Cisco router forwards packets from ingress to egress interfaces.

classful routing protocols   A routing protocol that does not carry subnet mask information in its routing updates.

classless   Operates without pre-defined classes. In networking, the pre-defined classes refer to the legacy Class A, B, C, and D network address ranges with pre-determined subnet masks.

classless routing protocols   A routing protocol that carries subnet mask information in its routing updates. Classless routing protocols can take advantage of VLSM and supernet routes.

console cable   A cable connected between the serial port of the host and the console port on the device.

convergence   Speed and ability of a group of internetworking devices running a specific routing protocol to agree on the topology of an internetwork after a change in that topology.

cost   An arbitrary value, typically based on hop count, media bandwidth, or other measures, that is assigned by a network administrator and used to compare various paths through an internetwork environment. Routing protocols use cost values to calculate the most favorable path to a particular destination: the lower the cost, the better the path.

D

data structure   A group of data elements stored together under one name. The adjacency database, link-state database, and forwarding database are all examples of data structures.

database description (DBD) packet   A packet used in OSPF that contains link-state advertisement (LSA) headers only and describes the contents of the entire link-state database. Routers exchange DBDs during the Exchange State of adjacency creation. A DBD is an OSPF Type 2 packet.

default gateway   Identifies the router to send a packet to when the destination is not on the same local network subnet.

default static route   A route that matches all packets and identifies the gateway IP address to which the router sends all packets for which it does not have a learned or static route.

designated router (DR)   OSPF router that generates link-state advertisements (LSAs) for a multiaccess network and has other special responsibilities in running OSPF. Each multiaccess OSPF network that has at least two attached routers has a DR that is elected by the OSPF Hello protocol. The DR enables a reduction in the number of adjacencies required on a multiaccess network, which in turn reduces the amount of routing protocol traffic and the size of the topological database.

Dijkstra's algorithm   The routing algorithm of the OSPF routing protocol.

directly connected network   A network that can be reached by the local router.

discontiguous network   A network that does not have a hierarchical scheme and thus has fragmented network addressing. It is impossible to summarize discontiguous networks.

distance vector routing protocols   Protocols that use either the Bellman–Ford algorithm or the DUAL Finite State Machine (FSM) (in the case of Cisco EIGRP) to calculate paths. A distance vector routing protocol requires that a router inform its neighbors of topology changes periodically.

Down state   The first OSPF neighbor state. It means that no information (Hello packets) has been received from this neighbor, but Hello packets can still be sent to the neighbor in this state.

DROTHER   A router that is neither the DR nor the BDR. DROTHERs are the other routers in the OSPF network.

DUAL Finite State Machine   The DUAL finite state machine embodies the decision process for all route computations. It tracks all routes advertised by all neighbors.

dynamic route   A remote network in a routing table that has been automatically learned using a dynamic routing protocol such as EIGRP or OSPF.

dynamic routing protocols   Allow network devices to learn routes dynamically. OSPF and EIGRP are examples of dynamic routing protocols.

dynamically assigned IP address   IP address information is provided by a server using the Dynamic Host Configuration Protocol (DHCP).

E

Enhanced IGRP (EIGRP)   Developed by Cisco, an enhancement to the legacy IGRP that provides routing protocol, EIGRP provides superior convergence properties and operating efficiency, and combines the advantages of link-state protocols with those of distance vector protocols.

equal cost load balancing   When a router utilizes multiple paths with the same administrative distance and cost to a destination.

Evaluation Right-To-Use (RTU) licenses   Evaluation RTU licenses are limited period-metered licenses that are valid for a predefined number of days. An RTU license scheme is an honor-based model for licensing. Licenses are not tied to a Unique Device Identifier (UDI), Product ID (PID), or Serial Number (SN).

event-driven updates   Sent out by link-state routing protocols after the initial flooding of link-state packets (LSPs), and only when there is a change in the topology. The LSP contains only the information regarding the affected link. Unlike some distance vector routing protocols, link-state routing protocols do not send periodic updates.

Exchange state   State in which OSPF routers exchange database description (DBD) packets. DBDs contain link-state advertisement (LSA) headers only and describe the contents of the entire link-state database.

ExStart state   State in which the routers and their DR and BDR establish a master/slave relationship and choose the initial sequence number for adjacency formation. The router with the higher router ID becomes the master and starts the exchange.

extended ACL   Filters traffic based upon multiple attributes, including protocol type, source IPv4 addresses, destination IPv4 addresses, source ports, and destination ports.

extended maintenance release (EM release)   Cisco IOS Software 15 release that is ideal for long-term maintenance, enabling customers to qualify, deploy, and remain on the release for an extended period. Provides approximately 40 months of total support. Incorporates features delivered in previous releases plus incremental new feature enhancements and hardware support.

Exterior Gateway Protocol (EGP)   A routing protocol used for routing between autonomous systems.

external route summarization   Route summarization that is specific to external routes that are injected into OSPF via route redistribution. Ensuring the contiguity of the external address ranges that are being summarized is important. Generally, only ASBRs summarize external routes. *See also* route summarization.

F

fast switching   The first packet is copied to packet memory and the destination network or host is found in the fast-switching cache. The frame is rewritten and sent to the outgoing interface that services the destination. Subsequent packets for the same destination use the same switching path.

feasibility condition   The feasibility condition is met when the receiving router has a feasible distance (FD) to a particular network and it receives an update from another neighbor with a lower advertised distance (reported distance) to that network. Used in EIGRP.

feasible successor   A next-hop router that leads to a certain destination network. The feasible successor can be thought of as a backup next hop if the primary next hop (successor) goes down. Used in EIGRP.

Flash   Nonvolatile storage that can be electrically erased and reprogrammed. It provides permanent storage for the IOS and other system-related files. Developed by Intel and licensed to other semiconductor companies.

floating static route   A static route used to provide a backup path to a primary static or dynamic route in the event of a link failure. Used only when the primary route is not available.

forwarding database   List of OSPF routes generated when an algorithm is run on the link-state database. Each router's routing table is unique and contains information on how and where to send packets to other routers. Can be viewed using the **show ip route** command.

FULL/BDR   An OSPF router that is fully adjacent with the indicated BDR neighbor. These two neighbors can exchange Hello packets, updates, queries, replies, and acknowledgments.

FULL/DR   An OSPF router that is fully adjacent with the indicated DR neighbor. These two neighbors can exchange Hello packets, updates, queries, replies, and acknowledgments.

FULL/DROTHER   A DR or BDR that is fully adjacent with a router that is neither the DR nor the BDR. These two neighbors can exchange Hello packets, updates, queries, replies, and acknowledgments.

Full state   State in which routers are fully adjacent with each other. All the router and network LSAs are exchanged and the routers' databases are fully synchronized.

fully specified static route   A static route in which both the output interface and next-hop address are identified.

G

Gateway of Last Resort   Used to direct packets addressed to networks not explicitly listed in the routing table. Also known as a default route.

global unicast addresses   Globally unique and routable IPv6 addresses.

H

Hello interval   Specifies the frequency, in seconds, at which a router sends Hello packets.

Hello keepalive mechanism   A small Hello message that is periodically exchanged to maintain adjacencies with neighboring routers. This means a very low usage of network resources during normal operation, instead of the periodic updates.

Hello packet   Type 1 OSPF packet used to establish and maintain adjacency with other OSPF routers.

High-Speed WAN Interface Card (HWIC)   Single-wide interface card that provides Cisco modular and integrated services routers with additional line-rate Layer 3 routed ports.

Hold time   The maximum time a router waits to receive the next Hello packet or routing update. Once the Hold time counter expires, that route will become unreachable.

I

Init state   OSPF state that specifies the router has received a Hello packet from its neighbor but the receiving router's ID was not included in the Hello packet.

interarea route summarization   Route summarization that occurs on ABRs and applies to routes from within each area. It does not apply to external routes injected into OSPF via redistribution. To perform effective interarea route summarization, network addresses within areas should be assigned contiguously so that these addresses can be summarized into a minimal number of summary addresses. *See also* route summarization.

Interior Gateway Protocol (IGP)   A routing protocol used for routing within an autonomous system (AS).

Interior Gateway Routing Protocol (IGRP)   Legacy Cisco proprietary routing protocol that was replaced by EIGRP.

Intermediate System-to-Intermediate System (IS-IS)   A dynamic link-state routing protocol that is based on a routing method known as DECnet Phase V routing. Routers are known as intermediate systems and exchange data routing messages using a single metric to determine the network topology. IS-IS was developed by the Organization for Standardization (ISO) as part of its Open Systems Interconnection (OSI) model.

internal router   Internal OSPF router that has all of its interfaces in the same area. All internal routers in an area have identical link-state databases (LSDBs).

IP address   The unique number ID assigned to one host or interface in a network.

L

legacy protocol   Routing protocol that is no longer used due to changed technologies. Examples are RIPv1 and IGRP.

level 1 parent route   A level 1 route in the routing table that has subnets "catalogued" under it. A level 1 parent route does not contain any next-hop IP address or exit interface information.

level 1 route   A route with a subnet mask equal to or less than the classful mask of the network address.

level 2 child route   A route that is a subnet of a classful network address.

link-local address   An IP address that is used for communications only within a network link. Packets sourced from or destined to a link-local address are not forwarded to other networks by routers. Link-local addresses play a significant role in IPv6.

link state   The status of a link, including the interface IP address/subnet mask, type of network, cost of the link, and any neighbor routers on that link.

link-state acknowledgment (LSAck) packet   Acknowledges receipt of LSA (link-state advertisement) packets. Link-state acknowledgment packets are Type 5 OSPF packets.

link-state advertisement (LSA)   Broadcast packet used by link-state protocols that contains information about neighbors and path costs. LSAs are used by the receiving routers to maintain their routing tables.

link-state database   A table used in OSPF that is a representation of the topology of the autonomous system. It is the method by which routers "see" the state of the links in the autonomous system.

link-state packet (LSP)   *See* link-state advertisement.

link-state request (LSR) packet   Used to request the pieces of the neighbor's database that are more up to date. Link-state request packets are Type 3 OSPF packets.

link-state router   A router that uses a link-state routing protocol.

link-state routing protocol   A routing protocol in which routers exchange information with one another about the reachability of other networks and the cost or metric to reach the other networks. Link-state routers use Dijkstra's algorithm to calculate shortest paths to a destination, and normally update other routers with which they are connected only when their own routing tables change.

link-state update (LSU) packet   Carries a collection of link-state advertisements one hop farther from its origin. Link-state update packets are Type 4 OSPF packets.

load balancing   The capability of a router to distribute traffic over all the router network ports that are the same distance from the destination address.

Loading state   OSPF state in which the actual exchange of link-state information occurs. Based on the information provided by the DBDs, routers send link-state request packets. The neighbor then provides the requested link-state information in link-state update packets. During the adjacency, if a router receives an outdated or missing LSA, it requests that LSA by sending a link-state request packet. All link-state update packets are acknowledged.

logical topology   The path over which the data is transferred in a network.

loopback address   The IP address assigned to a loopback interface. It could also be the local host loopback interface address on a host computer. In IPv4 this is the 127.0.0.1 address, while in IPv6 this is the ::1 address.

loopback interface   A software-only interface that emulates a physical interface. A loopback interface is always up and never goes down.

M

mainline train   A release of the Cisco IOS built from the bug fixes of a previous technology (T) train.

Message Digest 5 (MD5)   A widely used cryptographic hash function producing a 128-bit (16-byte) hash value, typically expressed as a 32-digit hexadecimal number. MD5 has been utilized in a wide variety of security applications, including to check data integrity.

Message Digest 5 (MD5) authentication   The most secure and recommended method of routing protocol authentication. MD5 authentication provides higher security because the password is never exchanged between peers. Instead, it is calculated using the MD5 algorithm. Matching results authenticate the sender.

metric   The quantitative value used to measure the distance to a given network.

multiaccess network   Network that allows multiple devices to connect and communicate simultaneously.

multiarea OSPF   In an OSPF network design, one large autonomous system (AS) is divided into smaller areas, to support hierarchical routing. All areas must connect to the backbone area (area 0).

N

neighbor   In OSPF, two routers that have interfaces to a common network. On multiaccess networks, neighbors are discovered dynamically by the OSPF Hello protocol.

neighbor table   OSPF table that lists all OSPF neighbor routers to which a router has established bidirectional communication. This table is unique for each router and can be viewed using the **show ip ospf neighbor** command.

nonbroadcast multiaccess (NBMA) network   Multiaccess network that either does not support broadcasting or in which broadcasting is not feasible. Examples of NBMA networks include Frame Relay and ATM.

Non-Volatile Random Access Memory (NVRAM)   Provides permanent storage for the startup configuration file (startup-config). NVRAM is non-volatile and does not lose its contents when power is turned off.

Null0 summary route   Another mechanism to prevent routing loops. EIGRP always creates a route to the Null0 interface when it summarizes a group of network routes because there is a risk of looping packets if a default route is also configured.

O

Open Shortest Path First (OSPF)   Link-state, hierarchical IGP routing algorithm proposed as a successor to RIP in the Internet community. OSPF features include least-cost routing, multipath routing, and load balancing. OSPF was derived from an early version of the IS-IS protocol.

OSPF area   A logical set of network segments (CLNS-, DECnet-, or OSPF-based) and their attached devices. Areas are usually connected to other areas through routers, making up a single autonomous system.

OSPF authentication   When configured on a router, the router authenticates the source of each routing update packet that it receives. This is accomplished by the exchange of an authenticating key (sometimes referred to as a password) that is known to both the sending and the receiving router. To exchange routing update information in a secure manner, enable OSPF authentication. OSPF authentication can either be none (or null), simple, or Message Digest 5 (MD5).

OSPF Hello and Dead intervals   The Hello interval is the frequency at which a router sends Hello packets, and the Dead interval is the length of time that a router waits to hear from a neighbor before declaring the neighboring router out of service. These parameters are configurable on a per-interface basis. Unlike the EIGRP intervals of the same name, the OSPF intervals must match or a neighbor adjacency does not occur.

OSPF states   Different states through which OSPF routers transition when adjacencies are being established. Specifically, OSPF routers transition through the Down state, Init state, Two-Way state, ExStart state, Exchange state, Loading state, and finally Full state.

OSPFv3   Version 3 of the OSPF routing protocol, used to support both IPv4 and IPv6 unicast address families.

P, Q

parent route   A level 1 route that has been subnetted. A parent route can never be an ultimate route.

passive interface   An interface that does not take part in the advertisement of routing information. The **passive-interface** command enables the suppression of routing updates over some interfaces while allowing updates to be exchanged normally over other interfaces. A neighbor adjacency cannot be formed over a passive interface. This is because link-state packets cannot be sent or acknowledged.

passive state   In EIGRP, the stable state to which a router transitions when it has identified the successor(s) for a certain destination.

periodic update   An update that is transmitted between routers at the end of a certain time period. The periodic update for RIP is 30 seconds.

physical topology   The arrangement of the cables, network devices, and end systems. It describes how the network devices are actually interconnected with wires and cables.

prefix length   Another name for a network prefix.

process switching   An older packet-forwarding mechanism still available for Cisco routers. In process switching the first packet is copied to the system buffer. The router looks up the Layer 3 network address in the routing table and initializes the fast-switching cache. The frame is rewritten with the destination address and sent to the outgoing interface that services that destination. Subsequent packets for that destination are sent by the same switching path.

Product Activation Key (PAK)   Serves as a receipt of purchase for an IOS image and is used to obtain a Software Activation License.

protocol-dependent modules (PDMs)   A feature of EIGRP in which individual modules are responsible for the tasks related to a specific routing protocol. EIGRP has PDMs for IP, IPX, AppleTalk, and IPv6.

quad-zero route   An IPv4 default static route. Referred to as quad-zero route because of its syntax of 0.0.0.0 for the network address and 0.0.0.0 for the subnet mask.

R

Random Access Memory (RAM)   Provides temporary storage for various applications and processes, including the running IOS, the running configuration file, various tables (e.g., IP routing table, Ethernet ARP table, etc.) and buffers for packet processing. RAM is referred to as volatile because it loses its contents when power is turned off.

Read-Only Memory (ROM)   Provides permanent storage for bootup instructions, basic diagnostic software, and a limited IOS in case the router cannot load the full featured IOS. ROM is firmware and is referred to as non-volatile because it does not lose its contents when power is turned off.

recursive lookup   Occurs when a router has to perform multiple lookups in a routing table before forwarding a packet.

reference bandwidth   The number, measured in Mb/s, that is used by routing protocols to calculate a route's metric. In OSPF, the default reference bandwidth is 100 Mb/s. Changing the reference bandwidth does not actually affect the bandwidth capacity on the link; rather, it simply affects the calculation used to determine the metric.

regular (non-backbone) area   An area that connects users and resources. Regular areas are interconnected through the backbone area. Regular areas are usually set up along functional or geographical groupings. By default, a regular area does not allow traffic from another area to use its links to reach other areas. All traffic from other areas must cross a transit area.

reliability   Indicates the dependability of the components that make up the network, such as the routers, switches, PCs, and servers.

Reliable Transport Protocol (RTP)   Responsible for guaranteed, ordered delivery of EIGRP packets to neighbors.

remote network   Network that can only be reached by forwarding packets to another router.

reported distance   In EIGRP, the total metric along a path to a destination network as advertised by an upstream neighbor in EIGRP.

RIPng   The IPv6 version of the RIPv2 dynamic routing protocol.

route summarization   The process of taking multiple contiguous routes and representing them with a single route statement.

Router Advertisement (RA) message   A message type used by an IPv6 router to provide IPv6 addressing information to clients. The router sends the message using the IPv6 all-nodes multicast address of FF02::1.

Router ID   A field in an OSPF Hello packet that is a 32-bit value expressed in dotted-decimal notation (an IPv4 address) used to uniquely identify the originating router.

Router Priority   Used in a DR/BDR election. The default priority for all OSPF routers is 1, but can be manually altered from 0 to 255. The higher the value, the more likely the router becomes the DR on the link.

Routing Information Protocol (RIP)   One of the oldest distance-vector routing protocols, employs the hop count as a routing metric. RIP is a legacy dynamic routing protocol.

routing protocol messages   Various types of messages used by routing protocols to discover neighboring routers, exchange routing information, and perform other tasks to learn and maintain accurate information about the network.

routing table   A data file in RAM that is used to store route information about directly connected and remote networks.

S

scalability   Indicates how easily the network can accommodate more users and data transmission requirements.

shortest path first (SPF)   Algorithm that uses accumulated costs along each path, from source to destination, to determine the total cost of a route. Commonly used in link-state routing algorithms. Sometimes referred to as Dijkstra's algorithm because it was developed by Edsger Dijkstra.

single-area OSPF   In an OSPF network design, all routers are in one area called the backbone area (area 0).

SPF tree   Topology tree to which a link-state routing algorithm adds a destination network after determining the shortest path to that network using the shortest path first algorithm (Dijkstra's algorithm).

split horizon   A technique for preventing reverse routes between two routers. Information about the routing for a particular packet is never sent back in the direction from which it was received.

standard ACL   ACL that filters traffic by using only the source IPv4 addresses.

standard maintenance release (T release)   Beginning with Cisco IOS 15.0, enables new IOS features to be delivered before the next extended maintenance release (EM release) becomes available.

static route   A remote network in a routing table that has been manually entered into the table by a network administrator.

statically assigned IP address   The host is manually assigned the correct IP address, subnet mask, and default gateway.

stub network   A network with only one exit point.

stub router   A router that has only one exit interface from the routing domain and forwards all traffic to a central or distribution router.

subnet mask   A dotted-decimal number that helps identify the structure of IP addresses. The mask represents the network and subnet parts of related IP addresses with binary 1s and the host part of related IP addresses with binary 0s.

successor   A neighboring router that is used for packet forwarding and is the least-cost route to the destination network. In EIGRP, a successor is chosen using DUAL from all of the known paths or feasible successors to the end destination.

summary route   Route summarization reduces the number of routes that a router must maintain. It is a method of representing a series of network numbers in a single summary address; for example, when multiple static routes that can be summarized with a common prefix length are replaced by one static route.

supernet route   A route that has a subnet mask less than the classful mask. A summary address is an example of a supernet route.

switched virtual interface (SVI)   Provides basic Layer 3 functions for a switch, which does not have a dedicated physical interface for IP addressing.

T

technology train   Prior to IOS 15, train that receives the same bug fixes as the mainline train but also receives new software and hardware features. Also called a T train.

Terminal emulation software   A software program required to establish a serial connection to the console port of a router.

TLV   In EIGRP, the data portion of the EIGRP packet. All TLVs (Type, Length, Value) begin with a 16-bit Type field and a 16-bit Length field. Different TLV values exist according to the router protocol.

topology diagram   Provides a visual reference that indicates the physical connectivity and logical Layer 3 addressing.

topology table   Contains information regarding EIGRP routes received in updates and routes that are locally originated. EIGRP sends and receives routing updates from adjacent routers to which peering relationships (adjacencies) have been formed. The objects in this table are populated on a per-topology table entry (route) basis.

Two-Way state   Designates that bidirectional communication has been established between two routers in OSPF. The term is also referred to as 2-Way state and occurs after the Init state. Bidirectional means that each router has seen the other's Hello packet.

type 1 router LSA   Contains a list of the directly connected interfaces, link types, and link states. All OSPF routers advertise their directly connected OSPF-enabled links in a type 1 LSA and forward their network information to OSPF neighbors.

type 2 network LSA   Contains the router ID and IP address of the DR, along with the router ID of all other routers on the multiaccess segment. Type 2 LSAs only exist for multiaccess and nonbroadcast multiaccess (NBMA) networks where there is a DR elected and at least two routers on the multiaccess segment. The type 2 LSA contains the router ID and IP address of the DR, along with the router ID of all other routers on the multiaccess segment. A type 2 LSA is created for every multiaccess network in the area.

type 3 summary LSA   Used by an ABR to advertise networks from other areas. ABRs collect type 1 LSAs in the LSDB. After an OSPF area has converged, the ABR creates a type 3 LSA for each of its learned OSPF networks. Therefore, an ABR with many OSPF routes must create type 3 LSAs for each network.

type 4 summary LSA   A type 4 summary LSA is generated by an ABR only when an ASBR exists within an area. Used by an ABR to advertise an ASBR to other areas and provide a route to the ASBR. All traffic destined to an external autonomous system requires routing table knowledge of the ASBR that originated the external routes. A type 4 LSA is generated by the originating ABR and regenerated by other ABRs.

type 5 AS external LSA   Describes routes to networks outside the OSPF autonomous system. Type 5 LSAs are originated by the ASBR and are flooded to the entire autonomous system and regenerated by other ABRs. A type 5 LSA link-state ID is the external network address.

U, V, W

ultimate route   A routing table entry that contains either a next-hop IPv4 address or an exit interface. Directly connected, dynamically learned, and local routes are all considered to be ultimate routes.

unequal cost load balancing   The capability of a router to distribute traffic over all the router network ports, even those that are different distances from the destination address. EIGRP supports unequal cost load balancing by using the **variance** command.

Unique Device Identifier (UDI)   Combination of the Product ID, Serial Number, and hardware version.

variable-length subnet masking (VLSM)   Allows for the use of different subnet masks for individual subnets, which allows a network space to be divided into unequal parts. With VLSM, the network is first subnetted, and then the subnets are subnetted again. This process can be repeated multiple times to create subnets of various sizes. Creates a more efficient use of address space.

vector   Identifies the direction of the next-hop router or exit interface needed to reach a destination network.

wildcard mask   A string of 32 binary digits used by the router to determine which bits of the address to examine for a match.

K-L

M

O

P